Coins in Rhodes

From the monetary reform of Anastasius I until the Ottoman conquest (498 - 1522)

Anna-Maria Kasdagli

Archaeopress Archaeology

ARCHAEOPRESS PUBLISHING LTD
Gordon House
276 Banbury Road
Oxford OX2 7ED

www.archaeopress.com

ISBN 978 1 78491 841 5
ISBN 978 1 78491 842 2 (e-Pdf)

This book is available direct from Archaeopress or from our website www.archaeopress.com

Contents

Part II. HOSPITALLER PERIOD (1309-1522)

List of Figures

List of Plates

Prologue

This study, in its early version, was a PhD Thesis submitted to the University of Athens. It is dedicated to the memory of Elias Kollias, Ephor of Byzantine Antiquities in the Dodecanese from 1978 until 1998, because without him it would never have been undertaken. However, it was put together in the hope that it will also benefit the archaeologists engaged in the rescue, protection and study of the local heritage in challenging times; without their contribution, the available numismatic information on Rhodes would have been poor indeed. I thank them all for their help at every stage of my research, for the information on excavated sites and finds and for their daily encouragement. It would be impossible to cite everyone by name without forgetting some.

Heartfelt thanks are also due to a host of others who administratively supported my research or gave practical assistance at various stages. Friends working in other fields, conservators, draughtsmen, computer specialists, architects, civil engineers, surveyors and photographers were available when needed and helped reduce errors and omissions concerning sites, finds, publications and various records. The Numismatic Museum in Athens was decisive for my development as a student of numismatics in the last twenty years through the advice of its expert staff and access to its specialist library. Finally, an important preparation for the analysis of Hospitaller coins was provided through a bursary of the British School at Athens in 1995 under its then Director Martin Jessop Price, which gave me the opportunity to study the Rhodian coins kept at the Museum of the Order of Saint John, Clerkenwell.

The guidance of my PhD Committee of Professors Sophia Kalopissi-Verti, my supervisor at the University of Athens, outstanding numismatist Vasso Penna of the University of the Peloponnese and a veteran of the Numismatic Museum in Athens, and medievalist Florentia Evangelatou-Notara, has been decisive in the avoidance of several pitfalls. I am grateful to all those who enabled me to present the material from Rhodes and apologize, to them and to the reader, for the errors that I could not avoid.

Anna-Maria Kasdagli
Ephorate of Antiquities of the Dodecanese
2017

Introduction

Rhodes and archaeology

Antiquarian interest in Rhodes has deep roots. Already in the Middle Ages educated visitors tried to trace evidence of its celebrated ancient past. Later on, the geographical location of the island, and of the town and its harbours in particular, attracted the Western travellers who replaced the medieval pilgrims on the sea-routes between Europe and the Middle East.[1] Romanticism revived interest in the Crusaders and their castles, while the rise of the bourgeoisie and of colonial ambitions encouraged the collection of antiquities. For the diplomats, career soldiers, antiquaries and collectors of the 19th and early 20th centuries, Rhodes had everything: a strategic location, easy access, a mild climate and adequate harbours, many standing monuments of the past and its ancient renown, which promised exciting discoveries.

Visitors like the Belgian colonel Rottiers (1826), French politician and antiquary Eugène Flandin (*c.* 1844) and Prussian Albert Berg (1853) published descriptions of Rhodes illustrated with engravings of various monuments; the important, and also illustrated with a number of sketches by the author, personal diary of Swedish MD Johannes Hedenborg (1854),[2] who spent his retirement in Rhodes, lies still unpublished in the local archaeological library. Other writers, such as Ludwig Ross (1845, 1852), Victor Guérin (1856), Charles Thomas Newton (1865), Gustave Schlumberger (1878), Édouard-Henri Furse (1889), Édouard Biliotti and the abbé Cottret (1881), Guy Sommi-Picenardi (1901) and Louis Fradin de Belabre (1908), dealt more systematically with the history of Rhodes and its antiquities; most of them were also active in the hunt for collectible antiquities synonymous with early archaeology. The architecture of the Hospitaller town was thoroughly explored by Frenchman Albert Gabriel in a two-volume work entitled *La cité de Rhodes, Architecture Militaire* and *Architecture civile et religieuse* (1921/1923). The breadth and quantity of scholarly publications about medieval Rhodes up to the last quarter of the 20th century was summarized and integrated in the presentation of its cultural history by Elias Kollias in 1994.[3]

In the 19th century, the town of Rhodes consisted of the medieval walled settlement, exclusively inhabited by Turks and Jews, and of Christian parishes scattered outside the medieval fortifications, between stretches of gardens and farmsteads. Two of the ancient harbours were still in use, although shrunk in size due to sedimentation: the commercial harbour, the ancient 'great harbour', flanked by the medieval town wall to the west and south; and Mandraki, north of the medieval town, where the fortified Ottoman arsenal was located. Muslim cemeteries spread over the sloping outer banks of the medieval fortifications. Among the Christian parishes, locally known as *marassia*, Niochori, the northern one, had a church dedicated to the Latin rite in addition to its Orthodox one, as some of its inhabitants were Western technicians who worked at the arsenal or European diplomats and merchants. The other *marassia*, each with its own church, spread in an arc from the southwest of the medieval settlement to its southeast, near the coast, thus: St. John, Ayioi Anargyroi (SS Cosmas and Damian), St. Anastasia, Metropolis, St. George 'Ano', St Nicholas and St George 'Kato'.[4] Further south was the Orthodox church and cemetery of St. Demetrius. In the last years of the 19th and the early 20th century a number of Greek schools were added to the other public buildings of the *marassia*.[5]

In the course of the 20th century, the material remains of the past were particularly affected by political developments. The decline of the Ottoman empire encouraged the colonial aspirations of Italy, which occupied Rhodes in 1912 by force of arms.[6] Apart from the Danish mission at and around Lindos (1902-9/ 1913-14), systematic archaeological exploration in Rhodes began during the Italian occupation of the island (1912-1943).[7] Until World War II, the Italians made use of archaeological discoveries in order to promote the role of Rome in the history of the island as an ideological tool of empire.[8] The medieval Great Hospital of the Knights of St. John became the Archaeological Museum, soon filled with excavation finds and antiquities purchased from the local population. The

[1] Among them celebrated personalities such as Jean de Thévenot (1655), the count of Choiseul-Gouffier (1776), Claud-Etienne Savary (1779), Joseph von Hammer (1803), Chateaubriand (1806), the count of Marcellus (1820), Joseph-François Michaut and Jean-Joseph-François Poujoulat (1830-31), Joseph d'Estourmel (1832), Lamartine (1835), William John Hamilton (1836) etc.
[2] Stefanidou 2001.
[3] Kollias 1994: 174-180.
[4] Gabriel 1921: 1-7; Papachristodoulou 1972: 401-402; Konstantinopoulos 1986: 238-242. For the parish churches see Dellas 2012.
[5] Maria 2008.
[6] Tsirpanlis 1998.
[7] Morricone 1965: 743-744. Coulié and Filimonos 2014: 16-40. Most of the portable antiquities unearthed in 19th c. excavations were sent to Britain (the British Museum), Italy (Florence) and Denmark.
[8] Tsirpanlis 1998: 79 ff.

FERT Archaeological Institute was set up and furnished with a specialist Library which would be a precious legacy for later archaeologists. The exploration of various sites was presented in the *Annuario della Regia Scuola Archeologica di Atene* and the periodicals *Clara Rhodos* and *Memorie*; an archaeological map of the island was published by Raffaele Umberto Inglieri in 1930.

Italian architects and archaeologists like Giuseppe Gerola, Pietro Lojacono, Amedeo Maiuri, Giulio Jacopi and Cesare Brandi contributed to large-scale excavations and restoration projects which still dominate the urban landscape and some sites in the countryside. The Ottoman cemeteries were cleared from the perimeter of the medieval fortifications, which was turned into public parks. Beyond the ring of parkland, the Italian rulers of Rhodes engaged in a broad building programme which houses most public services to this day, particularly in the harbour zone. Large public buildings, hotels, housing for the Italian military and administrators, markets and factories, and two new Latin churches were built, forming the principal nodes for the new urban grid of Rhodes, which also incorporated the *marassia* and older roadways (Figure 1).[9] The urban projects in the new colonial capital, the effort to associate the island's past with Italy for political reasons and the enhancement of archaeological sites of natural beauty, required extensive excavations of which only a few were documented,[10] according to the norms of the period.

In 1947, after World War II and the unification of the Dodecanese Islands with Greece, Greek archaeologists undertook the challenge of keeping up with the expansion of the town. Rhodes was being transformed into a major tourist attraction, bringing in much needed hard currency at a time when civil war was lingering on the mainland. The rapid rate of land development eventually led to rescue excavation by state employees in over 1,500 urban properties, in accordance with state law; thus a large part of the ancient city and its necropolis were gradually investigated. The street grid, with several public buildings, humble housing and mansions, its infrastructure, industrial installations such as casting pits and workshops, fortifications and the dwellings of the dead around them were brought to light.[11] The undoubted quality and dedication of the archaeologists who participated in this gigantic task, which is still in progress, has harvested an immense amount of material for the study of local history and society across several centuries.[12]

In the historic centre, continuously occupied since ancient times and today comprising the walled medieval settlement, rescue excavation was limited and, with a few exceptions, was carried out from the 1970s onwards. Within the fortifications of the protected medieval town,[13] large-scale excavations have been carried out in some of the areas where the Allied air raids of World War II had destroyed the medieval buildings. Smaller-scale exploration has formed part of the restoration and consolidation process in a number of standing buildings as well as in the interior and grounds of medieval churches.[14] From the late 1980s major restoration projects on the fortifications and urban historic buildings were jointly funded by the Greek state and the European Union. Modern restoration practices involve thorough study of surviving structures and their consolidation; this required the cutting of exploratory trenches using archaeological techniques in order to preserve the maximum amount of data. The information yielded by such soundings modified earlier assumptions relative to the development of the town,[15] but the significant moveable finds brought to light have not yet been systematically examined.

The Roman period, which connects the Hellenistic with the Byzantine era, is problematical for the archaeology of the city of Rhodes. Selective examination of Roman monuments was undertaken in the Italian period and refined by later scholars; however, an integrated study of the Roman city during the Early Christian centuries has not been attempted; large-scale correlation of architectural remains with other kinds of evidence has yet to be pursued and the pace and spatial aspect of the decline of the ancient city have yet to be traced systematically.[16] So far, at least

[9] Livadiotti and Rocco 1996.

[10] Published in various Italian periodicals but mainly in the local archaeological periodical *Clara Rhodos* (1928 ff.) See also Livadiotti and Rocco 1996.

[11] Kondis 1958: 146-158; Konstantinopoulos 1970; Dietz and Papachristodoulou 1988; *Ρόδος 2.400 Χρόνια* 1999; Philemonos-Tsopotou 2004; Giannikouri 2013; Patsiada 2013.

[12] The progress of archaeological investigation is to be found scattered in specialist publications and the *Chronika* section of the yearly *Archaiologikon Deltion*.

[13] Since 1988 the medieval town is a UNESCO designated World Heritage Site. Manoussou-Della 2001: 76.

[14] In some cases, archaeological excavation does not reach the lower strata when something important higher up has to be preserved, or when conditions become unsafe due to the proximity of standing masonry.

[15] Manoussou-Della 2001: 64 ff.; *15 χρόνια έργων αποκατάστασης στη Μεσαιωνική Πόλη της Ρόδου*, Athens 2007; *Μεσαιωνική πόλη Ρόδου, Έργα Αποκατάστασης 2000-2008.*

[16] An attempt to correlate moveable finds with structural remains across the city has recently been made by A. Katsioti (under publication, Archaeopress), in her examination of the sites where Late Roman lamps have been found; but this is only a start.

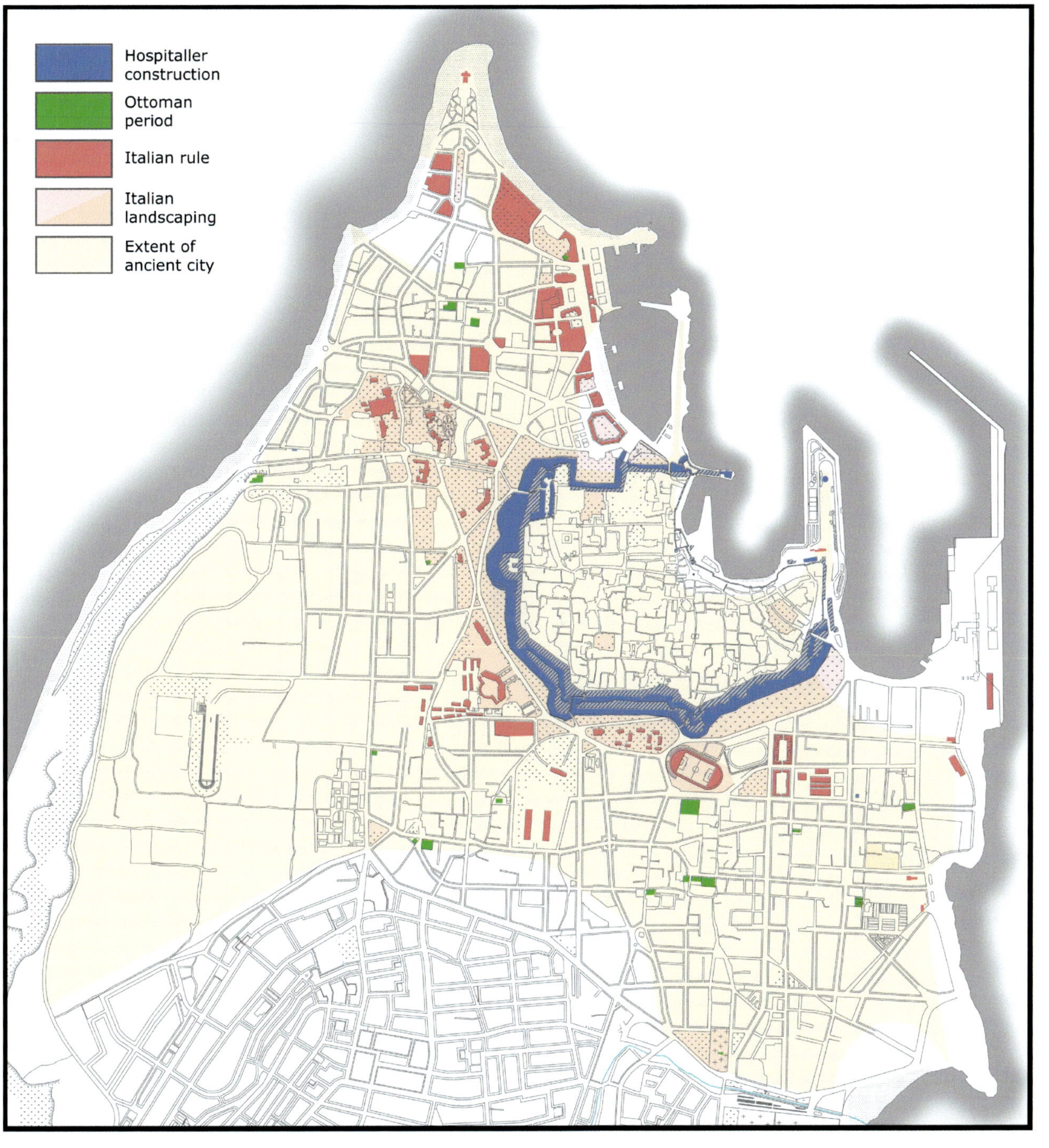

Figure 1: Italian urban remodelling in the town of Rhodes.

seven Early Christian basilicas have been located in the area covered by the ancient city;[17] their later phases come within the date-range of the present study.

Rhodes had shrunk drastically by Early Byzantine times. In the 7th century, a small part of the ancient city located on rising ground overlooking the two principal harbours was fortified (Figure 2, B). In the Byzantine period, although Rhodes was for a time a provincial capital and then an important naval base, it was rarely mentioned in the written sources. The Byzantine town is hard to discern in most archaeological sites, because it is hidden below standing Hospitaller buildings or was destroyed by their foundations, which deliberately sought the stable substrate of ancient constructions. In troubled times like the 7th or the 13th century, the history of the place and its inhabitants

[17] Manoussou-Della 2014. For the ancient substrate see n. 12 and Philemonos-Tsopotou 2004: 21-33.

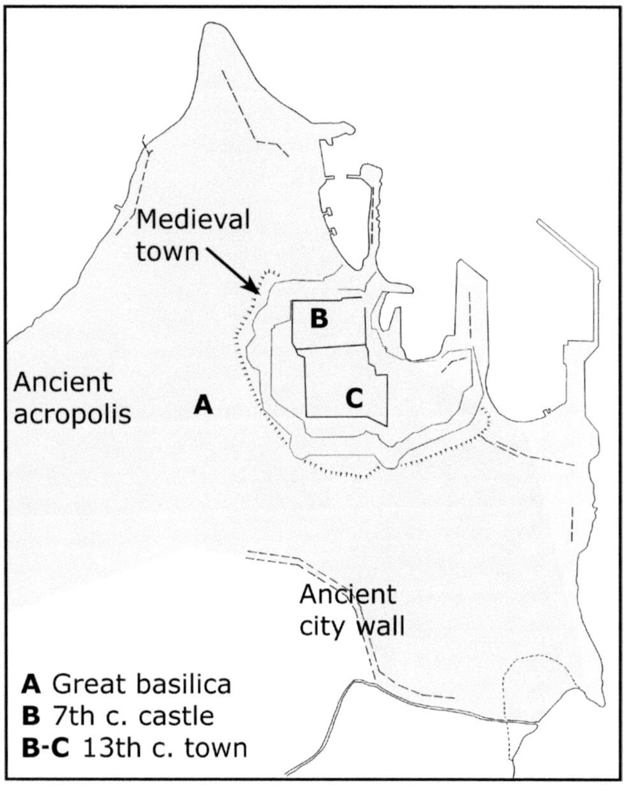

Figure 2: The urban nucleus from Hellenistic times to 1522.

is rather guessed that observed. From the 11th century, the walled settlement began to expand again (Figure 2, C), a process which continued in the Hospitaller period. Until the 14th century, historical sources provide limited and fragmentary information, mostly concerning events that affected the Byzantine state and more general political and military developments such as the Crusades.

In 1309, Rhodes was conquered by the Order of the Hospital, thus becoming the capital of a singular island state which survived until 1522. The stout Hospitaller defences with their broad and deep dry moat, preserved to this day, did not merely destroy the stratigraphy of the ground they stand on: the Knights, like their Byzantine predecessors, systematically quarried ancient structures in the vast expanse of ruins that spread outside the walls for building material to use in their own constructions, especially the fortifications. The massive disturbance caused by successive defensive structures, Byzantine and Hospitaller, which involved the recycling of older building material, the digging of great trenches and the massing of earthworks and sloping banks, is both a serious difficulty and an opportunity not sufficiently exploited: the fortifications cut through the ancient substrate but, at the same time, reveal various of its features in cross-section at a number of locations.

In the countryside of Rhodes, excavations have generally been limited to the sites of Early Christian basilicas, rescuing archaeological remains in developments involving construction within various villages or large seaside hotels; such sites seem to have emerged in Late Antiquity, particularly in agricultural areas. When the Byzantines lost control of the sea to the Arabs in the second half of the 7th century, these settlements disappeared. In addition, a number of deserted medieval villages in the interior have still to be explored. Even so, a number of archaeological sites have been investigated and new ones located; progress has also been recently made in the study of the pottery and other finds,[18] providing valuable information about Rhodes which sometimes does not accord with mainstream political developments or seems independent of them. Thus a background has been prepared which may be immensely enriched by the specialized study of the masses of material collected from excavations, fieldwork and the chance finds brought in by private individuals or seized from illegal traffickers of antiquities.

Subject-matter and structure

The present study covers the Christian coins so far treated by conservators and recorded from the period beginning with the reform of emperor Anastasius I (AD 498) and ending with the Ottoman conquest of Rhodes (1522) which are kept in the collection of the Ephorate of Antiquities of the Dodecanese (Figure 3). They mostly derive from archaeological excavations or are chance finds casually picked up by people. Most of the excavation finds were unearthed in the 1970s, '80s and '90s. Thus, the chronological boundaries are the reform of the copper coinage generally recognized as the beginning of Byzantine numismatics, and the conquest which ended the use of Christian petty coins on the island.

The work has two objectives: first, to present the material as fully as possible, in order to make it accessible to other scholars and, secondly, to draw the maximum of information from the available coin sample[19] for the political and social history of Rhodes during the ten centuries separating the Anastasian reform from the Conquest of 1522.

[18] Cf. Triandafyllides 2015; Michaelidou 1994 and 2014; Katsioti 2016.

[19] The term 'local coin sample' is used here to refer to the total of coins available to this study.

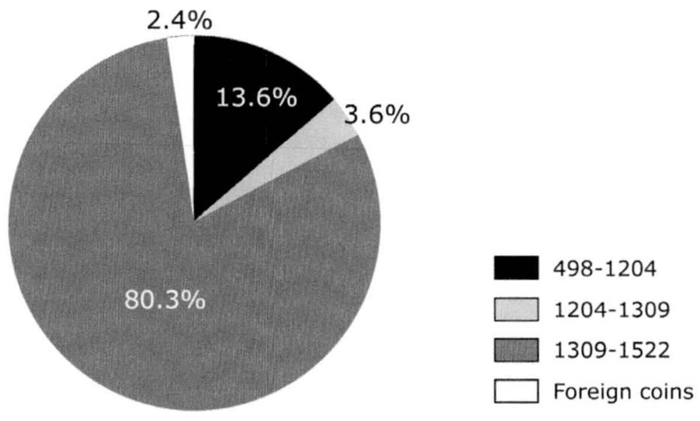

Figure 3: Chronological distribution of the coins covered by the study.

The coins presented and examined below are dealt with in two parts. The first part contains the material from Byzantine Rhodes (498-1309) and the second of the Hospitaller period (1309-1522). The Byzantine part is divided into two sections, reflecting the provenance of the coins. For several centuries the money available for daily transactions on Rhodes came from the imperial Byzantine mints. Of course, besides the scarcity of copper coins encountered in most of the Byzantine provinces between the 8th and 10th centuries,[20] local numismatic events emerged from time to time, when the need for coin apparently coincided with the temporary interruption in communications between Rhodes and the Byzantine capital. Thus the first section contains the following chapters:

- The 6th and 7th centuries
- The period from the late 7th century to 969
- The era of the anonymous *folles* (969 - 1092)
- The period from the monetary reform of Alexius I (1092) to 1204.

The second section, the 13th century, begins with the fall of Constantinople to the armies of the Fourth Crusade and ends with the conquest of Rhodes by the Knights Hospitaller in 1309. This is a transitional period, characterized by political instability and centrifugal tendencies. These characteristics resulted in the circulation of various imitations of imperial trachea and the operation of a local mint for copper. The petty coinage of the empire of Nicaea is rarely found in Rhodes, although Byzantine political and cultural influence remained dominant.

Each chapter contains, alongside the presentation of the relevant coins, a summary of available information on local history and the broader developments which might be expected to have influenced the island; special characteristics are noted, and a cautious attempt is made at interpreting the numismatic evidence.

The second part of the study deals with the Hospitaller period, from 1309 to 1522, when the medium for petty cash transactions was locally issued. Coin finds increase considerably; there are also increased numbers of foreign coins, probably indicative of the significance of overseas trade and the multiethnic character of the urban population and ruling class.

The approach to the Hospitaller period is different, due to the characteristics of the material which, although quantitatively dominant (Figure 3), derives from a much shorter period and includes important evidence from hoards. An introductory section on the coinage of the Latin East, the Order of the Hospital and a concise account of the production of its mint are followed by a description of the petty coinage, including an attempt to revise and refine coin types and their dating. Crucial for the understanding of coin production and typology is the examination of two large hoards with a *terminus a quem* most likely in the first quarter of the 15th century. The presentation of the period is concluded with the monetary reform of grand master Pierre d'Aubusson (*c.* 1490) and the numismatic evidence for the commercial ties of Rhodes with Western Europe and the Latin East.

The concluding chapter of the study attempts to summarize the changes in numismatic circulation on Rhodes from the 6th to the 16th century, with some more general comments on ongoing research, comparing the sample from Rhodes to other geographical locations in the eastern Mediterranean.

The history of the research

The focus of numismatic research in Greece is the Numismatic Museum at Athens. With its rich collection, important publications[21] and specialist library, it has enabled interested scholars and archaeologists to specialize and contribute to numismatic research. The Friends of the Numismatic Museum Society have organized a number of specialist conferences, providing a much needed platform for discussion and a permanent record by the publication

[20] Metcalf 1979: 50; Hendy 1985: 640-645; Morrisson 2010: 106 ff. On Rhodes, it begins *c.* 670 and retreats in the 11th century.

[21] Galani-Krikou *et al.* 2002; Kokkas and Nikolaou 2005.

of the proceedings.[22] Knowledgeable coin collectors and professionals have made their own contribution to the numismatics of Byzantium and Latin Greece through the publications of the Greek Numismatic Society and its annual periodical, the bilingual *Nomismatika Chronika*, whose first issue appeared in 1972.

Coins, and particularly coins of low purchasing value, have for long been accepted as important evidence for the dating of archaeological contexts, and of household pottery in the period starting from the decline of Roman cities until the end of the Ottoman period. However, while other kinds of documentary evidence, like archival material, have been used extensively to trace the individual portrait of a region, numismatics in Greece have lagged behind in this respect. This is partly due to the necessarily brief presentation of archaeological discoveries in the most important and comprehensive periodical dedicated to archaeological exploration, the *Chronika* section of the *Archaiologikon Deltion*, where the excavations of each year by every regional archaeological bureau (Ephorate) are presented in turn. The comparatively small number of coins found in a rescue excavation cannot be of much use for anything but dating. For the numismatic evidence to make sense in a broader context it is necessary for the sample to be sufficiently large to support argument, as in the large scale explorations conducted by the foreign Schools of Archaeology[23] or the various University departments engaged in research of this nature. Also, although the comparison between the numismatic profile[24] of different sites is a key part of the research, in extant publications the approach to the coinage is not consistent.

In Rhodes, the rich coin collection assembled before World War II by the Italian administration, part of which was on display in the Archaeological Museum, disappeared at the end of the war. An incomplete handwritten *Catalogo del Medagliere* is still preserved in the Library of the Ephorate of Antiquities of the Dodecanese where, after 824 ancient and Roman pieces, 25 Hospitaller coins are also listed.[25] However, some coins kept in storerooms, archives and desk drawers, escaped the fate of the bulk of this material; they include the silver *gigliato* of grand master Elion de Villeneuve (1319-46) found in a storeroom in an envelope with a pencilled note in Italian or the gold *solidus* of Byzantine emperor Basil I (867-86) found appended to a document dated 1917. It is quite possible that some of the coins now inventoried in the internal catalogue of the Ephorate without mention of provenance were also found in the Italian period. However, the fate of most of the Byzantine and Hospitaller coins undoubtedly brought to light in the Italian excavations remains a mystery. Thus, most of the coins of the archaeological collection of Rhodes examined here derive from the hundreds of excavations carried out by state archaeologists in the town after Rhodes became officially part of Greece in 1947,[26] from two large hoards discovered in obscure circumstances in the first half of the 20th century, from chance finds handed in by conscientious locals and from pieces seized from antiquities smugglers. It has to be said that the coin finds from an indeterminate number of excavated sites from the late 1990s to the present have yet to be treated and inventoried, but the currently available sample forms a solid basis for discussion.

The author's engagement with the coins of Rhodes began in 1988, as part of a wider drive to deal with the backlog of inadequately recorded finds in the storerooms of the Archaeological Service, under the direction of Elias Kollias, Director of the 4th Ephorate of Byzantine Antiquities which, from its headquarters of Rhodes, exercised a broad remit for the protection of Byzantine and later antiquities and heritage in the Dodecanese Prefecture.[27] As the inventory progressed, it became possible to compare the coin evidence with other sources for local history. Certain patterns began to emerge, as well as intriguing discrepancies with accepted interpretations and, with them, the desire to explore further and make sense of the accumulating data. From the year 2000 this led to the appearance of a number of papers by the author related to the coin evidence from Rhodes,[28] which coincided with contributions to the numismatic history of Rhodes by other scholars.[29] During the numismatists' Fourth Meeting, focusing on *Coins in Rhodes and Its Asia Minor* Peraia, (Cos, 30 May-2 June 2003), Panayota Psarri presented a communication on coin finds from the Rhodian countryside and Julian Baker one on coin circulation in the Dodecanese Islands between 1100 and 1400. Very important comparative material from Byzantine Cos was presented by Ersi Brouskari and Sophia

[22] Periodical *Obolos*.
[23] Cf. Grierson 1965c and *idem* 1966.
[24] I.e. the unique features of the *corpus* of locally found coins regarding ratios between coins of different periods and denominations.
[25] Mostly gold and silver coins (14 gigliati, 6 aspers, 3 sequins and two billon deniers, inv. nos 825-849). No Byzantine coins are mentioned.
[26] See Appendices, List of Excavated Properties and Sites with Coin Finds dated 498-1522.
[27] Under the Italian occupation of Rhodes responsible for the local antiquities was the Istituto FERT, founded in 1927 and directed, in turn, by A. Maiuri, G. Jacopi, L. Laurenzi and L. Morricone; in 1947, the latter handed over the Istituto and its appurtenances to the first Greek Ephor of Antiquities in the Dodecanese, I. Kondis, when Italy formally ceded the Dodecanese to Greece. In 1978, the Archaeological Service in the Dodecanese split into the XXII Ephorate of Prehistoric and Classical Antiquities and the 4th Ephorate of Byzantine Antiquities; they were merged again in 2014.
[28] Kasdagli 1992: 53-60; *eadem* 1996: 319-334; *eadem* 2000: 267-274; *eadem* 2002; *eadem* 2006a: 253-264; *eadem* 2006b: 325-338; *eadem* 2006c: 31-70; *eadem* 2007: 422-432; *eadem* 2010: 159-174.
[29] See *Obolos* 8-9.

Didioumi (4th-12th c.) During the Fifth Meeting, on *Coins in the Aegean Islands* (Mytilene, 16-19 September 2006), Andreas Mazarakis presented the first part of his study on the coins of Hospitaller Rhodes (1310-1476), which was later expanded to include the entire Hospitaller period in a separate publication.[30]

Increasing familiarity with the material and recent relevant publications raised questions that demanded a more methodical and comprehensive review of the coins of Rhodes. The need to include as many coins as possible in the study was time-consuming; but a generous study leave of three years by the Greek Ministry of Culture (2010-2012) permitted the updating and digitizing of the internal medieval coin catalogue of the Archaeological Ephorate of the Dodecanese, which reached a total of about ten thousand entries. An additional year's sabbatical (2015) enabled the author to put together this analysis, which includes a first attempt at setting the Byzantine and medieval coins from Rhodes in a broader context. As was expected, its contents substantially revise the views expressed by the author in earlier publications; and it is encouraging that often they seem to enhance and complement the interpretations recently proposed by other scholars studying different kinds of archaeological evidence like pottery, wall paintings and architectural remains.

Methodology

The usefulness of coins for dating purposes and, as a source of evidence, to the historian, has often been misunderstood.[31] Their role in everyday exchanges between private individuals in modern times makes it easy to forget that, for a very long time, this function was of secondary importance for the rulers. In fact, coinage was always produced under the strict supervision of the issuing authority, in order to cover mostly administrative needs, in the broader sense: to support, in various ways, a bureaucratic system and the institutions that kept it going, to promote political and military control, regularize daily interaction between soldiers and the local population they had to deal with, and enable the distribution of alms. The importance of coinage as a tool of state authority is reflected in the sentences passed on those caught counterfeiting or otherwise interfering with the official coin supply.[32]

Gold and silver pieces that escaped the recycling net of the state could have a much longer career than the copper due to their intrinsic value; while more careful striking and the symbolism of their representations encouraged their use as jewellery. Thus, the presence of individual gold or large silver coins in an archaeological context is often of limited significance for dating purposes. Moreover, the accidental loss of such pieces is relatively rare, as their value ensured care would be taken to keep them safe. Their presence in the form of hoards is much more significant, because the discovery of a hoard is usually associated with extraordinary circumstances which prevented its recovery by the original owners. For a single hoard this might be due to personal misadventure[33] but a series of hoards in a particular region is probably due to political instability and military action. In such circumstances, their dating is secure and their composition provides information for the impact of political developments to the wealthy and the administration, including mint production.[34]

In contrast, the low value of a copper coin increases its chances of getting lost or mislaid, although hoards of copper coins also occur ('hoarding' is probably not always the proper term for them). However, the presence of petty coin hoards usually has a different explanation than that of gold or silver, as it reflects different mechanisms and situations such as inflation, natural disasters, recall of the coins for recycling or, simply, carelessness. Low value usually ensured circulation within the geographical and chronological boundaries of the issuing authority. Thus, in combination with the natural durability of their fabric, frequent chance losses make petty coins valuable for dating purposes in archaeological contexts in periods when other written evidence consists of the much rarer seals and other inscribed artefacts.

[30] Mazarakis 2010. His work is of limited relevance to the present study, because it has a theoretical approach focusing on metrology, moneys of account and the role of Hospitaller coins in the economy.

[31] The modern analysis of coin finds follows the pioneering methodology of scholars such as Philip Grierson, John Kent and Michael Metcalf, all highly productive in the last quarter of the 20th century.

[32] For example, it seems that in Byzantium technicians employed by the imperial mints and the moneychangers (*katallaktai* or *argyramoivoi*) who played a key role in the distribution of copper coins might, at times, be lured into 'corrective' action when demand substantially overshot the official supply of coin. Hahn and Metlich 2000: 6. Hendy 1985: 253, 324-328. In fully monetized periods some taxes were paid exclusively in coin of high value (*charagma*) and others in smaller denominations, while the change (*strophe*) was paid by the state in copper pieces. The *katallaktai* were the middlemen who supplied the public with the required denominations.

[33] Such as the gold hoard Rhodes/1998, which is probably evidence for the tragic conclusion of a trip in the high road leading from the 12th century town to the west coast of the island. Christodoulidis 1998; Papadopoulou 2010: 175-176.

[34] Metcalf 2009: 144: *'A single hoard will offer ambiguous evidence; when a chronological sequence of several hoards provides a consistent story, its evidence is highly reliable.'*

Ease of identification generally makes copper coins handy for dating archaeological contexts. However, dating a context by a single coin find is often risky because, particularly in urban sites inhabited for a long time, the stratigraphy is seldom undisturbed. The disturbance need not be due to human action: creatures active underground, like earthworms or rats, and even the roots of long-disappeared trees, may help coins, especially the heavier ones, to travel downwards, creating confusion even in rural contexts. Moreover, clumsiness and mischance may befall at every step of the long journey of coin finds from the trowel to the desk of the coin specialist. Caution is therefore advisable if the dating evidence of a lone coin cannot be corroborated by some other means.

The larger the size of the coin sample in a particular site, the less significant occasional errors will be. This is important, because besides disturbed contexts and handling mistakes, the condition of the coins does not always permit precise identification. The sample supplied by a particular area may be studied independently from other finds, to answer questions about the relative monetization of the local society in particular periods, a factor often associated with the urbanization level of a site.[35] It may also pinpoint the centre of daily monetary exchanges in a wider area, the fluctuations of monetary circulation through time and the degree of control exercised by the central authority on the periphery of a state. In addition, it allows comparison of different sites, in order to explore issues of broader historical significance. The employment of various methodological tools such as losses per year,[36] the ratio between different denominations, the representation of different mints in the local sample, the wear pattern on the coins, the composition of the local 'numismatic profile'[37] and the comparison to other sites are useful in many ways: for example, the evaluation of coins of unknown provenance is much easier once the local numismatic profile is established, and even the derivation of coins seized from traffickers may be determined with relative accuracy.

* * *

The decision to explore the coin evidence from Rhodes across a span of ten centuries, in spite of the difficulties presented by the large number of coins and the varying degree of wear without recourse to particular excavation contexts, was taken with deliberation. The independent examination of a particular type of find is much simpler and, the larger the sample, the more likely it is that quantitative analysis will be reliable. A single coin is not much use, but the distribution on the map of all the coins of its type will produce information on the social and administrative situation; while comparisons between coin distributions at different periods will reveal much more and be very useful to scholars working with other sites or other kinds of archaeological evidence. Moreover, chance errors tend to disappear if a sample is large enough, while errors in methodology can be spotted, and compensated for, more easily. Naturally, it is necessary to take into account more general problems related to the circumstances of recovery and the condition of the coins.

The analysis of the material is based on two main premises supported by notable numismatists. The first is the significance of losses per year as an indicator of the circulation of copper and has been employed with particular success by David Metcalf and by others following in his footsteps.[38] Other scholars have occasionally expressed doubts,[39] or treated it with too much caution,[40] but with time its reliability has gained it acceptance. The second is the primary function of coin as a tool of government in reference to Byzantium clearly expressed by Wolfgang Hahn, who stressed that it was meant to facilitate the interaction of the state with the general population, regarding taxation and the supply of the armed forces[41] and other representatives of the government.[42] Thus, in the period under consideration, and particularly until 1204, the coin finds -or lack of them- should primarily be used as evidence of state policy and only secondarily as a marker for economic activity. Of course, the availability of coin facilitated exchanges between members of the public, particularly in urban settings, but this was not a primary concern for bureaucrats. This, to a lesser degree, is also true for Hospitaller Rhodes; what made the difference was the close proximity of rulers and ruled in the peculiarly cosmopolitan urban environment of the island capital. Moreover, the Hospital had strong motives to make life easier for pilgrims and other travellers and was therefore more responsive to the public need for petty cash ('black money'). Besides, the minting of fiduciary coin could be profitable for the public purse when social conditions created a need for frequent small-scale exchanges.

[35] Metcalf 2009: 145.
[36] Losses per year represent the quotient of the division of the number of coins of a particular ruler by the number of regnal years; it is used to keep track of fluctuations in coin circulation. Other time intervals may be used if more appropriate.
[37] The peculiarities of the local sample in comparison to other areas are represented by its 'numismatic profile', which is essentially the breakdown of its content into percentages across time.
[38] Metcalf 1979; *idem* 2009: 141-146.
[39] Mostly historians like Vryonis 1963: 291-300.
[40] Numismatists like Philip Grierson 1965c.
[41] Hendy 1985: 416, 646; Grierson and Travaini 1998: 41; Morrisson 2002: 911 ff.; Curta 2011: 68-92.
[42] Hahn and Metlich 2000: 7-8. This case has been taken much farther by social anthropologist David Graeber 2011.

The comparison with other parts of the Byzantine empire is helpful in weeding out general phenomena in order to look more closely into the peculiarities of the local numismatic profile.[43] Unfortunately, even the most useful publications of extensive excavations by the various Schools of Archaeology, Universities and other research agencies within and without Greece present difficulties. The oldest obviously suffer from dated identifications which have since been revised. However, these later, corrective contributions are scattered in a variety of publications and languages, which are not always easily accessible. Moreover, the presentation of a large number of coins is usually concise, preventing revision of the material according to recent scholarship without returning to the coins themselves. Finally, the plates of these publications are selective, showing legible specimens or some coins considered important by the author, but not the bulk of the material which might be more relevant to students of other regions. The condition of the coins, particularly the wear pattern, is seldom mentioned.

In this study an attempt has been made to present the material comprehensively and discuss its significance for each period in association with the historical background. More weight has been given to the examination of the coins, since the views of scholars on the broader subject and its background are likely to undergo further modifications. Many of the observations made here are not interpreted, or an interpretation is suggested with caution, in order to avoid forced arguments.

In the presentation of the material, site finds are often dealt separately from the rest of the coins within a group, whenever they are thought to present a more rounded view as, for example, in the ratio between various denominations for the period 498-668. When calculating losses per year, an effort is made to leave out hoarded coins, while the better preserved coins serve in more detailed analyses like the representation of the various mints under each emperor or more closely dated fluctuations in circulation. This ensures a fuller exploitation of the sample in order to reduce the possibility of statistical error.[44] The presentation is assisted by graphs and tables employing simple statistical approaches. For the comparisons of the Rhodian coins to those from other sites, where sample sizes vary widely, the numismatic profile (percentage of the total representing each period or emperor) for each site has been preferred, to facilitate the drawing of comparison graphs.

Integrating the evidence of the coins with the historical background faced two hurdles: the scarcity of information for Byzantine Rhodes itself in the written sources and the selective account of events by modern historians and, even more so, by the primary sources: events not directly relevant to the perceived flow of history tend to be omitted in authoritative works written with particular aims in mind although they may be able to throw some light on phenomena which have left traces in the local archaeological record. Unfortunately, the authority of major historical works in the portrayal of broader tendencies encourages the unwary to project interpretations based on wider trends, which may not be useful at the local level. For this reason, each chapter includes an extensive section attempting to trace the influence of events on the administrative setting Rhodes belonged to, in an effort to fill in some of the gaps in local history.

The attempt to link the numismatic evidence with political and military events is mostly based on recent secondary sources, because primary accounts often contain dating discrepancies the author lacked the expertise to deal with.[45] The choice of these works has been influenced by the fullness of their coverage of primary sources and relevant bibliography and their internal consistency as, for instance, in the case of the Arab invasion of Syria in the reign of Heraclius. A basic problem in the balancing of various sources of information is due to the difference of three or four months between the start of the Byzantine and Muslim calendar. The start of military campaigns is easier to date, because they generally began in the spring; and naval actions, particularly relevant to an island setting, even later. Their conclusion, which was often the result of *force majeure*, is harder to determine and frequently ended in tragedy due to bad weather. In any event, particularly for the second half of the 7th century, making a choice between alternative schedules is difficult, and some doubts must remain.

The material

The vast majority of the coins collected by the Ephorate of Antiquities in Rhodes are of low value. Most are chance losses or small parcels often found in disturbed layers. Gold and large silver coins are few indeed: 35 gold coins are

[43] The examination of coin circulation in other sites after the 12th century would have been desirable, but the variety of the coins in different locations and the fragmentation of political authority make the attempt not worth the effort, at least at present. For the problems of comparing coin samples of different regions see Guest 2012.

[44] Metcalf 1979: 11 ff.

[45] Cf. Conrad 1992: 317-401.

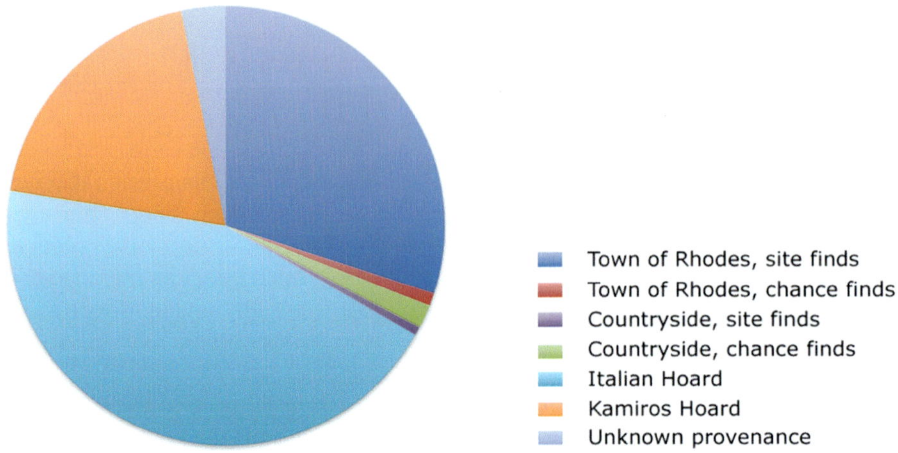

Figure 4: Provenance of the coins covered by the study.

included in the collection (of which two are debased *hyperpyra*), as well as 27 silver[46] and four of electrum. The rest of the site and chance finds are of copper or billon. It is also worth mentioning that 18 gold and two silver coins are of unknown provenance,[47] while eight of the gold pieces were presented by a native of the village of Salakos.[48] The remaining 17 gold, 13 silver and four electrum coins are single finds from excavations or chance finds of known provenance. As the gold and silver issues of the period under consideration are very poorly represented in the collection, they are mentioned without particular discussion because they are of no statistical significance and cannot be readily integrated into the main body of the material.[49] No attempt has been made to examine them in comparison to hoards and collections already published by other scholars and kept outside Rhodes, because the study of gold and silver requires a different approach and more finds.

The overwhelming majority of the inventoried Christian coins stored in the depots of the Archaeological Service or on display at the Palace of the Grand Master[50] were found on the island and were, when they were in circulation, the local medium of everyday monetary transactions. To date, the internal catalogue of the Ephorate of Antiquities contains about 10,200 pieces, which have been conserved by specialists and dated;[51] but an uncertain number of still untreated coins remain in the Service depots, a state of affairs common to most of the Ephorates of Antiquities in Greece and, the author suspects, wherever large-scale rescue excavations are carried out around the world. Of the treated coins, some came from other islands of the Dodecanese or are issues dated after 1522 and therefore of no relevance here. The remaining 9,555 pieces belong to six categories:

1. Archaeological site finds (2,845 pieces) derived from 180 excavated property plots or monuments situated within the town of Rhodes, including small purses of coins found in disturbed layers.
2. Chance finds (89 pieces) of known provenance from the town of Rhodes.
3. Chance finds from the countryside, most handed in by private citizens or archaeological inspectors (164 pieces).
4. Finds from 14 excavated sites in the countryside (63 pieces).
5. Two large Hospitaller hoards found on Rhodes under circumstances not properly documented. The first consists of 4,247 pieces and is known as the 'large hoard of the conservation lab' or the 'Italian period hoard'. According to information by Elias Kollias, it was discovered in the first half of the 20th century in the environs of a medieval building thought to have been the Hospitaller mint which still stands to the east of the Grand Masters' Palace.[52] The second hoard, comprising 1,834 pieces, was found in Kamiros on the west coast of the island, some 40 kilometres SW of the town.[53]

[46] Of which 14 derive from three hoards: Town of Rhodes/1990 (Kasdagli 1992), Paradeissi/[Italian period] (Kasdagli 1996), Town of Rhodes /1994 (Kasdagli 2006b).

[47] At least one of them was found in the Italian period.

[48] I. Varellis. It is probable that they originally belonged to two different lots: the first perhaps included the three *solidi* of Justinian I and the second three *solidi* of Heraclius and two *tremisses* of Phocas.

[49] Metcalf 2009: 144-145.

[50] Exhibition *Rhodes from the 4th Century AD to Its Capture by the Ottoman Turks (1522)*, 2004: 44-47.

[51] Some less precisely, due to poor state of preservation.

[52] Kasdagli 2013.

[53] It was accompanied by a later note of the 1960s, which was a partial copy of a decayed original.

6. Coins of unknown provenance, including seizures of illegally trafficked antiquities; some of them may be either chance finds collected just after World War II or from excavations undertaken during the Italian occupation of Rhodes. Pieces handed in by people active in other Dodecanese islands were left out of this group; others which, according to information by Elias Kollias and retired archaeological inspectors,[54] were found by farmers in the countryside, have been included in the chance finds from the countryside (category 3 above). Thus, 313 pieces (13 seized coins, 151 handed in by private citizens and 149 without documentation) are left in this category. They were included in the study because very few of them are likely to have been found outside Rhodes: generally, coins from other islands have remained in the local museums (of Cos, Calymnos, Symi and Kastellorizo) where they have been inventoried, even though they may have received treatment in Rhodes. Besides, it is unlikely that from a total of 3,473 pieces (leaving aside the two large Hospitaller hoards) a small fraction of 9% would be of particular statistical significance.

Of course, it is worth comparing the sample derived from chance finds with the picture derived from excavation coins in order to exercise appropriate caution when drawing conclusions. Chance finds are generally larger and better preserved that excavated coins, because corroded or small pieces are not so easily spotted by accident. From 553 chance finds, 147 (26%) are medieval deniers and obols of the period 1309-1522, with an average weight of less than 0.7 grams. However, of those, 45 are kept in the sacristy of the parish church of the village of Archangelos and the possibility that they derive from one or two small hoards is likely. If the Archangelos group is left out, the percentage of this period drops to 20% of the chance finds. For reasons explained in detail below, to reduce as far as possible the imbalance in the comparison between chance and excavated finds, post-1204 coins should be excluded from the weight graph.[55] In this, chance finds are represented by the paler line while excavation coins by the darker one:

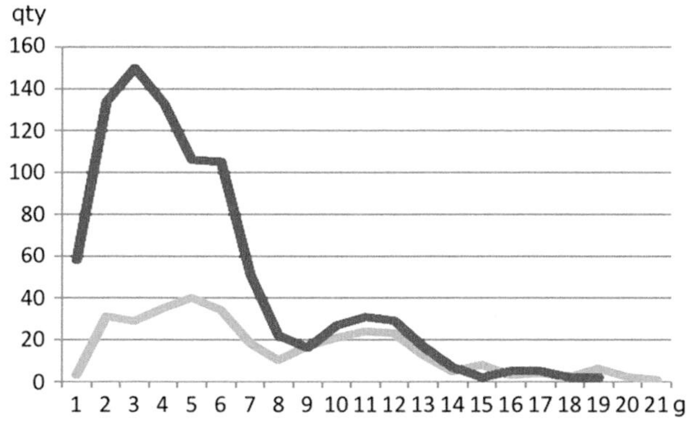

Figure 5: Comparison of site and chance finds by weight.

It is obvious that the proportion of chance finds relative to the total number of coins of a certain weight increases with weight. A second graph (Figure 6), with the percentages of increasing weight makes this clearer.

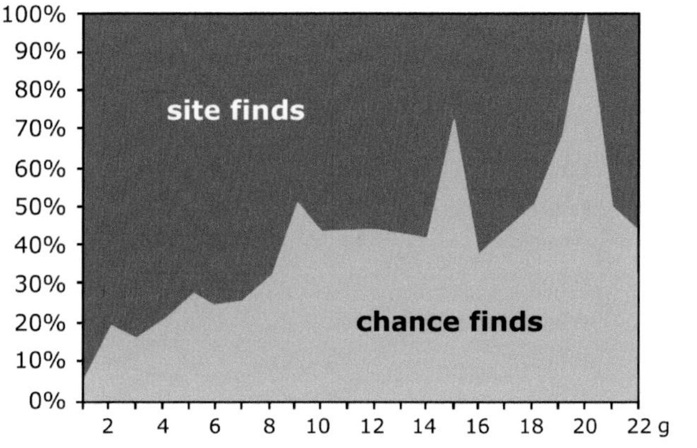

Figure 6: Comparison of the ratio of chance against site finds according to weight.

The calculation of losses per year is not without its problems: apart from the difficulty of dating with precision worn scyphate coins, and the fact that some of the coins of unknown provenance may be from old excavations, an indeterminate number of small purses deposed as grave offerings is concealed among the coins recovered from disturbed contexts in excavated churches of the medieval town (13th c. onwards); due to repeated use of the graves, these deposits have been mixed up.[56]

The following table, showing concisely the percentages of coins of each period in a number of churches which have yielded over 50 coins, is instructive:

[54] Special thanks are due to Emeritus Ephor of Antiquities Dr. I. Papachristodoulou, retired archaeological inspector P. Misodoulakis and Mr. K. Pharmakides.

[55] It comprises coins whose weight ranges from less than one to 20 grams.

[56] The regularity of this phenomenon in Rhodes and the type of the coins preclude the possibility that the graves were a convenient hiding place for the savings of the living, a practice recorded elsewhere. Avramea 2001: 15. For funerary coin deposits outside Greece see Travaini 2004.

	SITE	498 - 1204	1204 - 1309	1309 - 1522	Uncertain	Coin total
1	St Michael's (Demirli) with Haliloglou - Konstantinidis plots	9,8%	12,2%	76,3%	1,6%	558
2	SS Constantine & Helena with Minatsis plot	20,5%	25,1%	50%	4,3%	342
3	Panaitiou St.	11%	4,2%	87,8%	-	310
4	Pekmetzis plot	75,4%	15,2%	8,8%	0,6%	171
5	St Artemius and Nikolis plot	15%	1,8%	83,2%	-	167
6	St Mary of the Castle	77,5%	4,2%	12,5%	5,8%	120
7	Asprakis, Maravelias and Hasapoglou plots	57,8%	14,7%	26,6%	0,9%	109
8	Hatziandreou plot (great basilica of Rhodes)	72%	1,2%	25,6%	1,2%	82
9	St Spyridon	12%	9,3%	78,7	-	75
10	St Mary of the Burgh	1,6%	-	98,4%	-	63
11	St Mark	7,1%	14,3%	78,6%	-	56

Figure 7: Percentages of excavated coins by period in key sites.

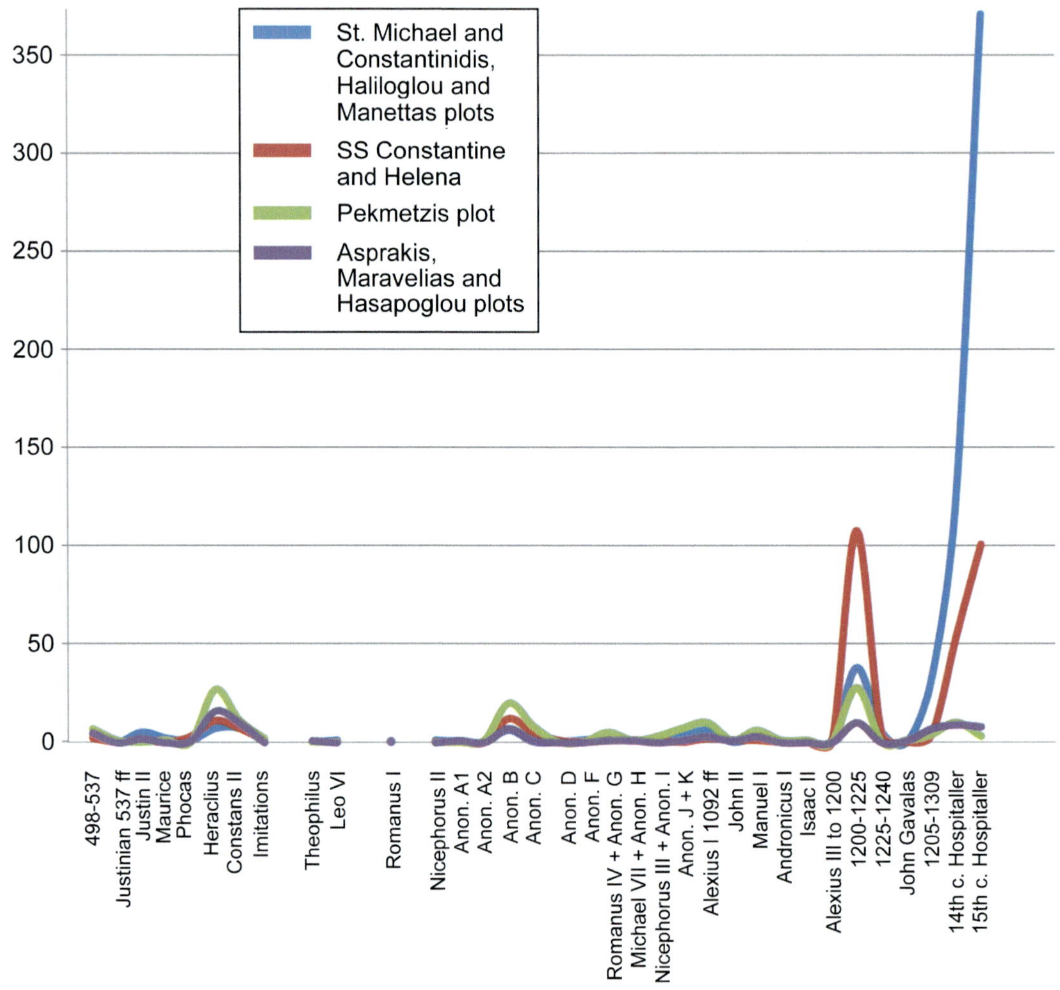

Figure 8: Comparison of coin finds from secular and religious sites.

In churches with burials dating from the 13th to the early 16th century, the percentage of coins from the period 1204-1522 always exceeds 75% of the total. St Michael's, built on top of an Early Christian basilica, was probably the Orthodox cathedral of the Hospitaller period and succeeded a smaller medieval church: this explains the elevated number of imperial Byzantine coins. The site of Panaitiou St., which includes the conventual church of the Order of St John, is an extreme case; although most of the graves in that church are without burial offerings, a single secular burial furnished with a variety of grave goods also contained about 190 small coins, representing 56.3% of the coin finds from the entire site. The Hatziandreou plot outside the medieval town, on the east slope of the ancient acropolis, contains the great Early Christian basilica of Rhodes; the Hospitaller coins found on the site probably mark the presence of crews quarrying building stone for the Hospitaller fortifications from its ruins. St Mary of the Castle is not a real exception either: only a small part of it has been excavated, and the focus of the dig was the holy water spring underneath the sacristy sealed off in Hospitaller times. However, in the Asprakis, Maravelias and Hasapoglou plots, adjacent to each other, there was no church and the site was excavated to a depth of five metres down to Hellenistic levels; and in the Pekmetzis plot, where burials are earlier, the percentage of post-1204 coins is low. Of course, many of these sites have not been archaeologically exhausted, but this does not undermine to a significant degree the exaggerated representation of the later period in the coin sample (Figure 8).

If the two large Hospitaller hoards, which together make up 64% of the material from Rhodes, and the chance finds are subtracted from the coin sample, the chronological distribution of the coins is modified, in comparison to Figure 3, as follows:

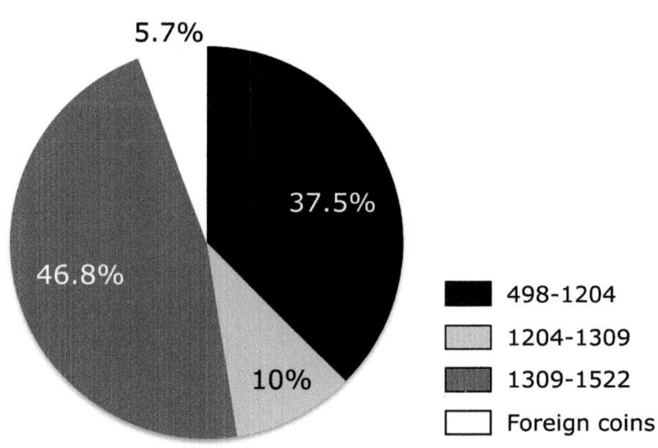

Figure 9: Chronological distribution of site finds.

Although uneven in length, the three periods reflect the history of Rhodes and each of them has its own special features. The majority of foreign coins belong to the period after 1204, and most of them date from the Hospitaller period. Of course, it is necessary to divide the presentation of the material in smaller instalments when particular characteristics dictate a modified approach. This has determined the structure of each chapter. Thus, the coins of the intervals 498-668, 969-1025 and 1092-1204 are analyzed emperor by emperor, while those of 668-969, 1025-1092 and 1204-1309 are examined alongside broader political, administrative and economic developments. The Hospitaller period is explored in greater depth because of the quantity and originality of the available material: the introductory section is followed by the presentation of the petty coinage of the 14th and 15th centuries, in much greater detail than ever before through the exploitation of key evidence from hoards. The brief *excursus* into the foreign coin finds constitutes a glimpse into the overseas contacts of Rhodes. The concluding chapter, apart from a summary of the new information made available in this study and a note on the work still to be done, contains comparisons with other areas of the Byzantine empire with substantial coin finds, an exercise of wider interest because it is also useful as a control of various published interpretations of the numismatic evidence.

The Bibliography contains most of the reading which helped the arguments in the text to take shape, although some of it is not directly cited. The appendices include lists of the land plots which produced the Byzantine and Hospitaller finds and maps with their location on the ground (Maps I and II), as well as the coins from each plot. A few important assemblages of coins are also included, as well as maps with the spatial distribution of coins of different periods (Maps III-VIII)[57]. The Catalogue contains almost all the recorded coins up to 1309, a representative selection of Hospitaller petty coin types and all the foreign coins. With some exceptions due to technical problems, all the coins in the Catalogue also figure in the Plates. Throughout the text and notes, bold figures refer to each coin's number in the Catalogue and Plates.

[57] Individual pie charts for each site which has yielded more than one coin help contrast the representation of different periods covered by each map; a tile shape indicates a hoard or singular context, the number within referring to the number of coins involved.

PART I. BYZANTIUM
(498 - 1309)

Period of the Imperial Mints (498-1204)

1. The 6th and 7th Centuries

850 coins date from the period between the monetary reform of Anastasius I in 498 and the death of Constans II in 668, an interval of 170 years; they represent 67% of the imperial Byzantine coins on the island. The numismatic dominance of the early period is remarkable. Most of the emperors of the period are represented in the sample: only coins from the joint rule of Justin I and Justinian I (April to June 527) and that of Constantine III and Heraclonas, and of Heraclonas alone (February to September 641) are missing. Figure 10 compares the representation of each emperor in the coins. Excavation finds are distinguished from the rest, of known and unknown provenance, because this is of some significance and will come up again. In absolute numbers, the representation of each emperor may be broken down as follows:

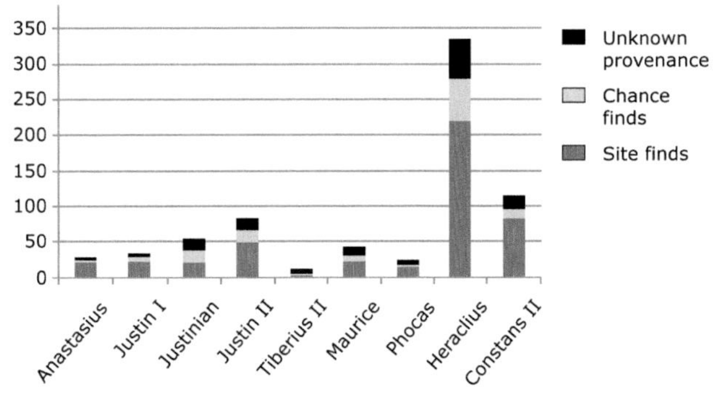

Figure 10: Number of coins by emperor, 498-668.

	Coins	Conversion into nummi	Losses per year	Losses per year in nummi
Anastasius I, [498] - 518	29	396	1.45	19.8
Justin I, 518 - 527	36	691	4	76.7
Justinian I, 527 - 565	59	1,453[58]	1.4[58]	37.3[58]
Justin II, 565 - 578	84	1,582	6.5	121.7
Tiberius II, 578 - 582	11	235	2.2	47
Maurice, 582 - 602	42	1,140	2	54.2
Phocas, 602 - 610	26	547[59]	3[59]	68.4[59]
Heraclius, 610 - 641	337	11,518[60]	10.6[60]	371.6[60]
Constans II, 641 - 668	123	4,154[61]	4,3[61]	159.8[61]

Figure 11: Coins by emperor and losses per year, 498-668.

Losses per year are considered an indicator for the relative velocity of circulation during an emperor's rule. The conversion of the number of pieces into *nummi* is intended to overcome the varying representation of different denominations. However, the first column also includes gold pieces and a small hoard of 18 copper pieces concealed about 660, which, naturally, are not included in the losses per year.

Besides the precisely identified coins there are some, mostly excavation coins whose worn condition has allowed only partial identification:

	Coins	Conversion into nummi	Percentage of the total of coins of the relevant period
Pentanummia 498-610	65	325	48.9 %[62]
Other doubtful 498-610	22	384	7 %
Doubtful 610-668	9	172	2.4 %

Figure 12: Inadequately dated coins, 498-668.

[58] Leaving out 5 solidi from the total on the left column. Gold coins are omitted from column 3, since with gold it is not possible to distinguish chance losses from hoarding.
[59] Leaving out two tremisses from the total on the left column.
[60] Leaving out two solidi from the total on the left column and 14 copper pieces from a hoard (Gavoyannis plot, medieval town of Rhodes).
[61] Leaving out five solidi, one semissis and two tremisses from the total on the left column, and four copper pieces from Gavoyannis hoard.
[62] Of the total representation of the denomination.

The reason that partially identified pieces of the period 610-668 are far fewer in number than those for the interval between 498-610 is due to the relative dearth of smaller denominations which are more vulnerable to corrosion. The late doubtful identifications consist of just two folles, two half-folles, three quarter-folles and a dodecanummium, while the partially identified pieces of the period between 498-610 include, besides the pentanummia with a christogram with illegible obverse legend which should be split between Justin I and Justinian I, three folles, seven half-folles, four quarter-folles, 28 pentanummia and seven dodecanummia. Thus, the dating problems of a sizeable proportion of the sample from the period 498-610 should be kept in mind, while the problem practically disappears under Heraclius and Constans II, where the partially legible pieces form a very small proportion of the total.

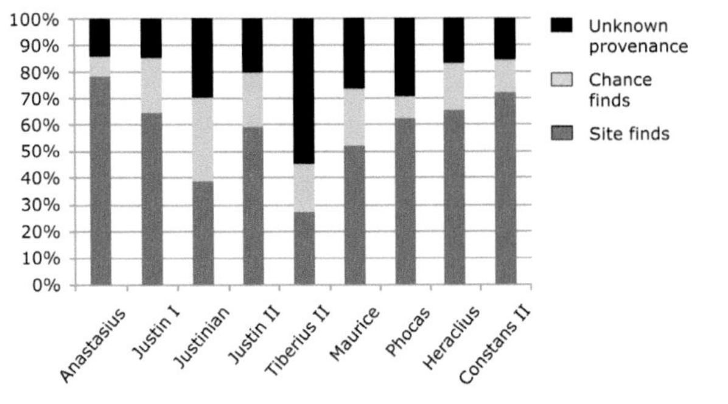

Figure 13: Percentages of coin provenance by emperor, 498-668.

A significant proportion of pieces handed in by private individuals among the coins of a particular emperor should also be treated with caution, especially if his total is modest. A typical example is Tiberius II (Figure 13). This raises questions not only for Tiberius, whose coins of unknown provenance exceed 50% of the total; but also for Maurice, Phocas and, more importantly, Justinian I. This phenomenon is partly due to the circulation of large and impressive folles at this time, which are easily noticed by laymen and are frequently picked up as surface finds: in excavation spoil, after ploughing or heavy rain such pieces, with a diameter often exceeding 3 cm and a weight ranging between 15 and 25 grams, are hard to pass by. Besides, in the case of Tiberius, the total sample is very small- a mere 11 coins. In this case even one deliberate acceptance by staff of a coin handed in by a member of the public may be of disproportionate significance. It is a common experience amongst archaeologists serving in regional offices to be confronted by copper coins of the period 498-668 handed in by private individuals for a modest cash reward. The inevitable bureaucratic procedure for the acquisition of coins of essentially insignificant worth often makes staff reluctant to receive them, since there is always a healthy degree of doubt as to their provenance[63], while members of the public are also often inclined to think that the staff -or the State- are out to exploit them by offering too small a reward. Thus issues which are rarer, and thus more welcome, may easily be disproportionally represented in the total of non-excavation coins. With these limitations in mind, the coins of each emperor will be examined in turn.

Anastasius I (491 - July 518)

The efficient administration of Anastasius, formerly a career bureaucrat specializing in state finance, is generally recognized. The relative encouragement he showed to urban entrepreneurship was balanced by stringency towards the countryside. By the end of his reign a reserve of 320,000 centenaria of gold had built up, a sum which must be considered huge, particularly in a period when the value of gold was much higher than today. The emperor undertook his reform of the copper coinage in 498, immediately after he had successfully dealt with the rebellious Isaurians.[64] Until then, the available petty cash consisted of tiny *nummi* or *minimi*,[65] which apparently changed hands by the fistful, if we are to judge by the term *follis* (purse) employed for the new large forty-nummus piece which entered circulation in 498, alongside subsidiary denominations of twenty- and ten-nummus pieces. The reform of the copper coinage aimed to facilitate the implementation of a number of new regulations concerning taxation, salaries and the state purchase of commodities at set prices drawn between 491 and 498.[66]

Folles	Half-folles	Quarter-folles	Pentanummia	Minimi
7	3	1	7	11

Figure 14: The coins of Anastasius.

[63] This mistrust is not excessive: the coins may be the result of clandestine operations and their disposal in the illegal traffic of antiquities considered not sufficiently rewarding. It is also possible for these coins to have been found in Asia Minor or even further away: Grierson, 1965c, mentions the practice of Western antiquities sellers to return coins of low value to the East in order to tempt tourists. Besides, large numbers of recent imitations circulate throughout the Near East, some of which may easily fool those not sufficiently experienced to identify them.

[64] Ostrogorsky 1980: 64-68.

[65] Frequently the two terms are treated as interchangeable. The term minimus is generally preferred for these tiny coins, because the metrology indicates that some at least might be equivalent to two nummi. Here minimus refers to the denomination, while nummus indicates the unit of the system.

[66] Hahn and Metlich 2000: 13-15.

A problem relating to the coins of Anastasius in Rhodes concerns the 11 minimi found on the site of the great basilica of Rhodes at the Hatziandreou plot, most in the fill of a drain but not, apparently, in a group (PL. 2). They represent 38% of the pieces of this emperor, although less than 5% if his total is converted to nummi[67]. They tend to influence unduly the emperor's statistics based on the number of coins, and it is not possible to date them relative to the pivotal date of 498, as Anastasius ascended the throne in 491 and the only copper he issued before 498 were minimi. Of course, the production of minimi continued throughout the reign, that is to say for another 21 years, which means than there is a 3:4 chance of their belonging to the period after 498. This, as well as the fact that they expose a weakness in statistics based on the number of coins, have led to their inclusion into the period under examination in this study. For Anastasius, at least, losses per year are better expressed in nummi (19.8) than by the number of coins (1.4).[68]

The rest of Anastasius' coins (PL. 1-2, Figure 14) are seven folles, three half-folles, a quarter-follis and seven pentanummia. Four of the folles are chance finds of which one was found in the countryside without further details regarding provenance, while for the other three there is no information at all. A half-follis and the unique quarter-follis are chance finds from the town of Rhodes; another half-follis is of unknown provenance. The other 12 pieces were found in archaeological sites: four (two folles and two pentanummia) in the medieval town and seven from excavations outside the medieval walls, five of them in the wider area of the great Early Christian basilica of the Hatziandreou plot where the 11 minimi were also discovered.

The following are also to be noted: Officina E dominates the -admittedly small- sample of the folles by a ratio of 5:1, with the only other officina present being A (a single specimen). In the fully legible pentanummia officina B predominates by a ratio of 2:1. One pentanummium (**17**) seems to date from the period 512-517 (Constantinople), but stylistically is more akin to the output of Nicomedia, while the character accompanying the value numeral is not clear- it might be either B or N. Another pentanummium (**18**) shows dots in the field on either side of the horizontal stroke of the E, but the letter in the position of the officina is a problem: it might be A, Δ, or even N.

Finally, the ratio between excavation folles and smaller denominations (half-folles, pentanummia and minimi) is 3 : 1 : 6 : 11 (by number of coins) or 1 : 0.3 : 2 : 3.6. Seven of the excavation coins are securely dated after 515, while another four between the years 512-517.

This is a rather poor representation, which reflects the decline of the ancient city. It should not be forgotten that in Late Antiquity Rhodes, which from approximately AD 300 was the capital of the *Provincia Insularum*, was struck by destructive earthquakes under Antoninus Pius in 142,[69] Constantius in 344/5[70] and Zeno.[71] About the middle of the 5th century it had been attacked by the Vandals,[72] while in 469/470 it had been plundered by the Isaurians.[73] Obviously the 5th century had not been easy for the island, and its misfortunes were crowned by the great earthquake of AD 515. Anastasius repaired the city wall (apparently reduced in extent) and drains, harbours and baths,[74] but the general condition of the city in his times must have been depressing, as coins of the emperor were only recovered in the environs of the great basilica and the 'great harbour', the most important of the five ancient harbours (excavations of the Maravelias and Hasapoglou plots).

Justin I (July 518 - August 527)

The coin finds of Justin I show some improvement. His reign is represented by 36 coins (PL. 3-4, Figure 15). Of those three (two folles and a minimus) come from excavations in the countryside,[75] more specifically from the villages of Kremasti, Mesanagros and Tholos respectively. Two chance finds come from the environs of the village of Archangelos (a follis and a half-follis). There are also five pieces of unknown provenance (two folles and three pentanummia). The remaining 25 are from the town of Rhodes, 20 from archaeological excavations and four chance finds (the latter one half-follis and three pentanummia).

[67] Assuming that a minimus was valued at 2 nummi.
[68] For the significance of petty coin hoards see Curta 2011: 77 ff.
[69] Aelius Aristeides [1898]: 72-95; Papadopoulos 2014: 56-77.
[70] Papadopoulos 201: 78-79.
[71] Papadopoulos 2014: 79.
[72] Under Theodosius II (408-450) or Marcian (450-57). Bury 1958: 257 n. 2: Nestorius, [Panegyris Herakleidou ek Damaskou, c. 451], 331.
[73] Under Leo I (457-74): Leo had failed to disband all the independent corps of the bucellarii, Isaurians and armed slaves in the previous year. Lenski 1999: 451 n. 194.
[74] John Malalas [1831]: 406; Papadopoulos 2014: 79-82.
[75] For the coins in the countryside see Appendices, Coin finds of the period 498-1522 and Map VIII.

	Folles	Half-folles	Pentanummia	Minimi
Constantinople	10	2	14	
Nicomedia	1		1	
Antioch		1		
Thessalonica		1		
?	2		3	1
TOTAL	**13**	**4**	**18**	**1**

Figure 15: The coins of Justin I.

The less important mints of Nicomedia, Antioch and Thessalonica are represented by four coins. The mint of Constantinople is dominant, with 26 coins, while six partly legible coins (two folles and three pentanummia) cannot, with certainty, be assigned to a particular mint. Among the folles officina E is still the most common, but no longer dominant: there are also two pieces of officina Γ, and one each of officinae A and Δ. In the fully legible pentanummia no officina stands out: there are three of officina A, two of B, four of Γ and two of Δ.

The distribution of the coins across the town is similar to that under Anastasius, with greater dispersal in the medieval town and the majority of those found outside the walls in the wider area of the great basilica of Rhodes. Losses per year amount to 4 or, rendered in nummi, to 76.7. Finally, the ratio between excavation folles and lesser denominations (half-folles and pentanummia) is 9 : 2 : 13 or 1 : 0.2 : 1.4.

Justinian I (August 527 - November 565)

The 'Justinianic prosperity' was at least partly due to the cautious fiscal policy of Anastasius I and the gold reserve that emperor had amassed.[76] Justinian embarked on the reconquest of imperial territories in the West, although the cost in resources was as great as its negative impact on the reconquered regions; in the east the emerging Persian threat was contained and large-scale rebuilding took place in the provinces, bolstering local economies, at least temporarily. Nevertheless, the demographic blow dealt by the bubonic plague[77] was succeeded, in the closing years of Justinian's reign, by new problems in both foreign policy and the economy.

The 56 coins of Justinian (PL. 5-9) include five gold solidi. These were all handed in, but a provenance from the town of Rhodes is recorded for three of them. They are all dated between 542 and 565; one is from officina Z and the other four from officina I. Two fifths of the copper coins of the emperor were minted in Constantinople (21 pieces, 41%), but there are also 12 from Antioch (23%), seven from Nicomedia (13%), three from Cyzicus (6%), two from Thessalonica (4%), and one each from Alexandria and Sicily (2% each).

	Solidi	Folles	Half-folles	16N	12N	Quarter-folles	5N
Constantinople	5	13	3			3	2
Nicomedia		4	3				
Cyzicus		3					
Antioch		6	3				3
Alexandria					1		
Thessalonica			1	1		1	
Sicily							1
?		2	2				
TOTAL	**5**	**28**	**13**		**1**	**3**	**6**

Figure 16: Coins securely dated to the reign of Justinian I.

Of the folles, six belong to officina B; officina E follows with four. However, the important thing is that under Justinian, from 538 onwards, the regnal year was added on the coins and other large denominations; this enables

[76] Laiou 2002: 12.

[77] The first epidemic of 541/542 was followed by others: in 558, when the dome of the church of Hagia Sophia was under repair, the plague reappeared in the capital. Rosen 2007: 290-293.

us to follow fluctuations in circulation more precisely than before. From the period before 537 there are only three folles, three half-folles an a 16-nummus piece. Then we have:

YEAR	Constantinople	Nicomedia	Cyzicus	Antioch	TOTAL
538/539 (XII)	1				**1**
539/540 (XIII)	2	3			**5**
540/541 (XIIII)		1			**1**
541/542 (XV)	5	2	1		**8**
542/543 (XVI)	1				**1**
543/544 (XVII)	1				**1**
546/547 (XX)	1				**1**
547/548 (XXI)	1			1	**2**
548/549 (XXII)			1		**1**
550/551 (XXIIII)				1	**1**
551/552 (XXV)			1		**1**
553/554 (XXVII)	1				**1**
556/557 (XXX)				1	**1**
558/559 (XXXII)				1	**1**
559/560 (XXXIII)				1	**1**
560/561 (XXXIIII)	1				**1**
563/564 (XXXVII)				1	**1**
564/565 (XXXVIII)		1			**1**

Figure 17: Dating of Justinian's coins after the reform of 538 (pentanummia excepted).

There are peaks in years 13 (539/540) and 15 (541/542), and a steep fall afterwards, the low level being maintained until the end of the reign. The break is most likely due to the great plague which spread through the empire in 542, and had lasting consequences.[78] Also interesting is the representation of the mint of Antioch from 548 on.[79]

There are only 21 excavation coins, of which one comes from the Kymisala site near Monolithos in south Rhodes. Of the 32 coins handed in, half are of unknown provenance; of the 16 whose provenance is recorded, 9 come from the town of Rhodes and 7 from the villages of Archangelos (3 pieces), Yennadi (2 pieces), Kalathos and Lardos. It is typical that of the stray finds 20 are folles of large size, weighing between 15 and 25 grams. The impressive appearance of the coins must have been the main reason that we have a comparatively high number of stray finds which dominate the sample. If a quantity of smaller denominations equivalent to that of the site finds, which have not been picked up, corresponds to them, the actual rate of losses per year of 1.4 (or 37.3 nummi) should be adjusted upwards. As it is, both indices are higher than those of Anastasius, but lower than those of Justin II. The dispersal in the countryside is higher, while distribution within the medieval walls is more regular.

The denomination ratio in the excavation coins (half-folles, quarter-folles, pentanummia) is 8 : 7 : 3 : 2 or 1 : 1 : 0.4 : 0.25. However, it should be stressed here that the ratio for the pentanummia is undermined by the inability to adequately identify a considerable number of pieces. The problem affects the type with a worn profile bust on the obverse shared between the three first emperors of the period, preventing us from precisely assigning the coins to the right ruler; but also the even more common type with a christogram on the reverse, which was issued by both Justin I and Justinian. A closer look at the problem follows, because of the abundant issue of this denomination by the following emperor, Justin II; his statistics are disproportionally higher because of a shift in the iconography, with the emperor's portrait replaced by his monogram, which made his pentanummia unmistakable even when badly preserved.

[78] Even follis **78**, which was pierced and used as a pendant (commemorative?) might be associated with the dramatic consequences of the plague, as it bears the date 541/542.

[79] Antioch had been devastated by the Persians in 540. Its mint opened temporarily in 542/543, during the plague, but operations broke off again until 546/547. Hahn 1973: Prägetabelle VIII.

Pentanummia with dating problems (512-565)

The difficulty of properly identifying the 26 pentanummia with a profile bust on the obverse and E on the reverse (PL. 22) affects the statistics of four emperors: Anastasius I, Justin I, Justinian I and Maurice (see also Figure 18), while that of the 37 pieces with a christogram on the reverse (Pl. 10) affects only Justin I and Justinian but is, due to its large representation in comparison to other types of these emperors, of greater importance. The statistics of Justinian are more affected, because none of the types he issued were exclusive to his reign: the one with the christogram which was issued until 537 and the one with the E later on were also used by other emperors.

More particularly, in 512 Anastasius began the circulation of pentanummia with a profile imperial bust on the obverse and the value E on the reverse. In 517 dots were added to the lower field on either side of the horizontal stroke of the E; after his death in July 518, Justin I continued with this variant until about 522. At this time the central mint issued a third type, with its initials CON (=Constantinople) added to the reverse. Experimentation continued after 522, with the issue of five other types, of which three do not concern us here, since they have yet to be found on Rhodes. These were followed by the two first types with the christogram, of which the second displays dots in the lower field, on either side of the vertical stroke of the P. Five types issued in five years, i.e. until 527, probably indicate a yearly type shift although, at the moment, the possibility that some of them may have entered circulation concurrently cannot be excluded. When the other eastern mints began to produce pentanummia, Antioch shortly after 512, Nicomedia about 517, Thessalonica in 518 and, finally Cyzicus in 538, the issues of Antioch and Thessalonica were easy to distinguish from those of the capital. Those of Nicomedia were distinguished by a N in the place of the officina mark and those of Cyzicus, yet to be found on Rhodes, by the characters K/Y (Justinian) and K (Maurice). Thus, of the coins of the first type it is generally harder to identify those issued in Constantinople.

	Theoretical weight of folles	Average weight of folles found on Rhodes	Theoretical weight of pentanummia	Average weight of pentanummia found on Rhodes
Anastasius I, 512-18	18.04	15.5	2.25	2.25
Justin I, 518-27	18.04	15.7	2.25	2.08 (2.29+1.87)
Justinian I, 527-38	18.04	18	2.25	-
Justinian I, 538-42	23.19	21.25	3	
Justinian I, 542-50	21.64	18.5	2.7	1.81
Justinian I, 550-[552]	18.04	17.2	2.25	
Justin II, 565-78	15.46	12.2	1.9	1.7
Tiberius II, 578-82	13.53	11	1.7	1.7
Maurice, 582-602	13.53	10.2	1.7	1.4[26]

Figure 18: Comparison of theoretical weight of Constantinopolitan issues with the average weight of Rhodian specimens (folles-pentanummia).

In the major part of the period when the two types of interest here were issued, 144 pentanummia were produced from a pound (324 grams) of copper. The theoretical weight of the coins was about 2.25 grams in the intervals between 512 and 522, 538 and 552[81] and 582 to 602.[82] The pentanummia with a christogram but without the dots at lower field continued in production under Justinian until 538, with the same weight. In 538, the reform that introduced the regnal year on the folles, half-folles and quarter-folles, the weight of copper coins was increased for a while. Thus, from 538 to 542, pentanummia were issued at 108 pieces to the pound, with a theoretical weight of 3 grams, and from 542 to 550 at 120 pieces to the pound, with a theoretical weight of 2.7 grams. From 550 the theoretical weight of the pentanummia had returned to 2.25 grams. Under Justin II the weight was slightly reduced to 1.9 grams and under Tiberius II from an initial 2.25 grams it was gradually reduced to 1.7 grams, to level off there under Maurice. Unfortunately, even if the coins leaving the mind had been accurately adjusted to the theoretical weight, something that did not happen, the variation in weight is of little help in dating the relatively badly preserved excavation finds of Rhodes. Morrisson has published a table comparing, among other things, the theoretical weight of the folles with the average weight encountered in excavation pieces from the Athenian Agora.[83] In the same way, it is possible to

[80] Value derived from a single specimen.

[81] Justinian may have ceased to issue pentanummia after 552. Hahn and Metlich 2000: 58.

[82] Hahn 1973; Hahn and Metlich 2000.

[83] Morrisson 1989: 248, Pl. 2.

draw comparisons with the Rhodian finds, both the more securely identified folles and the pentanummia, in order to expose the magnitude of the problem (Figure 18).

In the table above the folles serve as a control: their identification and dating are easier, and the loss of weight through corrosion is relatively lower. Even there, however, the smaller the representation in the sample, the less secure are the results: the single follis of Justinian dating from before 538 happens to be in very good condition and thus much closer to the theoretical weight of the issue in comparison to the other results in the relevant column, where the gap between theoretical and average weight ranges from 2 to 3.3 grams. Of course, this gap may partly be due to the tolerance accorded by the mint to variations in the weight of individual coins and from one ruler to the next, but this, in the larger denomination, should not be too great.

The last column, with the pentanummia of Rhodes, is deeply problematic. The tolerance of variations between individual coins leaving the mint would be comparatively greater in the smaller coins which, in addition, are more susceptible to deterioration. In some of the types shared between different emperors, the only reliable basis for identification is the obverse inscription with the imperial name, which is usually illegible: most of the time, even the length of the inscription cannot be estimated. The value recorded for the finds of Anastasius, precisely equivalent to the theoretical weight, is obtained from coins in fine condition of a particularly legible type (imperial bust/ E with dots). The value for Justin I would have been higher than the theoretical weight of the issue had it been based only on coins of this type (2.29 grams). However, as there are also coins of another of his types (christogram with dots at lower field compartments), which may be identified even when more worn (1.8 grams), his average falls to the more realistic value of 2.08 grams. Unfortunately for Justinian, the pentanummia he issued before 538 bear no distinguishing mark to tell them apart from those of Justin I without dots at the lower field compartments; the same holds true for his post-538 pentanummia which, as a type, were also issued under Anastasius, Justin I and Maurice. It may be more likely that an unassigned piece weighing over 2.25 grams belongs to the period 538-550, but this would also depend on the circulation of his pentanummia in comparison with his predecessors'. Besides, there are only two such pieces in the local sample,[84] while we already have five pieces of comparable weight from the reigns of Anastasius and Justin I. Thus, unfortunately, the weight of the pentanummia fails as a criterion for a precise identification.

Of greater interest for the identification of worn pentanummia seems to be the diameter which, unfortunately, has not been so systematically studied. Variations in the size of the flans are treated by scholars as an aspect of style. Naturally, the diameter by itself is not sufficient. If, however, other features are taken into account, eight coins may be assigned to Maurice, or even Heraclius, due to the broad, irregular flan and coarse style.[85] Of the rest, the limited number of letters in the legend signifies that four pieces probably belong to Justin I,[86] while for the opposite reason two more may be assigned to Anastasius.[87] Four coins belong to the type with the dots between the horizontal stroke of the E, and therefore to the interval 517-522, without sufficient evidence to determine the emperor, either Anastasius or Justin I,[88] while nine coins remain without precise identification, of which one was minted in Nicomedia,[89] and therefore was issued after 517. One more is worth noticing because the A in the position of the officina mark is placed on its side, base outwards (**356**).

12 of the pentanummia with a christogram on the reverse definitely belong to the reign of Justin I: nine because they bear dots in the lower central compartments of the field,[90] one because the inscription is legible and another one because of its short length. Two were issued by officina A, one by B, two more from officina Δ, two from either A or Δ, one possibly from Γ. Still another may belong to the mint of Nicomedia. Of the 37 which remain unidentified due to wear or off-centre striking, on 22 the officina letter is legible, so it is certain that they were minted in Constantinople. The odd thing is that of these 22 pieces 9 belong to officina A, another 12 to B and just one to officina Γ. In both the A and B groups the quality of the dies is variable, while the possibility of 'unofficial' minting cannot be excluded for some of the coins. Of the last 15, 14 are mostly illegible and their condition does not even permit the identification of the place of issue, while one is struck off-centre.

[84] **358** and **366**.
[85] **343, 348, 351, 357, 359, 363, 368** and **369**.
[86] **345, 355, 366** (variant with dots on either side of the middle stroke of the E) and **350**.
[87] **352** (with dot on either side of the central stroke of the E) and **367**.
[88] **347, 352, 354 and 364**.
[89] **344**.
[90] **47, 48, 49, 51, 52, 53, 54, 55** and **64**. Oddly, **64** bears a single, clear dot only in the lower left compartment of the field.

Justin II (November 565 - September 578)

The reign of Justin II is represented in Rhodes by 84 copper pieces (PL. 11-14), derived from six mints. There are also one follis and five pentanummia whose place of issue cannot be identified due to the bad state of preservation:

	Constantinople	Nicomedia	Cyzicus	Antioch	Alexandria	Thessalonica	?
Folles	8	9	3	1			1
20N	6	1		1		15	
12N					1		
10				1			
5N	24	4	3			1	5
TOTAL	**38**	**14**	**6**	**3**	**1**	**16**	**6**

Figure 19: The coins of Justin II.

16 folles, 12 half-folles, a quarter-follis and five pentanummia are chance finds and, of those, six folles, seven half-folles, the quarter-follis and three pentanummia are of unknown provenance. Losses per year amount to 6.4 coins or 120 nummi. It is worth noting the presence of the mint of Thessalonica, whence derive two thirds of the half-folles; moreover, these coins have been found all over the town, most of them in archaeological excavations. Also, two thirds of the unusually large number of pentanummia were minted in Constantinople. In the excavation finds the ratio of folles against other denominations (half-folles and pentanummia) is 8 : 13 : 30 coins or 1 : 1.6 : 3.7. There are two to three pieces from every regnal year except for the first and the last, apart from year 5 (569/70), which is represented by eight pieces, and years 9 and 10, represented by a single coin each (Figure 20).

The coins are distributed across the town, over the entire medieval settlement and the area round the great basilica outside the medieval walls, but also in enclaves to the north, the immediate west and to the south of the medieval town.[91] Nine chance finds were picked up in the town, without reference to a more precise location. There are also two pieces handed in by people who cited as find spots Rodini and Faneromeni in the periphery of the town and one piece excavated in a private plot 10 km south of the town. Other chance finds come from the villages of Afandou, Lardos, Yennadi and, possibly, Archangelos.

The significant increase in coin circulation in the city under Justin II, particularly in comparison with that under his predecessor after 542, is a general phenomenon possibly partly reflecting the reorganization of tax-collecting mechanisms which raised the ire of contemporary historiographers against the imperial couple.[92] The peak in coin circulation associated with the year 569/570 is rather harder to explain. The sources of local history are silent, while the only event of that year commented upon was the embassy of Zemarchos, *magister militum per Orientem* to Sogdiana. This embassy was part of Justin's attempt to put pressure on the Persians' flank and must have used the northern road to Samarkand, across the Black Sea, Transcaucasia and Caspian Sea, in order to avoid the Persians. Thus, this episode cannot be connected to Rhodes. However, the island was on the sea-lane towards Egypt and the Red Sea, a pathway the Byzantines must have used at this time to support the Christian king of Ethiopia in his effort to establish his dominance over the south of the Arab peninsula which, in 570, caused a Persian campaign in that part of the world.[93] Perhaps the numismatic evidence is an echo of imperial involvement in this affair.

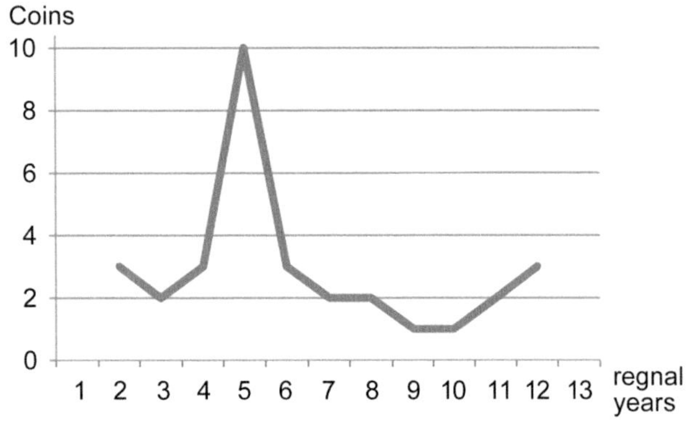

Figure 20: Distribution of precisely dated coins of Justin II by regnal year.

[91] See Appendices, Map III.

[92] It seems that empress Sophia was the dominant personality driving the effort to repair state finances after the spending sprees of Justinian's later years. Theophanes [1839]: 374; Hendy 1985: 226.

[93] Greatrex and Lieu 2002: 137; Savvides 1985: 68-69, 166. The Arab peninsula was of importance because of its gold and silver mines. Heck 2010: 100-101.

Tiberius II (September 578 - August 582)

Tiberius II essentially ruled the empire from December 574, after he was made caesar, under the watchful eye of the empress Sophia. However, the copper coins continued to display the figures of Justin II and Sophia until Justin's death on 5 October 578.[94] Excepting the half-folles of Thessalonica, where the obverse with seated imperial pair as well as the numeral K on the reverse were preserved throughout the reign, new types of folles and smaller denominations were introduced, with the value expressed in Latin numerals, and a new denomination appeared, the thirty-nummus piece. Unfortunately, the regnal year was preserved only on the folles, further obscuring the significance of the meagre representation of Tiberius in the coin evidence from Rhodes.

	Constantinople	**Nicomedia**	**Antioch**	**?**
Folles	3		1	
Triakontanummia		1		
Quarter-folles		1		2
Pentanummia				3
TOTAL	**3**	**2**	**1**	**5**

Figure 21: The coins of Tiberius II.

It consists of just 11 pieces (PL. 15): four folles, three minted in Constantinople and one in Antioch; one thirty-nummus piece and a quarter-follis from Nicomedia; and two quarter-folles and three pentanummia whose place of issue is impossible to determine due to the condition of the coins. Of these only three (A follis, a quarter-follis and a pentanummium) come from excavations in the town, from sites outside the medieval walls: one north of the medieval settlement, a second in association with the great basilica and the third a little further south. Another follis and a quarter-follis were picked up across the town, but the exact find spots are unknown. There is no reference to provenance for the remainder, although three of them were handed in by an inhabitant of the village of Lardos in the south of the island[95]. There are also two excavated quarter-folles which might belong either to Tiberius or to the later emperor Phocas, who revived the type, but the condition of the coins does not allow greater precision. As things stand, neither the ratio of excavated folles against the smaller denominations (1 : 1 : 1), nor the figure of losses per year (2.2 coins/ 53 nummi) are reliable due to the overall small number of coins known to have been found in the town: 45.4% of the total or, expressed in nummi, 39,6% (105 nummi from a total of 265).

Maurice (August 582 - November 602)

The efforts of the empress Sophia to restore imperial finances after the costly campaigns and grandiose building programme of Justinian were followed by the reckless populist policy of Tiberius II. Thus, when Maurice ascended the throne, harsh economic measures were required to support the military response to a variety of external threats: Avars and Slavs in the Balkans, the Lombards in Italy and the Persians in the east.

His rule is represented on Rhodes by 45 copper coins (PL. 16-18), as follows:

	Constantinople	**Nicomedia**	**Cyzicus**	**Antioch**	**Thessalonica**	**?**
Folles	9	2	4	5	1	
Half-folles	2	1		3	2	6
Quarter-folles	7			1		
Pentanummia	2					
TOTAL	**20**	**3**	**4**	**9**	**3**	**6**

Figure 22: The coins of Maurice.

24 are excavation finds, 10 are chance finds from recorded find spots and 11 are of unknown provenance. Three of the chance finds come from the area of Archangelos and a half-follis from the archaeological excavation at Tholos

[94] Tiberius appeared as co-emperor only on solidi minted between 26 September and 5 October. Hahn 1975: Pl. 10.

[95] They are the thirty-nummus piece of Nicomedia, the Antiochene follis and a pentanummium, handed in by K. Lengos (Record BE 2316, 1967).

(Sanctuary of Apollo Erethimios). The other chance finds are from the town and, for the first time, the area of the great basilica, although represented by six coins, is no longer dominant in the general sample. Ten finds turned up in the area within the medieval walls, in scattered locations, and another nine to the north, west and south of the medieval town. Among the archaeological site finds the ratio of folles against other denominations (half- and quarter-folles and pentanummia) is 10 : 5 : 7 : 2 (1 : 0.5 : 0.7 : 0.2) and losses per year come to 2.1 or, in nummi, 26.2.

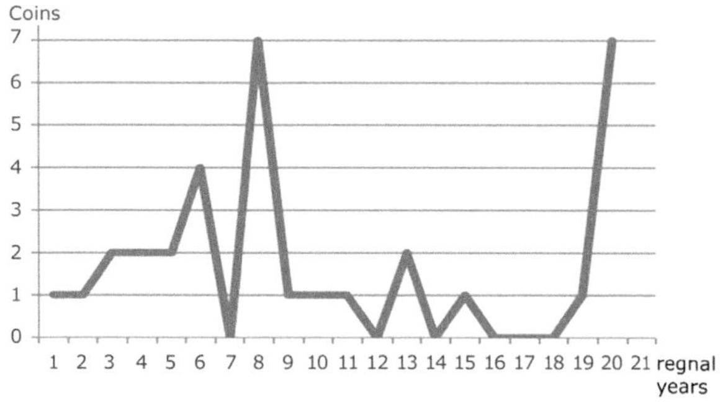

Figure 23: Distribution of precisely dated coins of Maurice by regnal year.

Under Maurice the coin types of the period before Tiberius were revived with small variations; thus, the regnal year also appears on the half-folles. The temporal distribution of the precisely dated coins is set out in Figure 23. It is obvious that, apart from the peaks of years 7 and 20 (588/589 and 601/602), more coins circulated on Rhodes in the first decade of the reign than in the second. In 588/589 the Persians conquered Martyropolis and Philippicus, the *magister militum per Orientem*, was unable to stop them. He was replaced by Comentiolus, who won a decisive victory at Sisauranum, near Nisibis.[96] In the following year, the Persian ruler Hormizd was deposed and his son Chosroes II managed to secure the throne with Byzantine help, closing this chapter of Perso-Byzantine conflict in 591. However, throughout Maurice's reign, the major field of military operations was in the Balkans. Successive inroads by Avaro-Slavic groups, with a series of clashes and truces which, usually, involved generous handouts to persuade the invaders to withdraw, give an impression of general confusion which seemed to clear somewhat in 599, with significant Byzantine successes against the Avars, Slavs and Gepids.[97] It is ironic that the emperor's preparations for decisive action in the winter of 602 resulted in the military uprising which brought Phocas to the throne and facilitated the spread of the Slavic element in the Balkan peninsula. The spike observed in monetary circulation on Rhodes in 601/602 possibly reflects the increased movement of supplies from Egypt and Cyprus towards the troops deployed in the Balkans.

Phocas (November 602 - October 610)

From a strategic point of view, the contribution of Phocas was disastrous: he led the rebellion which put an end to Byzantine control in the Danube and gave Chosroes II an excellent pretext to upset the balance of power in the eastern provinces of the empire. 26 coins in the collection of the Archaeological Service in Rhodes bear his name (PL. 19-20), including two gold tremisses.

	Constantinople	Nicomedia	Cyzicus	Antioch	Alexandria	?
Tremisses (AV)	2					
Folles	2	1	1	2		1
Half-folles	5	1	2	1		1
Quarter-folles				2		3
Pentanummia						1
Dodecanummia					1	
TOTAL	**9**	**2**	**3**	**5**	**1**	**6**

Figure 24: The coins of Phocas.

Seven of them are of unknown provenance while the two gold coins are chance finds from the town. A half-follis was found on the site of an Early Christian basilica excavated at the village of Mesanagros in south Rhodes and another was a chance find from the area of Archangelos. In the town, the area of the great basilica is represented by six coins, the walled town by seven, and another one was found outside the walls to the northwest. The ratio of excavated folles against other denominations (half- and quarter-folles and pentanummia) is 1 : 7 : 5 : 1 and the figure for losses per year 3 coins or 67.7 nummi.

[96] Greatrex and Lieu 2002: 171.
[97] Morrisson 2007: 429-430.

Phocas resurrected some of the coin types with Latin numerals introduced by Tiberius II, presumably to highlight the return to an open-handed fiscal policy after the elimination of Maurice. The regnal year appears on some half-folles of Nicomedia and Cyzicus,[98] but is missing from those of Constantinople and all quarter-folles. The precisely dated coins compose Figure 25.

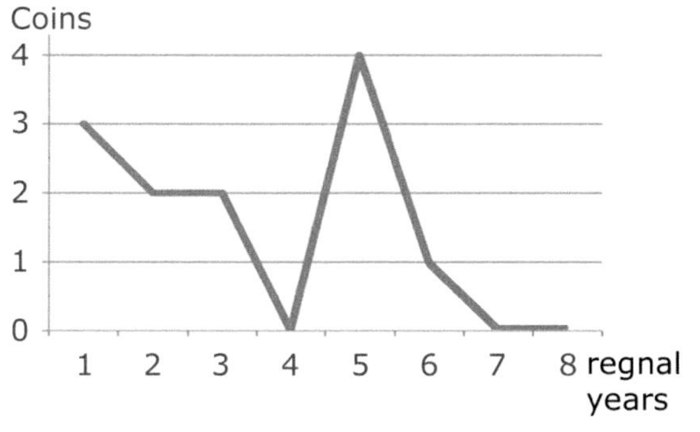

Figure 25: Distribution of precisely dated coins of Phocas by regnal year.

Increased coin circulation under Phocas is noted in other regions of the empire, and the absence of coins from years 608/609 and 609/610 is probably due to the uprising of the Heraclii which caused the central government to lose control of Egypt when Nicetas, nephew of Heraclius the Elder conquered it in 608.[99] Thus, losses per year should be adjusted to 4 coins or 91.2 nummi, double the figure of Maurice. As the phenomenon is widespread, it may well be linked to more systematic payment of soldiers' stipends, which had caused a major grievance under Maurice and prepared the ground for Phocas' accession to the throne.[100]

From the years 498-610, besides the pentanummia already discussed, date the following 20 coins, whose precise dating was made impossible by wear (PL. 21-22):

- Three folles of Constantinople dated *c.* 498-537.
- Five pentanummia, of which two minted in Nicomedia, dated *c.* 507-537, and two of Thessalonica.
- Four quarter-folles, of which two dated *c.* 578-608.
- Seven dodecanummia.
- A small billon (?) coin with frontal bust on the obverse and CN on the reverse (1/4 *siliqua*?)

Heraclius (October 610 - February 641)

From the 31 regnal years of Heraclius 340 coins have been recorded so far in Rhodes (PL. 23-45), including two gold solidi. One of them is a site find excavated within the medieval town and the other is recorded as a chance find from the town without greater precision.[101]

	CON	NIKO	KYZ	SEL	ICAVR	Neapolis	ΑΛΕΞ	ΘΕC	KRT	?
Solidi	2									
Folles	218	25	8		1	1		5		15
30N	2									
20N	22	1	1	2				9	1	10
12N							7			
10N	1	1						4		
6N							4			
TOTAL	**245**	**27**	**9**	**2**	**1**	**1**	**11**	**18**	**1**	**25**

Figure 26: The coins of Heraclius.

Of the 338 copper coins, 272 are folles, 47 half-folles, six quarter-folles, seven dodecanummia, four hexanummia and two 30-nummus pieces. No pentanummia issued by Nicomedia and Cyzicus have been found to date. 223 pieces are excavation finds. Leaving out of the reckoning 36 hoarded coins,[102] five Alexandrian dodecanummia and four hexanummia, the following ratio results between the different denominations: 140 : 34 : 4 or 1 : 0.24 : 0.03. It is

[98] Cf. **312** for an example of an undated half-follis of Cyzicus, although it must have been minted in 602/603. Hahn 1975: Prägetabelle XI.
[99] Greatrex and Lieu 2002: 187.
[100] The popularity Phocas enjoyed with the army was made clear during the revolt of the Heraclii. Kaegi 1981: 124.
[101] As on Figure 28 below, the mints are represented by their abbreviated signatures on the coins in order to save space, excepting Neapolis in Syria, which is distinguished by the less representative single letter N.
[102] From the excavation of the Gavoyannis and Kambouropoulos plots. See Selected assemblages I and II at the end of the volume.

possible to refine these ratios further, taking advantage of the conventional dates of the six different classes of Heraclian folles:[103]

Class		Denomination Ratio	
1:	years 1 - 3 (610-612)	18 : 3 : 2	or 1 : 0.16 : 0.11
2:	years 3 - 5 (613-615)	44 : 4 : 1	or 1 : 0.09 : 0.02
3:	years 6 - 14 (615-624)	11 : 4 : 1	or 1 : 0.36 : 0.09
4:	years 15 - 19 (624-629)	1 : 1 : -	or 1 : 1 : -
5a:	years 20 - 21 (629-631)	2 : 1 : -	or 1 : 0.5 : -
5b:	years 22 - 29 (631-639)	56 : 12 : -	or 1 : 0.21 : -
6:	years 30 - 31 (639-641)	7 : - : -	or 1 : - : -

Figure 27: Changes in the ratio between different denominations of Heraclius.

Naturally, half- and quarter-folles cannot be dated as accurately as the folles, as they are more carelessly struck and more worn; thus, one follis and nine half-folles included in the overall ratios are missing from Figure 27. Also, seven half-folles of Constantinople (629-641) have been placed in class 5b relying on statistical probability and weight. Even so, keeping in mind the difficulties of the sample, it is interesting to note that the decrease in the circulation of the smaller denominations is not regular: class 2 has fewer half-folles than one would expect, and there are also fewer quarter-folles in comparison to classes 1 and 3.

The role of the mints is important for the interpretation of these findings. Apart from the dominance of the mint of the capital, Thessalonica appears again after its almost complete disappearance from Rhodes in the interval 678-710. It still seems to specialize in smaller denominations, but now the ratio between denominations (folles, half-folles and quarter-folles) is more balanced: 1 : 1.8 : 0.8. The temporary mints of Seleucia, Isaura and Neapolis in Syria also make their appearance, the first with two half-folles, while we also encounter a single coin from Carthage dated 616/617, to remind us of Heraclius' attempt to move his headquarters to Libya at a time of singular distress. A glance at the dated coins is instructive:

<table>
<tr><th>Year</th><th>CON</th><th>NIKO</th><th>KYZ</th><th>SEL</th><th>ICAVR</th><th>Neapolis</th><th>ΑΛΕΞ</th><th>ΘEC</th><th>KRT</th></tr>
<tr><td>I</td><td></td><td>3</td><td></td><td></td><td></td><td></td><td></td><td></td><td></td></tr>
<tr><td>II</td><td>5</td><td>1</td><td>5</td><td></td><td></td><td></td><td></td><td></td><td></td></tr>
<tr><td>III</td><td>28</td><td>5</td><td>4</td><td></td><td></td><td></td><td></td><td>4</td><td></td></tr>
<tr><td>IIII</td><td>8</td><td>9</td><td></td><td></td><td></td><td></td><td rowspan="6">8</td><td>1</td><td></td></tr>
<tr><td>V</td><td>5</td><td></td><td></td><td></td><td></td><td></td><td>3</td><td></td></tr>
<tr><td>VI</td><td>10</td><td></td><td></td><td></td><td></td><td></td><td>1</td><td></td></tr>
<tr><td>VII</td><td>1</td><td>1</td><td></td><td>1</td><td>1</td><td></td><td></td><td>1</td></tr>
<tr><td>VIII</td><td>1</td><td>1</td><td></td><td>1</td><td></td><td></td><td>3</td><td></td></tr>
<tr><td>VIIII</td><td>1</td><td></td><td></td><td></td><td></td><td></td><td>1</td><td></td></tr>
<tr><td>X</td><td>4</td><td></td><td></td><td></td><td></td><td></td><td></td><td>2</td><td></td></tr>
<tr><td>XV</td><td>2</td><td></td><td></td><td></td><td></td><td></td><td></td><td></td><td></td></tr>
<tr><td>XVI</td><td>3</td><td></td><td></td><td></td><td></td><td></td><td></td><td>1</td><td></td></tr>
<tr><td>XVII</td><td></td><td>1</td><td></td><td></td><td></td><td></td><td></td><td></td><td></td></tr>
<tr><td>XX</td><td>16</td><td></td><td></td><td></td><td></td><td rowspan="7">1</td><td rowspan="7">3</td><td>1</td><td></td></tr>
<tr><td>XXI</td><td>3</td><td></td><td></td><td></td><td></td><td></td><td></td></tr>
<tr><td>XXII</td><td>5</td><td></td><td></td><td></td><td></td><td></td><td></td></tr>
<tr><td>XXIII</td><td>15</td><td></td><td></td><td></td><td></td><td></td><td></td></tr>
<tr><td>XXIIII</td><td>10</td><td></td><td></td><td></td><td></td><td></td><td></td></tr>
<tr><td>XXV</td><td>15</td><td></td><td></td><td></td><td></td><td></td><td></td></tr>
<tr><td>XXVI</td><td>9</td><td></td><td></td><td></td><td></td><td></td><td></td></tr>
<tr><td>XXX</td><td>9</td><td></td><td></td><td></td><td></td><td></td><td></td><td></td><td></td></tr>
<tr><td>XXXI</td><td>2</td><td></td><td></td><td></td><td></td><td></td><td></td><td></td><td></td></tr>
</table>

Figure 28: Chronological distribution of Heraclius' coins.

[103] Hahn 1981: Prägetabelle III.

In this table the rise of Nicomedia up to year 4 (613/614) is observable, and then intermittent presence up to year 16 (625/626);[104] while the coins of Cyzicus are concentrated in years 2 and 3. The presence of Thessalonica is relatively stable up to year 20, when that mint closed down. The presence of specimens from the temporary mints associated with the Persian campaigns supports contacts between Rhodes and Asia Minor or Syria in this difficult period. The piece from Neapolis (*c.* 630)[105] should not be a surprise: obviously Rhodes was again an important stopping place along the sea route to Egypt and Palestine after the final victory over the Persians in 628, a fact attested by the comfortable representation of the Alexandrian mint between 628 and 641.

The Alexandrian coins of this period are difficult to date. Although this cannot be proved, perhaps some of these coins may be dated to the interval between years 27 and 29, the apparent 'third numismatic gap' on Figure 29. The two other gaps observed between years 11 to 14 and 16 to 19 are probably due to the temporary loss of Egypt, which returned to Byzantine hands in 629,[106] because Rhodes was a main stop in the route linking the capital with its African grain supply.

The presence of coins of years 15 and 16 from Constantinople and Nicomedia indicate that contact with the region of the capital was not completely broken off, even during the celebrated siege of the latter in 626. Of course, seven coins are not much, and the 'second gap' which follows shows there were problems; but it is impossible to say whether this is due to a military event affecting Rhodes or just the temporary loss of Egypt. Scholars have not reached a consensus about the date of the Persian raid on Rhodes, placed by some between 614 and 617 and others between 623 and 626.[107] If this raid took place when communication with Constantinople was already difficult, the silence of Byzantine historiographers and the absence of a destruction layer associated with coins are both easy to explain. In the interval 614-617, the numismatic picture on the island is different, as is clearly shown by Figure 29, with the absolute number of dated coins.

The highest peak occurs in year 3 (612/613) and then the number of coins declines. The peak mostly consists of class 2 folles from Constantinople, which circulated widely from year 3 to year 5 of Heraclius (613-615). More specifically, there are 30 pieces of this class, of which 22 minted in Constantinople and five in Nicomedia while three more are too worn to identify the mint. There are also six Constantinopolitan folles of other classes, four folles of Cyzicus and three fractional coins from Thessalonica, a half-follis and two quarter folles. 43 losses per year are very hard to explain merely from the abundant supply of a particular type, when the already high yearly average of Heraclius is 10.9 (or, expressed in nummi, 384.8). The 'inflationary' tendency remarked elsewhere in this period is not adequate

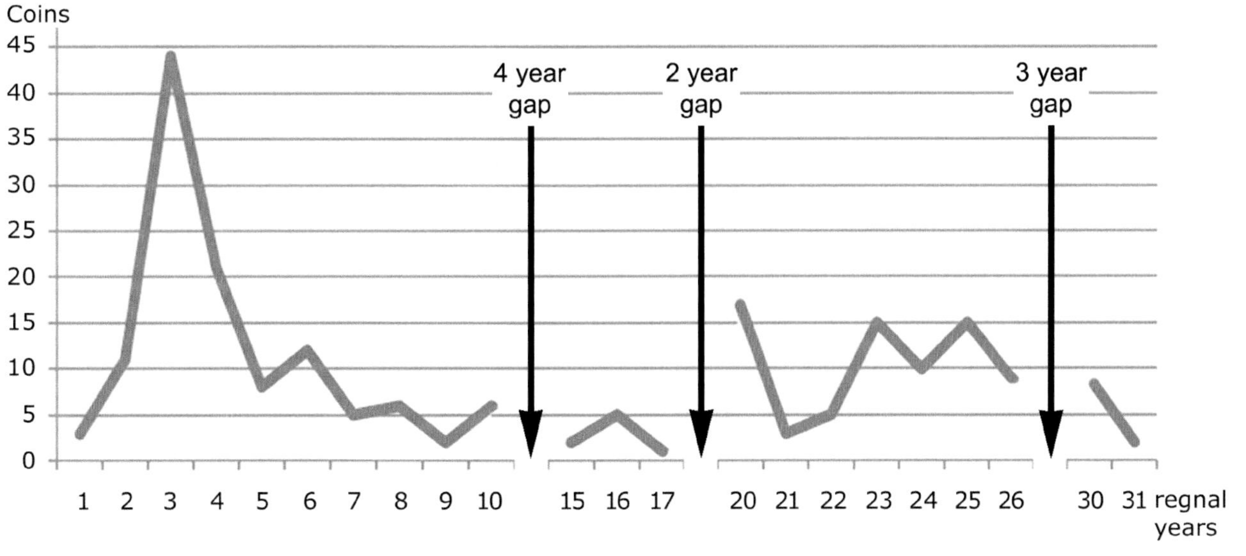

Figure 29: Distribution of dated coins of Heraclius by regnal year.

[104] On another follis of Nicomedia of the period 615-624, the regnal year is not legible (**644**).
[105] The precise dating of these issues is uncertain, but they certainly fit within the interval between 629 and 636 (battle of Yarmouk). Hahn 1981: 108-110. However, the piece was counterstruck c. 633. Grierson 1968: I, 56.
[106] Greatrex and Lieu 2002: 199, 307; Savvides 2007: 481-484.
[107] Greatrex and Lieu 2002: 226; Savvides 2007. Arab sources place it in 622/623, 'first year of the Prophet', which coincides with the 'first numismatic gap'. For the archaeological traces of the Persian raids in general see Russell 2001.

either, because it does not apply only for this specific year. A rise in mint output is mentioned elsewhere for year 3;[108] we do, however, need to ascertain how far the local phenomenon exceeds the wider tendency. Unfortunately, the publication of the large numbers of coins from the Athenian Agora predates the division of Heraclian folles into six classes and conflates classes 2 and 5.[109] 131 pieces are recorded from the Agora, inclusive of class 5 and smaller denominations displaying two standing figures, representing 56.5% of the coins of Heraclius in the catalogue. The corresponding numbers from Rhodes are 230 coins, equivalent to 68.8% of the total for the emperor, and the obverse type for class 2 folles and half-folles (Constantinople and Nicomedia) covers 100 pieces. Of those, 85 belong to just three years.[110] The 12% difference between the two sites is a strong indication that the sample of Rhodes is not typical.

Anyhow, the abundance of coins from the interval 613-615, which up to date has not been linked to any destruction layer, may perhaps be interpreted differently: in 613, the Byzantines made their first attempt to deal with the Persians. While Philippicus, brother-in-law of Maurice, led a diversion in Armenia, the emperor, his brother Theodore and cousin Nicetas joined forces in Syria, where they were eventually defeated.[111] The role of Rhodes in the preparation and supply of this campaign and, perhaps, after its unfortunate end, the evacuation of the troops and refugees destined for the capital should be considered as certain.

A relatively high number of losses is also noted in years 20, 23, 24 and 25. The high figure of year 20, 17 coins, is not so much due to the size of the folles: three out of ten are chance finds, but this ratio is smaller that that for the following year. We know, however, that Heraclius visited the Holy Land in the spring of 630, and Rhodes possibly contributed to the logistics of this visit. In view of the fall in monetary circulation of years 21 and 22, the stability of the three years that followed requires some explanation, but the written sources are not helpful. The Arab invasion in *Palaestina III* is dated to the autumn of 633. In February 634 Byzantine forces led by the *patricius* Sergius were defeated twice and Heraclius, then at Homs, sent his brother Theodore against the Arabs with a strong army. Another defeat at Ajnaidin followed and, in March 635, the enemy was outside Damascus. By the end of that year, the best part of the Syrian hinterland was controlled by the invaders, with the exception of a few urban centres. In August 636 the battle at Yarmuk put an end to Byzantine control in the region. These developments possibly explain the numismatic evidence from Rhodes, which was involved in the supply of the troops. Nevertheless, the drop in circulation of year 26 may reflect a more general lack of coin and supplies, a factor which has not particularly engaged scholars exploring the causes for the failure of Byzantine armies in Syria. This lack might well provide an explanation for the reports of pillaging Byzantine soldiers which alienated local populations.[112]

It has been noted elsewhere that the sequence of types or, even, the regnal year on a coin, is not always reliable for its precise dating:[113] Constantinopolitan coins of class 2 (613-615) are sometimes dated to year 2[114] and coins of class 3 (615-624) to year 5;[115] while class 1 (610-612) continues into year 3[116] and class 2 to year 6.[117] It may be that dies, both of the obverse and reverse, were used until they wore out to cut costs. However, the use of older types is much more common on the obverse, at a ratio of 4:1. An alternative explanation, offered by Hahn,[118] is the possibility that the authorities occasionally might tolerate 'private minting' in order to cover the need for coin; however, these coins from Rhodes show no evidence supporting this theory.

Examination of the officinae on the Constantinopolitan coins, which dominate the sample, for the years better represented, results in the following:

[108] Cf. the material from Sardis: year 2, 8 specimens; year 3, 46 specimens; year 4, 30 specimens; years 5 and 6, 17 specimens each; Bates 1971, 6-7. Later classes of Heraclius have not been recovered at Sardis.

[109] Thompson 1954: 70. She groups together classes 3, 4 and 6.

[110] Some of the 15 half-folles may be coterminous with the folles of classes 3 and 4, covering a period of 17 years. The 30 pieces of class 2 from year 30 are those with a legible regnal year. However, this class includes a fair number of worn coins which raise the average for the 613-615 three year period further. A comparative proportion of the worn pieces must belong to year 3, for which the number of 43 coins is the lowest possible figure of yearly losses.

[111] Greatrex and Lieu 2002: 189, 301.

[112] Papadopoullos 2006: 237-238. The dating and sequence of events in that volume seems more complete than in other works, which date the Arab invasion to 634. See also Schulze 2006: 2. For the problematic background see Kaegi 1981: 150-153.

[113] See also Grierson 1968: I, 182-183; Hendy 1985: 415.

[114] **394, 395.**

[115] **457.**

[116] **382, 384, 385, 386, 387, 388.**

[117] **430, 431, 432, 433, 434, 435, 436, 437.**

[118] Hahn and Metlich 2000: 6.

Year	Class	officina A	officina B	officina Γ	officina Δ	officina E
3	1 2	1 3	7	1 6	4 1	1 4
4	2			3	3	
5	2				4	
6	2 3	[1]		2 2	1 1	1 1
20	5a	3	4		2	1
23	5b	6	2	1-2	2	
24	5b		3	1	2	
25	5b	5	3	3	1	

Figure 30: Distribution of Constantinopolitan coins of Heraclius by officina.

It appears that officina Δ was particularly prone to the issue of 'irregularly' dated coins of year 3, while most of the coins of the next class (class 2) came from officinae B and Γ. In year 5 only officina Δ is represented, while in year 6 officinae Γ-E seem to have supplied equal quantities of regularly and irregularly dated pieces.

Four coins of Heraclius are countermarked. The single follis from Neapolis in Syria (**661**), minted after 629, bears Grierson's type F countermark[119] which, unless used for a number of years, dates the piece to *c.* 633. The same countermark appears on a corroded and basically unidentified follis (**707**). This countermark has been associated with the Byzantine troops in Syria at the time of the Arab conquest.[120] A half-follis of Constantinople, also minted after 629 (**615**), bears a countermark that may be either type F or Arab. Finally, a follis from Constantinople (**551**, class 5), is countermarked with a cruciform monogram which, although not fully legible, belongs either to Grierson's type G or, more likely, type H: in any case, it probably dates from transitional year 641.[121]

The large number of Heraclian coins, which may partly be due to inflationary tendencies, ensured their dispersal across the town of Rhodes, within and outside the medieval fortifications. New nuclei of finds appear, both in the northern parish of Niochori, to the north of the medieval settlement, and the area of Acandia to the south; several pieces have also been found along the roads leading to the countryside. However, the most important feature is the recession in the area round the great basilica of Rhodes (*c.* 30 coins) in comparison to the rise in the area now enclosed by the medieval walls, with a focus on the Pekmetzis plot (27 coins) but also other important sites (Maravelias/Asprakis and Hasapoglou plots, properties on Athinas Square etc.)[122]

A small hoard containing 14 coins of Heraclius alongside later issues was discovered in the Gavoyannis plot in the medieval town.[123] In the Kambouropoulos plot, near the village of Trianda (Ialysos), 22 pieces of Heraclius were recovered from ossuaries, together with two coins of Constans II. These coins may be reckoned as part of the losses per year since they were used singly as burial offerings and were therefore withdrawn from circulation within a relatively limited interval from their time of issue.[124] Coins of Heraclius have also been found in excavations at the villages of Tholos (sanctuary of Apollo Erethimios), Charaki and Mesanagros (Early Christian basilicas). Ten more villages in the countryside are represented by chance finds: Archangelos, Asklepio, Hagios Isidoros, Vati, Yennadi, Kalavarda, Kamiros, Kattavia, Lindos and Monolithos. It is clear that, inflationary or otherwise, the copper coinage of Heraclius circulated throughout the island and that its distribution in the town reflects important changes in the latter's spatial organization.

Constans II (September 641 - September 668)

When Constans ascended the throne Syria, Palestine, Armenia and Egypt had already been overrun by the Arabs, who were also threatening Anatolia. In his times, through the initiative of Muawiya, governor of Syria and later caliph (661-680) and founder of the Umayyad dynasty, the Arabs built a strong fleet and, gradually, the Byzantines

[119] Type 2 of Schulze and Schulze 2006: 4 and 16, with revision of dating.
[120] *Op. cit.*, 20, 24.
[121] Grierson 1968: I, 55-56.
[122] For the location of excavated plots see Appendices, Map II.
[123] Appendices, Selected Context I. For the excavation see Archaiologikon Deltion 32: 357. The hoard was found in area IV.
[124] Appendices, Selected Context II. Archaiologikon Deltion 52: 1155-1157. These coins are probably burial offerings, according to excavator Nika 2006: 57 and, *eadem*, 2014: 333-358.

lost control of the sea. The crisis caused by imperial monotheletism worsened, causing political instability in Libya and Italy. The effort to control the Slavs in the Balkans was short-lived, while the emperor's decision to get personally involved in Italy and Sicily, abandoning Constantinople, dislocated the machinery of the state.

A total of 122 coins have so far been recorded from the reign of Constans (PL. 46-52). Eight are of gold: five solidi, a semissis and two tremisses, of which only one solidus is of known provenance although handed in by a private citizen. The copper coins are 101 folles, seven half-folles, four quarter-folles and two dodecanummia. Leaving aside six hoarded pieces,[125] we get 4 losses per year, or 149 nummi. The ratio between folles and smaller denominations is 63 : 6 : 3 or 1 : 0.1 : 0.05, close to that of Heraclius, although it is not possible to break it down further, due to the bad condition of the half-folles.[126]

Unfortunately, the copper issues of Constans are particularly ill-struck, and the precise dating of his coins frequently difficult. More than one class of folles correspond to some regnal years, some of them limited to a particular year while others cover a longer time-span. Moreover, coins have yet to be assigned to some years. The table below shows the classes of the emperor's Constantinopolitan folles with their current dating and representation among the Rhodian material:[127]

<table>
<tr><th>Class</th><th>Year</th><th>Date</th><th colspan="2">Number of folles</th></tr>
<tr><td>1</td><td>1 - 2</td><td>Jan.-Sept. 642</td><td>7</td><td rowspan="6">8
(Class 1 or 4)</td></tr>
<tr><td>2</td><td>2</td><td>642/643</td><td>4</td></tr>
<tr><td>2bis</td><td>3</td><td>642/643</td><td>30</td></tr>
<tr><td>3</td><td>3</td><td>642/643</td><td>1</td></tr>
<tr><td>3bis</td><td>3</td><td>642/643</td><td>-</td></tr>
<tr><td>4</td><td>4 - 7</td><td>645/646 - 647/648</td><td>14</td></tr>
<tr><td>5</td><td>11 - 14</td><td>651/652 - 654/655</td><td>7[71]</td><td rowspan="3">1
(Class 5 or 6)</td></tr>
<tr><td>5bis</td><td>11, 13</td><td>651/652, 653/654</td><td>2</td></tr>
<tr><td>6</td><td>15 - 16</td><td>655/656 - 656/657</td><td>5</td></tr>
<tr><td>7</td><td>15 - 17</td><td>655/656 - 657/658</td><td>6</td><td></td></tr>
<tr><td>8</td><td>15 - 17</td><td>655/656 - 657/658</td><td>-</td><td></td></tr>
<tr><td>9</td><td>19 - 21, 23</td><td>659/660 - 660/661, 663/664</td><td>4</td><td></td></tr>
<tr><td>10</td><td>25</td><td>665/666</td><td>-</td><td></td></tr>
<tr><td>11</td><td>27</td><td>Sept. - Nov. 668</td><td>6</td><td></td></tr>
</table>

Figure 31: Distribution of Constans II folles by class.[128]

This material displays a remarkable phenomenon, the dominance of class 2bis ('INPER CONST'), an issue not commonly found elsewhere apart from Cyprus,[129] as well as a number of problems of which the most obvious is the inability to identify with precision eight coins, confusing our information relative to losses for years 1 to 7. A second problem is the low but persistent presence of imperial issues after the assumed Arab conquest various scholars have supported. Since, however, certain years are represented by more than one class, while others share a single one, we need to include as many coins as possible in the presentation of losses per year, leaving out hoarded coins and adding other denominations dated with reasonable accuracy. Thus, the laws of probability have been employed:

[125] Gavoyannis plot (4 pieces) and Kambouropoulos plot (2 pieces).
[126] The quarter-folles were issued from year 19 onwards; a 30-nummus piece appeared after year 23. Hahn 1981: Prägetabelle VII.
[127] According to Hahn 1981.
[128] One of the pieces of class 5 (**794**) bears the fully legible date XЧ, equivalent to 655/656. In Figure 32 it is placed in year 15.
[129] Foss 2008: 21; Metcalf 2009: 153. Typically, it is missing from Grierson's 1968 table of classes, Grierson1968: II, 409. Grierson 1982: 111, added three new types (2bis, 3bis, 4bis); Hahn 1981 has one more (5bis).

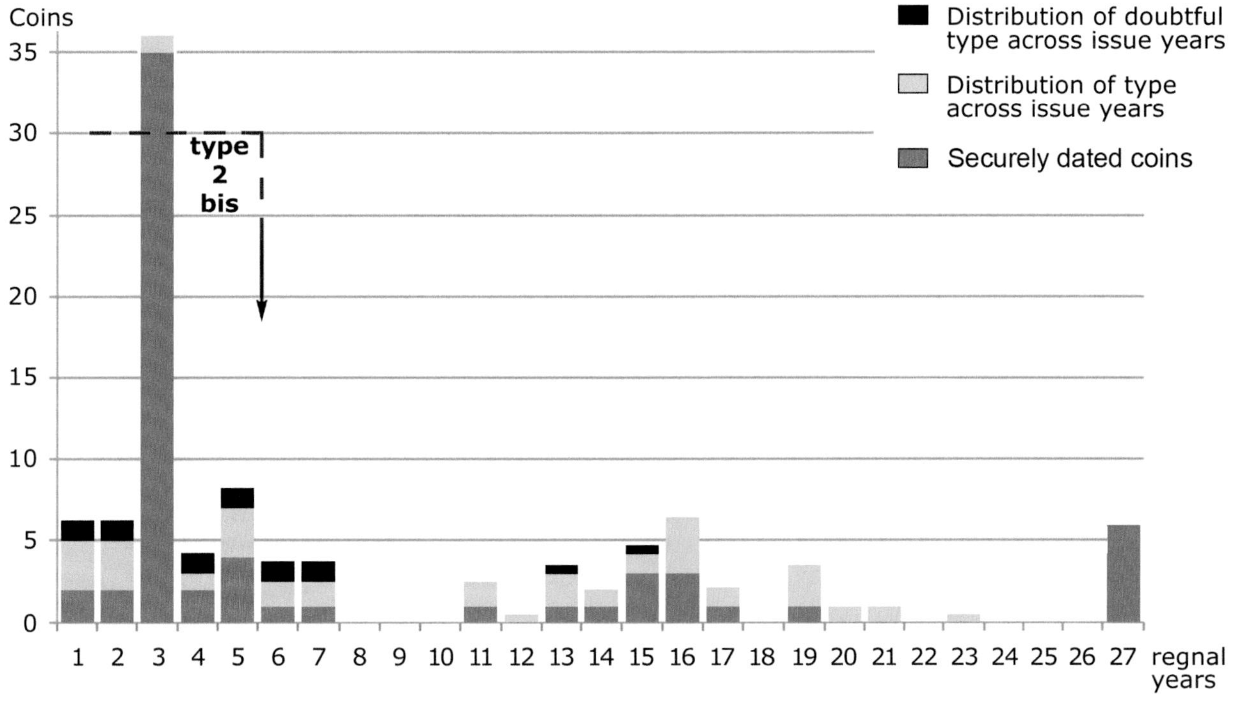

Figure 32: Distribution of coins of Constans by regnal year.

In the graph above, coins of a particular class without a legible date have been equally distributed between the regnal years they are known to cover, unless some of these years are better represented in the sample. For example, the eight folles which may belong to either class 1 or class 4 were shared between the two classes at a ratio of 1:3, because the dated coins also show this ratio; then, the share of each class was distributed between the years it was issued. In all cases, years with more precisely dated coins are proportionally favoured in the distribution of the less precisely dated pieces. The object of this procedure is to counter, as far as the sample allows, the effects of careless striking and wear, and seek moderate or hidden tendencies in coin circulation; although some blurring is inevitable.

The graph shows gaps between years 8 to 10, 18 to 22 and 24 to 26. The absence of coins from years 8 to 10 and also years 18, 22 and 26 is noted by Hahn,[130] so the only gap particular to Rhodes is year 25 (665/666). Of course, the steady decline after year 3 significantly reduces the statistical significance of such observations, but it does no harm to make a note of them. Thus, we are left with the very high representation of year 3 which, excepting a single sufficiently legible follis of class 3, consists of class 2bis folles and four half-folles with the same obverse. Year 4 is represented only by two dodecanummia from Alexandria, and the semblance of stability in years 5 to 7 may well be illusory, concealing another single peak. There is probably another rise, not particularly marked, between 655 and 657 and, in the years following, vestigial presence until the last months of Constans' reign (September-November 668), where there is a sudden peak reaching, if not exceeding, the figure for the start of the reign. So far, classes 3bis (year 3), 8 (years 15 to 17) and 10 (year 25) have not been found on Rhodes.

The numismatic peak at the end of the reign consists of six class 11 folles; it probably reflects a fleet mission linked to the death of the emperor, or the return of imperial troops from Sicily. Anyhow, it cannot be proved that the scarcity of coin on Rhodes in the last decade of Constans was due to enemy action. Administrative causes are most probably responsible, in association with the strategic marginalization of the island after the emperor moved to the West.

The written sources are not always helpful in the interpretation of this picture. It may well be that the respectable representation of the first two years is a result of the exile of Martina and her sons to Rhodes after the coup of September 641 and then the withdrawal of Byzantine officials and troops after the surrender of Egypt to the Arabs:

[130] Hahn 1981: Prägetabelle VII.

the fleet left Alexandria, toward Cyprus and, presumably, then Rhodes on the way north to Constantinople, on 12 September 642.[131] The spike of year 3, a feature shared only by Rhodes and Cyprus, is undoubtedly linked to the preparations of the campaign to retake Egypt. Indeed, class 2bis may have been issued specifically for the expenses of that campaign. Other classes, corresponding to one or more years, may have been issued to serve specific needs.[132] After the murder of Umar (end of 644), the new caliph Uthman had recalled general Amr ibn al-'As, conqueror of Egypt, giving the Byzantines an opening for effective military action. In 645, a powerful Byzantine fleet sailed from Rhodes under the command of *augustalis* Manuel the Armenian and took Alexandria by surprise; the mint was temporarily reopened, issuing dodecanummia like the two found on Rhodes. However, Amr was recalled, defeating Manuel at Nikiou and retaking Alexandria in the summer of 646 (end of Constans' year 5). Manuel was killed in that action and only a few of his troops managed to board the Byzantine ships and escape.[133]

The participation of the naval base on Rhodes in the general mobilization of the fleet caused by the conquest of Syria by the Arabs[134] and after the final loss of Egypt in 646 is certain. In 649 Constantia in Cyprus fell to the Arabs and the entire island was plundered by the new fleet of Muawiya who, in 653/4, raided Cyprus, Rhodes, Cos and Crete.[135] In 654 or 655 Constans was heavily defeated in the 'Battle of the Masts' off Phoenix (Neorion), which is associated with the conquest (or raiding) of Rhodes by the Arabs who, then, sailed north towards Constantinople, only to have their fleet destroyed by a storm.[136] However, the sequence and precise dating of events in the region, including the assault on Rhodes, is confused.[137] The murder of caliph Uthman in Medina (656) initiated a civil war (first *fitna*) which lasted until 661 and obliged Muawiya to turn his attention to the Middle East, probably abandoning his foothold on Cyprus.[138] The reduction of the pressure on the eastern front allowed Constans to turn his attention to the Balkans. In 658 he campaigned against the Slavs, settling large numbers of them in Anatolia. While he was wrapping up his affairs in the Balkans (658) the Arab succession crisis continued and, in order to buy time, Muawiya sought a truce which was concluded in 659. This truce, which lasted three years and was observed by both sides, included indemnity payments to the Byzantines but enabled Muawiya to become caliph.[139] In these circumstances, an occupation of Rhodes between 656 and 662 by the Arabs is unlikely.

In 661 Constans began a two-year tour of Greece whence, in the spring of 663, he sailed to Tarentum. After a campaign against the Lombards in Benevento and a brief visit to Rome, Constans established his headquarters in Syracuse and remained there until his death five years later. His presence in Sicily probably curtailed Arab activity in the region,[140] but from 663 onwards Anatolia suffered from successive destructive raids. His absence also caused political instability, most notably on the occasion of the rebellion of Shapur, general of the Armeniacs, in 667 or 668.[141]

From the Battle of the Masts until the death of Constans, Rhodes is absent from the written sources, while new raids in the Aegean are not mentioned, although after 663 pressure on Byzantium's eastern borders mounted steadily. If, indeed, the island was under Arab occupation for some time, this might explain the reduction in coin circulation observed after classes 6 and 7 (Figure 32); if so, the diffuse coin presence should be concentrated just before the key naval encounter at Neorion, marking the activation of the naval base, provided that the Arab occupation of the island followed the destruction of the Byzantine fleet. It seems more likely, though, that the numismatic downturn after 665 simply reflects administrative shortfalls under a government split by the lengthy absence of Constance and lack of strategic incentive.

About 640, local imitations of Byzantine folles had made their appearance in Arab-held Syria.[142] These imitations do not differ substantially from the Byzantine originals concerning either the weight or the flans. The older ones copy issues of Heraclius and, less often, of Phocas. More specifically, the imitations issued by the local administration

131 Ostrogorsky 1980: 115. One destination does not exclude the other.
132 3bis, 4bis, [5bis], 11. See Hendy 1985: 417-420, 661.
133 Stratos 1972: 44-45, 51-53; Butler 1902: 334, 465-475. Ostrogorsky (1980: 115) writes that Manuel survived and escaped by sea.
134 Cosentino 2007: 584 ff.
135 This raid may have also affected Chios. Nikolaou 2010: 82. For Arab raids on Rhodes in this period also see Savvides 1995: 13-19.
136 Cosentino 2007: 589-593.
137 Stratos, 1972, thought Constans endeavoured to prevent the Arabs from obtaining timber for ships' masts, thus explaining the name 'Battle of the Masts' given the encounter by Arab historians. However, more recently, the battle has been linked to an attempt against Constantinople by the Arabs in 654. O'Sullivan 2004: 67-88; Cosentino 2007: 590-592; Metcalf 2009: 400-418.
138 Papadopoullos 2006: 263.
139 Although he used the title from 660, full recognition of Muawiya as caliph by the Arabs took place after the death of Ali (caliph, although problematically, from 656 to 661).
140 Sicily was relentlessly plundered after his death, when his armies were withdrawn. Stratos 1974: 22-24.
141 Stratos 1974: 256-257; Haldon 2003: 62; Treadgold 1997: 320-323.
142 Pottier 2008: 87-155.

controlled by the Arabs copied Grierson's classes 3, 5 and 6,[143] and are dated by Pottier and his collaborators between 640 and 646.[144] After those came imitations of two particular obverses of Constans' folles.[145] The first group of imitations, with a facing bust, copies the coins already linked to the Byzantine attempt to recover Egypt and is dated by Pottier *c.* 645-647.[146] A subgroup of this, with the date XX on the reverse, is placed between 658 and 663.[147] The second group, which enjoyed much wider circulation and influenced the first Syriac issues with Arab emblems and script, is dated by scholars between 647 and 670.[148]

Coin **840** could, perhaps, belong to the second group of Heraclius' imitations (Class II), although it is more likely that its irregular appearance is due to overstriking. Among the numerous pieces of classes 1, 2bis and 4 of Constans it is not easy to distinguish Arab imitations, due to the inferior quality of the striking and the poor condition of a number of coins. However, for the time being, only one piece,[149] with the letter N reversed (И), seems to be an Arab imitation from Syria. A dodecanummium with the letters IB mirror-wise may also have been issued under Arab rule (PL. 53).[150]

A curious site find is a clumsy imitation copying a follis of year 1 or 2 of Phocas (seated imperial pair/ m).[151] This type has been used in Arab-Byzantine emissions in Syria- e.g. in Scythopolis (Beit She'an), Jerash and possibly Abila,[152] but the Rhodian piece is much flimsier and it is likely that it was an indirect copy, through a type II.3 Arab imitation which, if contemporary with the rest of its group, is dated between 642 and 646. It is doubtful that this piece came from Syria. If it is not an imitation of the period 610-641, and was minted on Rhodes, perhaps it strengthens the view supporting a brief occupation of Rhodes after 654. However, it is not impossible that it is later in date, belonging to a broader group of post-668 imitations.

To the period 610-668 are also dated the following coins, whose precise identification is not possible due to wear (PL. 53):

- Three folles
- Two half-folles
- Three quarter-folles
- One dodecanummium
- One unidentified small coin, perhaps a quarter-follis or late follis of Constans.

Constantine IV (September 668 - summer[153] 685)

From 663 onwards attacks in Anatolia became a regular feature and culminated in the establishment of Arab forces in the Propontis under Constantine IV. The occupation of the islands flanking the Anatolian littoral thus became necessary for the supply by sea of the Moslem troops wintering in Bithynia. The conquest of Rhodes by an Arab fleet led by Junada ibn Abu-Umayya al-Azdi, is recorded to have taken place the same year as that of Tarsus, dated ca. 672/673 or shortly after.[154] It also seems that the Arab occupation of Rhodes did not end with the treaty of 679; the orders for the recall of its garrison and the destruction of a fortress built to protect it 'from the constant harassment of the Byzantines' was ordered in late April of 680, after the death of Muawiya, by his successor Yazid I (May 680 - November 683).[155]

The 'seven year long' occupation of Rhodes should then be dated to the interval 673-681 and not earlier. There is numismatic evidence that seems to support this. Archaeological excavation in Rhodes has brought to light six coins

---

[143] Grierson 1982: 108, Pl. 5.
[144] Pottier 2008 (classes I and II): 97, 103.
[145] Grierson 1982 (classes 2bis, frontal bust, και 1/4, standing emperor): 111 and 112, Pl. 6.
[146] Pottier 2008 (class III.1): 104.
[147] Pottier 2008 (class III.2): 105.
[148] Pottier 2008 (class IV): 110.
[149] **856.**
[150] **857.**
[151] **848.**
[152] Goodwin 2005: 39; Foss 2008: 52-54, 141.
[153] Stratos 1974: 162-163.
[154] Stratos 1974: 33; Savvides 1995: 16-19; Bosworth 2002: 66. In 672 three Arab fleets wintered in the regions of the Karavisianoi (Cilicia, Lycia and Lydia) while a fourth, from Egypt, sailed just before the Byzantine fleet got there. The Byzantines merely plundered the Nile Delta. Christides 1984; Treadgold 1997: 325. This possibly means that in 672 the naval base on Rhodes was inoperative. Pryor and Jeffreys 2006: 26-27.
[155] Treadgold 1997: 327; Pryor and Jeffreys 2006: 27. There is also a view that Yazid was forced to abandon Rhodes and Crete when the army of the governor of North Africa Uqba ibn Nafi, Amr's nephew and founder of Cairouan, was defeated by the Berbers in 682/3. Wikipedia, articles Yazid I and Uqba ibn Nafi.

copying Constans' class 1 or class 4 (PL. 53).[156] They have thin flans, whose style recalls that of another piece bearing a Cypriot countermark,[157] although they are better struck than the flimsy imitation of the follis of Phocas mentioned above.[158] The countermarked piece[159] possibly circulated in Cyprus before the treaty following the breaking of the siege of Constantinople in 678.[160] The six pieces of Rhodes, perhaps contemporaneous with the Cypriot coin, are probably indirect copies of the folles of Constans; that is to say, they copy the Syrian imitations Alan Walmsley calls 'Byzantine Proxy II' and circulated between 650 and 670.[161] If this is true, they must be a kind of emergency money minted on Rhodes for local use during the Arab occupation of the island between *c.* 673 and 680. Four of the coins were found in excavations in the medieval town, one in the area of the great basilica of Rhodes (Hatziandreou plot) outside the medieval walls and still another was handed in by a member of the public but may have been found in the countryside. It should be noted that the coin with the Cypriot countermark, although probably a product of similar circumstances, imitates another class of Constans. To this family of emergency issues associated with the campaign of Muawiya against Constantinople must also belong two pieces published by Tony Goodwin.[162]

During the reign of Constantine IV, Byzantine control over the region of Rhodes was restored after the end of the long Arab siege of Constantinople (674-678)[163] and the treaty that followed between the emperor and Muawiya. However, to date, no coins minted by Constantine have been found on Rhodes.[164] Four folles of Constans II (one of class 5, two of class 11 and one half-legible of class 5-7) and the already mentioned coin imitating a follis of Constans II on a thin flan, bear countermarks with a monogram Grierson associated with Constantine IV.[165] This countermark is exclusively linked to Cyprus[166] and its presence on Rhodes cannot be a coincidence.

The history of the two islands in this period is full of problems, but it is certain that both Rhodes and Cyprus were under Arab control for some time, at least between 672/3[167] and the end of the siege of Constantinople in 678.[168] It would be reasonable to conclude that, after the treaty between Constantine IV and Muawiya, a mint operated in Constantia which called in the various coins currently in circulation, both issues of Constans II and Arab imitations, and authenticated them with a countermark. Some of this currency reached Rhodes, either around 680, perhaps in the process of the administrative reorganization of the islands after the departure of the Arabs or, less likely, about 691/2, the assumed date for the transfer of Cypriot settlers to Justinianopolis, presumably in order to restore former population levels in Bithynia which must have suffered severely from the invaders' operations.[169] If the latter holds true, the presence of the countermarked coins in Rhodes could be associated with the transport of settlers from Cyprus to Justinianopolis.

The dating of the countermark in the reign of Constantine IV has recently been questioned by Michael Metcalf who, through the analysis of the Soloi/1927 and Larnaca/1858 hoards, as well as finds from Paphos (Saranda Kolones), has been led to the conclusion that this countermark was used for a number of years, from 651 onwards, up to the beginning of the reign of Constantine IV.[170] The acceptance of Metcalf's interpretation regarding the dating of the countermarks with a monogram which might represent either Constans II or his successor, or even the mint of Constantia itself, does not pose an obstacle for the use of the countermark in Cyprus after 678. Of course, if he is right, the countermarked imitation of a Constans follis on a thin flan found on Rhodes may have been struck before 672/3 and have nothing to do with the Arab occupation of that decade or with the local imitations of Rhodes. In general, the issue of imitations on thin flans for some time, either by the Arabs or as a local reaction to the lack of coin in Rhodes and in other parts of the empire should not be ruled out. However, if the phenomenon is not linked to the Arab presence it should also be encountered in regions never occupied by the invaders.

---

156 **849**, **850**, **851**, **852**, **853** and **854**. **852** and **853** share the same die, but they are all stylistically similar.

157 Grierson 1968: I, 57; Metcalf 2009: 171-175.

158 Above, n. 151.

159 **855**. Probably an imitation of class 2bis, although the obverse is illegible. Cf. Metcalf 2009: 167-168.

160 The treaty is dated to 678/679. Stratos 1974: 51-52; Cheynet 2006: 8.

161 These emissions imitate issues of Constans. Walmsley 2010: 25-26.

162 Goodwin 2005: 34, no. 5 and 6.

163 Treadgold 1997: 325-327; Papadopoullos 2006: 265-266. Based on a philological analysis of the relevant passage of Theophanes' Chronographia, an attempt has recently been made to redate (and reduce in length) this siege of Constantinople by the Arabs in 668, making it coincide with the rebellion of Shapur. Prigent 2010: 167 n. 57, 176.

164 12 solidi which, together with two of Constans an one of Justin II, comprised the older part of the double hoard Lindos/1902. Balling 1963: 13-41.

165 **796** (class 5), **819** and **820** (class 11), **835** (class 5-7) and **855** (imitation).

166 Grierson 1968: I, 57, type I countermark; Grierson 1982: 121; Metcalf 2009: 171-175.

167 Stratos 1974: 31-35; Kaegi 1992: 248.

168 For Rhodes the most likely date is 681 or later. Above, 59 and footnote 156.

169 For the vicissitudes of Cyprus in the second half of the 7th century. See Papadopoullos 2006: 246 ff.

170 Metcalf 2009: 172-173, 200.

Conclusion

The distribution of coin finds of the period 498-668 within and without the medieval walled settlement (Figure 33) shows that, in the 6th and 7th century, the greatest resistance to urban decline outside the later fortifications was displayed around the great basilica of Rhodes on the lower slope of the ancient acropolis, west of the medieval town (see Figure 2, A). In this area, the circulation of copper coins continued until the fourth decade of the 7th century and was then reduced to scattered items until the end of the reign of Constans (Figure 33). Nevertheless, the concentration of the majority of the coins found outside the walls in particular enclaves indicates that the decline of the ancient city had begun much earlier, and that its consequences were already felt in the late 5th century.

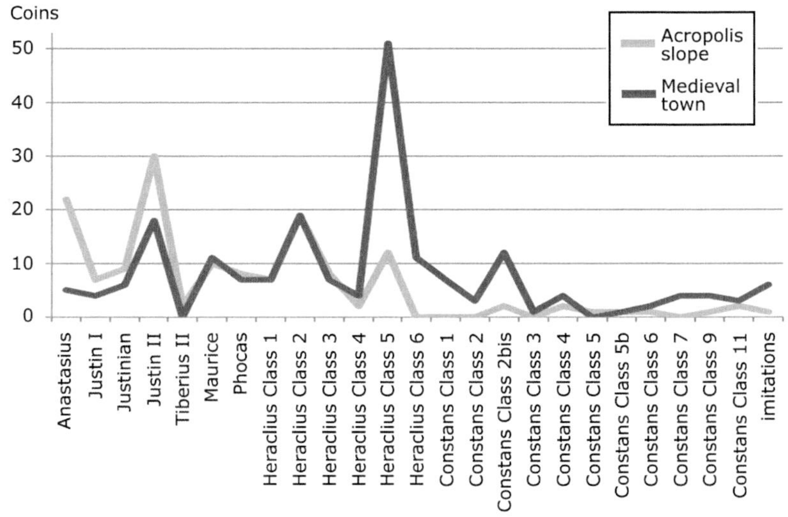

Figure 33: Comparison between the finds from the east slope of the ancient acropolis and the medieval town.

It is clear that the loss of Egypt and Syria, due to the economic exhaustion of the empire, reduced the strategic and commercial significance of Rhodes. The mobilization of enemy fleets in the region, of interest to the Arabs when they set their sights on Constantinople but also for the supply of shipbuilding timber, must have influenced the middle-range carrying trade. The destruction of the Byzantine fleet at the Battle of the Masts, with grave losses in craft an men, must have seriously affected the inhabitants of Rhodes, further afflicted by the advent of Junada in 672/3. With the removal of Constans II to Sicily, Rhodes was marginalized. A recent attempt has been made to reduce the significance of the Arab conquest of Rhodes under Constantine IV, and the attack of Junada in particular, which, it is suggested, may have taken place as late as 679.[171] This view mostly relies on estimations of the general significance of Rhodes for Byzantium, and the supposed development of a literary *topos* concerning the impoverishment of Rhodes at this time. Archaeological exploration and the numismatic evidence, however, seem rather to support the Arab historiographers. For the rarity of coin finds from the centuries following, different explanations are likely true but, in the last decades of the 7th century, the close of the period just examined, the condition of the celebrated ancient city must have been disheartening.

[171] Conrad 1992: 317-401; Bosworth 2002: 66. The occasionally exaggerated caution of Conrad is also noted by Metcalf 2009: 117.

2. Late 7th Century - 969

The coins

From the departure of the Arabs from Rhodes until the first appearance of an anonymous follis (class A1) issued, by general agreement, under John I Tzimisces (969-996), there is a space of three centuries when 25 emperors sat on the throne of Byzantium, including the second reign of Justinian II. Of those, only ten (in bold characters below) are represented in Rhodes (PLS. 54-55), by a mere 26 coins, of which three are solidi:

Emperor	Dates	Length of reign	Number of coins
Justinian II	**685-695**	10	1 (AV, unknown provenance)
Leontius	695-698	3	
Tiberius III	698-705	7	
Justinian II	705-711	7	
Philippicus	711-713	2	
Anastasius II	**713-715**	1+	1 (follis, stray find in the town)
Theodosius III	715-717	2	
Leo III	717-741	24	
Constantine V	741-775	34	
Leo IV	775-780	5	
Constantine VI	780-797	17	
Irene	797-802	5	
Nicephorus I	**802-811**	9	1 (follis, unknown provenance)
Stauracius	811	2 months	
Michael I	811-813	2	
Leo V	813-820	7	
Michael II	**820-829**	9	1 (follis, unknown provenance)
Theophilus	**829-842**	13	4 (folles, site finds)
Michael III	842-867	25	
Basil I	**867-886**	19	4 (2 AV stray finds from Lindos and Kattavia, and 2 folles: 1 site find and 1 of unknown provenance)
Leo VI	**886-912**	26	3 (folles: 2 of unknown provenance, 1 site find)
Alexander	912-913	1	
Constantine VII	**913-959**	46	2 (folles: 1 site find and 1 of unknown provenance)
Romanus I	**920-944**	24	7 (folles: 3 of unknown provenance, 4 site finds)
Romanus II	959-963	4	
Nicephorus II	**963-969**	6	2 (folles: 1 site find and 1 of unknown provenance)

Figure 34: Coins from Rhodes, 685 - 969.

The earliest of them is a solidus of Justinian II bearing the bust of Christ on the obverse.[172] In this period Arab coinage also became a means of religious propaganda: it is said that the intention of caliph 'Abd al-Malik to pay the annual indemnity due to the Byzantines[173] in his new gold coins bearing the *kalima* (Islamic Article of Faith) outraged Justinian; this is supposed to have led him to break the treaty with the Arabs in 692.[174] The solidus of Justinian II and two of the three folles until 829 are of unknown provenance. Site finds begin with a small peak under Theophilus[175] and then are minimal except for a similar peak under Romanus I. The problem with the folles

[172] Grierson (1982: 98) associates this type with the Quinisext Ecumenical Council, which resulted in a new schism with Rome. Ostrogorsky 1980: 139.

[173] This treaty is dated to the beginning of the reign of Justinian II, replacing an earlier one dated 678. Treadgold 1997: 332; Papadopoullos 2006: 266.

[174] Theophanes [1839-41]: 558-9; Broome 1985: 11-13, mentions a gold dinar of the type in question dated 693 (H 74). Ilisch (2010: 126-137) places the circulation of the new dinars in 696 (H 77).

[175] Hendy (1985: 645) believed that the changes perceptible under Theophilus were based on reforms of Nicephorus I. See also Niavis 1987: 61, 111-113, 264-265.

handed over by private individuals is that they are locally rare and it is possible that this fact encouraged their acquisition by the Ephorate without too many questions; and that these coins of uncertain provenance make up 50% of the total for the period under consideration. If all are included, the following graph ensues:

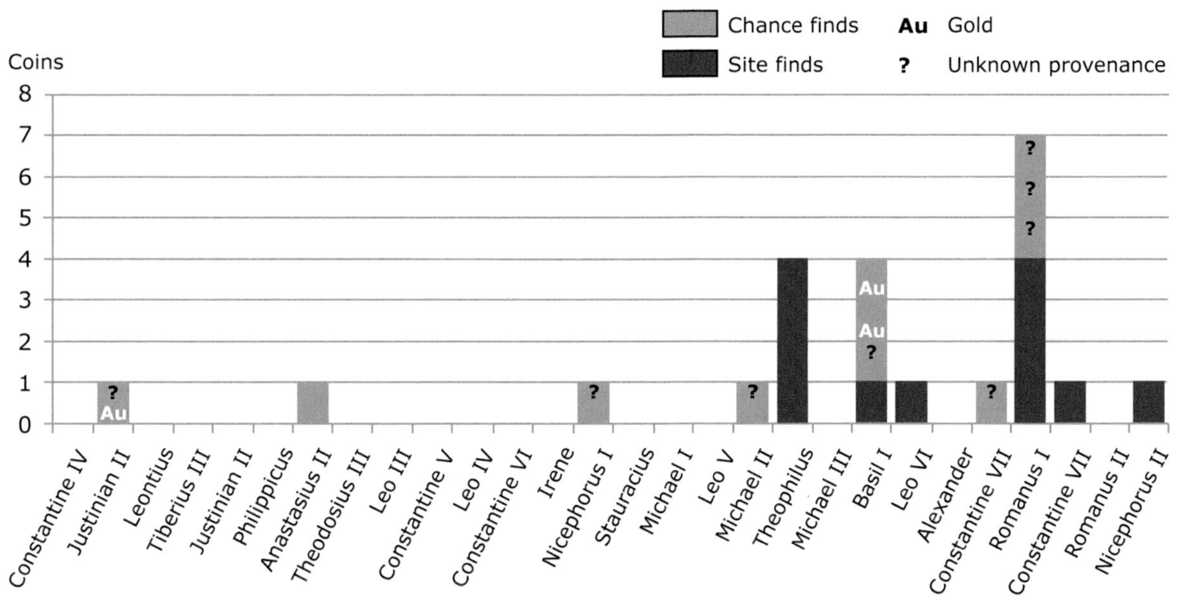

Figure 35: Distribution of coins of the period 668-969 by emperor.

This is a simple count of all coins. If the gold is excluded and a graph of losses per year is attempted (Figure 36 below), the disappearance of the copper from circulation is striking. Up to Michael II there are only three specimens, and the 'rise' under Theophilus is absurd in comparison with the period before 668. Indeed, if the single coin of Anastasius II is associated with the presence in Rhodes of the Byzantine fleet in 715, the contrast with the third year of Constans is in the order of 1:45.

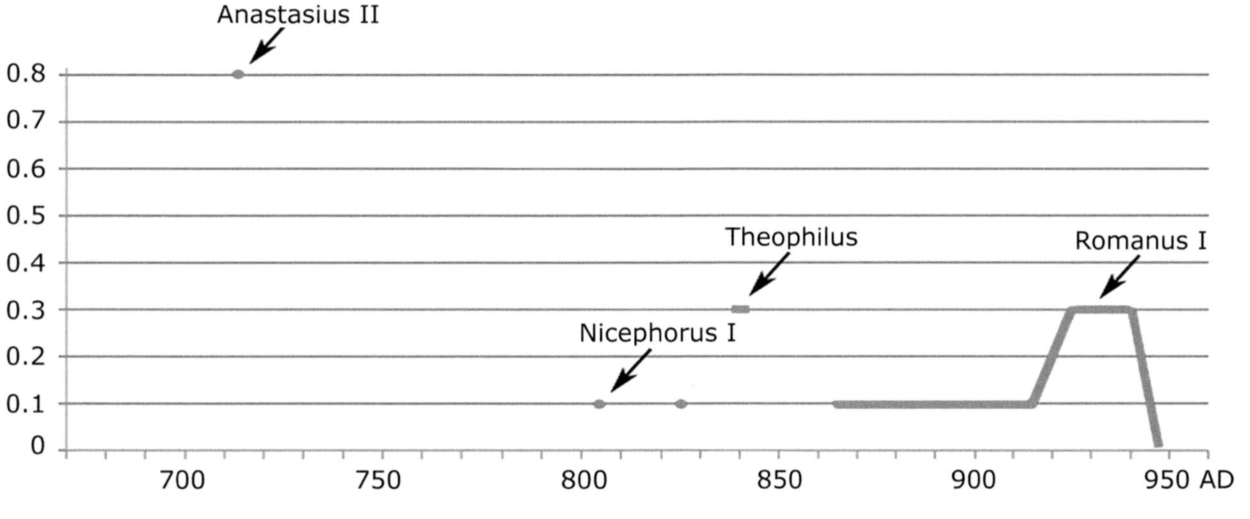

Figure 36: Losses per year, 668 - 969.

The absence of copper in Rhodes is not local in character but a well-established phenomenon of the Byzantine provinces which, in most sites, begins in the last decades of the 7th century and is associated with the general reorganization of the state. This overhaul, after the heavy losses of territory in the Middle East, north Africa and the Balkans, with the consequent loss of income from taxes, was effected under considerable pressure from an assortment of problems. The need to curtail spending while facing external danger from several directions, led to the establishment of new territorial units, the *themes*, where the role of the military dominated. Institutions like the *apothekai*, imperial *commercia* and military lands ensured the survival, equipment and supplies of the armies and fleet in the provinces at a lower cost and without the need for the use of copper coins, whose circulation was generally limited to the capital and temporary administrative headquarters.[176]

The historical background

From the 7th to the 10th century the Byzantine empire had to deal with a number of political crises, aggravated by economic problems. The geographical location of Constantinople and its strong walls repeatedly protected the administrative headquarters from external and internal enemies. The central authority was reinforced, but the financial exploitation of the periphery became harsh and its protection difficult. The decline of its cities, a phenomenon of Late Antiquity, worsened and reached its logical conclusion with the abandonment of some urban centres and the removal of their inhabitants to more secure locations in the hinterland. Fortified settlements and mountain passes would delay invading armies until the thematic troops could intervene effectively, while Byzantine diplomacy often incited attacks at the enemy's rear by third parties. However, when the coordinating central authority could not respond properly for whatever reason, the problems in the provinces became acute and serious losses in territory and men could be expected. Every political, military or administrative stumble an emperor committed could spark a succession crisis, or social unrest within the capital, exacerbating an already dangerous situation and further exhausting the resources of the state.

The first major crisis occurred at the end of the 7th century, at a time of administrative and defensive reforms whose management required a light hand, something Justinian II clearly lacked. He alienated the aristocracy with his agrarian policy and the common people with heavy taxation, and chose to break an advantageous truce with the Arabs in 692, when the second civil war among the latter was just over.[177] This resulted in a heavy defeat at Sebastopolis (692/3) and the imprisonment of Leontius, general of the Anatolikon theme, for two years. As soon as he was freed, Leontius rebelled and deposed Justinian. This initiated a period of political instability which undermined the effectiveness of the state and gave external enemies the opportunity to establish themselves within Byzantine territory. The violent final elimination of Justinian caused an invasion by the Bulgars who had been his allies. Philippicus, his successor, was also removed by an uprising. The only coin found in Rhodes from these troubled times is a follis of Anastasius II, who endeavoured to prepare for the coming clash with the Arabs[178] with the muster of forces in Rhodes; the troops rebelled and after six months of civil war he was deposed.[179] Theodosius III, his reluctant successor, was soon succeeded by the able general of the Anatolikon theme Leo III the Isaurian in 717.

Leo III repulsed the Arabs who invested Constantinople by land and sea in the same year. As before, the assault on Constantinople apparently brought about the pillage of Rhodes, possibly in the spring of 718 by the Egyptian fleet on its way to the besieged capital.[180] At the beginning of his reign Leo also put down uprisings in Macedonia and Sicily. From 726 on, the Arabs raided regularly at the eastern front until 740, when the Byzantines won a great victory at Akroïnon. His son, Constantine V, proved an exceptional military leader. He began his reign by coping with the dangerous uprising of Artabasdus and recovered territories in Syria; in 747 the general of the Cibyrrheotes defeated the Arab fleet off Cyprus. Soon after, the collapse of the Omayyad dynasty and the transfer of the seat of the caliph from Damascus to Baghdad[181] lowered the pressure along the eastern borders of the empire. In his time we have the first appearance of select troops (*tagmata*) fighting alongside the thematic armies.[182]

The second critical period began in 780, with the long minority of Constantine VI. When he came to power in 790, he proved unequal to the task; his mother Irene seized the reins of government and had him blinded (797). Trying to curry favour with her subjects through extensive tax exemptions, she caused the state finances to collapse. Arabs and Bulgars humiliated the Byzantine troops, forcing the empire to pay heavy indemnities in exchange for a truce and Irene finally lost control 802. She was succeeded on the throne by former bureaucrat Nicephorus I, who imposed effective, if onerous, economic measures.

---

[176] Hendy 1985: 640-645; Morrisson 2001.
[177] Second *fitna*, 680-692.
[178] Bury 1889: 371-372.
[179] Theophanes [1839-41]: 590-591; Bury 1889: 372; Ostrogorsky 1980: 154-155.
[180] Theophanes [1839-41]: 609. Suleiman had died in the autumn of 717; the lack of food in the besieging army the following spring must in part have been due to the breakdown of provisioning by sea.
[181] By the fist Abbasid caliph, Abul 'Abbas al-Saffah (750-754).
[182] Haldon 1999: 78.

Nicephorus was unfortunate in his dealings with external enemies[183] and in 806 caliph Harun al-Rashid[184] forced him to accept a humiliating treaty.[185] With this campaign of al-Rashid is associated an Arab raid on Cyprus and, in September 807, Rhodes was plundered, although the fortified town held out.[186] In 811 Nicephorus was killed fighting against the Bulgars. His son Stavracius, seriously wounded, was dethroned shortly before succumbing to his injuries by his brother in law, Michael I Rhangabe. In Michael's reign the Byzantines were forced to recognize Charlemagne as *basileus*, in exchange for part of the Dalmatian littoral he had held from the time of Irene. In 813, the Bulgar khan Krum defeated the Byzantine army at Adrianople after Leo the Armenian, *strategos* of the Anatolikon ran away; soon after, Leo managed to become emperor. Fortunately for him, Krum died in 814 and the situation in the Balkans calmed down. Matters also improved in the East because, after the death of al-Rashid, the caliphate was rent by civil war until 827.[187] Leo was murdered in 820 and the accession of Michael II the Amorian put an end to the succession crisis.

His most serious threat came from the rebellion of Thomas the Slav (821-823) who, with the support of the naval themes of the Aegean and the Cibyrrhaiotes laid siege to Constantinople. The destruction of the thematic fleets in this rebellion lost the empire control of the Aegean sea and, in 828, the Arabs conquered Crete.[188] At about the same time, the uprising of Euphemius in Sicily led to an Arab invasion of the island. The Arabs took Palermo in 831, under Theophilus,[189] who faced Arab raids throughout his reign.[190] It seems that, in his times, apart from the imperial mint in Constantinople, another mint was operating, perhaps in Thessalonica; it was probably active until 904 and is associated by scholars with the establishment of the theme of Thessalonica.[191] In spite of the constant campaigning, at the death of Theophilus the imperial coffers had a surplus of 1,090 *centenaria* of gold.[192] His issues are the first imperial coins to turn up as site finds in Rhodes after Constans II.

Byzantium was competently governed during the minority of his son Michael III by empress Theodora;[193] the gradual recovery of the empire was expressed by increased daring on the eastern front: in 853, a Byzantine fleet destroyed Damietta[194] and a fresh attack followed a year later. Michael's adult reign stands out for its cultural efflorescence but was also marked by a schism with the Church of Rome under patriarch Photius, the first Russian raid (860) and the loss of most of Sicily. In contrast, at the eastern front important victories were achieved.[195] In 867, Michael III was murdered by his favourite Basil, the founder of the Macedonian dynasty.

Under Basil I, Arab raids in Dalmatia were successfully countered by the imperial fleet at Ragusa[196] and the problem of the Paulicians was finally solved with the conquest of Samosata. Bari surrendered to the Byzantines in 876[197] but the Arabs took Syracuse in 878.[198] About 900 an Arab penetration into Cilicia, conducted in tandem with a naval operation along its littoral, was contained by general Nicephorus Phocas the Elder but Arab corsairs from Syria plundered Demetrias in 902 and Thessalonica in 904. A reorganization of the fleet followed[199] and the Byzantines defeated the Arabs in the Aegean sea in 905 and plundered Laodicea in 910. However, the attempt to retake Crete in 911 failed and, on its way back, the Byzantine fleet was surprised by the Arabs and destroyed in 912.[200]

During the minority of Constantine VII, the Byzantine army was repeatedly defeated by the Bulgar tsar Symeon (893-927) and, finally, the *drungarius* of the imperial fleet Romanus Lecapenus ascended the throne through the

183 Scholars have not reached an agreement about the effectiveness of the campaign against the Slavs in the Peloponnese; officially they were not an external enemy. Curta 2014.
184 In 796 the caliph had transferred his headquarters from Baghdad to Raqqah in Syria.
185 Apparently, however, the balance of Nicephorus' policy vis-a-vis the Arabs was positive. Treadgold 1988: 144-146.
186 Theophanes [1839-41]: 749.
187 Fourth *fitna*.
188 These Arabs were not controlled by Syria: at least some of them were political refugees from Spain. Clot 2004: 91; Lev 1984: 223.
189 Euphemius had asked the Tunisian Aghlabids for military aid. F. M. Crawford 1907: II, 71-74; Lev 1984: 226.
190 By caliph al-Mu'tasim (833-842).
191 Morrisson 2002: 914. It may be that production, contemporaneous with the establishment of the theme of Thessalonica, was interrupted after the capture of the city by Leo Tripolites in 904. Hendy 1985: 424-426.
192 34.5 tons or 7.8 million solidi. Hendy 1985: 224-225.
193 Backed by her brothers Bardas and Petronas, magister Sergius Nicitiates and logothete of the drome Theoctistus.
194 Because the Egyptians supported the Arabs of Crete. Ostrogorsky 1980: 218-222; Lev 1984: 224.
195 Cheynet 2006: 22; Ostrogorsky 1980: 217, 219, 223-232; Dagron 2002: 431.
196 Ragusa was the headquarters of a provincial fleet which protected the region from the Arabs, who besieged the town in 886. Cheynet 2006: 450.
197 Bari was held by the Arabs from 847 (emirate under Kalfun and successors, Kreutz 2011: 38). Its siege by Louis II the German lasted from 866 to 871, when he was assisted by a blockade by the Byzantine/Slav fleet. Wickham 1981: 62, 154-155. In 876 the Byzantines took Bari. Theophanes Continuatus II [2011]: 55. For the relations between southern Italy and Byzantium from that date on, see also Gay 1904.
198 Cheynet 2006: 25; Ostrogorsky 1980: 233-239.
199 Lev 1984: 225.
200 Cheynet 2006: 28; Ostrogorsky 1980: 255-259.

marriage of his daughter to the young Constantine.[201] In 923 or 924,[202] the Byzantine fleet defeated the Arabs off Lemnos. General John Curcuas took Melitene in 931, but in 938 was defeated at the Euphrates by Saif-ad-Daulah, emir of Aleppo. In 941 the Rus raided the east side of the Bosphorus before being contained by Curcuas; while in 943 a Russian expedition to the Danube under Igor aided by the Pechenegs concluded with a treaty which allowed Curcuas to pursue further successes on the eastern front. The reign of Romanus I ended with the ill-conceived coup of his sons who were soon after arrested and exiled, one in Rhodes the other in Samothrace.[203]

The policy of Romanus I in support of small property holders was continued by Constantine VII.[204] In 949 a new attack on Arab Crete failed, while clashes with the Arabs continued in North Syria and Mesopotamia. Crete was finally recovered under Romanus II by Nicephorus Phocas the Younger, in 960-961. The following year Phocas returned to Syria where he took Aleppo and, in 963, after the death of Romanus, ascended the throne through his marriage to the widowed empress Theophano. Phocas overturned the agrarian policy of his predecessors but reinforced the institution of the military lands while setting limits to the property held by the Church; he also imposed strict controls on urban economic activity. In 963-965 he was campaigning in Cilicia and after that in Syria, where Antioch was taken in 969, shortly before his murder by John Tzimisces.

Control of the sea and Rhodes

The early large fleets Constans II brought together to face the Arabs[205] apparently consisted of squadrons both from Constantinople and from the coastline of the provinces. The *strategos* of the *Karabisianoi,* that is to say of the war fleet, is mentioned in the sources from about 680 until 711. From then on, and possibly from 717 onwards, it seems that the administrative separation of the fleet of the capital from the provincial ones proved more efficient. The first naval theme, the Cibyrrhaiote, to which Rhodes belonged, already existed in 732, when its *strategos* is first mentioned.[206] At this time defence of the sea was in three tiers: a) the fleet of the capital (*vasilikon ploimon*) b) the provincial fleets (*thematikon ploimon*) and c) the squadrons of the thematic coastlands. The arsenals, ships and equipment were distributed all over the empire, but the bulk was concentrated in the capital itself and the harbours of the Propontis. The crews of the provincial fleets were enlisted on the same terms as the soldiery of the thematic armies.[207]

The use of the term Dark Ages for the 8th and 9th centuries in Byzantium is nowadays going out of fashion. Nevertheless, where Rhodes is concerned, it is aptly descriptive. During this obscure period, which also includes part of the 7th and the 10th century, the town and island are mentioned almost exclusively in connection with raids, sea-battles and uprisings. During the 9th and 10th centuries it seems that Rhodes was the base of a *drungus* and the second in importance harbour of the theme, after its capital Attaleia.[208] The fragmentary historical record preserves the adverse consequences of the island's geographical location. The loss of Egypt and Syria and the 'neutrality' of Cyprus[209] removed most of its economic importance, while the establishment of the Cibyrrhaiote theme reduced its administrative role. Moreover, every time the Arabs mounted an expedition against Constantinople or advanced as far as south-western Asia Minor, Rhodes was raided or temporarily occupied as a matter of course. Besides, the proximity of Crete after 828[210] increased insecurity in the south Aegean. Although there is no consensus about the precise date of the Arab conquest of Crete, possible raiding of the Rhodian hinterland is unlikely to have been particularly noticed in the general mayhem and may have thus been unrecorded.

The main function of Rhodes in those times was as a naval base and arsenal,[211] but the maintenance of the fleet was not always a priority for the central government; nor was state attention always beneficial for the inhabitants

[201] Cheynet 2006: 29; Ostrogorsky 1980: 262-265.
[202] Lev 1984: 237.
[203] Cheynet 2011: 114-116; Ostrogorsky 1980: 265-278.
[204] Ostrogorsky 1980: 272-276, 280; Lefort 2002: 282; Toubert 2002: 384.
[205] Cosentino 2007: 577. For the Byzantine fleet see also Pryor and Jeffreys 2006.
[206] Concerning the Aegean Sea, it was followed by the establishment of the themes of Hellas and Samos. The existence of a 'Karabisian' theme, which several 20th c. scholars have accepted as the precursor of the Cibyrrhaiote theme, is in doubt. Antoniadis-Bibicou 1966: 63-98.
[207] Cheynet 2006: 156.
[208] Antoniadis-Bibicou 1996: 94. Treadgold 1995: 66-67, 74-75, 108.
[209] Dikigoropoulos 1958: 94-114; Papadopoullos 2006: 269-278; Zavagno 2013: 3-3; Metcalf 2009: 478-486, 496-497, 575-576.
[210] Scholars have expressed various views on the date of the Arab conquest of Crete. The opinion based on the date of the siege of Alexandria, which was held by the Arabs from Al Andalus, by Abd'Allah, general of caliph al-Ma'mun, who drove them out, seems the most reliable. Malamut 1989: II, 72-75; Treadgold 1988: 251-254.
[211] Cf. Al-Masudi [1863]: 423, 'Cette île est située en face d'Alexandrie, à la distance d'une nuit de navigation, c'est là que commence le pays des Francs. Aujourd'hui, en 332 de l'hégire [AD 943], Rhodes est un arsenal où les Grecs construisent leurs vaisseaux de guerre...'

of the naval themes.[212] Theophanes, for example, numbers the legislation of Nicephorus I concerning the naval lands of the Cibyrrhaiote theme among the evils that emperor inflicted on his subjects;[213] while the participation of the Cibyrrhaiotes in the uprising of Thomas the Slav under Michael II (821-824) may have been a reaction to imperial policy. The destruction of the thematic fleets in this civil war seems to have enabled the invasion of Sicily by the Aghlabids (from 826 onwards) and the conquest of Crete by Arabs from al-Andalus (*c.* 828). During the Arab-Byzantine conflict in Anatolia, Rhodes must have served the Byzantines as a stage for the supply of the troops by sea, at least when the action involved the wider region of Cilicia.[214]

A great deal has been written concerning the neglect of the Byzantine navy by the state. However, without the pressure of immediate danger, the maintenance of a fleet was expensive. Also, keeping crews in training was dangerous both for the men and the equipment,[215] not just from accidents but also because of the sudden shifts in the weather.[216] Besides the upkeep of personnel, even if no actual shipbuilding took place, the ships had to be beached at regular intervals to be scraped clean and caulked; and ropes, sail, masts and oars replaced. This would have required *corvées* in the Rhodian hinterland -Rhodes still had abundant shipbuilding timber- and the contribution of rope makers, the supply (or weaving) of sail cloth, and the management of large storerooms if not also roofed ship sheds. Even if the raw materials for the maintenance of the vessels were available locally, something that may be doubted, the technical knowhow must have suffered from raids, defeats, natural disasters and plagues and had to be fostered and renewed.

The topography of the town of Rhodes in this period has been examined by Katerina Manoussou-Della.[217] However, we know very little about its organization and commercial role. It is thought that the arsenal operated in the northernmost harbour, the modern Mandraki. This is very likely, because this harbour had the same function both in antiquity and, later, under the Ottomans. The arsenal was, in any case, the main reason that the exposed site of the town was never abandoned, in a period characterized by the frequent abandonment of coastal settlements and the relocation of the inhabitants in defensible inland sites. The existence of the arsenal meant that the workmen and their families had to live nearby, for reasons of both convenience and security. In times of danger, as in 807, these people could take shelter in the Early Byzantine castle, even though some of them may have been living outside its walls. Also, given the straitened circumstances of the empire, the arsenal personnel, the oarsmen and permanent garrison must have been granted arable land in order to maintain themselves.

Part of the experience of the sailors of the fleet must have been bred in their daily contact with the sea as fishermen or crews of traders, while the simplest way to lower the cost of the arsenal's upkeep was to make it available for the repair of commercial craft at a price, a practice also known from the Ottoman period. Some of the handful of copper pieces of this period found in Rhodes may be due to this auxiliary activity. However, in times of insecurity and inadequate care by the central authority, the decline of the arsenal must have been rapid. Perhaps this factor contributed to the uprising of the soldiers of Opsikion in Rhodes in 715: they cut down the unfortunate general logothete Ioannes who was in charge of the planned expedition against the Arabs and then sailed along the Anatolian coastline in search of a new emperor.[218]

Byzantine historians mention Rhodes directly only four times from the end of the 7th century on: in association with the revolt of 715, the Arab raids of 718 and 807,[219] and the exile of Stephanus Lecapenus in 945,[220] before his final removal to Lesbos, where he died in 963. The history of the island can be traced only indirectly, through general developments and their impact on the naval theme of the Cibyrrhaiotes to which Rhodes belonged. Besides

212 Ahrweiler 1966: Appendice III, 419-439.

213 Theophanes [1839-41]: 757, ninth 'vexation'. Niavis 1987: 106. The eighth 'vexation', concerning the imposition of a tax on the purchase of slaves in the Dodecanese implies that slaves and other loot from successful encounters with the Arabs were sold in the harbour of Rhodes. It seems that the assertion of al-Masudi in the 10th century about its function as a gateway to Byzantium was equally valid 150 years earlier. Niavis 1987: 102-105.

214 The strategic significance of Cilician rivers such as the Pyramus (Ceyhan) for control of the region around Mopsuestia and the Cygnus (Berdan) for Tarsus needs to be explored, in view of the situation in Egypt, where the fleet was partly employed to control the country. Kubiak 1970: 48-50.

215 The vulnerability and cost of vessels is also discussed by naval treatises of the period. Christides 2002: 93.

216 This characteristic of the Aegean is internationally recognized by modern yachtsmen.

217 Chapters V and VIII of her Doctoral Thesis (2014).

218 Theophanes [1839-41]: 590-591. It is obvious that the rebels lacked a leader. Treadgold (1997: 344) believes that the men of Opsikion held a grudge since the blinding of George Boraphos, their count, two years earlier. It is possible that the taxatoi of Opsikion also had other grievances. Savvides 1985: 150. Theodosius III, who gained the throne in this way proved incompetent and soon abdicated.

219 Savvides 1995: 20-21.

220 Under guard by four dromons with crews of 120 men and one *ousia* during the 949 expedition against Crete. Constantinus Porphyrogenitus [1829]: 665; Malamut 1989: II, 600.

the few direct references, the following events associated with the Cibyrrhaiote theme may be reasonably assumed to have affected Rhodes itself:

- The capture, by the Cibyrrhaiote fleet, of the ships of Artabasdus off Abydos, when he sent them for help to the caliphate during his bid for the throne (741-743).[221]
- The victory of the *strategos* of the Cibyrrhaiotes over the Egyptian fleet in the bay of Keramaia in Cyprus *c.* 747.[222]
- The expedition of the *patricius* Theodore against Elpidius in Sicily with a large fleet, probably from the Cibyrrhaiote theme, in 781.[223]
- The defeat of the Cibyrrhaiote fleet in the gulf of Attaleia and the execution by the enemy of its *strategos*, Theophilus, in 790.[224]
- The legislation of emperor Nicephorus I concerning the naval lands (*nautika ktemata*) in the Cibyrrhaiote theme.
- The uprising of Thomas the Slav (821-823) and his support by the naval themes, which led to the destruction of their fleets.
- The conquest of Crete by the Arabs *c.* 828.
- The attempt of Krateros, *strategos* of the Cibyrrhaiote theme, to retake Crete in 828, with a fleet of the naval themes.[225]
- The recruitment of *tessarakontarioi* by Nicetas Ooryphas and their establishment in the Cyclades in 829.[226]
- The destruction of the Arab fleet of Crete in 841.[227]
- The destruction in a storm at Cape Gelidonya of a large Arab fleet prepared by caliph Mu'tasim to attack Constantinople shortly before his death, in 842.[228]
- The attempt to recover Crete *c.* 843 by Theoctistus.[229]
- The destruction of Damietta by the Byzantine fleet in 853.[230]
- Raid against Damietta in 854.[231]
- Raid against Pelusium (Farama) in 859.[232]
- The attempt by *caesar* Bardas to recover Crete in 866.[233]
- The activity of Arab corsairs in the 9th and early 10th century.
- The Arab campaign in Cilicia, in combination with a naval expedition along its coast, which was checked by Nicephorus Phocas the Elder in 900.
- The reorganization of the Byzantine fleet, which defeated the Arabs in the Aegean in 905 and the raid against Laodicea in 910.
- Himerius' attempt to recover Crete in 911 and the destruction of his fleet by the Arabs near Chios in 912.
- The crowning of Romanus Lecapenus, *drungarios ton ploimon*, as senior emperor in 920.
- The attempt of Constantine Gongylas to recover Crete in 949.
- The campaigns of John Curcuas in northern Syria in 949.
- The defeat of the Arab fleet of Tarsus by the Basil Hexamilites, *strategos* of the Cibyrrhaiotes, in 956.[234]
- The reconquest of Crete by future emperor Nicephorus Phocas in 962.
- The Cilician campaign of Nicephorus II in 963-965.
- The recovery of Cyprus by Nicephorus II in 965.
- The Syrian campaigns of Nicephorus II in 966-969.

---

[221] The intervention of the thematic fleet so close to the capital is due to the fact that Artabasdus was in possession of Constantinople, where the royal squadron was based. Treadgold 1997: 357-358.
[222] Kubiak 1970; Malamut 1989: I, 107; Papadopoullos 2006: 276.
[223] Treadgold 1988: 67.
[224] Treadgold 1988: 93-95, 348.
[225] Bury 1912: 289-290.
[226] Treadgold 1988: 257.
[227] Treadgold 1988: 240.
[228] Wikipedia, article Mu'tasim.
[229] Bury 1912: 291-292, (Cont. Georg., 814).
[230] Bury 1912: 292. Grégoire 1933: 515 ff.
[231] Kubiak 1970: 59.
[232] *Op. cit.*
[233] Bury 1912: 170-171. In a campaign where both Michael III and the caesar Bardas participated the absence of the most important naval theme would have been extraordinary. Whether the fleet actually reached Crete after the murder of Bardas by Basil (where the opinion of Grégoire is worth considering, *op. cit.*), is not so important.
[234] Theophanes Continuatus VI [1863]: col. 469; Pryor and Jeffreys 2006: 399-400.

Recapitulating, a first recovery of the thematic fleet of the Cibyrraiotes is observed about 740, followed by a severe blow in 790 and, a generation later, prolonged weakness due to the consequences of the revolt of Thomas the Slav, in combination with increased insecurity caused by the Arab presence on Crete after 828. The endeavour of Nicetas Ooryphas to contain the Arabs of Crete and the destruction of their fleet in 841 was followed, a year later, by the destruction of the Syriac fleet, securing an interval of quiet. From 853 until 866 large Byzantine fleets including the thematic fleet of the Cibyrrhaiotes, are active in Egypt, Crete and Cyprus, indicating significant recovery. A reduction in the role of the fleet is observed under Basil I and control of the Aegean is lost again, resulting, most notably, in the plundering of Demetrias in 902 and Thessalonica in 904 by Syrian corsairs. The ensuing reorganization in 905 brought about some successes until 912, when the fleet was destroyed off the island of Chios by Arab corsairs, on its way back from another attempt to recover Crete. It is probable, judging from the location of the Byzantine disaster, that the Cibyrrhaiote squadron had already split off to return to its headquarters thus escaping the fate of the imperial squadron. It is, however, unlikely that its luck held in the disastrous expedition of Gongylas, again against Crete, in 949. Nevertheless, by 956 the thematic fleet had recovered and must have played a supportive role in the great campaigns in Cilicia and northern Syria under Romanus II and Nicephorus II Phocas.[235]

To conclude, it is obvious that *c.* 700, if not during the last quarter of the 7th century, Rhodes had been incorporated in the reforms which allowed the Byzantine provinces to maintain armies, and then fleets, without the use of copper coin.[236] The organization of the themes and the institutions of the military lands and *apothekai*[237] obviated the need for cash at the local level, at least where small scale exchanges were concerned. It may well be that the interruption in the supply of copper coin by the central authority for administrative reasons intensified the downturn of the local economy and then inhibited growth, as it did elsewhere, once external threats had receded.[238]

Scholars note a gradual recovery in monetary circulation during the 9th century,[239] while some even question the range of the disappearance of petty cash in the Byzantine provinces during the 'Dark Ages'.[240] However, increased circulation in specific sites like 9th century Amorium, are due to localized factors mostly having to do with the involvement of central government.[241] Rhodes is a classic example of the opposite. We cannot even speak of an emerging recovery in the 9th century, although the reign of Theophilus is represented by four coins, most of them much corroded. Minting quality has possibly something to do with this, in which case Rhodes may have come into contact with the 'provincial mint' operating at this time.[242] We have no coins from the reign of his successor, Michael III, although Rhodes probably participated in the expeditions of the thematic fleets in 843, 853 and 866, since very little copper was struck during his reign.[243] Only a single piece belongs to the time of the 956 expedition and none date from 962, when the entire Byzantine fleet was involved in the assault upon Crete. Numismatic circulation, if it can so be called, is at negligible levels under Basil I, Leo VI and Constantine VII (0.1 losses per year); while a 'spike' comparative to that of Theophilus appears under Romanus I, although we have no information on the activities of the thematic fleet at the time. Then the figure drops again to a very low 0.3 under Nicephorus II.

It is thus clear that the arsenal of Rhodes, and the walled town attached to it, operated within an administrative framework which did not require daily transactions in small currency.[244] So far, the numismatic evidence does not support the presence of a consumer-oriented urban environment. We should probably visualize, for this period, the existence of a settlement maintained for a particular purpose and mostly supported by its own hinterland or, in difficult times, through measures taken by the local military commander.[245]

235 For the Byzantine fleet under Nicephorus Phocas see also Liutprand of Cremona [1881]: 915.
236 Treadgold 1995: 24; Laiou 2010: 63-64. For the broader canvas of these developments see Haldon 1995: 232-253; *idem* 1999: 71 ff.
237 Hendy 1985: 640-645. Ragia 2011: 197-200, 221, 244.
238 Cf. Guillou 1974; Metcalf 1979: 15.
239 Metcalf 1979: 18 ff.,
240 Lightfoot 2002: 229-239.
241 E.g. Amorium was the birthplace of Michael II and the headquarters of Constantine V for years.
242 Morrisson 2002: 914.
243 Grierson 1973: I, 459-460.
244 Angold 1984b: 6-7; Haldon 1999: 249-250.
245 Cf. Hendy 1989: 13-15; Haldon 1999: 84. For the difficulties in the interpretation of urban Byzantine sites in this period see also Russell 1986.

3. The Period of the Anonymous Folles (969 - 1092)

John I (December 969- January 976)

Like Nicephorus II Phocas, John I Tzimisces spent most of his reign campaigning against external enemies. In 966, and in order to concentrate his attention on the eastern front, Phocas had encouraged the Russian prince Sviatoslav (964-972) to attack the Bulgars from the north. By the summer of 969, Sviatoslav was in control of much of Bulgaria and demanded that the Byzantines abandon the Balkans altogether, before being defeated at Arcadiopolis. In 971, the Byzantine army led by Tzimisces in person, drove Sviatoslav out and Bulgaria was annexed by the empire.[246] At this time Tzimisces took measures against the growing power of great landowners, also curtailing the freedom of movement of small farmers.[247] In 972 he led an expedition into Mesopotamia, while from 974 until his death he was campaigning in Syria and Palestine against the Fatimids, taking strong cities like Damascus, Caesarea, Beirut, Sidon and Acre.

The rule of John I Tzimisces is, from nearly every aspect, a continuation of the policies of Nicephorus II. However, his reign is marked by the circulation of the first folles of the so-called anonymous series (PL. 56), which was to dominate circulation through the best part of the 11th century. As these coins do not bear the name of the issuing emperor, numismatists refer to the various classes using successive letters of the alphabet. They have been sequentially dated by overstrikes, either by a later anonymous class or by some eponymous issue, since in the second half of the 11th century the anonymous series was complemented by folles bearing the names of various emperors. Naturally, as their study progressed, the date of some anonymous classes was revised.[248] Now the more primitive version of Class A, known as A1, is assigned to John I, represented in the Rhodian finds by four pieces, corresponding to 0.57 losses per year. Although modest, the figure represents a rise from the 0.3 of Nicephorus II.

Basil II (January 976-December 1025)

The military successes of the mid-10th century were due to remarkable leadership and the emergence of the tagmatic armies, composed of well-trained and equipped professional soldiers.[249] The importance of the thematic troops was seriously reduced. On the death of John I, the succession passed to the two young sons of Romanus II. The eldest, Basil II, was only 18 years old and his inexperience encouraged veteran generals Bardas Sclerus and Bardas Phocas, representing powerful landowning clans, to claim the throne through a civil war which lasted, on and off, until 989 allowing the Bulgars to regroup and found a new sovereign state. Part at least of the thematic fleet had sided with Bardas Sclerus, but was easily neutralized by Basil's imperial squadron.[250] As the *tagmata* had supported the rebels, Basil II had to turn for assistance to Vladimir, ruler of Kiev[251] and employ Russian troops which, later, became the nucleus of his own expeditionary forces. The troubles Basil II encountered in the first two decades of his long reign strongly influenced his later policies and had a serious impact on the choices available to his successors. From 991 until about 994 and from 1001 to 1014 his attention was turned towards Bulgaria, which was again annexed by the Byzantine state in 1018. In between, and after the capitulation of the Bulgars, Basil turned to the east, securing the recent Byzantine conquests in Syria and annexing part of Armenia and Georgia to the empire.[252]

These acquisitions were divided into themes and the eastern borderlands into smaller units, under the command of dukes. Conquered parts of Cappadocia, Cilicia and northern Syria were settled by Armenians.[253] Basil's campaigns were carried out by tagmatic troops, and the emperor promoted the commutation of the thematic *strateia*, which could provide only lower grade soldiers.[254] He also did not hesitate to employ Venetian shipping as transport for his

[246] Haldon 2004: 156-171.
[247] Ostrogorsky 1980: 294-295.
[248] Grierson and Travaini 1998: 42. On certain points there is no full agreement, because some emperors are not linked to a particular coin type, while certain issues of the second half of the 11th century are assigned to rebels or different mints. The identifications here are mostly based on the publications of Grierson and Hendy.
[249] Haldon 2004: 153-154.
[250] At least the part of the fleet based in Attaleia. Metcalf 2009: 507.
[251] Vladimir (980-1015) wed Anna Porphyrogenita, sister of Basil, and was baptized.
[252] Cheynet 2006: 37-38.
[253] Angold's criticism of Basil's policy (Angold 1984b: 10-11) is problematic. The expansionist drive had been initiated by his predecessors and had its own dynamic. The settlement of Armenians in conquered areas was the application of a traditional solution born out of necessity for the restoration of regions devastated by war and taxation; while it undermined, as did other measures taken by the emperor, the dangerous power of the Anatolian magnates. The integration of the Bulgars and Armenians could only have been achieved given sufficient time and stability. Friction between Armenians and Orthodox in Cappadocia was expressed in religious terms but was probably due to shifts in power at a local level.
[254] Cheynet 2006: 277.

army.[255] He sought, with various measures, to reduce the influence and economic power of the great landowners, whose influence on the military could cause problems and threaten the central authority. At the same time, he tried to protect small landholdings from the *dynatoi*, transferring part of the financial burden of taxation to the latter (*allelengyon*). In spite of the massive military expenses, the efficiency of the administration and the new measures of Basil II resulted in the accumulation of a gold reserve which, in 1025, amounted to 200,000 'talents'.[256]

The folles of Basil II (PL. 56-58) preserved on both sides the main design bequeathed by John I. However, there was significant improvement in minting quality (class A2), the weight of the coins increased, and a series of 'secret marks' was introduced.[257] On Rhodes, 23 folles of class A2 have been identified so far; of those, only six are site finds. This is the result of the impressive size of the coins, some of which weigh over 15 grams. The anonymous A2 class is thought to have also covered the three years after Basil's death when his brother Constantine VIII reigned alone (1025-1028). Grierson has distinguished about fifty variants of class A2, based on their obverse and reverse 'secret marks'.[258] In the Rhodian coins, not always sufficiently well preserved to be securely classified, at least ten of his types have been identified, as follows: 3 (five pieces), 8, 12 (or 21 or 34), 14 (or 22, or 35, or 41), 14b (or 24), 27 (two pieces), 31,[259] 32, 34 (or 35-40), 39, 41 (two pieces) and 47 (one or two pieces). Losses per year are about the same as for the reign of John I, or perhaps a shade lower (0.44), if the three years of the reign of Constantine VIII are taken into account.

It has recently been maintained that, after the conquest of Crete (961), the fleet was neglected and its role limited to the pursuit of Arab corsairs. The commutation of military service in the naval themes is taken for granted, although not adequately supported by the available evidence. It is thought that under Basil II and after him the reduced capability of the fleet was supplemented by the enlistment of allies like the Venetians, who presented a cheaper alternative to the maintenance of the thematic fleet.[260] This view is too sweeping. The conquest of Crete, considered as a *terminus*, came before the great campaigns of the reign of Nicephorus II and was followed by the full assimilation of Cyprus by the empire (964), ending three centuries of theoretical neutrality for the island. At this time, besides the Syrian corsairs, the Byzantines had to deal with the rising power of the Fatimids, something which would have been very difficult without the existence of a fleet.[261]

The historiography of the period is not particularly helpful about the contribution of the navy, whose role was overshadowed by the spectacular successes of the land armies and the dominant image of the soldier-emperor in the public consciousness.[262] Indeed, the fleet was not particularly suited for the transport of heavy cavalry and the sumpter beasts required in the campaign routes between Asia Minor, Armenia, the Euphrates and Syria. Many of the animals and most of the supplies must have been collected by the expeditionary forces along the way. Nevertheless, given that the Byzantine campaigns were highly planned affairs, whenever the action moved closer to the coast the presence of the navy must have been particularly helpful. During yearly campaigning the fleet could carry relatively quickly and at relatively low cost supplies, siege equipment, timber and reinforcements, remove the injured, refugees and captives and cover the rear of the army. The best documented collaboration between the Byzantine army and navy was the blockade of Sviatoslav at Dorostolon in 971 and, in this case, the fleet involved must have been that of the capital. However, the fact that in 975 John I established a chain of coastal themes in Syria is obviously connected to the presence of the Cibyrraiote fleet in the region.[263] Besides, the reference to the admirals of the themes who backed the uprising of Bardas Sclerus in 976[264] is an indication that the collaboration of the army and navy in the eastern provinces must have been regular before the death of Tzimisces. It is true that in the Scleros uprising their participation did not amount to much against the fleet of the capital.[265] Because of this incident, the absence of the thematic fleets from the accounts of the rest of the reign of Basil II might be explained

[255] Chrysobull of 992, under doge Pietro Orseolo II (991-1009). Tuma 1984; Nicol 2004: 67-70. The enlistment of Venetian assistance may imply deliberate neglect of the thematic fleet which had supported rebellious magnates in the early part of the reign: Basil did not forget quickly.
[256] Hendy 1985: 225.
[257] Grierson 1982: 205-208. Grierson 1973: II, 644 ff.
[258] The number of varieties probably indicates correlation with regnal years, including the time Constantine VIII was sole emperor, after Basil's death.
[259] With three dots above the reverse legend.
[260] Cheynet 2006: 266.
[261] E.g. in Sicily, although the defeats on land and sea of the Byzantine expeditionary force under Manuel Phocas (964-965) led to the abandonment of the attempt to recover possession of the island by Nicephorus II; and concerning the control of northern Syria from 969 (establishment of the new Fatimid capital in Cairo) onwards. For the powerful Fatimid fleet as well as the capabilities of the Byzantine navy during the second half of the 10th c. see Lev 1984; Bramoullé 2008.
[262] Haldon 1999: 243-244; Morris 1988: 87 ff.
[263] At Gabala (Jableh), Balanaia (Banyas), Laodicea and Antaradus. Treadgold 1995: 36.
[264] Treadgold 1997: 513-514.
[265] Zonaras [1897]: 543.

by a deliberate neglect born of the emperor's mistrust. It is not impossible, however, that Basil had a change of mind later on, perhaps in the last years of his reign when he began considering action against the Arabs in Sicily.

Successors (1028 - 1092)

The important administrative changes of the 11th century and the increased political instability of the interval between the great soldier-emperors and the monetary reform of 1092, render the interpretation of the available evidence more complex. An understanding of the broader context is necessary for the interpretation of the testimony of the coins in Rhodes which, in this period, is particularly interesting.

Constantine VIII apparently withdrew the privileges hitherto enjoyed by the Venetians after the downfall of doge Otto Orseolo, who sought refuge in the Byzantine court.[266] Constantine died three years after Basil II, bequeathing the throne to his son in law, Romanus III Argyrus. Argyrus represented the interests of the Constantinopolitan nobility, but tried to continue the aggressive military policy of the soldier emperors in Syria and Egypt, although lacking in both experience and skill. His two Syrian campaigns in 1030 and 1032 failed miserably and the situation was salvaged by the general George Maniaces, who took Edessa in 1031.[267] A great expedition against Egypt in 1033 was repulsed with heavy losses, while between 1031 and 1034 the provinces were hit by famine.

The murder of Romanus III brought to the throne Michael IV the Paphlagonian, the next husband of empress Zoë; before his untimely death, he led a campaign in the Balkans to deal with the rebellion of Peter Delyan (1040-41), an incident due to the imposition of taxation in money rather than kind in Bulgaria, a move which reversed the policy of Basil II. This is probably an indication of the consequences brought about by the more general abandonment of the tax and land policies of Basil II and the endeavour of his successors to curry favour with the populace in the capital while at the same time granting privileges to the urban nobles. After the attempt of Michael V Calaphates to rule without the backing of Zoë, the empress married again, bringing into power Constantine IX Monomachus in 1042. During his rule, the annexation of the Armenian kingdom of Ani was the final stage of the territorial expansion of the empire, pursued in Sicily by George Maniaces from 1038 to 1042.[268]

In 1042, increased taxation, but possibly also friction with the local governor Theophylactus, led to the revolt of the *katepano* of Cyprus Theophilus Eroticus.[269] In 1043, year of the Maniaces rebellion, a Russian attack against Constantinople inaugurated a period of new problems with external enemies. In 1047, another uprising, that of Leo Tornices, coincided with the appearance of the Pechenegs on the south bank of the Danube. Administrative reforms between 1043 and 1047 had reinforced central control on the provinces, undermining the local military commanders.[270] The disappointing performance of the army of Iberia against the Seljuk Turks in 1048-9 led to its dissolution. After this, the war with the Pechenegs strained the budget, leading to austerity measures in 1053-1055 and to appreciable debasement of the gold coinage.[271] The 1054 schism with the Roman church[272] would have serious political repercussions in the years following. Michael VI Stratioticus (1056-57) favoured the capital's bureaucrats, irritating the provincial aristocracy which managed to replace him with Isaac I Comnenus after a bloody battle at Nicomedia. In spite of the pitiful state of the army, Isaac managed to check the Pechenegs and Hungarians in the north and the Seljuks on the eastern border. He resorted to cuts in salaries and other measures in order to restore the empire's defensive capability, but the reorganization of the army required the abolition of the administrative structures set up in the reign of Constantine IX; Isaac's efforts gradually led to political isolation and, finally, his resignation in 1059.[273]

---

[266] Otto Orseolo, doge from 1009 to 1026, was the son of Pietro II Orseolo, who had signed the first treaty with Basil II in 991. At the time the Orseolo tried to establish hereditary claims on Venice, an ambition betrayed by a series of dynastic marriages: the wife of Otto was a daughter of Geza of Hungary, in 1004 his brother John had married Maria Argyra, 'niece' of Basil II, while one of their sisters was wed to the son of Svetoslav Suronja, ruler of Croatia (997-1000). Staley 1910: 50-54. Nicol (1988: 46) considers impossible the relationship with the emperor. However, Helena, wife of Constantine VIII and daughter of Alypius, came from a prominent Constantinopolitan family and a close family tie with the Argyroi is not at all unlikely. This might partly explain the choice of Romanus Argyrus as heir of Constantine. If Otto Orseolo was exiled in 1026, he was received in Byzantium by Constantine VIII and not Romanus III who, according to Nicol, repealed Venetian trading privileges.

[267] Treadgold 1995: 215. Savvides 2004: 33-38.

[268] Savvides 2004: 43-49, 53-57.

[269] Metcalf 2009: 502-503.

[270] For the consequences on the fleet see Ahrweiler 1966: 159.

[271] Ostrogorsky 1980: 333; Hendy 1985: 509; Morrisson 2011: 69, 71.

[272] The violent rupture was mostly due to the dominant personalities of pope Leo IX, legate Humbert of Silva Candida and patriarch Michael Cerularius, but also to the ambivalent attitude of Constantine IX. Ostrogorsky 1980: 319, 335-337.

[273] Angold 1984: 57.

Under his successor Constantine X Ducas (1059-67) control passed again into the hands of the bureaucrats of Constantinople, with disastrous results for the provinces. Serious territorial losses to the Normans in South Italy, the Hungarians, Pechenegs, Uzes and Cumans in the Balkans and to the Seljuks in the east took place. The collapse of the eastern borders and the fall of Caesarea to Alp Arslan in 1067 finally brought to the throne Romanus IV Diogenes (1068), who had distinguished himself against the Pechenegs. His first two campaigns in the east were quite successful, but in 1071 he was betrayed on the battlefield at Manzikert by Andronicus Ducas and the subsequent heavy defeat led to his deposition and death. The political victory of the bureaucrats of the capital under Michael VII Ducas Parapinaces (1071-78) led to desperate practices in search of money and the ineptness of the central government caused a series of uprisings in various parts of the empire.

To sum up, between 1041 and 1081, the reduction of income from taxes was exacerbated by the multiplication of remunerative offices. The squandering of the gold reserve left by Basil II[274] encouraged the production of luxury goods, commerce and the Constantinopolitan guilds, but also inspired political instability, as anyone desiring political or financial advantage had to curry favour at court. In essence, the government adapted itself to the ambition of the upper classes in the capital, ignoring the needs of the rest of the empire and paying no mind to its protection.[275]

In the provinces the farming of continually increasing taxation gradually drove the peasants into bondage to the great landowners, as the *dynatoi* were largely able to avoid the payment of taxes.[276] The thematic troops were absorbed by the agrarian substrate[277] and the *tagmata* were abandoned in order to save money and weaken the provincial nobility. This forced the state to resort to foreign mercenaries who, after 1071 were mostly Turks; when these were called upon to garrison fortified settlements they found themselves in a position of strength and gradually built up a network of principalities and alliances, while the exploitation of the Anatolian plateau passed into their hands. The only hope of survival for the aristocracy of the eastern provinces lay now in getting control of the capital and, after the short reign of the aged Nicephorus III Botaneiates, Alexius I Comnenus gained the throne in 1081 with the support of the Ducas clan and of Nicephorus Melissenus, another rebel, thus ensuring dynastic stability.

The empire was already at the edge of a precipice, and would remain there for another twenty years. Alexius was obliged to neglect Anatolia and the Aegean for ten years, in order to safeguard the European lands of the empire, where control had not been quite lost. He first had to deal with the Normans, who had taken Dyrrachium in October 1081 and then the Bogomils and the Serbs. Against the Normans he had the support of Venice, but in order to ensure it he granted important trading privileges to the Republic (1082). When the Pechenegs joined forces with the Bogomils and besieged Constantinople in 1090-91, Alexius enlisted the help of the Cumans, because of the lack of Byzantine troops.[278] The situation in Asia Minor had turned critical, as Tzachas, emir of Smyrna with connections to the Anatolian hinterland, had managed to put together a fleet and occupied all the major islands along the littoral, from Lesbos in the north to Rhodes in the south.[279] Tzachas backed the Pecheneg attempt against Constantinople with his navy, and the warning did not go unheeded. This time the emperor did not seek Venetian help but built a new fleet which, under the leadership of John Ducas, recovered the islands in 1092 and then went on to suppress uprisings on Crete and Cyprus.[280]

From 1028 until 1092, the class A folles were followed (PLS 58-67) by at least 11 more classes (B to L), although those accepted as imperial issues minted in Constantinople were classes B (Romanus III), C (Michael IV), D (Constantine IX), E-F (Constantine X), G (Romanus IV), H (Michael VII), I (Nicephorus III), J and K (Alexius I, before 1092).[281] From 1059 to 1081 this series was supplemented by signed folles of emperors Constantine X, Romanus IV, Michael VII and Nicephorus III (PLS 68-70). No copper coins are assigned to emperors Michael V (1041-42), Zoë (1042), Theodora

[274] Ostrogorsky 1980: 327; Hendy 1985: 225-226.
[275] Angold 1984: 73-74.
[276] Hendy 1969: 54-55.
[277] An effort to revive or reorganize the thematic armies in the East was made by Romanus IV. Treadgold 1995: 116, 218.
[278] Angold (1984: 127) notes the disparate forces under Alexius at the battle of Mt. Levunium in 1091, stressing its 'feudal' element.
[279] Malamut 1989: 91. Savvides 1995: 23-25.
[280] The *Alexiad* covers the attacks of Tzachas on the islands in four different chapters: VII 8, VIII 3, IX 1-9 and XI 5; the occupation of Rhodes by the emir of Smyrna is mentioned, but not the date of its recovery by Alexius. In XI 5 it seems to say that when the Crusaders were on the way to Antioch, i.e. in 1097, Rhodes (and Chios!) were still held by Tzachas. Considering the arguments in Gautier 1970, which firmly date the reconquest of the islands by John Ducas in 1092, and the fact that he would hardly have moved against the rebels of Crete and Cyprus without first securing Rhodes, this is highly unlikely. It seems that Anna Comnena was recapitulating, in order to explain why Alexius was following his own agenda while the Crusaders were in difficulties: the rest of the passage deals with the Byzantine offensive of 1097 against Smyrna and various cities in the Meander area held by the Turks. For a concise account see Zonaras [1870]: 239. For the dates see Malamut 1989: I, 91 ff, 116-117; Pryor and Jeffreys 2006: 101.
[281] According to more recent attributions.

(1055-56), Michael VI (1056-57) and Isaac I (1057-59). In addition, the relevant bibliography includes imitations of classes A2,[282] B,[283] C and J. Class A2 imitations are thought to be contemporary to the official issues but this, unfortunately, does not hold true for class B, some imitations of which have been dated to the reign of Alexius I.[284] Some imitations of classes C and J are associated with the Normans in southern Italy.[285] The case of class B is complicated with reference to Rhodes, because a great many class B pieces found on the island are so worn that it is impossible to tell whether they are imperial issues or imitations (PLS 58-62). Moreover, these coins are clipped and their condition places them in a group alongside several pieces of class C (PLS 62-63), and signed folles of Romanus IV (PL. 68).

Thus, in the following table, the coins of the period are not presented simply by emperor: they are also divided into anonymous and signed types, while the coins belonging to the clipped and worn group are placed separately, within brackets, since they were presumably in circulation for a much longer space. For this reason, they are not included in the column of losses per year.

Emperor	Dates	Anon. Class	Number of coins	Signed folles	Number of coins	Total	Losses per year
John I	969-976	A1	4			4	0.6
Basil II Constantine VIII	976-1025 1025-1028	A2	23			23	0.44
Romanus III	1028-1034	B	6 [+84]			6	1
Michael IV	1034-1041	C	6 [+25]			6	0.7
Constantine IX	1042-1055	D	4			4	0.3
Constantine X	1059-1067	E F	2 3	Class 1 Class 2	2 3	10	1.3
Romanus IV	1068-1071	G	2		2 [+17]	4	1
Michael VII	1071-1078	H	7		2	9	1.5
Nicephorus III	1078-1081	I	13	El AE	2[41] 12	27	6.2
Alexius I	1081-1092	J K	8 17			25	2.3

Figure 37: The coins of Rhodes, 969 - 1092.

Leaving aside, for the moment, the coins within brackets, there is a total of 117 pieces, of which two are of electrum.[287] 57% of the total are site finds. Of the class B coins, one is overstruck on class A2,[288] and one of class C is overstruck on class B.[289] Another piece combines a class C reverse to a class D obverse, but it is uncertain whether it is a hybrid, an imitation[290] or an overstrike. Two out of three pieces of class D are also problematical: on one the back of the throne seems absent,[291] while another is probably an imitation, since the letter S on the legend is shaped like a Z.[292] Of the class H coins one is struck on a thin flan and another on a follis of Theophilus.[293] Two of the class J coins are overstruck on folles of Nicephorus III and one on a follis of Constantine X. Two of the class K coins are overstruck on class J and a third on a thin flan. Another piece, with a class D obverse, bears on the reverse a cross similar to that of class I.[294]

The graph below shows losses per year for the fully identified folles from 969 to 1092. Until the reign of Romanus IV it ranges between 0.4 and 1, with a significant drop under Constantine IX, when the value drops to the level of

[282] Grierson 1973: II, 674-675.
[283] Grierson 1973: II, Pl. LV.
[284] Around 1090. Grierson 1973: II, 674-675, 680-681.
[285] The first between 1060 and 1080 and the second between 1081 and 1087. Grierson and Travaini 1998: 42.
[286] The debased histamena of Nicephorus III are not included in the losses per year.
[287] **1118** and **1119**. The second is a site-find.
[288] **914**.
[289] **1006**.
[290] **1035**. Due to the design of the jewelled cross.
[291] **1038**.
[292] **1031**. However, this coin does not resemble at all the Italian imitations published by Grierson and Travaini 1998: Pl. 5, 61-62 and Pl. 7, 89-90.
[293] **1048** and **1051** respectively.
[294] **1133**.

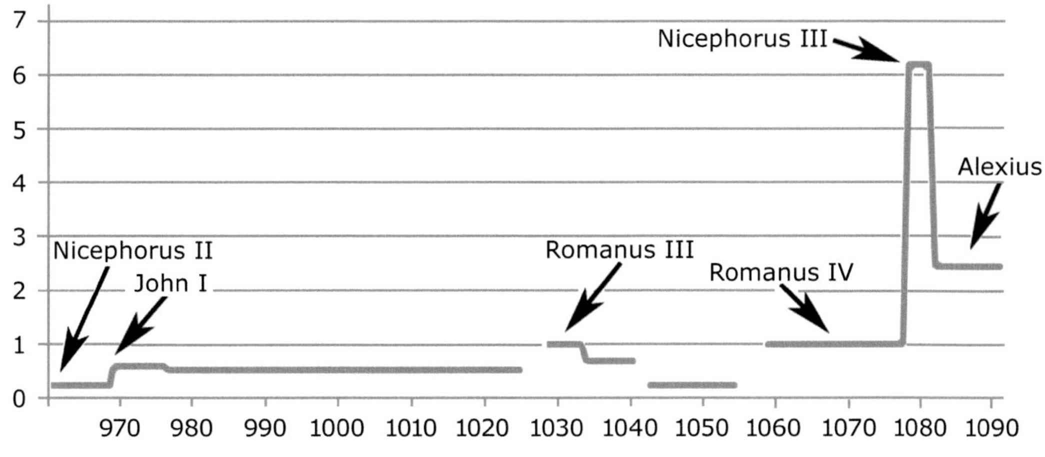

Figure 38: Losses per year, 969- 1092.

Nicephorus II. The high value for Nicephorus III is encountered elsewhere,[295] and is considered inflationary, but other explanations associated with administrative changes should not be excluded.

From the accession of Alexius I (4 April 1081) until 1092, anonymous folles of classes J and K circulated on Rhodes, where the ratio between them is 1 : 2 (8:17). During the early years of his reign Alexius was bound by the demands of the Norman peril and his control over the eastern Aegean was correspondingly weak. In 1085, with the death of Robert Guiscard in Cephalonia, pressure on the western front decreased. The replacement of class J by class K is thought to have taken place in 1087.[296] This means that the years 1087-1089[297] until, that is, the activities of Tzachas severed communication between Rhodes and the empire, saw a considerable rise in monetary circulation. This phenomenon might be linked to the presence of tax collectors or, more likely, to some impact of the Turkish danger, perhaps an attempt by the Byzantine authorities to mobilize against his expansionist policy which has not been recorded in the written sources. In the second case, the data may be read as a spike dated *c.* 1088.

The problem of the worn folles

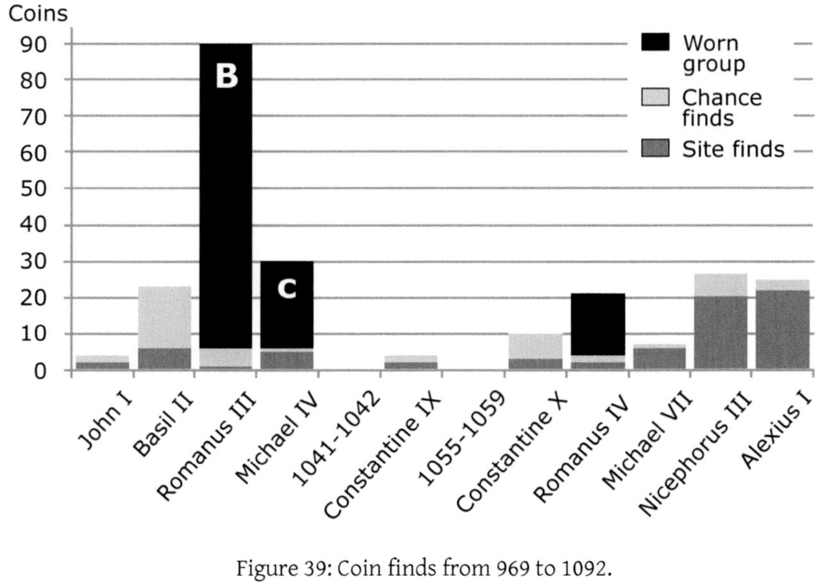

Figure 39: Coin finds from 969 to 1092.

The collection of the archaeological Service in Rhodes holds a further 129 11th century folles which cannot be incorporated in the preceding analysis without serious thought, because they share certain common characteristics which set them apart from the rest of the material. Of those folles 84 apparently belong to anonymous class B, 25 to anonymous class C and 17 are signed folles of Romanus IV Diogenes. Most of the coins in the group (84%) are site finds but all are clipped and worn to a point that we cannot really tell whether they are official issues or imitations.[298] This

[295] Metcalf 1979: 65-66, 7; Bates 1971; Woodward 1929.
[296] Hendy 1999: I, 191.
[297] The problems of Alexius I with the Pechenegs dated from 1086-7. Angold 1984: 109-110.
[298] Grierson 1973: II, 680-681.

seems to be a purely local phenomenon.[299] The importance of this singular group in relation to the rest of the material is made clear Figure 39.

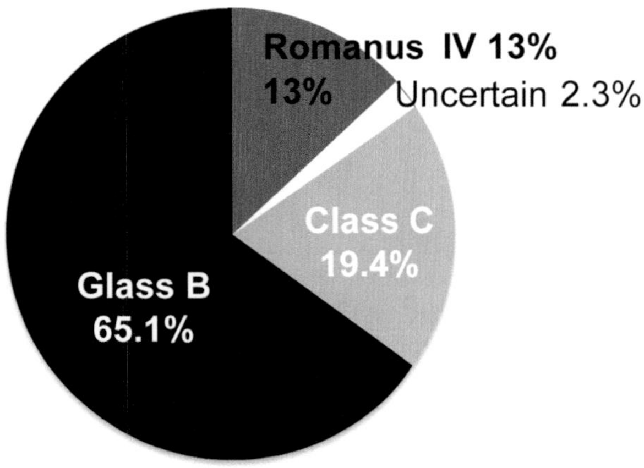

Figure 40: 11th century worn folles.

Of course, the distribution of the worn coins in the chart is likely to mislead, since most of them must have been lost long after they were put into circulation and some time after they were clipped, too, considering the amount of wear they suffered afterwards.[300] The chart also shows increased representation of site finds towards the end of the period. This is mostly due to the generally lower quality of the later issues, which are not as noticeable as the folles of Basil II and his immediate successors. The worn folles present the most intriguing numismatic problem of the 11th century in Rhodes. The composition of the group of 129 worn pieces is shown Figure 40. The wear on all the coins fits a particular pattern: the cross on the reverse has served as a guide for the clipping and afterwards most of the coins remained in circulation long enough for the image of Christ on the obverse to be completely effaced.[301] Unfortunately, most of the features distinguishing official issues from the imitations of Class B published by Grierson are concentrated on this side.[302] On the reverse Grierson points out elements commonly encountered on imitations: misshapen b and L, and angular S. However, too much metal has been removed from the sides of the clipped pieces of class B for the b and even the L to be clearly visible. Examination of the S, the only remaining clue, does not reveal pieces with the S in a particularly angular form. Thus, the possibility that the worn class B pieces are imitations, early or late, cannot be confirmed. Figure 41, comparing the weight of the Rhodian coins with the published specimens of the Dumbarton Oaks Collection, reflects not only the clipping but also the degree of wear of the former (Figure 41).

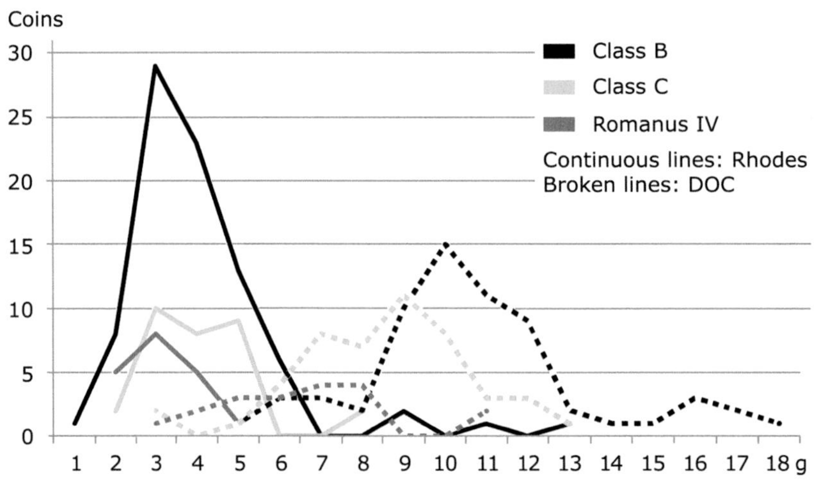

Figure 41: Weight comparison of anonymous classes B and C and signed folles of Romanus IV in Rhodes and Dumbarton Oaks.

[299] Even though, usually, coins in such condition generally do not appear in publication plates. The author's attempts to locate similar pieces elsewhere resulted in only two pieces, clipped but not with the degree of wear typical of Rhodes. One has been published by Heidemann (2002: 466, D) and the other belongs to a British collection without provenance information.

[300] Most are single finds, but some were burial offerings (e.g. those of the Minatsis plot).

[301] Bust of Christ Emmanuel on anonymous class B and the signed issue of Romanus IV, Christ Antiphonetes on anonymous class C.

[302] Grierson 1973: II, 680-681. For the variations of class B see also Zervos 2003.

It is shown that in comparison with the sample from the American collection, most of the Rhodian class B coins have lost over two thirds of their weight, while those of class C and the signed folles of Romanus IV at least half of it, even if the coins of Dumbarton Oaks weighing more than the average are excluded. Had the obverse of the worn coins been deliberately effaced and the traces of the intervention subsequently worn away, the brief occupation of the island by Tzachas in c. 1090 would immediately come to mind. However, this is not likely because it would be pointless to remove the divine image from the obverse only to carefully preserve the cross on the reverse. The careful handling of the cross during clipping is obvious:

Figure 42: Clipping of the 11th century worn folles.

The clipped anonymous class B coins are oval or oblong in shape, because the elongated Latin cross had to be preserved; the rest are usually rounder or squarish in shape, because of the Greek cross on the reverse. Indeed, in some specimens of anonymous class C, the effort to preserve the letters of the invocation IC |:| XC / NI |:| KA in the field led to the removal of more metal from the top and bottom of the reverse. Besides, among the numerous specimens of class B we encounter coins in various stages of wear after the clipping and those less worn preserve traces of Christ's bust on the obverse. Therefore we may be certain that the effaced obverse is the result of its originally shallower relief. It is not known whether the clipping itself took place in Rhodes or elsewhere. Taking into account the comparative number of specimens, and pending similar proof from elsewhere, it will be assumed for now that it happened in Rhodes.[303]

This reasoning raises questions: have we to deal with a single numismatic event or with more than one? Or was it an ongoing process involving local officials, responsible for both the clipping and the velocity of circulation betrayed by the wear of the coins? The simple answer would be that these coin types arrived on the island in response to specific administrative needs at times when the demand for petty cash and/or raw metal was high. Under Romanus III there was a failed expedition against Egypt in 1034 as well as campaigns in Syria and, as shown in the chapter dealing with the period 498-668, coin circulation in Rhodes was heavily affected by events concerning Egypt, due to its location and the presence of the arsenal. In the reign of Michael IV began the enterprise for the reconquest of Sicily conducted by George Maniaces, which probably caused a similar response. Lastly, Romanus IV was campaigning in Syria and Cilicia in 1068 and 1069. The support of a fleet is not mentioned in the sources, but the same is true for the campaigns of Nicephorus II, John I and Basil II in the same region. In their time its organization and upkeep relied on Middle Byzantine mechanisms, which did not require exchanges in petty cash. It seems, however, that in the 1030s things changed. Basil II had encouraged the commutation of the *strateia* and, probably, other structures associated with the provincial arsenals had also been affected. When operations in the arsenal of Rhodes intensified with the preparations for the Egyptian expedition, at least part of the work might require the payment of wages. It is not necessary, however, to visualize changes in the operation of the arsenal in order to explain the influx of coin. At the time, most Byzantine troops were already mercenaries and a brief stay on the island when travelling by sea, perhaps due to adverse weather, could be sufficient to explain the presence of small change locally.

It is thus clear that towards the middle of the 11th century the use of petty cash was replacing provincial institutions that had functioned with remarkable efficiency in the 9th, 10th and early 11th century, reviving phenomena last encountered in Rhodes under Constans II. A second look at Figure 39 confirms the dysfunction of the state in the area around Rhodes, both after 1041 and after 1069. It is obvious that a need for small change was already developed in the town, and that the lack of it was strongly felt. However, supply of coin by the state fell behind demand, at least after 1041, resulting it the serious wear seen on the coins of anonymous classes B and C already in circulation.

[303] The recovery of a clipped coin in Syria (above, n. 298) may easily be explained by the role of Rhodes in the campaigns of Romanus III.

The same happened in the interval after 1070 until, under Nicephorus III, large quantities of copper coins entered circulation. Thus, the increase in mint output under Nicephorus in comparison with his predecessor Michael VII is not necessarily a sign of inflation: it may merely have been a response to demand, facilitating the maintenance of soldiers or other social groups. The production and supply of this coinage may even have been profitable for the treasury.

To the issues of Nicephorus III were added, before Tzachas took the town in *c.* 1090, the two anonymous classes of Alexius I. For this reason also, it is impossible to link the worn folles group with the brief occupation of Rhodes: as we will see, after the numismatic reform of 1092, the new copper tetartera circulated widely and the need for coin was not so acute. It is possible that some of the worn pieces remained in circulation after 1078 but most of them must have been lost earlier, since the worn pieces could hardly compete with the new issues. It is, therefore, possible to incorporate the worn folles group to the other losses per year. This is done in the simplest possible way, based on the following premises: a) That the clipping took place soon after the issue of the coins, b) that losses afterwards were at a steady rate and c) that most of the worn coins were no longer in circulation at the time of Nicephorus III. The losses per year of the worn group according to these premises may be superimposed on the data of Figure 38 thus:

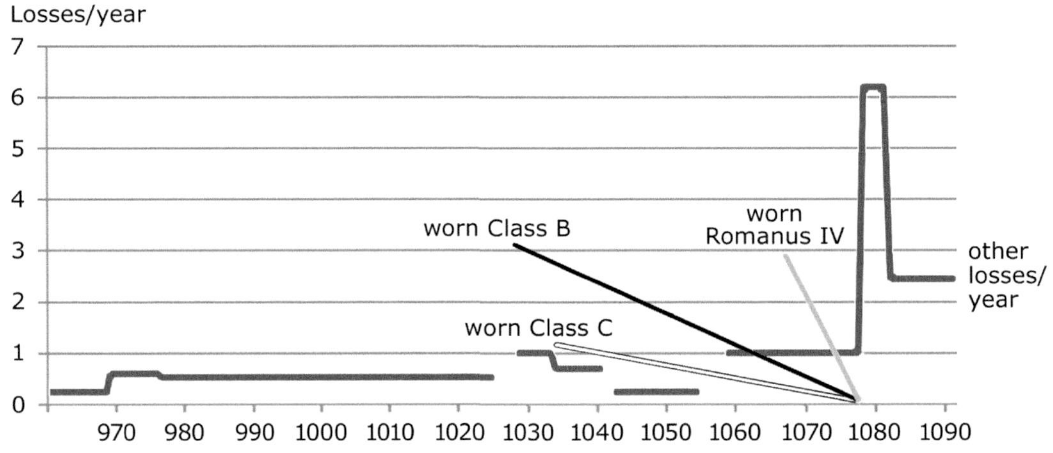

Figure 43: Working hypothesis for the incorporation of the worn coins into losses per year.

This approach may be refined through the use of more sophisticated statistical tools and bolstered by the precise measurement of wear on the coins. For present purposes, though, the simple conversion of the losses per year graph is achieved by adding to the total of finds from each subsequent reign the percentage of worn coins assumed to have been lost in it. The picture that emerges in this way should reflect more closely the circulation of the copper folles on Rhodes after 1030 (Figure 44).

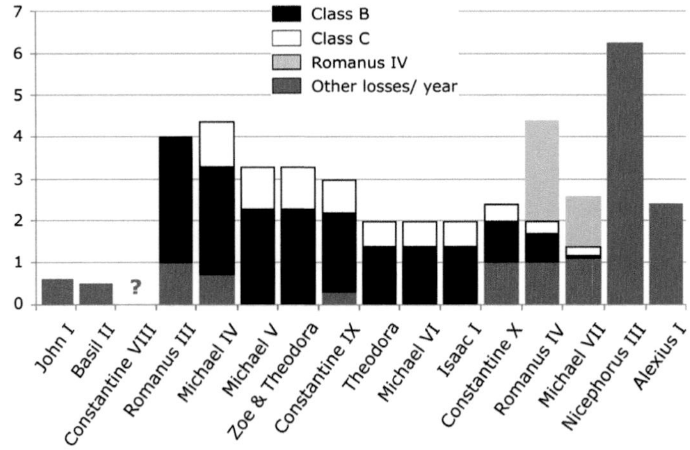

Figure 44: Losses per year from 969 to 1081 after the addition of the worn folles.

Apart from other inherent methodological weaknesses, this *schema* conceals fluctuations in the circulation of coin which cannot be detected with the information available. Nevertheless, the increase of coin circulation from the 1030s onwards is substantial, reaching, or even exceeding, the values of the period between 498 and 668: the relevant figure under Nicephorus III is at the same level as under Justin II (6.5), while the values for Romanus III, Michael IV and Romanus IV around the level of Constans II (4.3). It is clear that the monetization of the economy has recovered from the hiatus of the previous three centuries and, in mid-century, is showing a dynamism driven by local conditions and not by the central government.

The methodical clipping of the much used coins under examination is very interesting.[304] It appears that the general dysfunction had affected the supply of raw materials like copper, and that unknown agencies took steps to meet local needs through this intervention on the official currency. It is unfortunately hard to say whether the clipping took place on arrival of the new coins or shortly after, perhaps during the payment of wages or the collection of dues in the local market. Nor is it possible to ascertain if the clipping served private interests, the operation of the arsenal or some other need. We also do not know, although this may be solved as the numbers of finds rise with time, how systematic the clipping was across different reigns and if it affected other classes rare on Rhodes. For the moment, the evidence supports three phases: the first, and most widespread, apparently occurred very shortly after the arrival of class B on Rhodes and was probably applied by the local administrator. The success of the measure, and possibly the continued presence of this official at his post in the following reign, led to the clipping of class C. The clipping of the signed folles of Romanus IV a generation later imitated the earlier practice, but the presence of the original source of inspiration was not necessary, since the results of his industry were still in circulation. Of course it is possible, although hard to prove, that some specimens were clipped elsewhere, or by private individuals. It is, however, certain that clipping had stopped when the issues of Nicephorus III entered circulation[305] and that this local phenomenon did not reappear.

* * *

To sum up, cities occupying key locations in the Anatolian plateau were already prosperous in the 9th century, their economy relying on the animal market and animal produce. The comparatively numerous coin finds in such sites testify to the administrative importance of fortified nodes during the campaigns against the Arabs. But in the second half of the 11th century local conditions favoured the establishment of Turkic settlers which, gradually, reached down to the coast, cutting off from their hinterland cities like Attaleia which, by the time of the second Crusade, relied on supplies arriving by sea.[306] The collapse of the organization and defense system in the provinces and the replacement of the thematic troops and *tagmata* by mercenaries must have temporarily encouraged the use of coin in the towns they guarded. In Greece, the development of cities like Athens, Corinth, Thebes[307] and Sparta,[308] associated with the growth of manufacture, is mostly observed in the 11th century.[309] The importance of the naval base of Athens, perhaps more important than that of Rhodes in this period, should not be overlooked.

In 1035, under Michael IV, Arab corsairs raided the coastland of the Thrakesion theme and were neutralized by the *strategos* of the Cibyrrhaiotes. The fleet of 1035 may have been put together in 1033-1034, during the preparation of the Egyptian expedition of Romanus III (1034) or even earlier, to support the campaigns in Syria, explaining the large numbers of anonymous class B folles found in Rhodes. Possibly, it was the absence of the Cibyrrhaiote fleet in Egypt that permitted the Arab raid on Myra in 1034. It is natural to suppose that in 1038 the Cibyrrhaiotes participated in the transport of Maniaces and his men to Italy, which was marked in Rhodes by the class C folles; after this, however, there is no further mention of the thematic fleet. Presumably, the central government had lost interest in the thematic naval bases as much as in the troops, although the naval *strateia*, due to its low cost, was apparently maintained until the reign of Michael VII.[310]

The increased circulation of folles under Nicephorus III and, to a lesser degree, under Alexius I in the period up to 1090 (2.8 losses per year) may reflect an administrative response beneficial for Rhodes as well as for the central government. The development of the town is noticeable from the second quarter of the 11th century. The causes of this are not yet known; they may have been related to increased traffic in the harbour of Rhodes, either for

[304] Roughly squared coins of class B have been found elsewhere, something possibly due to mint practice; but the clipping of the coins in Rhodes is much more drastic.
[305] The coins of Michael VII are too few for reliable conclusions, as are those of Constantine IX and Constantine X earlier.
[306] Vryonis 1996: 130-244; Laiou 2001: 166.
[307] Galani-Krikou 1993b-c; *eadem* 1995; *eadem* 1996; *eadem* 1997; *eadem* 1998a; *eadem* 1998b.
[308] Angold 1984: 64-66; Hendy 1989: III, 16-17.
[309] Or earlier. See Laiou-Thomadaki 2006: 98 ff.
[310] Cheynet 2006: 156; Ahrweiler 1966: 377.

military or for commercial reasons, but only research in other fields of material culture may throw some light on the matter. In any case, the maintenance of the fleet had lapsed, allowing the emir of Smyrna to occupy the islands of the eastern Aegean without particular difficulty *c.* 1089. After the empire recovered control of the islands, *c.* 1092, some at least of the naval bases of the old naval themes were revived, to service the new centrally controlled navy.[311]

The first part of the reign of Alexius I ends with the reconquest of the islands of the eastern Aegean in 1092. Two points set it apart from the efforts of Isaac I and Romanus IV. The first is the strengthening of the position of the emperor, which relied on the imperial clan and most notably his mother, Anna Dalassena, who managed to control the political situation in the capital during Alexius' lengthy absences on campaign.[312] The second concerns the handling of external dangers; Alexius made the right choices at the proper time and his resolve did not weaken in spite of frequent failure. The role of the Comneni clan has been much criticized. However, the concentration of wealth in the hands of his extended family allowed the emperor to consolidate his position, and deal with the inefficiency which burdened the financial resources of the state and crippled defense.

311 The office of the *megas dux* of the fleet was created especially for John Ducas, giving him full control of military forces in the Aegean. His operations in the region continued for a number of years, building up an extensive administrative framework. He became responsible for the best part of naval organization and, given its concentration in the Aegean, he was also granted control of the provinces of Hellas and Crete. Angold 1985: 128-9.

312 Angold 1984: 131.

4. From the Monetary Reform of Alexius I (1092) to 1204

In 1092, Alexius engaged in a monetary reform much more substantial than that of John I, or even Anastasius I, as it affected not just the copper coins but currency of all values including gold. The political situation and the relations of Byzantium with its neighbours are fairly clear, although the historical sources are unequal and conceal social and economic developments which contributed, after the fall of the Comnenian dynasty, to separatist tendencies. Towards the end of the 12th century, the incapacity of the central authority led to the loss of control not only of the provinces but also of the populace in Constantinople, with lamentable results. This process concluded, in the early years of the 13th century, with the conquest of the Byzantine capital by the armies of the Fourth Crusade. Numismatic circulation in general, but also the picture provided by the coins of Rhodes in particular, is directly related to shifts in imperial policy.

The reform of Alexius I and Rhodes (1092-1118)

From the start, Byzantine coinage belonged to the trimetallic system, comprising the gold solidus, the silver milliaresion which, although not minted in great quantities also served as a unit of account for tax purposes, and the copper follis, in an equivalence ratio of 1 : 12 : 288. Its collapse, dated between 1042 and 1092, was followed by the minting of various denominations in gold (*hyperpyron*), electrum (*aspron trachy*), billon (*aspron trachy*) and copper (*tetarteron* and possibly *half-tetarteron*) from 1092 onwards. This was misunderstood by Western contemporaries, who increasingly came into contact with the empire after 1095, and by the older generation of Byzantine scholars. The Latins were used to coins whose value was directly related to their precious metal content and were particularly suspicious of Byzantine alloy coins, while Byzantinists considered them a sign of decline.

In fact, the monetary reform of Alexius I sought to regularize the situation on the ground, in order to facilitate the collection of taxes and meet other needs such as salaries and the transfer of large sums.[313] The elucidation of the new system was partly based on metrological tables of the coins themselves[314] and partly on a document incorporated in a manuscript dated to the last quarter of the 12th century,[315] known under the title *Palaia kai nea logarike*. It is a Byzantine exposition of the reckoning and payment of taxes in coin, before and after the monetary reform of Alexius I, dated *c.* 1135.[316] It also includes reports of tax collectors, queries they addressed to the central administration and the solutions redacted in response. It is a highly technical text which, interpreted by Michael Hendy,[317] links the monetary reform of 1092 with the more efficient collection of taxes. It is calculated that the two together resulted in a fourfold increase of state revenues from taxation.[318]

Before the reform, the main tax (land tax) had to be paid in *charagma* (coins of precious metal) if it exceeded two thirds of a solidus, and the difference (change, *strophe*) was returned in copper folles. The debasement of the solidus to a third of its original value at the peak of the monetary crisis (1071 onwards) led to its employment as the unit of account for the calculation of tax even after the reform: the main tax had to be paid in electrum, while secondary taxes could be paid in copper. In reality, the taxpayer had to pay the main tax in *charagma* and at least part of his other taxes in billon. The new system comprised the following denominations and equivalences: 1 gold hyperperum = 3 electrum trachea = 48 billon trachea = 864 tetartera.[319] An electrum trachy was worth 4 milliaresia of the old accounting system, or 96 folles, although both these units no longer existed in coin form.[320] It is thought that the new system was fully employed in tax collection around 1108/9.[321] Around the middle of the 12th century began the debasement of the billon trachy, which gradually became a fiduciary coin[322] while, after 1185, it was the turn of the electrum trachy, due to the worsening political situation and the inefficient handling of the economy.[323]

---

313 Angold 1984: 132-133.
314 Cf. Hendy 1969: 10-13.
315 Dated by Svoronos 1960: 79, shortly after 1182/3.
316 Svoronos 1960; Laurent 1960: 283.
317 Hendy 1969: Chapter 6.
318 Harvey 1989: 89-90; Morrisson 1979: 419-464.
319 It is thought that the first tetartera were of lead, while tetartera of Constantinople afterwards were of billon, in contrast to those of Thessalonica which were of pure copper. Hendy 1999: I, 197-200.
320 Hendy 1985: 516. The relationship of the tetartera to larger denominations seems to have been mutable: Grierson 1982: 17.
321 Hendy 1969: 57.
322 Under John II its silver content was 7-6%. Under Manuel it wavered between 6 and 4.5%, under Isaac II it dropped to 3-2.5% and under Alexius III was c. 3-2%. Hendy 1999: I, 45.
323 Hendy 1969: 19.

It is interesting that the monetary reform of Alexius I coincides with the recovery of the eastern Aegean islands. This was obviously a time of increasing confidence: Alexius now could afford to handle matters which would improve the efficiency of government in the long term. After the Pechenegs and Tzachas, the emperor turned again to the Balkans in order to deal with the Serbs. However, he was obliged to interrupt his campaign in 1094, in order to face the Cumans in Thrace. The navy established to counter Tzachas was then employed to subdue rebellions on Crete and Cyprus and then for the reconquest of the Anatolian coastland and part of its hinterland.[324] From 1096 onwards, it was also employed to follow the course of the First Crusade, intervening at need. At this time the recovery of Cyprus and the siege of Antioch must have increased significantly the importance of the naval base of Rhodes. Thus, the delayed participation of Venice in the Crusade does not seem to have caused problems on the island when the Venetian fleet wintered in its harbour in 1099/1100.[325]

After the surrender of Nicaea in 1098, the Seljuk capital had been transferred to Iconium. The consolidation of Kilij Arslan's position after the defeats of the Crusaders in Anatolia in 1101[326] interrupted the land route connecting Constantinople to Syria, further reinforcing the importance of the sea rout to the Holy Land. In 1103 a Pisan fleet failed to take Rhodes after losing an encounter with a Byzantine squadron near Patara; this event highlights the complications inherent in the presence of Italian crusading fleets in the Aegean.

In spite of the problems caused to imperial diplomacy by crusading Normans, the Byzantine presence in Syria was supported by the navy. In 1103 the Byzantines assisted in the siege of Tripoli while in 1104 the defeat of the Crusaders by the Turks at Harran allowed the emperor to retake Tarsus, Adana and Mamistra, as well as Laodicea and other harbours in Palestine. The strengthening of the Byzantine position in Syria forced Bohemond, the prince of Antioch, to counterattack in the Balkans. After three years of preparations, backed by systematic anti-Byzantine propaganda in Western courts, he landed in Avlona and invested Dyrrachium in 1107. However, the enterprise failed and he was obliged to sign a treaty with Alexius at Devol (September 1108). In the years following Alexius strove to consolidate his eastern borders with campaigns in Bithynia and Mysia in 1116-7, where he checked a raid by Malik Shah, sultan of Iconium, and gained a substantial victory at Philomelion.

In 1111 the emperor sought a treaty with Pisa, probably in order to regularize a hitherto unpredictable factor and balance the influence of Venice which was developing into a monopoly.[327] The increased pressure in the Aegean caused by western flotillas required constant vigilance: in 1112 five Genoese galleys raided the region of Abydos and four of them were eventually captured by the imperial fleet. These galleys were the vanguard of a squadron also including Lombard and Pisan vessels.[328] *Ad hoc* Latin marauding and alliances, often arranged by individual adventurers and not the cities of their origin, were inspired by the prospect of loot and the fluctuating relations between the Italian naval powers, usually linked to the struggle for control of Eastern markets in various regions and not only in the Aegean. However, as long as the Byzantine fleet preserved a strong presence in the Aegean, the chances of serious consequences from this state of affairs remained limited.

It is significant that, so far, no trachea issued by Alexius after the monetary reform of 1092 have been found in Rhodes. In contrast, his smaller denomination, the tetartera (PLS 70-73), have been found in some quantity and in a number of varieties. This is rather surprising, since the tetartera are known to have dominated circulation west of the Aegean, while the billon trachea further east.[329] Possibly, this is due to Rhodes being assigned to the administrative structure set up to support the new Byzantine navy under the *megas dux* and, partly, the use of tetartera as a medium of exchange in the markets organized for the supply of the Crusaders.[330] Apart from some challenging identifications, the post-reform reign of Alexius I is represented by the following:

[324] Haldon 1999: 95-96. Conquest of Smyrna, Ephesus (2,000 captives were settled on the islands), Sardis, Philadelphia, Laodicea, Choma, Lampe. Comnena [2001]: XI 5, 4-5.

[325] Before heading for Myra, where the Venetians picked up the remnants of the relics of saint Nicholas. Seamen from Bari had stolen a march on them in 1087, but recent anthropological examination has confirmed that the bones now kept in the two Italian cities belong to the same skeleton: http://www.stnicholascenter. org/pages/relics-in-the-lido-of-venice/. The Venetian fleet then sailed to the Holy Land, where in July 1100 it assisted in the reduction of Haifa. Nicol 2004: 104-108.

[326] Runciman 1981: 18-31.

[327] Mission of curopalates Basil Mesemerius. Laiou 2001: 178.

[328] Comnena [2001]: XIV, 3.

[329] In small hoards of Comnenian petty coins in mainland Greece tetartera and half-tetartera dominate. Touratsoglou *et al.* 1979: 366-368. Penna 1996a: 212-218. In Bulgaria, however, aspra trachea are dominant, a fact that Hendy 1985: 436-437, ascribed to the production and supply of particular denominations within the boundaries of large administrative divisions.

[330] The new infrastructure supporting the fleet lay in the provinces of Hellas and the Peloponnese. Angold 1984: 128-129. Hendy 1985: 431. In 1974, the discovery of a hoard containing tetartera of John II and Manuel I in southern Turkey should be interpreted differently: the presence of tetartera dated after the policy change of John II regarding the finances of maintaining the fleet may be due to the presence of crusader armies in the region. O'Hara 1975: 61, 68. See also Laiou 2001: 169.

Mint	Denomination	Type	Variety	Number of coins
Constantinople	Tetartera	2nd coinage	A	1
			C	2
			D	2
Thessalonica	Tetartera	2nd coinage		10
		3rd coinage		9
		4th coinage	a1 [Zervos IIIa?]	7
			Zervos IIIb	8
'Unknown Greek mint'	Half tetarteron			1
TOTAL				**40**

Figure 45: Reform coins of Alexius I.

Unfortunately, although we know the sequence of the various types of tetartera, and can make educated guesses about their places of issue, we still cannot date them accurately.[331] Moreover, a further obstacle to the proper assessment of coin circulation in Rhodes between 1092 and 1118 is the tetarteron type bearing a jewelled cross on the obverse, generally known as the Fourth Coinage of Thessalonica. In Rhodes this type is represented by a comparatively significant number of coins (about 40 pieces),[332] most of which in a poor state of preservation. This is a serious problem because the type was widely imitated, while it is possible that some of the imitations may be considerably later than the official issues: the wide circulation of the type may suggest that it could serve as a model for quite a while.[333]

19 coins of this type were probably struck in the imperial mint. Eight of the better preserved specimens belong to Zervos' variant IIIb.[334] Ten more share the characteristic button at the centre of the jewelled cross of Zervos' variant IIIa, but in half of them the stepped base of the cross is not visible, probably due to the condition of the coins. In addition, the reverse legend is generally worn off, while the cross on the *globus cruciger*, in three cases where it is fairly distinct, is composed by four dots and not five. For the rest, the engraving of the dies, the weight and the position of the axes on the coins (0 or 6), are consistent with the official issues. Nevertheless, if the official IIIa variant is held to always display a *globus cruciger* with a five-dot cross, then at least two thirds of the Rhodian jewelled cross tetartera must be considered as imitations for various reasons, as follows:

Variety	Description	Weight	Axes	Number of coins
a1	Button on the crossing of the jewelled cross. The rays start outside its outline.	2.7-3.2 g (except for incomplete specimens)	0 or 6	7
a2	The same	1.5-1.7 g	0 or 6	3
b1	Jewelled cross without steps, X over crossing without rays. Maltese cross on l. of reverse field and on the globus cruciger.	3.5 g	0	1
b2	Jewelled cross without steps, X over crossing with rays. Maltese cross on l. of reverse field and on the globus cruciger.	2.5 g	6	1
c	Jewelled cross without steps, X over crossing with rays.	1.7 - 2 g	7, 11	2
d	Jewelled cross, X over crossing without rays. Thin flan, rough design.	1.3 g	10	1
e	Jewelled cross, button on the crossing, rays. Thin flan, rough design.	0.6 g	-	1
f	Rough design, jewelled cross with rays. Perhaps more than one type.	3-4.7 g (except for incomplete or worn specimens)		7 [8]
g	Transposed letters on obverse.	3 g (worn)	-	1
h	Coarse design on both sides, button without rays on the crossing of the jewelled cross, false letters in the compartments of the field, follis-sized.	5.3 g	6	1

Figure 46: Imitations of 4th coinage of Thessalonica tetartera of Alexius I.

331 Hendy 1999: I, 199.
332 Including five very worn specimens as well as a grossly made follis-sized piece.
333 Papadopoulou 2005: 145-162. See, however, Baker 2007: 220, 225-227.
334 Hendy 1999: I, 236-237 and II, Pl. VII 40a; Zervos 2009: 483-488.

Variant **a** above (perhaps related to Zervos' IIIa) is split in two groups according to weight; possibly **a2** could be an imitation of **a1**. Variants **c** to **h** should be considered as imitations either because of the low quality of the striking (**d**, **h**), or the reduced weight (**c**, **e**), while variants **b1** and **b2** recall specimens minted in Greece by the Venetians which have been assigned a date *c.* 1204.[335] It is possible that variant **a1** is an official issue of Alexius I, since it seems to have been imitated in pieces either of reduced weight (**a2**), or of singularly gross fabric and design (**h**); the matter must remain open until specimens of variant **a** are identified from other sites. Most -if not all- of the imitations found on Rhodes must have been produced elsewhere: their condition does not allow firm conclusions, but the impression is that we have to do with a variety of styles and origins. The excavational record dating the 'Corinthian' imitations to the early 13th century,[336] if not misleading, cannot possibly affect the majority of the Rhodian specimens which belong to other variants. The imitative tetartera of Rhodes could be associated with Venetian commercial activity under Alexius or a little later, when Byzantine coins were again in short supply, and are unlikely to belong in the 13th century.[337]

Nearly all of the coins, including the imitations, are site finds. Only one was found in the countryside; the rest were recovered in the town of Rhodes, most within the medieval walls. According to the relevant bibliography, 34 pieces are from the mint of Thessalonica, five from Constantinople and one from the 'unknown Greek mint' thought to have operated at Thebes or some other of the then rapidly developing towns of mainland Greece.[338] In any case, this latter find is significant because it seems that, so far, no other specimens of the type have been recorded east of the Aegean.[339]

Besides these, five folles minted in Trebizond by the Gabras span the transition from the 11th to the 12th century (PL. 74); all are site finds from the walled medieval town. Three of them are assigned by Hendy[340] to the 1080s (types 2 and 3), and two more to *c.* 1100 (types 7 and 8).

John II (15 August 1118 - early April 1143)

After the Byzantine treaty with Pisa, the accession of John II caused further offence to Venice, as the new emperor refused to renew the trading privileges the Republic considered as its due. This could have serious consequences for the Venetian economy which, till that point, mostly relied on its commercial ties with Byzantium and Egypt. Thus, the Byzantine rebuff was treated by doge Domenico Michiel as a *casus belli*. The Venetian reaction was combined with an expedition to Syria, where the king of Jerusalem Baldwin II had asked for aid. In 1122, after three years of preparations, a great fleet left Venice commanded by the doge in person, and laid siege to Corfu. However, the worsening situation in Syria obliged the doge to abandon this objective and depart for Palestine in early 1123. In the East, he drove a hard bargain with the Latins, obtaining commercial privileges which somewhat shifted Venetian interests in the eastern Mediterranean, and then assisted the Christians in the siege of Tyre (1124). On the way back, the fleet began a systematic campaign of devastation in the Aegean. Rhodes was the first Byzantine possession to be attacked, because, it was said, the locals had refused to supply the Venetian fleet while Michiel was already in financial trouble.[341] Historians do not quite agree on the details, but it seems that after Rhodes the Venetians attacked Andros and Chios, where their fleet spent the winter of 1124/1125, also attacking Lesbos. Next spring, making their way towards the Adriatic, the Venetians attacked the Peloponnese and Cephalonia, finally getting home loaded with plunder. This show of force obliged John II to review his policy towards the Republic, renewing its commercial privileges.

The dominant feature of the reign of John II was the safeguarding of imperial territories through constant campaigning in the East and the Balkans. In 1119-20 he was fighting in the Meander valley.[342] In 1122 he crushed the 'Pechenegs'[343] who had crossed the northern frontier and then, until 1128, he turned against the Serbs of Rascia and the Hungarians who backed them.[344] From 1130 until 1136 the emperor was campaigning in Anatolia against

[335] Papadopoulou 2005: 151, IIc(i)-(ii) cross to l. of reverse field, and table XIV,12 (globus cruciger).
[336] Papadopoulou 2005.
[337] With the possible exception of variants b1 and b2, if the dating by Papadopoulou is corroborated.
[338] Hendy 1999: I, 131.
[339] Papadopoulou 2005: 151-153.
[340] Hendy 1999: I, 427-428.
[341] The refusal of the Rhodians may have been due to the inability of the Venetians to pay: during the siege of Tyre, the doge had had to issue 'leather money' to get by. Heyd 1885: 195; Malamut 1989: I, 98, 119.
[342] Angold 1984: 153; Hendy 1999: I, 244.
[343] According to Angold (1984: 153), they were probably Cumans.
[344] Angold 1984: 153-154. The emperor settled defeated 'Pechenegs' and Serbs in the eastern provinces, where they had the obligation to serve in the army but also paid taxes. Ostrogorsky 1980: 391-392.

the emirate of Melitene. In 1137 he led an expedition against Cilician Armenia,[345] an ally of the Crusaders, and took Tarsus, Adana and Mamistra, obliging Raymond of Poitiers, prince of Antioch, to recognize his suzerainty. In 1138 he led an expedition in Syria with the reluctant participation of the Latins and laid siege to Shaizar (Larissa). In 1139 he was in the Sangarius region and in 1140 he invested Neocaesarea; while his last campaign in Cilicia (1142-3), aimed to bring Latin-held northern Syria under his control.

The campaigns of John II focused on territories away from the coast and the need for naval support was consequently reduced. Thus, the financial policy required for the support of the army and the accumulation of a gold reserve led to increased centralization; one of his measures was to transfer the monies collected for the maintenance of the Aegean fleet to the central treasury.[346] The long-term consequences of the rapid development of Italian cities and of their savage competition against each other for the safety of the Eastern Mediterranean shipping lanes could not be predicted by the reformers in the Constantinopolitan administration, probably due to the still relatively limited importance of Western commercial activities for the empire and the high cost of naval bases in the provinces. It seems that at this time the imperial strategy for the defence of the coastlands was the use of a land army in combination with strongly fortified coastal settlements which could be controlled more effectively by local governors or *pronoiarioi*.[347] Even the confirmation of the privileges of Pisa in 1136 may not have been aimed against Venice but at the increasing power of the Normans, traditional enemies of Byzantium, in south Italy.[348] As a result Byzantium failed to protect is extensive coastline and the Aegean islands. The raid on Patmos by 'Spanish Saracens' was not a good omen for developments in the Aegean.[349] Their appearance was a reminder that the seafarers of the Italian cities were not the only foreigners active in the region.[350]

The reign of John II, considered by many scholars as the apogee of the Comnenian period, is remarkably poorly represented in the coins from Rhodes. Only five pieces have been recorded so far (PL. 74), as follows:

Mint	Denomination	Type	Variety	Number of coins
Constantinople	Aspron trachy (Bi)	2nd coinage	A	1
	Tetartera	A		3
Thessalonica	Tetarteron	B		1

Figure 47: The coins of John II.

They are all site finds from the interior of the medieval town, and the sample is still dominated by tetartera. The representation of the mints, though, has been reversed. It seems that all the coins are dated between 1122 and 1137.[351]

Manuel I (April 1143-24 September 1180)

Manuel I by and large continued the policies of his father, although his flamboyant personality, together with the several and varied written sources available for the reign and the disastrous quarter-century that followed, have affected its interpretation. Manuel endeavoured to respond to the increased expectations of his clan, the public and the foreigners who sought his support in an increasingly complex web of political and economic interests. In his times pressure increased on various fronts: the union of Sicily and south Italy under king Roger II (1130-54), the negative consequences of the Second Crusade, the Muslim recovery in Anatolia, the increasing arrogance of the Venetians and the vicious clashes between Italian merchants even in his own capital, the involvement with Latin Syria and the increased importance of relations with the German emperor were matters requiring vigilance and careful handling. The involvement of many rulers with the Latin East made the wealth of his court a first-class diplomatic tool, and promoted an imperial ideology which was not new in its essentials.

345 One of the interesting features of this campaign was the relocation of the entire population of Tell Hamdun (modern Toprakkale) from Armenia to Cyprus.
346 Harvey 1989: 112 and n. 140.
347 Oikonomides 2010: 232-240; Hendy 1999: I, 245.
348 Probably because Pisa participated in a coalition against Roger II of Sicily, whose authority over south Italy was being consolidated at the time. John's diplomatic and financial support of this coalition, which included pope Innocent II and German emperor Lothair, aimed to safeguard Byzantine possessions in South Italy and contain Norman power.
349 Malamut 1989: I, 120. The reference in the archives of Patmos is dated between 1127 and 1157, so that the episode might have taken place under Manuel; but this does not change its significance.
350 For example, from the 12th c. on, the Catalans were added to the powerful Norman fleet.
351 Hendy 1999: I, 250-251.

At the beginning of his reign, Manuel could use the reserve amassed by his predecessor in order to consolidate his authority and cope with external dangers. The development of the Second Crusade (1147-49) while Roger II was establishing his power in South Italy created a particularly dangerous situation whose immediate consequence was the loss of Corfu and the pillaging of Athens, Thebes, Corinth and Modon by the Normans. The reinforcement of the fleet in 1148[352] was a first response to the threat of a new Norman invasion of the Balkans and the power of the Sicilian fleet. In any case, the emperor had to focus his resources on the military situation in the Balkans while keeping a watchful eye on the events of the Crusade in Asia.

The Crusaders conveniently blamed their failure on the lack of imperial support, reinforcing the mistrust of the pope and the West towards the 'schismatic Greeks'. Manuel's only diplomatic gain in those years was the friendship struck with Conrad III of Germany (1138-52) during the Crusade.[353] This helped forge a front against the Normans, but Conrad died in 1152 and the 1155-6 Byzantine campaign in Italy frightened the pope and Venice and offended the new German emperor Frederick I Barbarossa. The campaign against the Normans would have safeguarded the western Balkans but Manuel's army was abandoned by his allies and defeated at Brindisi in 1156. In 1157, when the Byzantines were starting a new campaign against the Normans from Ancona, the Sicilian fleet plundered Euboea and in 1158 took Almyros before peace was made between Manuel and William I of Sicily.

Between 1159 and 1169, Manuel's attention was turned to Syria. The plundering of Cyprus by the prince of Antioch in 1156 led to an estrangement between the Byzantines and the Latins, reinforcing the position of Nur ad-Din, Seljuk ruler of Aleppo. A new alliance with the Latins was achieved in 1158, through the marriage of Baldwin III of Jerusalem to Theodora, niece of Manuel. Manuel combined this alliance with a campaign in Cilicia and the submission of the king of Armenia. In 1161 Manuel married Mary, daughter of the prince of Antioch, and in the same year the Antiochenes took part in Manuel's victorious campaign against the Seljuks in Anatolia.[354] In the years following, the emperor's influence lessened Seljuk pressure on the Latin states. In 1167 Amalric I, the new king of Jerusalem, married Maria Comnena, another niece of Manuel, and agreed to participate in a major Byzantine assault against the waning power of Egypt. This would safeguard the rear of Christian Syria, but Latin ill-will led the enterprise, which took place in 1169, to fail. A diplomatic journey of Amalric to Constantinople in 1171 led to a new alliance against Egypt. Indeed, a fleet prepared by Manuel sailed to Acre in 1177, but disagreements between king Baldwin IV of Jerusalem and Philip I, count of Flanders, cancelled the campaign.

Meanwhile, the grant of trading privileges to Genoa in 1155[355] had displeased the Venetians and, in 1162, they plundered the Genoese quarter in Constantinople with the help of the Pisans.[356] In 1170, after a new agreement between Manuel and the Pisans, the Venetians plundered the Pisan quarter. The aftermath of the rivalry between Italian merchants even reached Rhodes where, as in other islands, the local authorities seem to have favoured the Venetians against the newly arrived Genoese.[357] After a new attack on the Genoese quarter in Constantinople Manuel had all Venetian citizens in his territories arrested, and seized their property.[358] Escaping Venetians plundered Lesbos, Chios and Rhodes and the following year Venice sent a powerful fleet to the Aegean. This forced the emperor into negotiations, but while waiting for Manuel's decision in Chios their fleet was struck by a plague, which was brought back to Venice. In 1173, the Venetians joined Frederic I in the siege of Ancona and in 1175 allied themselves to William II of Sicily. Ironically, both Manuel and Frederic suffered heavy defeats in 1176: the former at Myriocephalon by Kilij Arslan, sultan of Iconium,[359] and the second by the Lombard League at Legnano. In 1179, a year before his death, Manuel agreed to reimburse the Venetians for their financial losses of 1171[360] and obtained an unexpectedly favourable peace treaty with Kilij Arslan, considering the importance assigned by historians to the defeat at Myriocephalon.[361]

352 Magdalino 1993: 53, 138.

353 Magdalino 1993: 46-53.

354 When Manuel sought Latin mercenaries in Rhodes in 1161, it must have been for this campaign. The presence of mercenaries in Rhodes was due to the fact that the port was a station on the sea-lane to the Holy Land.

355 To stop the Genoese fleet from supporting the Normans. Epstein 1996: 72, 79.

356 It was followed by a war between Pisa and Genoa (1162-75). In the same period, after the plundering of Milan by Frederic I, the Genoese sought his favour and their relations with Byzantium cooled. Epstein 1996: 76, 78.

357 Before 1174, Andronicus, dux of Rhodes, confiscated the goods of Genoese merchants. Malamut 1989: I, 173, 325; II, 445, 506. The same thing had taken place on Crete. Rhodes remained in the Cibyrraiote theme until 1147 and afterwards had its own dux. Malamut 1989: I, 325.

358 Hendy 1985: 593.

359 In 1173, Frederic had made friendly overtures to Kilij Arslan. Angold 1984: 183; Magdalino 1993: 98.

360 For the date see Brand 1968: 20.

361 Magdalino 1993: 98-100.

Manuel's reign has been held by many to have exhausted the resources of the empire.[362] According to Nicetas Choniates, Manuel made excessive use of the *pronoia*, while the provinces were burdened by the presence of mercenaries. Contemporary written sources complain of heavy taxation and the continuous plundering of the Aegean littoral, generally ascribed to the abolition of the provincial squadrons by John II.[363] Manuel did put together three large fleets (1148, 1168 and 1176-7), for expeditionary purposes; but they intercepted foreign marauders only occasionally. If, however, his policies were so disastrous, it is odd that the state held together for four decades. The explanation is probably to be found in the prosperity of the empire at this time and, perhaps, in the estimation of Michael Hendy concerning its economy.[364] In his concise presentation of Manuel's reign,[365] Hendy touches upon the supposed decrease of available gold, as the hoarding of gold appears to decrease in the second half of the 12th century, being replaced by electrum[366] and billon hoards. Hendy thought that this was partly due to the need to spread the available gold more widely due to economic development and therefore the more widespread use of coin with a reduced gold content. Another factor which possibly intensified the phenomenon was the *pronoia*: a portion of the taxes earlier collected by the state had been allotted to individuals who, in turn, provided services (e.g. soldiers). Thus, part of the state income from the exploitation of the land and other sources now bypassed the central administration, limiting the recycling of precious metals by the mint. This may well have negatively affected the availability of small change, since one way coins of lower value were put into circulation was through the *strophe* received by the citizens when they paid their taxes. The reduction in the circulation of coins of low value is observable in Rhodes, but not just for the reign of Manuel: it is more serious under John II.

The number and variety of coin finds in Rhodes increases under Manuel (PL. 74-76). He is the only emperor of the 12th century also represented by a gold coin:[367]

Mint	Denomination	Type	Variety	Number of coins
Constantinople	Hyperpyron		II	1
	Aspra trachea (El)[56]	1st coinage	B	1
		2nd coinage	B	2
	Trachea (Bi)	4th coinage	D	2
			?	7
	Clipped trachea (Bi)[57]	2nd coinage		1
		3rd coinage		3 or 4
		4th coinage		2 to 4
	Tetartera	1st coinage		2
			D	1
Thessalonica	Tetartera		A	1
			B	1
'Unknown Greek mint'	Half-tetartera		A	1
			B	1

Figure 48: The coins of Manuel I.

It should be remarked that only nine of the billon trachea are likely to have circulated in Rhodes during his lifetime. The other nine are clipped and most of them belong to the 'neatly clipped trachea' group, and must have reached Rhodes twenty years after his death. The appearance of such coins is thought to be due to official clipping carried out in Constantinople and is dated *c.* 1200.[370]

362 Ostrogorsky 1980: 391-4.
363 Although, in 1158, the monks of Patmos complained that they had been raided by the Greek praktor of Samos, one Pegonites. Magdalino 1993: 139 n. 128.
364 Harvey 1989; Hendy 1985: 590-602.
365 Hendy 1999: I, 275-280.
366 Cf. Balling 1963 for Rhodes and Metcalf 2009: 533 for Cyprus.
367 Derived from a small hoard. Christodoulides 1998: 951; Papadopoulou 2010: 174-187.
368 204 aspra trachea (El) of Manuel I form the bulk of the double hoard Lindos/1902, but its concealment should probably be dated to the last decade of the 12th century. Balling 1963: 13-14.
369 The obverse on three of these trachea is illegible from wear and the orientation of the axes uncertain.
370 Hendy 1999: I, 45-46, 59-66.

It is worth noting that the non-clipped trachea of the emperor all belong to the 4th coinage. There are also five tetartera, of which three from Constantinople and two from Thessalonica, and two half-tetartera, of types A and B of Hendy's 'unknown Greek mint'.[371] It is obvious that the proportions of trachea and tetartera have changed, clearly through the depreciation of the billon trachea in comparison to the coins of higher value. The representation of the mints has also changed: the rise of Constantinople, already observed under John II with a proportion of 4:1, under Manuel rises to 10:1. The type D tetarteron of Thessalonica shows a variant of the imperial costume.[372]

Hendy also attempted to date the issues of Manuel I;[373] according to his work, the distribution of the emperor's unclipped coins across the reign is as follows:

Dates	AV	El trachea	Bi trachea	Tetartera	½ tetartera	TOTAL
1143 - 1152		1		2	1	4
1152 - c. 1160	1	2		2	1	6
c. 1160 - c. 1164				1		1
c. 1164 - 1167						
1167 - 1180/1183			8			8

Figure 49: Dating of the coins of Manuel I.

It is clear that the shift from tetartera to the billon trachea was accomplished after 1167, when the equivalence with the hyperpyron had altered significantly.[374] The presence of Manuel's billon trachea on Rhodes in this period may be associated with the Egyptian expeditions of 1169 and 1177.[375]

Alexius II (September 1180 - October 1183) and Andronicus I (September 1183 - 12 September 1185)

There are no coins from the brief reign of Alexius II under the guardianship of his mother Mary of Antioch, although it is likely that the last types of Manuel I were still being issued.[376] The regency of Mary and the favour she showed to foreigners created social tensions in the capital and divided the aristocracy; territorial losses were suffered in the Balkans and Anatolia. In the spring of 1182 Andronicus Comnenus, first cousin of Manuel I, camped in Chalcedon and incited a popular uprising which turned against the Latins in Constantinople, with general slaughter and plundering. With the assistance of *megas dux* Andronicus Contostephanus he took charge of the capital and, in September 1183, was crowned co-emperor. Two months later Alexius II was murdered.

Andronicus tried to protect the poor and the provinces from government corruption and the exploitation of powerful landowners, whom he pursued with deliberate cruelty. His reign was also troubled by the invasion of king Bela III of Hungary in 1183, the loss of Rascia, the establishment of the usurper Isaac Comnenus in Cyprus in 1184 and, finally, an invasion by William II of Sicily, who took Dyrrachium in June 1185 and plundered Thessalonica that August. On 12 September, an uprising of the panicking populace in Constantinople cost Andronicus his life.

Three billon trachea of Andronicus' type B of Constantinople have been found in Rhodes (PL. 76). One is pierced at the rim and another is incomplete.

Isaac II Angelus (12 September 1185 - August 1195)

The reign of Isaac II is noted for the squandering of public money, the reckless sale of offices and the increase of corruption. The tax burden on the provinces increased, leading to a series of rebellions. Militarily, the Norman threat in 1185 was successfully dealt with by the general Alexius Branas but was soon followed by a revolt in Bulgaria which resulted in a peace treaty and the establishment of the second Bulgarian empire. In 1187 Isaac attempted to recover Cyprus, but his fleet was defeated and captured by Sicilian admiral Margarito of Brindisi. In 1189 a peace treaty with the Normans restored lost territories to the empire. However, in the same year Isaac, due to a pact with Saladin, refused to facilitate the passage of the crusading army of Frederick I Barbarossa through his territory;

[371] Hendy 1999: I, 131, 284; Hendy 1969: 126-130. See, however, Touratsoglou *et al.* 1989: 372-373.
[372] **1239**.
[373] Hendy 1999: I, 287.
[374] From 1: 48 to 1:120. Hendy 1999: I, 287.
[375] Magdalino 1993: 74, 97.
[376] Hendy 1999: I, 287.

Frederick occupied Philippopolis and plundered Thrace, thus obliging Isaac to change his mind. In 1190 Isaac was defeated by the Bulgars and recognized the Serbian state.

Besides the loss of Cyprus, Isaac faced a series of rebellions by disaffected subjects: in 1185 by Alexius Branas, in 1188-9 by Theodore Mankaphas at Philadelphia and, finally, after another defeat by the Bulgars at Arcadiopolis, his brother Alexius in 1195.

An incident typical of the situation in the Aegean under Isaac II was played out in and about Rhodes. In 1192, the Genoese corsair Guglielmo Grasso, in collusion with a Pisan ship, entered the harbour of Rhodes as a merchant and pillaged the harbour neighbourhood. Then he ambushed a Venetian flotilla carrying an embassy of Saladin, slaughtering the crews and the Greek and Syrian merchants on board, and captured a Sicilian vessel carrying a Byzantine embassy from Cyprus.[377]

The coinage of Isaac II (PLS 76-77) is represented by 29-32[378] trachea: one is of electrum and the rest of billon.[379] However, only nine are likely to have circulated in Rhodes in his time. The rest are clipped, and seven or eight of them belong to the neatly clipped category and must have reached Rhodes under Alexius III.[380] Clipping and the condition of almost all the coins make a confident attribution hazardous. The diameter of the neatly clipped trachea ranges from 19 to 23 mm.[381] However, the coins of Rhodes include eight more pieces which, although much reduced in size (17.5-14 mm), share two features of the neatly clipped trachea, namely the careful circular clipping and the respect to the imperial figure at the centre,[382] so that they may represent the final stage of the official clipping in the capital, shortly before 1203.

To a more irregular style of clipping, also possibly systematic, belong three specimens much reduced in size and cut from the rim of coins not previously clipped. The position of the axes on three of them is regular, implying an official original minting, but the clipping manner recalls examples from the coinage of John Comnenus-Ducas in the 13th century.[383] Finally, two more carelessly clipped, although larger pieces may not be issues of Isaac but type B 'faithful copies'.[384] The clipping of the remaining six coins may have been carried out anywhere, including Rhodes. It is quite likely that the small size of the more heavily clipped pieces represents an attempt to bring them closer in size to western petty coins; this may have occurred even after 1204.

A trachy and a tetarteron of Isaac Comnenus, 'tyrant' of Cyprus from 1185 to 1191,[385] have also turned up in Rhodes (PL. 76). Both seem to belong in the later issues of his six-year rule from his central mint.[386] The finds are of interest because they may be evidence for contacts between Rhodes and Cyprus at a time the two islands presumably belonged in different camps: Isaac Comnenus was backed by the Normans of Sicily who defeated the Byzantine expeditionary fleet of 1187.

Alexius III Angelus ([August] 1195 - 17 July 1203)

Under Alexius III corruption reached new peaks and there was widespread want in the provinces due to heavy taxation; money continued to be wasted when it was not paid out to avoid attacks by foreign enemies. Defeats by the Bulgars, whose raids reached central Greece, continued in 1196-7. In Anatolia Mankaphas raided the Byzantine borders aided by the sultan of Iconium. From 1198, a chrysobull of Alexius allowed the Venetians to trade freely throughout the Aegean.[387] However, the inability of the Byzantines to police the seas resulted in heavy Venetian losses caused by Genoese and Pisan corsairs.[388] Alexius tried to limit their depredations by hiring the services of other adventurers: he sent John Steiriones, a Calabrian, against the Genoese Gaffore, while in 1201 a piratical fleet from Sicily was repulsed by a hired Genoese corsair. Under these conditions, separatist tendencies within the empire intensified.[389]

---

[377] Laiou 2001: 157-159. A little later Grasso became count of Malta, a possession of the kingdom of Sicily (1197- 1203). Dalli 2006: 97-98.

[378] Four pieces, **1251**, **1278**, **1279** and **1280** may be type B faithful copies.

[379] 31 if **1251** is discounted.

[380] **1259**, **1260**, **1261**, **1262**, **1263**, **1264**, **1265** and perhaps **1266** (diam. 18.5 mm).

[381] Hendy 1999: II, Pl. LIV: B.3a.12=23 mm, 3f.21=21 mm, 34.7=19 mm, 3c.22=20 mm, 3c.24=21 mm, 3d.3=22 mm.

[382] Hendy 1999: I, 59.

[383] **1275, 1276, 1277, 1278.** Cf. Hendy 1969: Pl. 41 no. 10, 15-16, 18 and Pl. 44, no. 1-10.

[384] **1279** and **1280**.

[385] For his career and descent see Hendy 1999: I, 354.

[386] Hendy 1999: I, 356.

[387] Malamut 1988: I, 174.

[388] Angold 1984: 290.

[389] Ahrweiler 1966: 288-292; Pryor and Jeffreys 2006: 122; Ostrogorsky 1980: 403; Haldon 1999: 96.

Fifteen or sixteen[390] coins of Alexius III have been inventoried in Rhodes (PL. 78). In the finds from his period the evolution of systematic clipping, with the gradual reduction of the diameter, is clear. The smallest five specimens have not been clipped as carefully as the rest although an effort was still made to preserve the figure (or face) of the emperor, so they probably do not belong with the four smallest clipped pieces of Isaac II. The presence of a reverse variant with three dots on the upper part of the *loros* on three pieces with regularly oriented axes should be noted.[391]

To the coins that entered circulation under Alexius III should be added 7-10 clipped pieces of Manuel I and 15 of Isaac I. It must also be mentioned that most of the coins of the Angeli from Rhodes are site finds, and all of them billon trachea. Thus, between 1200 and 1203 losses per year shoot up to a value of 11. This may be a symptom of crisis, or due to factors such as increased activity in the harbour and the presence of corsairs or mercenaries, as well as the delayed arrival of his coins in the island.

* * *

Coin circulation derived from losses per year for the 12th century may be displayed in some detail, through the more precise dating now available for coins of John II, Manuel I and Alexius III. If, to these, the early years of Alexius I are added, before his monetary reform, and the reign of Nicephorus III for the sake of comparison, a more informative picture ensues:

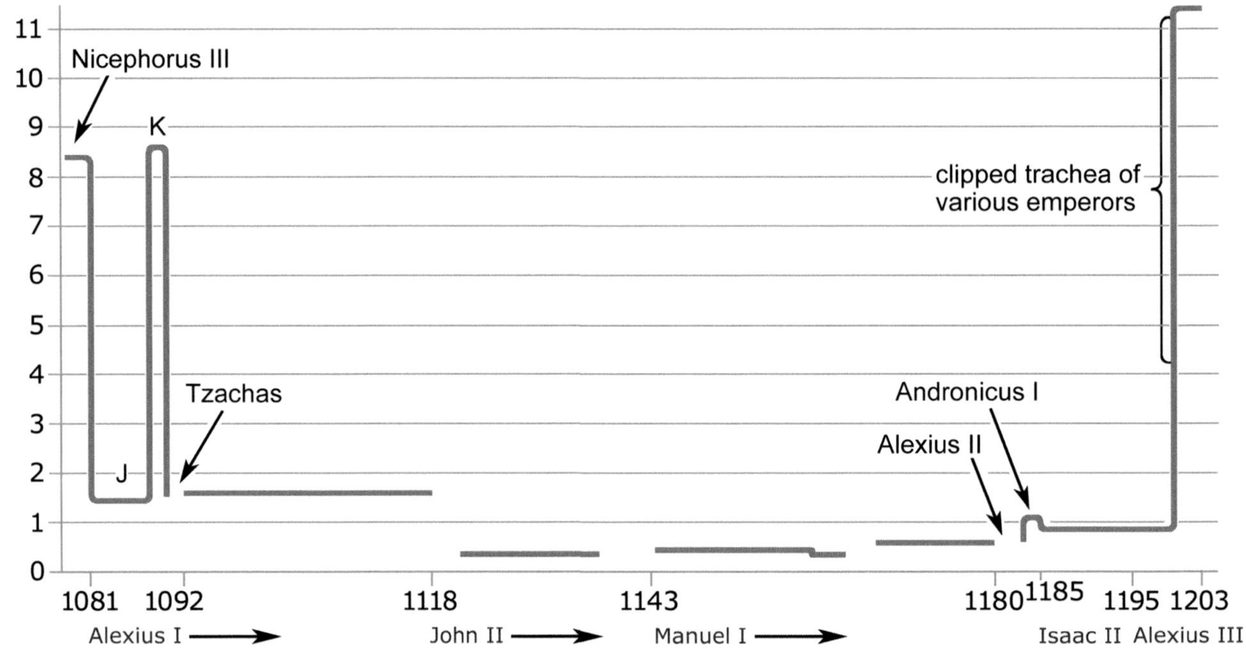

Figure 50: Losses per year of billon and copper coins between 1078 and 1203.

There are peaks under Nicephorus III, probably of administrative origin, under Alexius I before the occupation of the islands of the eastern Aegean by Tzachas of Smyrna, and under Alexius III in the years *c.* 1200-1203. There are also gaps in the numismatic evidence at the start and end of the reign of John and in the interval *c.* 1164-67 under Manuel. Moreover, perhaps the last part of the reign of Manuel I should contain two substantial peaks in years 1168 and 1176-7, when the expeditions against Egypt (1169, 1177) were under preparation, or the in concentration of troops and/or supplies due to the geographical location of Rhodes. It is clear that, until 1118, there is increased monetary circulation probably due to a number of factors: the campaign for the recovery of the Anatolian littoral with the support of the fleet, the supervision of events in Syria and the wintering of the Venetian crusader fleet in Rhodes in 1099/1100, and the more efficient collection of taxes after 1108. This is supported by the fact that three successive coinages of Thessalonica are respectably represented in Rhodes. The supply of coin from Thessalonica may be associated with the administrative reorganization of the coastal provinces of the Aegean in order to support

[390] **1293** may be a class B faithful copy.

[391] **1287**, **1288**, **1297**.

the fleet which played an important part in the territorial and political recovery of the empire under Alexius I. In any case, it is tempting to link the second coinage with the Anatolian campaign, the third coinage with the appearance of the Crusaders, particularly in the years 1098-1100, and the fourth with the new order, after the tax reform came into full effect after 1108.

The death of Alexius introduces a period of reduced monetary circulation covering the reigns of John II and most of Manuel I. A small increase is observed after 1167, which may be a transient event associated with the Byzantine expeditions against Egypt. If Figure 50 is compared to Figure 44, or even Figure 38 of the previous chapter, the picture obtained seems to break with the well-documented steady economic development of the 11th and early 12th centuries.[392] What we have is a rise in circulation until the period of Alexius which is then curtailed until the last quarter of the 12th century. Of course, economic prosperity may not necessarily result in the increased circulation of petty coins; but small-scale exchanges in coin may hint at the manner and social impact of economic development, such as increased urbanization. These hints are missing from Rhodes from the middle years of the 12th century, if it is assumed that the lack of coin under John II was somewhat mitigated by Venetian imitative tetartera copying those of his predecessor.

At both ends of this interval the island received large crusader fleets. In 1099/1100 the Venetian fleet wintered there, while at the end of April 1191 the fleet of Richard the Lionheart spent ten days there to recover from the effects of a violent storm. We have no further information about the first episode, but the silence of the sources probably means that the needs of the Crusaders were met without particular problems. It is likely that the local authorities had been alerted in time or that the Byzantine fleet was at hand to bring in added supplies. In contrast, the chronicler of Richard I in 1191 was impressed by the extent and quality of the ruins of the ancient city but mentioned recently abandoned monasteries amongst the ruins and a sparse population. He did not mention the Byzantine fortified settlement by the harbour and noted the poverty of the local market in foodstuffs, in spite of the island's fertility:

> Chapter XXVII. Of the winds that were at one time calm, at another agitating the sea, and the dangers which King Richard sustained as far as Crete, and from Crete to Rhodes.
> *(...) The wind, which slackened not all night, at dawn of day drove our fleet violently upon the island of Rhodes: there was no port, and the surf stretched along the shore; however, we enjoyed there our rest the better for having wished for it so earnestly, from that day until the following Monday, when we put in at Rhodes. Rhodes was anciently a very large city, not unlike Rome; though its extent can scarcely be estimated, there are so many ruins of houses and portions of fallen towers still standing, and such wonderful remains of walls and buildings of admirable workmanship. There are also a few monasteries still remaining out of so many ancient edifices, for the most part deserted, though formerly inhabited by such numerous societies of monks. The site of so great a city, though by time laid waste, proves the former existence of a large population; but very few inhabitants were found there now who could sell us food. But as the king was indisposed, we tarried there a few days, during which he waited the arrival of the ships that had wandered out of their course and lost us, and the galleys which followed him. He made inquiries also about that cruel tyrant, emperor of Cyprus, who was wont to detain the pilgrims who put in at his port.*
>
> Chapter XXVIII. Of the departure of King Richard from Rhodes, through the gulf, and of the arrival of the queen at Cyprus. *Having spent ten days at Rhodes, which is a very fertile and productive island, they went on board, and set out on their voyage on the 1st of May...*[393]

The apparent contradiction between the absence of produce and the perceived fertility of the land might be explained by the collated nature of the source[394] but also by the season, when the grain was still unripe and the weather did not favour fishing. The arrival of the Crusaders appears to have been fortuitous, but in any case a stay of ten days was not scheduled. However, the plunder of Rhodes by the Venetians in 1124, due to their vengeful mood and the reluctance (or inability) of the locals to receive their fleet,[395] must have seriously affected the island. Another blow, less violent but more insidious in the long term, must have been the measure introduced by John Poutzes, *megas logariastes* of emperor John II (and of Manuel I later): the revenues from the maritime lands were no longer directly passed to the fleet, but *'paid into the treasury, which was supposed to meet future naval requirements. At this stage, commutation had not been completed but after the reform the islands no longer provided manned warships.'*[396]

392 Cf. Harvey 1989: 244-68; Laiou 2002: II, 759; Magdalino 1993: 24-25.
393 Richard of Holy Trinity, chapters 27-28.
394 Cf. Morgan 1973: 60 ff.
395 Nicol 2004: 114.
396 Harvey 1989: 112. See also Magdalino 1993: 139; Hendy 1999: I, 245-246; Malamut 1988: I, 88.

This centralization certainly upset the operation of provincial naval stations and shipyards which, it should not be forgotten, supported a variety of trades which contributed to the urban character of the associated settlements. It is also likely that these arsenals, officially or unofficially, had also served private shipping at a price, thus contributing further to the local economy.

The lack of coin after 1118 may well be due to the presence of *pronoia* holders,[397] which should have limited the need to import the copper coins necessary for the payment of the *strophe* by tax collectors. There are a number of candidates among the local *dynatoi*, the Gavalas, Alopoi, Katakalon, Bardas or Armenopouloi who, because they were not associated with the high Comnenian aristocracy, are rarely mentioned in the written sources. Nevertheless, given their dominant position on the island after 1204, and their long association with Rhodes, the Gavalas are the most likely choice.[398] The *pronoia*, raiding and curtailment of the role of the local arsenal are probably sufficient to explain the serious reduction in coin circulation. The incident in the harbour of Rhodes involving Guglielmo Grasso[399] a year after the visit of the English king, betrays the impotence of the local authorities towards the end of the century. There is an impression that Rhodes, like other provincial centres, was waiting for the dissolution of the central authority in order to take advantage of the opportunities provided by economic development in the Mediterranean at this time.[400]

[397] For the effects of the *pronoia* on monetary circulation in general: Cheynet 2006: 132-133; Oikonomides 2002: 1042 ff.

[398] It is possibly not a coincidence that in the 10th century Stephen Lecapenus was exiled in Rhodes: he had married into the Gavalas family. For the aristocratic landowners of Rhodes from the 10th to the 13th century see Katsioti and Archontopoulos 2000: 384-5 and n. 59.

[399] The actions of Grasso, considered by their immediate victims, the Byzantines and Venetians, as plain piracy, could also be differently interpreted: the problems with Frederic Barbarossa had led Isaac II and the Venetians to negotiations with Saladin, which Western privateers might consider as sufficient cause to treat them as legal targets.

[400] Cf. Magdalino 1993: 147.

The 13th century (1204 - 1309)

Rhodes is not mentioned in the text of the *Partitio Romaniae*, the agreement drawn between the Crusaders after the conquest of Constantinople in 1204.[401] It is reasonably inferred that Rhodes was not ceded to anyone because it was no longer under Byzantine control. Local ruler Leo Gavalas, or perhaps his father, had become independent from 1203; when, that is, Alexius III Angelus was deposed by the Latin allies of Alexius IV, or even earlier.[402] This may mean either that Gavalas owed his position to Alexius III and felt no obligation towards his supplanter, or that he had seized the chance to break away from the empire, like other local potentates in the Byzantine provinces: during the last twenty years of the 12th century the oppression of Constantinople had caused widespread disaffection partly due, according to historians, to heavy taxation and partly because the central government inhibited the growth of the Byzantine economy, appropriating resources which aroused the ambitions of local magnates. At a time of increasing administrative dysfunction, the provinces had good reasons to prefer local rulers of limited power who had vested interests in the prosperity of the society under their control, were familiar with local conditions and problems and were more accessible to their subjects.

Irrespective of the date his rule began, it seems that Leo Gavalas managed to preserve his independence until c. 1225. In this he was helped by the impotence of Theodore I Lascaris, who had to face both the Latins of Constantinople and the Byzantines of Trebizond, not to mention the Turkish presence in the Anatolian hinterland. From 1225 until his death in 1240, Leo was, more or less reluctantly,[403] subject to the emperor of Nicaea, the highly capable John III Ducas Vatatzes. Relations with Nicaea became even closer when he was succeeded by his brother John, who at some point was *megas droungarios* of John III, to whom he was related through marriage.[404] In 1248, the Genoese took the Rhodians by surprise and occupied the town; it was recovered shortly before his death by Nicene forces.[405]

In 1250, after the death of John Gavalas, the administration of the island passed into the hands of a series of appointees representing the emperor of Nicaea who, in 1261, recovered Constantinople. The return of the Byzantine capital to Constantinople again distanced Rhodes from the central administration and the local governors were often allowed to act independently, albeit under increasing insecurity. This situation apparently continued until the early 14th century, when the deliberate planning and persistence of Foulques de Villaret, master of the Order of the Hospital, led to the permanent loss to the empire of Rhodes itself and of the neighbouring islands (1309).

The Gavalas period (1204-1250)

The 13th century was a time of transition for Rhodes, as the influence of its Byzantine overlords fluctuated. Our knowledge for the first half of the century is fragmentary, while from 1250 onwards we can scarcely cite the names of some of its governors. We also know very little about local society, although in the last quarter of the century the settlement of Turcomans on the island was favoured by the rivalry between the corsairs employed by the Byzantine emperors to control the Aegean. The political instability is reflected in the coins, which present a number of difficulties. It is believed that the official high-value currency was the hyperpyron of Nicaea. In Rhodes, however, with the exception of two hoards of which one was never examined by a specialist, archaeological finds are limited to the silver of Cilician Armenia and the Seljuk sultanate of Iconium.[406] In the billon and copper, the empire of Nicaea is very poorly represented (PL. 78): it consists of two trachea of Theodore I and two trachea and one tetarteron of

[401] Miller 1908: 27-31; Oikonomides 1992: XX; Penna 2010b: 18, 34. Interestingly, Naxos is also absent from the Partitio Romaniae; Marco Sanudo hastened to occupy it around 1205, as a vassal of the Latin emperor of Constantinople. Koumanoudi 2005: 248-249.

[402] In the recent bibliography there is no consensus for the precise date Rhodes broke away from Byzantine central control: see Savvides 1987: 306-307. Gavalas seems to have held other islands in the SE Aegean, at least for a time. However, it is not certain that Leo himself was the man who broke away from Constantinople since, according to Nicephorus Blemmydes, a contemporary ([1984]: 56), his 'right to rule did not derive from the state but was a paternal legacy, passed on by his ancestors'. Cf. Hendy 1999: II, 648-649. Hendy's view that John or Stephen Gavalas, who appear in the sources of the late 12th century, may have founded the lordship of Rhodes, seems reasonable.

[403] In 1233, Leo rebelled and Nicene troops plundered the countryside of Rhodes; John III recalled those troops in order to deal with Latin trouble in Bithynia. The following year a treaty of mutual support was drafted between Leo and the Venetians, who were concerned about an attack of Vatatzes on Crete. However, in 1235-6 he is supposed to have taken part with his ships in the siege of Latin-held Constantinople by John III and Ivan II Asen of Bulgaria. Savvides 1987: 309-321.

[404] Langton 1978: 134-135.

[405] Savvides 1983: 420-423.

[406] Kasdagli 1996: 329, 331. One consisted of gold coins of John II, Michael VIII and Andronicus II, and was found near the village of Damatria in the early years of the Italian occupation of Rhodes. The other, found relatively recently at an unknown location, included a hyperpyron of John III. The Paradissi hoard includes dirhem of Kay-Khusraw II (1237-46), Kay-Khusraw III (1265-8) and Masud II (1282 ff). The countermarked dirhem shown on Schlumberger's plates IX (8) and XIX (16, 17) belong to Kay-Khusraw II and Masud II.

John III, while three other trachea may be issues of Nicaea but are absent from the relevant bibliography (PL. 87).[407] In contrast, Latin imitative trachea (PLS 80-86), particularly the small-module issues, are very common; a few 'faithful copies' have also been found, most of them of type C (PL. 79). The rest of the local sample is made up of local issues of the Gavalas brothers and the officials who succeeded them as imperial appointees after 1250. However, there are also coins of disputable date and origin, some at least of which may have been minted locally.

Obviously, in this period the copper did not enter circulation through the traditional mechanisms of the imperial administration and was probably no longer associated with taxation.[408] Also, the issuing authority is not always clear. This institutional break is accompanied by other problems: which coins should we consider 'local' or 'valid currency' and which are foreign? How are we to explain the abundance of Latin and other imitative trachea? When and for what reasons did a local mint begin to operate? What is the sequence and dating of the locally minted issues? Which were their immediate models? The attempt to tackle such topics must be preceded by a review of the available material. A rough sorting of the adequately identified petty coins is set out below, in descending sequence according to the relative representation of each group:

	Specimens	**% of the total**
Latin imitative trachea, small module	133	43.6
Anonymous Rhodian 'tetartera'	94	30.8
'Tetartera' of Leo Gavalas	29	9.5
Latin imitative trachea, large module	15	4.9
Imitations of Nicene imperial issues	12	3.9
Faithful imitations of Byzantine trachea	9	2.9
'Tetartera' of John Gavalas	5	1.6
John III Ducas Vatatzes	3	0.9
Theodore I Lascaris	2	0.6
Other Byzantine	3	0.9
TOTAL	**305**	

Figure 51: Coins of the 13th century in Rhodes.

This shows that the Latin imitative small-module trachea dominate. However, their importance in the sample is overstated because 40% of those (53 coins) come from a single site, the church of SS. Constantine and Helena in the medieval town, and were once the contents of purses buried as grave offerings. Unfortunately, they derive from shaft graves disturbed by successive burials, possibly family tombs. From the same church also come 66% of the large-module Latin imitatives, and 42% of type C 'faithful copies'. This phenomenon, which probably signifies that the church was a node of reference for a particular group of people in the town, must be taken into account in any further analysis of the numismatic evidence. The following graph displays the presence of small-module Latin imitatives by type, but also the relative significance of this archaeological site for the general evaluation of the Rhodian coins of this period (Figure 52).

An interesting feature of this graph is that relatively few worn pieces ('?') have been found on the site, pointing to the fact that most of the coins recovered were interred fairly soon after entering circulation. It is worth noting that no other site shows a similar concentration, and that about three quarters of the coins from the first half of the 13th century come from a deep shaft (possibly family) grave in the north aisle of the church.[409]

Small-module Latin imitative types C and F have not been found in the church. The absence of class B faithful copies or large-module Latin imitatives of types A, B, F and H of Constantinople and A of Thessalonica are of lesser significance, because they are much scarcer finds overall. Besides, perhaps the large-module pieces were seldom included in the funerary purses, although they may have been used as single offerings. The detailed representation of these issues is as follows:

[407] **1479, 1480** and **1482.** To date, a trachy of Theodore Comnenus-Ducas of Thessalonica (1303) and two trachea assigned to Andronicus I Gido of Trebizond (**1304, 1305**) have also been recovered (PL. 79).

[408] Hendy 1999: II, 453.

[409] Papavassileiou 1992: 677-688, Figure 5. See Appendices, Selected Contexts IV.

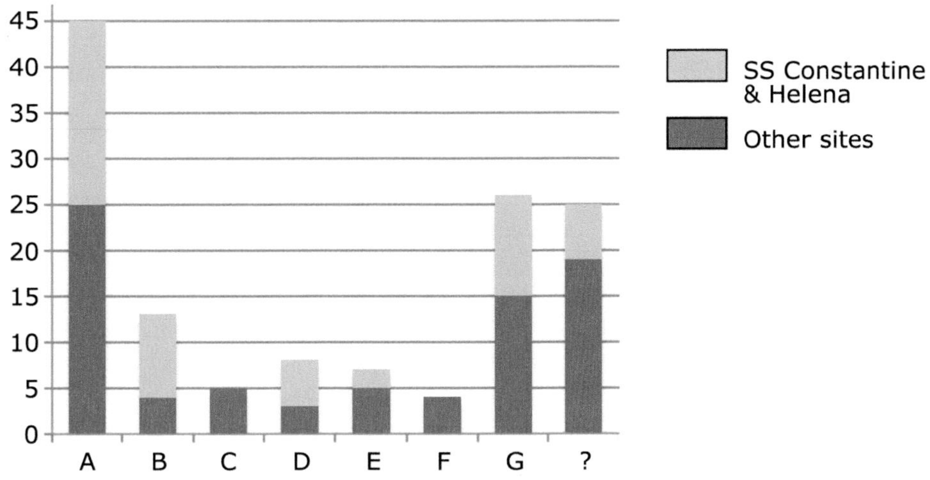

Figure 52: Small module Latin imitatives of types A-G in Rhodes.

	Total of coins	SS Constantine and Helena
'Faithful copies', type B	2	-
'Faithful copies', type C	7	3
Latin imitatives, large module, Constantinople, type A	1	-
Latin imitatives, large module, Constantinople, type B	1	-
Latin imitatives, large module, Constantinople, type C	3	2
Latin imitatives, large module, Constantinople, type D or E	1	1
Latin imitatives, large module, Constantinople, type F	1	-
Latin imitatives, large module, Thessalonica, type A	2	-
Latin imitatives, large module, Thessalonica, type B	3	2
Latin imitatives, large module, Thessalonica, type C	3	2
Imitations of Nicene coins	10	4

Figure 53: Comparison of large module imitative trachea from SS Constantine and Helena with the total for the group.

Among the coins found at SS Constantine and Helena is one of the two coins assigned by recent publications to Andronicus I Gido of Trebizond (1222-1235) found in Rhodes (PL. 79).[410] The interpretation of the numismatic evidence from the church is based on the assumption that the small-module Latin imitative trachea were issued, most likely in Constantinople, by the Venetians from 1204 onwards.[411] The dominance of these coins in the Rhodian sample of the first half of the 13th century testifies to the dynamic representation of Venetian interests on the island well before the treaty between Leo Gavalas and Venice in 1234. Indeed, if their presence in Rhodes is taken together with the absence of Rhodes from the document of the *Partitio Romaniae*, it is likely that the economic relations forged by the 1170s between the Venetians and the *archontes* of Rhodes[412] assisted Gavalas' bid for independence *c.* 1203, safeguarding the new *status quo* from possible claims by other Crusaders. For this early period it is not necessary to focus on the person of Leo Gavalas, whose authority came by right of inheritance. The title of caesar on his signed coins also mentioned in the treaty of 1234 with Venice was possibly a reward for his submission to Nicaea *c.* 1225, or imperial confirmation of his authority by John III.

Before 1225, the principal medium for small-scale transactions must have been the small-module Latin imitative trachea; which does not mean that they were then immediately withdrawn from circulation. Their excessive

[410] Penna 1997: 8 and n. 6, with bibliography. Elsewhere classed as Latin imitatives, large module, type H (cf. Hendy 1999: II, 678).

[411] Penna 1997; Hendy 1999: II, 670-672.

[412] Andronicus, dux of Rhodes, had seized the goods of Genoese merchants some time between 1155 and 1174. The same had happened in Crete, implying the influence of the main competitors of Genoa at a time when the Ligurian metropolis was trying to expand its business in the Aegean. Malamut 1989: I, 325 and II, 445, 506.

concentration in the church of SS Constantine and Helena might mark the religious focus of the active Venetian presence in the town; or, at least, of their Greek representatives. It seems that the church, or some earlier religious foundation, already existed on the site in the 11th century, judging from a funerary coin deposit of 15 11th-century anonymous folles found in a grave a few yards to the east. It is possible that an earlier church once stood on the site;[413] but the extant building was probably built in the early 13th century, perhaps under Alexius III.[414] The use of the church by Venetians or their collaborators is strengthened by the fact that coin finds drop to a minimum after the death of Leo Gavalas. The ties of his brother John with the imperial court at Nicaea need not have been forged after Leo's death. In 1241 there is a mention of *droungarios* John Gavalas,[415] while Venetian sources cite an unknown Gavalas as the commander of the Nicene fleet besieging Latin Constantinople in 1235/6.[416] If this Gavalas was John, brother of Leo, already a high-ranking official of John III of Nicaea, he was not bound by the treaty of Leo with the Venetians in 1234. Moreover, this interpretation would explain his marriage into the Vatatzes family,[417] which would ensure Byzantine control over Rhodes in the long term.

John, as a courtier of Vatatzes, did not share his brother's priorities. He probably spent little time in Rhodes and this might explain the relative scarcity of his signed Rhodian coins. His absence from Rhodes in 1248 exposed the town to the opportunistic Genoese, who occupied it. Under John Gavalas, Venetian influence must have waned; after 1250, with the arrival of an imperial representative as governor, it must have been minimal. Later on, the favour shown to the Genoese by Palaeologan emperors Michael VIII and Andronicus II removed Rhodes definitely from the sphere of Venice; although finds of Venetian *quartaroli* from the town (PL. 148) show that contacts with the Republic were not broken.[418]

According to the numismatic evidence, the church of SS Constantine and Helena was used again for burials after 1330, under Hospitaller rule, when grave offerings of small purses of coins occur both in the 14th and the 15th centuries. The coins confirm the different history of the church from the also numismatically significant church now known as St Michael's and in Ottoman times called the Demirli Mosque: even excluding the coins of grave B and others reasonably supposed to derive from grave offerings from the finds of SS Constantine and Helena, the differences between the two foundations are significant (Figure 74).

The eponymous coins of Leo Gavalas (PL. 89-90) probably entered circulation in 1225, after the successful campaign of John III in Rhodes. They are thin, flat coins probably analogous to the *follari* and *tartarones* of contemporary Latin sources.[419] The legend '*kaisar* Gavalas/ *doulos* of the *basileus*' on them appears to advertise a new situation.[420] There are two main variants with corresponding dies. The first (A) bears the ligature ȣ (TOY) on the reverse[421] and is represented by 13 pieces; while the second (B)[422] apparently by another 13, making allowances for the wear of some of the coins. Another specimen with a variant A reverse is from a different obverse die (A1), while we also have two other coins of which the first bears another obverse variant (C, reverse only partly legible) and the second a different variant of the reverse (D, obverse partly legible). The switching of dies on both sides of an issue is not unusual; but in the present case the dominance of two dies for each side and the rarity of the rest, although all the coins are single finds from various sites, might be explained by the variable durability of dies. In total there are 29 coins of Leo[423] which, assuming they circulated between 1225 and 1240, represent 1.6 losses per year.

413 Excavation of Minatsis plot. Nika 1992; *eadem* 1993: 572; Baker 2006: 352.

414 Coin circulation on the site in the 12th century is represented by two tetartera of Alexius I and a half-tetarteron of Manuel I. From the period 1200-1203 (where most of the systematic clipping of the Constantinopolitan trachea took place) at least three clipped coins of Isaac II were recovered from the site. See relevant Appendix, 195.

415 Langton 1978: 134-135 and n. 70, 442. Along with the Tarchaniotai, who had been involved in the conspiracy of 1224, *megas droungarios* John Gavalas had trespassed on the property of the monastery of Lembos, located between Nymphaion and Smyrna and restored by John III, who supported the monks against his nobles (Miklosich and Müller 1871: 254-255). Apart from using military force against Rhodes in 1225, Vatatzes may have lured Leo's brother to change sides.

416 Langton 1985: 110-113. If it was John Gavalas who commanded the Nicene fleet against Constantinople in 1235, the policy of Leo in the years 1233-6 is perfectly consistent.

417 Savvides 1988: 202.

418 Heyd 1885: II, 436-448. Afterwards the Venetians concentrated their efforts on the island of Cos. Luttrell 1997: 740-742. At least two of the eight quartaroli bear the name of doge Giovanni Dandolo (1280-9).

419 Touratsoglou *et al.* 1989: 368.

420 Hendy 1999: II, 649. It does not seem likely that the title of caesar was granted to Leo by the Latins, who had no reason to confer it, or by Theodore I, who hardly had the means to control the ruler of Rhodes: the building of the Nicene fleet was an achievement of John III.

421 Schlumberger 1878: Pl. VIII, 18; Hendy 1999: II, Pl. XLVIII, AE1.1 and 1.3.

422 Schlumberger 1878: Pl. VIII, 17; Hendy 1999: II, Pl. XLVIII, AE1.1 and 1.2.

423 The specimen missing from the list is only partly legible.

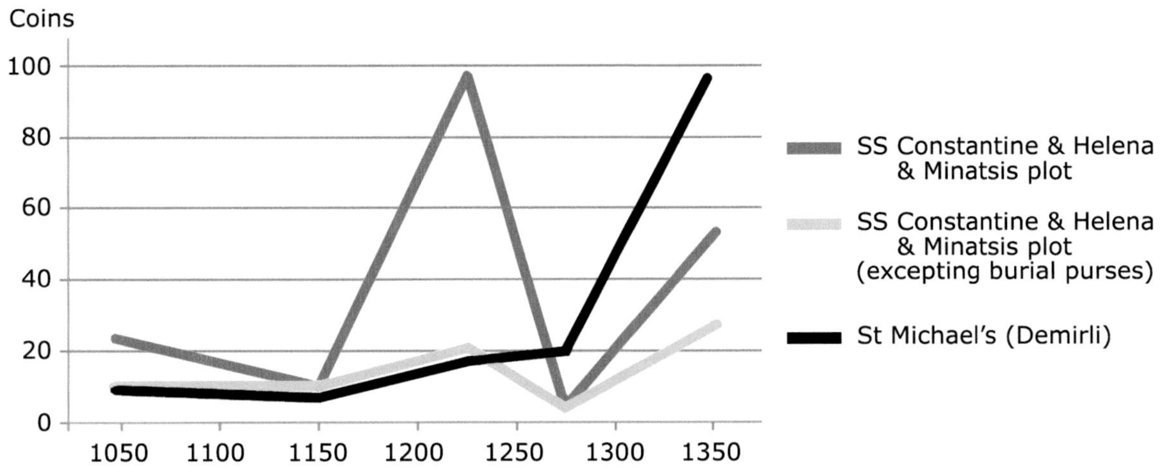

Figure 54: Comparison of finds from the churches of SS Constantine and Helena and St. Michael's.

The signed issue of John Gavalas (PL. 90), similar in fabric and style with that of Leo, bears the legend ΩΙ(άννης) Ο ΓΑΒΑΛΑC / Ο ΑΥΘΕΝΤΗC ΤΗC ΡΟΔΟΥ. The reversed abbreviation of his first name is preceded by an eight-pointed star and followed by a small fleur-de-lys, the emblem of Nicaea. Only five of his coins are included in the collection of the Ephorate of the Dodecanese. Of those, two share the same dies on both sides; a third has the same obverse. A fourth piece has different dies on both sides from the others. Although the sample is small, what they convey about the local mint is quite regular. Leaving out the two years Rhodes was under Genoese occupation, there are 0.6 losses per year, much lower than for his predecessor.

Apart from the published Latin and faithful imitative trachea, the finds from Rhodes include two, apparently hitherto unknown, types of Byzantine-style trachea of the Nicene period, with individual technical features (PL. 87). The first type, provisionally A_p, is represented by at least ten specimens from various dies, most of them unfortunately corroded to some degree.[424] They form a distinctive group because the reverse bears a representation of a standing emperor being crowned by the Virgin, while the shape of the flan is quite unusual, with a pronounced angle between the central sunk area and the smooth flaring rim. The figures are stocky and the emperor's dress recalls that on Nicene type A of Theodore I, except that the belt is styled like the collar.[425] On two specimens the emperor holds a labarum in his right hand but on a third the staff ends in three dots forming a triangle. The obverse bears a bust of Christ. Although the diamond-pattern *loros* first appears under Theodore I, it is also used under John III.[426] Moreover, on two of the pieces the characters [H] / Θ are visible at the lower left of the reverse field, recalling the *signa* used on the gold of John III.[427] For these reasons, and also because the representation of the emperor crowned by the Virgin is found among the coins of John III but not of Theodore I,[428] the immediate model of type A_p should probably be sought in the coinage of John III.

The second type, provisionally B_p, is represented by two specimens[429] sharing the same reverse die (the obverse is completely illegible on one of them), and also appears completely unknown to scholars. It represents a standing emperor holding labarum and globus cruciger, whose crosslet is composed of dots. The imperial dress borrows features of the dress of John III as shown on type A (El), mint of Magnesia:[430] from his figure are copied the collar and *loros* above the waist, and from the garment of St Constantine at his side the part below the waist, with the

[424] Four of the pieces were found in the church of SS Constantine and Helena.
[425] Hendy 1999: II, 459-460 no. 5a and Pl. XXVII, 5a.4.
[426] Hendy 1999: II, 491 no. 20 and Pl. XXXI, 20.
[427] Hendy 1999: II, 478-479. Alternatively, these characters may be read as the initials H Θ[εοτόκος] (=the Virgin). Theoretically, the type could have been modelled on type A of the second coinage of John Ducas of Thessalonica (1237-c. 42), Hendy 1999: II, XLII,7, but we have no evidence of relations between Rhodes and Thessalonica in this period.
[428] Hendy 1999: II, 483 and Pl. XXIX. The design with the Virgin crowning the emperor first appears under Manuel I (cf. Hendy 1999: I, Constantinople, 4th coinage, Pl. XV), and again on Latin imitative large module type F. Grierson 1982: 270.
[429] **1477** and **1478.** One is a site find from the town, the other was found in the acropolis of Phileremos overlooking the modern village of Trianda (Ialysos).
[430] Hendy 1999: II, 491 no. 20 and Pl. XXXI.20.

characteristic almond-shaped jewels on the *loros*. The obverse apparently bears a bust of Christ similar to that of local imitative type A_P.

Although the pieces of type B_p are not in good condition, it is clear that, in the matter of style, the type is much finer than group A_p. It might even be an official type of John III which has escaped the attention of scholars, since a great many types of billon trachea are already known from his reign; the only problem is that the Rhodian specimens show no trace of an inscription. Type A_p is very likely a local coinage, probably of Leo Gavalas, as 40% of the coins (4 pieces) were found in the church of SS Constantine and Helena.[431] Thus, if the A_p coins are added to the signed pieces of Leo, losses per year are raised from 1.6 to 2.3. If his signed coins cover the period from 1226 onwards, and are succeeded by the similar coins of his brother John, then the anonymous trachea of Rhodes were issued before 1226.[432]

Rhodes from 1250 until its conquest by the Knights Hospitaller (1309)

From 1250 onwards, the local mint continued to operate but its numerous issues are anonymous or, at best, only suggest the issuing authority. In reality, in is not yet generally accepted that they are all later than the signed Gavalas coins. The basic bibliography for these coins is still the relevant chapter in Gustave Schlumberger's venerable publication *Numismatique de l'Orient latin*, with its very helpful illustrations.[433] Schlumberger considered 32 types of anonymous 13th century coins he had encountered as Rhodian issues, since most of the coins had been found on the island. Some resembled the signed coins of the Gavalas brothers, or were linked by similarities in design, style and fabric. Thirty types of Schlumberger, which will be reviewed below as issues of the second half of the century,[434] are distributed in his plates as follows:

Pl. VIII, nos. 21, 22, 23, 24, 25, 27, 28, 29, 30, 31
Pl. IX, nos. 1, 2, 3, 4, 5, 6, 7, 9, 10, 11
Pl. XIX, nos. 12, 13, 14, 15, 18, 20
Pl. XX, nos. 23, 24, 26, 27

Of those, nine have yet to find their way to the local archaeological collection,[435] while three further types have been found. Thus, the production of the local mint as a whole must have included about forty types and variants. Schlumberger also assigned to Rhodes a countermark encountered on silver *dirhem* of the sultanate of Iconium. His conclusions have been cautiously adopted by later scholars to varying degrees,[436] with some expressing different opinions on specific points.[437] Typology and certain differences in technique have been used to support theories which question the Rhodian origin of the coins.[438] An important weakness of such criticisms is that they rely on the examination of a limited number of pieces of doubtful origin, since they belong to coin collections.

Most of the 92 conserved coins kept by the Ephorate in Rhodes are single site finds, and none of them belong to an identifiable hoard. The limited number and the wear of finds has not permitted the distinction between obverse and reverse for any type. They are all flat, thin and light coins, usually weighing about a gram or less, vulnerable to corrosion. They are easy to identify even when worn to illegibility, from the technique of their production: strips of copper foil 15-20 mm wide were cut into squares and a more rounded shape was achieved by clipping the corners, often resulting in roughly octagonal flans. In their technique, size and weight, but not the designs, the Rhodian coins resemble local issues of mainland Greece found both in 13th century hoards and singly.[439] In spite of the often poor state of preservation and limited numbers of finds, the variety of the Rhodian coins is remarkable. Most of them fit into six groups separated by typological relationships (Figure 55).

The first group (PL. 92), which comprises three types, bears on one side a pair of Bs facing each other with a crosslet between them. The other side is dominated by a fleur-de-lys, which in the first type is plain and set within a beaded

[431] Five more were found outside the medieval walls and one is kept in the sacristy of the parish church of the village of Archangelos.
[432] Alternatively, although less likely, they may be an issue of the 1230s, when Leo was again distancing himself from the empire of Nicaea.
[433] Schlumberger 1878: 214-221 and Pls. VIII, IX, XIX, XX.
[434] Type VIII, 26 is a tetarteron of Nicaea. Hendy 1999: II, Pl. XXXVIII, 7.3, 7.8. The word ΔΟVΛΟS on type VIII, 16 recalls the coins of Leo Gavalas.
[435] The following: Pl. VIII, 27 and 28, IX, 1, 2, 9, 10 and 11 and XX, 23 and 24. A specimen representing one of the types not found on Rhodes so far (IX, 10), is kept in the Numismatic Museum in Athens, cat. no. 5699.
[436] Grierson 1982: 255; Hendy 1999: II, 648-650; Grierson and Bellinger 2006: I, 87.
[437] Iliescu 1989: 49-52; Bendall and Broome 1985.
[438] For example, the assignment of some issues to Samos (Iliescu 1989: 49) is not supported by the evidence of Saulnier 1985.
[439] Baker 2007, with bibliography.

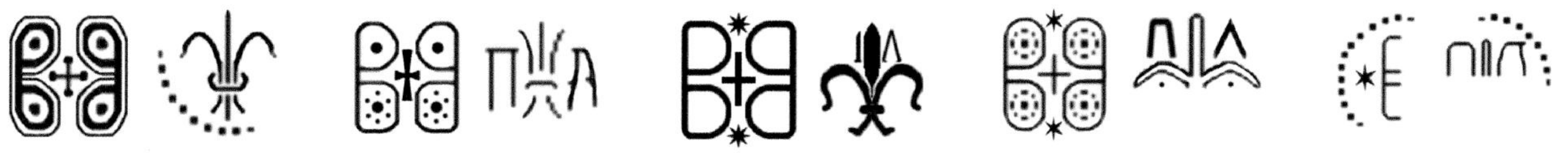

Figure 55: Local issues of the period 1250-1309, group 1.

circle.[440] The Bs of this type are formed by strings of beads, surrounded by a thin outline, and contain a bead in each loop. They copy the design of an anonymous tetarteron of Nicaea,[441] but with a crosslet set between them. The lily, emblem of saint Tryphon, patron of the city of Nicaea,[442] first appears on its own on a tetarteron of Theodore II (1254-1258).[443] Thus, it is likely that the type combining the facing Bs and lily was minted in Rhodes under Theodore II.

The Bs of the second type are linear, but their lower loops contain a rosette composed of dots, while under the lateral petals of the fleur-de-lys on the other side are set the letters Π and A or Λ.[444] The third type seems to comprise at least two varieties. In the finds from Rhodes it is represented by only three incomplete pieces, whose reading is facilitated by a coin in better condition kept at the Numismatic Museum.[445] The Bs on one side may have loops decorated by dots and be flanked by stars, either placed laterally near the rim or at top and bottom of the design. On the other side the letters Π and Λ are arranged above the lateral petals of the lily, which may curve downwards over decorative dots. The initials ΠΛ (or ΠA) presumably signify the dynastic change in the empire of Nicaea in 1258, when Michael VIII Palaeologus ascended the throne. They probably entered circulation between 1258 and 1261: before, that is, Nicaea ceased to be the Byzantine capital.

The second group (PL. 93) on one side shows the letters B(ασιλεύ)C and on the other a combination of letters, either free-standing or arranged in the quarters of a cross. There are at least two types. Most common is the one bearing on one side a ligature of the letters M, X, A and Λ, with a curved abbreviation stroke above.[446] The ligature almost certainly represents the name Michael and refers to emperor Michael VIII (1259-82),[447] whose brother John held Rhodes, possibly in *pronoia*, between 1261 and 1273 or 1275.[448]

Figure 56: Local issues of the period 1250-1309, group 2.

Six coins of the same group have letters arranged in the quarters of a cross,[449] but their poor state of preservation makes it impossible to distinguish whether they represent one or more types. In all of them the letter on the upper left quarter appears to be an A, or a ligature with A. Another A, or an Λ, occupies the top right quarter. In two cases the letter in the lower left quarter seems to be a Π; in the lower right, also in two cases, probably a B. Schlumberger's coin VIII, 22 clearly belongs to this group and, apparently, he also encountered difficulties in deciphering it: no B occurs on the upper right quarter of any of the six coins kept in Rhodes, while in the lower right quarter a partially preserved B was read as a Γ. It is thus quite likely that at least on some of the coins we have an arrangement of the letters later composing the very common ligature of the imperial surname encountered on *assaria* of Andronicus II,[450] with the B(ασιλεύς) replacing the Γ of Schlumberger.

---

440 **1555, 1556, 1557, 1559, 1560, 1561, 1562.** Cf. Schlumberger 1878: Pl. VIII, 25. **1565** is a plainer variant of the type.

441 Either of John III or Theodore II. Hendy 1999: II, 536 and Pl. XXXVII, 7.

442 Grierson and Bellinger 2006: I, 92.

443 Hendy 1999: II, Pl. XXXVI, 13b.

444 **1563**, Schlumberger 1878: XX, 27.

445 Inventory No. N.M.A. 5713. The Rhodian pieces are **1566** and **1567**. Cf. Schlumberger 1878: IX, 11, obviously a variant of the type. This specimen preserves an interesting detail on the obverse, where the quarters of the central crosslet are decorated with dots.

446 **1574, 1575, 1576, 1577, 1578, 1579, 1580, 1581, 1583.** Cf. Schlumberger 1878: Pl. XIX, 14.

447 Lianta 2009: 55.

448 Savvides 1988: 206-208 and n. 32-34.

449 **1583, 1584, 1586, 1582, 1587, 1588.** Cf. Schlumberger 1878: Pl. VIII, 22 and Hendy 1999: II, 650 (2).

450 And in the same sequence, as noted by Lianta 2009: 44. See also Grierson and Bellinger 2006: II, Pl. 38, no. 661-670, Pl. 40, nos. 702-703, 712-716.

Another piece, partially preserved, may be associated with this group: it shows on one side the letters B and C, although back to back, and on the other side, within a circle, the letters A and Π, probably in the top quarters of a cross (**1590**). If the type with M(ι)XA(η)Λ dates from the later part of the reign of Michael VIII, then the others might belong to the rule of his successor, Andronicus II (1282-1328).

The third group (PLS 91, 94) on one side bears a cross pattée and dots in the four quarters, a design which appears in imperial issues under Andronicus II,[451] but is much older among Latin issues.[452] There are two types: the first on the other side shows a single B[453] and the second two Bs back to back.[454] The coins with the single B could be earlier, since the B as a main design appears in the period of Nicaea and, later, perhaps also on coins of Trebizond.[455] To the same group might belong the type bearing a single B on either side, sometimes accompanied by one or two stars or a crosslet:[456] on two pieces of this type the accompanying crosslet is decorated with a dot in each quarter.[457]

Figure 57: Local issues of the period 1250-1309, group 3.

Schlumberger also presents a specimen of the type with back-to-back Bs without dots in the quarters of the cross.[458] A piece bearing a cross pattée on either side may be a mule of this variant. Back-to-back Bs first appear on assaria of Andronicus II which entered circulation after 1294, at the time Michael IX was co-emperor.[459] Thus, it is reasonable to suppose that the coins of the group with back-to-back Bs circulated in Rhodes after 1294. This interpretation has consequences for the dating of a separate phenomenon first discussed by Schlumberger and systematically examined by Bendall and Broome.[460] It concerns a countermark encountered on dirhem of the Seljuks of Iconium of the period 1264-1290.[461] The two scholars express reservations both for the circulation of Seljuk coins in Rhodes and for their countermarking on the island, although they suspect their presence in a hoard from the Rhodian countryside brought to light in the period of the Italian occupation.[462] However, in the same area another hoard has been found, also containing Seljuk silver, while a counterstruck dirhem of Masud II, handed in by a local, is part of the archaeological collection.[463] Moreover, the countermark in question, showing on one side a pair of Bs back to back, and on the other a lozenge decorated with dots, also appears on a Rhodian copper issue of the group following.

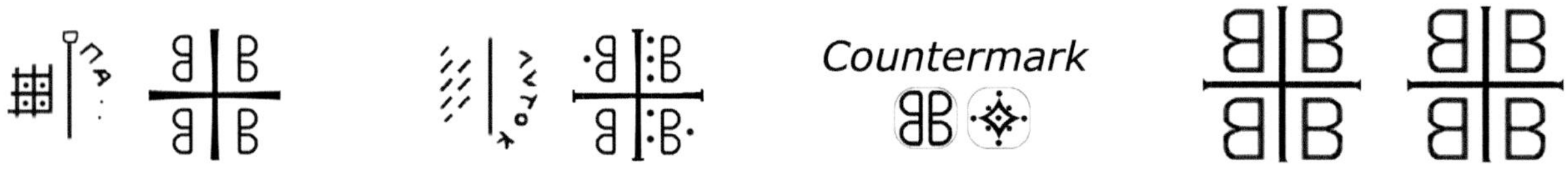

Figure 58: Local issues of the period 1250-1309, group 4.

The principal feature of this fourth group (PLS 93, 95), is a cross whose quarters are occupied by four Bs turned outwards from the main vertical axis. This arrangement appears considerably later on imperial issues and was

[451] On tornesia of doubtful date (Grierson and Bellinger 2006: II, Pl. 33, no. 551) and on a half-basilikon (Grierson and Bellinger 2006: II, Pl. 32, nos. 549-550).
[452] Like issues of Cyprus and the Normans, which could have been the models of the Rhodian group. Cf. Metcalf 1995: 190 Figure 19 (1192-4), Pl. 26, nos. 655 -657, Cypriot deniers and obols (1218-32).
[453] **1545, 1546, 1547** with a single B. The Numismatic Museum in Athens has another coin of this type, from the Jerusalem Collection (a gift of the Patriarchate).
[454] **1599, 1600, 1601, 1602, 1603, 1604** with Bs back-to-back. Cf. Schlumberger 1878: Pl. VIII, 29, XIX, 20.
[455] Wroth 1911: Pl. XLII, 7-8. This theory is confirmed, as will be shown below, by an overstruck coin (Figure 60, **1556**).
[456] **1548, 1549, 1550, 1551, 1552, 1553.** Cf. Schlumberger 1878: VIII, 29 and XIX, 20; Grierson 1982: Pl. 87, 1394.
[457] **1548, 1549.**
[458] Schlumberger 1878: Pl. XIX, 15. Cf. **1605.** A plain cross also appears on tornesia of Andronicus II. Grierson and Bellinger 2006: II, Pl. 33, nos. 552-557.
[459] Assaria of class XVI, Grierson and Bellinger 2006: II, Pl. 39, no. 692 and Thessalonican trachea, Grierson and Bellinger 2006: II, Pl. 42, no. 750.
[460] Bendall and Broome 1985.
[461] Of Kay-Khusru III (1264-1282) and Masud II (c. 1282-1305).
[462] Brandi 1938: 10. The hoard contained 48 gold coins of John II (34 pieces), Michael VIII (13 pieces) and Andronicus II (1 piece) and 39 silver 'Muslim' coins of the period 1239-1311, probably Seljuk.
[463] Six Seljuk (1 of Kay-Khusru II, 1237-46, 1 of Kay-Khusru III and the rest probably of Masud II) along with four Armenian tram of Levon I (1199-1226). The countermarked dirhem is **1598.** Kasdagli 1996: 323, 331-333.

adopted by the Gattilusi dynasty of the island of Lesbos.[464] One type of the group bears on the other side the figure of a standing emperor and a circumferential inscription where only some letters from the words AVTOK[PATOP.. or ΠA[Λ... are legible in the extant specimens. The type occurs in two variants: the second has various decorative dots flanking each B.[465] Four of the six coins of the type carry the countermark described above.

The second type[466] repeats the main feature of the group on both sides and is cut on larger flans. A possible degradation of this type is represented in a series of coins with a cross flanked by four Bs on either side (PL. 96). In some pieces all the Bs on one side are turned outwards forming a lozenge.[467] But the cutting of the dies and the striking are very shoddy and at least some of the letters are irregularly placed, either vertical or turned inwards.

The fifth group (PLS 95, 96) is also distinguished by the arrangement of four Bs round a cross, but they are turned towards the centre of the coin forming a lozenge. This layout is also found on class XVI Constantinopolitan trachea of emperor Andronicus II Palaeologus (1294 ff.)[468] One of the types in the group bears on the other side a monogram containing the letters B, N or Z, P, T or Γ and A.[469] It is found in more than two variants, in one of which the monogram appears corrupted while another is distinguished by its elegant design and decorative dots.[470] However, this monogram seems to be an adaptation of the design on the class XVII Constantinopolitan trachea, which bear on one side the indictional year NB (=1303/4).[471] Thus, this Rhodian type could well date from *c.* 1304.

Figure 59: Local issues of the period 1250-1309, group 5.

The other type, recorded in two variants, also has a cross with four letters arranged in the quarters. In the first variant three of the letters are arranged radially, their tops towards the centre of the flan, while the fourth, the letter Γ in the lower right quarter, is set parallel to the cross, thus fixing for us the vertical axis of the side. As the radial arrangement of the other letters could support a circular sequence for the reading, we most likely get O, Θ, Δ and Γ or Θ, O, Γ and Δ. In the second variant,[472] this side is a mirror image of the previous one with the difference that the Γ has been altered into a C turned outwards, that is again out of line in comparison with the other three letters. It could well be due to the careless copying by the die-cutter of the first variant: besides, the second variant is generally less carefully made than the first.[473]

In the numismatic material of the Palaeologan period of Rhodes there are some issues which cannot be included in the groups above. One type bears on one side a B with a star and on the other a Latin cross between the letters Π and L (PL. 92).[474] Both cross and letters are decorated with spiky projections, resembling another type, smaller in size, with a Greek cross ornamented with thorns on one side and on the other a B, possibly after another letter.[475] The interesting thing is that one of the two specimens of the first type is clipped, perhaps to match the size of the second type. In another type, of the same size as the smaller of the two just described, the letter Λ accompanies a ligature of Π and A, while the other side bears the letters BA, giving a development of the Palaeologan surname.[476] Another piece of roughly equal size shows a ligature of H and E or T on one side and XE on the other (PL. 96).[477]

464 Grierson and Bellinger 2006: I, 87-88. Back-to-back Bs occupy the upper quarters of the cross on a trachy of Andronicus II, dated after 1294 (class III trachy, Grierson and Bellinger 2006: II, Pl. 35, no. 596).
465 All countermarked, except **1591**. Cf. Schlumberger 1878: IX, 4-6, without a countermark. Second variation, without a countermark, **1596**, **1597**.
466 Schlumberger 1878: Pl. VIII, 23.
467 Cf. Schlumberger 1878: Pl. VIII, 24 and XIX, 13.
468 Grierson and Bellinger 2006: II, Pl. 36, no. 618-621. The Rhodian issues lack the 'rays' of the cross.
469 Cf. also Schlumberger 1878: 220, 'note additionnelle'.
470 **1628** and **1629**, cf. Schlumberger 1878: Pl. IX, 3. **1630**, **1631**, **1632**, **1633** and **1634** belong to a plainer variation. **1635** is a shoddy specimen, showing a pair of Bs back-to-back, with the slanting connecting line between them reversed (cf. Schlumberger Pl. XX, 26).
471 Grierson and Bellinger 2006: I, 85 and 5.2: Pl. 36, no. 622.
472 Schlumberger 1878: Pl. VIII, 30; Grierson 1982: Pl. 87, no. 1395
473 In this group belongs another Rhodian coin (**1638**), with the four inward slanting Bs on both sides.
474 Cf. Schlumberger 1878: Pl. IX, 7.
475 **1570**, **1571**.
476 **1572**. Cf. Schlumberger 1878: Pl. VIII, 31.
477 **1639**.

A piece with an A on one side, read as a ligature of Γ and A and assumed to belong to the Gavalas is much too shoddy and stylistically foreign to their securely dated coins.[478] If we can depend on Schlumberger's design, it seems similar to specimens of group 3. Another piece, illegible on one side, seems to copy the cross with a B on the crossing encountered on a tornesion of Andronicus II[479] - here, however, we have a Latin cross (PL. 94). Finally, a piece with the same design on both sides, although stylistically related to the two first types of group 3, resembles a coin of Salerno of the mid-12th century (PL. 91).[480] And, if this seems improbable, the BC of group 2 also resembles a type of Salerno, as does the radial arrangement of the letters on the second type of group 5.[481]

The groupings whose description has just been completed depend almost entirely on similarities of design between various types and the assumption that, whenever a local issue bears a design strongly resembling an imperial type, it is most likely that the local moneyer used the imperial coin as an inspiration. This is not always a safe assumption since, in the case of group 4, the local use of the main design predates its adoption by the imperial mint by half a century.[482] Also, a number of local designs are absent from imperial issues; and when they are present, we really have no way of working out how long it took for the local mint to pick them up. Naturally, it is reasonable to assume that, the narrower the gap between the circulation of model and derivative, the closer the ties between the central government and its local representatives were likely to be.

The first type of group 1 is most likely contemporary to Theodore II due to the presence of the fleur-de-lys on one side, while the other two, and a third published by Schlumberger and yet to turn up in Rhodes since his lifetime (Pl. VIII, 27), to the interval 1258-61, before the recovery of Constantinople by the Byzantines demoted the status of Nicaea. The issues of group 5 may fairly confidently be assigned to the post-1294 period and the same may be said for the group 3 type bearing on one side a pair of back-to-back Bs: they both copy designs which appear on imperial issues dated to the joint reign of Andronicus II and his son Michael IX (1294-1320). For the countermark stamped on pieces of the first type of group 4, Bendall and Broome give as *terminus post quem* 1290, a date drawn from the use of this countermark on a *dirham* of Masud II, sultan of Iconium. The same countermark may well be roughly contemporary to the type of group 3 bearing the two Bs back to back. Beyond this point it would be difficult to go without the precious evidence of overstruck pieces **1556** and **1627**:

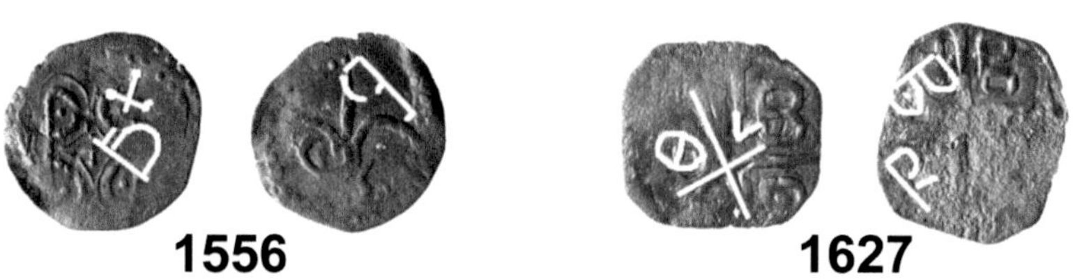

Figure 60: Overstruck coins of the period 1250-1309.

1556 belongs to a type already assigned to the reign of Theodore II (1254-8). Underneath it, however, an earlier strike is clearly visible: it shows a B on both sides, belonging to a type included in the third group, due to its resemblance with the type bearing a single B on one side and a cross with pellets in the quarters on the other. This type, in turn, is placed alongside the type with a pair of Bs and dates after 1294. However, this *impasse* is illusory. The design typical of the third group, the cross with pellets in its quarters, was borrowed by the imperial mint from Frankish models after 1294. It is also encountered on obols of Henry I of Cyprus (1218-53),[483] a contemporary of emperor John III Vatatzes. Thus, it is quite possible that the copper of Cyprus served as a model for a copper issue on Rhodes in the years 1250-54. The single B, appearing on the other side of the coins with the cross, and also in an associated issue on both sides (an example of this is the understrike of **1556**), is modelled on an anonymous Nicene tetarteron probably belonging to the coinage of John III. The connection between the two types is confirmed by the presence of the crosslet with dots in its quarters next to the single B on one side of the type with a single B on either side.[484] Thus, group 3 includes both early and later issues of Rhodes.

1627 is an overstrike of the second type of group 4 on the group 5 type bearing in the quarters the letters O, Θ, Δ C. It is thus clear that part of group 4 contains some issues earlier than group 5 and some interpolated in it.

---

[478] **1640.** Cf. Schlumberger 1878: Pl. VIII, 21 and Hendy 1999: II, 650 (1).

[479] **1606.** Cf. Grierson and Bellinger 2006: II, class III, Pl. 33, no. 558.

[480] **1554**, and Schlumberger 1878: Pl. XIX, 18. Cf. Grierson and Travaini 1998: Pl. 19, no. 322.

[481] Cf., respectively, Grierson and Travaini 1998: Pl. 18, no. 298 and Pl. 20, nos. 330-333.

[482] These are the four outward-looking Bs flanking a cross of Rhodian 'group 4', provisionally dated to c. 1290-1304. The same arrangement is encountered on a politikon of John V (c. 1345). Grierson and Bellinger 2006: I, 87; Lianta 2009: 275, no. 865.

[483] Metcalf 1995: Pl. 26, Nos. 655-657.

[484] There is a variant of this type where the B on one side is accompanied by a star, recalling **1554**, which resembles a coin of Salerno. This raises the question of the possible impact on Rhodes of the close relations maintained between John III and Latin emperor Frederick II.

Dating the types with greater precision and associating most of them with particular governors faces insuperable gaps in the historical sources. After the death of John Gavalas we ignore the names of the governors of Rhodes until 1261, when the island was bestowed to John Palaeologus, the brother of emperor Michael VIII. John Palaeologus held the island for at least a decade, and modern scholarship is not in agreement as to its end, which should most likely be placed a little before 1273.[485] To this time probably belong some of the early experimentations with the Palaeologid monogram on issues without the fleur-de-lys of Nicaea.[486]

According to modern historians, John Palaeologus was succeeded by one Krivikiotes, *katepano* of Rhodes, who already held the post in 1273, and is remembered in the sources as a collaborator of corsairs and a serious threat to Venetian interests.[487] The next lord (*dominus*) of Rhodes was John dello Cavo, a corsair of Genoese origin born on the island of Anaphe,[488] *megas doux* of Michael VIII from 1275.[489] It seems, however, that he took actual control of Rhodes in 1278 with the help of the Turcomans from Makre, who supported his rule in exchange for possession of the eastern part of the island. It appears that his authority was challenged by a pirate called del Moro, also Genoese, who had his eye on Rhodes from 1270 and may have held it briefly before the establishment of dello Cavo.[490]

Serious doubts have been expressed about the replacement of dello Cavo by Andrea Moresco, another Genoese corsair, in 1282.[491] They are reinforced by the dedication in a codex of the Biblioteca Laurentiana of Florence bearing the date 1284, to one *pansebastos* Michael, 'great *archon* of the East and *kephale* of the island of Rhodes and of the Cycladic islands surrounding it'.[492] Genoese brothers Andrea and Lodovico Moresco appear in the sources later, in 1303, as privateers in the waters of Corfu; Andrea entered the service of Andronicus II in 1304. He soon made an impression and received Carpathos as a fief by the emperor. In May 1306 Vignolo Vignoli, an uncle of the Moresco brothers, entered into an agreement with Foulques de Villaret, master of the Order of the Hospital, for the conquest of Rhodes and smaller Dodecanese islands which purportedly the emperor had ceded to him or his nephews but the family had not been able to take possession of: at this time Carpathos and Cos were apparently controlled by the Venetians, enemies of Andronicus II; while the only part of Rhodes granted to Vignoli by the emperor was the *casale* of Lardos.

Thus, it is impossible to confirm that Krivikiotes remained in control of Rhodes until 1278.[493] Also, it is not clear how long dello Cavo held the island. The coins of group 2 and the countermarked type of group 4 should, nevertheless, belong to the interval 1273-1294. It may be that the type with the monogram of Michael VIII was employed by Krivikiotes to promote his authority after the retirement of John Palaeologus from public life, due to financial misconduct.[494] The typological affinity of group 2 could be considered as evidence for the dating of its other two types to the period before 1278, although this would leave only the oldest type of group 4 for the interval 1278-1294.

The late type of group 3 and the countermark resembling it, the second type of group 4 and group 5 in its entirety were most likely issued after 1294. The late type of group 3 must be the earliest, followed by the ΟΘΔΓ type of group 5, then the ΟΘΔC type of the same group and, lastly, the second type of group 5. These types possibly cover the decade up to 1304, since the group 5 type with the monogram probably dates from 1304-5, and its variants reach up to 1307, if the crude type with the irregularly arranged Bs on both sides is considered an emergency coinage of the years 1307-1309.[495]

The picture drawn by groups 3, 4 and 5 indicates a much more complicated political background that the one reconstructed so far by modern historians- that is the succession of dello Cavo by the Moresco in 1282 and their control of Rhodes until at least 1306. The late type of group 3 introduces the pair of back-to-back Bs, which may belong to the period after 1294 if the designer was inspired by an imperial prototype.[496] This issue may be

485 For John see also Magdalino 1976.

486 **1567**, **1568**, **1569**, **1570**, **1571** and **1572**, as, perhaps, type 3 of group 2.

487 Luttrell 1997: 739, n. 9; Morgan 1976: 416, 423, 429.

488 Between 1269 and 1277 his name is mentioned 19 times (!) in the 1278 list of attacks against shipping associated with Venetian interests. Morgan 1976: 427-432.

489 Geanakoplos 1959: 211.

490 Savvides 1988: 212.

491 Savvides 1988: 214; Luttrell 1997: 740, n. 11.

492 Evangelatou-Notara 2000: 111-112.

493 He had probably lost control of the island a little earlier, since dello Cavo had to enlist Turcoman assistance.

494 Savvides 1988: 208, n. 32.

495 At the time, while laying siege to the town, the Knights of St John were taking control of the countryside.

496 If it is assumed that the pair of back-to-back Bs first appeared on Rhodian coins, earlier than on imperial emissions, its issue could possibly be dated a few years earlier, bearing in mind that the countermark which followed cannot be earlier than 1290, according to the analysis in Bendall and Broome 1985.

contemporary with the countermarking of the early group 4 type and all the dirhems of the Iconium Seljuks still in circulation on the island. The first type of group 5 introduces four letters which may belong to a name, surname, or be the initial letters of a four-word sentence; the third type of the same group, perhaps after the intervention of the second type of group 4,[497] displays a new monogram which is then progressively degraded. All this shows that, starting with the third type of group 3, probably dated c. 1295, until the Hospitaller conquest of Rhodes in 1309, we may well be dealing with a sequence of at least four individuals in the control of the town, as follows:

VII. Issuing authority of the 3rd type of group 3, possibly identical to the countermarking authority
VIII. Issuing authority of the 1st type of group 5 (ΟΘΔΓ)
IX. Issuing authority of the 2nd type of group 5 (ΟΘΔC)
X. Issuing authority of the 2nd type of group 4
XI. Issuing authority of the 3rd type of group 5 (monogram)
XII. Issuing authority of the 3rd type of group 4

The countermark validating the coins of the first type of group 4 and the Seljuk silver (above, I) may be associated with a change in the political situation which reduced Muslim influence on the island, since the Latin-inspired motif of the cross pattée with pellets in the quarters oh the third type of group 3 seems a reflection of crusader ideology. It is worth noting that between 1294 and 1309, an interval of 16 years, we encounter an equal number of local types if we also count their variants. This may mean that in this period the local mint assumed the imperial practice of a yearly change of coin type. We also have an increase in the influence of imperial designs on the Rhodian types, although no Rhodian issue copies an imperial type exactly, something that seems to have been avoided on purpose. The design with the four back-to-back Bs on either side at this time is an innovation not encountered on imperial coins.

The lengthy but necessary analysis of the activity of the Rhodian mint after 1250 results in the following table, where the proposed dating of the various types is summarized, each type given a new sequential numbering (first column) which is also used in the Plates:

Type	Group	Dating	Specimens	Total	Losses per year
1	3		3		
2	3	1250 - 1254	6	10	2
3			1		
4		1254 - 1258	7	7	1.4
5		1258 - 1261	1	4	1
6			3		
7			3		
8		1261 - c.1272	2	6	0.5
9			1		
10	2	c.1273 - c.1278	9	9	1.5
11	2		6		
12	2	1278 - c.1294	1	14	0.9
13	4		7		
14	3		6		
15			1		
16	5	c.1294 - c.1304	6	28	2.8
17	5		7		
18	4		8		
19	5	c.1304 - c.1307	8	8	2
20	4	1307 - 1309	3	3	1

Figure 61: Chronological distribution of local issues of the period 1250-1309.

* * *

[497] Type 18 (PL. 95) may be later than type 19 (1304 ff.), but is placed there because of overstruck **1627**.

Putting together the data from 1204 to 1309, results in the following graph of losses per year, if the small-module Latin imitatives from burial offerings in SS Constantine and Helena are removed from the sample:

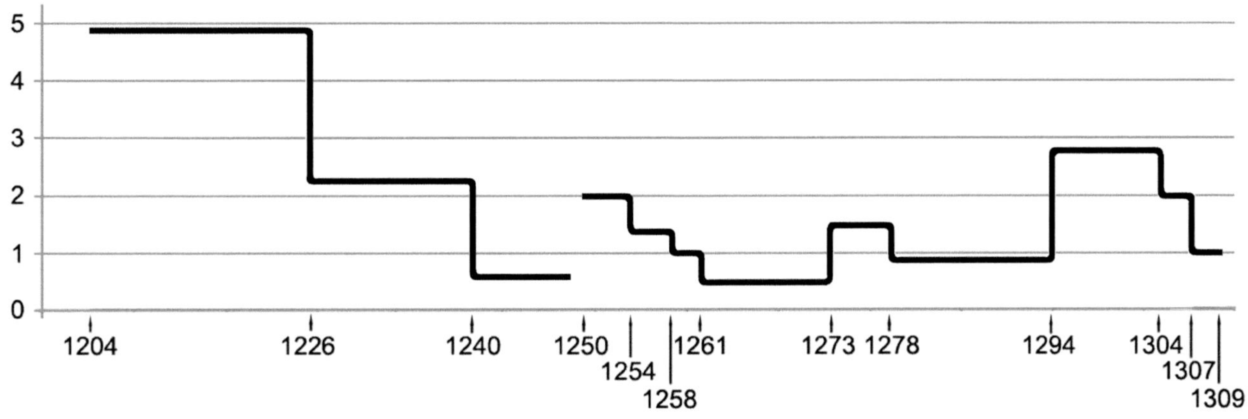

Figure 62: Losses per year in the period 1204-1309.

The higher values are concentrated at the beginning and, to a lesser extent, the end of the 13th century. These are times where historical evidence is singularly scarce. The silence of the written sources associated with the administrative centres of the region is, perhaps, telling: the absence of external control was probably advantageous for the traffic in the harbour and the development of urban functions in the town of Rhodes. Nevertheless, the implied impact of imperial issues on the local mint between 1294 and 1307 raises questions concerning the influence of Constantinople and the way it was expressed in the island society. Beyond this, it is possibly not coincidental that a dearth of small coin is observed when the island was probably held in *pronoia* by John Palaeologus. The low representation of John Gavalas has already been discussed.

In conclusion, the datings suggested in table 16 are not definitive or, indeed, particularly narrow or all equally backed by evidence. However, there is no evidence that any of the issues included have anything to do with the Gavalas period. In the first half of the 13th century, local needs in small change were first met by imported Latin imitative types, particularly the small-module range, and then by the signed issues of Leo and John Gavalas. The anonymous local A_p trachea may date from before 1226, but in is uncertain whether they were issued by Leo Gavalas or his assumed predecessor. In Rhodes the thin, polygonal, flat coins circulated only in the second half of the 13th century and the early years of the 14th.

The adoption of non-Byzantine designs, also encountered in imperial issues from the late 13th century onwards is, of course, more pronounced in Rhodes where the presence of Latin seamen, merchants, travellers and settlers was proportionately more influential. The possibility of connections with south Italy raised by the appearance of some types, and the casual mention of a clash between Sicilians and Venetians in Rhodes *c.* 1300,[498] probably betrays that a significant Sicilian presence in the town itself may have been overshadowed by the dominant role of Venice and Genoa in the Aegean in the broader historical perception.[499] Perhaps, at times, Latin moneyers worked for the local lords, if we judge from affinities with coins of Cyprus and south Italy and also from the occasional mishandling of Greek lettering, particularly towards the end of the period. Besides, the operation of the local mint was presumably intermittent, while production must have been regulated by a series of contracts. In any case, the requirements of the lords of Rhodes or their representatives on local, itinerant or purposely imported metalworkers concerning the quantity, quality and design of the coins must have varied greatly according to circumstance.

[498] Luttrell 1997: 742.

[499] The presence of Sicilians in the Eastern Mediterranean is possibly related to Byzantine foreign policy during the second half of the century, which led to the Sicilian Vespers in 1282, dooming the plans of Charles of Anjou against Byzantium. Geanakoplos 1959: 329-371; Runciman 1982: 201-213. Epstein (1992: 269, 271-272) merely implies the significance, and possibly the development, of commercial ties between Sicily and the East after 1282, as his book deals with the Late Middle Ages.

Part II. HOSPITALLER PERIOD (1309-1522)

Preface

The 11th century proved particularly difficult for the inhabitants of the Holy Land and for Latin pilgrims as well. From 1004 until 1012, Fatimid caliph al-Hakim imposed harsh measures on religious minorities. The compound of the Holy Sepulchre was destroyed in 1009 and was rebuilt, in a reduced scale, by Byzantine emperor Constantine IX Monomachus between 1042 and 1048, after prolonged negotiations between the Byzantines and Ali az-Zahir, al-Hakim's successor.[500] During the early part of the reign of caliph al-Mustansir, conditions for pilgrims improved somewhat, although the dangers facing Latin travellers are highlighted in the story of the Great German Pilgrimage that took place in 1064-65.[501] Conditions deteriorated again with the Seljuk conquest of Palestine (1073-98), a time of slaughter and raiding. The fluid situation in the region combined with political and social developments to bring about the First Crusade. This novel undertaking of Latin Europe mobilized disparate forces that reached the East in successive waves, between 1096 and 1102. Thus, Western coins appear in the wider region in substantial numbers after 1095. They are generally silver deniers which usually bear on one side a cross within a circle surrounded by a legend. Those most commonly encountered are those of Lucca, Valence, Chartres and Poitou, but coins of other French towns and of Normandy also turn up occasionally. Two pieces from Lucca, one of Normandy and one of Chartres are the earliest to have so far been found in Rhodian archaeological excavations.[502]

After the conquest of the Holy Land (1097-99), the Crusaders started issuing their own coin. In Antioch and Edessa the earlier coins[503] were in the Byzantine style,[504] while in the kingdom of Jerusalem petty coinage was western in style from the first.[505] Later, while gold still copied Islamic dinars, the issue of billon deniers became generalized[506] and elements that, after the Fourth Crusade, were adopted in Cyprus and Latin Greece, made their appearance. At about this time also began the issue of copper so-called obols. Some of the designs on Latin coins were even adopted by the imperial mints of Nicaea[507] and then of Constantinople. Such examples are the cross pattée within a circle, often cantoned with dots, platelets or other objects such as stars or crescents, the fleur-de-lys, the castle and other buildings. Small pieces of silver were the means of exchange most familiar to the Crusaders who settled in Palestine and later in former Byzantine territories. According to Metcalf,[508] the first local issues of Palestine in the Latin style entered circulation about 1136, and the last in the 1280s, probably at Tripoli. After the Third Crusade (1189-92), local issues circulated alongside European coins, mostly from France and Sicily. On Cyprus, Latin issues appear *c.* 1192 and the earliest of them bears the name of Guy, 'king of Jerusalem' and lord of Cyprus.

At first, the larger coins of Jerusalem and Cyprus imitated Arab dinars and hyperpyra respectively. Since the denier was, to the Latins, a small silver coin, the imitations of Fatimid dinars of the kingdom of Jerusalem and of Tripoli, and the scyphate coins of the kingdom of Cyprus were generally called bezants, qualified with some specific.[509] Between 1216 and 1259, silver dirhem imitating Arab coins were also issued in the Holy Land.[510] The first large silver coin to arrive in the East was the Venetian *grosso*, first issued by doge Andrea Dandolo (1192-1205); it was widely copied in the Balkans, where various unofficial imitations are also encountered.[511] Gold was first minted in Genoa and Florence in 1252, and the earliest Venetian ducats entered circulation in 1285.[512] Crusader silver *gros* were only issued in Tripoli, between 1251 and 1287.[513] *Gros grands* were steadily produced in Cyprus from the reign of Henry II (1285-1324), while their halves appeared under Hugh IV (1324-59).[514]

---

[500] The relevant treaty had been signed by Romanus III. The increased danger for pilgrims even after the death of al-Hakim is evident in the career of Fulk Nerra, count of Anjou (970-1040), who went on pilgrimage four times: in 1003, 1008 1035 and 1038. Bachrach 1993: 25. The last two journeys were undertaken with a strong armed escort. Halphen and Poupardin 1913, in Van Houts 1985: 549 and P. Larousse, *Grand Dictionnaire Universel du XIX siècle*, vol. 8 (1872): 661-662, entry Foulques. For recent revisions see Bachrach 1993 and Sumption 2003: 140. The organization of mass pilgrimages for reasons of security is repeated in the sources: for example, around 1026, Richand, abbot of St. Venne, led seven hundred pilgrims, at the expense of Richard II, duke of Normandy (963-1026). Van Houts 1985: 551.

[501] Annales Altahenses maiores 1848: 815-817. Van Houts 1985: 559.

[502] **3134**, **3135**, **3137** and **3137** respectively.

[503] Until about 1130 and 1150 respectively.

[504] **3143** is a specimen found in Rhodes.

[505] Production of the eponymous deniers of the kingdom began under Baldwin III (1143-63), but the anonymous type inscribed MONETA REGIS may be earlier. Metcalf 1995: 52 ff., pl. 9 and 10.

[506] E.g. **3144**, a denier of Sidon.

[507] See above, 75-76.

[508] Metcalf 1995: 149.

[509] Metcalf 1995: bizancios auri saracenatos 46, bizancios saracenatos regis Hierusalem 43, biçantios de Acri iusti ponderis 47, crusader bezants of Tripoli 151, bisanti d' oro copoluti di Cipri 180. Also Pegolotti [1936]: bizanti di Alessandria 71, bizante di Tunisi 131, bizanti di Tripoli (N. Africa) 134.

[510] Metcalf 1995: 98-104.

[511] Touratsoglou and Baker 2002: 204-235.

[512] Stahl 2000: 28 ff.

[513] Under Baldwin VI (1251-75) and Baldwin VII (1275-87). Metcalf 1995: 149 and Pl. 20.

[514] Metcalf 1995: 199-205.

Large gold and silver coins circulated alongside all kinds of Western style deniers, the latter being more suitable for everyday transactions. The first deniers of the Latin East adopted designs inspired by Western issues, but then various new, characteristic types evolved, under the influence of political developments and the emblems of local rulers. From 1205 to about 1232, one side of the Cypriot deniers adopted a variant of the Genoese denier, obviously reflecting the influence of the Ligurian metropolis on the politics and economy of the Crusader States. In the duchy of Athens, an early denier type also copies the characteristic 'gate' of the Genoese *denaro* between 1240 and 1258.[515] In the principality of Achaia emissions probably began about 1245, with obols also influenced by the Genoese denier.[516] After 1262 these types were replaced by issues copying the design of the deniers of the French city of Tours (*tornesi, deniers tournois*); their minting apparently continued until 1350. Gradually, an increasing number of unofficial imitations was added to official issues. The production of these imitations possibly continued until the last decades of the 14th century.[517]

Coins of Cyprus and Armenia are occasional finds on Rhodes, as well as Italian small change of the 13th and early 14th centuries (PLS 147, 148, 150), such as the billon denaro and copper *quartaro* of Genoa, the *denaro* of Ancona and the already mentioned copper quartarolo of Venice (*c.* 1200-1330). On Crete and the other Venetian possessions in the Aegean it appears that, after 1335, the dominant petty type was the *soldino*, which was replace by the *tornesello* towards the end of the century.[518] Both types bore on one side the lion of St. Mark. Tornesi were also briefly minted on Venetian Tenos (1303-11) and on Chios, a Genoese possession.[519] At neighbouring Mytilene, the Genoese also used the type of the denier tournois,[520] but mostly preferred heraldic designs reflecting, among others, Byzantine prototypes. The strongest impact of the Genoese *denari* in the Eastern Mediterranean during the 14th century is observed in Hospitaller Rhodes.

The Order of St John

The origins of the military order of St John, otherwise known as the Order of the Hospital, lie in the Holy Land before the First Crusade, where the members of a religious foundation maintained a hospice for indigent pilgrims, with a church dedicated to saint John the Almoner. After the Christian conquest of Jerusalem, their organization was recognized as an independent Order by pope Paschal II in 1113. The Order's assistance to pilgrims needing hospitality and nursing care was rewarded with generous gifts by lay and religious magnates, and it soon acquired extensive properties in Palestine and the pilgrims' countries of origin in Western Europe.[521] The early rule of the Order dates from the first half of the 12th century, while in the second half its military character was already well developed.

Gradually, the role of the Order of St. John in the defence of the Latin states in the East grew, and the Hospitallers held a number of important fortresses. Alongside the Order of the Temple, the Hospital became a protagonist in the politics of these states, without relinquishing its contribution to the welfare of pilgrims. The hospital maintained by the Order in Jerusalem could shelter and look after several hundred people at any one time,[522] while Israeli archaeological excavations at Acre have revealed a model hospital building and other facilities on an impressive scale.[523] The Hospitallers also maintained hostels and hospices in Western Europe along main pilgrimage routes and in harbours used by ships bound for the Holy Land.

In 1291, after the fall of Acre, last foothold of the Crusaders in Palestine, the Latin refugees, the surviving Knights of St John amongst them, sought refuge in Cyprus. Hospitaller headquarters were set up at Colossi, near Limassol and, like the Templars, the Hospitallers got involved in the internal politics of the kingdom.[524] Both Orders held extensive lands in the West, while their expulsion from the Holy Land was considered by many Europeans as a moral failing. In 1305, the election of French pope Clement V gave king Philip IV the Fair the opportunity to move against the Templars, to serve both financial and political ends. The Templar leadership did not realize the seriousness of the danger in time, and were caught by surprise when Philip had all members of the Order in France arrested in

[515] Metcalf 1995: 244 and Pl. 37, 861.
[516] Cf. Metcalf 1995: Pl. 25, Pl. 38, No. 882-883; Pesce and Felloni 1976: 14.
[517] Metcalf 1995: Pl. 44; Tzamalis 1981: 122.
[518] Stahl 2000, 45-46, 60-63. Many torneselli have been found on Rhodes, but no soldini.
[519] Tornesi between 1324 and 1329 (Metcalf 1995: 291) and 1348-1498 (Mazarakis 2003: 162, 175, 194, 197).
[520] Schlumberger 1878: Pl. XVII, 15-17.
[521] Riley-Smith 1967: 36 ff.
[522] Kedar 1998: 3-26.
[523] *Hadashot Arkheologiyot, Excavations and Surveys in Israel* 14-18, 1995-1998.
[524] The involvement of the Hospitallers and the Templars in the politics of Cyprus at this time is examined by Hill 1948: II, 198-201; Riley-Smith 1967: 203-214; Luttrell 1972; *idem* 2003: 75; Edbury 1991: 112; Papadopoullos 1995: 739 ff.

1307. Other European rulers followed suit and the forcible dissolution of the Temple was accomplished (1312).[525] In contrast to Jacques de Molay, master of the Templars, Foulques de Villaret, the master of the Hospital, avoided an open rift with the French king and sought new independent headquarters for his Order in the East. In 1306, he came to an understanding with Genoese adventurer Vignolo Vignoli, which resulted in an invasion of Rhodes, the occupation of important strongholds in the island's hinterland and, in spite of the efforts of Byzantine emperor Andronicus II, the surrender of the island's capital to Villaret in 1309.[526]

The conquest of Rhodes by the Hospitallers caused a break with the island's past, but also brought about a transformation of the Order itself.[527] For the first time, although under papal suzerainty, the Knights of St John acquired political autonomy and heterodox subjects. They could sign commercial agreements and treaties, maintain harbours and crews for their vessels, collect taxes and mint their own coins. Their lands in the West provided a substantial income (*responsiones*) which permitted them to improve the defences of their island state without unduly oppressing the indigenous population. Their dependence on the West was not only financial: most of their manpower came from the Latin West, while the conflicts between Western rulers tended to cause internal strains within the ranks of the international Order. This became marked during the election of a new grand master and in the chapters general required to take place at intervals by the Order's statutes.

Papal intervention could have more serious consequences for the Knights and their island state. The pope frequently used the Order as a pawn in his political chessboard, without overly concerning himself with the consequences to this distant Christian outpost in a period when Muslim might was in the ascendant. Moreover, the pope could use his leverage with the Knights to bolster up his own bankers or encourage the ambitions of individuals that undermined the control of the Order on its properties in the West.[528] Relations with their overlord complicated the situation within the Order during the period of the papal schism, although the support of the Holy See was at times essential for the Hospital.

Promotion of their image in the West was a constant preoccupation for the Knights, who sought to present their activity in the East within the setting of crusader ideology and Christian charity. After military spending on both defensive and offensive objectives, the upkeep of hospitals and other welfare institutions on Rhodes and elsewhere was a heavy drain on their budget but ensured the goodwill of moralists and the royal courts of Europe. The Hospital took part in every crusading enterprise in the eastern Mediterranean and maintained close ties with Cyprus and Cilician Armenia,[529] offering military and diplomatic support to both these states in their struggles against Egypt and the Turks. Hospitaller vessels patrolled the area of the modern Dodecanese, but also the waters off Cerigo and the Northern Sporades. To control the sea they also used Latin corsairs, particularly Catalans, while their endeavour to limit the supply of arms and related materials to Muslim powers brought them into conflict with Venice.

Rhodes became an important centre for the carrying trade, particularly for Westerners who wished to avoid Venetian harbours: after Sicily, ships from Catalonia, the South of France and Italy usually stopped in Rhodes on their way to Cyprus or Egypt. The spoils and slaves acquired in raids by the Knights and their allies generally ended up in the market of Rhodes. The Hospital also encouraged the local production of sugar and soap, and provided asylum and the chance for permanent settlement to Christian refugees from Syria and Anatolia. The town of Rhodes gradually expanded, and its population comprised, besides the local Greeks, Latins, Jews, Armenians and Syrians, as well as many slaves from the Balkans and the East.

In the 14th century the Order consolidated its hold on the neighbouring islands and engaged in campaigns and raids aiming to curtail the expansion of Muslim power. For a substantial interval (1374-1402) they held Smyrna; they attempted to acquire a foothold on the Peloponnese and, after the Christian armies were crushed at the battle of Nicopolis in 1396, undertook the ransom of Christian prisoners. From the early 15th century, the peril from the East grew apace. In 1402 Tamerlane drove the Knights out of Smyrna and they, soon after, raised the strong fortress

[525] Barber 1978; Seward 1995.

[526] Luttrell 2003: 76, 171, 198. For the foreign policy of Andronicus II see Laiou 1972.

[527] For a concise but balanced account see Luttrell 1975 and Rossi 1975. The coverage of the Order's history on Rhodes is uneven. Delaville Le Roulx, Luttrell, Tsirpanlis and Vatin have thoroughly explored parts of the political history, infrastructure and social background of Hospitaller Rhodes. Epigraphics, architectural projects and the study of the Order's activities in Latin Europe have put the period into perspective. However, even now, the venerable *Dell' Istoria della Sacra Religione, and Illustrissima Militia di San Giovanni Gierosolimitano* of Hospitaller historian Giacomo Bosio (1544-1627), is a necessary tool for the understanding of the period.

[528] Such as Juan Fernandez de Heredia from 1348 until 1376, who caused serious problems for masters Gozon, Corneillan, Pins, Berenger and Juilly, until his own accession to the mastership. Delaville Le Roulx 1913: 124-198; Bonneaud 2004: 134.

[529] Where they also held lands. Delaville Le Roulx 1913: 17; Riley-Smith 1967: 103. The pope was particularly concerned about the fate of Armenia, whose rulers had embraced the Latin creed under Leo I (1198-1219).

of St. Peter (Bodrum), at Halicarnassus.[530] In 1444 Rhodes was besieged and seriously threatened by a Mamluk force from Egypt.[531] Afterwards, it was the rising power of the Ottomans that posed the danger. The smaller Hospitaller islands and the Rhodian countryside were repeatedly raided by Turkish flotillas, although the fortresses of the hinterland usually provided the inhabitants with adequate shelter. The strong fortifications of the town of Rhodes and sound leadership caused the siege of a large army sent by Mehmed II the Conqueror to fail in 1480, causing a sensation throughout Europe. Rhodian prosperity apparently continued for a further forty years and, in 1510, the Order's fleet defeated the Mamluks at Alexandretta, dooming Egyptian efforts to control Portuguese inroads in the Indian Ocean.[532] The Hospitaller period of Rhodes ended with the successful siege of Suleiman II the Magnificent in 1522. The Knights surrendered upon terms and, when they departed from Rhodes, a substantial part of the urban population left with them, and was eventually to settle in Malta[533].

Rhodes was ruled by 19 grand masters of the Order of St. John:

	Name	Reign	Tongue
1	Foulques de Villaret	1309-1319	Provence
2	Helion de Villeneuve	1319-1346	Provence
3	Déodat de Gozon	1346-1353	Provence
4	Pierre de Corneillan	1353-1355	Provence
5	Roger de Pins	1355-1365	Provence
6	Raymond Berenger	1365-1373	Provence
7	Robert de Juilly	1373-1377	France
8	Juan Fernandez de Heredia	1377-1396	Spain
9	Philibert de Naillac	1396-1421	[Auvergne]
10	Antoni de Fluvià	1421-1437	Spain
11	Jean de Lastic	1437-1454	Auvergne
12	Jacques de Milly	1454-1461	Auvergne
13	Pere Ramon Zacosta	1461-1467	Spain
14	Giovanni-Battista degli Orsini	1467-1476	Italy
15	Pierre d'Aubusson	1476-1503	Auvergne
16	Emery d'Amboise	1503-1512	France
17	Guy de Blanchefort	1512-1513	Auvergne
18	Fabrizio del Carretto	1513-1521	Italy
19	Philippe Villiers de l'Isle-Adam	1521-1523	France

Figure 63: The masters of the Hospital in Rhodes, 1309-1522.

Hospitaller minting

The techniques of coin production in medieval Europe, also used in the Hospitaller mint of Rhodes are familiar to coin specialists, who describe them in detail.[534] Some scholars have complemented the study of coins with experimentation in die-cutting and testing alloys.[535] The process required particular competence in the sinking of dies; blanks of suitable size and the correct alloy would be prepared and introduced between the dies, and a less skilled worker would hammer in the design.

The method for the mass production of blanks was not always the same. Greater care was taken with gold or silver blanks, and even with good quality billon, but the preparation of copper blanks for the low value obols was much more casual. It seems that, usually, thin sheets of metal were cut into blanks of the proper diameter with shears

[530] Luttrell 1986; De Vaivre 2009.

[531] For the economic and political consequences of the threat from the East see Bonneaud 2012.

[532] The Mamluks were in Syria to acquire timber for the building of a fleet for the Red Sea with Ottoman help. Vatin 1994: 300, 317-319. If the project had been realized, it could may have put an end to the Portuguese occupation of the strategically important island of Socotra off Yemen (they had taken it in 1507) and prevented their settlement in Goa (1510), thus affecting the penetration of Europeans in the Indian Ocean. For the historical background Boxer 1977: 15-64, 106 ff.; Fonseca 2008.

[533] Brockman 1969.

[534] Balog 195; Sellwood 1962; Forbes 1971; Grierson 1975; Cooper 1988; La Nièce and Craddock 1993.

[535] Sellwood 1962: 56-65; Stewart 1969: 269-289; Grierson 1975: 97-110; Esty 1990: 205-221.

or round 'pastry cutters', and the weight finely adjusted after striking.[536] Unfortunately, most of the silver coins of Rhodes, both those recovered from archaeological sites and those in numismatic collections, are clipped to some extent, a phenomenon which may be due to mint but also illegal practices. Thus, it is difficult to establish the intended diameter and method of production of these blanks. However, there are indications for the use of a circular cutter for the billon deniers of Rhodes which, when in reasonable condition, show a much more regular outline than the obols. It is also obvious that the blanks of the deniers were blanched by bathing in acid, a technique common for this type of coin.[537]

Blanks for the obols could be produced either by passing the molten metal through a sieve over water, turning the liquid metal drops into ovoids which were then hammered flat; or by cutting pieces off a metal rod and then hammering them. In Rhodes, for the obols of the 14th century the first method seems to have been preferred, judging from the usually irregularly elliptical shape of the flans. In the 15th century, this technique may have been used, but there are also issues with flans probably produced from square-sectioned rods (PLS. 140, 142, 144).[538]

The dies were of steel, worked while heated with engraving tools such as burins and punches, some of them for various letters or the main design of each side. The dies were fixed on iron bars and the lower die (*standard* or *staple*), further from the striking hammer, was often fixed on an anvil. The 'hammer' or *trussell* die, conventionally used for the reverse of a type, was more clearly impressed and wore down much faster than the staple used for the more complex obverse. Thus, for every staple die, two or three trussel dies had to be made. The process of striking did not require particular skill. If carried out carelessly, however, the die might be struck off-centre on the blank and some of it fail to impress, something quite common in the obols examined, particularly those of the 14th century, but rare in the billon and silver. Carelessness might also result in double-striking (if a coin slipped on the die) or brockage (when a coin got stuck on the die and its design was impressed on the coin struck after it). No regular orientation of die axes is observable in the petty coins of the Hospitaller period.

The die sinkers included small variations in the designs which could be employed to keep track of production; thus, a set of trussel dies with the corresponding staple might define a particular 'type'. However, in order to cut cost, dies were frequently used until they became too worn and, normally, one die from a particular set would continue in use for a while after the die for the other side had been changed. This may help to arrange a series of 'types' in chronological order (*linkage*) or, at least, to ascertain the way dies were employed in the mint: sequentially until they wore out (*single-sequence continuous usage model*)[539] or in other ways such as in the *die-box model*,[540] where an obverse die might be used with any of three reverses simultaneously, or when two or more sets were used simultaneously and interchangeably when other factors, such as relative wear, might influence frequency of use.

The rate of wear for a die was related to the hardness of the flans. If they were struck when still warm, but not too hot, the lifespan of dies might be extended, but the chances of coins getting stuck on a die increased, affecting the quality of the emission and slowing down the work, particularly in small denominations. In the obols of Rhodes occasional brockage and some 'stretched' specimens imply that striking directly followed the hammering of the blanks or, at least, that the blanks were reheated before striking. The life of a worn die could be extended by recutting with an engraving tool.

At the close of the 14th century and the early years of the 15th, petty coins in Rhodes were recycled by simple overstriking, for reasons obviously linked to the additional time and cost required for the production of new blanks, or in order to prevent the reduction of the silver content by the moneyers. Less systematic, but not rare, was the overstriking of large foreign silver coins with a local equivalent,[541] but such pieces are not present in the Archaeological Collection of Rhodes.

The moneyers (*monetarii*) who sank the dies and made the blanks had skills similar to those of gold- and silversmiths and often worked in both trades, particularly when coin production was intermittent or limited. There is evidence for itinerant coiners and workshops in general[542] and also in Rhodes.[543] Two contracts between the Order of the

[536] Sellwood 1962: 60-63.
[537] Grierson 1975: 106.
[538] Both obols and imitations which might be considered as jetons.
[539] Esty 1990: 206.
[540] Esty 1990: 208.
[541] Cf. Kasdagli 2002: RF?, 47 (Roger de Pins), R6/5, 49, R6/11, 51 και R6/14 (Raymond Berenger), R8/9, 58, R8/13, 59 (Juan Fernandez de Heredia), R9/12, 68 (Philibert de Naillac).
[542] Grierson 1975: 100; Stewart 1971: 266; Grierson and Blackburn 1986: 95-100; Allen 2012: 25, 92.
[543] Demetrios Markezis, goldsmith (*aurifaber*) and magister monete of the Hospital, was a native of Chalkis on Euboea. He settled in Rhodes and,

Hospital and one George Markezis, concerning the operation of the mint by the latter, are preserved in the Archives of Malta. The first is dated 1 February 1450, under master Jean de Lastic,[544] and entrusted the operation of the mint *in lo loco dentro lo Castello acostumato*[545] to Markezis, upon specific terms.

Among other things, Markezis would provide the necessary equipment (*massaricie et ferramenti et stampe*) and undertook its maintenance at his own expense. He and his staff would work only in the premises of the mint (*lauorare dela picola cossa alla grande in lo ditto locho et non in altra parte, di note o de jorno, lui o li soi lauoranti*).[546] Markezis, together with the supervisors of the mint, would ensure the quality of the alloy for the issue of gold and silver coins. As master of the mint, he could not refuse to convert into coin any quantity of metal brought in by individuals. After the preparation of the correct alloy, the number of coins to be produced had to be declared in the *Castellania*. The permit issued by the Castellania would have to be presented by Markezis at the Palace, in order to obtain the dies which would be handed over either by the grand master or his seneschal. The dies would be carried to the mint by someone enjoying the master's trust, who would remain there and supervise the work. The quality of the new coins would be checked at the Castellania by the officers responsible before the new coins could be delivered to the owner. If a problem was noticed concerning quality, Markezis would have to take them back, melt them down and repeat the process. Markezis would keep a percentage of the coin produced, part of which would be paid to the grand master. It is worth noting that, when gold was struck, the master was entitled to two thirds of the profit, while from the issue of silver only a fifth. The production of the coins should be completed within one day (*dal jorno che l'auera receuuto l'oro o l'argento per monetarlo*) and six *marks* of silver were the lowest limit of a day's production (*se devera rendere al manco ogni jorno marchi sey d'argento*).

The document is concerned with the issue of gold and silver, and not with that of petty coin. Thus, we do not know how the system worked for the smaller denominations in relation to the management of dies and the profit. It is clear from the first document that this was not the first contract between Markezis and the Order. It is therefore reasonable to assume that the Hospitaller mint operated through contracts. What happened if there was no one suitable to run the mint is not clear. Certainly, foreign gold and silver could be accepted, but the lack of petty coin was not as easy to deal with and must have caused difficulties in the local market, as is shown by a document dated 28 April 1488.[547]

Rhodian silver and gold[548]

Without the agreement with Vignolo Vignoli, the Hospital may have missed the opportunity to conquer Rhodes.[549] Nevertheless, after 1309, Genoese influence on the new island state waned.[550] The first Hospitaller issues under Foulques de Villaret, were silver gros and half-gros, bearing on one side the design of the master's seal.[551] Thus, the coins which had entered circulation in France during the reform of St Louis after the Seventh Crusade were preferred to locally available or Genoese models. In any case, when the Knights of St John took Rhodes, *gros grands* and *gros petits* were already circulating in Cyprus.[552] Today Villaret's silver coins are extremely rare.

The revolt of his subordinates in the summer of 1317 obliged Villaret to retreat first in the citadel of Lindos and then to the court of king Robert of Naples. From there, through Genoa, he reached the papal court at Avignon in

according to a document in the Archives of Malta, married a local woman of the *marinarii* class about 1400. His son Georgios was in the same trade in the mid-15th century. Tsirpanlis 1995: 452-454, document 157. In 1478, the master of the Hospital's mint was a Catalan. Mannucci 1987: 298.

[544] Tsirpanlis 1995: 523, document 199. The second contract, dated 1 December 1454, under grand master Jacques de Milly, is still unpublished.

[545] The palace complex also included outbuildings now lost or isolated from the main structure. The mint should have been located as far as possible from the living quarters, because of the noise. A. Gabriel, 1923, 91, believed, inaccurately, that the building traditionally considered the Hospitaller mint was entirely modern. Actually, this building, although drastically modified under Italian rule (1912-43), dates from the period of master Antoni Fluvià and is contemporary with the early building phase of the auberge of the Spanish tongue (information by architect Dr. George Dellas).

[546] The prohibition to produce coins outside the premises of the mint may be an indication that such infringements had occurred earlier. Perhaps the anonymous gros issued by James of Cyprus in 1456, during his sojourn in Rhodes, were produced outside the mint by the moneyers employed there. Pitides 1988.

[547] Mannucci 1987: 295.

[548] This chapter is mainly based on studies of private and public collections in the West, some kept in major institutions such as the Cabinet de Medailles in Paris, The Ashmolean Museum in Oxford, the British Museum and the Museum of the Order of St John at Clerkenwell, London. Most of the Hospitaller coins now in the West came from Anatolian hoards. Cf. Gitta Kastner, *Auctiones* 15 1985; Sotheby's 1997: 101-105; Kasdagli 2002. The Sant Pere de Rodes/1989 Catalan hoard is an exception. Marot *et al.* 1999.

[549] Delaville Le Roulx 1913: 10-11; Zachariadou 1983: 11-12; Luttrell 2003: 75, 193.

[550] Schlumberger 1878: 223. Luttrell 1975: 287; *idem* 1997: 737-761. Part of the slab of the Vignoli family tomb has been found (above 133); from the same period we also have a funerary inscription from the tomb of a John Gavalla: the fact that members of these two families still lived in Rhodes does not mean that they preserved any political influence in Hospitaller times.

[551] Metcalf 1995: 296-297; Mazarakis 2010: 11.

[552] Metcalf 1995: 200-205.

August 1318, in order to confront before the pope the accusations of his Order and their representative, Maurice de Pagnac, elected by the Convent to replace him. After deliberations which took several months Pagnac was deposed, Villaret persuaded to retire and, in June 1319, Helion de Villeneuve, prior of Provence, succeeded him as master.[553] Villeneuve stayed in the West for thirteen years, dealing with the Order's economic troubles with the support of pope John XXII, and settling various problems concerning the properties inherited by the Hospital after the dissolution of the Temple in 1312.

The regular operation of the Hospitaller mint is conventionally dated from Villeneuve's arrival in Rhodes in 1332. Large silver *gigliati* and their halves, known as *aspers*, were issued under his rule.[554] The first gigliati, also known as *carlini*, had been minted in the kingdom of Naples in 1303, in the reign of Charles II. Robert the Wise, his successor, expanded the issue of the denomination in Provence, where Villeneuve seems to have been involved in the process.[555] This explains the use of the type in the reorganization of the Hospitaller mint soon after.[556] The new coins bore on the obverse the master's kneeling figure before a patriarchal cross on steps, and on the reverse the floriated cross typical of the gigliati, with an escutcheon of the Order replacing the central petal of the fleur-de-lys finials of the cross. The circumferential legend +FR(ater) ELION(us) D(e) VILANOVA D(e)I GRA(CIA) M(agiste) R /+OSP(i)TAL(is) S(ancti) IOh(ann)IS I(he)R(usa)L(emita)NI Q(onven)TV(s) RODI ran continuously from the obverse into the reverse. The obverse of the Rhodian gigliati linked the coinage of Villeneuve with that of Villaret and was also a borrowing from the master's seal:[557]

Figure 64. Hospitaller silver coins (after Schlumberger)
1. Villaret gros. 2. Villeneuve gigliato.

The aspers were identical with the gigliati in appearance but smaller in size, with more abbreviations in the legend. The collection of Rhodes includes a single gigliato of Villeneuve derived from the pre-war local Italian collection, and one of his aspers, found by archaeologists in the medieval town (PL. 97).[558]

The regular issue of gigliati continued under Villeneuve's successors until Antoni de Fluvià (1421-37), with a brief reappearance under grand master Giovanni Battista degli Orsini (1467-76).[559] From the times of Roger de Pins (1355-65) a heraldic badge or shield of the issuing master of the Hospital appeared in the obverse field behind the figure of the master; and from the times of Juan Fernandez de Heredia (1377-96) onwards 'secret signs' were also added to the field. In the second half of the 14th century the production of aspers was reduced[560] and, under Heredia, the denomination was replaced by lighter *tierces* with the same design. It seems that the tierces circulated widely and the Archaeological Collection in Rhodes contains four of these pieces.[561] Under Philibert de Naillac (1396-1421), Heredia's successor, the production of tierces seems to have been significantly curtailed, since until now only a single coin, a site find from the medieval town, has found its way into the local collection.[562]

553 Delaville Le Roulx 1913: 17-18, 51.
554 Luttrell 2003: 54-56.
555 A contract for their issue was signed in 1330 at the residence of Helion de Villeneuve in Villeneuve-les-Avignon. Grierson 1965c: 49. Villeneuve served as seneschal of Robert in Provence. Metcalf 1995: 297.
556 In more recent publications it is assumed that the production of gigliati in Provence began in 1320 or earlier (Baker 2006: 364 and n. 68). However, it is difficult to detach the reform of the Rhodian coinage from the arrival of Villeneuve in Rhodes.
557 Schlumberger 1878: 242.
558 **1658** (gigliato), **1659** (asper). In the handwritten Catalogo del Medagliere of the Italian period, which is not a complete inventory of the Italian collection, are entered a gigliato and an asper of Villeneuve, although the latter is not **1659**, which was brought to light much later.
559 According to the Catalogo del Medagliere, the Italian collection of the Museum of Rhodes in the Italian period also included three gigliati of Roger de Pins (1355-65), seven of Heredia, one of Naillac and one of Fluvià.
560 In Western collections are described aspers of masters Déodat de Gozon (1346-53), Roger de Pins and Raymond Berenger (1365-1373), and a single issue under Orsini. Mannucci 1983: 292-293.
561 **1660**, **1661**, **1662**, **1663**.
562 **1664**. Schlumberger 1878: 254.

Towards the end of the 14th century, the minting quality of silver gradually deteriorated and the crisis peaked under Naillac;[563] significant improvement in minting quality is observed under his successor, Antoni Fluvià. Jean de Lastic (1437-54) and his successors Jacques de Milly (1454-61) and Pere Ramon Zacosta (1461-67) issued silver pieces which replaced the tierces and are known as *giannetti*, since they bore the figure of St John the Baptist on the obverse.[564] The years 1377-1460 were a period of financial and numismatic crisis for the Order: Europe suffered a silver famine[565] while the ambitious plans of Heredia on mainland Greece led to his capture by John Bua Spata, ruler of Arta, in 1378. His ransom was a large one, at a time when the danger from the East was increasing.[566] The Order responded to the threat with a series of fortification works, in Rhodes and in the other possessions of their state. The failure of a siege of Rhodes by the Mamluks of Egypt in 1444 led to the reinforcement of the town walls, but the enormous expense caused unrest in the Convent.[567]

From the times of Fluvià gold sequins were also issued by the Rhodian mint, modelled on the Venetian ducat.[568] The silver was reformed by grand master Pierre d'Aubusson about 1490.[569] The new money included large *lire*, inspired by coins like the *testoni* of Milan, and their halves, bearing on one side St John the Baptist and on the other the arms of the grand master. The Collection of Rhodes comprises two gold sequins, one of Milly, found in the medieval town, and another of grand master Fabrizio del Carretto (1513-21) which may be an Italian find;[570] a half-lira of this master may also be an Italian find.[571] From two late Hospitaller hoards come one more lira and six half-liras of Carretto (PL. 97).[572]

Petty coins

According to Francesco Balducci Pegolotti, agent of the Bardi bankers of Florence, at the time of his report on Rhodes in his work *La prattica della mercatura*, dated between 1332 and 1336,[573] billon deniers circulated alongside the gigliati and aspers. The equivalence was 1 gigliato = 2 aspers = 32 deniers. These deniers, usually anonymous, were identified by 19th century scholars and are the commonest site-find for the 14th century in the town.[574] The excavational coins also comprise small copper pieces which, to avoid confusion with the billon pieces, will henceforth be termed obols; although their 15th century equivalents are called *denarii parvi* in contemporary sources.

In 1458, under grand master Jacques de Milly (1454-1461), William Wey, an English cleric from Exeter College in Oxford, visited Rhodes on pilgrimage. In his *Itineraries*, he included coin equivalences between the places he passed through which were first discussed, in what concerns Rhodes, by Frederick Hasluck.[575] 'Deniers' were still in circulation, but the equivalences had changed: 1 gigliato = 1.5 giannetto = 48 deniers (*At Rodys ye shal haue gylotys an jouettys and asperys. A gylote ys worth a jouett and halfe, a jouett is worth xxxij denars of Rodys*). Finally, the record of a Council decree dated 28 April 1488 refers to the issue of petty coins by grand master Pierre d'Aubusson: *pro moneta cudenda. Preterea quia Civitas habundat hominibus et non reperitur pecunia minuta fuit deliberatum quod est necessarium ut Reve.mus D.us Magr. cudere faciat quatrinos vel parvos denarios pro sua convenientia.*[576] It covers both billon deniers (*denarii quatrini*) and obols (*denarii parvi*). Aubusson's billon deniers of 1488 are signed and easy to identify, but it is not the same with the obols. Judging from the name, each denier was worth four obols.

Schlumberger refers to the petty coins of the Hospital in two places of his chapter on the currency of Hospitaller Rhodes. The first cites Pegolotti and concerns issues he dates in the early 14th century, before the rule of de Pins (1355-65), following the opinion of Paul Lambros.[577] The second passage, more extensive, is entitled *Deniers anonymes des grands maîtres*, but describes and discusses copper issues he himself had collected in Rhodes, which he considered later than those of Roger de Pins and earlier than the signed billon of Aubusson, without attempting

[563] Oddly, among the various issues of Naillac gigliati, there is one which stands out from the rest regarding minting quality. Kasdagli 2002: 64, variant d, R9/6, R9/16.
[564] Mannucci 1982: 343-350. One giannetto of Lastic is a site-find (1665); another figures in the Catalogo del Medagliere.
[565] Day 1978; Spufford 1988a: 339 ff.
[566] Particularly after the battle of Nicopolis (1396).
[567] Bonneaud 2012: 22-43.
[568] No gold coins of master Pere Ramon Zacosta are known. A 14th century attempt to mint gold by Déodat de Gozon (1346-53) and Pierre de Corneillan (1353-5), had petered out. Metcalf 1995: 299.
[569] It seems that Aubusson engaged in a series of experimentations with the coinage. Mannucci 1987; Mazarakis 2010: 47-48, 53-56.
[570] **1666** and **1667** respectively.
[571] **1675**.
[572] Rhodes/1990, Kasdagli 1992: 53-60 (**1670-1674**); and Rhodes/1994, *eadem* 2006b: 325-338 (**1668-1669**). See also Psarologaki and Zerlendis 1996.
[573] Luttrell 2003: 54-56.
[574] Schlumberger 1878: Pl. X, 3.
[575] Hasluck 1912-1913: 179-181.
[576] Mannucci 1987: 295-296.
[577] Schlumberger 1878: 241.

greater precision.[578] His intuition has now been confirmed by two major hoards found in Rhodes in the first half of the 20th century.

The first hoard, also known as the 'Italian hoard' or 'Lab hoard', comprises 4,247 pieces and apparently came to light when the Italians were landscaping the area round the Palace of the Grand Master. Between 1937 and 1940 the Palace was partially rebuilt and underwent drastic alterations in order to serve as a summer residence of the king of Italy.[579] To create the necessary garden setting, an entire Hospitaller neighbourhood was levelled to the east of the Palace. Only one building was spared near the Palace and must have originally belonged to the medieval palace compound.[580] Local tradition has it that this structure once housed the Hospital's mint. It was certainly in a suitable location, adjacent to the west face of the wall dividing the Collachio (upper town) into two segments, at a distance of merely 55 metres east of the palace.[581] The operation of the mint there would be under the immediate control of the ruler, without causing too much disturbance with its furnace and hammering. It is reported that the hoard in question was found in the vicinity of the supposed mint, if not actually inside it.[582] The original part of this building may be slightly later than the concealment date of the hoard, although barrel vaults are difficult to date and the association of Fluvià with its construction may be significant. In any case, the surviving building could easily have occupied the site of an earlier one with the same function.

The second major hoard, of virtually identical composition to the first, comprises 1,834 pieces. It was *'brought in* [to the Archaeology Offices] *by the German Wagner from Kamiros'*, is the statement in Greek on a 1960s label which had, apparently, replaced the degraded original find note, possibly written in a different language when it was no longer fully legible. Thus, the hoard was found in Kamiros, a locality on the island's west coast about 40 km distant from the town of Rhodes, but further information is lacking. The absence of a first name together with the fact that the very common name of Wagner may easily have replaced the similar but unusual Wagener, raises the suspicion that the find was brought in at the orders of Otto Wagener, military commander of Rhodes in 1944-1945.[583] Thus, the hoard may have been discovered in 1944, when the German army was setting up long-range gun batteries near Kamiros to cover the sea passage between Rhodes and the neighbouring island of Chalki. If it was found then, since the coins were of base metal they were handed over by Wagener to the FERT Archaeological Institute, precursor of the Greek Archaeological Service in Rhodes.

A preliminary examination dates the two hoards in the early 15th century, either towards the close of the rule of Philibert de Naillac (1396-1421), or in the early years of his successor, Antoni de Fluvià (1421-37). This dating is based on foreign coins from both hoards[584] and from other internal evidence which will be examined in detail further on. The two finds were not savings hoards, but most likely collections of pieces recalled for recycling.[585] Apart from a limited number of foreign denier-type coins, a Byzantine coin of Constans II and a tierce of Heredia, the content of the two hoards is divided into two categories of coins: one belongs to the older group distinguished by Schlumberger and his contemporaries, while the other consists almost entirely of pieces overstruck at least once. Concisely, the content of the two hoards is presented below in Figure 65.

The obol types placed by Schlumberger in his second group[586] are completely missing from the hoards. This is proof that his views about the chronological separation of the two groups were correct: to be more precise, his second group of small coins belongs to the period after 1421. The condition of the coins in the two hoards is not particularly good and most of them are not fully legible due to wear, faults in striking or overstriking. The sorry condition of many overstruck pieces is balanced by the wear of the older deniers and obols, which Schlumberger assigned to the predecessors of Roger de Pins, i.e. before 1355.

In spite of their wear, the coins from the hoards are in a better state of preservation than the site finds from the period most of which are corroded to some degree. About 1570 small coins of the Hospitaller period have been recovered in archaeological excavations in Rhodes (Figure 66).

---

578 Schlumberger 1878: 267-268. For a discussion of Schlumberger see also Metcalf 1995: 302-303.

579 Livadiotti and Rocco 1996: 241-242.

580 Today it houses the carpentry workshop of the Archaeological Service.

581 Manoussou-Della 2007: 334-335 and pl. 291 (T); *eadem* 2014: 77 (Figure 16), 119, 122.

582 Personal communication by Elias Kollias.

583 He succeeded Ulrich Kleemann in October 1944, but was in Rhodes from July of that year: www.lexikon-der-wehrmacht.de.

584 For the Kamiros hoard a quattrino of Mantua (Francesco I Gonzaga, 1382-1407) and a tornesello of doge Antonio Venier (1382-1400). For the Italian hoard, a copper coin of Francesco II of Mytilene (1384-1403), seven torneselli of Andrea Venier and a Portuguese *real de 10 soldos* of king John I (1385-1443).

585 As will be shown below, many of them were of billon.

586 That is, the period after de Pins but before Aubusson. Schlumberger 1878: 267.

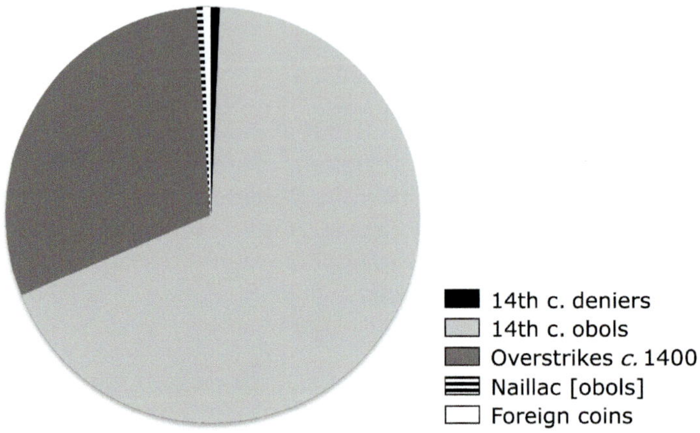

Figure 65: Composition of the two major Hospitaller hoards of Rhodes.

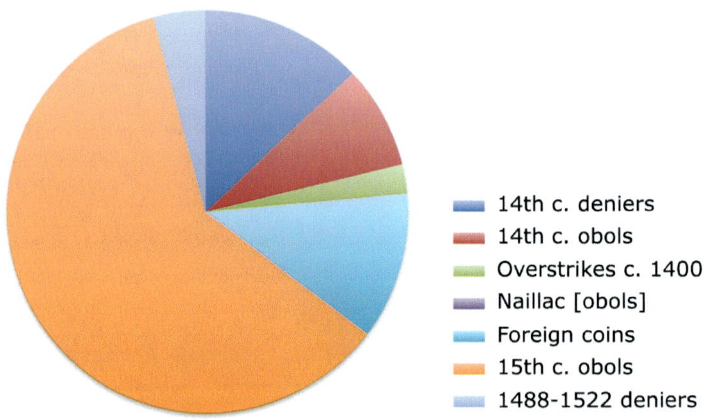

Figure 66: Site-finds of the Hospitaller period from the town of Rhodes.

These also include contemporary foreign coins which found their way to Rhodes such as torneselli and denier-type coins of the Latin East, Cyprus, Italy and other Western lands. As was explained in the Introduction, many of the Hospitaller coins were found in the excavation of churches, and probably derive from disturbed funerary deposits. In only one case it is reasonably certain that the recovered coins belong together. It concerns 185 pieces found in a richly furnished burial in the church of St John in the Collachio, the conventual church of the Hospital.[587] The resulting problem in estimating losses per year as an indicator of coin circulation has already been discussed.[588] Even without this problem, it is difficult to make any but the roughest estimates because most of the site finds are anonymous issues whose dating is uncertain. Thus, it is necessary to attempt a dating for these coins closer than the broad divide between the 14th and the 15th century, to establish the different types and, if possible, their chronological sequence. To do this, the material has been divided and examined under the following four headings:

- 14th century deniers
- Overstruck coins
- 14th century obols
- 15th century obols

Site finds are more relevant for the study of the deniers of the 14th century and the obols of the 15th but corrosion was a barrier to in-depth investigation. The two major hoards are of exceptional value for the study of 14th century

[587] Kasdagli 2009; *eadem* 2013: 211-212.

[588] See above, Introduction, 11-13. The only extensive archaeological excavation without a church in the medieval town is that of the Asprakis-Maravelias-Hasapoglou plots, with a total of 27 Hospitaller coins.

obols and overstrikes, although they also provide evidence which may contribute to the elucidation of problems concerning 14th century deniers as well.

1. 14th century billon deniers

Apart from gros and half-gros, Foulques de Villaret issued anonymous billon deniers bearing on one side a castle with three towers and on the other a cross pattée, within beaded circles.[589] The circumferential legend read +·S(an) C(t)I· IOhA(nn)IS·B(aptista)· / +·MAG(ist)R(i)· hOSPITAL(is). The model for these deniers has been sought in *keratia* of Chios dated between 1314 and 1319, showing a similar castle.[590] However, such a castle also features on an anonymous denier type of the duchy of Athens dated 1309-1311.[591] Given the financial and political crisis Villaret was facing in 1317,[592] the denier of the duke of Athens seems a likelier prototype. Otherwise, a common model might be sought elsewhere for all three issues.

The deniers of Villaret may have remained in circulation for as long as two decades. Today they are very rare; archaeological excavation in Rhodes has brought to light two of them (PL. 98).

After the monetary reform of Villeneuve, from the 1330s on, it is certain that, alongside the large silver pieces, deniers were also in circulation, providing the means for small daily transactions (PLS 98-102). As in the times of Villaret, these deniers were anonymous. The main design on the obverse was a 'Genoese gate' (*janua*) within a circle, with a dot on the right side of the field which sometimes helps identify partially illegible specimens, since it is not encountered on similar coins outside Rhodes; the circumferential legend +CIVIS·RODI accompanies the janua. On the reverse the legend +MAG(ist)R(i)·hOSPITAL(is) is arranged round a circle enclosing a cross pattée.

The anonymous billon deniers circulated in a number of variants. In a preliminary sorting attempt, two types were distinguished: in type I the main design is enclosed in a smooth circle. The main design of the finest variant of type I is shown in Figure 67.[593] This variant, with a visibly higher silver content, may well have been the first to be issued, since Gresham's law ensures that finer coins will disappear from circulation when in competition with pieces worth the same nominally but of lower intrinsic value. This early variant is distinguished by the rather thick, smooth circle enclosing the main design, and the form of the legend is ✠CIVIS·RODI / ✠MĀGR· hOSPITĀL'. In some well-preserved specimens of the variant the outer circle round the rim is also visible; in most it has been lost, often possibly through filing to remove some of the metal (Figure 68). The vertical strokes of the janua are generally thick, and the lettering is composite. A second variant marks a change in the form of the letter A, from Ā to Ħ, but the circle round the main design is still smooth. In some specimens the ending of the legend is altered to ĦL;, and a final dot stop follows the ligature.[594]

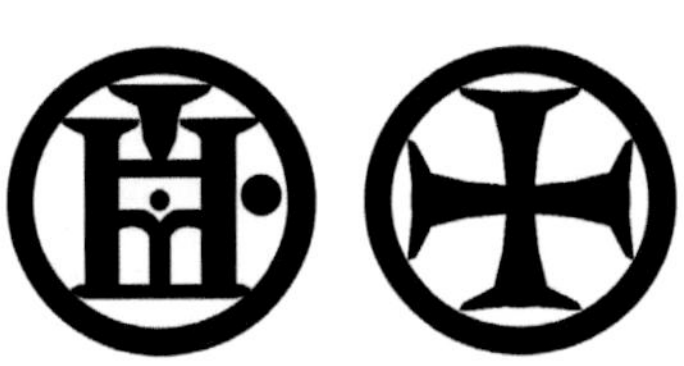

Figure 67: Central design of anonymous billon denier of Rhodes (type I).

Figure 68: Composite lettering on early deniers.

Later issues, assembled in type II, have a visibly reduced silver content and have suffered more from corrosion. The verticals of the janua are thinner and the main design less carefully engraved; the circle round it is usually beaded. Different variants show only some of these features, but the condition of the coins does not allow systematic analysis. Variations in the legend are also observable, some shown below:

---

[589] Metcalf 1995: 296-297.
[590] Schlumberger 1878: 243 and Pl. XIV 23, 24; Mazarakis 2010: 16-17.
[591] Metcalf 1995: 290 (Chios), 245 and Pl. 37 No. 868 (duchy of Athens).
[592] Schlumberger 1878: 243; Delaville Le Roulx 1913: 11-25; Luttrell 1993: 78.
[593] The design was lifted from **1680**.
[594] Cf. **1800**, **1802**, **1817**, **1818** (PLS 100-101).

]ⲤⲒⲨⲒS[595]
· ✠ · Ⲥ…[596]
• ✠ • Ⲥ…[597]
○ ✠ ○ ⲤI… / [ⲘⲀGR…[598]
· ✠ · ⲘⲀGR…[599]
]ⲘⲀGR·OSPITⲀ[

Unfortunately, the coins are not fully legible and it is not possible to recover a complete design from any variant due to the limited sample currently available. Besides the anonymous issues, Schlumberger noted deniers carrying the badge of Roger de Pins, a pinecone, to the left of the field next to the janua. Most of the Pins signed deniers (PL. 103) show a general affinity to the anonymous type II billon.

Another type of billon denier, unknown to Schlumberger, bears a tiny fleur-de-lys at the end of the obverse legend (PL. 103). This type should most probably be assigned to Robert de Juilly (1373-77), whose arms bore a floriated cross (*croix fleurdelisée*), for whom a badge in the form of a lily would seem more appropriate. When the first specimen that came to light was published, the badge was described as an alder or oak leaf, but the discovery of other specimens has helped clear the point.[600] Among recently treated coins three more specimens of the type were found; now the existence of at least two variants of the obverse and two of the reverse has been established: the published first specimen has an annulet in the field to the right of the janua, while the other three bear a dot; on three of the pieces, the stop between the words in the legend is a colon rather than a single dot. The legends of the four pieces are set out below:

✠[·]ⲤI[VI]S[·]RODI⚜ / ✠ⲘⲀGR·hOSP[TⲀL] **(1891)**
✠[:]ⲤIVIS : RODI⚜ / [ ]ⲘⲀGR·hOSPITⲀ… **(1892)**
✠…RODI⚜ /]ⲘⲀGR:h… **(1893)**
✠ : ⲤIVIS : RODI[⚜] / ✠ⲘⲀGR·hOSPIT… **(1894)**

The other features of the type include elegant design, a smooth circle round it and a needle at the top of each vertical of the janua. This is probably the latest billon denier of the 14th century and has been found as an understrike in the Italian and Kamiros hoards.

The first anonymous billon deniers were issued under Helion de Villeneuve, but they may have preceded the gigliati. They were modelled on Genoese coins, and could conceivably have been designed purposely for acceptance by Genoese. In 1320, according to chronicler Giovanni Villani (*c.* 1280-1348),[601] the Knights dealt successfully with a serious Turkish attempt to attack Rhodes:

> *Nel detto anno [1320], uno Amiraglio di Turchia, venendo per prendere l'Isola di Rodi, la quale tenea la magione dell' Hospedale, con più di 80. tra Galee & altri legni di Saracini, il comandatore di Rodi con 4. Galee & 20. altri piccoli legni, & con l'ajuto di 6. Galee di Genovesi, che tornavano d'Erminia* [Armenia], *combatterono co' detti Saracini, & sconfisserli, & gran parte de' detti legni presono e profondarono. Appresso andarono a una Isoletta* [Tilos][602], *ch' era ivi presso, dove havevano (b) posto più di dieci mila Turchi per metterli in su l'Isola di Rodi ; & tutti li presono i Christiani, & uccisero i vecchi, & i giovani vendero per ischiavi.*

This was the second collaboration of the Hospital with the Genoese after some years of tension: in 1318, grand preceptor Albrecht von Schwarzburg had attacked the Turks of Altoluogo (Ephesus) with the backing of the Zaccaria of Chios. The assistance provided by the Genoese to Schwarzburg and Gérard de Pins[603] in 1320 must have been substantially rewarded, in view of the numerous slaves taken. An anonymous issue to serve such a purpose, during an emergency, was unlikely to cause problems because of the master's absence from Rhodes. If this is how things

595 Cf. **1813, 1814, 1818, 1850** (PLS 101-102); and as understrikes in **2002, 2010, 2012, 2015, 2019** (PL. 109).
596 Cf. **1802, 1851** (PLS 101, 103); as understrikes in **1992, 1994, 2001** (PL. 106).
597 As understrikes in **1996, 1999** (PL. 106).
598 **1861** (PL. 102); as understrikes in **1989, 1990, 1993, 2005, 2008, 2013** (PL. 106).
599 Cf. **1843** (PL. 101).
600 Kasdagli 1996: 333.
601 Muratori 1728: chapter CXVII, column 501.
602 Zachariadou 1983: 14. Tilos is 37 nautical miles due west of the town of Rhodes.
603 For Schwarzburg see Luttrell 1975: 287 ff.; and *idem*, 2003: 13, 16. Pins had been appointed lieutenant of the master by the pope in 1317, after the flight of Foulques de Villaret from Rhodes. Delaville Le Roulx 1913: 14.

happened, the extreme rarity of the coins of Villaret is more easily explained, and the spread of the new coins would have been facilitated by the success of the enterprise and the distribution of the spoils. Another point strengthens the case for an early issue of the janua deniers under Villeneuve. They were replaced by a signed type sometime under Roger de Pins (1355-65), since his early gigliati were also without the badge, which makes its appearance in his late issues. The anonymous deniers had entered circulation before Pegolotti wrote his section on Hospitaller Rhodes[604] and, at some point, as will be shown below, they must have been in use alongside the obols which, being of lower value, should show a higher rate of chance losses. However, in the site finds the ratio between billon deniers and obols is 4:3. Thus, the farther ahead the introduction of the deniers, the easier it is to explain this disparity. The main weakness of this interpretation lies in the possibility that some anonymous deniers may have been issued after the signed coins of Pins: it is therefore, at present, only a working hypothesis. Nevertheless, the letters in the legends of the earliest deniers are different from those on the silver of Villeneuve: the characteristic Ħ appears in later issues of the billon.

In contrast to site finds, the two major hoards contained only 41 anonymous deniers and three signed Pins pieces, against 4,096 obols. As we will see below, most of the deniers which had not been withdrawn from circulation earlier due to their higher silver content, were recycled, probably in the times of Heredia, by simple overstriking. It seems certain, however, that the anonymous deniers had largely disappeared from circulation by the 1380s at the latest.

2. 1377-1421 overstrikes

The fate of the 14th century deniers is made clear in the composition of the two major Hospitaller hoards. Concisely, it is as follows:

	ITALIAN HOARD	KAMIROS HOARD
14th c. deniers (Bi)	**28** (0.6%)	**13** (0.7%)
14th c. anonymous obols (AE)	**2840** (66.9)	**1256** (68.5%)
Pins (1355-65) deniers (Bi)	1 (0.02%)	2 (0.1%)
Berenger (1365-73) obols (AE)	24 (0.6%)	10 (0.5%)
Juilly (1373-7) deniers (Bi)	-	-
14th c. obol imitations (AE)	21 (0.5%)	9 (0.5%)
'Coarse' overstrikes [Bi]	586 (13.7%)	235 (12.8%)
Naillac (1396-1421) deniers, type 1	6 (0.1%)	4 (0.2%)
'Clumsy' overstrikes [Bi]	701 (16.5%)	295 (16%)
Naillac deniers, type 2	8 (0.2%)	-
Foreign	28 (0.6%)	7 (0.4%)
Illegible	2 (0.04%)	3 (0.15%)
Other	2 (0.04%)	-
TOTAL	**4,247 pieces**	**1,834 pieces**

Figure 69: Composition of the two major Hospitaller hoards.

In both hoards, 30% of the contents is made up of overstruck coins which are easily sorted into two categories. The first ('coarse' issues) is overstruck mostly on Hospitaller deniers, although the understrike is not always visible (PLS 104-108).[605] The overstrike is a coarse version of the obols of Schlumberger's early group. The obverse shows a thickly drawn châtel with the circumferential legend +MA(gi)STRI OSPET(alis), starting with a crosslet situated below the base of the châtel, which usually has an annulet within; the reverse has annulets in two opposed quarters of the cross, whose form draws closer to the Maltese version, and the conclusion of the obverse legend which reads IERUSALEM(itani) (cf. Figure 70, 1). This first category is represented by 821 pieces from both hoards. In 262 of those (32% of the total) the obverse legend is completely illegible. Of the better preserved coins, 337 (41% of the total) have annulets in the first and fourth quarter of the reverse cross, while in the other 222 (27% of the total), the annulets occupy the second and third quarter (ratio of 3:2). The shoddy striking makes it difficult to distinguish

[604] In 1336 at the latest. Luttrell 2003: 54-56.

[605] In both hoards this category represents 14% of the total. In the Italian hoard, with 586 pieces, legible traces of the understrike are preserved on 243 coins. In the Kamiros hoard, with 235 pieces, 139 preserve legible remnants of the understrike. An in-depth study of these coins could add to the information gathered from site-finds about the variants of the billon deniers. The understrikes of this category also include some foreign issues as in the case of **2042**, **2043** and **2044** (PL. 107).

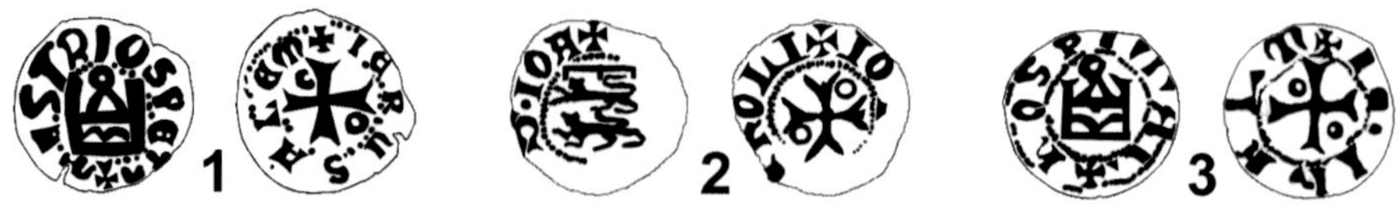

Figure 70: Petty coinage, 1377-1421: 1. Anonymous denier overstrike c. 1377-1421). 2. [Obol] with Naillac arms. 3. Anonymous Naillac overstrike.

variants, but there are at least four versions of the châtel, of which one is much better designed than the other three.[606] It is not certain that the die-cutter of these overstrikes used punches: most of the dies could have been produced with simple engraving.

Among the understrikes of this category we find signed deniers assigned to the mastership of Juilly,[607] so it dates from the period after 1377, probably under Heredia. Pins signed deniers are also found as understrikes, but most of the overstruck pieces were originally anonymous Rhodian deniers. The fact that the reverse of the overstrike displays the annulets distinguishing 14th century obols could be interpreted as an indication that the distinction between deniers and obols faded after 1377.

The châtel typical of the second category of overstrikes ('clumsy' overstrikes, PLS. 110-115) is drawn with thinner lines and the legend starts below it. There are a number of variations, stylistically very similar, but with different inscriptions; the dominant distinguishing feature is the fact that the coins have been overstruck at least twice, making the legends particularly hard to read. In a few specimens traces of the original billon type are still visible. However, repetitive overstriking may well conceal the fact that the original type was usually a billon issue.[608] The legends of this group are usually variants of +hOSPITAL S/ IO IhRLM O, spread over both sides of the coins (Figure 70, 3). The legend may start on either side of the coin and the following variations have been confirmed so far, although there are others, only partially legible:

No.	Obverse (châtel)	Reverse	Identified pieces
1	+ONIT · S[B]O...	+OSPITAL[· S · IO ·]	16
2	+ONIT · SBO...	+IO · IhRLM · O	10
3	+[h]OSPITA...	+[·]S · IO · IhRLM ·	9
4	+OSPITAL · [M]	+IO · IhRLM · O	57
5	+IO · IhRLM · O	+[h]OSPITAL · [M]	55
6	+IO · IhRLM	+IO · IhRLM	5
7	+hO · IhRLM ·	+IO · IhRLM · O	25
8	+hOSPITAL...	+hOSPITAL...	21

Figure 71: Legends of Naillac overstrikes in the two major Hospitaller hoards.

A variation bears, exclusively on the châtel side, the obscure legend +ONIT·SBO·LM. This heavily abbreviated inscription may, perhaps, be read as O(ste)N(d)IT S(uper)BO L(u)M(ine)[609] and may be linked to the abbreviations on the other side of the coin, which refer to the Order. Invocations also appear on gigliati of the time, which could be considered, given the circumstances, as emergency issues and were also very ill-struck.[610] On the pieces with this 'obverse', the side with the cross bears either the first or the second half of the usual version of the legend. Although most of the types in this category are anonymous, there is an exception, precious for their dating, with the legend +PhI(li)BERTI M(agistri) on the side of the châtel (PL. 109).[611] This is, of course, Philibert de Naillac, the successor of

[606] Cf. **1903**, **1904**, **1905** etc. for the more numerous first variant; **1921**, **1984** and **1926** for the second, where the châtel resembles an open square (see also Figure 70, 1) and no annulet is discernible inside; **1928** and **1932** for the third, with an attenuated châtel; and **1941** and **1942** for the fourth, where the châtel is smaller in size and better formed (PLS 104, 106).

[607] **1958**, **1959**, **1960**, **1961**, **1962**, **1963** and two more pieces, Italian hoard; **1964**, **1965**, Kamiros hoard (PL. 105).

[608] In some cases a first group overstrike is legible, under the later clumsy type. However, we also find coins of the clumsy group overstruck by another type of the same group.

[609] 'May the light from on high enhance...' Many thanks to Dr. Eleni Kalkani-Passali for her assistance in the interpretation.

[610] Such as SANTA CROSE AIUTA M, SANTA CROSE FAbE, IN NOMINE DEI SANTA CROSE AMEN, SANTA CRO AIUT AU MAIST OPI. Beckenbauer 1973, 83-88 and 1978/1979. Metcalf 1995: 300-301.

[611] On the side with the cross, with annulets in the second and third quarters, the legend is +IOANES IER[O](sa)L(emitan)I. The same abbreviation

Heredia, and the consignment of all the types belonging to this category to his mastership is justified by the affinity with his badly struck gigliati, although this is not the only available evidence.

A few specimens of an eponymous small coin of Naillac, where the arms of the master (*two lions passant in pale, a label of three pendants*) replace the châtel, were found in both hoards (Figure 70.2, PLS 108, 109), but some of them are overstruck with anonymous types of the second category, although they do not seem to contain any silver.[612] The carefully designed type with the arms of Naillac is an innovation and some of the coins were struck on new blanks.[613] Presumably, this type went into circulation concurrently with the only fine, but relatively rare, gigliato of the master[614] and may represent a transient attempt to improve minting quality. However, it is not proven that the signed coins circulated before all the overstrikes of Naillac: one of the specimens also preserves the imprint of a die belonging to the fist category of overstrikes (**2087**). Unfortunately, the condition of the coin does not allow us to decide which of the two impressions is the understrike and the dating of the first category of overstrikes remains open: it may have belonged either to Naillac, or to his predecessor, Juan Fernandez de Heredia. Two anonymous types of Naillac, not fully reconstructed, carry a legend with the segment IOANES IE..., and may be very close in date to this signed type of the master.[615]

In spite of the quantity of overstruck coins in the two large hoards, their representation among the site finds is relatively small. If the coins of Schlumberger's second group are removed from Figure 66, the comparison to the content of the two major hoards is instructive:

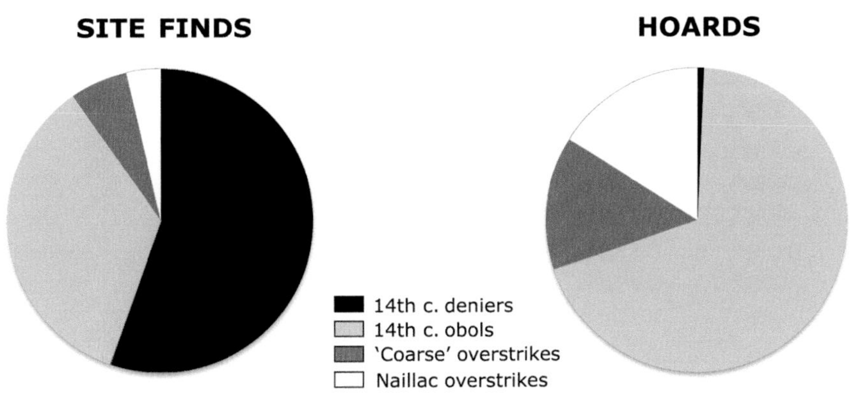

Figure 72: Comparison of representation by category between site finds and the two major Hospitaller hoards.

The hoards reflect the situation of a specific point in time in the early decades of the 15th century, while the site finds are an aggregate, representing a multitude of stray losses and burial offerings, from Villeneuve to Naillac. Each underlines different issues but may serve as a control for the other.

The hoard evidence proves that the Hospital engaged in the recall of small change on at least three occasions and that the objective was recycling (Figure 73). On the first occasion, probably under Heredia, Rhodian billon deniers, anonymous and signed, as well as a few foreign pieces, were recalled and restruck with the dies of the 'coarse' overstrikes. It is hardly a coincidence that at this time the quality of the silver also declined.

On the second occasion, under Naillac, older deniers, including the 'Heredia' overstrikes, were recalled and restruck with a series of 'clumsy' types, most of which were anonymous. These types resemble, especially in the lettering and low striking quality, the 'emergency' gigliati of the master.[616] The variety of these types indicates that this recall may have been a lengthy process.

occurs in the gigliati of the master bearing an invocation on the other side.

612 Only chemical analysis could answer this question, as many of the Genoese gate billon deniers seem to have contained a low amount of silver.

613 Not all: **2079** seems overstruck on a Cypriot denier.

614 See above, n. 563. Gigliati of this type are not published either by Bernareggi (1964: 119-136) or by Beckenbauer (1973: 68-88). They are also absent from Sotheby's 1997 catalogue.

615 **2108**, **2109**, **2110**.

616 Kasdagli 2002: 64-67.

The third recall included all the overstruck deniers, all the 14th century obols and the few deniers which had hitherto escaped overstriking. This action probably prepared the ground for a monetary reform, towards the end of Naillac's rule or, more likely, under his successor, Antoni de Fluvià, who is known to have restored the minting quality of the gigliati[617] and introduced the first gold sequins. The recycling evidence is summarized below:

RECALL	OVERSTRIKE	DATE
Billon Hospitaller deniers and some foreign coins	Coarse types	After 1377, under Heredia or Naillac
Coarse overstrikes and eponymous deniers with Naillac arms	Clumsy overstrikes (generally overstruck more than once)	Naillac (1396-1421)
14th c. deniers and obols, including the overstruck issues and some foreign coins	Melting down for the issue of new 15th c. types	After 1403[119] or under Fluvià (1420s)

Figure 73: Recalls of issues based on the two major Hospitaller hoards.

We have to conclude that the first group of obols, which Schlumberger limited to the first half of the 14th century, continued in circulation until the early 15th century. Otherwise, it would be difficult to explain its dominant presence in the two major hoards. It remains to consider when the obols were first issued, and how the various types related to each other. The two major hoards, which contribute valuable information on coin circulation at the turn of the century, are crucial for our understanding of the obols.

3. *14th century copper obols*

Pegolotti makes no mention of a denomination lower than the denier, which probably means that the anonymous obols of Rhodes (PLS 116-133), of pure copper, entered circulation later than the deniers. It might be suggested that their low value made them irrelevant for commercial exchanges, but the argument is weak. Moreover, there are good reasons to believe that the obols entered circulation at a time when the deniers were already familiar tender. Nevertheless, the inscriptional and stylistic affinities between the two coins, balanced by the care taken to make it easy to tell them apart, signify that the coins circulated concurrently for a while.

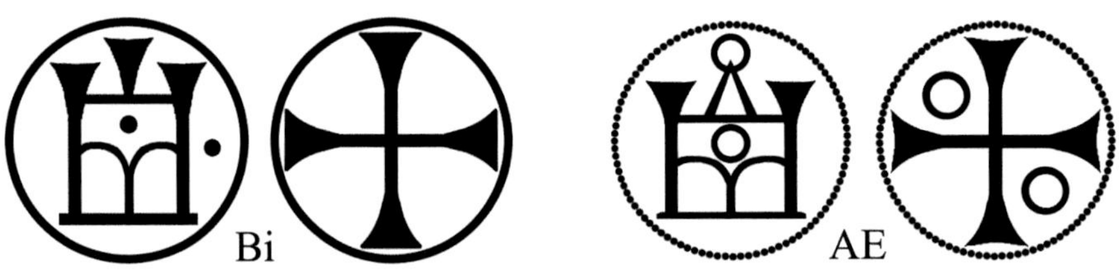

Figure 74: Simplified designs of early denier (left) and obol (right).

It is obvious that the building on the obverse of the obols, called a *châtel* by numismatists, is a modified janua, borrowing its pointed roof from the deniers tournois, with the addition of an annulet at the top. Annulets on two opposed quarters of the reverse field also helped to make obols distinctive. The obverse of the obols bore the legend +CIVITAS RODI(S) (instead of CIVIS) and the reverse +MAG(iste)R OSPITAL(IS) (without the h at the start of the second word). It is worth noting that the annulets on the reverse were borrowed from the *Amalricus* type obols of the kingdom of Jerusalem which, although named after king Amalric (1163-74), continued in circulation into the 13th century.[619] The following common features strengthen the relation between the Rhodian obols and the Amalricus type: (a) the switch of the annulets from quarters 1 and 4 to 2 and 3 in some issues, (b) their occasional replacement by platelets, (c) the variety of stops in the legends and (d) the weight which, in most specimens, is

---

[617] Schlumberger 1878: 255. The production of gigliati under Fluvià seems to have been limited (Metcalf 1995: 301; Sotheby's 1997: 104), but this does not undermine the reforming hypothesis.

[618] The date 1403 derives from a coin of Francesco II of Mytilene in the Italian hoard (**3343**) but may be extended, since *quattrini* of Francesco I Gonzaga (**3328**, Kamiros hoard) continued to be issued in Mantua until 1407. However, dating the two hoards *c.* 1443, the end of the reign of John I of Portugal (**3324**, Italian hoard), is not likely because then the absence of foreign issues of the first quarter of the 15th century, especially the deniers of Alfonso of Sicily (1416 ff.) frequently turning up as site finds in Rhodes, would be hard to explain.

[619] Metcalf 1995: 59-71 and Pl. 11.

roughly half a gram. Various stops (·, :, ∘, ⁚, ꝏ) recall issues of Genoa, probably the homeland of at least some of the moneyers who worked in Rhodes in the 14th century.[620]

To date, 129 14th-century obols have been recorded from archaeological excavations in Rhodes. With few exceptions, they are in poor condition (PLS. 134-138), discouraging analysis. However, the 4,096 obols of the Italian and Kamiros hoards, although generally very worn, are much more legible that the site finds. Careful examination led to the identification of many variations in details, leading to interesting conclusions about their production and relative chronology.

The first thing to note is that, in both hoards, two thirds of the total are anonymous copper obols of the 14th century (see Figure 72). There is also a signed type of master Raymond Berenger, unknown to Schlumberger, which has yet to turn up in excavations and is identified by the escutcheon at the end of the obverse legend (PL. 133); this escutcheon is found on all the gigliati of that master. The signed type was published some years ago, after a cursory examination of the Italian hoard.[621] The systematic inspection of both hoards revealed a total of 34 specimens.[622] At least two variants of the obverse can be reconstructed from these pieces, but only one for the reverse, as follows:

Obverse: châtel, +CIVITAS∘RODIS⛉
Reverse 1: cross with annulets in quarters 1 and 4, +MAGR∘SPITALI∘
Reverse 2: cross with annulets in quarters 2 and 3, +MAGR·OSPITALI⁚

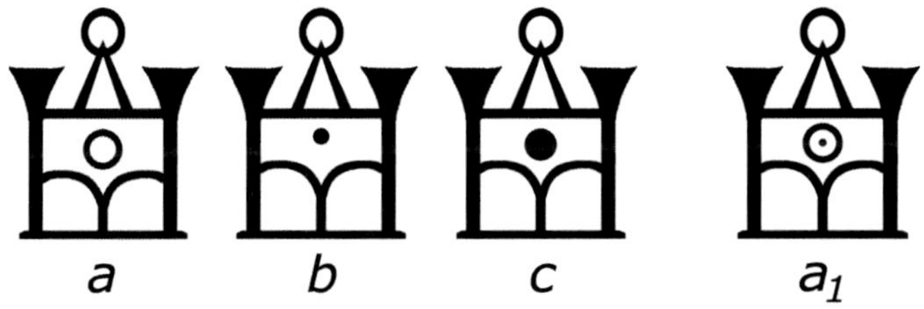

Figure 75: 14th century obols. Main variants of the châtel.

The 14th century obols come in a bewildering number of varieties. The differences between them occur both in the main design and in the details of the legend. On the châtel side (Figure 75), the annulet above the double arch within the building is often replaced by a dot or a platelet:

On the reverse (Figure 76), the annulets occupy either the first and fourth quarters of the cross, or the second and third. Occasionally, annulets are replaced by platelets:

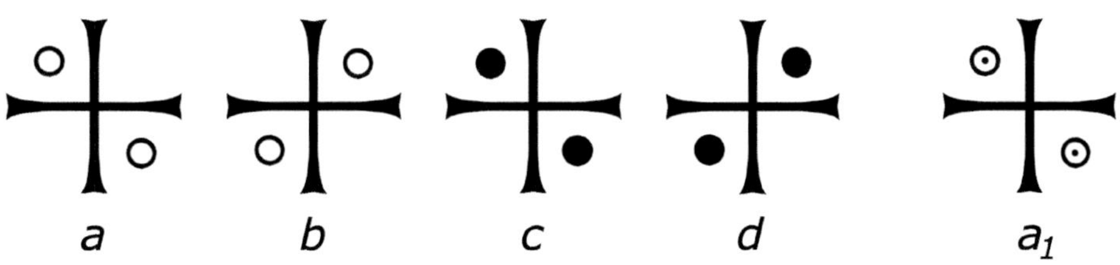

Figure 76: 14th c. obols. Main variants of the cross.

Figure 77: 'Juilly' obol. Obverse and reverse designs.

A variant of the annulet with a central dot, occasionally seen on either side of some variants, could be due to the engraving technique (Figs. 75-76, a_1). It is hard to assign any of the types to a particular ruler. A possible exception may be a group with platelets on the cross side, which stands out among the rest of the 14th century obols (Figure 77, PL. 132). The châtel on the reverse is very distinctive: its triangular roof is topped by a platelet, and there is a dot within the triangle as well as above the arches. In addition, thin needles protrude from the top of the vestigial towers or 'uprights'.

[620] *Corpus Nummorum Italicorum* I, Casa Savoia, 1910; Pesce and Felloni 1976; Baldassarri 2011: 37, Figure 7.
[621] Kasdagli 1996: 327-328.
[622] 23 in the Italian hoard and ten in the Kamiros hoard; all are illustrated on PL. 133 except **2732**.

This last feature also occurs in the billon deniers with the Juilly badge (fleur-de-lys).[623] The obols in question also share another characteristic of most of Juilly's deniers, the use of a colon as a stop in the legends. Moreover, they are the commonest obol types found in the two major hoards, probably due to the fact that they were the last to be issued, most likely under Juilly or, at a stretch, under Heredia.

The first observations concerning the details of the various types were made when the coins were entered in the relevant internal inventory of the Ephorate. There is a close stylistic relationship between the many variants which, excepting the issues assumed to belong to Robert de Juilly, does not encourage an analysis based on the evolution of die design, a criterion often found to be particularly misleading in numismatics anyway.[624] However, it was of the first importance to look for the time-span and rate of production of the obols, since two generations of moneyers could easily have worked for the Hospital's mint between 1332 and 1373. To answer this question it was necessary to sort out the many types[625] and locate common features which could serve as indicators for their sequential arrangement.

The procedure employed for the sorting of the types was based on a number of observations and the selection of indicators was dictated by practical considerations. Small differences were noted both in the main design and in the legends decorated with numerous kinds of stops. The legend on either side always starts with a crosslet pattée. On the châtel side, the two main versions differ in the final letter (+CIVITAS RODI or +CIVITAS RODIS) but there is also another version where the two words are joined as CIVITARODIS. On the side with the cross there are three variants of the second word: OSPITAL, OSPITALI or OSPITALIS, although the first word, MAG(iste)R is always abbreviated in the same way. The stops usually appear between the words and at the end of the legend, and are the following:

- One (•, ˙ , .), two (:), three (⁖, ∵, ⁘, ⁝) or four dots (⁘, ⁛ , ⁞)
- One, two or three annulets (°, ∘, ⸰, ⁂)
- A cogwheel, alone (✿) or flanked by a raised dot on either side (˙✿˙).

A single dot sometimes serves as replacement of a single letter (OSPIT˙LIS, OSPITAL˙S), while occasionally it also appears between the initial crosslet and the word following (e.g. +˙MAGR...) The letter L, often rendered as Ŀ or/ and in a ligature with the preceding A (ĦĿ) when at the end of the word (OSPITAL) is frequently joined to the final stop as a flourish, e.g. as Lᒋ, L:, Lᒋ•, L: or Lᒋ⁘. There are a number of versions for the letter A (Λ̄, Ā, Ⱥ, Ħ).[626] O is sometimes joined to D in the word RODI (ŒD), possibly due to crowding; while D is, on occasion, blurred or *doubled.* These, and other less apparent variations in the legends, are complicated by striking errors: the die may be larger than the flan, or struck off-centre or glancingly (so that part of the legend has not imprinted), or worn or, through use, have gathered filings or other dirt which clogs some details filling, for example, the inside of letters such as D and A.

The potentially high number of legend variants, particularly on the reverse, initially discouraged analysis based on them. The main design of both sides was much more manageable since its basic variants were easy to spot, probably on purpose. The side with the cross can easily be split into four main versions: there are either annulets or platelets in opposed quarters, either the first and fourth, or the second and third (Figure 76a-d). However, the results were too lopsided, as may be seen from the table below, where the various types in the Italian and Kamiros hoards are sorted according to the four versions of the reverse main design:

Variants of reverse design	Types (#)	Number of types	Percentage
Annulets in quarters 1 and 4	18, 18a, 12, 6, 20, 19, 20b, 24, 25, 26, 29, 10, 3, 2, 7, 23, 23a, 32, 34, 24a, 32, 34, 24a, 24b, 1, 4, 23b, 30, 53, 99, 57, 80, 47, 41, 48a, 50, 64, 90, 95d, 95, 89a, 96, 45, 141, 142, 143, 59, 60, 81, 87, 116, 116a, 116b, 117, 117b, 118, 119, 120, 121, 86, 122, 125, 114a, 114b, 88c, 44, 44a, 52, 52a, 136, 143a, 52d, 52e, 52f, 80a, 72, 72a, 77, 130, 127, 128, 131, 149, 114, 152, 157, 163, 163b, 163c, 146, 145, 151, 155, 160, 161, 161a, 88, 162,	98	75%
Annulets in quarters 2 and 3	166, 167, 172, 174	4	6%

[623] Kasdagli 1996: 326-327 and Eik. 8.

[624] Stewart 1969.

[625] For the purposes of this study 'type' represents the pieces sharing the same combination of obverse and reverse. Henceforth, the numbering of types is preceded by a # (hash).

[626] The character Ⱥ is not used in the transcription of the legends. When the A is open, a bold, underlined Λ̄ is used instead.

Variants of reverse design	Types (#)	Number of types	Percentage
Platelets in quarters 1 and 4	178, 178a, 182, 183, 183a, 185, 187, 188, 191, 192, 194, 194a, 194b, 194c, 205	15	10%
Platelets in quarters 2 and 3	199, 200, 201, 202	4	9%

Figure 78: Correspondence of reverse design variants and types.

Obviously, if three-fourths of the sufficiently legible obols fall within one reverse design variant, the exercise is not particularly helpful. The more complex punch was, undoubtedly, the one used to reproduce on the dies the design of the châtel. The existence of such punches is proven by the fact that various types share a particular châtel design, which gradually deteriorates through the use of the punch on heated metal, as shown by cases where the die reproduces a slanting châtel, or one whose base curves downwards.[627] The adoption of the obverse design as a basic criterion seems simpler, at first glance, since there are only three main versions, depending on the presence of a dot, an annulet or a platelet inside the châtel. If the legible coins are sorted accordingly, we get the following result:

Obverse design variants	Types (#)	Number of types	Percentage
Châtel with annulet inside	53, 99, 57, 80, 47, 41, 48a, 50, 64, 90, 95d, 95, 89a, 96, 45, 141, 142, 143, 59, 60, 81, 87, 116, 116a, 116b, 117, 117b, 118, 119, 120, 121, 86, 122, 125, 114a, 114b, 88c, 44, 44a, 52, 52a, 136, 143a, 52d, 52e, 52f, 80a, 72, 72a, 77, 130, 127, 128, 131, 166, 167, 194, 194a, 194b, 194c,	60	44%
Châtel with platelet inside	149, 114, 152, 157, 163, 163b, 163c, 146, 145, 151, 155, 160, 161, 161a, 88, 162, 172, 174	18	18%
Châtel with dot inside	18, 18a, 12, 6, 20, 19, 20b, 24, 25, 26, 29, 10, 3, 2, 7, 23, 23a, 32, 34, 24a, 32, 34, 24a, 24b, 1, 4, 23b, 30,178, 178a, 182, 183, 183a, 185, 187, 188, 191, 192,	38	29%
'Juilly type' châtel with dot inside	199, 200, 201, 202, 205	5	9%

Figure 79: Correspondence of obverse design with types (#) and numbers of coins.

The situation appears more balanced that in the preceding table, but this is not enough. In reality, things get more confusing because, in some cases, the interior of the annulet gets filled due to the clogging of the punch used for the sinking of the die, turning into a platelet. It could be supposed that the presence of platelets is entirely due to this process, but careful examination shows that we often have separate small punches for the platelets, whose diameter varies slightly from that of the annulets.

Despite such drawbacks, the early processing of the coins was based on the variants of the main designs. Then the coins which were worn too much to preserve a useful part of the lettering were put aside; the remaining 1,742 obols, 43% of the total from both major hoards, were further sorted according to the inscriptional details, also taking into account flaws and peculiarities displayed by particular dies or punches. Of the reasonably preserved obols used in the analysis described below, 60% derive from the Italian hoard and the rest are from the Kamiros hoard. This ratio should be sought as a yardstick for the verification of most of the types identified through the analysis, and of the emissions to which they are likely to belong.[628]

After sorting the coins according to the design of the cross, each of the four resulting groups was then split further using the central distinctive mark inside the châtel: dot, annulet or platelet. This was done to reduce as far as possible the quantity of coins that would then have to be compared according to the variations of the legends, in order to get to the number of obverse and reverse variants. In spite of the wear from long use and the careless striking,[629] it was finally possible to reconstruct 18 variants for the obverse, including the two belonging to the late issues assigned to Robert de Juilly or, less likely, to Juan Fernandez de Heredia. More particularly, there are 16 variants of the legend, but the mark inside the châtel adds at least two more to the obverse. The main problem

[627] Cf. **2630** (PL. 128) and **2380** (PL. 118) respectively.
[628] An emission should be said to include more than one type (pair of matched dies): the set of reverses is associated to a particular obverse should be included.
[629] The problem mostly lies in the fact that the hammering of most coins was, to some degree, off-centre. This probably means that the staple was not fixed on a stable surface.

here is the likelihood that the annulet was changed into a platelet through the wear of punches and dies.[630] No less than 53 variants of the reverse legend were identified,[631] and they may increase in the future, when all the coins contained in the two hoards are carefully examined. Taking into account variations of the cross, the obverse variants rise to 54.

It should be stressed that the above numbers do not correspond to actual dies but to groups of coins sharing a sufficient number of similarities in their details to ensure that a particular obverse or reverse is distinct from any other recorded in this study, although some of the recorded variants are indeed represented by a single die. The combination of a particular legend and main design variant on both sides of a coin determine the type (#) to which the coin belongs. The singularities of particular punches and the wear of the dies were also very helpful in the final stages of the sorting process, although their possibilities have not been exhausted.[632]

The first point established by the analysis is the average ratio of 1:3 between the variants of obverse and reverse, confirming that the obverse was indeed the side with the châtel. Even without the systematic recording of the dies, this indicates that for each staple die there were probably two to three trussels, the variation dependent on shifts of practice or accidents in the operation of the mint. Removing the five late types distinctive from the rest, from the combination of 15 obverse and 49 reverse variants a maximum of over 700 combinations would be possible, assuming that all dies were available at the same time. Naturally this does not happen, but over a hundred types have been identified so far.

In the early phases of the sorting, the apparent number of types was almost double but was gradually reduced when familiarity with the identifying features of each type grew. Thus, successive emendations resulted in the deletion of several initial type numbers (#), while others had to be further divided, the # number being preserved with the addition of letters.[633] To avoid mistakes, no attempt has been made to renumber the types, since the present sorting has not exhausted the possibilities of the available material. Nevertheless, the work is sufficiently advanced to reach significant conclusions which further progress is unlikely to overturn.[634]

The 104 types identified so far are not equally represented in the current sample; indeed, there is wide variation in the representation of even the five late types, as may be seen in Figure 80.

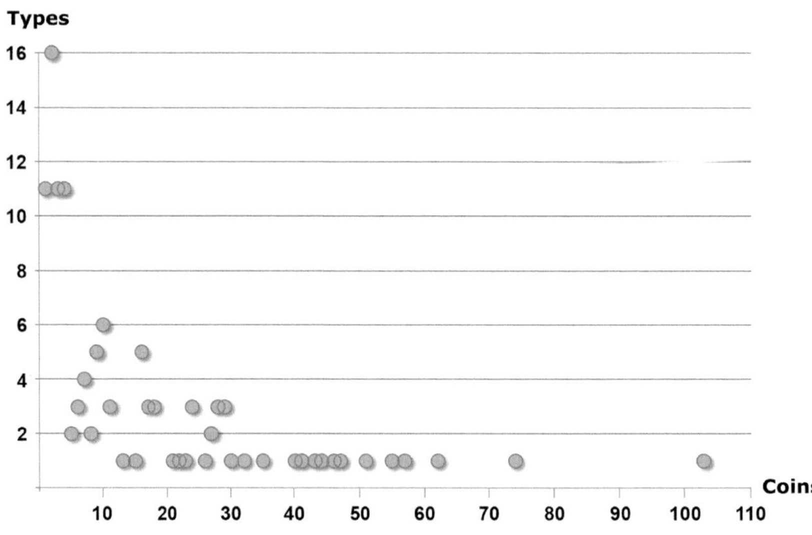

Figure 80: Representation of 14th c. obol types in the legible selection from the large hoards.

[630] Cf. **2622** and **2623** (PL. 128, #44).
[631] This number includes the four types of the 'Juilly' obols.
[632] Recording all the letter punches and marking the progressive wear of every die, both necessary to determine the number of dies, was not attempted in the present study, whose focus was the establishment of the broader picture.
[633] E.g. #183 and #183a or #24a and #24b.
[634] One of them concerns the sequencing of the types which, as will be seen, requires caution in the final numbering, which could only follow the identification of the dies.

64 of the types are represented by less than ten coins each, piling up at the left side of the graph. One third of the total of types is defined by only one to three pieces. At the other end, the commonest late type assigned to Juilly is represented by 103 pieces at the far right of the graph. The other four types of the late group are much less common, with 24, 17, 16 and 4 pieces respectively. In total, these five types correspond to 164 coins, 9% of the sample and this dominance is probably due to their late date. Another 15 types are represented by 30-74 pieces each. It would be natural to assume that the rarer types were earlier that those better represented, but it would be a mistake to assume that successive emissions were of equal size. The disparity in the representation of the various types imposed the need for further exploration, with the assistance of technical or stylistic affinities which might define further groups of types. It is also not unlikely that the low representation of some types is due to the early decommissioning of some dies, perhaps because of faulty making or careless handling. The detailed description of types which follows begins with the variations of the obverse, which are discussed according to legend, since this provides greater detail.

The obverse, or châtel side, of the 14th c. obols dated includes the following legend variants:

✠ᑕIVITΛS∘RODI
✠ᑕIVITAS∘RODI
✠ᑕIVITΛS∘RODI·
✠ᑕIVITAS∘RODI∘
✠ᑕIVITAS∘RODI∴
✠ᑕIVITΛS∘RODI˙✿˙
✠ᑕIVITAS∘RODIS
✠ᑕIVITAS·RODIS˙
✠ᑕIVITΛS∘RODIS
✠ᑕIVITAS∘RODIS:·
✠ᑕIVITAS∘RODIS∘
✠ᑕIVITΛRODIS
✠SIVITAS∘RODI·
✠SIVITAS∘RODI:·
✠ᑕIVITΛS:RODI
✠ᑕIVITΛS:RODI·

i. Legend ✠ᑕIVITΛS∘RODI (PLS 116-117)

Occurs in three versions (I, II and III). In the first (I) two die versions are distinguished by legend, where D occurs either joined to O (ᑕD) or appears doubled. The second version (II) is distinguished by the form of the twin arches inside the châtel, which look like the transverse section of an open book (Figure 81a).

Figure 81: Selected variants and transformations of the châtel.

In both these versions the mark above the double arches is a dot. Version I is found in types #6 and #29 (variant with ᑕD), #18, #18a and #26 (variant with doubled D). However, versions I and II were also used concurrently: they occur together in types #12, #19/20 and #25. It is possible, of course, that a more in-depth study of the material will reveal that the two variants also occur together in more of the above types.

The third version (III), found in types #53 and #149, is characterized by the châtel, which has been impressed with two different punches whose only differences are an imperfection above the left end of the base in the first and the fact that the arches in the second are very low. The châtel in type #53 bears an annulet mark inside, above the arches. In type #149 a platelet replaces the annulet. However, as both punches occur both in types #53 and #149, while the reverse legend is also the same, the two types must have been issued together. It is possible that the platelet of type #149 was a result of the clogging of the annulet punch inside the châtel.[635] This interpretation is also supported by the percentage of the identified coins of the two types in the two hoards:

#53: Italian Period Hoard 70%, Kamiros Hoard 30%
#149: Italian Period Hoard 33%, Kamiros Hoard 67%

The sum of both types results in a ratio of 1:1 between the two hoards.[636]

[635] It seems that ring-shaped punches were used in the engraving of the châtel prototypes, for the mark inside as well as the top of the triangular roof.
[636] To reach the expected ratio between the two hoards, deriving from their relative size, at least another type should be added to the particular

At the end of the inscription a small raised dot in type #6 may be due to a die imperfection. Details helpful for the sorting of the reverses of types #10, #20b and #24, which bear the same legend, are unclear due to lack of specimens.

ii. Legend ✠ϹIVITHS∘RODI (PLS 118-119)

At least two châtel punches have been used, the mark inside being an annulet; they seem to coexist in types #41, #47, #50, #57, #64, #80, #95, #95d and #96. More characteristic is the one (Figure 81c) where the right arch has a hooked right end not properly joined to the right vertical (tower) of the châtel. Thus, is some specimens this end is broken off, resulting in an incomplete arch.[637] Another châtel punch has higher arches, the one on the left squarish in shape and broader than the right.[638] The deterioration of the die in the legend, due not only to wear but also to the adherence of filings, is obvious in some specimens.[639]

iii. Legend ✠ϹIVITΛS∘RODI· (PL. 120)

Shared among four types, #45, #141, #142 and #143. The châtel, identical in all of them, has an annulet inside and, oddly, a dot to the right field (Figure 81b), an idiosyncrasy it shares only with the janua on the obverse of the billon deniers of the period. In all four types the crosslet at the start of the reverse legend is flanked by dots. Also, the D on the obverse is doubled, but not identical to that encountered in a variant of obverse i (I). As far as the condition of the coins allows, it seems that only one die was responsible for this obverse.

iv. Legend ✠ϹIVITHS∘RODI∘ (PL. 120)

Four types, #59, #60, #87 and #194c. Two different punches for the châtel, which bears an annulet within. In some specimens of the first variant (a) the lower part of the roof triangle has an imperfection due to the deterioration of the punch. In the second variant (b) the verticals of the châtel splay somewhat upwards. Variant b appears alongside a in types #60 and #194c. The variant b châtel is usually so worn that the annulet is not clear and, in some cases, might be read as a platelet. Oddly, two pieces belonging to variant b, one of type #60 and the other of type #194c,[640] seem to bear a dot in the right field next to the châtel, as in obverse iii, although the design of the châtel is clearly different. In type #59 only variant a has been recorded so far; while in #87, represented by only two specimens, variant b has been used.

v. Legend ✠ϹIVITHS∘RODI⸎ (PL. 121)

Three types, #178, #178a and #188. Possibly a single die, in which the châtel recalls variant iv b, although the mark inside it is a dot and not an annulet.

vi. Legend ✠ϹIVITΛS∘RODI·∘· (PLS 121-123)

This legend is shared by many types. Most of them (#86, #116, #116a, #116b, #117, #117b, #118, #119, #120, #121, #122, #125, #194 and #194a) bear an annulet mark inside the châtel. Three types, however, #163, #163b and #163c, have a platelet instead, and the châtel punch used in the sinking of their die shows other peculiarities, such as a roof annulet inclining to the right and the right side of the roof triangle blurred.[641] The obverse legend in types #163 and #163c, and perhaps also in #163b, has a doubled D, similar -if not identical- to its parallel in obverse iii.

It is clear that two distinctive châtel punches have been used, of which the one with the annulet mark, in some specimens of types #118, #119 and #120 and all the coins of types #117b, #194 and #194a,[642] has an additional characteristic, probably due to accident: a thin line joins the base of the roof triangle with the upper left splaying part of the right tower. Thus, the production sequence of types must be #86/ #116/ #116a/ #116b→#118 / #119/ #120→#194/ #194a.

---

emission. The Italian hoard (Figure 69) contained 2,840 anonymous obols, while the Kamiros hoard 1,256, that is to say a ratio of 7:3. However, differences in the relative preservation of the coins in the two hoards does not permit the same ratio in identifications: the actual ratio for identified coins is nearer to 5:3.

[637] Cf. #47 (**2372, 2373**), #50 (**2375**), #80 (**2395**).

[638] #41 (**2364, 2368**), #47 (**2369**).

[639] Cf. **2390** (#80) which evolves into **2382** (#50).

[640] **2432** and **2435** respectively.

[641] This could be a reason to split this obverse in two, if the evidence of obverse xii did not exist (below).

[642] To date, type #117b is represented by a single specimen (**2479**), while type #194a by two (**2485, 2486**).

vii. Legend ✠CIVITAS◦RODIS (PL. 124)

Shared between types #2, #7, #23, #24a, #24b, #182 and #187. The mark inside the châtel, probably from a single die, is a dot. Perhaps type #166, with an annulet inside, shares the same legend, but it is represented by a single specimen (**2532**), not fully legible.

viii. Legend ✠CIVITAS·RODIS· (PL. 125)

Types #114, #152, #157, #172 and #174. The châtel in this group is not well preserved, but in some specimens looks more compact in comparison to others, where it appears to splay upwards. When fully legible, with two exceptions, the diacritical mark inside the châtel is a platelet.[643]

The precise (raised) placement of the dot at the end of the legend possibly connects this obverse to obverse ix. In any case, there are at least two dies, without counting details in the legend. Two reverses, those of types #114 and #174, occur in both variants of the signed obverse of Raymond Berenger. Thus, obverse vii probably dates from the years 1365-73.

ix. Legend ✠CIVITAS◦RODIS· (PL. 126)

Only type #114b, probably from a single die, with an annulet inside the châtel. Type #88c, with only three partly legible specimens, may also belong here.

x. Legend ✠CIVITAS◦RODIS⁖ (PL. 126)

Types #1, #4, #23b and #183. Perhaps type #183a also belongs to the group, but the identified specimens do not provide sufficient evidence. The relationship between the other types is strengthened by a particular feature, which was probably an engraving error on the châtel punch. This is a slanting line starting from the upper right corner of the châtel interior and ending at the base of the central support of the double arch. It does not appear on all the specimens, allowing for the use of two dies concurrently. The diacritical mark inside the châtel is a dot.

xi. Legend ✠CIVITAS◦RODIS◦ (PL. 127)

Types #30, #185, #191 and #192. A single die. The diacritical mark in the châtel is a dot.

xii. Legend ✠CIVITARODIS (PLS 127-130)

Used in several types. #44, #44a, #52, #52a, #52d, #52e, #52f, #72, #72a, #72b, #77, #80a, #136, #143a and #192 bear an annulet inside the châtel, while #88, #145, #146, #151, #155, #160, #161, #161a and #162 have a platelet instead. At first glance, there are three châtel punches with an annulet inside and one more with a platelet. However, careful examination shows that there are only two punches, which were altered through use.

The first punch (Figure 81 d_1) is characterized by the preservation of part of the guiding lines for the drawing of the châtel, which joined the ends of the base with the opposite upper inner corners, whose projected crossing marked the location of the diacritical annulet. The other feature of this version of the châtel is the annulet at the top of the roof triangle, leaning slightly to the left (types #44a, #72, #72a, #77). While in use, and probably during the production of types #44 and #80, an elongated filing got stuck on the punch, parallel and a little above the base of the châtel on the left side: it projects outwards as far as the beaded circle bordering the field of the main design (Figure 81 d_2). In this condition the punch was also used for types #52, #52a, #52, #52d, #52e, #52f, #136 and #143a. The presence of more than one die is betrayed by the varying thickness of particular letters in the legend.

During the production of type #44, another châtel punch was employed (Figure 81 e_1), which also preserved the remnants of the guiding diagonals at the endings of the base. The diacritical mark inside is again an annulet, but the annulet on top of the triangular roof leans heavily to the right. Next, during the sinking of a die for type #145a, the annulet mark was clogged and became a platelet. Soon after, the blurring of the right slope of the roof appeared: it is evident in types #88, #145, #146, #151, #155, #160, #161, #161a and #162 (Figure 81 e_2). It should be noted that the

[643] The first exception concerns a piece of type #174 (**2551**) with illegible legend, although the annulet inside is particularly clear. The second concerns site-find **2852** (PL. 137) which, although in mediocre condition, probably belongs to type #172.

same punch, in its worn phase, was also used for types of obverse vi. One of the dies produced with this punch in its late stage is made distinctive by a thorny projection on the inner side of the vertical of the letter D.

xiii. Legend ✠SIVITHS∘RODI· (PL. 131)

Types #127, #128, #130, and #194b. One die, with a châtel punch characterized by low asymmetrical arches within, and by an unusually prominent annulet mark.

xiv. Legend ✠SIVITHS∘RODI⁝ (PL. 131)

A single type, #131. Limited sample, but the châtel punch has higher arches and a smaller annulet than obverse xiii.

xv. Legend ✠CIVITAS:RODI (PL. 132)

Types #199, #201, #202 and #205. The form of the châtel changes, as well as the style. This is probably the work of a new engraver. The verticals ('towers') are substantially thicker and straighter; on their splayed tops thin 'needles' are visible. The roof triangle has a broader base, a small dot inside, and the annulet at the top is replaced by a platelet. The mark within the châtel is also a dot. The open A of the legend recalls earlier reverses 11, 17, 43-44, but the lettering looks generally coarser.

xvi. Legend ✠CIVITAS:RODI· (PL. 132)

Only one type, #200. The châtel punch is in the same style with that of obverse xv, but the building itself is narrower.

The variants of the reverse legend are far more numerous than those of the obverse, and the list may not yet be complete, due to the wear of the available material. So far, 53 have been recorded as follows in Figure 82.

The variants of the reverse legend will be cited below using Arabic numerals (without the # symbol), to avoid confusion with the variants of the obverse, where minuscule Latin numerals are used. It should be kept in mind that the combination of the two is one of the basic distinctions of a type, albeit not the only one, because two types bearing the same legend may differ from each other as to the main design. A specific variant of the reverse legend is not necessarily associated with a single variant of the cross, or of the obverse. Still, the reverse legend usually occurs only in association with a particular variant of the cross, thus permitting the use of its numeral for the definition of the type as far as the reverse is concerned.[644] Its association with more than one obverse (*linkage*) provides evidence that may assist in the chronological succession of the types. Of the recorded reverse legend variants, 27 (recurring variants) are associated with more than one variants of the obverse or accompany more than one variants of the reverse.[645] Given their significance, they are described and discussed before the remaining reverse legends.[646]

Recurring reverse variants

1. Legend ✠MAGR· OSPITAL

Appears in types #44a (PL. 127), #45 (PL. 120), #117b (PL. 122) and #146 (PL. 128), all belonging to the cross variant with annulets in the 1st and 4th quarter. Types #44a, #45 and #117b bear on the obverse a châtel with an annulet as a diacritical mark inside, while type #146 has on the obverse a châtel with a platelet inside.

In type #44a a dot is probably present between the crosslet and the M at the start of the legend. In type #45, the châtel is accompanied by a dot on the right field. The available sample is not sufficient for the full reconstruction of type #117b: the first A in the legend is completely illegible. In type #146, the L at the end of the legend in some pieces seems decorated with more than one dot, but this may be a result of the degradation of the die.

644 Excepting legends 15, 16 and 35.
645 They are nos. 1, 2, 3, 5, 7, 8, 10, 11, 13, 14, 15, 16, 17, 18, 19, 21, 22, 28, 29, 30, 31, 34, 35, 41, 43, 44 and 47.
646 The solitary variants are nos. 4, [6], 9, 12, 20, 22a, 23, 24, 25, 26, 27, 27a, 30a, 32, 33, 36, 37, 38, 39, 42, 45, 46, 48, 49, 50, 51.

1	+MΛGR·OSPITΛLı·	27	+·MΛGR[ ]OSPIT[AL]I·
2	+MΛGR°OSPITΛLı°	27a	+·MΛGR[ ]OSPITALI[·]
3	+MΛGR·OSPITΛL⁝	28	+·MΛGR✿OSPITALI·
4	+M[Λ]GR·OSPIT[Λ]Lı[·:]	29	+MAGR°OSPITALI·
5	+MAGR°OSPITALı·	30	+MAGR°OSPITALI·:
6	+MAGR°OSPITALr·	30a	+MAGR°OSPITA[LI·:]
7	+MAGR·OSPITALı·:	31	+MΛGR·OSPITΛLıIS
8	+MAGR·OSPITALr⁝·	32	+MΛGR°OSPIT[AL]IS
9	+MΛGR°OSPITALı°	33	+MΛGR°OSPITΛLIS
10	+MΛGR°OSPITΛLıI·	34	+MAGR·OSPITA[Lı]IS·
11	+[MΛ̲GR°OSPITALI·	35	+MAGR°OSPITALIS
12	+MΛG...OSPITΛLı·[I	36	+MΛGR·OSPITALIS
13	+MΛGR°OSPITΛLıI°	37	+MΛGR°OSPITALIS
14	+MΛGR·OSPITΛLıI°	38	+MAGR°OSPITALIS
15	+MΛGR·OSPITΛLıI8	39	+MAGR°OSPITALIS·
16	+MΛGR°SPITΛLI°	41	+MAGR°OSPITALIS::
17	+MΛ̲GR°OSPITALI·:·	42	+MAGR°OSPITALıIS°
18	+MΛ̲GR°OSPITA[Lr·I·:·]	43	+MΛ̲GR°OSPITALS:
19	+MΛ̲GR°OSPITA[LI°	44	+MΛ̲GR°OSPITAL·S
20	+MΛGR°OSPITALıI°	45	+MΛGR°OSPIT̄·LıIS
21	+MAGR·OSPITALI·	46	+MΛGR°OSPIT̄·LıI·S
22	+MAGR°OSPITALıI·	47	+MΛGR°OSPIT̄·LıIS·
22a	+MAGR°OSPITΛLıI°	48	+MΛGR·OSPITΛLı
23	+MAGR°OSPITALI°	49	+MΛGR:OSPITΛLı
24	+MΛGR°OSPITALI·	50	+MAGR:OSPITALı⁝
25	+MΛGR°OSPITALI·:	51	+MΛGR:OSPITΛLıI·
26	+MΛGR°OSPITALI°		

Figure 82: Variants of the reverse legend.

2. Legend +MΛGR°OSPITΛL°

Occurs in types #52 (PL. 129), #53 (PL. 117), #149 (PL. 117) and #151 (PL. 129). They all belong to the cross variant with annulets in the 1st and 4th quarter. The two first bear on the obverse a châtel with an annulet inside, while the other two have a platelet.

In type #52 there are at least two dies, since the position of the annulet in the 4th quarter is not the same in all the coins.[647] The reverse of some specimens of type #53 is marked by the entrapment of filings at the end of the legend.[648] At least two dies are also present in type #149, of which the more common has a centrally placed annulet in the 4th quarter. In some specimens, the annulet in the 4th quarter is larger.[649] Type #151 looks more worn than the others, and on some coins the lower half of the vertical of the cross seems shorter.

3. Legend +MΛGR·OSPITΛL⁝

Occurs in types #44 and #145 (PL. 128), which belong to the cross variant with annulets on the 1st and 4th quarter. The first has an annulet mark inside the châtel on the obverse, while the second has a platelet. Some specimens of both types share the same die, whose identifying feature is the top of the letter R. This strengthens the hypothesis put forward in the case of obverse xii.

647 Cf. **2631, 2635.**
648 Cf. **2352, 2354, 2355.**
649 Cf. **2361, 2362.**

5. Legend ✠MAGR◦OSPITAL ·

Occurs in types #47 (PL. 118), #130 (PL. 131), #1 (PL. 126) and #2 (PL. 124). They all belong to the cross variant with annulets in the 1st and 4th quarter. The first two bear on the obverse a châtel with an annulet within, while in the other two the diacritical mark is a dot.

The ending of the #47 legend is clearly L·. Two dies are distinguishable; in one the ending of the legend is compressed, while in the other the final dot is larger. #130 is similar to #47. It also has two dies, distinguished by the form of the final serif in the L, and its decorative dot. Some pieces of #1 and #2 are problematic: they might belong to a separate variant, since the final L is incomplete. It might end in a curve connected to the dot following, perhaps with the addition of another dot above the curve, where the die struck off the flan. There could be at least three variants: L·, L or L·.

8. Legend ✠MAGR· OSPITAL∵

Found in types #50 (PL. 118) and #12 (PL. 116). They both belong to the cross variant with annulets in the 1st and 4th quarter. The first bears on the obverse a châtel with an annulet inside, while the second has a dot instead. The reverse of both types has been struck from the same dies, at least three of them; they may be distinguished from each other by the arrangement of the final ornament in the legend: in the first its four dots are irregularly arranged, in the second the ornament appears compressed and in the third there are only three dots.

10. Legend ✠MΛGR◦OSPITΛLI·

Found in types #52a (PL. 129), #120 (PL. 122), #160 (PL. 129), and #163b (PL. 122), belonging to the cross variant with annulets in the 1st and 4th quarter. The first two have an annulet within the châtel on the obverse, while the others have a platelet (cf. obverse i, III).

11. Legend ✠MΛGR◦OSPITALI[·]

Found in types #57 (PL. 118) and #4 (PL. 126). They both belong to the cross variant with annulets in the 1st and 4th quarter. The first shows an annulet within the châtel on the obverse, while the second has a dot instead. The first A of the legend is open, a form also present in variants 17, 43 and 44 of the reverse.

13. Legend ✠MΛGR◦OSPITΛLI◦

Occurs in types #136 and #155 (PL. 130), #157 (PL. 125) and #194 (PL. 122). The first three belong to the cross variant with annulets in the 1st and 4th quarter and the fourth to the cross variant with platelets in the same quarters. #136 and #194 have on the obverse a châtel with an annulet inside, which in #155 and #157 is replaced by a platelet.

17. Legend ✠MΛGR◦OSPITALI∵

Occurs in types #18 (PL. 116), #23 (PL. 124), #23b (PL. 126) and #80 (PL. 119), all belonging to the cross variant with annulets in the 1st and 4th quarter. The first A in the legend is open, a form also occurring in variants 11, 43 and 44. On the obverse all bear a châtel with a dot inside. Two dies have been used for the reverse of #23, of which one shows a split at the end of the right branch of the cross. The same cross punch has been used in the reverse of type #18, rotated 90° counterclockwise. Type #23b also probably shares the same die as type #18, although the upper dot in the group of four composing the final ornament of the legend lies off the flan.

21. Legend ✠MAGR· OSPITALI·

Occurs in types #59 (PL. 120), #64 (PL. 118), #127 and #131 (PL. 131). They all belong to the cross variant with annulets in the 1st and 4th quarters; on the obverse they bear a châtel with an annulet inside. There are two dies in type #59, distinguishable by the difference in the thickness of the final letter I. Type #64 also shows a thick I. The four types show stylistic affinity, with graceful finials on the cross, although the sample is not sufficient to establish the details of type #131.

22. Legend ✠MAGR◦OSPITALI·

Occurs in types #60 (PL. 120) and #128 (PL. 131), both belonging to the cross variant with annulets in the 1st and 4th quarter, and bear on the obverse an annulet inside the châtel. In two specimens of type #60 the right branch of the cross is shorter,[650] so two dies were used in its striking. This does not seem to hold true for type #128.

28. Legend ✠[·]MĀGR☼OSPIT[AL]I·

It occurs in types #143 (PL. 120) and #143a (PL. 128), which belong to the cross variant with annulets in the 1st and 4th quarter and show an annulet inside the châtel on the obverse. However, the châtel is accompanied by a dot at the right field. In type #143a there are two dies, differing in the placement of the cogwheel used as a stop between the words of the legend. The commonest of them was also used in type #143. Another feature shared between the two types is the dot between the crosslet at the start of the legend and the M following.

29. Legend ✠MAGR◦OSPITALI·

Occurs in types #6 (PL. 116) and #7 (PL. 124). They belong to the cross variant with annulets in the 1st and 4th quarter and on the obverse have a châtel with a dot within.

30. Legend ✠MAGR◦OSPITALI·⁚

Occurs in types #80a (PL. 128), #125 (PL. 123) and #19/20 (PL. 117). They all belong to the cross variant with annulets in the 1st and 4th quarter. The first two bear on the obverse a châtel with an annulet inside, which in the third is replaced by a dot. In type #19/20 two dies are distinguished by the arrangement of the three dots at the end of the legend.

31. Legend ✠MĀGR·OSPITĀLIS

Occurs in types #121 (PL. 121), #161 (PL. 130), #163 (PL. 121) and #26 (PL. 116). They all belong to the cross variant with annulets in the 1st and 4th quarter. The first shows on the obverse a châtel with an annulet within, the two following a châtel with a platelet and the fourth one a châtel with a dot inside. All the types have small-sized annulets in the quarters of the cross. The available sample for type #26 is not sufficient for the establishment of a full description.

34. Legend ✠MAGR· OSPITALIS·

Occurs in types #183a (PL. 126), #187 (PL. 124), #188 (PL. 121) and #194b (PL. 131). They all belong to the cross variant with annulets in the 1st and 4th quarter. The first three show on the obverse a châtel with a dot within, while the last has an annulet instead. The placement of the final dot in the legend, either centrally or raised, should rather be considered the feature of a die.

35. Legend ✠MAGR◦OSPITALIS

Occurs in types #87 (PL. 120), #30 (PL. 127), #178a (PL. 121), #182 (PL. 124), #183 (PL. 126), #185 (PL. 127) and #194c (PL. 120). Types #87 and #30 belong to the cross variant with annulets in the 1st and 4th quarter, while the rest to that with platelets in the same quarters. Types #87 and 194c show on the obverse a châtel with an annulet within, while the rest have a dot instead. There are two versions of type #185, of which one has a dot at the end of the legend, and at least three dies, since the platelets in the quarters of the cross in **2585** are smaller than in the others of the type. In type #194c there is probable evidence of blanks struck while warm.[651] The sample for type #30 is not sufficient to establish all its details.

[650] **2428** and **2429**.

[651] In **2435** and **2436** the cross is more compressed than in **2437** although the typically squashed dividing annulet in the legend is shared by all three specimens.

36. Legend ✠ᗰΛGR·OSPITΑL:IS

Occurs in types #52e (PL. 129), #88c (PL. 126), #122 (PL. 121), #88 (PL. 130) and #163c (PL. 122). They all belong to the cross variant with annulets in the 1st and 4th quarter. The first three bear on the obverse a châtel with an annulet within, replaced in the other two by a platelet.

41. Legend ✠ᗰΑGR◦OSPITΑL:IS⁚⁚

Occurs in types #95d (PL. 119) and #20b (PL. 117). They both belong to the cross variant with annulets in the 1st and 4th quarter. The first bears on the obverse a châtel with an annulet within, and the second with a dot. Type #20b is represented by a single specimen.

43. Legend ✠ᗰΛ̲GR◦OSPITΑL:S:

Occurs in types #95 (PL. 119), #10 (PL. 117) and #24a (PL. 124). All three belong to the cross variant with annulets in the 1st and 4th quarter of the cross, and were apparently struck with the same die, judging from the placement of the annulet in the 4th quarter of the cross. The first A of the legend is open, a form also encountered in types 11, 17 and 44. The first type bears on the obverse a châtel with an annulet within, while the other two have a dot instead.

44. Legend ✠ᗰΛ̲GR◦OSPITΑL:'S

Occurs in types #96, #24 (PL. 119) and #24b (PL. 124). All three belong to the cross variant with annulets in the 1st and 4th quarter. The first A of the legend is open, a form also encountered in types 11, 17 and 43. The first type bears on the obverse a châtel with an annulet within, while the other two have a dot instead. The die of type #24b seems to have also been used for the reverse of type #96, judging from the peculiarity in the annulet of the 1st quarter.

47. Legend ✠ᗰΛGR[◦]OSPIT·L:IS·

Occurs in types #52d (PL. 129), #116a (PL. 123) and #162 (PL. 129). All three belong to the cross variant with annulets in the 1st and 4th quarter. The first two bear on the obverse a châtel with an annulet within, while the last has a platelet instead. Type #162 has two variants, of which one shows a dot at the end of the legend.[652]

Solitary variants

[45]. Legend ✠ᗰ[Λ]GR· OSPIT[Λ]L[•⁚]

Type #142. Annulets in the 1st and 4th quarter of the cross. On the obverse (iii), the diacritical inside the châtel, which is accompanied by a dot to the right field, is an annulet.

6. Legend ✠ᗰΑGR◦OSPITΑL·

Type #41 (PL. 118). Annulets in the 1st and 4th quarter of the cross. On the obverse (ii) the diacritical mark is an annulet.

9. Legend ✠ᗰΛGR◦OSPITΑL◦

Type #117 (PL. 123). Annulets in the 1st and 4th quarter of the cross. On the obverse (vi), the diacritical mark is an annulet.

12. Legend ✠ᗰΛG…OSPITΛL·[I

Type #194a (PL. 122). Platelets in the 1st and 4th quarter of the cross. On the obverse (vi), the diacritical mark is an annulet.

[652] **2649.**

14. Legend +ᗰΛGR·OSPITΛLI°

Type #172 (PL. 125). Platelets on the 2nd and 3rd quarter of the cross. On the obverse (viii), the diacritical mark is an platelet.

20. Legend +ᗰΛGR°OSPITĦLI°

Type #118 (PL. 122). Annulets in the 1st and 4th quarter of the cross. On the obverse (vi), the diacritical mark is an annulet.

22a. Legend +ᗰĦGR°OSPITΛLI°

Type #114b (PL. 126). Annulets in the 1st and 4th quarter of the cross. On the obverse (ix), the diacritical mark is an annulet.

23. Legend +ᗰĦGR°OSPITĦLI°

Type #178 (PL. 121). Platelets in the 1st and 4th quarter of the cross. On the obverse (v), the diacritical mark is a dot.

24. Legend +ᗰΛGR°OSPITĦLI·

Type #72 (PL. 127). Annulets in the 1st and 4th quarter of the cross. On the obverse (xii), the diacritical mark is a dot.

25. Legend +ᗰΛGR°OSPITĦLI ⁖

Type #77 (PL. 127). Annulets in the 1st and 4th quarter of the cross. On the obverse (xii), the diacritical mark is an annulet.

26. Legend +ᗰΛGR°OSPITĦLI°

Type #72a (PL. 127). Annulets in the 1st and 4th quarter of the cross. On the obverse (xii), the diacritical mark is an annulet.

27. Legend +·ᗰΛGR[ ]OSPIT[ĦL]I·

Type #141 (PL. 120). Annulets in the 1st and 4th quarter of the cross. On the obverse (iii), the diacritical inside the châtel, which is accompanied by a dot to the right field, is an annulet.

27a. Legend +·ᗰΛGR[ ]OSPITĦLI[·]

Type #119 (PL. 122). Annulets in the 1st and 4th quarter of the cross. On the obverse (vi), the diacritical mark is an annulet.

30a. Legend +ᗰĦGR°OSPITĦ[LI ⁖]

Type #191 (PL. 127). Platelets in the 1st and 4th quarter of the cross. On the obverse (xi), the diacritical mark is a dot.

32. Legend +ᗰΛGR°OSPIT[ĦL]IS

Type #86 (PL. 123). Annulets in the 1st and 4th quarter of the cross. On the obverse (vi), the diacritical mark is an annulet.

33. Legend +ᗰΛGR°OSPITΛLIS

Type #161a (PL. 130). Annulets in the 1st and 4th quarter of the cross. On the obverse (xii), the diacritical mark is an platelet.

37. Legend ✠ᗰΛGR◦OSPITAL'IS

Type #52f (PL. 128). Annulets in the 1st and 4th quarter of the cross. On the obverse (xii), the diacritical mark is an annulet.

38. Legend ✠ᗰAGR◦OSPITAL'IS

Type #25 (PL. 116). Annulets in the 1st and 4th quarter of the cross. On the obverse (i), the diacritical mark is a dot.

39. Legend ✠ᗰAGR·OSPITAL'IS·

Type #29 (PL. 116). Annulets in the 1st and 4th quarter of the cross. On the obverse (i), the diacritical mark is a dot.

42. Legend ✠ᗰAGR◦OSPITAL'IS◦

Type #192 (PL. 127). Platelets in the 1st and 4th quarter of the cross. On the obverse (xi), the diacritical mark is a dot.

45. Legend ✠ᗰΛGR◦OSPIT'·L'IS

Type #116 (PL. 123). Annulets in the 1st and 4th quarter of the cross. On the obverse (vi), the diacritical mark is an annulet.

46. Legend ✠ᗰΛGR◦OSPIT'·L'I·S

Type #116b (PL. 123). Annulets in the 1st and 4th quarter of the cross. On the obverse (vi), the diacritical mark is an annulet.

48. Legend ✠ᗰΛGR· OSPITΛL

Type #200 (PL. 132). Platelets in the 2nd and 3rd quarter of the cross. On the obverse (xvi) late châtel variant (Juilly or early Heredia) with dot inside and within the roof triangle.

49. Legend ✠ᗰΛGR:OSPITΛL

Type #199 (PL. 132). Platelets in the 2nd and 3rd quarter of the cross. On the obverse (xv) late châtel variant with dot inside and within the roof triangle.

50. Legend ✠ᗰAGR:OSPITAL'·˙

Type #201 (PL. 132). Platelets in the 2nd and 3rd quarter of the cross. On the obverse (xv), late châtel variant with dot inside and within the roof triangle.

51. Legend ✠ᗰΛGR:OSPITΛLI·

Type #202 (PL. 132). Platelets in the 2nd and 3rd quarter of the cross. On the obverse (xv) late châtel variant with dot inside and within the roof triangle.

The distribution of the recurring variants of the reverse per obverse legend are shown below in Figure 83.

Only 11 of the obverse legends appear on the table, those associated with recurring legend variants. Three more are not shown because, so far, they have not been found associated with recurring reverse legends or are not helpful because they are very poorly represented in the sample. They are the following:

(ix) ✠CIVITΛS◦RODIS·
(xi) ✠CIVITAS◦RODIS◦
(xiv) ✠SIVITAS◦RODI:·

To save space, the late group assigned to Juilly or Heredia has been omitted, since it is distinct from the earlier obols. On the other hand, the legend of the signed obols of Berenger has been included, because it shares two reverse

	1	2	5	8	10	11	13	15	16	17	21	22	28	29	30	31	34	35	36	41	43	44	47
+CIVITΛS∘RODI		■		■						■				■	■	■				■	■	■	
+CIVITHS∘RODI			■	■		■				■	■									■	■	■	
+CIVITΛS∘RODI•	■												■										
+CIVITHS∘RODI∘											■	■						■					
+CIVITHS∘RODI✿																	■	■					
+CIVITΛS∘RODI·∘·					■		■								■	■			■				■
+CIVITHS∘RODIS			■							■				■			■	■			■	■	
+CIVITHS•RODIS'					■		■	■	■														
+CIVITHS∘RODIS:•			■			■				■							■	■					
+CIVITHS∘RODIS∘	■																						
+CIVITΛRODIS	■	■			■		■						■		■	■			■				■
+SIVITHS∘RODI•			■								■	■					■						
+CIVITHS∘RODIS✿								■	■														

Figure 83: Distribution of recurring reverse variants per obverse inscription.

legends with anonymous issues. The legends on the table were ordered according to resemblances in the order of the characters in the legend, the plainer variants placed first. If this arbitrary order is changed, bringing closer obverses which share the same reverse variant, the modified table is instructive:

	1	2	5	8	10	11	13	15	16	17	21	22	28	29	30	31	34	35	36	41	43	44	47
+CIVITΛS∘RODI•	⊠												⊠										
+CIVITΛRODIS	⊠	⊠			⊠		⊠						⊠		⊠	⊠			⊠				⊠
+CIVITΛS∘RODI·∘·					⊠		⊠								⊠	⊠			⊠				⊠
+CIVITHS•RODIS'					⊠		⊠	⧅	⧅														
+CIVITHS∘RODIS✿								⧅	⧅														
+CIVITΛS∘RODI		⊠		⧇						⧇				⧇	⊠	⊠				⧇	⧇	⧇	
+CIVITHS∘RODI			⧇	⧇		⧇				⧇	⧇									⧇	⧇	⧇	
+CIVITHS∘RODIS			⧇							⧇				⧇			⧇	⧇			⧇	⧇	
+CIVITHS∘RODIS:•			⧇			⧇				⧇							⧇	⧇					
+CIVITHS∘RODI✿																	⧇	⧇					
+SIVITHS∘RODI•			⧇								⧇	⧇					⧇						
+CIVITHS∘RODI∘											⧇	⧇						⧇					

Figure 84: Modification of Figure 83 as to the order of the obverse legends.

Two main groups of reverse legend variants are now distinguished. The first (cross-hatched squares), includes those associated exclusively with the first four legend variants of the obverse but, in three cases, with the fifth (ignoring the Berenger obverse). One subgroup (slashed squares) represents the two recurring reverse variants which the fourth obverse legend variant shares with the Berenger signed types. The second group (circle-in-square) begins in the fifth legend variant of the obverse, but is exclusively associated with all the rest.

It is clear that the fifth obverse inscription belongs to a transitional obverse, but it is necessary to ascertain if the succession of the variants is from top to bottom or the reverse. The fact that the plainer legends belong to the transitional phase proves that relative simplicity is not a valid criterion. Besides, the numbering of the reverse variants also does not follow a chronological sequence: so far, it is also ordered according to the order of the characters and the increased complexity of the variants. Thus, another modification is useful, to reduce scattering. The result is shown on Figure 85.

The ordering of the reverse variants could be arranged differently, as could the ordering of the obverses on either side of the dividing arrow. This is probably not an accident: although we are not dealing with dies here, but with

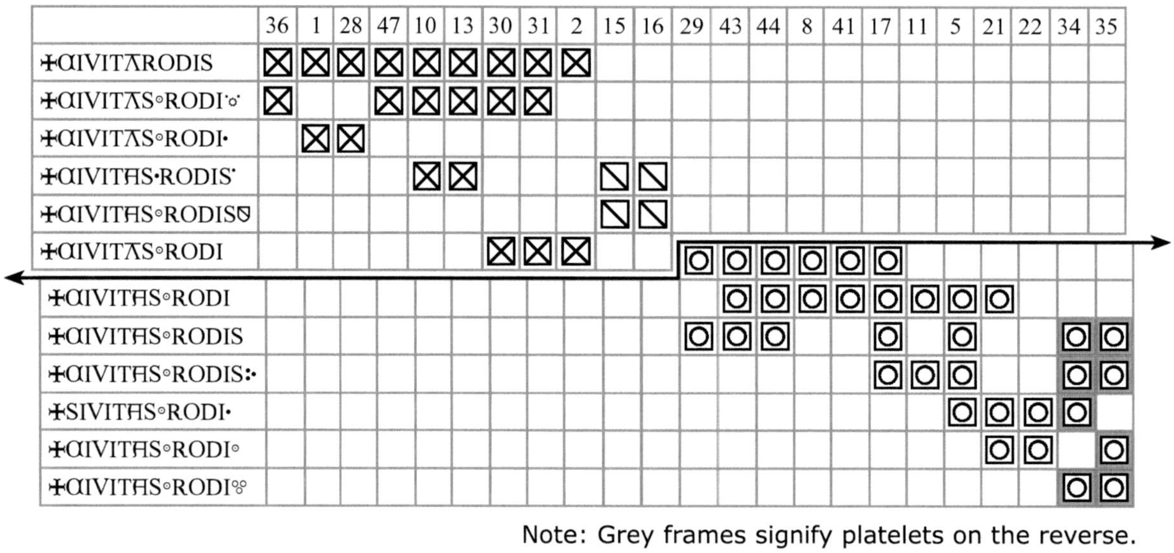

Figure 85: Modification of Figure 84 mainly as to the order of the reverse legends.

variants where specific versions of the obverse are associated with a number of specific reverse legends, we get a glimpse of something similar to the *die-box model*. According to this model, the dies of the reverse were kept in a box when work ceased and, when it was resumed, were used interchangeably with the fixed staple.[653] In the case of Rhodes, a more confusing procedure seems to have been practiced since, on occasion, at least two staples seem to have been in use at the same time or, perhaps, interchangeably. It appears that the staples were not fixed in place during striking, and that they, also, were kept in a separate box and made available either simultaneously or at intervals by one or more strikers. When this happened, it is not unlikely that the most important reason for the selection of a particular die was its condition.

There are, however, two distinct phases in the production of the obols and the writer's opinion is that Figure 85 depicts fairly accurately the order of production: the obverses above the dividing arrow are older than those below it. This is supported by a number of points:

- The introduction of the new copper denomination required dynamism, reflected in the number of reverse variants associated with the second and third obverses, and also with the number of solitary types associated with them. This is shown clearly in the table below, where the two late obverses have also been included (Figure 86, in green).
- The use, at first, of an annulet within the châtel in order to enhance the differences between the obol and the billon denier. The dot as a mark within the châtel first appears with the transitional obverse legend +ƆIVITΛS∘RODI and is exclusively adopted in the late types (green in Figure 86) which are linked to the Juilly deniers and form a distinct group.
- Wider use of platelets in the reverse variants of the second group of Figure 86. In the first group, platelets in the first and fourth quarter of the cross are associated only with the latest phase of the use of a particular châtel punch.[654] In the second group, the annulets on the reverse are combined with five obverse variants and appear in twelve types.[655] The platelets may have derived from the degradation of annulets in dies and punches and then morphed as an alternative mark, eventually monopolizing the reverses of the late, third group of obols.

Within the three main groups, the order of the obverse variants is provisional, but relies on a series of clues. For example, the obverse placed first (iii) displays a dot on the field to the right of the châtel, a feature copied from the billon deniers of Rhodes which afterwards disappears. This obverse shares two reverses with the obverse next in line (xii) (Figure 87), which seems to have continued in use for a considerable time alongside the third obverse, vi. The fourth obverse (ix) is represented by few specimens and so far its association is confirmed with only one reverse variant (36), which first appears with earlier obverses xii and vi. The fifth obverse (vii) is also associated

[653] Esty 1966: 207-208.
[654] Types #194 and, possibly, #194a (obverse vi) which belong to the first group.
[655] Types #178, #178a, #182, #183, #183a, #185, #187, #188, #191, #192, #194b, #194c.

	Obverse legend	Types (#) with links	Solitary types (#)	Percentage of legible specimens
xii	+CIVITΛRODIS	14	9	52,6%
vi	+CIVITΛS∘RODI·∘·	10	7	
iii	+CIVITΛS∘RODI·	2	2	
ix	+CIVITΛS∘RODIS·	1		
viii	+CIVITAS·RODIS·	4	1	
i	+CIVITΛS∘RODI	3	1	
		6	1	38%
ii	+CIVITAS∘RODI	7	2	
vii	+CIVITAS∘RODIS	7		
x	+CIVITAS∘RODIS:·	5		
xiii	+SIVITAS∘RODI·	4		
xiv	+SIVITAS∘RODI:·	1		
iv	+CIVITAS∘RODI∘	4		
v	+CIVITAS∘RODI∘∘	2	1	
xi	+CIVITAS∘RODIS∘	2	2	
xv	+CIVITΛS:RODI	4		9,6%
xvi	+CIVITΛS:RODI·		1	

Figure 86: Number of types (#) per obverse legend.

with obverses xii and vi through reverses 10 and 13, but shares two more reverses, 15 and 16, with the signed obols of Raymond Berenger. Thus, it provides a key for the dating of the series. The first group is completed with four types of transitional obverse i (#53, #149, #19 and #26) which are linked, through reverses 2, 30 and 31, with obverses xii and vi.

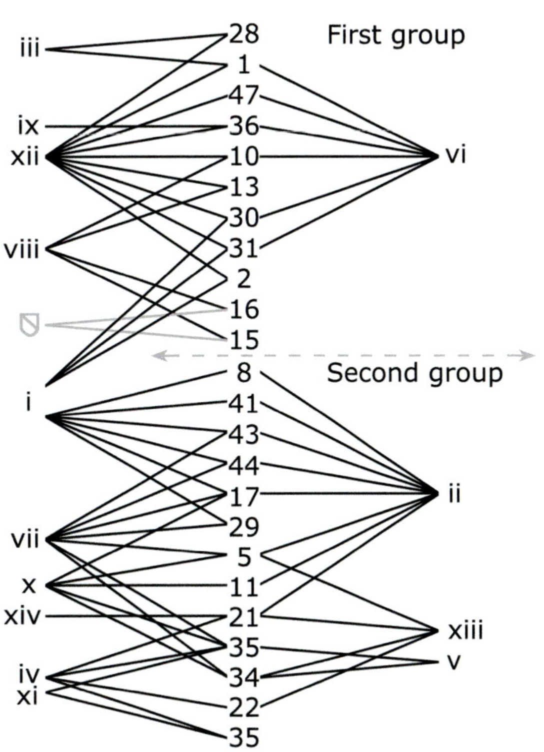

Figure 87: Linkage of obverses and reverses in the 14th century obols.

The remaining reverses associated with obverse i are the first ones in the second group. Four of them (17, 41, 43 and 44) also occur with the next obverse, ii, and three (17, 43 and 44) carry on with obverse vii, the next in line. Obverses ii and vii also share reverse 5. Obverse vii shares with the next one, x, reverses 17 and 5 and two more, 34 and 35. Closing the circle, obverse x also shares with ii reverse 11, while obverses xiii, xiv and v share reverse 21 with obverse ii. Thus, the second part of the production of obverse i and obverses ii, vii and x must be part of a second complex web of interchangeable dies. Vestiges of this web (reverses 5, 21, 35 and 34) are associated with obverses xiv, xiii, iv, v and xi, alongside reverses 22 and 42. In the production of obverses vii, xiv, xiii, iv, v and xi, most reverses with legend variant 35[656], and all the types with reverse 34, bear platelets instead of annulets in the first and fourth quarter of the cross.

Platelets in the first and fourth quarter also appear on the reverse of one of the third group types (49), whose châtel is distinctive in both form and style and has already been associated with the signed deniers of Robert de Juilly. However, it is certain that it shares the same obverse (xv) with reverses 50, 51 and 52 and probably the same legend

[656] Reverse 35 has annulets instead of platelets.

with reverse 52: all these have platelets in the second and third quarters of the cross, an innovation of this group. The other obverse of the group, xvi, clumsier than xv, is associated with only one reverse, 48.

This anonymous group should probably be assigned to the rule of Robert de Juilly despite his brief tenure of the mastership. Local conditions at the time may well have made the minting of obols profitable and it should be recalled that Juilly was an experienced administrator.[657] Alternatively, if these rather clumsy issues copied certain elements of this master's billon, but entered circulation a little later, they may belong in the early years of Heredia.

In any case, since minting quality deteriorated after 1377, the maximum time-span for the production of the competently crafted issues of deniers and obols in the 14th century cannot have exceeded 60 years, even if it is assumed that the early anonymous deniers were issued by Gerard de Pins, lieutenant of Villeneuve. In 1320, as has already been mentioned, the Knights put together a squadron supported by Genoese galleys in order to repulse an expedition against Rhodes mounted by the Turcomans of Menteshe.[658] Perhaps this operation required the issue of small coin to reward Genoese crews and this would explain the adoption of the Genoese gate as a design. Obols, however, were a fiduciary denomination and it is therefore unlikely that they entered circulation before the arrival of Villeneuve in Rhodes in 1332, so the time-span for their issue is reduced by at least 10 years.

The introduction of the anonymous obols in the local market, sometime after the issue of the early deniers, must have been undertaken with deliberation, as the deniers were intrinsically worth more than the obols. The two denominations had to be easy to distinguish from each other for the Hospital to avoid being accused of chicanery. Thus, it seems that the use of the annulets on the reverse served this purpose; and the annulets within and on top of the châtel may have done the same for the obverse, along with the triangular roof. Later, when the locals were familiar with the new denomination, the annulet on the obverse lost this significance and became just another feature which could be altered to serve internal purposes in the mint.

Since the early issues of Berenger are placed towards the end of the first group of obols (Figure 87), the types of the second group should be distributed between Berenger and his successor, Robert de Juilly, within the years 1365-77. Similarly, the best part of the first group must date from the period before 1365. This is probably confirmed by the unequal representation of solitary types between the two groups, as we could expect the earlier issues to be less well represented in the sample:

	Obverse legend	*Linked types (#)*	*Solitary types (#)*	*Total of specimens*
iii	✠CIVITΛS∘RODI·	#45 (32), #143 (23)	#141 (10), #142 (2)	67
xii	✠CIVITΛRODIS	#52 (41) + #151 (10), #52a (32) + #160 (27), #52d (9)+ #162 (10), #136 (9) + #155 (4), #52e (16), #80a (4), #143a (4), #88 (35), #161 (8), #44a (7)	#44 (17) + #145 (18), #52f (2), #72 (10), #72a (3), #77, #192, #146 (17), #161a (2)	286
vi	✠CIVITΛS∘RODI·∘·	#121 (4) + #163 (10), #122 (24) + #163c (9), #120 (55) + #163b (4), #116a (11), #117b (2), #125 (4), #194 (16),	#86 (9), #116 (7), #116b (3), #117 (16), #118 (11), #119 (2), #194a (2)	189
ix	✠CIVITΛS∘RODIS·	[#88c] (3)		3
viii	✠CIVITHS·RODIS·	#114 (28), #152 (3), #157 (2), #174 (29)	#172 (74)	136
i	✠CIVITΛS∘RODI	#53 (26), #149(21), #26 (3), #19 (61)	#29 (57)	168
		#12 (47), #6 (4), #18 (6), #10 (2), #20b, #24 (2)	#25 (48)	110
ii	✠CIVITHS∘RODI	#47 (28), #50 (24), #57 (3), #80 (40), #95 (27), #95d (7), #96 (4)	#41 (16), #64	149
vii	✠CIVITHS∘RODIS	#2 (15), #7 (6), #23 (11), #24ab (8), #182, #187 (22)		63
x	✠CIVITHS∘RODIS⁖	#1 (51), #4 (7), #23b (13), #183 (10), #183a (2)		83
xiii	✠SIVITHS∘RODI·	#127 (44), #128 (9), #130 (18), #194b		72
xiv	✠SIVITHS∘RODI⁖	#131 (3)		3

[657] Delaville Le Roulx 1913: 181.
[658] Villani [1728]: 501; Delaville Le Roulx 1913: 78-79; Zachariadou 1983: 11-14.

	Obverse legend	*Linked types (#)*	*Solitary types (#)*	*Total of specimens*
iv	✠ƆIVITAS∘RODI∘	#59 (30), #60 (62), #87 (2), #194c (3)		97
v	✠ƆIVITAS∘RODI⁘	#178a (5), #188 (28)	#178 (29)	62
xi	✠ƆIVITAS∘RODIS∘	#30, #185 (46)	#191 (4), #192 (6)	57
xv	✠ƆIVITAS:RODI	#199 (24), #201 (103), #202 (17), #205 (4)		148
xvi	✠ƆIVITAS:RODI·		#200 (16)	16

Figure 88: Distribution of types (#) per obverse inscription (more than one specimen per type within parentheses).

Figure 88 preserves the colours representing each group; the number within brackets after the type (#) number represents the number of identified specimens of the type, if there are more than one. In total, the first group is represented by 849 identified pieces (50% of the total), the second group by 696 (41%) and the third by 164 (9%). Thus, if the second group and the last types of the first belong to Berenger and, perhaps, Juilly, the compact character of the first group implies that most, if not all of its types, belong to the rule of Roger de Pins (1355-65) and, at a stretch, his immediate predecessors. This dating must be fairly accurate, since the small fiduciary coins for local use gained general acceptance at about the middle of the 14th century. In Rhodes at least, if not elsewhere, such coins may well have been accepted under the social pressures generated by the Black Death (1347-53), which must have enhanced the role of charity for the support of survivors. The plague struck Rhodes in 1348 under Gozon, and again in 1361-2 under Pins,[659] whose alleviating policies earned him the *sobriquet* 'L'aumonier'. It is tempting to take this literally, and assign the entire first group to Roger de Pins, the second to Raymond Berenger and the third to Robert de Juilly.

The reduction of the window for the issue of the obols to 1347-1377 or even 1355-77, is reinforced by the excavational data. As a rule, the lower the value of a coin the higher the chance to encounter it as a site find, unless there are other factors at play.[660] However, among the 14th century site finds from Rhodes, the billon deniers are much more common than the copper obols. The coin profile of the two major hoards probably reflects the situation at some point between 1420-1430, but with some processing may give insights for earlier times. Simplifying and modifying somewhat the data of Table 70, we can compare them with site finds:

	LARGE HOARDS	SITE FINDS
Anonymous 14th c. deniers (Bi)	41 (0.7%)	208 (50.6%)
Anonymous 14th c. obols (AE)	4096 (68.2%)	143 (34.8%)
Pins (1355-65) deniers (Bi)	3 (0.04%)	12 (2.9%)
Berenger (1365-73) obols (AE)	34 (0.6%)	-
Juilly (1373-77) deniers (Bi)	-	7 (1.7%)
Coarse [Bi] issues	853 (14,2%)	25 (6%)
Naillac (1396-1421) deniers, type 1	10 (0.2%)	1 (0.2%)
Anonymous Naillac overstrikes	964 (16%)	15 (3.6%)
TOTAL	**6,001 pieces**	**411 pieces**

Figure 89: Comparison between site finds of the period 1330-1421 and the contents of the two major Hospitaller hoards.

The difference in the respective size of the samples from the hoards and archaeological excavation may be overcome by the use of percentages on the total of each category. The gap between 0.7% and 50.6% is spectacular. Even if the later overstrikes are added to the deniers in the sample from the hoards, the billon count reaches 31% of the total. It thus approaches the ratio of 3:1 between copper and billon, which is not too far from the 4:1 ratio valid towards the end of the 15th century between the smaller denominations issued by grand master Pierre d'Aubusson. However, in the site finds reflecting chance losses and the disturbed funerary purses, the ratio is still an unsatisfactory 1:1.4. If the overstrikes of the turn of the century are added to the billon deniers, the ratio (1:1.7) is not significantly altered. The imbalance in the site finds may, however, be very simply explained by the fact that, for a considerable time,

[659] Tsiamis *et al.* 2011: 195.
[660] An example of this is the coin evidence from Byzantine Rhodes, when the issue of copper was an administrative tool.

only billon was available for small transactions.[661] The innovative introduction of the master's badge on the coins under Roger de Pins, including the billon deniers, may be an indication of a broader review of mint practice which produced the first obols.

A more precise dating of the copper is not possible; but with the first group of obols a large number of types of uniform style produced by a particular team of *monetarii* entered circulation. These men must have continued working for the Knights at least until the beginning of the rule of Juilly, when the dies for this master's billon were made. The less well crafted obols of the third group associated with the Juilly deniers by features such as the needles on top of the verticals and the colon as a stop in the legend were the work of a new die sinker active in the 1370s.

The success of the obols produced until, very likely, 1377, and the need for them, are confirmed by the presence of imitations (PL. 139). They must have circulated in larger numbers than the Berenger obols, since they have occasionally turned up as site finds, while no Berenger signed obols have done so yet. 34 such imitations have been found in the major hoards. The only punch used in the making of their dies seems to have been the one for the beading of the circle round the main design. Apart from other flaws in the engraving, the badly-formed letters are very noticeable, as is the often inverted S. Differences in quality seem to imply the activity of more than one maker. It is impossible to say whether these imitations circulated alongside the regular issues or somewhat later. However, they were not modelled on the third group, and their use of the rare cogwheel stop characteristic of type #143 (Figure 88), assumed to have been issued at the start of the first group, indicates an early date.

4. Petty coinage between c. 1422 and 1522

The documentary evidence for the coinage of the Hospital between *c.* 1422 and 1522 is fragmentary, and is summarized as follows, with some input from the coins themselves:

> *c.* 1421-30: Recall of all the petty coins which circulated before 1421. First gold sequins issued by Fluvià.
> 1450: Contract between the Order and moneyer Markezis for the striking of gold and silver in the mint. Gigliati are no longer struck; a smaller silver piece, the *giannetto*, has replaced them under Lastic.
> 1454: Reform of the operation of the Hospitaller mint after the first Chapter General of grand master Jacques de Milly.[662]
> 1458: Report of pilgrim William Wey on the equivalence of deniers to giannetti, gigliati and the Venetian ducat.
> 1461-67: Possible interruption of striking gold under Pere Ramon Zacosta, who imposed onerous economic measures.
> 1467-76: Issue of sequins and gianneti under Giovanni-Battista degli Orsini, and temporary revival of the gigliato.
> 1488: Issue of petty coins under Pierre d'Aubusson.
> *c.* 1490: Reform of the silver coinage by Aubusson.

The two major hoards of the Hospitaller period are evidence of a radical change in the production of the Rhodian mint, which included the wholesale recall of older coins. A number of reasons could lie behind the reform: the replacement of a variety of older coins with different silver contents, the opportunity to remove what silver they contained at a time of bullion famine,[663] or the promotion of a new, purely fiduciary coin which could be profitable to the moneyers and the Order because of the increased need for small change in the town.

The recycling of which the Italian and Kamiros hoards were a part probably dates from the third decade of the 15th century. Presumably, the Naillac anonymous issues bearing the invocations associated with the external threat circulated in the first decade of the new century marked by the loss of Smyrna in 1402. They may have been used to pay the labourers engaged in the work for the construction of the imposing Naillac tower at the entrance of the harbour of Rhodes and even the Castle of St Peter at Bodrum before 1408.[664] It is doubtful that they were issued later, since Naillac left Rhodes for the West in 1409 and did not return until October 1420.

---

661 Also, the picture of the final recall of the petty coins of the 14th century presented by the two large hoards must have been influenced by the gradual withdrawal from circulation of the deniers, due to Gresham's Law.
662 The unpublished document of 1454 concerns the issue of gold and silver coins by George Markezis, like the 1450 contract published by Tsirpanlis, which it closely resembles. Archives of the Order of Malta, 365. For the text and its preliminary reading thanks are due to Dr. Anthony Luttrell.
663 Spufford 1988: 361.
664 Luttrell 1986: 144, note 13; De Vaivre 2009: 601.

In 1421 Naillac was succeeded by Catalan Antoni Fluvià, whose career had evolved in the East and had been serving in Rhodes since 1387. The election of the new master took place in the Convent of Rhodes without external intervention and it seems than his experience and ability were the deciding factors. It is already known that Fluvià issued the first gold sequins copying both sides of the Venetian ducat, a coin whose minting continued until the end of the Hospitaller period.[665] In contrast to his predecessors, Fluvià remained in Rhodes for the duration of his 16-year rule and focused his attention on the administration and various long-term problems. Assisted by a number of Catalans he had placed in key posts in Rhodes, he succeeded in pushing forward a substantial building programme involving the town's defences and various public buildings through careful management of his resources, without rousing hostility within the Order.[666]

The recall of the old coinage probably took place in the early part of his rule, since no coins of Alfonso I of Sicily (1416-58),[667] common enough as site finds, have been found in the two hoards. The new types of petty coins would have been handy for the payment of wages to the workmen who were kept busy in the construction of the new town wall also under the successors of Fluvià, masters Jean de Lastic (1437-54) and Jacques de Milly (1454-71), at least until 1457.[668] It is likely that, in Fluvià's recycling, the silver of the 14th century billon was removed from the metal, since the petty coins of the 15th century were of pure copper until the times of Aubusson. These coins (PLS. 140-143) are termed obols here, since they still show the châtel[669] on one side and the cross with annulets in opposite quarters on the other.

Local causes were partly responsible for the financial straits experienced by the Hospital under Lastic, including the cost of extending the town wall. They provoked unrest among Lastic's subordinates and Zacosta, who succeeded him, had to be particularly strict in money matters and was, naturally, labelled a miser. In Western Europe, the widespread silver famine, due to the exhaustion of the silver mines in Bohemia toward the end of the 14th century and, in the 1450s, the Ottoman conquest of the Serbian and Bosnian mines, peaked between 1457 and 1465.[670] At intervals, the lack of bullion also affected the gold. New mining operations began in the Alps and in Saxony in the 1470s, restoring the issue of coin. As the natural flow of silver was from north to south and from west to east, it is possible that the entire episode of scarcity and recovery reached Rhodes with a certain time lapse. The lack of silver must have encouraged the use of fiduciary coin for small exchanges.

The contracts between the Hospital and Markezis concerned the issue of gold and silver; they are of passing interest here, principally because of the clause limiting the practice of striking coin to the premises of the Mint. In this matter, additional information is provided by the historian of the Order Giacomo Bosio regarding the reasons that led Milly to a reorganization of the Mint: *E desiderando* [Milly], *che i danari, che si battevano in Rodi; liberamente in ogni Luogo spendere si potessero; e che volentieri, in tutti gli altri Stati ricevuti fossero; riformò la lega delle monete, e costituì nuovi ordini, e Capitoli sopra la Zecca.*[671] Here the word *danari* does not refer to deniers, whose circulation was limited within the boundaries of the island state, but larger denominations, which were not up to international standards. It is, of course, difficult to believe that problems in foreign exchange would not rebound on coin circulation locally, because Hospitaller Rhodes was not self-sufficient in various basic commodities. In any case, the issue of fiduciary deniers by Fluvià and his successors is certain, since Wey mentions that, when he visited Rhodes under Milly, 32 deniers equalled one giannetto and 48 one gigliato. These equivalences indicate that the value of the denier had dropped considerably from the times of Pegolotti (32 deniers = 1 gigliato), but this is not surprising since the 'deniers' of the mid-15th century were actually copper obols. The distinction between *quattrini* and *denari parvi* in the document of 1488 is clear.[672]

Although still anonymous, the 15th century obols (PLS 140-143) bear different legends from their 14th century predecessors. In the table below, the main varieties are set out:

[665] To date, only sequins of Pere Ramon Zacosta have not been recorded. The first known sequin of grand master Lastic was published in 1983. Mannucci 1983: 289.

[666] Bonneaud 2004: 134-152. In contrast to his successor Jean de Lastic who, admittedly, also had to face the expenses incurred in the siege of Rhodes by the Mamluks of Egypt in 1444. Bonneaud 2012: 22-43.

[667] Also known as Alfonso V of Aragon, again from 1416, and as Alfonso I of Naples from 1442.

[668] This is the date when the new walls of Rhodes were completed, according to the inscription celebrating the event, still in situ on the fortifications. Gabriel 1921: 98.

[669] With a single exception, type 1 in Figure 90, which shows a Genoese gate instead.

[670] Spufford 1988a: 339-362.

[671] Bosio 1629: II, 249.

[672] Mannucci 1987: 295-296.

Type	Châtel [obverse]	Cross [reverse]	Exemplar
[1]	+MΛGISTRI·OSPITΛLIS, janua	+IEROSΛLEMITΛNI RODI	**2965**
[2]	+MΛGISTRI·OSPITΛLIS	+IEROSΛLEMITΛNI ROD'	**2953**
[3]	+...PI...LI·S, + below	+OSPITΛ...SSIO	**2981**
[4]	+OSPITΛLIS S IO	+M OSPITΛLIS S IO	**3001**
[5]	+CONUENTUS RhODI	+OSPIT[A]LIS...	**3005**
[6]	+CONUENTUS R[ ]O...	+IERVSΛLE...	**2946**
[7]	[MAGI]STEROSPIT[A	+MAGISTERO...L	**2948**
[8]	+...ALISIE[RU]	+OSPI...[L]	**3009**
[9]	+CON[U]...ODI	+CO[N]VENT[ ]S	**3011**
[10]	+CONUENTU...ODI	+IE...ΛRO[D:]	**3010**
[11]	+CONUE[NTO RODI	+OSPITALIS IERVSALE[M]	**2920**
[12]	+CONUENTUS RhODI	+MAGISTER·OSPITALIS·	**3013**

Figure 90: 15th century obol legends.

Most of the legends belong to groups which comprise specimens with slight differences between them in both legend and main design. The legends are not equally represented in the available sample. Indeed, they seem less significant than those of the 14th century for sorting the various groups of coins, because 15th century die-sinkers took greater freedoms with the design of related issues mixing, for example, janua with châtel ([1]/[2]) or starting the legend below or above the châtel ([3]/[4]). Most coins are site-finds and their generally mediocre state of preservation makes it hard to sort them into types. Stylistic differences between them indicate work by different moneyers who served the Hospital's mint under contract, at different times. There are no overstrikes, so their chronology is very hard to establish without additional evidence.

Four major groups emerge: [1]/[2]/[10], [3]/[4], [5]/[8]/[9]/[11] and [12]. Legends [6], [7], [5], [8], [9] and [10] are each represented by one to four coins only. The group including legends [1], [2] and, possibly, [10] is stylistically different from all the others in various ways, including the shape of the flans, which are more rounded than those of the rest and may have been produced with the same sieve-above-water technique most likely employed for the 14th century obols, while the blanks for the other groups seem to have been made from pieces of square-sectioned metal rods hammered flat. In spite of the use of both janua ([1]) and châtel ([2]) as the main design, the two issues also closely resemble each other in the long legends, tightly-packed lettering, crowded design and the use of the Λ form of A. **3010**, the only representative of legend [10], shows stylistic affinities with [1] and [2] but its inclusion in their group is tentative.

Group [3]/[4] is clumsily made; most of its reasonably legible coins belong to legend [4], which on the obverse begins over the châtel, but there are some specimens ([3]) in which the obverse legend starts below it. Both obverse designs are matched with two versions of the reverse legend, beginning either as +OSPIT or as +M · OSPIT... This group is clumsily made in comparison to the first, with brief and repetitive legends and carelessly engraved châtel punches with, most commonly, a dot inside.

Legends [6] and [7], represented by a meagre one and three identified specimens respectively, also seem stylistically related, although [7] bears platelets instead of annulets in the opposite quarters of the cross on the reverse. Legends [5], [8] and [9], all represented by a token number of identified specimens,[673] also show similarities to each other, particularly in the lettering, including the A form of the A, and the shape of the coins; but they also appear related to group [11], much better represented in the available sample. This, in its turn, is stylistically associated with the last group, [12]; this is even better represented in the sample, a fact related to a specific excavation context which offers the first independent clues for a dating sequence of the 15th century obols.

The quatrini which circulated in 1488 have been identified with the signed billon small coins issued by Aubusson and frequently found in archaeological excavations (PLS. 145-146). These deniers show on one side St John the Baptist holding a staff with a cross in his right hand and an open scroll in the left, with the legend S(anctus) IOhANN(e)S B(aptista) IERV(salemitanus) and on the other the cross moline of the Aubusson family arms with the circumferential legend f(rater) PE(trus) D'AVBVSSON M(agister) OSPIT(alis). Archaeological evidence may help identify the obols issued alongside the signed deniers of Aubusson.

[673] By four, one and two pieces respectively.

In 1856, the conventual church of the Hospital, St John the Baptist in the Collachio, then used as the principal mosque of the Ottoman town, was destroyed by a gunpowder explosion. After the salvage of reusable building material, particularly marble slabs from the floor, the site was levelled and a new school was raised on top of the earth-filled ruin. Limited exploration of the church was conducted during the Italian occupation of Rhodes by Pietro Lojacono between 1932 and 1934.[674] In 1988, the collapse of a revetting wall after heavy rain led to a new archaeological excavation on the site. In the central aisle, under the foundation of the *mihrab* added in Ottoman times before the sanctuary, a vaulted burial structure was brought to light. The tomb contained the only richly furnished burial discovered under the floor of the church. Apart from a few small bones, no skeleton was found although the fill did not seem disturbed; it is possible that this was the grave of a small child.[675] A quantity of iron nails pointed to the presence of a coffin and the furnishings recovered included a gilt silver pendant,[676] coral, pearl, rock crystal and glass beads, a small knife, a broken bone flute, a pair of dice, fragments of a painted glass vessel, copper sheeting, metal dress fastenings (a buckle, lacing tabs, round-headed pins, a hook), and about 190 small coins. The coins were not found massed together. However, although they were scattered in fill 40 cm thick, mixed with the other objects, most were concentrated in two areas. If we assume that most of the finds were originally inside the coffin, it is possible that at least two funerary purses containing the coins disintegrated before the wood of the coffin had rotted away, so that the coins were scattered inside.

It is possible that the rich burial was not the first to occupy the grave, but its unique character makes it unlikely that any of the coins or other finds belonged to another burial; all the more so, since none of the other Hospitaller burials in the church contained grave goods.[677] Thus, give or take an intrusive coin or two, the coins from the grave may be considered as a single deposit dated *c.* 1488-1503 by three signed deniers ('quatrini') of Aubusson. The composition of the deposit is as follows:

Type	Obol No.	Qty	%
Aubusson deniers (Bi)		3	1.6
Rhodian 15th c. obols, type +CONVENTUS RODI/+MAGISTER OSPITALIS	[12]	62	33
Rhodian 15th c. obols, type +CONVENTO RODI/ +OSPITALIS IERUSALE[M	[11]	16	8.5
Rhodian 15th c. obols, janua type	[1]	3	1.6
Rhodian 15th c. obols, type +MAGISTRI OSPITALIS/ +IEROSALEMITANI ROD	[2]	2	1
Rhodian 15th c. obols, type +OSPITALIS S IO	[4]	2	1
Rhodian 15th c. obols, type +CONVENTO RODI/ +CONVENTO	[9]	1	0.5
Rhodian 15th c. obols, type +MAGISTER OSPIT[A/ +MAGISTER O...L	[7]	1	0.5
Rhodian 15th c. obols, type +CONVENTU[S R]ODI/ +IE...A RhO[D	[10]	1	0.5
Rhodian 15th c. obol imitations		36	19.1
Rhodian 15th c. obols, uncertain type		40	21.3
Naillac overstrike		1	0.5
Rhodian 14th c. obols		3	1.6
Cypriot sixain (AR)		1	0.5
Sicilian deniers		5	2.7
Torneselli		3	1.6
Tornesello imitation		1	0.5
Venetian denier		1	0.5
Ancona denier		1	0.5
Naples denier		1	0.5
Mytilene denier		1	0.5
Chios tornese		1	0.5
Corroded Western coins		2	1

Figure 91: Conventual church of St. John/1995 burial deposit composition.

674 Livadiotti and Rocco 1996: 236, 238.
675 Evidence for the burial of children held in ward by the Hospital is preserved in funerary inscriptions. Cf. Kasdagli 2008: 186 and pl. 19.10.
676 Kasdagli 2009a: 283-285.
677 In contrast to other churches of the town, where deposits of small purses of petty coins are common. For the coins in the burial see also Appendices, Selected Context V.

Among the 15th century obols, the group better represented in the deposit is the one bearing the legend +CONUENTUS RhODI/ +MAGISTER·OSPITALIS· (group [12] in Figure 90, see also Figure 92.3). It appears in four variants, with an annulet or a dot within the châtel and with the annulets or platelets of the reverse either in the first and fourth quarter or in the second and third, without counting small differences in the legends. Its strong presence (at least 66 pieces) probably signifies that it should be identified with the *denari parvi* issued in 1488. Group [11], bearing the legend +CONUENTO RhODI/ + OSPITALIS·IERUSALEM, is represented by 17 coins and may be slightly later, or a bit earlier in date. Most of the other coins in the deposit must be earlier in date.

At present, only conjectures are possible for the dating of the other 15th century obol groups in Figure 90. At least three types preserve features looking back to issues dated before 1421:

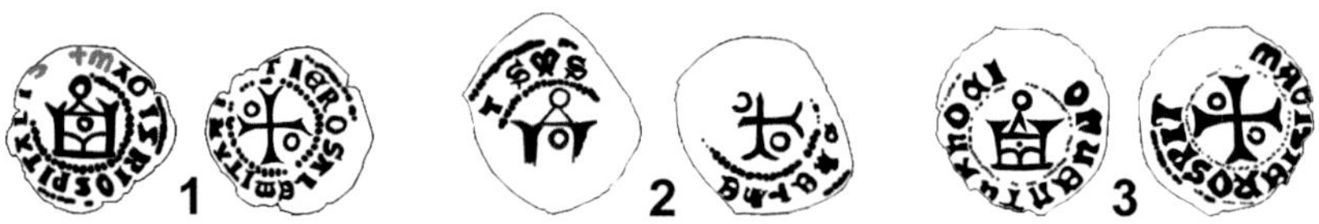

Figure 92: 15th c. obols: 1. Group [2]; 2. Imitation; 3. Group [12].

a. Group [1], with a Genoese gate instead of a châtel on the obverse, stylistically and in its legend akin to group [2], which has a châtel.

b. Group [3], where the obverse inscription starts below the base of the châtel, recalling the overstrikes of Naillac. Stylistically and in its legend this group resembles group [4], but also shows similarities to the broad category of coins not included in Table 37 because they bear nonsense legends, but are very common site finds and well represented in the funerary deposit of St John (Figure 92b and PL. 144).

c. Group [7], with platelets in opposite quarters of the cross on the reverse. It should be mentioned that groups [6] and [11], with similar legends, also seem to share the same elongated script, with most typical the letter L.

The general development of coin production in the 15th century seems to begin in a reforming spirit under Fluvià, but later gets into difficulties until its recovery under Aubusson, when the town had largely recovered from the damages inflicted by the siege of 1480 and the destructive earthquakes of 1481. With this course in mind, the following sequence is provisionally proposed for the main groups before [11] and [12], until new evidence is brought to light or the available material is studied in greater detail:

Groups [1] and [2] (cf. Figure 92.1) are assigned to Fluvià, since the recalled earlier issues must have been replaced by a substantial output of new coin.

Groups [3]-[4] follow; the first of them also revives an older feature, the legend starting below the châtel. However, they are soon swamped by quantities of imitations with nonsense legends without a crosslet, since the local authorities take no action while the need for small change has become pressing (Figure 92.2). It is possible that these imitations were first marketed as tokens or *jetons* (*méreaux*), to cover a different need, such as that for funerary offerings. The repeated characters MERMERMER... in the legend of the commonest types may well allude to the word méreau. Even when the inscription is indistinct, these imitations stand out because the verticals of the châtel do not project above the rectangle of the building and within it a large annulet is present above vestigial arches at the lower corners. It is worth noting that these imitations are a little heavier than the obols with meaningful legends. Although the imitations may have had a distinct function at first, the need for small change must have soon led to their wide acceptance as token coins; it seems that they circulated freely, as substitute obols, even after the issue of new *denari parvi* by Aubusson in 1488, at least for a while, since the funerary deposit from the church of St John contained at least 36 of these pieces. Their dating in relation to group [11] is problematical; this group could be contemporary to some of the imitations, or slightly later than [12].

Under grand master Emery d'Amboise (1503-1512), three types of signed billon deniers were struck, but so far only two of them figure in the archaeological collection of Rhodes (PL. 146). The first shows on one side the standing figure of St John the Baptist holding a Lamb, with the legend ECCE AGNUS DEI, and on the other a shield with the family arms of Amboise (*paly of six*) and the legend +F(rater) EMERICVS DAMBOISE M(agister). The second type bears on one side a Jerusalem cross cantonned with crosslets of St Andrew and the legend +F(rater) EMERICVS

DAMBOISE M(agnus) M(agister); on the other is a paschal Lamb above an exergue, with the legend EC(c)E A(g)NVS D(e)I [Q(v)I TO(llis)].

Twice as many deniers of Aubusson have so far been found in archaeological excavations as the two types of Amboise together: there are 54 Aubusson deniers against 22 of Amboise, of which 12 belong to the first type and 10 to the second. Thus, if it is assumed that the deniers of Aubusson entered circulation between 1488 and 1503, losses per year work out as 3.6. Under Amboise the figure drops to 2.4.

No deniers of grand master Fabrizio del Carretto (1513-21) are known; nor have we any evidence for the issue of obols from the times of Amboise to the end of the Hospitaller period in Rhodes, although it is not impossible that some of the anonymous types that have not yet been dated entered circulation in the 16th century. The apparent drop in the circulation of petty coins may be due to our inability to date the post-1420 obols as well as the apparent reluctance of the Order's officials to take requisite action under Carretto. Was this reluctance merely due to administrative dysfunction or did the Knights feel that the available coin was sufficient for the local market? Perhaps the assumption that Rhodes continued to increase in prosperity right up to the final siege of 1522 is overly optimistic. The long-term effects of the Plague epidemic that struck Rhodes between 1498 and 1500[678] have still to be systematically explored, while in the first decades of the 16th century the defence of its island state seems to have been the main preoccupation of the Hospital.

Foreign coins

During the Hospitaller period, coins were essentially of two kinds. Under certain circumstances, those containing a substantial amount of precious metal could be used as a medium of exchange abroad. The movement of silver coins from Western Europe to the East is a thoroughly studied phenomenon.[679] The movement of gold, generally from Africa to Europe and then, again, towards the East, is also a familiar pattern, and has left traces in Rhodes.[680] Medieval commercial treatises are full of references to exchange ratios between the gold and silver coins of every land that might be of professional interest to their authors,[681] and familiar coins such as the florin of Florence or the Venetian ducat. For small states, the issue of similar coins carried prestige but, in actuality, foreign gold and silver were welcome and generally circulated freely. Their value might be somewhat higher in their countries of origin, but they remained valuable anywhere and across time.

Gold and silver coins were useful for the transfer of capital, the bulk purchase of goods and the payment of tax, tribute or ransom. The daily needs of the urban population, the wages of labourers or itinerant craftsmen could generally be covered by lower denominations of billon and pure copper. These made life easier for the man in the street, and were quasi-fiduciary coins circulating within a narrow geographical compass. They were easily lost and are common as site finds. Until the late 14th century many of them still contained a token amount of silver and were known under various names: deniers, tornesi, pennies etc. The silver famine of *c.* 1390 and, again, after 1430 until *c.* 1465, helped establish the circulation of a purely fiduciary petty coinage.

In general, every sovereign authority had its own petty coins and powerful states like Venice could enforce a prohibition on the use of foreign issues in their domains although, in general, the control of petty coins seems to have been a priority during periods of crisis.[682] In any case, most of the foreign small coins turning up today in archaeological sites may well have fallen off the pocket of some traveller. It is therefore useful to examine their provenance, since it gives indications for the overseas contacts of the Rhodians and marks the stages along trade routes.

Among the coins of Hospitaller Rhodes, about 150 site or chance finds,[683] or 9% of the total, were struck elsewhere (PLS 147-154). The corresponding percentage in the Italian and Kamiros hoards is much lower, hardly reaching 0.6% (35 pieces). Naturally, it should not be forgotten that excavation coins derive from the entire Hospitaller period (1309-1522) and that some finds are even earlier. The two major hoards, on the other hand, consisted of the coins still in circulation *c.* 1421. For example, site finds include two silver deniers of Lucca (1004-1125), an English penny

[678] Papachristodoulou 1972: 355-357.
[679] Spufford 1988: 109-240.
[680] Papadopoulou 2010.
[681] Cf. the case of Pegolotti [1936].
[682] Instances of illegal bulk trading of black money are recorded from the peak of the bullion famine in the early decades of the 15th century. Cf. Spufford 1988: 360.
[683] Excepting gold and silver hoards.

(1180-1218),[684] a denier of Chartres and one of Normandy, both dating from the 11th century or earlier,[685] three pieces from Crusader mints in the Holy Land, the odd copper Armenian coin as well as a *tram* of the early 13th century, a Genoese denier of the 12th or 13th century, and eight Venetian quartaroli of the 13th century. In the two major hoards only a denier of Hugh III of Cyprus (1267-84) is definitely older than the Hospitaller conquest of Rhodes. For the rest, the provenance of the identified foreign coins is as follows:

Provenance	Finds	Major hoards
France	2 (1 AV)	
Armenia	1	
Genoa	1	2
Florence	1 (AV)	
Venice	4 (1 AV)	
Sicily	53	2
Naples	3	1
Majorca	1	
Minorca	1	
Portugal	1	1
Rome	2	
Papal issues	3	
Milan	1	1
Ravenna	1	1
Ancona	4	
Ascoli		1
Bologna		1
Mantua		1
Cyprus (Lusignan dynasty)	18	4
Cyprus (Genoese deniers of Famagusta)	5	5
Mytilene	4	1
Chios	2	1
Anatolian ducat imitations	2 (AV)	
Lepanto (Naupactus)	1	
Achaia	1	
Torneselli	36	8
Tornesello imitations	3	

Figure 93: Foreign coins.

Some comments are necessary regarding the data of Figure 93. To begin with, the five gold coins found in various sites confirm the widespread circulation of various foreign gold coins reported by the written sources.[686] Of the 53 Sicilian deniers, 49 belong to the Eagle/ Arms of Aragon type which circulated under Martin the Young (1402-9), Alphonso I (1416-58) and John II (1458-79). The significance of Sicily as a major stage in the sea route connecting Rhodes with the West, whence the Hospital drew most of its personnel and income, is obvious. The Sicilian deniers are more common even than the torneselli representing the closer-range contacts with the Venetian possessions in the Aegean sea (Cyclades, Euboea, the Peloponnese, Crete). It should be noted here that all the precisely identified torneselli from the two major hoards bear the name of doge Antonio Venier (1382-1400), while among the site finds Giovanni Dolfin (1356-61), Andrea Contarini (1368-82), Michele Steno (1400-13) and Agostino Barbarigo (1486-1501) are also represented. Among the less well preserved torneselli some may be near-contemporary imitations.

The significant presence of Cyprus is not to be wondered at, considering the close ties between the Order and the kings of Cyprus, although most of the coins date from the 14th century. Of greater interest is the presence of

[684] Perhaps a relic of the visit of Richard Lionheart and his fleet in April 1191.
[685] For the Normans in Byzantium before the First Crusade see Van Hout 1985.
[686] Cf. Mannucci 1987: 296.

Genoese deniers from Famagusta (1373-1464), adequately represented in both major hoards. The presence of Chios and Mytilene in the sample reflect the sea route to the Black Sea mostly served by Genoese ships. *Tornesi* from mainland Greece are very scarce,[687] particularly considering the discovery of a hoard consisting exclusively of such coins in 1927.[688] Perhaps, however, this hoard, concealed around the middle of the 14th century during the time of the Plague, was a traveller's purse.

Two things stand out: the first is the discreet presence of Venice itself, lost among the other Italian cities for most of the Hospitaller period. The second is the rarity of foreign coins after 1465: only three pieces have been identified so far, all from Venice.[689] This, taken together with the difficulty of identifying Rhodian small change for the early 16th century, raises questions that are difficult to answer.

[687] Except for the tornese of Lepanto and one which is probably an issue of the principality of Achaia, only two tornesi (**3309** and **3310**) have been found in excavations; their condition makes proper identification impossible.
[688] Baker 2006: 361, with bibliography.
[689] Two of doge Agostino Barbarigo (1486-1501); and a *bagattino* struck after 1500, which may have entered circulation after the fall of Rhodes to the Turks.

Overview - Conclusions

The comprehensive inventory of the Christian coins of the 4th Ephorate of Byzantine Antiquities began in 1988. Until 1990, about 1,750 treated coins had been inventoried, mostly derived from older excavations. Extra funding raised the number of treated coins to about 7,000; but the inventory stalled at about 4.5 thousand due to increased pressure in other aspects of archaeological work. Already from the year 2000, date of the first publication of numismatic material from the Ephorate after the finds from the Latin cathedral of medieval Rhodes,[690] certain local circulation patterns had been noted; the progress of the inventory served merely to enhance them, confirming the representative character of the early sample.[691] Thus, the present study began with more than a single objective. A full publication of the coins would enable local archaeologists and other scholars to integrate them in their research; the conundrum of dating the locally minted petty coinage from the 13th through the 15th century could be systematically tackled; and the causes behind local phenomena of circulation might become more clear. Issues of particular interest were:

- The significance of 7th century countermarks and imitations.
- The local spread of clipped and worn 11th century Byzantine anonymous folles of classes B and C and signed folles of emperor Romanus IV.
- The exclusive but substantial representation of the reformed coinage of emperor Alexius I by tetartera, and their imitations.
- The dating of the local Byzantine coinage of the 13th century.
- The dating of the anonymous petty coins of the Hospitaller period.

To answer questions regarding the first three points required a) the careful examination and inventory of all the treated coins in order to reduce the chances of sampling errors and b) the systematic reexamination of the historical background. Since direct mentions to Byzantine Rhodes in historical works are rare, an attempt was made to sort out events of wider significance which ought to have affected the town and island directly. Events not included in wider historical approaches because they are not linked to essential trends or did not have long-term or clear consequences were also reviewed. Such examples were the timing of the spread of Justinian's Plague, diplomatic failures like the policy of Justin II in the Arab peninsula, the influence on administrative shortcomings of the actions of particular emperors, generals and bureaucrats, or practical difficulties caused by technological or natural limitations which rendered the machinery of the state more vulnerable to imponderables like the weather and sudden pressure on the borders of Byzantium. The employment of such means for the interpretation of localized phenomena of monetary circulation cannot be very reliable. However, the numismatic evidence on its own rarely solves problems for the historian; and it is worth tracing likely correlations which may, eventually, complement the findings of other specialists.

The spatial distribution of 6th century coins (Appendices, Map III, with individual pie charts for each site yielding coins for both the 6th and 7th centuries) indicates that the decay of the ancient city was already advanced, and that its origins must be sought in the fifth century, if not earlier. Perhaps, eventually, the comparison of the spatial distribution of the already studied Hellenistic coinage[692] with the Rhodian imperial issues and Roman imperial coins which succeeded them[693] will provide a useful outline of the process of urban decline.

In the 6th century, according to the numismatic evidence, the greatest resistance to this decline is observed in the east slope of the hill of the ancient acropolis, with the great basilica of Rhodes -the second largest in Greece after St. Demetrius in Thessalonica- as its focus. Most of the few recovered coins of Anastasius I were found there; the low rate of circulation during his times shows that this decline cannot be due to the great earthquake of AD 515, since this struck Rhodes near the end of his reign. The relief measures taken by the emperor on behalf of Rhodes may have assisted a certain recovery which is marked by a rise in monetary circulation under his successor, Justin I (Figs. 11 and 95). The several unidentified pentanummia of the period may be responsible for the apparent slight decrease under Justinian I until 542, but the drop in circulation after 642, the year of the great plague, is the most significant feature of his reign.

[690] *Archaiologikon Deltion* 25: 518-527.
[691] Kasdagli 2000.
[692] Apostolou 1998; *eadem* 2003; Ashton 2001.
[693] Rerearch into the coinage of the period is under way: E. Apostolou, *The Numismatic history of Rhodes in the Roman Period.*

The increase in the availability of coin under Justin II is probably associated with the more efficient collection of taxes, although this need not be its only cause. The increased circulation of denominations lower than the follis also influences the general impression and probably facilitated small-scale exchanges and raised the probability of chance losses. Other factors, such as the gradual recovery after the great plague, or the efforts to contain the Persian advance in Syria, may well have contributed to the rise in coin circulation.

The subsequent drop may be attributed to the relaxation of financial control under Tiberius II, as the coins from his reign are very few. From Tiberius to Phocas there is a small but steady rise, which peaks suddenly and spectacularly in the first years of Heraclius. This phenomenon is obviously linked to a reorganization of the structures of government as well as the response to the Persian offensive. It is not a coincidence that another rise occurs towards the end of Heraclius' reign, with the Arab invasion of Palestine. The consequences of the increased strategic importance of the harbour of Rhodes are felt under Heraclius, later to develop into the primary reason for the survival and fortification of the coastal medieval settlement. The fact that more coins of the 6th century have been recovered from the area of the great basilica than from the harbour zone (Figure 33), a situation reversed in the 7th century, reinforces this interpretation. Further support is provided by a comparison with the available sample from the city of Constantia in Cyprus, whose geographical location was key for the supply of Byzantine troops in Syria. The sharp rise in monetary circulation under Heraclius is also present there, a feature absent from the analysis of the coin finds from other Cypriot sites such as, for example, Kourion.[694] The graph below emphasizes the similar development of the two harbours during the first half of the 7th century:[695]

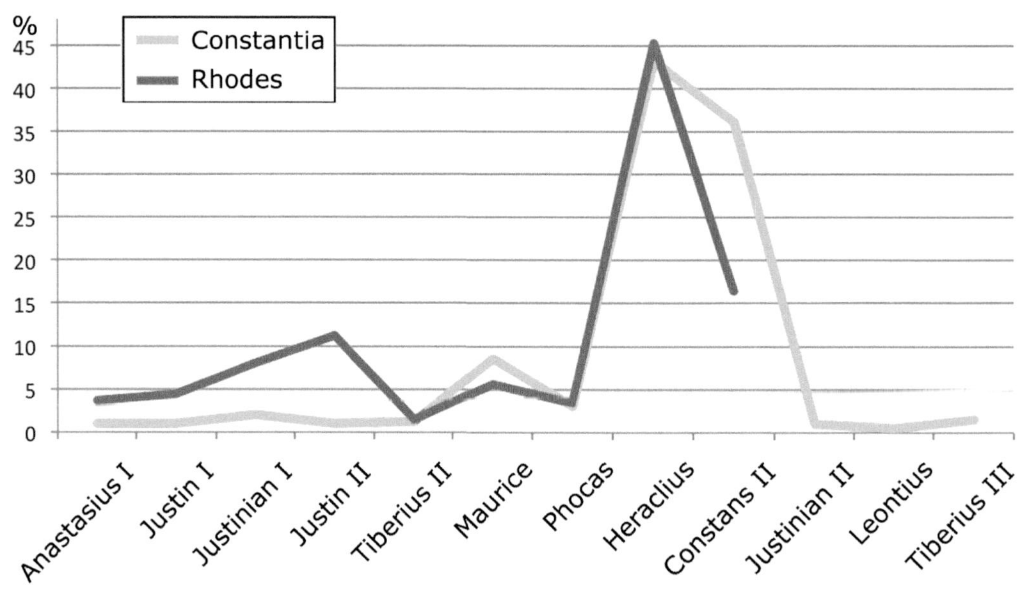

Figure 94: Comparison of Rhodes and Constantia numismatic profiles for the 6th and 7th centuries.

The comparison involves 744 coins from Rhodes and 714 from Constantia; it is based on the percentage of the total of finds issued in each emperor's name. Since the coins of Heraclius from Constantia are split between those before or after 629, it is not possible to see whether the Rhodes peak between 613 and 615 also occurs in the Cypriot city. It is certain, however, that if there is a corresponding peak, it will not be as sharp as in Rhodes, because the Cypriot sample from before 629 is just 28,5% of the emperor's coins, while in Rhodes the corresponding representation is 52,3%, and the coins from the interval 613-615 alone make up 28% of the coins of Heraclius. The analysis of the classes of Heraclius in Rhodes is presented in the graph below (Figure 95), together with the coins from the 6th century; losses per year are represented in nummi in order to reduce the impact of the variable representation of smaller denominations.

The result shows that in Rhodes coin circulation shot upwards in the first five years of Heraclius' rule, afterwards dropping to levels low even by 6th century standards. In the third decade of Heraclius the sample returns to the

[694] Metcalf 2009: 155-156.

[695] For the coin evidence from Constantia (714 finds), see Metcalf 2009: 211.

level of the emperor's first three years and continues relatively high until the end of the reign. It is obvious that the increase in circulation, in both Rhodes and Constantia, was the result of military action in Syria. However, it was not expressed in the two cities in the same manner; and inflationary tendencies are possible, given the increased availability of coin locally.

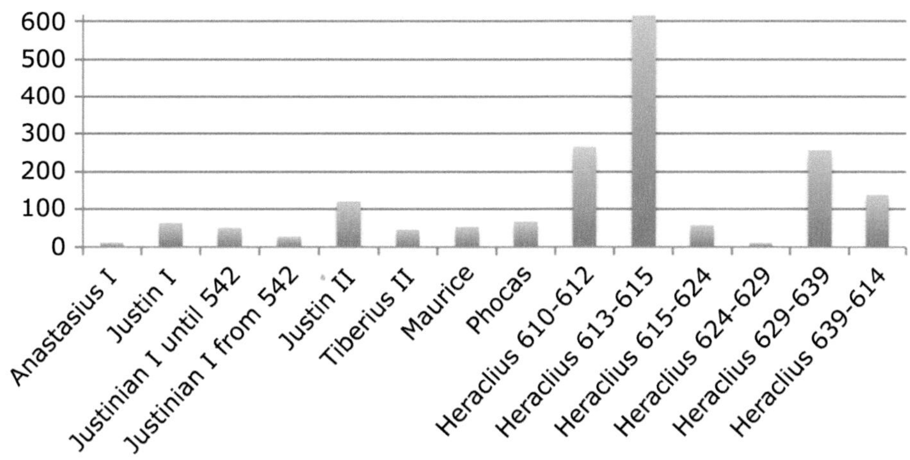

Figure 95: Losses per year expressed in nummi, 491-641.

The comparison with Constantia is of interest also in the times of Constans. The strong presence of the INPER CONST (2bis) class folles, due to the preparations for the campaign to recover Egypt, is a feature of the local sample in both places. In Constantia they make up 26% of the emperor's coins, but in Rhodes the percentage is higher still (35%), a fact that rules out the issue of the class in Cyprus.[696] In general, the differences between the numismatic profiles of the two sites may be ascribed to the fact that Rhodes was a strategically located naval base between Constantinople and Egypt, while Constantia was the outlet to a productive hinterland close to Syria. From 645 on, coin finds in Rhodes are reduced until the naval encounter at Phoenix (Battle of the Masts, *c.* 654); this is also associated with increased circulation, whose precise pattern cannot be assessed because of the poor state of preservation of several specimens. After the departure of Constans for Italy in 663, coin finds in Rhodes disappear. A spike at the end of the reign should probably be linked to movements of the fleet associated with the emperor's death. The evidence of the coins in the second half of the 7th century confirms that the military role of Rhodes had become dominant.

A small group of local imitations marks the brief occupation of Rhodes by the Arabs (*c.* 773-782). These flimsy and clumsy imitations are not direct copies of the coins of Phocas and Constans II; they copy the Arab pseudo-Byzantine issues imitating the imperial coins that circulated in Palestine until about 664.[697] The countermarks on finds from Cyprus, probably dating after 680, link political developments in the two islands. However, from the times of Constantine IV, the circulation of imperial copper coins in Rhodes ceases.

From the late 7th to the second quarter of the 11th century, the demonetization of the local economy is the principal characteristic of the numismatic profile of Rhodes.[698] The circulation of copper coins ceased completely in a very short time. From the period of Theophilus a limited number of folles reappears. However, the presence of coins remains rather sporadic from the mid-10th century until the 1030s,[699] although the importance of the naval base of Rhodes is recognized by the written sources. From *c.* 1030 onwards, coin circulation shoots up and the plentiful clipped and worn thin class B and C anonymous folles, and the eponymous, equally worn folles of Romanus IV, testify to the incipient need for petty coins, at a time when the central authority lacked the motivation to provide them regularly (Figure 44; Appendices, Map IV).[700] We do not know what factors had caused such a development in the town in the 10th and early 11th century, whether increased traffic in the harbour, military or otherwise, or a more general prosperity due to increased security; but it is obvious that the arrival of substantial quantities of copper coin to cover military needs under Romanus III and Michael IV was eagerly accepted, and that these pieces remained in circulation for at least three decades. The same welcome is signalled for the eponymous folles of

[696] Metcalf 2009: 152-153.
[697] Pottier *et al.* 2008: 115; Schulze and Oddy 2012: 187-200.
[698] The picture provided by the coin finds of Rhodes supports the chronological limits set by Metcalf 1979: 21.
[699] As the number of varieties of the anonymous A2 folles testifies: Grierson 1982: 208, var. 1, 3, 5, 8, 9, 14, 22, 24, 27, 31, 32, 39, 41, 47.
[700] They are either issues of Constantinople or imitations; their state of preservation does not allow distinctions between the two.

Romanus IV, which remained in circulation at least until the reign of Nicephorus III, who supplied the Byzantine provinces with large quantities of copper.

The expansion of the town beyond the south wall of the Collachio nucleus in the 11th century is clearly marked by the distribution of the coin finds. There is a fair chance that the earliest phase of the church of SS Constantine and Helena dates from this period. The problematic Minatsis plot hoard (Appendices, Selected Context III)[701] of 17 coins found in a grave most likely associated with this church consists of 14 worn 11th-century folles and three clipped 12th-century trachea; but there is no proof that we have to do with a single deposit, since graves of this period were frequently reused and the stable orientation of the burials meant that successive deposits of coins could come to occupy the same space. Also, the heavy wear on the 11th century issues is not particular to this hoard: few specimens of the plentiful anonymous Classes B and C are in better condition, and this wear pattern does not occur in the well-represented folles of Nicephorus III and Alexius I. Thus, a date in the 1070s is more likely for the deposit of the folles in this grave and provides our earliest evidence for both the existence of the church and for the local custom of depositing parcels of copper coins as grave goods.

Coin circulation remained comparatively high in Rhodes throughout the reign of Alexius I, presumably because of its increased strategic importance (Figure 50). After his monetary reform, the first indisputable imitations of imperial copper issues made their appearance in the town. The inclusion of Rhodes in the tetartera sphere of circulation, mostly extending to the west of the Aegean sea, may well be related to administrative adaptations related to the support of the new imperial fleet. A drastic reduction in coin circulation occurs under John II and may have encouraged the circulation of imitative tetartera; this reduction continues under Manuel I, in spite of the great fleets prepared for particular campaigns in 1148, 1168 and 1176-7 which may have raised the local coin sample. The reduction was probably due to the centralizing policy of John concerning the finances of the fleet and the spread of the *pronoia* during the 12th century. This led to the replacement of direct taxation paid in cash to the fisc with the payment of dues in various forms, including goods, produce and services, to the *pronoiarios*. During the 12th century, it gradually replaced the payment of salaries to officials of various ranks, resulting in a sharp fall in the income of the fisc, since much of it was diverted into private hands. The decrease in money transactions between the state and the general public limited the state's need for petty cash, which was mostly required for tax returns

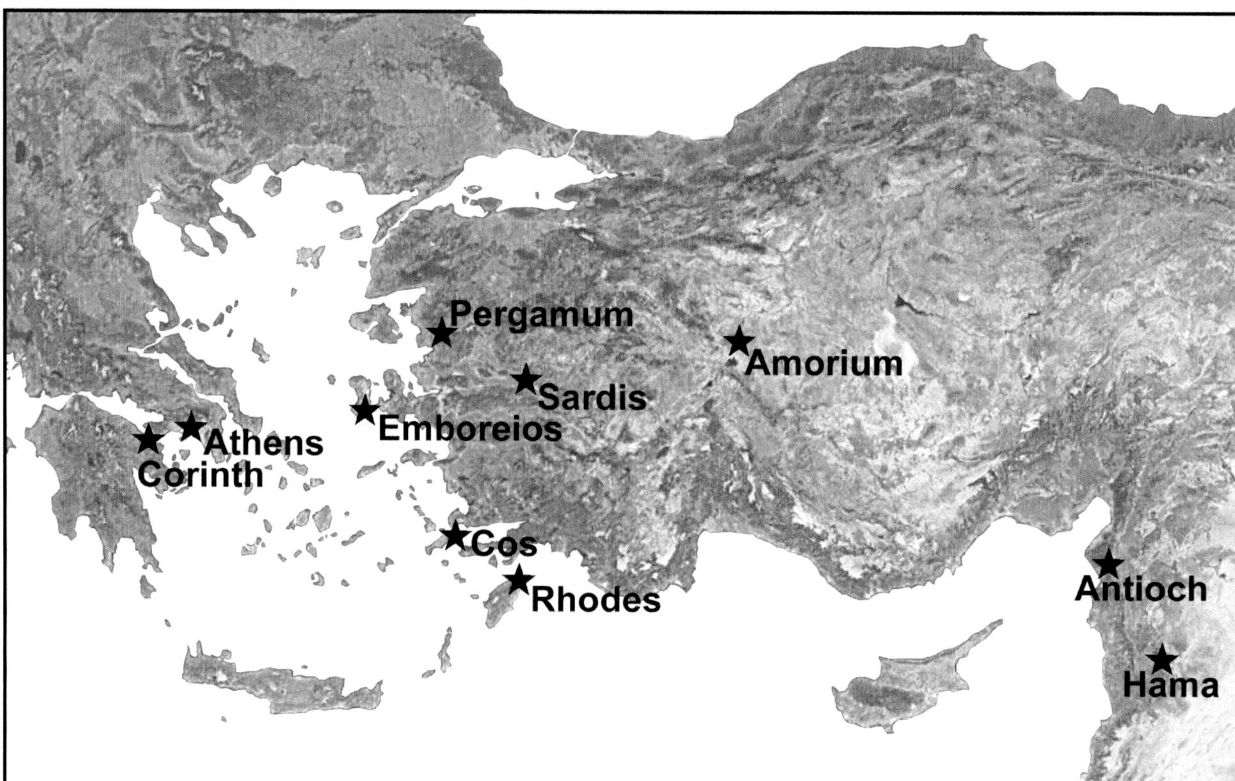

Figure 96. Geographical distribution of the compared sites.

[701] Nika 1993: 572; Baker 2006: 352.

and military spending, at least in the provinces. The state was also rid of the need to pay soldiers and craftsmen involved in defensive projects, since the responsibility for their upkeep devolved to middlemen.[702] It is telling that the next rise in monetary circulation accompanies the loss of control over the provinces by the central government at the close of the century.

* * *

A comparison with the coin sample of other regions of the Byzantine empire between 598 and 1204, exposes the way Rhodes functioned into the broader context and also provides methodological insights. Eight other sites are compared to Rhodes (Figure 96). The basic comparison is made between Rhodes and the main corpus of finds from the important excavations in Antioch, Sardis, Amorium, the Athenian Agora and Corinth (Figure 97).[703] These sites were chosen because they represent various geographical regions, have different histories and have produced sufficient quantities of coins to provide reasonably reliable information on monetary circulation.[704]

	Antioch	**Sardis**	**Amorium**	**Athens**	**Corinth**	**RHODES**
Anastasius I	634	48	3	31	7	29
Justin I	900	[46][16]	1	13	8	[49]
Justinian I	352	[187]	5	97	40	[76]
Justin II	176	188	4	207	85	84
Tiberius II	90	26	6	20	16	11
Maurice	128	179	7	25	9	45
Phocas	34	99	6	48	18	25
Heraclius	55	175	14	232	9	335
Constants II	81*	87	26	817	37	116
Constantine IV	-	2	6	30	4	-
Justinian II	-	1	6	7	-	-
Leontius	-	-	1	-	-	-
Tiberius III	-	-	6	1	-	-
Philippicus	-	-	-	61	-	-
Anastasius II	-	-	1	4	-	1
Leo III	-	-	4	22	-	-
Constantine V	-	-	1	1	-	-
Leo IV	-	2	4	1	-	-
Constantine VI	-	-	2	1	-	1
Irene	-	-	-	1	-	-
Nicephorus I	-	-	6	-	2	1
Michael I	-	-	-	-	1	-
Leo V	-	1	6	1	-	-
Michael II	-	2	12	2	2	1
Theophilus	-	2	18	4	23	4
Michael III	-	-	-	1	4	-
Basil I	-	-	4	17	50	2
Leo VI	1	6	9	81	158	3
Constantine VII	-	10	14	198	187	2
Romanus I	-	3	14	59	357	8
Nicephorus II	-	1	19	46	37	2

[702] Oikonomides 2002: 1042-6.
[703] As published by Waage 1952; Bates 1971; Katsari *et al.* 2012; Thompson 1954; and Edwards 1933. Corinth is represented only by the coins of the original publication, so as to preserve consistency in the identifications.
[704] There are weaknesses: we know, for example, that the representation of Theophilus at Corinth is six times higher than presented in the original publication (Metcalf 1973c: 182-183). Also, Figure 97 does not contain data from Cyprus because the picture there is confused due to the number of sites with dissimilar numismatic profiles. Cf. Metcalf 2009: 159.
[705] There are 39 identified coins of Justin I from Sardis and 35 from Rhodes, while those of Justinian I are 173 and 52 respectively. To those have been added the unidentified pentanummia at a ratio of 1:2, to avoid an excessive disparity between the representation of the two emperors.

	Antioch	Sardis	Amorium	Athens	Corinth	RHODES
John I (A1)	[28][17]	[3]	6	104	146	4
Basil II (A2)	[138]	[25]	63	519	679	24
Romanus III (B)	125	5	10	218	154	90
Michael IV (C)	80	6	29	154	96	31
Constantine IX (D)	8	-	8	104	18	5
Constantine X + E-F	57	6	24	105	221	10
Romanus IV + G	8	5	35	108	21	21
Michael VII + H	6	1	6	229	144	9
Nicephorus III + I	23	-	24	1036	500	24
Alexius I + J-K	29	-	1	1270	713	81
John II	1	-	-	145	138	5
Manuel I	-	-	-	3775	1509	26
Andronicus I	-	-	-	78	19	3
Isaac II	-	2	-	156	30	31[-22]
Alexius III	-	3	-	18	27	16[+22]
TOTAL	**2925**	**1121**	**412**	**10047**	**5157**	**1184**

Figure 97. Comparison of the coins from Rhodes to other sites.

Common features shared by most of the chosen sites may be taken as general characteristics, while deviations from them are most likely local phenomena possibly reflecting either historical events which may, or may not, be recorded in the written sources, or aspects of currency management as an administrative tool, or even factors and tendencies of the local economy and society. Comparisons may be made in three ways:

- Through the absolute number of coins of each emperor
- Through the calculation of losses per year
- Through the percentage of the total of each sample representing each emperor (numismatic profile).

The absolute number of coins of low value in any site is a correlation of the degree of monetization of small-scale daily exchanges and the extent of the explored area; while losses per year provide an index for variations in monetary circulation at a particular site through time. Combining the two shows the relative importance of the coinage in the life of a place. The numismatic profile, on the other hand, is the most convenient means of comparing different sites, because the size of each sample is of secondary importance, while differences are enhanced. In the processing of the data of Figure 98, pains were taken to separate general tendencies from features peculiar to a particular site, highlighting the case of Rhodes, and noting weaknesses due, for the most part, to dated identifications of particular groups of coins.

A lot of detail may be drawn for the period between 498 and 668 (Figure 98). Justinian is well represented in Rhodes, although less than Justin II, and the coins from Sardis[707], Athens, Corinth and Rhodes support a general increase in coin circulation under Justin II. A rise at this time is also observed in Antioch, but there it also continues under Tiberius II. A rise in coin numbers under Maurice and a subsequent drop under Phocas occurs in Antioch, Sardis and Rhodes. However, since losses per year are lower under Maurice, coin circulation is lower in Antioch,[708] Amorium, Athens and Corinth, picking up somewhat under Phocas (Sardis). In Rhodes losses per year show relative stability from Tiberius II to Phocas, between the peaks of Justin II and Heraclius. A new rise in coin numbers occurs under Heraclius (Antioch, Amorium, Athens,[709] Sardis, Rhodes) which, however, reckoned in losses per year, shows a

[706] In Antioch class A1 has been split from A2 following the ratio of Athens (17%) and in Sardis according to the ratio of Amorium (9%), the nearest geographical location.

[707] At Sardis there is a gentle but steady rise in circulation up to Justinian, a sharp peak under Justin II, a return to former levels under Tiberius and a new rise under Maurice and Phocas, followed by a decline. The main cause here must be the destruction of the city by the Persians in 616. For the significance and precise dating of the event see Greatrex and Lieu 2002: 195 and n. 99.

[708] The idiosyncrasies of Antioch, which had its own mint until 610, include the comparatively strong representation of Anastasius I, followed by a further rise under Justin I. This is followed by a decline briefly interrupted under Maurice. However, according to the losses per year, the peak under Justin I, probably due to the great earthquake of 526, is succeeded by an abrupt and substantial decline of circulation under Justinian and Tiberius II, and then a gradual fall until the Arab conquest in 637.

[709] Losses per year show that in Athens the increase in circulation under Heraclius was not very marked and the peak under Constans is due to that emperor's sojourn in the city in the winter of 662/663.

decline in circulation at Antioch, Sardis, Amorium and Corinth. The increase in Athens is slight, and only in Rhodes becomes a dominant feature. Under Constans II there is a further increase at Amorium, Athens and Corinth which, however, losses per year translate into a drop in circulation in Antioch, Sardis, Amorium and Corinth.[710] According to losses per year, the increase at Corinth and Amorium is small, while at Rhodes and Sardis there is a reduction, obviously due to the emperor's removal to the West after 663.

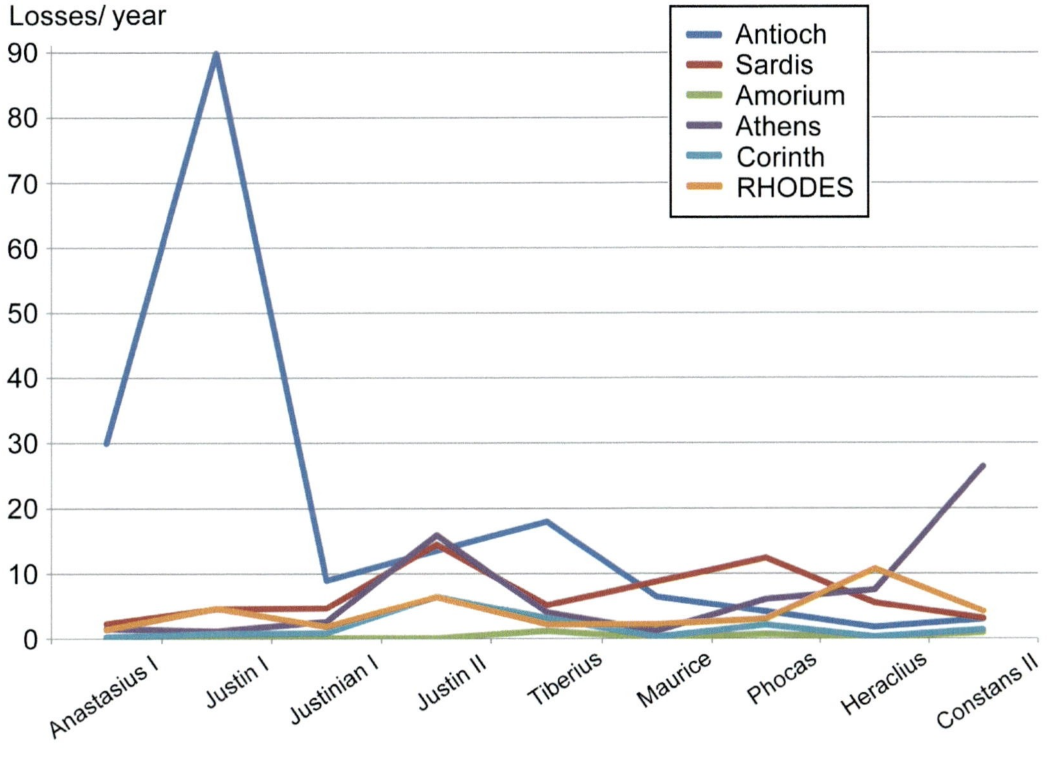

Figure 98: Comparison of losses per year between Rhodes and selected sites (498-668).

In the period 668-969 (Figure 99) there is a sharp demonetization of the economy from the late 7th century in Corinth, Sardis and Rhodes, and a serious reduction of coin circulation in Athens, where full demonetization occurs later, under Constantine V.[711] A slight rise in coin finds occurs in all the sites under Michael II and Theophilus (Amorian dynasty). After a new low under Michael III[712] the presence of coin increases everywhere from the times of Basil I onwards, most markedly in Athens and Corinth. Losses per year show that monetization of the local economy took place in Athens and Corinth under the early Macedonian emperors, although in Amorium the situation was reversed until the reign of Nicephorus II.[713] The figures for Rhodes at this time do not show a perceptible increase in circulation- merely a slight increase in sporadic finds.

The number of coins substantially increases in all the sites under Basil II, but this reflects the length of the reign and does not signify an increase in coin circulation (Figure 100). This occurs (Athens, Corinth, Antioch,[714] Rhodes) under Romanus III and wanes under Constantine IX. Afterwards there is a limited increase, with losses per year increasing in most sites until 1071; then they are reduced, except for Athens and Corinth, where the rise continues. Coin

[710] It is possible that the sample from Antioch includes Arab pseudo-Byzantine issues which, in 1952, were not yet distinguished from imperial issues. Research in this field has made great progress in the last two decades. See Goodwin 2005; Schulze *et al.* 2006; Pottier *et al.* 2008; Foss 2008; Haldon 2010.

[711] In Athens, where Philippicus (711-713) is well represented, coins of Leo III (717-741) also occur. Antioch lay beyond the Byzantine borders until its reconquest under Nicephorus II in 969.

[712] At Sardis there is a numismatic gap between Theophilus and Leo VI.

[713] The unbroken series of copper coins in Amorium at a time where they were rare in other sites (to date only coins of Philippicus, Irene, Michael I and Michael III have not turned up) was due to its strategic and administrative importance.

[714] Antioch was under Byzantine control until the revolt of Philaretus Brachamius (1078). Comnena: VI, 9. It was followed by its conquest by the Seljuks (1084) and the Crusaders (1098). Possibly, some of the coins published as tetartera of Alexius I are imitations, while the rest attest to the supply of the Crusaders by the Byzantine fleet.

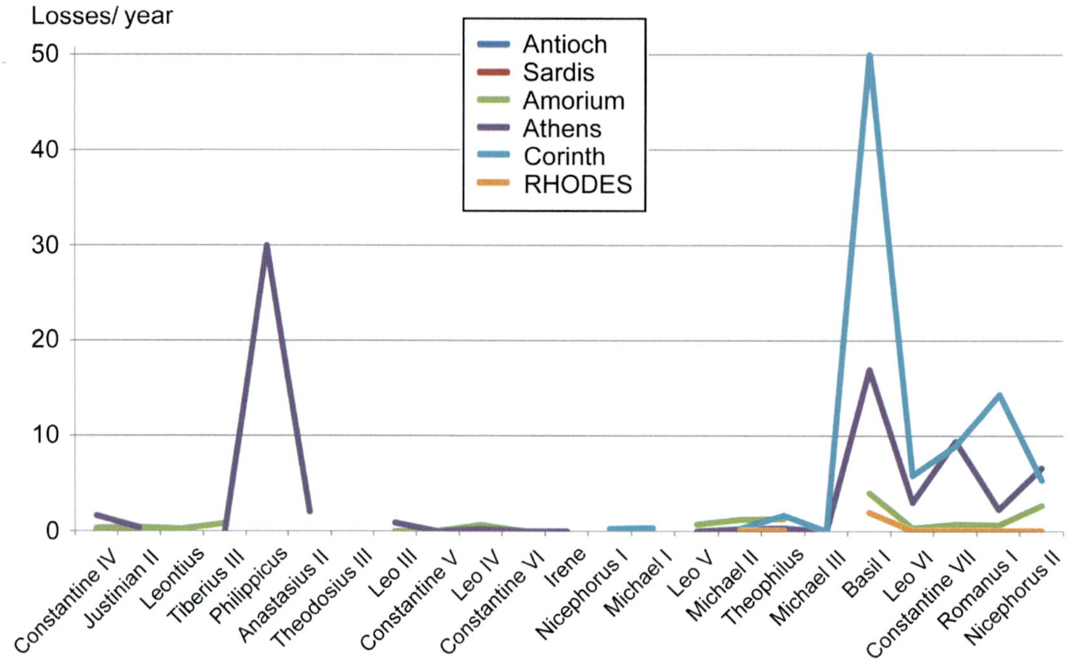

Figure 99: Comparison of losses per year between Rhodes and selected sites (668-969).

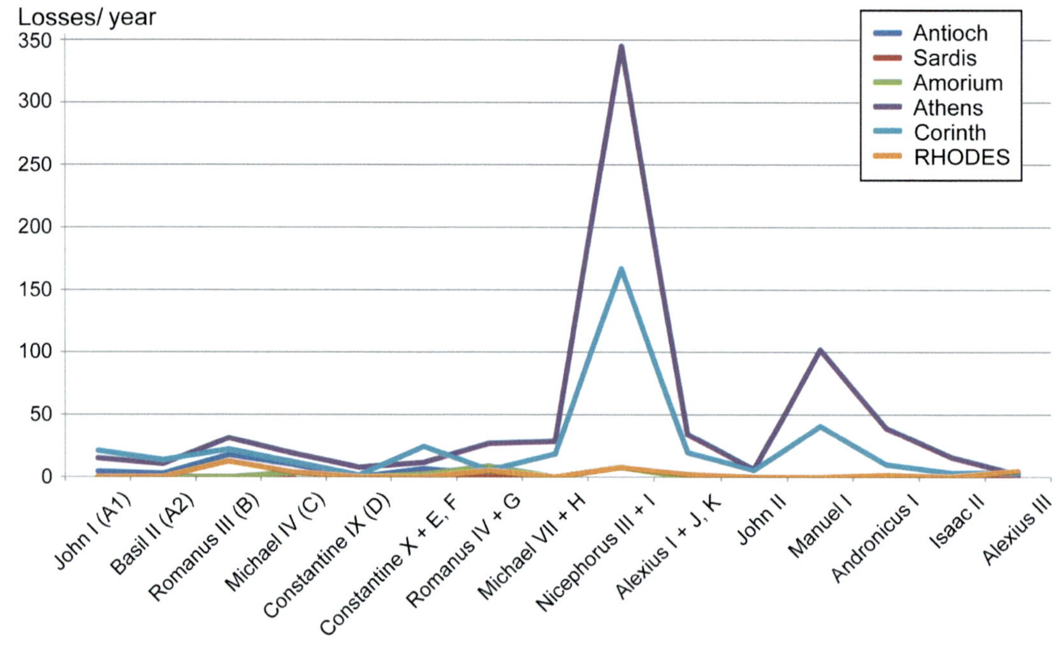

Figure 100: Comparison of losses per year between Rhodes and selected sites (969-1204).

circulation peaks in all the sites,[715] except Sardis,[716] under Nicephorus III where the rise is generally spectacular, with the exception of Rhodes, where the rise is less steep, and the succeeding fall under Alexius I more restrained. Afterwards, John II is respectably represented only in Athens and Corinth, although the subsequent sudden peak

[715] It is worth noting the presence of coins of Michael VII and Nicephorus III at Amorium, because it is assumed that the city was no longer in Byzantine hands after 1071. Vryonis 1971: 21.

[716] Sardis was seized by the Seljuks after 1071: and was recovered by megas dux John Ducas in 1097: Comnena: XI ,6. Nevertheless, there is a coin gap from 1071 until the times of Isaac II.

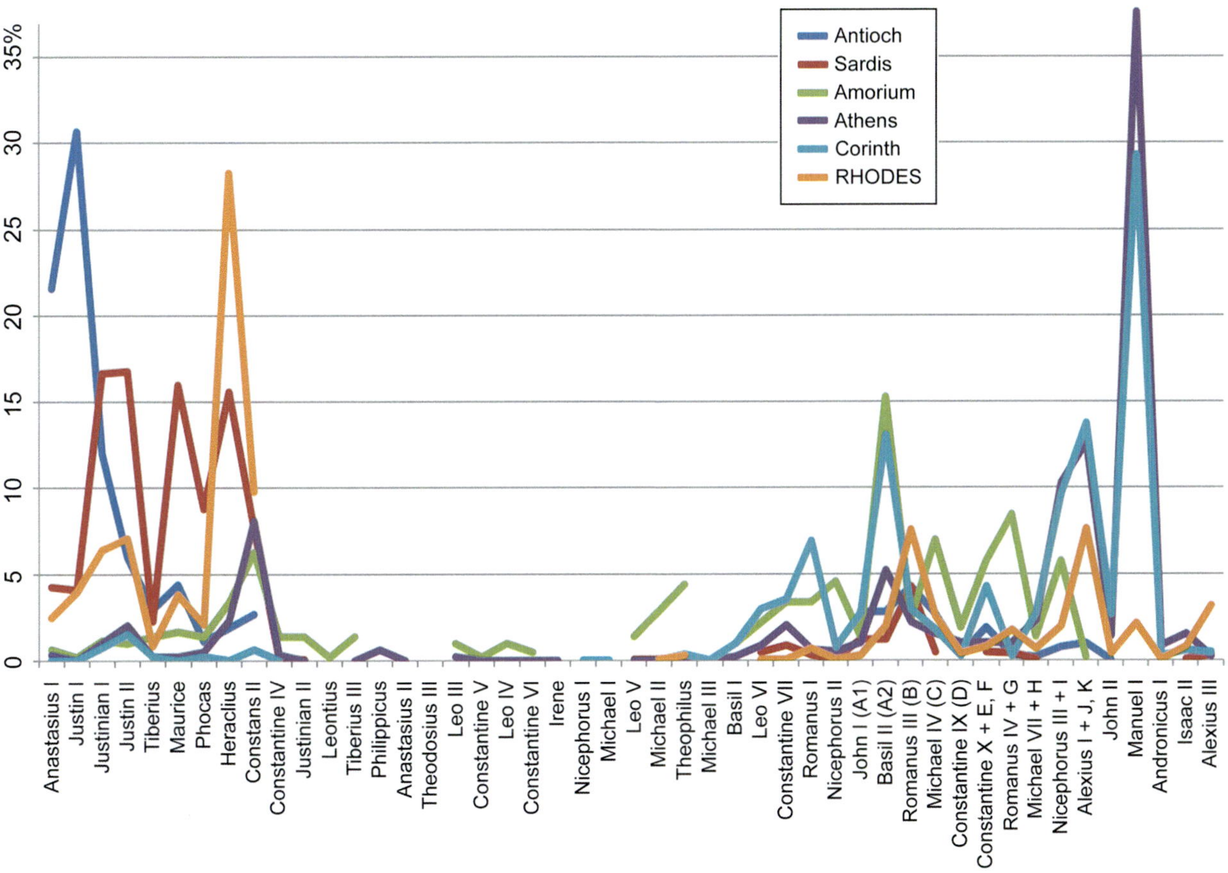

Figure 101: The numismatic profile of Rhodes compared to selected sites.

under Manuel I in the two sites may be partly due to the confusion between imperial issues and early 13th century imitations.[717] The steep rise observed in Rhodes under Alexius III is partly due to the inclusion of the neatly clipped trachea of his predecessors, since the clipping took place in the Byzantine capital *c.* 1200;[718] this modification has not been undertaken in the data from Athens and Corinth.

The numismatic profile of Rhodes from the 6th century to 1204 is compared with five major sites in Figure 101. Its most important features include the spectacular representation of Heraclius, which overshadows the also high representation of Constans II, and the peaks under Romanus III and Alexius I.

In recent years the relevant bibliography has been augmented by some sites whose corpus of coins is still small; although, for geographical reasons, its comparison to Rhodes is of special interest. In the Byzantine period, Cos and Chios were important stages along the sea lane connecting Rhodes to Constantinople. Figure 102 derives from the publication of the finds from Cos[719] and Emboreios on Chios.[720]

The numismatic profile drawn from the finds from Cos shows the following important differences from Rhodes:

- The percentage of the coins of Constans II is much lower.
- There are finds from the reigns of Leo III, Constantine V, Leo IV and Leo V, while Theophilus and Romanus I are missing.
- The representation of Leo VI and, to a lesser extent, of Constantine VII, is higher.
- There are no coins of Alexius I, John II, Andronicus I and Alexius III.

[717] The breakthrough for the interpretation of the imitative coins was made by Hendy in 1969, although the precise dating and origin of some imitations remains problematical. A recent revision of the data from Corinth confirms a rise in coin circulation. Penna 2010c: 410.
[718] Grierson 1982: 236-237.
[719] Brouskari and Didioumi 2006 (336 pieces).
[720] Ballance *et al.* 1989 (41 pieces).

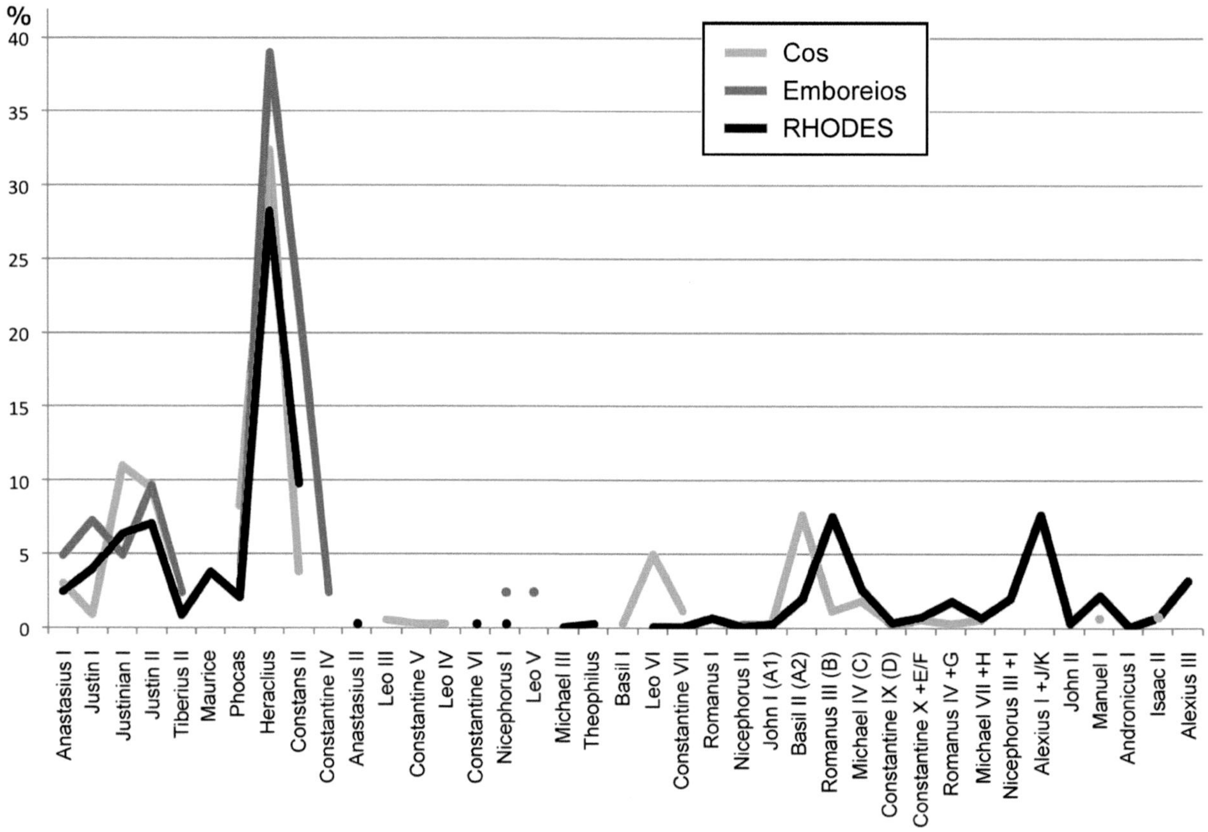

Figure 102: The numismatic profile of Rhodes compared to Cos and Emboreios on Chios.

Thus, Cos has already produced more coins of the period 668-969 than Rhodes, although the total number of coins is much smaller; and it does not participate in the rise of coin circulation between the 1030s and 1118. The only common feature of the two neighbouring islands is the dominant presence of Heraclius, a phenomenon also occurring at Emboreios on Chios, where the coin finds stop after 820.[721] Presumably, the crucial difference between Cos and Rhodes is the agricultural character of the former against the naval base of Rhodes. The importance of local features for the coin finds is also obvious in a comparison of Sardis to Amorion and Pergamum[722] in Asia Minor, cities which might have been expected to share more common features than they actually do since they belong to the same broad geographical region (Figure 103). Even without counting the peak under Constans, due to his restoration of Pergamum after the Persian raids, particular common features between the numismatic profiles of the three sites are not evident. In contrast, similarities can be found between sites distant from each other if they are situated in the same traffic route, as is the case with Rhodes compared to the two available Syrian sites, Antioch and Hama,[723] in the second half of the 6th century and the first half of the 7th (Figure 104).

The transitional 13th century is remarkable for the circulation of a wide variety of copper issues in the town of Rhodes and the operation of a local mint for the production of several of them. The main medium for daily exchanges in the town during the first fifteen or so years of the century, when Rhodes was possibly controlled by the father of Leo Gavalas, are the small module Latin imitative trachea, particularly types A and G, which imply a connection to Venetian activity from Constantinople. The finds from that time also include other trachea, like 'faithful' copies, large module Latin imitatives and, possibly, coins of Isaac II and Alexius III clipped to the size of a denier or even smaller.

* * *

[721] As also in Constantia, Cyprus (see above, Figure 94).
[722] Voegtli 1993.
[723] For Hama see Thomsen 1986.

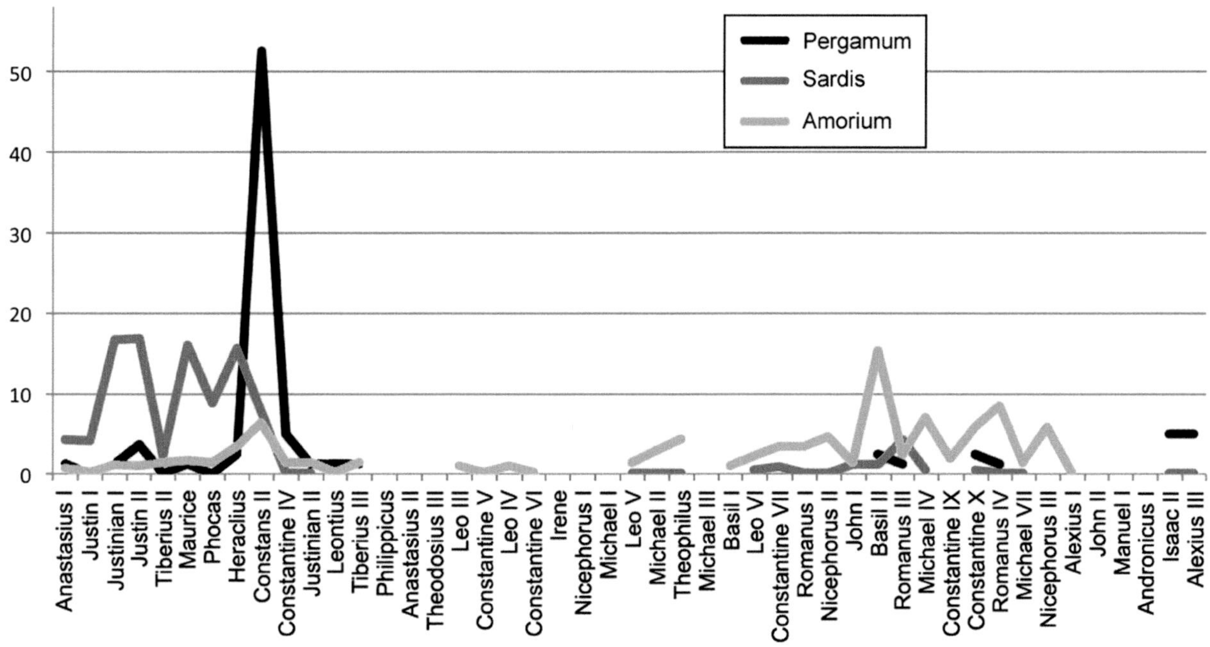

Figure 103: Comparison of the numismatic profiles of Pergamum, Sardis and Amorium.

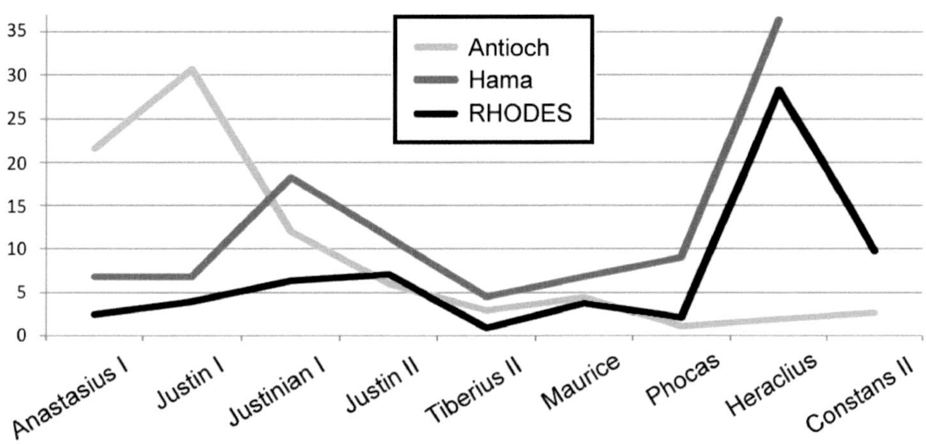

Figure 104: The numismatic profile of Rhodes compared to Syrian sites (6th - 7th c.)

It seems that in the Gavalas period imitative trachea were also minted in Rhodes: hitherto unknown and now presented for the first time, they bear a representation of the Virgin crowning an emperor. Besides a characteristic shape and style, these 'imitations' are influenced by trachea of Theodore I and John III Ducas-Vatatzes, Byzantine emperors of Nicaea. Their precise dating is problematical but they may conceivably have been issued before 1226. Another new type of trachy so far encountered only on the island is similar in style to Nicene trachea and could be either a local issue or a new Nicene type.

Leo Gavalas was responsible for the earliest signed Rhodian 'tetartera' of the 13th century, on thin, flat flans, which date after 1226, since he is qualified as *caesar*, a title granted him by Vatatzes. Similar coins were issued in the 1240s by his brother and successor John, although in limited numbers. From a numismatic point of view, the most important church of the first half of the 13th century is the one now known as SS Constantine and Helena in the medieval town of Rhodes. The finds from this site have provided valuable new evidence which has led to a reexamination of coin circulation in the first half of the century and of the Gavalas period on the island; thrown light on the history of the monument itself; and included new local types and other coins which have not been found elsewhere in the town so far.

From the end of the Gavalas period until the Hospitaller conquest of the island (1250-1309), losses per year fluctuated between about 0.5 and 2.8. The various local 'tetartera' issues of the half century were minted on behalf of a series of, at best, little known representatives of Byzantine emperors Theodore II, Michael VIII and Andronicus II. These coins are generally anonymous, or bear more or less ambiguous initials. Careful study of the designs, and comparisons to similar imperial emissions and near-contemporary coins from other lands, has led to a provisional dating sequence of twenty types, representing about 90% of the total of finds. This attempt is a more systematic and mature approach towards a topic which had engaged the author in the past, and thoroughly modifies earlier conclusions.[724] The reorganization of the local issues of the second half of the 13th century alters assumptions about some aspects of its political history, showing closer links with Constantinople in the last years of the 13th century and the beginning of the 14th than was previously supposed.

The spatial distribution of 13th-century coin finds in the town (Appendices, Map V) reflects the increased vigour of monetary circulation in the expanding town, particularly in the first half of the century. St Michael emerges as a significant religious site alongside SS Constantine and Helena and the two older foundations of the Pekmetzis church and the cathedral of St. Mary of the Castle and, apparently, overtaking in importance at least the first two of those in the second half of the century.[725] The earliest dated burials on the site afterwards occupied by the conventual church of St. John also belong to the second half of the century and belong to a church which was replaced by St. John of the Collachio; surprisingly, the site of St. Mark also emerges vigorously in the second half of the century, after coin finds dry up at SS Constantine and Helena.[726]

Comparing the evidence from Rhodes from 1204 onwards to other sites is unlikely to provide reliable information concerning coin circulation, at least for the present, due to the high percentage of burial offerings among the finds. The danger of overestimating the degree of monetization of the local economy from the 13th century onwards is serious (cf. Figure 7), although the increase during the first decades of the 13th century is substantial. According to the currently available excavation data, after a decline from the 1240s onwards, circulation seems to have picked up again *c.* 1330 (cf. Figure 8); and it remained at levels equal to those of the highest 13th century values for most of the Hospitaller period.

* * *

The last in the series of spatial distribution maps of the medieval town (VI) covers the Hospitaller town. The relative dearth of substantial secular excavation sites is regrettable; but if the current state of the monetary evidence clearly reflects the proliferation of religious foundations, the doubling of the available small change in the 15th century also seems certain. Churches where the coin finds include an undetermined number of coin purses are indicated by transparent pie charts.[727]

In comparison to the Byzantine period, the two centuries of Hospitaller rule in Rhodes are extremely well documented. Historical works[728] are backed by a plethora of documents from the Order's Archive on Malta, many survivals scattered in local archives across Western Europe,[729] dozens of travellers' accounts,[730] commercial records and treatises,[731] the remarkably preserved urban matrix of the medieval town of Rhodes[732] and hundreds of inscriptions and coats of arms.[733] Concerning the coinage of Hospitaller Rhodes, purely Western in character, the minting of silver and gold have been thoroughly studied,[734] although they are relatively rare. The main gap in our knowledge has been the dating of the petty coins, billon deniers and copper obols, most of which are anonymous. These coins are common finds in excavations, in Rhodes and most of the other Dodecanese islands; dating them precisely should enhance the usefulness of other finds recovered from the same contexts in the last forty years.

---

[724] Kasdagli 2006c.
[725] On the site of the cathedral, the lack of finds probably marks only the date the holy water spring was walled off, since the rest of the church has not been properly investigated. It may well be that a population increase resulted in contamination of the aquifer supplying the spring, since the substrate of the town is riddled with the tunnels of the ancient drain system which would facilitate the seepage of effluent from cesspits.
[726] The remnants of frescoes within St. Mark's date from the Hospitaller period.
[727] The 14th century hoard of 26 good quality billon deniers recovered from SS Constantine and Helena is atypical in its relative value.
[728] Cf. Bosio 1629; Delaville Le Roulx 1913; Vatin 1994; Luttrell 2003 and several articles.
[729] Cf. Tsirpanlis 1991: 11-21; *idem*, 1995; Luttrell 2003; Sarnowsky 2001: 11-16, 701-703.
[730] B. Waldstein-Wartenberg (†1992), unpublished compilation.
[731] Pegolotti [1936].
[732] Gabriel 1921 and 1923; Kollias 1994.
[733] Kasdagli 2009, with bibliography.
[734] Schlumberger 1878; Beckenbauer 1973; Mannucci 1982, 1983 and 1987; Metcalf 1995; Mazarakis 2010.

The study of the petty coins of the Hospitaller period has involved the examination of two major hoards of 4,247 and 1,834 pieces respectively, assembled *c.* 1420-1430 most likely in the course of a monetary reform; as well as chance finds and the usually corroded excavational coins. The separation into issues of the 14th and 15th/16th century was easy, but further analysis proved challenging. The large number of coins, the rather poor quality of the striking and the advanced degree of wear in many specimens led to errors in the early stages of the identification of the various types. Limiting the number of examined coins to those better preserved proved necessary for the analysis of the anonymous obol types. Even with the 1,700 or so pieces judged sufficiently well preserved to be useful to the study, growing familiarity with the details of various dies and the peculiarities of particular punches led to a series of revisions concerning the number of types and of the punches used for the sinking of the dies. Eventually, this examination yielded valuable evidence which, taken in conjunction with the ratios of site finds and the historical record, led to a number of conclusions.

After the deposition of master Foulques de Villaret (1319) his successor, Helion de Villeneuve, was busy in the West for several years; he only set foot on the island in 1332, and this event is accepted as the *terminus post quem* for the issue of new coin. The new billon deniers bearing a Genoese gate on the obverse are first mentioned by Pegolotti between 1332 and 1336. Their production began considerably earlier than that of the obols and may, indeed, have even preceded the arrival of Villeneuve in Rhodes. An early issue date for the deniers would go a considerable way in explaining the fact that the billon deniers are far more common as site finds than the 14th century obols, although the opposite should be expected from the relative value of the two denominations and the fact that the obols remained in circulation until the second decade of the 15th century. For a while, the anonymous deniers circulated concurrently with the obols. It is certain that the anonymous deniers were not produced by the craftsmen who made the anonymous obols, although the obols were definitely influenced by features of the local deniers. It is quite likely that different moneyers from Genoa were responsible for the early anonymous deniers, possibly dated *c.* 1320-35, and for the obols of the mid-century.

The issue of the obols seems to have begun in the times of the Black Death or immediately after. A great many types were apparently struck in a relatively short time, perhaps even between 1355 and 1377, with two or three obverse dies in use at the same time, and several more reverses. Most of this output probably falls within the rule of masters Pins and Berenger (1355-73); an important reason for their circulation may have been the necessity for alms to support those left destitute by the plague. The sinking of the dies was quite competent; to make them, the *monetarius* responsible made use of a series of simple and more complex punches, both for the main design and for the legends. The striking, however, is rather careless and there are questions on the resilience of the dies, perhaps due to the low quality of the metal: perhaps this was responsible for the uneven representation of the various types in the available sample- it may be that some dies were put out of commission much earlier than others.

Signed deniers entered circulation under masters Pins and Juilly. Pins introduced his personal badge on his deniers; an escutcheon of Berenger, his successor, appeared in a limited issue of obols since, perhaps due to financial problems, he does not seem to have struck any deniers.[735] Conceivably, Robert de Juilly (1373-77), probably responsible for the latest deniers bearing a fleur-de-lys badge, also issued the five distinctive late obol types which stand out stylistically from the rest of the 14th century copper. However, in the absence of corroborative evidence, it is safer to set broader margins for these late obols (1373-96) to include the period of master Juan Fernandez Heredia: their dies were certainly not the work of the craftsman responsible for the elegantly designed deniers of Juilly, although they incorporated some of their design features.

Towards the end of the 14th century, probably under Heredia (1377-96), anonymous and signed deniers were systematically recalled, together with foreign coins of similar size, and overstruck with a new, coarsely designed anonymous type, probably as part of a campaign to meet financial needs in a situation when the Rhodian mint was facing serious problems.[736] A new cycle of overstrikes is securely dated to the period of master Philibert de Naillac (1496-1521), which coincided with the peak of the crisis in the local mint. It was possible to date the new overstrikes through the identification of two new petty issues of this master, of which one bears the master's arms and the other his personal name. It is possible that the overstrikes of Naillac entered circulation before 1409, when the master left Rhodes for the West, where he remained until the last year of his life.

[735] Apparently the loot from Alexandria in 1365 was not sufficient to cover the cost of the expedition and make up for the difficulties in drawing the *responsiones* due from the West, judging from the proceedings of the Chapter General of 1370.
[736] At this time, the silver famine in Europe exacerbated the financial problems of the Order.

The recall of all the small coins just described, highlighted by the two major Hospitaller hoards of Rhodes, was most likely undertaken by master Antoni Fluvià (1421-37), who is known to have issued new types of coins. For the time being, the lack of securely identified hoards from the times of Fluvià onwards, and the corrosion of site-finds, prevent serious attempts to date the several types of obols which entered circulation until the end of the Hospitaller period in Rhodes, as most of them were recovered from regularly reused tombs whose fill is heavily disturbed. To date, only one deposit of coins discovered in the conventual church of St. John offers some useful indications for the sequencing of these obols, because participation in its discovery reassured the author about the integrity of the find. It is, however, clear that the development of the urban environment and the local market in the 15th century led to an increase in the circulation of petty coins, and to the appearance of quantities of imitative 'obols' before 1488. A limited number of imitations has also been identified for the 14th century, but the 15th century phenomenon was on an entirely new scale. The 14th century imitations are relatively few, clumsy and easy to distinguish from regular issues. This cannot be claimed for the 15th century, when the dividing line between imitations and official issues is not always clear.

At present, one group of imitations stands out: it consists of coins slightly heavier than the other 15th century issues, with nonsense legends and a châtel with vestigial 'towers' and an annulet within. These pieces are relatively well made, and the letters in the nonsense legends well formed, each with a separate punch. It seems that, in their design, too close a similarity to official issues was avoided while some of the letter punches may have been employed in the minting of coins with the perfectly legible legend +OSPITALIS S IO. It would appear that, at some point, craftsmen employed by the Order to produce obols turned to the independent production of tokens in order to cover a particular need, endeavouring to avoid accusations of counterfeiting. A model for such a practice may be found in the jetons with nonsense legends mass-produced about that time in the city of Nuremberg[737] and used as abacus counters or game tokens. The imitations of Rhodes, probably too small for an abacus and too numerous to explain as game tokens, are more likely to have been designed for a different use: perhaps in burial ritual offerings or, at any rate, ostensibly for this innocuous-seeming local custom. It is evident, however, that very soon the need for small change and the lack of response by the Order led to their adoption as token coins.

The presence of a distinct group of imitations and the care taken to stress its irregular character in comparison to contemporary coins of the 15th century does not mean that some truly low grade obols with meaningful legends were not, themselves, imitations. It is unlikely that the persistent need for small change caused only one unofficial attempt to meet it. The few surviving documents concerned with the Hospital's mint make it clear that it operated through a series of contracts with private individuals. Thus, at times, the local authorities may have tolerated the informal production of copper pieces of token value intended for the daily needs of the urban population. In the future, careful analysis of the site finds, with much patience and the contribution of new discoveries, may lead to the establishment of a sequence for these pieces and then proceed to differentiate official issues from likely imitations. In any case, new official obols and signed deniers entered circulation in 1488, under grand master Pierre d'Aubusson, to cover the shortfall which had encouraged the circulation of imitations. A little later, the reform of the silver coinage brought about the issue of strikingly designed large coins in the Renaissance style.[738]

Emery d'Amboise (1503-1512), Aubusson's successor, continued minting along the lines established by his predecessor. Besides gold sequins and Renaissance silver he issued three signed types of billon deniers. It is not known whether copper obols were also struck at this time; but it is certain that there was a substantial reduction in the volume of denier production: site finds of Aubusson show 3.6 losses per year, while those of Amboise 2.4, while only two of his types have so far been recovered from Rhodian excavations.[739] A few rare coins are known from the brief tenure of master Guy de Blanchefort (1512) but it is not at all certain that they ever circulated on Rhodes.[740] Under Fabrizio del Carretto (1513-20) the issue of deniers ceased, although the production of gold and silver continued normally. The last grand master of Rhodes, Philippe Villiers de l'Isle-Adam, was obliged to abandon Rhodes with the remainder of his forces after the surrender of the city in January 1523. Until then, he managed to strike standard type gold sequins and, apparently, some innovative pieces 19th century Western collectors managed to obtain in Rhodes.[741] However, the latest securely dated Hospitaller coins in the collection of the Archaeological Service in Rhodes are a sequin of Carretto and some large silver coins of the same master, most of which come from

[737] Mitchiner 1988; Kasdagli 1999: 121-123.
[738] After 1489, when Aubusson became a cardinal. For details see Mazarakis 2010: 45 ff.
[739] Schlumberger 1878: 253 and Pl. X, 25.
[740] Schlumberger 1878: 264 and Pl. XI, 13.
[741] Schlumberger 1878: 266-267 and Pls. XI, 15, 18, 20.

two hoards brought to light in archaeological excavations in the town in 1990 and 1994; at least one of those hoards dates from the fateful siege of 1522.[742]

A suspected reduction in petty coin circulation in the town of Rhodes after 1503 is hard to prove conclusively because of the anonymity of the obols. However, a drastic reduction is also observed in the number of foreign small coins dating from the second half of the 15th century, a trend whose causes are hard to assess without comparisons to the coin finds from other sites of the Eastern Mediterranean; the publication of the 14th and 15th century coins from other islands along the maritime routes of the Aegean held by the Latins, such as Lesbos, Chios and Samos, is highly desirable.

* * *

From the 6th to the 12th century, copper coinage was principally an administrative tool, although at times its wider significance for the local society and small-scale transactions reveals the structure and changes of the urban environment. However, rises in the numbers of coins on the island are usually associated with military needs of the central government in Constantinople. Conclusions concerning the size of the local economy without supporting evidence from gold are not particularly reliable, because the movement of goods in bulk is independent of the circulation of petty coins,[743] but possibly comparisons based on the number of single finds are not completely valueless: concerning daily transactions and, consequently, the degree of urbanization, in the 6th and 7th century Rhodes must have ranked nearer Sardis and Constantia, while in the 11th and 12th perhaps closer to Antioch, keeping in mind that most of the medieval town of Rhodes remains unexcavated. The dearth of coin finds from the 8th to the early 11th century is explained by institutional changes affecting the Byzantine provinces which permitted the operation of a naval base and arsenal in Rhodes without recourse to small change. From the 11th century until 1309, the periodic relaxation of central control often coincided with increases in the circulation of petty coins.

From 1309 until 1522, the Order of St. John exercised its rule on Rhodes directly and efficiently. The local ruler, the master of the Order, had an interest in the development of the urban character and prosperity of the local community which was acquiring, under the aegis of the multinational Order, a cosmopolitan hue. The monetization of the local market covered the needs of both pilgrims in transit and of that part of the population which made a living in the town or had recently or temporarily settled there. Under these circumstances, the smooth function of the market was, for the ruling elite, not only profitable but also necessary, in order to avoid resentment and unrest.

In contrast to the research carried out by foreign educational institutions in important sites like ancient Corinth or the ancient agora of Athens, archaeological exploration in Rhodes has had an essentially rescue character. The wide dispersal of plots of land excavated before they could be developed by the owners, together with the fact that the archaeologists could not choose where to excavate, mean that the investigation, although fragmented, was evenly distributed in most parts of the modern town and its suburbs.[744] The collected evidence now permits the confident forecasting of the archaeological significance of areas yet unexplored. Two categories of land have not been thoroughly investigated by archaeologists so far: a) Those built up during the Italian period in the first half of the 20th century or, earlier still, in the *marassia* created by the evacuation of the local Christians from the walled town after the Turkish conquest from 1523 onwards[745] and b) the zone of the medieval fortifications and standing secular buildings within, which have not yet been significantly altered. The coins occasionally picked up in the zone of the fortifications generally belong to the Hospitaller period or are later still: in any case, the degree of disturbance of the urban landscape in this zone means that such finds are only useful in broad statistical analyses.

Apart from the excavated churches within the medieval town, characterized by an unusual concentration of coin finds, other localized foci of increased petty coin losses have been identified outside the fortifications contemporary to them (Appendices, Map VII). Thirty-odd Hospitaller coins from the site of the great Early Christian basilica of Rhodes have been associated with quarrying for building material. Others occur along the main roads leading to the countryside from the gates of the town. The expansion of the Hospitaller town impacted on the ancient monuments surrounding it; and some of the old churches outside the walls[746] were demolished by the Knights in the

[742] Kasdagli 1992 and 2006b respectively. The owner of the second hoard was buried in a mass grave with his purse still attached to his waist.
[743] Cf. Metcalf 2009: 45.
[744] For the methodological importance of this factor see Metcalf 2009: 142.
[745] The nuclei of the marassia, with the exception of a few spots, have not been investigated by archaeologists (cf. Figure 1).
[746] The presence of a number of medieval churches outside the fortified settlement is mentioned in the written sources, the earliest of which is the chronicler of Richard the Lionheart's visit to Rhodes in 1192. See also Luttrell 2003: 288-289.

15th and early 16th century, in the fear that they might serve to shield besiegers from the Hospital's artillery. Thus, concentrations of Hospitaller coins outside the medieval town may mark the sites of some of these lost churches.[747]

Archaeological excavation in the Rhodian countryside (Appendices, Map VIII), has generally been limited to the sites of Early Christian monuments under the pressure of recent land development, both inside various villages and in coastal zones where large hotels proliferate. It appears that some coastal sites developed in Late Antiquity, mostly near productive agricultural areas, before Byzantium lost control of the sea in the second half of the 7th century. It is therefore natural for coins of the first half of the 7th century to dominate the limited sample, since they also circulated in the town in much greater numbers than those of the 6th century. Most of the coins from the countryside were handed in by locals. For the moment, the largest concentration of coins is recorded at the village of Archangelos, where the Hospital endeavoured to strengthen the defences in the area after catastrophic Ottoman raids in the 15th century.[748] This picture is likely to change in the near future, as a result of recent archaeological investigations in the south of the island which promise exciting discoveries.

Familiarity with the numismatic material has answered some questions only to raise others. It is odd that there are no Byzantine coins at all from the 14th century. And is the rarity of foreign coins after 1470 solely due to the gradual reduction in the number of mints in the Aegean and the Italian peninsula? The sorting and inventory of the -admittedly limited- number of Islamic coins of the period before 1522 found in archaeological sites has not even started: it would be very useful to compare them with the rest of the foreign coins, in order to recreate a fuller network of the commercial ties of Hospitaller Rhodes; and would also permit a more objective assessment of the significance of the Western coins found on the island. Also, very little is known about small-scale exchanges in the local market in the first twenty years of the 16th century.

The present study has not by any means exhausted the possibilities of the available material. However, with the assistance of excavation diaries, other burial deposits may, in time, be identified and contribute to a scheme for the sequencing of the 15th century obols. The examination of the less well preserved coins from the two major Hospitaller hoards may also prove useful, because the full identification of as may coins as possible will consolidate the picture provided by the quantitative representation of the various types. Although the bulk of the coin finds have already been treated and inventoried, there is still some numismatic material lying forgotten and unprocessed alongside other site finds stored in various corners of the Ephorate's depots. Tracking these strays will allow an assessment of the cost of cleaning them, and will hopefully set in motion the process for their integration into the available corpus. Finally, the revision of the old identifications of the finds from Corinth and Athens would greatly enhance the interest of comparisons with the Byzantine coins of Rhodes.

The most important and encouraging feature emerging from the study of the numismatic corpus of Rhodes in the period under discussion is its support and elaboration of archaeological evidence from other fields such as the Late Antique lamps,[749] which seems to reach the same conclusions about urban decline and the economic situation of the 7th century, while the study of church murals dated *c.* 1300 also shows closer ties with Constantinople that hitherto assumed.[750] The reexamination of other finds and vestiges of buildings from contexts containing coins assigned a closer dating in the present study may confirm or undermine some of the arguments presented here. However, such a task requires a reorganization of the excavation finds lying crammed and practically inaccessible in scattered depots; this need grows ever more urgent, since the excavation diaries and associated photographic record are fading along with the recollections -if not also the physical presence- of the excavators, who are still best qualified to interpret them.

[747] Kollias 2007: 284 and n. 12.
[748] The size of the published sample has been affected by the keen eyesight and cooperative attitude of particular inhabitants.
[749] Katsioti, under publication.
[750] Kefala 2015.

Bibliography

Abbreviations in the appendices and catalogue

ADelt *Archaiologikon Deltion, Chronika*
DOC *Catalogue of the Byzantine Coins in the Dumbarton Oaks Collection and in the Whittemore Collection*
DChae *Deltion of the Christian Archaeological Society*
MIB W. Hahn, *Moneta Imperii Byzantini*
PAE *Praktika Archaeologikes Etaireias*

15 χρόνια έργων αποκατάστασης στη Μεσαιωνική Πόλη της Ρόδου [15 Years of Restoration in the Medieval Town of Rhodes], 2007. Athens, Ministry of Culture.

Abulafia, D. 1987. *Italy, Sicily and the Mediterranean 1100-1400.* Aldershot, Ashgate.

Abulafia, D. 1993. *Commerce and Conquest in the Mediterranean 1100-1500.* Aldershot, Ashgate.

Aelius Aristides (AD 117-181), 1898. *Aelii Aristidis Quae Supersunt Omnia II* (B. Keil, ed.) Berlin, Weidmann: 72-91.

Ahrweiler, H. 1966. *Byzance et la Mer. La marine de guerre, la politique et les institutions maritimes de Byzance aux VIIe-Xve siècles.* Paris, Presses Universitaires de France.

Allen, M. 2012. *Mints and Money in Medieval England.* Cambridge, Cambridge University Press.

Angold, M. J. 1984a. *The Byzantine Aristocracy IX to XIII centuries.* Oxford, BAR International Series 221.

Angold, M. J. 1984b. *The Byzantine Empire 1205-1204.* London, Longman.

Angold, M. J. 1985. The Shaping of the Medieval Byzantine 'City'. *Byzantinische Forschungen* 10: 1-37.

Annales Altahenses maiores (11th c.), 1848. *Monumenta Germaniae Historica* 20, Hanover, Hahn.

Antoniadis-Bibicou, H. 1966. *Études d'histoire maritime de Byzance à propos du 'thème des Caravisiens'.* Paris, S.E.V.P.E.N.

Apostolou, E. 1998. *L'histoire monétaire de Rhodes pendant l'époque hellénistique.* Unpublished PhD thesis, Université Paris 4 Sorbonne.

Apostolou, E. 2003. Ελληνιστική Ρόδος. Η οικονομική της ιστορία μέσα από τη μελέτη των νομισμάτων της [Hellenistic Rhodes. Its economic history deduced from the study of the coinage]. *Obolos* 6: 6-30.

Armstrong, L., Elbl I. and Elbl M. (eds) 2007. *Money, Markets and Trade in Late Medieval Europe. Essays in Honour of John H. A. Munro.* Leiden, Brill.

Ashton, R. H. J. 2001. The Coinage of Rhodes 408 - *c.*190 BC. In A. Meadows and K. Shipton (eds), *Money and its Uses in the Ancient Greek World.* Oxford, Oxford University Press.

Astengo, C. 1957-8. Genova nella numismatica. *Italia numismatica.* Casteldario, Società Ligure di Storia Patria.

Astengo, C. 1961. Il denaro primitivo della zecca di Genova nei due secoli di sua emissione. In *Atti del Congresso internazionale di numismatica.* Rome, Istituto Italiano di Numismatica.

Archives of the Order of Malta. *The mint of the Order on Rhodes.* 365, f 1454.

Arles, A. 2009. *Entre monnayage officiel et faux-monnayage. La fabrication de la monnaie au marteau en France (XIIIe-XVIIe siècles). Approche physico-chimique, expérimentale et historique.* PhD thesis, Université d'Orléans 2009, ftp://ftp.univ_orleans. fr/theses/adrien. arles_2050.pdf

Auction Catalogue: The Grand Masters of the Order of the Hospital of St. John of Jerusalem at Rhodes (1307-1522), 101-105.

Auctiones 15, 18 Sept. 1985. 'Principauté d' Achaïe, Ile de Chio, Ile de Lesbos, Seigneurs des deux Phocées, Grands-Maîtres de l' ordre de Saint-Jean de Jérusalem à Rhodes, 1307-1522, Les Grands-Maîtres à Malte, 1530-1798'; 55-56.

Avramea, A. 1983. Νομισματικοί «θησαυροί» και μεμονωμένα νομίσματα από την Πελοπόννησο (ΣΤ' - Ζ' αι.) [«Trésors» monétaires et monnaies isolées du Peloponnèse (VI-VII siècles)] *Byzantina Symmeikta* 5: 49-90.

Avramea, A. 2001. Το νόμισμα στη βυζαντινή κοινωνία [The Coin in the Byzantine Society]. *Obolos* 5: 8-27.

Bachrach, B. S. 1993. *Fulk Nerra, the Neo-Roman Consul, 987-1040.* Berkeley, University of California Press.

Baker, J. and Ponting M. 2001. The Early Period of Minting of Deniers Tournois in the Principality of Achaia (to 1289), and their Relation to the Issues of the Duchy of Athens. *Numismatic Chronicle* 161: 207-254.

Baker, J. 2003. Coin Circulation in Early 14th Century Thessaly and South-Eastern Mainland Greece. In N. G. Moschonas (ed.), *Money and Markets in the Palaeologan Era*: 293-336. Athens, National Hellenic Research Foundation.

Baker, J. 2006. Some Notes on the Monetary Life of the Dodecanese and its Microasiatic Peraia, ca. 1100-1400. *Obolos* 8: 351-378.

Baker, J. 2007. Two Thirteenth-Century Hoards and some Site-Finds from Argos. *Numismatic Chronicle* 167: 211-233.

Baker, J. and Galani-Krikou, M. 2009. Further Considerations on the Numismatics of Catalan Greece, in the Light of the Athens Roman Agora (Lytsika) 1891 Hoards. In S. Drougou, D. Evgenidou, Ch. Kritzas *et al.*, Κερμάτια Φιλίας, Τιμητικός τόμος για τον Ιωάννη Τουράτσογλου: 457-472. Athens, Numismatic Museum.

Baker, J. and Stahl, A. 2013. Coinage and Money in the Morea after the 4th Crusade. In S. Gerstel (ed.), *Viewing the Morea: Land and People in the Late Medieval Peloponnese*: 457-472. Washington DC, Dumbarton Oaks Research Library.

Baker, J. 2015. Money and Currency in Medieval Greece. In N.I. Tsougarakis and P. Lock (eds), *A Companion to Latin Greece*: 217-254. Leiden/Boston, Brill.

Baldassarri, M. 2011. Le monete della Repubblica di Genova dal 1139 al 1814. In L. Travaini (ed.), *Il patrimonio artistico di Banca Carige. Monete, pesi e bilance monetali*: 34-47. Milan, Silvania.

Ballance, M., Boardman, J., Corbett, S. and Hood, S. 1989. *Excavations in Chios 1952-1955, Byzantine Emporio*. London, BSA Supplementary Volume No. 20.

Balling, J. 1963. A Byzantine Double Hoard from Lindos. *Nordisk Numismatisk Årsskrift*: 13-41.

Balog, P. 1955. *Notes on Ancient and Medieval Minting Technique. Numismatic Chronicle* Series 6, 15, 45: 195-202.

Barber, M. 1978. *The Trial of the Templars*. Cambridge, Cambridge University Press.

Barrandon, J.-N. and Bompaire, M. 1992. *Ecus d' or affaiblis, de 1417 à 1436. Revue Numismatique* 34: 100-150.

Bates, G. E. 1971. *Archaeological Exploration of Sardis, Byzantine Coins*. Cambridge Mass, Harvard University Press.

Beckenbauer, E. 1973. *Johanniterorden auf Rhodos*. Gitta Kastner Katalog 3, Ausgewählte Münzen. München, 22-23 Mai 1973: 68-88.

Beckenbauer, E. 1978/1979. Die unlesbaren Rückseitenlegenden einiger Gigliati des Johanniter-Grossmeisters Philibert de Naillac. *Jahrbuch fur Numismatik und Geldgeschichte* 28/29: 81-83.

Bedoukian, P. Z. 1962. *Coinage of Cilician Armenia*. Numismatic Notes and Monographs 147. New York, American Numismatic Society.

Belaubre, J. 1982. *Le trésor d' Uzès. Revue Numismatique* 24: 92-154.

Belaubre, J. 1987. Fiduciarisation du denier au moyen Age français (XIe-XVe s.). In G. Depeyrot and T. Hackens, G. Moucharte (eds), *Rythmes de la production monétaire de l'antiquité à nos jours*: 499-510. Louvain-La-Neuve, Université catholique de Louvain.

Bellinger, A. R. and Metcalf, D. M. 1959. A Hoard of Byzantine Scyphate Bronze Coins from Arcadia. *Numismatic Chronicle* Series 6, 19: 155-164.

Bendall, S. and Morrisson, C. 1979. *Un trésor de ducats d' imitation au nom d' Andrea Dandolo (1343-1354), Revue Numismatique* 21: 176-193.

Bernareggi, E. 1964. Gigliati del Gran Maestro dei Cavalieri di Rodi Philibert de Naillac. *Rivista Italiana di Numismatica e Scienze Affini* Series 5/LXVI, 12: 119-136.

Bendall S., and Broome, M. 1985. Seljuq Silver Dirhams with Palaeologan Countermarks. Oriental Numismatic Society Occasional Paper No. 20.

Bendall, S. 1977. The Mint of Trebizond Under Alexius I and the Gabrades. *Numismatic Chronicle* 17: 126-136.

Bendall, S. 1979. Some Further Notes on the Mint of Trebizond under Alexius I. *Numismatic Chronicle* 19: 211.

Bendall, S. 1981. A Follis of Alexius I of Trebizond. *Numismatic Circular* 89: 237.

Bendall, S. 1982. A New Twelfth-century Coin from the Mint of Trebizond. *Numismatic Chronicle* Series 7, 22: 163.

Biaggi, E. 1992. *Monete e zecche medievali italiane dal sec. VIII al sec. XV*. Torino, Montenegro.

Blemmydes Nicephorus (1197-1272), 1984. *Autobiographia*. Corpus Christianorum, Series Graeca 13. Turnhout, Brepols.

Bompaire, M. 1987. Les cadences de production (XIVe-XVIe s.), en France principalement. In G. Depeyrot, T. Hackens, G. Moucharte (eds), *Rythmes de la production monétaire de l'antiquité à nos jours*: 579-597. Louvain-La-Neuve, Université catholique de Louvain.

Bonneaud, P. 2004. *Le prieuré de Catalogne, le couvent de Rhodes et la couronne d'Aragon 1415-1447*. Millau, Études & Communication.

Bonneaud, P. 2012. Le difficile exercice du pouvoir par le maître Jean de Lastic 1437-1454. *Société de l'Histoire et du Patrimoine de l'Ordre de Malte* 26: 22-43.

Bosio, G. 1629. *Dell' Istoria della Sacra Religione, & Illustrissima Militia di San Giovanni Gierosolimitano*, vol. 2. Rome, Facciotti.

Bosworth, C. E. 2002. Arab Attacks on Rhodes in the Pre-Ottoman Period. In Y. Y. al-Hijji and V. Christides (eds), *Aspects of Arab Seafaring. An attempt to fill in the gaps of maritime history*: 63-72. Athens, Institute for Graeco-Oriental and African Studies/ Kuwait Foundation for the Advancement of Science.

Boxer, C. R. 1977. *The Portuguese Seaborne Empire 1415-1825*. London, Hutchinson.

Bramoullé, D. 2008. Activités navales et infrastructures maritimes: éléments du pouvoir fatimide en Méditerranée orientale (969-1171). In G. Fabre, D. Le Blévec, D. Menjot (eds), *Les Ports et la navigation en Méditerranée au Moyen-Âge*: 253-269. Paris, Le Manuscrit.

Brand, C. M. 1968. *Byzantium Confronts the West*. Cambridge Mass, Harvard University Press.
Brandi, C. 1938. La cappella rupestre del Monte Paradiso. *Memorie* 3: 9-18.
Brockman, E. 1995. *The Two Sieges of Rhodes*. New York, Barnes and Noble.
Brooke, G. C. 1932. *English Coins from the Seventh Century to the Present Day*. London, Methuen.
Broome, M. 1982. *A Handbook of Islamic Coins*. London, Seaby.
Brouskari, E. and Didioumi, S. 2006. Υστερορωμαϊκή και βυζαντινή Κως. Η συμβολή των νομισμάτων (4ος-12ος αι.) [Late Roman and Byzantine Cos: the Contribution of Coins (4th-12th Century)] *Obolos* 8: 297-323.
Brown, H. W. 1988. The Medieval Mint of Cairo. Some aspects of mint organisation and administration. In N. J. Mayhew and P. Spufford (eds), *Later Medieval Mints. Organization, Administration and Techniques*. The Eighth Oxford Symposium on Coinage and Moneraty History, Oxford 1988: 30-38. BAR International Series 389.
Bury, J. B. 1889. *A History of the Roman Empire from Arcadius to Irene (345 A.D. to 800 A.D.)* vol. 2. London, Macmillan.
Bury, J. B. 1912. *A History of the Roman Empire from the fall of Irene to the accession of Basil I (AD 802-867)*. London, Macmillan.
Bury, J. B. 1958. *History of the Later Roman Empire from the death of Theodosius I to the death of Justinian*, vol. 1. New York, Dover.
Butler, A. J. 1902. *The Arab Conquest of Egypt and the Last Thirty Years of the Roman Dominion*. Oxford, Clarendon.
Buttrey, T. V. 1993. Calculating Ancient Coin Production: Facts and Fantasies. *Numismatic Chronicle* 153: 342-352.
Buttrey, T. V. 1994. Calculating Coin Production II: Why It Cannot Be Done. *Numismatic Chronicle* 154: 341-352.
Cameron, A. and Conrad, L. I. 1992. *The Byzantine and Early Islamic Near East, 1: Problems in the Literary Source Material*. Princeton, Darwin Press.
Campaner y Fuertes, A. 1978. *Numismatica Balear*. Madrid/Palma, Gelabert.
Castan, C. and Cayon, H. P. 1980. *Las Monedas Hispano-Musulmanas y Cristianas, 711-1981*, Primera Parte, Monedas Hispanomusulmanas 92-898 Hégira (711-1492 J. C.) Madrid, Artegraf.
Castellani, G. 1925. *Catalogo della Raccolta Numismatica Papadopoli-Aldobrandini*. Venice, Civico Museo Correr.
Cheynet, J.-C. 2006. *Le monde byzantin, 2, L'empire byzantin: 641-1204*. Paris, Nouvelle Clio.
Christides V. 1984. *The Conquest of Crete by the Arabs (ca. 824): A turning point in the Struggle Between Byzantium and Islam*. Athens, Academy of Athens.
Christides, V. 2002. Arab - Byzantine Struggle in the Sea: Naval Tactics (7th-11th c. AD): Theory and Practice. In Y. Y. al-Hijji and V. Christides (eds), *Aspects of Arab Seafaring. An attempt to fill in the gaps of maritime history*: 87-93. Athens, Institute for Graeco-Oriental and African Studies/ Kuwait Foundation for the Advancement of Science.
Christodoulides, N. 1998. Ρόδος, Οδός Κ. Τσαλδάρη [K. Tsaldaris St.]. *Archaiologikon Deltion* 53, *Chronika*: 951.
Clot, A. 2004. *L'Espagne musulmane*. Paris, Perrin.
Comnena Anna (1083-1153), 2001. *Alexias*. Corpus Fontium Historiae Byzantinae 40. Berlin, De Gruyter.
Constantine VII Porphyrogenitus (905-959), 1829: *De Cerimoniis Aulae Byzantinae I. Corpus Scriptorum Historiae Byzantinae*. Bonn, Weber.
Conrad, L. 1992. The Conquest of Arwâd: a source critical study of the historiography of the Early Medieval East. In A. Cameron and L. I. Conrad (eds), *The Byzantine and Early Islamic Near East, I, Problems in the Literary Source Material*: 317-401. Princeton, Darwin Press.
Cooper, D. R. 1988. *The Art and Craft of Coinmaking. A History of Minting Technology*. London, Spink.
Corpus Nummorum Italicorum, Primo tentativo di un catalogo generale delle monete medievali e moderne coniate in Italia e da italiani in altri paesi, I-XIX, 1910-1940. Rome, Academia dei Lincei - C. Colombo.
Cosentino, S. 2007. Constans II and the Byzantine Navy. *Byzantinische Zeitschrift* 100/2: 577-603.
Coulié, A. and Filimonos, M. (eds) 2014: *Rhodes, XVe - Ve siècle avant J.-C. Une île grecque aux portes de l'Orient*. Exhibition Catalogue. Paris, Louvre/ Somogy.
Crawford, F. M. 1907. *Southern Italy and Sicily and The rulers of the South*. London, Macmillan.
Curta, F. 2011. *The Edinburgh History of the Greeks c. 500 to 1050. The Early Middle Ages*. Edinburgh, Edinburgh University Press.
Curta, F. 2014. Coins and Burials in Dark-Age Greece. Archaeological Remarks on the Byzantine "Reconquista". In R. Kostova (ed.), *Medieval Man and His World, Studies in Honor of the 70th anniversary of Prof. Dr. habil. Kazimir Popkonstantinov*: 55-102. Veliko Tirnovo.
Dagron, G. 2002. The Urban Economy, Seventh-Twelfth Centuries. In A. E. Laiou, (ed.), *The Economic History of Byzantium from the Seventh through the Fifteenth Century* vol. 2: 393-461.
Dalli, C. 2006. *Malta, the Medieval* Millennium. Valletta, Midsea Books.
Day, J. 1978. The Great Bullion Famine of the Fifteenth Century. *Past and Present* 79: 3-54.
Day, J. 1987. *The Medieval Market Economy*. Oxford, Blackwell.
Day, J. 1987. Les frappes de monnaies en France et en Europe aux XIVe-XVe siècles. In G. Depeyrot, T. Hackens and G. Moucharte (eds), *Rythmes de la production monétaire de l'antiquité à nos jours*: 537-555. Louvain-La-Neuve, Université catholique de Louvain.

Day, W. R. 2005. The petty coinage of Genoa under the early Doges 1339 - 1396. In C. Alfaro, C. Marcos and P. Otero (eds), *XIII Congreso internacional de numismática (Madrid, 15-19 septiembre 2003): Actas - Proceedings - Actes*: 1295-1304. Madrid, Ministerio de Cultura.

Delaville Le Roulx, J. M. A. 1913. *Les Hospitaliers à Rhodes jusqu'à la mort de Philibert de Naillac (1310-1421)*. Paris, Leroux.

Dellas, G. 2012. Οι σταυροθολιακές εκκλησίες της Δωδεκανήσου (1750-1924) [Cross-groined Vaulted Churches of the Dodecanese (1750-1924)]. *Dodekanesos* 7 (Jan.-June): 19-476.

De Roos, M. 1988. Men and Manners in a fifteenth-century mint. Mint personnel in Holland. In N. J. Mayhew and P. Spufford (eds), *Later Medieval Mints. Organization, Administration and Techniques.* The Eighth Oxford Symposium on Coinage and Moneraty History, Oxford 1988: 147-157. BAR International Series 389.

Dhénin, M. 1987. Quelques remarques sur le travail des graveurs de coins. In G. Depeyrot, T. Hackens and G. Moucharte (eds), *Rythmes de la production monétaire de l'antiquité à nos jours*: 543-457. Louvain-La-Neuve, Université catholique de Louvain.

Dietz, S. and Papachristodoulou, I. (eds) 1988. *Archaeology in the Dodecanese.* Copenhagen, National Museum of Denmark.

Dikigoropoulos, A. J. 1958. The political status of Cyprus AD 648-965. *Report of the Department of Antiquities, Cyprus* 1940-1948: 94-114.

Dumas, F. 1979. Les monnaies normandes (Xe-XIIe siècles) avec un répertoire des trouvailles. *Revue Numismatique* 6/21: 84-140.

Duplessy, J. 1988. Les monnaies concurrentes de Henri VI, roi de France et d'Angleterre, et de Charles VII. In N. J. Mayhew and P Spufford (eds), *Later Medieval Mints. Organization, Administration and Techniques*: 128-146. BAR International Series 389.

Edbury, P. W. 1991. *The Kingdom of Cyprus and the Crusades 1191-1374*. Cambridge, Cambridge University Press.

Edwards, K. M. 1933. *Corinth VI, Coins, 1896-1929*. Cambridge Mass., Harvard University Press.

Marot, T. *et al.* 1999. *El Tesoro de Sant Pere de Rodes, Una ocultacion de monedas de oro y de plata a principios del siglo XVI.* Barcelona, Museu Nacional d'Art de Catalunya.

Epstein, S. R. 1992. *An Island for Itself: Economic development and social change in late medieval Sicily.* Cambridge, Cambridge University Press.

Epstein, S. A. 1996. *Genoa and the Genoese, 958-1528*. Chapel Hill, University of N. California Press.

Esty, W. W. 1966. *The Theory of Linkage*. *Numismatic Chronicle* 6: 205-221.

Evangelatou-Notara, F. 2000. Χορηγοί, κτήτορες, δωρητές σε σημειώματα κωδίκων: παλαιολόγιοι χρόνοι [Patrons, owners, donors from notes on manuscripts of the Palaeologan period]. Athens, Parousia, Parartema 49.

Pegolotti Francesco Balducci (*fl.* 1310-47), 1936. *La Pratica della Mercatura* (ed. A. Evans). Cambridge Mass., Publications of the Mediaeval Academy of America 24.

Felloni, G. and Laura, G. 2004. *Genova e la storia della finanza: una serie di primati*? Genoa, Brigati.

Filimonos-Tsopotou, M. 2004. Η ελληνιστική οχύρωση της Ρόδου [The Hellenistic Fortifications of Rhodes]. Athens, Publications of the Archaiologikon Deltion 86.

da Fonseca, L. A. 2008. The Portuguese Military Orders and the Oceanic Navigations: From Piracy to Empire (Fifteenth to Early Sixteenth Centuries). In J. Upton-Ward (ed.), *The Military Orders Vol. 4, On Land and by Sea*: 63-73. Aldershot, Ashgate.

Forbes, R. J. 1971. *Studies in Ancient Technology*, vol. 8: 267-289. Leiden, Brill.

Foss, C. 2008. *Arab-Byzantine Coins, An Introduction, with a Catalogue of the Dumbarton Oaks Collection.* Dumbarton Oaks, Harvard University Press.

Gabriel, A. 1921. *La cité de Rhodes* I, *Topographie, Architecture militaire*. Paris, De Boccard.

Gabriel, A. 1923. *La cité de Rhodes* II, *Architecture civile et religieuse*. Paris, De Boccard.

Galani-Krikou, M. 1992a. Συμβολή στην έρευνα της κυκλοφορίας μεσαιωνικών νομισμάτων στο δεσποτάτο της Ηπείρου (1204-1449). In *Πρακτικά Διεθνούς Συμποσίου για το δεσποτάτο της Ηπείρου (Άρτα, 27-31 Μαΐου 1990)*: 125-161. Arta.

Galani-Krikou, M. *et al.* 1992b. 1η ΕΒΑ, Ανασκαφικές εργασίες. *Archaiologikon Deltion* 47, *Chronika*: 67-71.

Galani-Krikou, M. 1993a. Ελευσίνα, Νομίσματα. *Archaiologikon Deltion* 48, *Chronika*: 46-49.

Galani-Krikou, M. 1993b. Θήβα, Νομίσματα. *Archaiologikon Deltion* 48, *Chronika*: 83-85.

Galani-Krikou, M. *et al.* 1993c. 1η ΕΒΑ, Ανασκαφικές εργασίες. *Archaiologikon Deltion* 48, *Chronika*: 75-85.

Galani-Krikou, M. *et al.* 1995. 1η ΕΒΑ, Ανασκαφικές εργασίες. *Archaiologikon Deltion* 50, *Chronika*: 69-90.

Galani-Krikou, M. *et al.* 1996. 1η ΕΒΑ, Ανασκαφικές εργασίες. *Archaiologikon Deltion* 51, *Chronika*: 71-86.

Galani-Krikou, M. 1997. Θήβα, 10ος-15ος αι. Η νομισματική μαρτυρία από την Αγία Τριάδα [Thèbes: 10e-14e s. Le témoignage numismatique d'Hagia Trias]. *Byzantina Symmeikta* 11: 141-168.

Galani-Krikou, M. 1998a. Θήβα, 6ος-15ος αι. Η νομισματική μαρτυρία από το Πολιτιστικό Κέντρο [Thèbes 6ème-15ème siècle. Le témoignage monétaire du Centre Culturel]. *Byzantina Symmeikta* 12: 113-150.

Galani-Krikou, M. 1998b. Νομισματικοί θησαυροί των μέσων χρόνων από τη Θήβα [Medieval Hoards from Thebes]. *Deltion Christianikes Archaiologikes Etaireias* 20: 275-284.

Galani-Krikou, M. 2002. Νομισματική Συλλογή: Η Άμφισσα στους αιώνες μέσα από τα νομίσματα [Numismatic Collection: Amfissa across the centuries through the coins]. Amfissa Archaeological Museum.

Galani-Krikou, M., Nikolaou, Y., Oikonomidou, M., Penna, V., Touratsoglou I. and Tsourti H. 2002. *Σύνταγμα βυζαντινών θησαυρών του Νομισματικού Μουσείου* [Compendium of the Byzantine Hoards of the Numismatic Museum]. Athens, Numismatic Museum.

Gautier, P. 1970. Diatribes de Jean l'Oxite contre Alexis I Comnène. *Revue des Études Byzantines* 28: 5-55.

Gay J. 1904. *L'Italie méridionale et l'empire byzantin depuis l'avènement de Basile Ier jusqu'à la prise de Bari par les Normands 867-1071.* Paris, Fontemoing.

Geanakoplos, D. J. 1959. *Emperor Michael VIII Palaeologus and the West: a Study in Byzantine - Latin Relations.* Cambridge Mass., Harvard University Press.

Giannikouri, A. (ed.) 2013. *Όλβιος Άνερ, Μελέτες στη μνήμη του Γρηγόρη Κωνσταντινόπουλου* [*Olbios Aner*: Studies in Memory of Gregoris Konstantinopoulos]. Athens, Ministry of Culture and Sports, Archaeological Institute of Aegean Studies.

Goldthwaite, R. A. 2008. *The Economy of Renaissance Florence.* Baltimore, Johns Hopkins University Press.

Goodwin, T. 2005. *Arab-Byzantine Coinage, Studies in the Khalili Collection* vol. 4. London, Nour Foundation/ Azimuth.

Graeber D., 2011. *Debt. The First 5,000 Years.* New York, Melville House.

Greatrex, G. and Lieu, S. N. C. 2002. *The Roman Eastern Frontier and the Persian Wars II, AD 363-630.* Abingdon.

Grégoire, H. 1933. Études sur le neuvième siècle I. Un grand homme inconnu: le magistre et logothète Serge le Nicétiate. *Byzantion* 8: 515-534.

Grierson, P. 1952. *Pegged Venetian Coin Dies: Their Place in the History of Die Adjustment. Numismatic Chronicle* Series 6, 12: 99-105.

Grierson, P. 1954. A Note on the Stamping of Coins and Other Objects. In C. Singer *et al.* (eds), *A History of Technology II:* 485-492. Oxford, Clarendon.

Grierson, P. 1956. The Roman law of counterfeiting. In R. A. G. Carson and C. H. V. Sutherland (eds), *Essays in Roman Coinage Presented to Harold Mattingly*: 240-261. Oxford, Oxford University Press.

Grierson, P. 1957a. La moneta Veneziana nell' economia Mediterranea del Trecento e Quattrocento. In *La civiltà veneziana del Quattrocento*: 77-97. Florence; reprinted in P. Grierson 1979, *Later Medieval Numismatics (11th-16th centuries), Selected studies* XII. London, Ashgate.

Grierson, P. 1957b. The Coin List of Pegolotti. *Studi in onore di Armando Sapori*: 485-492. Milan; reprinted in P. Grierson 1979, *Later Medieval Numismatics (11th-16th centuries), Selected studies* XI. London, Ashgate.

Grierson, P. 1962. Numismatics and the Historian. *Numismatic Chronicle* Series 7, 2: i-xiv.

Grierson, P. 1965b: Le gillat ou carlin de Naples-Provence: le rayonnement de son type monétaire. In *Catalogue de l'Exposition "Centenaire de la Société française de numismatique (1865-1965)"*: 43-56; reprinted in P. Grierson 1979, *Later Medieval Numismatics (11th-16th centuries), Selected studies* XIII. London, Ashgate.

Grierson, P. 1965c: The Interpretation of Coin Finds (1). *Numismatic Chronicle* Series 7, 5: i-xiii.

Grierson, P. 1966. The Interpretation of Coin Finds (2). *Numismatic Chronicle* Series 7, 6: i-xv.

Grierson, P. 1968. *Catalogue of the Byzantine Coins in the Dumbarton Oaks Collection and in the Whittemore Collection, vol. 2. Phocas to Theodosius III 602-717.* Washington DC, Harvard University Press.

Grierson, P. 1971. The Monetary Pattern of Sixteenth-Century Coinage. *Transactions of the Royal Historical Society*, Series 5, 21: 45-60.

Grierson, P. 1973. *Catalogue of the Byzantine Coins in the Dumbarton Oaks Collection and in the Whittemore Collection, vol. 3. Leo to Nicephorus III 717-1081, Part 2, Basil I to Nicephorus III (867-1081).* Washington DC, Harvard University Press.

Grierson, P. 1975. *Numismatics.* London, Oxford University Press.

Grierson, P. 1982. *Byzantine Coins.* London, Methuen.

Grierson, P. and Blackburn, M. A. S. 1986. *Medieval European Coinage: with a Catalogue of the Coins in the Fitzwilliam Museum, Cambridge, 1: The Early Middle Ages (5th-10th centuries).* Cambridge, Cambridge University Press.

Grierson, P. 1991. *The Coins of Medieval Europe.* London, Seaby.

Grierson, P. and Travaini, L. 1998. *Medieval European Coinage: with a Catalogue of the Coins in the Fitzwilliam Museum, Cambridge, 14: Italy, part 3: South Italy, Sicily, Sardinia.* Cambridge, Cambridge University Press.

Grierson, P. and Bellinger A. R. 2006. *Catalogue of the Byzantine Coins in the Dumbarton Oaks Collection and in the Whittemore Collection, vol. 5.1, Michael VIII to Constantine XI, 1258-1453.* Washington DC, Harvard University Press.

Grierson, P. 2001. The Fineness of the Venetian Ducat and its Imitations. *Scritti Storici e Numismatici*: 317-326. Spoleto, Centro Italiano di Studi nell' Alto Medioevo.

Guest, P. 2012. The Production, Supply and Use of Late Roman and Early Byzantine Copper Coinage in the Eastern Empire. *Numismatic Chronicle* 172: 105-131.

Guillou, A. 1974. Production and Profits in the Byzantine province of Italy (tenth to eleventh centuries): an expanding society. *Dumbarton Oak Papers* 28: 89-109.

Hahn, W. 1973. *Moneta Imperii Byzantini,* vol. 1, *Von Anastasius I. bis Justinianus I. (491-565), einschließlich der ostgotischen und vandalischen Prägungen.* Vienna, Osterreichischen Akademie der Wissenschaften.

Hahn, W. 1975. *Moneta Imperii Byzantini,* vol. 2, *Von Justinus II. bis Phocas (565-610), einschließlich der Prägungen der Heraclius-Revolte und mit Nachträgen zum I. Band.* Vienna, Osterreichischen Akademie der Wissenschaften.

Hahn, W. R. O. 1980. A Sixth-Century Hoard of Byzantine Small Change from Egypt, and its Contribution to the Classification of African Minimi. *Numismatic Chronicle* 20: 64-70.

Hahn, W. 1981. *Moneta Imperii Byzantini,* vol. 3, *Von Heraclius bis Leo III. /Alleinregierung (610-720).* Vienna, Osterreichischen Akademie der Wissenschaften.

Hahn, W. and Metlich, M. A. 2000. *Money of the Incipient Byzantine Empire (Anastasius I - Justinian I, 491-565).* Vienna, Veröffentlichungen des Instituts für Numismatik und Geldgeschichte der Universität Wien.

Haldon, J. 1999. *Warfare, State and Society in the Byzantine World 565-120.* London, UCL Press.

Haldon, J. 2003. *Byzantium in the Seventh Century.* Cambridge, Cambridge University Press.

Haldon, J. 2001. *The Byzantine Wars. Battles and campaigns of the Byzantine Era.* Stroud, Tempus.

Haldon, J. (ed.) 2010. *Money, Power and Politics in Early Islamic Syria. A review of current debates.* Farnham, Ashgate.

Halphen, L. and Poupardin, R. (eds) 1913. *Chroniques des comtes d'Anjou et des seigneurs d'Amboise.* Paris, Piccard.

Harvey, A. 1989. *Economic Expansion in the Byzantine Empire 900-1200.* Cambridge, Cambridge University Press.

Hasluck, F. W. 1911-1912. On Imitations of the Venetian Sequin Struck for the Levant. *Annual of the British School at Athens* 18: 261-264.

Hasluck, F. W. 1912-1913. Contributions to the History of Levant Currencies. I. A Hoard of Mediaeval Coins from the Sporades, II. William Wey's Notes on the Coinage of the Latin Orient. *Annual of the British School at Athens* 19: 174-181

Hazlitt, W. C. 1900. *The Venetian Republic: Its Rise, Its Growth, and Its Fall 421-1797,* vol. 1, London, London and Black. http://babel.hathitrust.org/cgi/pt?id=hvd.hwk8tw;view= 1up;seq=372

Hazlitt, W. C. 1974. *The Coinage of the European Continent. Middle Ages - 20th century.* (ed. A. N. Oikonomides): 180-293. Chicago, Ares.

Heck, G. W. 2010. First Century Islamic Coinage: Mastering the Message from the Money. In J. Haldon (ed.), *Money, Power and Politics in Early Islamic Syria. A review of current debate:* 97-123. Farnham, Ashgate.

Heidemann, S. 2002. *Die Renaissance der Städte in Noedsyrien und Nordmesopotamien. Städtlische Endwicklung und wirtschaftliche Bedingungenin ar-Raqqa und Harran von der Zeit der beduinischen Vorherrschaft bis zu den Seldschuken*: 394-5. Leyden-Boston-Cologne, Brill.

Hendy, M. F. 1969. *Coinage and Money in the Byzantine Empire, 1081-1261.* Dumbarton Oaks Studies 12. Washington DC, Harvard University Press.

Hendy, M. F. 1985. *Studies on the Byzantine Monetary Economy 300-1450.* Cambridge, Cambridge University Press.

Hendy, M. F. 1999. *Catalogue of the Byzantine Coins in the Dumbarton Oaks Collection and in the Whittemore Collection, vol. 4, Alexius I to Michael VIII, 1081-1261.* Washington DC, Harvard University Press.

Hendy, M. F. 1983. The Goroslav hoard, the emperor Frederick I, and the monastery of Bachkovo. In C. N. L. Brooke, I. Stewart, J. G. Pollard, T. R. Volk (eds), *Studies in Numismatic Method presented to Philip Grierson*: 179-191. Cambridge, Cambridge University Press.

Hendy, M. F. 1989. 'Byzantium, 1081-1204': The Economy Revisited, Twenty Years On. In *The Economy, Fiscal Administration and Coinage of Byzantium* (Collected Studies): III, 1-48. Northampton, Variorum Reprints.

Heyd, W. 1885. *Histoire du commerce du Levant au moyen-âge*, 2 vols. Leipzig, Harrassowitz.

Hill, G. 2010. *A History of Cyprus*, vols. 2 and 3. Cambridge, Cambridge University Press.

Hoffmann, H. 1884. Les *monnaies royales de France depuis Hugues Capet jusqu'à Louis XVI.* Paris, Hoffmann.

Hohlfelder, R. L. 1978. *Kenchreai, Eastern Port of Corinth III*, The Coins. Leiden, Brill.

van Houts, E. M. C. 1985. Normandy and Byzantium in the Eleventh Century. *Byzantion* 55: 544-559.

Iliescu, O. 1989. Contribution à l' histoire des colonies génoises en Romanie aux XIIIe-XVe siècles. *Revue Roumaine d'Histoire* 1-2 (Jan.-June): 25-52.

Ilisch, L. 2010. Abd al-Malik's Monetary Reform in Copper and the Failure of Centralization. In J. Haldon (ed.), *Money, Power and Politics in Early Islamic Syria. A review of current debates*: 126-137. Farnham, Ashgate.

Inglieri, R. U. 1930. *Carta archeologica dell' isola di Rodi.* Florence, R. Istituto Geografico Militare.

Ireland, S. 2000. *Greek, Roman and Byzantine Coins in the Museum of Amasya (Ancient Amaseia), Turkey.* London, Oxbow.

Ives, H. 1954. *The Venetian Gold Ducat and its Imitations.* New York, American Numismatic Society.

Jacoby, D. 2005. The Economy of Latin Constantinople, 1204-1261. In A. Laiou (ed.), *Urbs Capta. The Fourth Crusade and its consequences. La IVe Croisade et ses conséquences*: 195-214. Réalités Byzantines 10. Paris, Lethielleux.

Jacopi, G. 1932. *Lo Spedale dei Cavalieri e il Museo Archeologico di Rodi.* Rome, Ministero Della Educazione Nazionale.

Jordanov, I. 1984. [*Coins and Circulation of Coins in Bulgaria of the Middle Ages*], *1081-1261*. Sofia, [Science and Art].

Kaegi, W. E. 1981. *Byzantine Military Unrest 471-843: An Interpretation*. Amsterdam, Hakkert.

Kaegi, W. E. 1992. *Byzantium and the Early Islamic Conquests*. Cambridge, Cambridge University Press.

Karabatsos, V. 2006. Η νομισματική παρουσία στην Κάρπαθο από την υστερορωμαϊκή μέχρι την ύστερη βυζαντινή περίοδο. Συμβολή στην ιστορία της Καρπάθου [The presence of coins on Carpathos from the Late Roman to the Late Byzantine Period. A contribution to the history of Carpathos]. *Obolos* 8: 283-295.

Kasdagli, A. M. 1992. Νέο νομισματικό εύρημα από τη Ρόδο [Hospitaller Silver Find in Rhodes]. *Nomismatika Chronika* 11: 53-60.

Kasdagli, A. M. 1996. Μεσαιωνική Ρόδος: Θησαυροί και σπάνιες κοπές [Mediaeval Rhodes. Hoards and Rarities]. In *Μνήμη Martin J. Price*: 319-334. Athens, Hellenic Numismatic Society.

Kasdagli, A. M. 2000. Χριστιανικά νομίσματα από τη Ρόδο. Μία πρώτη προσέγγιση [Christian Coins from Rhodes. An Introduction]. *Deltion tes Christianikes Archaiologikes Etaireias* 21: 267-274.

Kasdagli, A. M. 2002. *The Rhodian Coins at the Museum of the Order of Saint John, Clerkenwell*. Monographs of the Hellenic Numismatic Society 3, Athens.

Kasdagli, A. M. 2006a. Νομίσματα στα Δωδεκάνησα από τη μεταρρύθμιση του Αναστασίου (498 μ.Χ.) έως το 19ο αιώνα [Coins in the Dodecanese from the Reform of Anastasius to the 19th century]. *Obolos* 8: 253-264.

Kasdagli, A. M. 2006b. Ο θησαυρός της Παναγίας του Μπούργκου στη Ρόδο (1522) [The Hoard of Our Lady of the Borgo in Rhodes (1522)]. *Obolos* 8: 325-338.

Kasdagli, A. M. 2006c. Ροδιακές χάλκινες κοπές στο 13ο αιώνα. Μία απόπειρα ταξινομήσεως [Rhodian Copper Issues of the 13th centhry. An attempt at classification]. *Nomismatika Chronika* 25: 31-70.

Kasdagli, A. M. 2007. Η νομισματική κυκλοφορία στη μεσαιωνική πόλη της Ρόδου (8ος-16ος αιώνας) [Coin circulation within the walls of medieval Rhodes]. *15 χρόνια έργων αποκατάστασης στη Μεσαιωνική Πόλη της Ρόδου*: 422-432. Athens, Ministry of Culture.

Kasdagli, A. M. 2008. Funerary Monuments of Hospitaller Rhodes: an Overview. In J. Upton-Ward (ed.), *The Military Orders, Volume 4, On Land and by Sea*. Aldershot, Ashgate.

Kasdagli, A. M. 2009. Τρία μεσαιωνικά κοσμήματα από τις ανασκαφές της Ρόδου. Συμπεράσματα και προβλήματα της έρευνας [Three pieces of medieval jewellery from archaeological excavations in Rhodes: an investigation]. *Deltion tes Christianikes Archaiologikes Etaireias* 30: 283-284.

Kasdagli, A. M. 2010. Νομίσματα των μέσων χρόνων στην εκτός των μεσαιωνικών τειχών πόλη της Ρόδου [Coins of the Middle Ages Recovered in the Town of Rhodes outside the Medieval Walls]. *Obolos* 9 vol. 2: 159-174.

Kasdagli, A. M. 2013. Hospitaller Small Change: An Archaeological Perspective. In E. Buttigieg and S. Phillips (eds), *Islands and Military Orders, c. 1291-c. 1798*: 203-213. Farnham, Ashgate.

Kasdagli, A. M. 2015. Η νομισματική μαρτυρία στο ιερό του Ερεθιμίου Απόλλωνος κατά τη βυζαντινή περίοδο [The Sanctuary of Apollo Erethimios: The Byzantine Coins]. In P. Triantafyllidis (ed.), Ερεθιμία. Διαμόρφωση και ανάδειξη του Ιερού του Ερεθιμίου Απόλλωνος στον Θεολόγο Ρόδου. Rhodes, Ministry of Culture.

Katsari, C., Lightfoot, C. S. and Ozme, A. 2012. *The Amorium Mint and the Coin Finds. Amorium Reports 4*. Berlin, De Gruyter.

Katsioti, A. and Archontopoulos, Th. 2000. Το παρεκκλήσιο της οικογένειας των Αρμενόπουλων στη Ρόδο και η τέχνη του τέλους του 12ου αιώνα στα Δωδεκάνησα. In *Ρόδος 2.400 Χρόνια. Η πόλη της Ρόδου από την ίδρυσή της μέχρι την κατάληψη από τους Τούρκους (1523)*. Acts, vol. 2: 375-386. Athens, Ministry of Culture.

Katsioti, A. under publication, *The Lamps of Late Antiquity from Rhodes, 3rd-7th Centuries*. Oxford, Archaeopress.

Kedar, B. Z. 1998. A Twelfth-Century Description of the Jerusalem Hospital. In H. Nicholson (ed.), *The Military Orders, Vol. 2, Welfare and Warfare*: 3-26. Aldershot, Ashgate.

Kefala, K. 2015. *Οι τοιχογραφίες του 13ου αιώνα στις εκκλησίες της Ρόδου* [Thirteenth century wall paintings in the churches of Rhodes]. PhD thesis, University of Athens http://ebooks.epublishing.ekt.gr/index.php/chae/catalog/book/54

Kent, J. P. C. 1988. Interpreting coin-finds. In J. Casey and R. Reece (eds), *Coins and the Archaeologist*: 201-217. London, Seaby.

Kollias, E. and Michaelidou, M. 1997. Το μεσαιωνικό εργαστήρι επεξεργασίας ζάχαρης της Ρόδου [The medieval sugar refinery of Rhodes]. In Τεχνογνωσία στη Λατινοκρατούμενη Ελλάδα. Athens, ETBA.

Kollias, E. 1998. *The Medieval City of Rhodes and the Palace of the Grand Master*, 2nd Edn. Athens, Archaeological Receipts Fund.

Kollias, E. 2007. Αναζητώντας τα χαμένα μνημεία της μεσαιωνικής πόλης της Ρόδου [Searching for the lost monuments of the medieval town of Rhodes]. In *15 Χρόνια έργων αποκατάστασης στη Μεσαιωνική Πόλη της Ρόδου*: 283-296. Athens, Ministry of Culture.

Kondis, I. 1958. Zum antiken Stadtbauplan von Rhodos. *Athenische Mitteilungen des Deutschen Archäologischen Instituts* 73: 146-158.

Konstantinopoulos, G. 1970. Το ρυμοτομικόν σύστημα της αρχαίας Ρόδου [The street plan of ancient Rhodes]. *Athens Annals of Archaeology* 3: 52-55.

Konstantinopoulos, G. 1986. Αρχαία Ρόδος [Ancient Rhodes]. Athens, MIET.

Koumanoudi, M. 2005. The Latins in the Aegean after 1203: Interdependence and Interwoven Interests. In A. Laiou (ed.), *Urbs Capta. The Fourth Crusade and its consequences. La IVe Croisade et ses conséquences*: 247-265. Réalités Byzantines 10. Paris, Lethielleux.

Kreutz, B. M. 2011. *Before the Normans: Southern Italy in the Ninth and Tenth Centuries*. Philadelpia, University of Pennsylvania Press.

Kubiak, W. B. 1970. The Byzantine Attack on Damietta in 853 and the Egyptian Navy in the 9th Century. *Byzantion* 40: 45-66.

Laiou, A. 1972. *Constantinople and the Latins: the Foreign Policy of Andronicus II, 1282-1328*. Cambridge, Harvard University Press.

Laiou, A. 2001. Byzantine Trade with Christians and Muslims and the Crusades. In A. Laiou and R. Parviz Mottahedeh (eds), *The Crusades from the Perspective of Byzantium and the Muslim World*: 157-196. Dumbarton Oaks, Harvard University Press.

Laiou-Thomadaki, A. 2006. Μεταξύ παραγωγής και κατανάλωσης: Είχαν οικονομία οι βυζαντινές πόλεις; [Between production and consumption: Had Byzantine towns an economy?] *Praktika of the Athens Academy* 81 B: 85-120.

Laiou, A. E. (ed.) 2002. *An Economic History of Byzantium from the Seventh through the Fifteenth Century*, Washington D.C., Dumbarton Oaks Research Library and Collections.

Laiou, A. E. 2002. Political history. An outline. In A. E. Laiou, (ed.), *The Economic History of Byzantium from the Seventh through the Fifteenth Century* vol. 1: 9-28.

Lane, F. C. and Mueller R. C. 1985. *Money and Banking in Medieval and Renaissance Venice, vol. I, Coins and Moneys of Account*. Baltimore and London, Johns Hopkins University Press.

La Niece, S. and Craddock, P. (eds) 1993. *Metal Plating and Patination. Cultural, technical and historical developments*. Oxford, Butterworth-Heinemann.

Lambros, P. 1972. *Monete Inedite dell' Ordine di S. Giovanni di Gerusalemme in Rodi*. Athens, Bibliotheke Historikon Meleton 50, Numismatic Series 7.

Langton, J. S. 1978. *John III Ducas Vatatzes' Byzantine Imperium in Anatolian Exile, 1222-54: The Legacy of his diplomatic, Military and internal program*. PhD thesis, University of California Los Angeles.

Langton, J. S. 1985. The Forgotten Byzantino-Bulgarian Assault and Siege of Constantinople, 1235-1236, and the Breakup of the *entente cordiale* between John III Ducas Vatatzes and John Asen II in 1236 as Background to the Genesis of the Hohenstaufen-Vatatzes Alliance of 1242. In S. Vryonis Jr. (ed.), *Byzantine Studies in Honor of Milton V. Anastos, Byzantina kai Metabyzantina* 4. Malibu, Undena Publications.

Laurent, V. 1960. N. G. Svoronos, Recherches sur le cadastre byzantin et la fiscalité aux XIe et XIIe siècles ; le cadastre de Thèbes. Paris 1960. *Revue des* Études *Byzantines* 18: 281-284.

Lefort, J. 2002. The Rural Economy, Seventh-Twelfth Centuries. In In A. E. Laiou, (ed.), *The Economic History of Byzantium from the Seventh through the Fifteenth Century* vol. 1: 231-310.

Lenski, N. 1999. Assimilation and Revolt in the Territory of Isauria, from the 1st Century BC to the 6th Century AD. *Journal of the Economic and Social History of the Orient* 42/4: 413-465.

Lev, Y. 1984. The Fatimid Navy, Byzantium and the Mediterranean Sea 909-1036 CE/297-429 AH. *Byzantion* 54: 220-252.

Lhotka, J. F. and Anderson, P. K. 1989. *Survey of Medieval Iberian Coinages*. New York, Sanford J. Durst Numismatic Publications.

Lianta, E. 2009. *Late Byzantine Coins 1204 – 1453 in the Ashmolean Museum University of Oxford*. London, Spink.

Lianta, E. 2006. John II Comnenus (1118–43) or John III Vatatzes (1222–54)? (Distinguishing the Hyperpyra of John II from those of John III1). *Numismatic Chronicle* 166: 269-299.

Lianta, E. 2010. Ο 'θησαυρός' «Θεσσαλονίκη/2007» με βυζαντινά τραχέα από κράμα (bill.) του 13ου αι. μ.Χ. [The Thessaloniki/2007 Hoard of byzantine billon trachea of the 13th c.] *Nomismatika Chronika* 28: 51-64.

Lightfoot, C. S. 1995. A New Anonymous Follis from Amorium. *Numismatic Circular* CIII/10 (December): 376.

Lightfoot, C. S. 2002. Byzantine Anatolia: reassessing the numismatic evidence. *Revue Numismatique* 158: 229-239.

Liutprand of Cremona (*c.* 920-972), 1881. *Relatio de legatione constantinopolitana*: columns 909-938. J. P. Migne (ed.), *Patrologiae Cursus Completus* CXXXVI, Paris.

Livadiotti, M. and Rocco, G. (eds) 1996. *La presenza italiana nel Dodecaneso tra il 1912 e il 1948. La ricerca archeologica - La conservazione - Le scelte progettuali.* Catania, Prisma.
Lopez, R. S. 1956. Back to Gold, 1252. *Economic History Review* Series 2, 9: 219-240.
Lopez, R. S. and Raymond, I. W. 1990. *Medieval Trade in the Mediterranean World.* New York, Columbia University Press.
Lunardi, G. 1980. *Le monete delle colonie genovesi.* Genoa, Società Ligure di Storia Patria.
Luttrell, A. 1972. The Hospitallers in Cyprus after 1291. *Acts of the I International Congress of Cypriot Studies* vol. 2: 161-171. Nicosia, Hetaireia Kypriakon Spoudon.
Luttrell, A. 1975. The Hospitallers at Rhodes 1306-1421. In K. M. Setton and H. W. Hazard (eds), *A History of the Crusades III, The Fourteenth and Fifteenth Centuries*: 278-339. Madison, University of Wisconsin Press.
Luttrell, A. 1986. The Building of the Castle of the Hospitallers at Bodrum. In *The Mausolleion at Halikarnassos: Reports of the Danish Archaeological Expedition to Bodrum 2, The Written Sources and their Archaeological Background.* Aarhus, Aarhus Universitetforlag: 143-161. Reprinted in Luttrell, A. 1999. *The Hospitaller State on Rhodes and its Western Provinces, 1306-1462*, VI. Aldershot, Ashgate, Variorum Collected Studies.
Luttrell, A. 1997. The Genoese at Rhodes: 1306-1312. In L. Balletto (ed.), *Oriente e Occidente tra Medioevo ed Età Moderna. Studi in onore di Geo Pistarino*: 737-761. Genoa, Brigati.
Luttrell, A. 1999. Earthquakes in the Dodecanese: 1303-1513. In E. Zachariadou (ed.), *Natural Disasters in the Ottoman Empire, Halcyon Days In Crete III, A Symposium held in Rethymnon, 10-12 January 1997:* 145-151. Rethymnon, Crete University Press.
Luttrell, A. 2003. *The Town of Rhodes: 1306-1356.* Rhodes, Archaeological Receipts Fund.
Magdalino, P. 1976: Notes on the Last Years of John Palaiologos, Brother of Michael VIII. *Revue des Études Byzantines* 34: 143-149.
Magdalino, P. 1993. *The Empire of Manuel I Komnenos 1143-1180.* Cambridge, Cambridge University Press.
Malalas Ioannes (*c.* 491-578), 1831. *Chronographia.* Bonn, Weber.
Malamut, E. 1989. *Les îles de l'Empire byzantin, VIIIe-XIIe siècles*, 2 vols. Paris, Byzantina Sorbonensia 8.
Malloy, A. G., Fraley Preston, I. and Seltman, A. J. 1994. *Coins of the Crusader States 1098-1291.* New York, Attic Books.
Mannucci, M. 1979. Note sul sito delle due Focee e sulla zecca di Foglia Vecchia. *Quaderni Ticinesi di Numismatica e Antichità Classiche* 8: 335-344.
Mannucci, F. 1982. "Giannetti" dei Gran Maestri dell' Ordine di San Giovanni a Rodi. *Quaderni Ticinesi di Numismatica e Antichità Classiche* 11: 343-350.
Mannucci, F. 1983. Tre monete inedite dei cavalieri di San Giovanni a Rodi. *Quaderni Ticinesi di Numismatica e Antichità Classiche* 12: 289-294.
Mannucci, F. 1987. Sulle monete di Pietro d' Aubusson Gran Maestro dei cavalieri di San Giovanni a Rodi (1476-1503). *Quaderni Ticinesi di Numismatica e Antichità Classiche* 16: 293-301.
Manoussou-Della, K. 2001. *Medieval Town of Rhodes. Restoration Works (1985-2000).* Rhodes, Ministry of Culture (TDPEAE).
Manoussou-Della, K. 2014. Η πόλη της Ρόδου κατά τους μεσαιωνικούς χρόνους. Ο μετασχηματισμός των οχυρώσεων από την ύστερη αρχαιότητα έως την ιπποτική οχυρωμένη πόλη [The City of Rhodes in the Middle Ages. The transformation of the fortifications from Late Antiquity to the Hospitaller fortified town]. Unpublished PhD thesis, National Technical University of Athens.
Maria, M. 2008. Εκπαιδευτήρια της Δωδεκανήσου [Educational Institutions of the Dodecasnese]. Rhodes, Zitis.
al-Masʿūdī (Abu al-Ḥasan ʿAlī ibn al-Ḥusayn ibn ʿAlī, *c.* 896-956), 1863. *Les prairies d'or,* vol. 2, Paris, 423, 1864, vol. 3, 67 (947) http://archive.org/stream/lesprairiesdor02 masuuoft# page/422/ mode/2up
Mayhew, N. J. 1988. Irregularities in the Irish mint accounts, 1279-1284. In N. J. Mayhew and P. Spufford (eds), *Later Medieval Mints. Organization, Administration and Techniques.* BAR International Series 389: 87-96.
Mazarakis, A. 1992. Το νομισματοκοπείο της Χίου την περίοδο των Ζαχαρία 1304-1329 [The mint of Chios in the Zaccaria period 1304-1329]. *Nomismatika Chronika* 11: 43-50.
Mazarakis, A. and Kofopoulos, S. 1996. Οι Γατελούζοι: γενεαλογικές και νομισματικές αναθεωρήσεις [The Gattilusi: genealogical and numismatic revisions]. In *Πρακτικά: Οι Γατελούζοι της Λέσβου*: 189-221. Athens.
Mazarakis, A. 2003. Τα Νομίσματα της Χίου 1346-1566 [The coins of Chios 1346-1566]. Athens.
Mazarakis, A. 2006. *Zaccaria e Della Volta nell' Egeo Orientale*, 1268-1329. Atene, Circolo Numismatico Ligure "Corrado Astengo", Sezione della Società Ligure di Storia Patria.
Mazarakis, A. 2010. *A Survey of the Rhodian Coins of the Order of St John.* Athens.
Mazarakis, A. 2012. *Το δουκάτο της Βενετίας και οι απομιμήσεις του στην Ανατολή 14ος - 16ος αι.* [The ducat of Venice and its imitations in the East 14th - 16th c.] Athens.
Μεσαιωνική πόλη Ρόδου, Έργα Αποκατάστασης (2000-2008) [Medieval Town of Rhodes, Restoration Works (2000-2008)], 2008. Rhodes, Ministry of Culture (TDPEAE).

Metcalf, D. M. 1962a. The New Bronze Coinage of Theophilus and the Growth of the Balkan Themes. *American Numismatic Society Museum Notes* 10: 81-98.
Metcalf, D. M. 1962b. The Aegean Coastlands under Threat: Some Coins and Coin Hoards from the Reign of Heraclius. *Annual of the British School at Athens* 57: 14-23.
Metcalf, D. M. 1964. The Brauron Hoard and the Petty Currency of Central Greece, 1143-1204. *Numismatic Chronicle* Series 7, 4: 199-219.
Metcalf, D. M. 1965a. Bronze Coinage and City Life in Greece circa AD 1000. *Annual of the British School at Athens* 60: 1-40.
Metcalf, D. M. 1965b. *Coinage in the Balkans 820-1355*. Institute for Balkan Studies 80: Thessaloniki.
Metcalf, D. M. 1967. How extensive was the Issue of Folles During the Years 775-820? *Byzantion* 37: 270-310.
Metcalf, D. M. 1973a. The Peter and Paul Hoard: Bulgarian and Latin Imitative Trachea in the Time of Ivan Asen II. *Numismatic Chronicle* Series 7, 13: 144-172.
Metcalf, D. M. 1973b. Byzantinobulgarica: the second Bulgarian Empire and the problem of 'Bulgarian imitative' trachea before and after 1204. *Numismatic Circular* 81: 418-421.
Metcalf, D. M. 1973c. Corinth in the ninth century: the numismatic evidence. *Hesperia* 42: 180-251.
Metcalf, D. M. 1974. Byzantine Coins Minted in Central Greece under Basil II. *Nomismatika Chronika* 3: 21-24.
Metcalf, D. M. 1978. The tetarteron in the twelfth century. *Numismatic Circular* 86: 574-5.
Metcalf, D. M. 1979. *Coinage in SE Europe 820-1396*. Royal Numismatic Society Special Publication No. 11, London.
Metcalf, D. M. and Willis, P. J. 1979. Crusader Coins in the Museum of the Order of St. John, at Clerkenwell. *Numismatic Chronicle* Series 7, 19 (139): 133-138.
Metcalf, D. M. 1982a. Note on Some Hoards and Stray Finds from the Time of the Crusades. *Hamburger Beiträge zur Numismatik* 27/29 (1973-75): 67-83.
Metcalf, D. M. 1982b. The Gros grand and the Gros petit of Henry II of Cyprus, Part I. *Numismatic Chronicle* 142: 83-100.
Metcalf, D. M. 1983. *The Gros grand and the Gros petit of Henry II of Cyprus*, Part II. *Numismatic Chronicle* 143: 177-201, pl. 30-35.
Metcalf, D.M. 1984-5. A Twelfth-Century Hoard from the Sea dated by Coins of Raymond of Poitiers. *Israel Numismatic Journal* 8: 77-83.
Metcalf, D. M. 1985. A Hoard of Billon Trachea from the Empire of Nicaea, *c.* 1215/1220. *Hamburger Beiträge zur Numismatik* 30/32 (1976-78): 55-70.
Metcalf D. M. 1989. The value of the Amorgos and Thera hoards as a test case for the interpretation of sub-Byzantine trachea in the years around 1204. *Nomismatika Chronika* 8: 49-59.
Metcalf, D. M. 1990. The Currency of Lusignan Cyprus in the Years Around 1400 in the Light of a Coin Hoard Excavated at Polis. *Report of the Department of Antiquities Cyprus*: 241-284. Nicosia.
Metcalf, D. M. 1992. A Comment on the Circulation of Tornesia of Charles of Anjou, and their Chronology. *Nomismatika Chronika* 11: 27-31.
Metcalf, D. M. 1995a. *Coinage of the Crusades and the Latin East in the Ashmolean Museum Oxford*, 2nd Edn. Royal Numismatic Society Special Publication No. 28. London.
Metcalf, D. M. 1995b. Coins of the Latin princes of Antioch, 1098-1130, found at Corinth and Athens. *Nomismatika Chronika* 14: 77-78.
Metcalf, D. M. 1996. Faithful Copies and a Hoard Containing neatly-Clipped Trachea. In *ΧΑΡΑΚΤΗΡ, Αφιέρωμα στη Μάντω Οικονομίδου*: 177-186. Athens, Archaeological Receipts Fund.
Metcalf, D. M. 2000a. Mint-Activity in Byzantine Thessaloniki. In Το Νόμισμα στο Μακεδονικό Χώρο. *Obolos* 4: 171-182.
Metcalf, D. M. 2000b. *M. Hendy, Catalogue of the Byzantine Coins in the Dumbarton Oaks Collection and in the Whittemore Collection*, vol. 4. *Numismatic Chronicle* 160: 396-401.
Metcalf, D. M. 2001. Monetary recession in the Middle Byzantine period: the numismatic evidence. *Numismatic Chronicle* 161: 111-155.
Metcalf, D. M. 2009. *Byzantine Cyprus 491-1191*. Texts and Studies of the History of Cyprus 62. Nicosia, Cyprus Research Centre.
Michaelidou, M. 2014. *Βυζαντινή και μεσαιωνική εμφυαλωμένη κεραμική στη Ρόδο από τα τέλη του 10ου αι. έως το 1522: η μαρτυρία των ανασκαφικών ευρημάτων της πόλης* [Byzantine and medieval glazed pottery in Rhodes from the end of the 10th *c.* until 1522: the evidence of the archaeological finds of the town]. Unpublished PhD thesis, University of Athens.
Miklosich, F. and Müller, J. 1871. *Acta et Diplomata Graeca Medii Aevi Sacra et Profana IV*. Vienna, C. Gerold.
Miller, W. 1908. *The Latins in the Levant. A History of Frankish Greece (1204-1566)*. New York, Dutton and Co.
Mitchiner, M. 1988. *Jetons, Medalets and Tokens Vol. I. The Medieval Period and Nuremberg*. London, Seaby.
Morgan, G. 1976. The Venetian Claims Commission of 1278. *Byzantinische Zeitschrift* 69: 411-438.

Morgan, M. R. 1973. *The Chronicle of Ernoul and the Continuations of William of Tyre*. Oxford, Oxford University Press.

Morricone, L. 1965. Rodi. In G. Trecanni (ed.), *Enciclopedia dell'arte antica classica e orientale VI*. Roma, Istituto della Enciclopedia italiana: 743 ff.

Morris, R. 1988. The two faces of Nikephoros Phocas. *Byzantine and Modern Greek Studies* 12: 83-115.

Morrisson, C. 1970. *Catalogue des monnaies byzantines de la Bibliothèque Nationale*, 2 vols. Paris, Bibliothèque Nationale.

Morrisson, C. 1979. La logarikè: réforme monétaire et réforme fiscale sous Alexis 1er Comnène. *Travaux et Mémoires* 7: 419-464.

Morrisson, C. 1989. Monnaie et prix à Byzance du ve au viie siècle. *Réalités byzantines* 1: 239-260. Paris, Lethielleux.

Morrisson, C. 1992. Constantinople et la monnaie byzantine. *Dossiers d'Archéologie* 17 (November): 54-59.

Morrisson, C. 1995. La diffusion de la monnaie de Constantinople: routes commerciales ou rites politiques? In C. Mango, G. Dagron, G. Greatrex (eds), *Constantinople and Its Hinterland*. Papers from the Twenty-Seventh Spring Symposium of Byzantine Studies, Oxford: 77-89. London, Routledge.

Morrisson, C. 2001. Survivance de l'économie monétaire à Byzance (VIIe-IXe siècle). In *Οι σκοτεινοί αιώνες του Βυζαντιου (7ος - 9ος αι.)*: 377-410. Athens, National Research Foundation.

Morrisson, C. and Bendall, S. 2001. Monnaies de la fin de l' empire byzantin à Dumbarton Oaks: un catalogue de référence. *Revue Numismatique* 157: 472-493.

Morrisson, C. 2002. Byzantine Money: Its Production and Circulation. In In A. E. Laiou, (ed.), *The Economic History of Byzantium from the Seventh through the Fifteenth Century* vol. 3: 909-966.

Morrisson, C. (ed.) 2004. Le Monde Byzantin I. L'empire romain d'orient (330-641). Paris, Nouvelle Clio.

Morrisson, C., Popovic, V., Ivanisevic, V. *et al.* 2006. Les trésors monétaires Byzantins des Balkans et d'Asie Mineure (491-713). *Réalités byzantines* 13: 559-71. Paris, Lethielleux.

Morrisson, C. 2007. La fin de l'antiquité dans les Balkans à la lumière des trésors monétaires des VIe et VIIe siecles. Académie des Inscriptions & Belles-Lettres, Comptes rendus, 151/2 (April-June): 663-684.

Mélanges Cécile Morrisson, Travaux et Mémoires 16, 2010.

Morrisson, C. (ed.) 2012. *Trade and Markets in Byzantium*. Washington D. C.

Morrison, C. 2014. La place de byzance dans l'histoire de l'economie medievale (717 env. -1204): methodes, acquis, perspectives. In D. Barthelemy - J.-M. Martin (eds), *Richesse et croissance au Moyen-Age. Orient et Occident*: 11-30. Paris, Centre de recherche d'histoire et civilisation de Byzance.

Mosser, S. McA. 1935. *A Bibliography of Byzantine Coin Hoards*. New York, Numismatic Notes and Monographs 67.

MÜNZEN UND MEDAILLEN AG, Basel 30, 5 Nov. 1965, 'Émirs d' Asie Mineure, Seigneurs de Rhodes, Les Grands Maîtres à Malte etc.': 65-68.

Niavis, P. 1987. *The Reign of the Byzantine Emperor Nicephorus I (AD 802-811)*. Athens, Basilopoulos.

Nicol, D. M. 1988. *Byzantium and Venice*. Cambridge, Cambridge University Press.

Nightingale, P. 1988. «The king's profit»: trends in English mint and monetary policy in the eleventh and twelfth centuries. In N. J. Mayhew and P. Spufford (eds), *Later Medieval Mints. Organization, Administration and Techniques*. BAR International Series 389: 61-75.

Nika, A. 1992. Οικόπεδο Μηνατσή [Minatsis plot]. *Archaiologikon Deltion* 47 (1992), *Chronika*: 674-675.

Nika, A. 1993. Οικόπεδο Μηνατσή [Minatsis plot]. *Archaiologikon Deltion* 48 (1993), *Chronika*: 571-572.

Nika, A. 2006. Τάφοι-οστεοφυλάκια της παλαιοχριστιανικής βασιλικής στην Ιαλυσία της Ρόδου. Συνδυαστικά δεδομένα αρχαιολογικών και ανθρωπολογικών ερευνών [Tombs-ossuaries of the Early Christian basilica at Ialysos, Rhodes. Convergent archaeological and anthropoligical research data]. In *Human Evolution and Population Biodiversity in SE Europe, 2nd International Congress of Anthropology, Athens, 5-7 June 2006*: 57. Athens, Hellenic Anthropological Association.

Nika, A. 2014. Χάλκινες πόρπες από τη Ρόδο. Εξαρτήμαρτα ένδυσης 'φοιδεράτων' ή Βυζαντινών; [Bronze Buckles from Rhodes. Byzantine or 'Foederati' Dress Accessories?] In P. Triantafyllidis (ed.) *Σοφία άδολος. Τιμητικός τόμος για τον Ιωάννη Χρ. Παπαχριστοδούλου*: 333-358. Rhodes, Ministry of Culture and Sports.

Nikolaou, Y. 2004a. Νομισματική κυκλοφορία στη βυζαντινή Θεσσαλία (6ος-14ος αι.) [Coin circulation in Byzantine Thessaly (6th-14th c.] In *Το νόμισμα στο θεσσαλικό χώρο. Νομισματοκοπεία, κυκλοφορία, εικονογραφία, ιστορία. Αρχαίοι - Βυζαντινοί- Νεότεροι Χρόνοι*. Πρακτικά Συνεδρίου της 3ης Επιστημονικής Συνάντησης: 571-588. Athens, Friends of the Numismatic Museum.

Nikolaou, Y. 2004b. Numismatic Circulation in the Aegean Islands during the Seventh Century. In G. Livadas (ed.), *Festschrift in Honor of V. Christides. Graeco-Arabica*, vols. 9-10: 291-309.

Nikolaou, Y. 2010. Συμβολή στη νομισματική κυκλοφορία των νησιών του Αιγαίου κατά τον 7ο αι. Ο «θησαυρός» Χίος/1998 [The Chios/1998 Hoard]. *Obolos* 9, vol. 2: 77-93.

Oeconomides, M. and Drosoyanni, P. 1989. A Hoard of Gold Byzantine Coins from Samos. *Revue Numismatique* Series 6, 31: 145-182.

O'Hara, M. D. 1975. Notes on recent Byzantine hoards. In *Coin Hoards I*: 67-68. London, Royal Numismatic Society.
Oikonomides, N. 1992. La décomposition de l'empire byzantin à la veille de 1204 et les origines de l'empire de Nicée: à propos de la "Partitio Romaniae". In *Byzantium from the Ninth Century to the Fourth Crusade*. Aldershot, Ashgate, Variorum: XX.
Oikonomides, N. 2002. The Role of the Byzantine State in the Economy. In In A. E. Laiou, (ed.), *The Economic History of Byzantium from the Seventh through the Fifteenth Century* vol. 3: 973-1058.
Oikonomidou-Karamessini, M. 1985. Τρεις «θησαυροί» του 13ου αιώνα του Νομισματικού Μουσείου Αθηνών [Three 13th century hoards of the Numismatic Museum, Athens]. *Byzantina* 13: 983-1001.
Ostrogorsky, G. 1980. *History of the Byzantine State*. Oxford, Blackwell.
Papachristodoulou, Ch. 1972. *Ιστορία της Ρόδου, από τους προϊστορικούς χρόνους έως την ενσωμάτωση της Δωδεκανήσου (1948)* [History of Rhodes, from prehistoric times to the incorporation of the Dodecanese (1948)]. Athens, Stege Grammaton kai Technon Dodekanesou.
Papadopoli-Aldobrandini, N. 1893-1907. *Le monete di Venezia*, vols. I-IV. Venice, F. Ongania.
Papadopoullos, Th. (ed.) 1995. *Ιστορία της Κύπρου* [History of Cyprus], vols. 4-5. Nicosia, Archbishop Makarios III Foundation.
Papadopoullos, Th. (ed.) 2006. *Ιστορία της Κύπρου* [History of Cyprus], vol. 3. Nicosia, Archbishop Makarios III Foundation.
Papadopoulos, G. A. 2014. *Ρόδος. Οι Σεισμοί και τα Τσουνάμι από την Αρχαιότητα μέχρι Σήμερα* [Rhodes. Earthquakes and Tsunamis from Antiquity to the Present]. Athens, Ocelotos.
Papadopoulou, P. 2005. Un trésor monétaire de trachéa de billon du XIIe siècle provenant de Butrint (Albanie). In C. Alfaro, C. Marcos and P. Otero (eds), *XIII Congreso Internacional de Numismatica, Madrid 2003, Actas*: 1231-1236. Madrid, Ministerio de Cultura.
Papadopoulou, P. 2005. Tétartèra d'imitation du XIIIe siècle: à propos du trésor de Durres (Albanie). *Revue Numismatique* 161: 145-162.
Papadopoulou, P. 2010. Χριστιανοί και Μουσουλμάνοι στη Μεσόγειο: με Αφορμή το Θησαυρό Ρόδος/1998 [Christians and Muslims in the Mediterranean: In Light of the Rhodes/1998 Coin Hoard]. *Obolos* 9/II: 174-187.
Papaefthymiou, E. G. and Touratsoglou, I. 2013. *Olokotinon. Studies in Byzantine Numismatics and Sigillography in Memory of Petros* Protonotarios. Athens, Hellenic Numismatic Society.
Papageorgiadou-Banis, Ch. and Giannikouri, A. (eds) 2008. *Sailing in the Aegean. Readings on the economy and trade routes*. Athens, National Research Foundation.
Patsiada, V. 2013. *Μνημειώδες ταφικό συγκρότημα στη Ρόδο. Συμβολή στη μελέτη της ελληνιστικής ταφικής αρχιτεκτονικής* [A Monumental Tomb Complex in the Necropolis of Rhodes. A contribution to the study of Helllenistic funerary architecture]. Athens, Archaeological Receipts Fund.
Penna, V. 1993. Το Βυζάντιο και οι λαοί της κεντρικής και ανατολικής Ευρώπης: η νομισματική μαρτυρία (Η' - ΙΑ' αι. μ. Χ.) [Byzantium and the peoples of central and eastern Europe: the numismatic evidence (8th-11th century)]. In N. G. Moschonas (ed.), *Η επικοινωνία στο Βυζάντιο,* Πρακτικά Β› Διεθνούς Συμποσίου: 651-656. Athens, National Research Foundation.
Penna, V. 1995. A Rare Justinian Half-follis of Pontic Provenance. *Deltio Kentrou Mikrasiatikon Spoudon* 11: 86-92.
Penna, V. 1996a. Η ζωή στις βυζαντινές πόλεις της Πελοποννήσου: η νομισματική μαρτυρία (8ος-12ος αι. μ.Χ.). In *Μνήμη Martin Jessop Price*: 195-264. Athens, Hellenic Numismatic Society.
Penna, V. 1996b. Ανδρόνικος Α' Κομνηνός: Νομισματικά παραλειπόμενα [Andronicus I Comnenus: Numismatic omissions]. In ΧΑΡΑΚΤΗΡ, *Αφιέρωμα στη Μάντω Οικονομίδου*: 231-242. Athens, Archaeological Receipts Fund.
Penna, V. 1997. Βυζαντινό νόμισμα και λατινικές απομιμήσεις [Byzantine coinage and Latin imitations]. *Τεχνογνωσία στη λατινοκρατούμενη Ελλάδα*. Athens, Politistiko Technologiko Idryma ETBA.
Penna, V. 1999. Κατάσχεση Κομοτηνής 1996: μελέτη στην κοπή και στην κυκλοφορία των υπερπύρων του Ανδρονίκου Β [The 1996 Komotini sequestration: a study in the minting and circulation of the hyperpyra of Andronicus II]. In K. Nikolaou (ed.), *Ο Μανουήλ Πανσέληνος και η εποχή του*: 159-176, Athens, National Research Foundation.
Penna, V. 2001. Νομισματικές νύξεις για τη ζωή στις Κυκλάδες κατά τους 8ο και 9ο αιώνες [Numismatic hints for life in the Cyclades in the 8th and 9th century]. In E. Kountoura-Galaki (ed.), *Οι σκοτεινοί αιώνες του Βυζαντίου (7ος - 9ος αι.)*: 398-413. Athens, National Research Foundation.
Penna, V. 2002a. *Το Βυζαντινό Νόμισμα: Μέσο συναλλαγής και έκφραση αυτοκρατορικής προπαγάνδας / Coinage: Medium of transaction and manifestation of imperial propaganda*. Nicosia, Bank of Cyprus Cultural Foundation.
Penna, V. 2002b. Numismatic circulation in Corinth from 976 to 1204. In In A. E. Laiou, (ed.), *The Economic History of Byzantium from the Seventh through the Fifteenth Century* vol. 2: 655-658.
Penna, V. 2006. *Χαλκούς, ένεκα αλλαγής. Ο άγνωστος κόσμος των χάλκινων νομισμάτων* [Chalkous for everyday dealings]. Athens, Benaki Museum. 'sdfds'

Penna, V. 2009. 'Θησαυρός' Πάρου/1999. Επανεξέταση των 'πιστών απομιμήσεων' [Paros/1999 Hoard. A re-assessment of the 'faithful/direct copies']. In S. Drougou, D. Evgenidou, Ch. Kritzas *et al.* (eds), *Κερμάτια Φιλίας, Τιμητικός τόμος για τον Ιωάννη Τουράτσογλου*: 507-514. Athens, Numismatic Museum.

Penna, V. 2010a. Χρήμα και αγορά στην Αχαΐα κατά τον 13ο αιώνα: Η μαρτυρία των νομισματικών θησαυρών [Money and market in Achaia during the thirteenth century: the testimony of the hoards]. In E. Saranti (ed.), *Δύμη, Φραγκοκρατία - Βενετοκρατία - Α' Τουρκοκρατία*, Πρακτικά Συνεδρίου: 87-112. Dyme.

Penna, V. 2010b. Κοινωνία και οικονομία στο Αιγαίο κατά τους βυζαντινούς χρόνους (4ος-12ος αι.) [Society and economy in the Aegean in Byzantine times (4th-12th c.] *Obolos* 9/II, 11-42.

Penna, V. 2013. Η μαρτυρία των νομισμάτων και των σφραγίδων [The evidence of the coins and seals]. In G. Sakellarakis (ed.), *Κύθηρα, Το μινωικό ιερό κορυφής στον Άγιο Γεώργιο στο Βουνό 3: Τα ευρήματα*: 419-462. Athens, Athens Archaeological Society.

Pennas, Ch. and Samoladou I. 2010. Βυζαντινά και μεσαιωνικά νομισματικά ευρήματα Κυκλάδων [Byzantine and medieval coin finds from the Cyclades]. *Obolos* 9/II: 135-156

Pesce, G. (ed.) 1963. *Monete genovesi*. Milano, Libri Artistici.

Pesce, G. and Felloni, G. 1976. *Genoese Coins*. Genoa, Stringa Publications.

Pitidis, Th. 1988. Το ανώνυμο κυπριακό γκρος [The anonymous Cypriot gros]. *Nomismatika Chronika* 7: 25-29.

Poey d'Avant, F. 1858. *Monnaies féodales de France*. Paris, Bureau de la Revue Numismatique Française.

Porteous, J. 1997. *The John J. Slocum Collection of Coins of the Crusades*. London, Sotheby's 6 & 7 March 1997.

Pottier, H., Schulze, I. and Schulze, W. 2008. Pseudo-Byzantine Coinage in Syria under Arab Rule (638-c. 670). Classification and Dating. *Revue Belge de Numismatique* 154: 87-155.

Prigent, V. 2010. La Sicile de Constant II: l'apport des sources sigillographiques. In *La Sicile de Byzance à l'Islam. Études réunies par Annliese Nef et Vivien Prigent*: 157-187. Paris, De Boccard.

Protonotarios, P. N. 1978. A contribution to the attribution of the 6th century Byzantine imitative issues, the so-called «moneta militaris imitativa». *Nomismatika Chronika* 5-6: 71-74.

Protonotarios, P. N. 1991. Η νομισματοκοπία της αυτοκρατορίας της Τραπεζούντας (1204-1461) [The coinage of the empire of Trebizond (1204-1461)]. In M. Koromila (ed.), *Οι Έλληνες στη Μαύρη Θάλασσα από την εποχή του Χαλκού ως τις αρχές του 20ου αιώνα*: 300-304. Athens, Politistiki Etaireia Panorama.

Pryor, J. and Jeffreys, E. M. 2006. *The Age of the ΔΡΟΜΩΝ: the Byzantine navy ca. 500-1204*. Leiden/Boston, Brill.

Psarologaki, A. and Zerlendis, M. 1996. *Ταφές και ταφικές κατασκευές στην εκκλησία της Παναγίας του Μπούργκου*, στη μεσαιωνική πόλη της *Ρόδου* [Burials and tombs in the church of St. Mary of the Borgo in the medieval town of Rhodes]. In *16ο Συμπόσιο Βυζαντινής και Μεταβυζαντινής Αρχαιολογίας και Τέχνης, Α*θήνα 17-19 *Μ*αΐου 1996, Πρόγραμμα και Περιλήψεις *Ε*ισηγήσεων και *Α*νακοινώσεων: 82-83. Athens, Christian Archaeological Society.

Psarri, Y. 2006. Νομίσματα των παλαιοχριστιανικών χρόνων από την ύπαιθρο της Ρόδου [Monnaies paléochretiennes de la campagne de Rhodes]. *Obolos* 8: 267-280.

Ragia, E. 2009. The Geography of the provincial administration of the Byzantine empire (ca. 600-1200): I. 1. The *Apothekai* of Asia Minor (7th-8th c.) *Byzantina Symmeikta* 19: 195-245.

Ragia, E. 2011. The Geography of the provincial administration of the Byzantine empire (ca. 600-1200): I. 2. *Apothekai* of the Balkans and of the islands of the Aegean Sea (7th-8th c.) *Byzantinoslavica* 69: 86-113.

Ρόδος 2.400 χρόνια. Η πόλη της Ρόδου από την ίδρυσή της μέχρι την κατάληψη από τους Τούρκους (1523) [Rhodes 2,000 Years. The town of Rhodes from its foundation until the Turkish conquest (1523)], 2 vols. 1999. Athens, Ministry of Culture.

Rhodes from the 4th c. AD to its Capture by the Ottoman Turks (1522). Palace of the Grand Master, 2004. Athens, Archaeological Receipts Fund.

Richard of Holy Trinity (*c.* 1220, formerly attributed to Godefroy de Vinsauf). *Itinerarium Peregrinorum et Gesta Regis Ricardi*. http://www.yorku.ca/inpar/ richard_of_holy_ trinity.pdf

Riley-Smith, J. 1967. *The Knights of St John in Jerusalem and Cyprus 1050-1310*. London, Macmillan.

Rosen, W. 2007. *Justinian's Flea*. New York, Viking.

Rossi, E. 1975. The Hospitallers at Rhodes 1421-1523. In K. M. Setton and H. W. Hazard (eds), *A History of the Crusades III, The Fourteenth and Fifteenth Centuries*: 314-339. Madison, University of Wisconsin Press.

Runciman, S. 1981. *A History of the Crusades*, 3 vols. Harmondsworth, Peregrine/Penguin.

Russell, J. 1986. Transformations in Early Byzantine Urban Life: The Contribution and Limitations of Archaeological Evidence. In *The 17th International Byzantine Congress, Major Papers*: 137-154. New Rochelle, New York, Caratzas.

Russell, J. 2001. The Persian Invasions of Syria/Palestine and Asia Minor in the Reign of Heraclius: Archaeologicalm Numismatic and Epigraphic Evidence. In In E. Kountoura-Galaki (ed.), *Οι σκοτεινοί αιώνες του Βυζαντιου (7ος - 9ος αι.)*: 41-71. Athens, National Research Foundation.

Saulnier, J.-M. 1985. *Catalogue des monnaies byzantines de Thasos*. Unpublished study, École Française d'Athènes.

Savvides, A. 1983. Η ελληνική δυναστεία των Γαβαλάδων και η ελληνοϊταλική διαμάχη για τη Ρόδο το 13ο αιώνα [The Greek dynasty of the Gabalas and the Greco-italian struggle for Rhodes in the 13th c.] *Byzantina* 12: 407-425.
Savvides, A. 1985. *Το οικουμενικό βυζαντινό κράτος και η εμφάνιση του Ισλάμ, 518-717 μ.Χ.* [The oecumenical Byzantine state and the appearance of Islam, AD 518-717]. Athens, Estia.
Savvides, A. 1987. *Βυζαντινά στασιαστικά και αυτονομιστικά κινήματα στα Δωδεκάνησα και στη Μικρά Ασία 1189-c. 1204 μ.Χ.* [Byzantine rebellions and uprisings in the Dodecanese and Asia Minor 1189-*c.* 1204]. Athens, Domos.
Savvides, A. 1988. Rhodes from the End of the Gabalas Rule to the Conquest by the Hospitallers, A. D. *c.* 1250-1309. *Byzantinos Domos* 2: 100-231.
Savvides, A. 1995. *Η βυζαντινή Ρόδος και οι Μουσουλμάνοι* [Byzantine Rhodes and the Muslims], 2nd Edn. Athens, Trochalia.
Savvides, A. 2004. *Γεώργιος Μανιάκης. Κατακτήσεις και υπονόμευση στο Βυζάντιο κατά τον 11ο αιώνα* [George Maniaces. Conquests and undermining in 11th *c.* Byzantium]. Athens, Periplous.
Savvides, A. 2007. Σχετικά με την περσική επιδρομή κατά της Ρόδου επί Ηρακλείου [Concerning the Persian raid on Rhodes under Heraclius]. In *Ρόδος 2400 Χρόνια*, vol. 2: 481-484. Athens, Ministry of Culture.
Schlumberger, G. 1878 (*Supplément* 1882). *Numismatique de l'Orient latin.* Paris, Leroux.
Schulze, W., Schulze, I. and Leimenstoll, W. 2006. Heraclian countermarks on Byzantine copper coins in seventh-century Syria. *Byzantine and Modern Greek Studies* 30/1: 1-27.
Schulze, W. and Oddy, A. 2012. Terminology for the transitional coinage struck in 7th century Syria after the Arab conquest. In T. Goodwin (ed.), *Arab-Byzantine Coins and History. Papers presented at the Seventh Century Syrian Numismatic Round Table held at Corpus Christi College, Oxford on 10th and 11th September 2011*: 187-200. London, Archetype.
Sellwood, D. 1962. Medieval Minting Techniques. *British Numismatic Journal* 31: 57-65.
Seltman, A. J. 1964a. A Hoard of Venetian Torneselli. *Numismatic Chronicle* Series 7, 4: 283-285.
Seltman, A. J. 1964b. A Hoard of Rhodian Gigliati. *Numismatic Chronicle* Series 7, 4: 287-291.
Seltman, A. J. 1974. The Monagri Hoard. In *The Church of the Panagia Amasgou, Monagri, Cyprus, and Its Wallpaintings. Dumbarton Oaks Papers* 28: 347-349.
Seward, D. 1995. *The Monks of War. The Military Religious Orders* (revised edition). London, Penguin.
Sidiropoulos, K. 2000. Münzfunde und Münzumlauf im spätrömischen und protobyzantinischen Kreta. In *XII Internationaler Numismatischer Kongress Berlin 1997, Akten*: 840-852. Berlin, Staatliche Museen zu Berlin.
Sidiropoulos, K. 2000. Νομισματικά ευρήματα [Coin Finds]. In P. G. Themelis (ed.), *Πρωτοβυζαντινή Ελεύθερνα, Τομέας* 1, vol. 2: 261-287. Rethymnon, Ancient Eleutherna Museum.
Sidiropoulos, K. 2002. Η νομισματική κυκλοφορία στην υστερορωμαϊκή και πρωτοβυζαντινή Μεσσήνη. Τυπικό παράδειγμα ή ιστορική εξαίρεση; [Coin circulation in Late Roman Messene and Olympia. Urban and agricultural space in the western Peloponnese. Typical example or historical exception?] In P. G. Themelis and V. Konti (eds), *Πρωτοβυζαντινή Μεσσήνη και Ολυμπία, Αστικός και αγροτικός χώρος στη Δυτική Πελοπόννησο*, Πρακτικά του Διεθνούς Συμποσίου, Αθήνα 29-30 Μαΐου 1998: 99-124. Athens, Institute of Byzantine Research.
Sidiropoulos, K. 2004a. Νομισματική ιστορία της ρωμαϊκής και πρωτοβυζαντινής Κρήτης (67 π.Χ. - 827 μ.Χ.): Testimonia et desiderata [Numismatic history of Roman and Early Byzantine Crete (67 BC - AD 827): Testimonia et desiderata]. In M. Livadioti and I. Simiakaki (eds), *Creta romana e protobizantina,* Atti del Congresso Internazionale (Iraklio, 23-30 settembre 2000), vol. 1: 193-223. Padua, Bottega d'Erasmo.
Sidiropoulos, K. 2004b. Κνωσός, Colonia Iulia Nobilis Cnosus, Μακρύτειχος: τα νομισματικά ίχνη της ιστορίας [Knossos, Colonia Iulia Nobilis Cnosus, Maktyteichos: the numismatic traces of hisoty]. In *Το Ηράκλειο και η περιοχή του. Διαδρομή στο Χρόνο. Ιστορία, αρχαιολογία, λογοτεχνία, κοινωνία*: 635-671. Heraklion, Crete University Press.
Sidiropoulos, K. 2006. Αργύριον αξικόν: νομισματικές εκδόσεις και «θησαυροί» [Argyrion Axikon: numismatic publications and hoards]. In *Ο Μυλοπόταμος από την αρχαιότητα ως σήμερα. Περιβάλλον - Αρχαιολογία - Ιστορία - Λαογραφία - Κοινωνιολογία*, Πρακτικά Διεθνούς Συνεδρίου: 147-165. Rethymnon, Istorike kai Laografike Etaireia Rethymnou.
Spahr, R. 1982. *Le Monete Siciliane dagli Aragonesi ai Borboni (1282-1836).* Basle/Graz, Association internationale des numismates professionnels.
Spufford, P. 1988a. *Money and its Use in Medieval Europe.* Cambridge, Cambridge University Press.
Spufford, P. 1988b. Mint Organization in late medieval Europe. In *Later Medieval Mints. Organization, Administration and Techniques.* In N. J. Mayhew and P. Spufford (eds), BAR International Series 389: 7-29.
Spufford, P. 2002. *Power and Profit: The Merchant in Medieval Europe.* London, Thames and Hudson.
Stahl, A.M. 1985. *The Venetian Tornesello. A medieval colonial coinage.* New York, American Numismatic Society.
Stahl, A. M. 1988. The mint of Venice in the thirteenth century. N. J. Mayhew and P. Spufford (eds), *Later Medieval Mints. Organization, Administration and Techniques,* BAR International Series 389: 97-127.
Stahl, A. M. 2000. *Zecca: The Mint of Venice in the Middle Ages.* Baltimore, Johns Hopkins University Press.

Stahl, A. M. 2013. The Mediterranean Melting Pot: Monetary Crosscurrents of the Twelfth through the Fifteenth Centuries. In M. S. Brownlee and D. Gondikas (eds), *Renaissance Encounters: Greek East and Latin West*: 241-62. Leiden, Brill.

Staley, E. 1910. *The Dogaressas of Venice.* London, Laurie.

Stefanidou, A. 2001. The Medieval Town of Rhodes Based on Johannes Hedeborg's Manuscript (1854). *Mediterranean Archaeology and Archaeometry* 1: 69-77.

Stewart, I. 1969. Style in Medieval Coinage. *Numismatic Chronicle* Series 7, 9: 269-289.

Stewart, I. 1971. Scottish Mints. In R. A. G. Carson (ed.), *Mints, Dies and Currency: Essays Dedicated to the Memory of Albert Baldwin.* Oxford

Stewart, J. R. 2002. *Lusignan Cyprus and its Coinage*, 2 vols. Nicosia, Bank of Cyprus Cultural Foundation.

Stratos, A. 1972. *Το Βυζάντιον στον Ζ' αιώνα, τ. Δ', Κωνσταντίνος Γ'(642-668)* [Byzantium in the 7th *c.* vol. 4. Constantine IV (642-668)]. Athens, Estia.

Stratos, A. 1974. *Το Βυζάντιον στον Ζ' αιώνα, τ. Ε', Κωνσταντίνος Δ' (668-687)* [Byzantium in the 7th *c.* vol. 5. Constantine IV (668-687)]. Athens, Estia.

Sumption, J. 2003. *The Age of Pilgrimage. The Medieval Journey to God.* Mahwah NJ, Paulist Press.

Svoronos, N. G. 1959. *Recherches sur le cadastre byzantin et la fiscalité aux XIe et XIIe siècles ; le cadastre de Thèbes. Bulletin de correspondence hellénique* 83/1: 1-145.

Theophanes (6th *c.*) 1839. *Chronographia I.* Bonn, Weber.

Theophanes Continuatus II (10th *c.*) 2011. *Vita Basilii Imperatoris.* Corpus Fontium Historiae Byzantinae 42. Berlin, De Gruyter.

Theophanes Continuatus (10th *c.*) 1863. *Historiae Byzantinae scriptores post Theophanem.* J. P. Migne (ed.), *Patrologia Graeca*, vol. 109. Turhnout, Brepols.

Thompson, M. 1954. *Coins from the Roman through the Venetian Period, The Athenian Agora II,* The American School of Classical Studies at Athens. Princeton, Princeton University Press.

Thomsen, R. 1986. *Hama, Fouilles et Recherches de la Fondation Carlsberg 1931-1938 III, 3, The Graeco-Roman Coins*. Copenhagen, Fondation Carlsberg.

Toubert, P. 2002. Byzantium and the Mediterranean Agrarian Civilization. In In A. E. Laiou, (ed.), *The Economic History of Byzantium from the Seventh through the Fifteenth Century* vol. 1: 377-991.

Touratsoglou, I. 1973. Unpublished Byzantine Hoards of Billon Trachea from Greek Macedonia and Thrace. *Balkan Studies* 14/1: 131-166.

Touratsoglou, I. 1974 The Aiani Hoard of Billon Trachea. *Athens Annals of Archaeology, Symmeikta* 7/3: 433-435.

Touratsoglou, I. 1975. «Θησαυρός» άσπρων τραχέων από τα Βραστά Χαλκιδικής [Hoard of aspra trachea from Vrasta, Chalkidiki]. *Athens Annals of Archaeology, Symmeikta* 8/1: 124-130.

Touratsoglou, I. and Loverdou-Tsigarida, K. 1976. Ρωμαϊκοί και βυζαντινοί νομισματικοί 'θησαυροί' από το Βορειοελλαδικό χώρο στην Εφορεία Βυζαντινών Αρχαιοτήτων Θεσσαλονίκης [Roman and Byzantine coin hoards from Northern Greece in the Ephorate of Byzantine Antiquities of Thessaloniki]. *Archaiologikon Deltion* 31: 23-48.

Touratsoglou, I. 1981. «Θησαυρός» άσπρων τραχέων/1983 από την Άρτα [A hoard of aspra trachea/1983 from Arta]. *Archaiologikon Deltion* 36: 209-226.

Touratsoglou, I. 1987. L'atelier monétaire de Thessalonique au quatorzième siècle après J.-C.: le rayonnement d'un centre artistique avant de déclin de l'empire. In D. Davidov and R. Samardzic (eds), *L'Art de Thessalonique et des pays balkaniques et les courants spirituels au XIV siècle*: 183-192. Belgrade, Insitute of Balkan Studies.

Touratsoglou, I., Tsourti-Kouli, H. and Galani-Krikou M. 1989. Ο θησαυρός "Κομοτηνής"/ 1979(;) Συμβολή στην κυκλοφορία των τεταρτηρών του ΙΒ' αι. μ.Χ. [The "Komotini"/1979(;) Hoard. A contribution to the circulation of the 12th century tetartera.] In Ch. Bakirtzis (ed.), *First International Symposium for Thracian Studies, "Byzantine Thrace" Image and Character*, vol. I: 366-428. Amsterdam, Hakkert.

Touratsoglou, I. and Baker J. 2002. Byzantium of the Venetians, Greece of the 'Grossi'. In Ch. A Maltezou and P. Schreiner (eds), *Βυζάντιο, Βενετία και ο ελληνοφραγκικός κόσμος (13ος-15ος αιώνας),* Πρακτικά του Διεθνούς Συνεδρίου που οργανώθηκε με την ευκαιρία της εκατονταετηρίδας από τη γέννηση του *R. J. Loenertz o.p.* Βενετία *1-2* Δεκεμβρίου *2000*: 204-235. Venice, Greek Institute of Byzantine and Post-Byzantine Studies in Venice.

Touratsoglou, I. 2002. La monnaie byzantine aux XIIe-XIIIe siècles et le témoignage des trouvailles de Grèce: à propos d' un ouvrage récent. *Revue Numismatique* 158: 385-404.

Travaini, L. 2004. Saints and Sinners: Coins in Medieval Italian Graves. *Numismatic Chronicle* 164: 1-16.

Treadgold, W. 1988. *The Byzantine Revival 780-842*. Stanford, Stanford University Press.

Treadgold, W. 1995. *Byzantium and Its Army, 284-1081*, Stanford, Stanford University Press.

Treadgold, W. 1997. *A History of the Byzantine State and Society*. Stanford, Stanford University Press.

Triantafyllidis, P. (ed.) 2015. *Ερεθιμία. Διαμόρφωση και ανάδειξη του Ιερού του Ερεθιμίου Απόλλωνος στον Θεολόγο Ρόδου* [Erethimia. Ordering and enhancement of the sanctuary of Apollo Erethimios at Theologos, Rhodes]. Rhodes, Ministry of Culture.

Tsanaka, A. and Doukas, K. 2009. Βυζαντινά νομίσματα από τα Βρύα Χαλκιδικής [Byzantine coins from Vrya, Chalkidiki]. In S. Drougou, D. Evgenidou, Ch. Kritzas *et al.* (eds), *Κερμάτια Φιλίας, Τιμητικός τόμος για τον Ιωάννη Τουράτσογλου*, vol. 1: 517-538. Athens, Numismatic Museum.

Tsiamis, C., Poulakou-Rebelakou, E., Tsakris, A. and Petridou, E. 2011. Epidemic waves of the Black Death in the Byzantine Empire 1347-1453 AD. *Le Infezioni in Medizina* 3: 195.

Tsirpanlis, Z. 1970. *Μελέτες για την ιστορία της Ρόδου στα χρόνια των Ιπποτών* [Studies on the history of Rhodes under the Knights Hospitaller]. Thessaloniki, Dodecanisiaka Analekta 1.

Tsirpanlis, Z. 1991. *Η Ρόδος και οι Νότιες Σποράδες στα χρόνια των Ιωαννιτών Ιπποτών (14ος-16ος αι.)* [Rhodes and the Southern Sporades under the Knights Hospitaller (14th-16th c.] Rhodes, Archaeological Receipts Fund.

Tsirpanlis, Z. 1995. *Ανέκδοτα έγγραφα για τη Ρόδο και τις Νότιες Σποράδες από το αρχείο των Ιωαννιτών Ιπποτών 1421-1453* [Unpublished Documents for Rhodes and the Southern Sporades from the Archive of the Knights Hospitaller 1421-1453]. Rhodes, Archaeological Receipts Fund.

Tsirpanlis, Z. 1998. *Ιταλοκρατία στα Δωδεκάνησα 1912-1943* [The Italian Occupation of the Dodecanese 1912-1943]. Rhodes, Archaeological Receipts Fund.

Tuma, O. 1984. Some Notes on the Significance of the Imperial Chrysobull to the Venetians of 992. *Byzantion* 54: 358-366.

Tzamalis, A. P. 1981. *Τα Νομίσματα της Φραγκοκρατίας 1184-1566* [The Coins of the Frankish Period 1184-1566]. Athens, Noummio.

Tzamalis, A. P. 1990. Η πρώτη περίοδος του τορνεζίου. Νέα στοιχεία από ένα παλαιό εύρημα [The first period of the tornese. New evidence from an old find, Part One]. *Nomismatika Chronika* 9: 101-131.

Tzamalis, A. P. 1991. Η πρώτη περίοδος του τορνεζίου. Νέα στοιχεία από ένα παλαιό εύρημα. Μέρος Β' [The first period of the tornese. New evidence from an old find, Part Two]. *Nomismatika Chronika* 10: 43-66.

Tzamalis, A. P. 1994. Το «εύρημα» της Ήλιδος/1964 [The Elis/1964 Hoard]. *Nomismatika Chronika* 13: 65-74, 82-84.

Tzamalis, A. P. 2004. Η «Πριγκιπέσσα Ιζαμπώ» και οι άνδρες της. Επανεξέταση ενός παλαιού νομισματικού μυστηρίου [Princess Isabeau and her husbands. Reexamination of an old numismatic puzzle]. *Nomismatika Chronika* 23: 59-67.

de Vaivre, J.-B. 2009. Essai de chronologie des campagnes de construction du château Saint-Pierre (Bodrum, Turquie). *Academie des Inscriptions & Belles-Lettres, Comptes rendus des séances avril-juin*: 601-622.

Valakou, P. 2010. Νομίσματα της Γενουατοκρατίας στη Χίο (1346-1566). Η συλλογή του Βυζαντινού Μουσείου Χίου [Coins of the Genoese period in Chios (1346-1566) The collection of the Chios Byzantine Museum]. *Obolos* 9, vol. 2: 109-118.

Valakou, P. 2012. Νομίσματα των Zaccaria (1304-1329) στη συλλογή του Βυζαντινού Μουσείου Χίου [Coins of the Zaccaria in the collection of the Chios Byzantine Museum]. *Nomismatika Chronika* 30: 45-58.

Vatin, N. 1994. *L'Ordre de Saint-Jean -de-Jérusalem, l'Empire ottoman et la Méditerranée orientale entre les deux sièges de Rhodes 1480-1522.* Louvain-Paris, Peeters.

Villani Johannes (*c.* 1276-1348), 1728. *Historia Universalis.* In *Rerum Italicarum Scriptores* vol. XIII: cols. 9-1004. Milan, Muratori.

Voegtli, H. 1993. *Die Fundmünzen aus der Stadtgrabung von Pergamon.* Berlin-New York, Deutsches Archäologisches Institut.

Vryonis, S. 1963. An Attic hoard of Byzantine gold coins (668-741) from the Thomas Whittemore collection and the numismatic evidence for the urban history of Byzantium. *Zbornik Radova Vizantoloskog Instituta* 8/1: 291-300.

Vryonis, S. 1971. The Decline of Medieval Hellenism in Asia Minor and the Process of Islamization from the Eleventh Through the Fifteenth Century. Berkeley-Los Angeles-London, University of California Press.

Waage, D. B. 1952. Greek, Roman, Byzantine and Crusaders Coins. *Antioch-on-the-Orontes IV,* Part Two. Princeton, Princeton University Press.

Waldstein-Wartenberg, B. *European Travellers in Rhodes, 1322-1534.* Unpublished compilation.

Walmsley, A. 2010. Coinage and the Economy of Syria-Palestine in the Seventh and Eighth Centuries CE'. In *Money, Power and Politics in Early Islamic Syria. A review of current debates*, Haldon J. (ed.), Farnham, 21-44

Wickham, C. 1981. *Early Medieval Italy*. London, Macmillan.

Woodward, A. M. 1929. Byzantine Coins. In R. M. Dawkins (ed.), *The Sanctuary of Artemis Orthia at Sparta*. London, Macmillan.

Wroth, W. 1908. *Catalogue of the Imperial Byzantine Coins in the British Museum*, vols. I-II. London, British Museum.

Wroth, W. 1911. *Catalogue of the Coins of the Vandals, Ostrogoths and Lombards and of the Empires of Thessalonica, Nicaea and Trebizond in the British Museum*. London, British Museum.

Zachariadou, E. 1983. *Trade and Crusade*. Venice, Library of the Hellenic Institute of Byzantine and Post-Byzantine Studies 11.

Zavagno, L. 2013. Two hegemonies, one island: Cyprus as a middle ground between the Byzantines and the Arabs 650-850 A.D. *Reti Medievali Rivista* 14/2: 3-30.

Zervos, O. H. 2002. A Barbarous Hybrid Tetarteron of the time of Alexios I Komnenos. *Nomismatika Chronika* 21: 101-102.

Zervos, O. 2003. The Substantive Varieties of Anonymous Folles of Class B. *Nomismatika Chronika* 22: 63-66.

Zervos, O. H. 2004. A note on three unusual counterfeit deniers tournois from Corinth Excavations. *Nomismatika Chronika* 23: 75-79.

Zervos, O. H. 2005. A little-known iconographic variant of a copper tetarteron of John II Komnenos. *Nomismatika Chronika* 24: 61-63.

Zervos, O. H. 2006. Additional notes on the copper tetarteron issue of John II Komnenos. *Nomismatika Chronika* 25: 17-20.

Zervos, O. H. 2008-9. Corrections to Hendy's Description in DOC IV of two Issues of Provincial Coppers of Alexios I Komnenos. *Nomismatika Chronika* 27: 47-51.

Zervos, O. H. 2009. A new variant of the copper tetarteron with "jeweled cross" of Alexius I Comnenus. In S. Drougou, D. Evgenidou, Ch. Kritzas *et al.* (eds), *Κερμάτια Φιλίας, Τιμητικός τόμος για τον Ιωάννη Τουράτσογλου*, vol. 1: 483-488. Athens, Numismatic Museum.

Zonaras Ioannes (11th-12th *c.*), 1897. *Epitome Historion*, vol. 3. Bonn, Bekker.

Appendices

List of excavated properties and sites with coin finds dated 498-1522

New Town of Rhodes (below, Map I)

1. Acropolis, south of the temple (1973)
2. Angelidis plot, St. Kotiadi St.[751]
3. M. Angelou plot, Sk. Zervou St.[752]
4. Aivalis plot, Theotokopoulou St.[753]
5. Amygdalas plot, Laïka Ayiou Ioannou (1966)
6. Anastasiadis plot, corner of Nikitara and Athinagora Streets[754]
7. Atsidis plot, Alexandrou Papagou St.
8. Avgerinos plot, Navarinou St.[755]
9. Ayakatsikas plot, Lindou Avenue 31 side-street.[756]
10. Ayakatsikas plot, Kodringtonos St.[757]
11. Bekir-Minettos plot, corner of Diagoridon and Kennedy Streets[758]
12. Charalambous plot, corner of Venetokleon and St. Kazoulis Streets[759]
13. City wall, junction of Kanellopoulou and Grigoriou 5ou Streets (1977)
14. Damianos plot, 4 Charalambous St.[760]
15. Diagoras Stadium, Vyronos St. (1967)
16. Dontas-Dilaverakis plot, Parthenopis St. (1973-4)
17. Doxopoulos plot, Volonaki St.[761]
18. Emboriko Epimeliterio (TEE) plot, Ethelonton Dodekanision St.[762]
19. Emmanouïl plot, Charalambous St.[763]
20. Ethnikis Trapezis plot, Kyprou Sq.[764]
21. Filippou plot, Navarinou St.[765]
22. Fotaras-Despotakis plot, Lindou Ave. (Epta Vayes)[766]
23. Ganotakis plot, Cheimarras St.[767]
24. Geniki Techniki plot, Ayiou Ioannou St.[768]
25. Geronikolas-Doulgaroglou plot, Laïka Ayiou Ioanni[769]
26. Gerontas plot, Aeschini St. (1981)[770]
27. Giahias plot, Lindou Avenue (1967)[771]
28. Giakras-Hatzimichalis plot, M. Petridi St.[772]
29. Giallousis plot, Kanellopoulou St.[773]
30. Giamis plot (Hotel Despo), Vasilissis Sophias St. (G. Lambraki St.)[774]

[751] Archaeological diary 151: 119-131.
[752] ADelt 19 (1964): 473.
[753] ADelt 19 (1964): 472.
[754] ADelt 20 (1965): 579, 591,
[755] ADelt 29 (1973-4): 951-5.
[756] ADelt 29 (1973-4): 959.
[757] ADelt 19 (1964): 472; ADelt 34 (1979): 429.
[758] ADelt 29 (1973-4): 957.
[759] ADelt 19 (1964): 471-2.
[760] ADelt 18 (1963): 323; ADelt 19 (1964): 466; ADelt 43 (1988): 583-585.
[761] ADelt 29 (1973-4): 954.
[762] ADelt 18 (1963): 322.
[763] ADelt 18 (1963): 323; ADelt 19 (1964): 466.
[764] ADelt 22 (1967): 530-1.
[765] ADelt 32 (1977): 352-6.
[766] ADelt 31 (1976): 386.
[767] ADelt 21 (1966): 449-50.
[768] ADelt 47 (1992): 618; ADelt 48 (1993): 511-5; ADelt 49 (1994): 768-9.
[769] Archaeological diary 3a: 211-218; PAE 1960: 281.
[770] Archaeological diary 145: 117.
[771] ADelt 22 (1967): 536-8.
[772] ADelt 30 (1975): 363.
[773] ADelt 30 (1975): 369.
[774] ADelt 22 (1967): 517.

31. Giannakopoulos-Voudouris plot, corner of Kennedy and Cheimarras Streets[775]
32. Gikas plot, corner of Pindou and Th. Sofouli Streets[776]
33. Greek Tourist Organization (EOT) plot, corner of Ethnarchou Makariou and Alexandrou Papagou Streets (1959)
34. Hastas plot, corner of Kanada and Bevin Streets[777] (1968)
35. Hatziandreou plot, corner of P. Mela and Cheimarras Streets[778]
36. Hatzioannou plot, Lindou side-street (1990)
37. Hatzistamatis plot, Agias Anastasias St.[779]
38. Hotel 'Soleil', corner of Dimokratias and E. Venizelou Streets[780]
39. Iatridis-Katsaras-Kakas plot, corner of Megalou Konstantinou and Garibaldi Streets[781]
40. Ioannidis-Salvaris-Volonakis plot, Kennedy St.[782]
41. Kafetzidakis plot, Alexandrou Diakou St. (1962)
42. Kaloudis plot, 15A Voulgaroktonou St.[783]
43. Karayannis plot, P. Rodiou St.[784]
44. Katavenakis plot, corner of Kodringtonos and Athinagora Streets[785]
45. Katsaras plot, corner of Amerikis and 25 Martiou Streets[786]
46. Kavasilas plot, St. Kotiadi St.[787]
47. Kazoulis-Alevras plot, Akramitou St.[788]
48. Kazoulleion Highschool for Girls, Venetokleon St.[789]
49. Kiousoglou plot, 29 Ethelonton Dodekanision St.[790]
50. Koilias plot, 47 Ayiou Georgiou St.[791]
51. Konstantinidis-Kakas plot, Pavlou Mela St.[792]
52. Konstantinidis-Kakas plot, corner of St. Kazouli and A. Panagouli Streets[793]
53. Kostaridis plot, corner of Vyronos and Kanada Streets[794]
54. Kostaridis plot, corner of P. Mela and Voreiou Ipeirou Streets[795]
55. Kouros plot, corner of Pavlou Mela and Cheimarras Streets[796]
56. Kozas plot, Pavlou Mela St.[797]
57. KYP plot, Ayion Anargyron St.[798]
58. Kypriotis plot, corner of Amarantou and 28is Oktovriou Streets[799]
59. Kyramariou plot, corner of Kanada and Kolokotroni Streets[800]
60. Linardos plot, Agiou Ioannou St.[801]
61. Mantas plot, corner of 33 Kanada St. and Bevin St.[802]
62. Maravelias plot, 3 R. Feraiou St.[803]
63. Ts. Matthaiou plot, Kizil Tepe, betw. Aischini and Konstantinou Ydraiu Streets[804]

775 ADelt 34 (1979): 418-9.
776 ADelt 24 (1969): 459
777 ADelt 34 (1979): 429-30.
778 ADelt 23 (1968): 442-3; ADelt 24 (1969): 464-7; ADelt 25 (1970): 527; ADelt 26 (1971): 552-555; ADelt 34 (1979): 473; ADelt 54 (1999): 994-5; ADelt 61 (2006): 1341-2.
779 ADelt 22 (1967): 520-1.
780 ADelt 18 (1963): 324.
781 ADelt 28 (1973): 610-4.
782 ADelt 22 (1967): 515-6.
783 ADelt 32 (1977): 366-7.
784 Archaeological diary 122: 15-17, 24, 31-33, 40, 42, 46-7, 53.
785 ADelt 20 (1965): 589.
786 ADelt 29 (1973-4): 970-2; ADelt 30 (1975): 369.
787 ADelt 42 (1987): 608.
788 PAE 1960: 282.
789 ADelt 32 (1977): 360-1.
790 ADelt 22 (1967): 533.
791 ADelt 19 (1964): 473.
792 ADelt 23 (1968): 437-8.
793 ADelt 33 (1978): 397.
794 ADelt 43 (1988): 593-4; ADelt 44 (1989): 472-4; ADelt 45 (1990): 467; ADelt 46 (1991): 445-9.
795 ADelt 19 (1964): 466.
796 ADelt 34 (1979): 473.
797 ADelt 20 (1965): 593-4.
798 ADelt 25 (1970): 511-14.
799 ADelt 21, (1966): 442-3; ADelt 22 (1967): 534.
800 Archaeological diary 13: 185 ff.
801 ADelt 34 (1979): 421-2.
802 ADelt 29 (1973-4): 948.
803 ADelt 18 (1963): 323.
804 ADelt 34 (1979), 443.

64. Menexelis plot, corner of P. Mela and Diagoridon Streets[805]
65. 'Mnemeion Aspidos', Afroditis St.[806]
66. E. Moschos plot, Papalouka St.[807]
67. Moustakis plot, Diagoridon St.[808]
68. Myriallakis-Papamanolis plot, corner of Iroon Polythechneiou and I Kazouli Streets[809]
69. Myriallis plot, Konstantinou Palaiologou St.[810]
70. Neas Zilandias St. (Th. Sofouli) (1955)
71. Oikonomidis-Ioannidis plot, 19 Th. Sofouli St.[811]
72. Pachos House, G. Efstathiou St.[812]
73. Panagiotakis plot, Parthenopis St. (1980)
74. Panopoulos plot (R26), Pindou St.[813]
75. Papachristodoulou plot, 17 Ethnarchou Makariou St.[814]
76. Papachristodoulou plot, Tsaldari St.[815]
77. Papadopoulou plot, Agiou Ioannou St. (1970)
78. Papageorgiou-Hastas-Voyatzis plot (R40), Grigoriou 5ou St.[816]
79. Papagiannakis plot, Grigoriou 5ou St.[817]
80. Papaioannou-Stavrias plot, Fleming St.[818]
81. Papapanagiotou plot, corner of Kanada and Athinagora Streets[819]
82. Papastamatis plot, corner of Pindou and Enoplon Dynameon Streets[820]
83. Pappou plot, Th. Sofouli St.[821]
84. Petridis plot, corner of Iroon Polytechneiou and I. Kazoulli Streets (1966)[822]
84a. Petridis plot, corner of P. Mela and Navarinou Streets[823]
85. Platis plot, P. Mela St.[824]
86. Politou-Hatzistratis-Koutsomanolis plot, corner of Konstantinou Ydreou and Papamanoli Streets[825]
87. Rodini
88. Priest Roussos plot, Komninon side-street[826]
89. Sambanis plot, P. Mela St.[827]
90. Sarikas-Moskis plot, A. Panagouli St. (8 Pring. Alexias St.)[828]
91. Simixis plot, Cheimarras St.[829]
92. Skordos plot, Pindou St.[830]
93. Skoumbourdis plot, St. Kazouli St.[831]
94. Soihan-Minettos plot, corner of Th. Sofouli and Cheimarras Streets[832]
95. Sotirakis plot, P. Mela St.[833]

805 ADelt 20 (1965): 594.
806 ADelt 28 (1973): 637.
807 Archaeological diary 73.
808 ADelt 23 (1968): 438.
809 ADelt 25 (1970): 507.
810 ADelt 23 1968): 433; ADelt 28 (1973): 608-10.
811 Archaeological diary 76: 222; Archaeological diary 86: 1-50.
812 PAE 1958: 235-8.
813 PAE 1959: 186-9.
814 PAE 1960: 275-8.
815 ADelt 35 (1980): 536, 538
816 ADelt 23 (1968): 447; ADelt 24 (1969): 453; ADelt 25 (1970): 500 ff.; ADelt 26 (1971): 534 ff.; ADelt 34 (1979): 430.
817 ADelt 30 (1975): 366.
818 ADelt 34 (1979): 413-5.
819 ADelt 46 (1991): 462.
820 ADelt 19 (1964): 465-6; ADelt 20 (1965): 594; ADelt 21 (1966): 449-50.
821 ADelt 47 (1992): 617.
822 ADelt 22 (1967): 516, 535. Dates in parentheses not agreeing with the bibliographical information indicate recovery independent of the published excavation.
823 ADelt 35 (1980): 530.
824 ADelt 26 (1971): 541.
825 ADelt 33 (1978): 402-3.
826 ADelt 20 (1965): 593.
827 ADelt 18 (1963): 324; ADelt 19 (1964): 465.
828 ADelt 29 (1973-4): 955-7.
829 ADelt 42 (1987): 679-80.
830 ADelt 23 (1968): 439.
831 Archaeological diary 156.
832 ADelt 18 (1963): 324; ADelt 19 (1964): 466; ADelt 39 (1984): 311.
833 ADelt 21 (1966): 449.

96. Soulounias plot, Amerikis side-street[834]
97. Stavrias-Laos plot, extension of Agiou Nikolaou St.[835]
98. Synetairismou II development, S. Venizelou St.[836]
99. Tourkalis plot, corner of Ethelonton Dodekanision and 25is Martiou Streets[837]
100. Tsigaridis plot, 48 Athinagoras St.[838]
101. Tzedakis plot, Cheimarars St. (1982)[839]
102. Valakis-Volonakis plot, corner of Navarinou and Cheimarras Streets[840]
103. Valsamoulis plot, Rodini (1962)[841]
104. Venetokleion Highschool for Boys, Palaiologou St.[842]
105. Viotechnon plot, corner of Kanada and Kolokotroni Streets[843]
106. Water Authority (DEYAR) trench, P. Tsaldari St.[844]

Medieval Town of Rhodes (below, Map II)

1. Argyrokastrou Square[845]
2. Aristofanous St.
3. Asprakis plot, Platonos St.[846] (1976 ff.)
4. Auberge of the *tongue* of Spain, Ippoton St.[847]
5. Bastion of St. George, sector of the *tongue* of Auvergne[848]
6. Bastion of Carretto[849]
7. 'Castellania' (Public Library), Ippokratous Sq.[850] (1988)
8. Chrysochoou plot, 147 Menekleous St.[851]
9. 2 Demosthenous St.
10. Gate of St. John, Fluvian bulwark and bastion of Aubusson[852]
11. Gate of St. Paul[853]
12. Gavoyannis plot, 147D Menekleous St.[854]
13. Giouloglou Plot, corner of Apellou and Protogenous Streets[855]
14. Haliloglou plot, Athinas Sq.[856]
15. Hasapoglou plot, Platonos St.[857]
16. Hatzilazarou plot, corner of Pythagora and Sofokleous Streets[858]
17. Holy Apostles (Imaret), corner of Ippodamou and Sokratous Streets[859]
18. Holy Trinity (Dolapli), Dimosthenous St.[860]
19. Hospice of St. Catherine, corner of Thiseos St. and Peisidorou Sq.[861]
20. Installation of drain network in the medieval town (DEPOS)[862]
21. 21 Ipparchou St.

[834] ADelt 38 (1982): 388.
[835] ADelt 28 (1973): 633-4.
[836] ADelt 22 (1967): 531-3; ADelt (1968): 433, 438-9; ADelt 29 (1973-4): 954.
[837] ADelt 18 (1963): 322 (Cairo Palace Hotel).
[838] ADelt 35 (1980): 532.
[839] ADelt 42 (1987): 587-9.
[840] ADelt 29 (1973-4): 951-4.
[841] Archaeological diary 7: 119.
[842] ADelt 26 (1971): 535-9.
[843] ADelt 23 (1968): 433, 438-9.
[844] ADelt 53 (1998): 951.
[845] ADelt 56-59 (2001-4): 374.
[846] Archaeological diary 96.
[847] ADelt 53 (1998): 994-6; ADelt 54 (1999): 988; ADelt 56-59 (2001-4): 374-8.
[848] ADelt 49 (1994): 815; ADelt 50 (1995): 823-4; ADelt 52 (1997): 1148-9; ADelt 53 (1998): 991.
[849] ADelt 56-59 (2001-4): 385-7.
[850] ADelt 43 (1988): 669.
[851] ADelt 43 (1988): 657-60.
[852] ADelt 48 (1993): 571; ADelt 49 (1994): 816.
[853] ADelt 56-59 (2001-4): 387-8.
[854] ADelt 32 (1977): 357.
[855] ADelt 47 (1992): 673; ADelt 52 (1997): 1147-8.
[856] ADelt 47 (1992): 675-7.
[857] ADelt 19 (1964): 467-8; ADelt 25 (1970): 507-11.
[858] ADelt 42 (1987): 672-3.
[859] ADelt 52 (1997): 1150.
[860] ADelt 34 (1979): 473-5.
[861] ADelt 43 (1988): 653-7; ADelt 44 (1989): 516-8; ADelt 48 (1993): 590; ADelt 49 (1994): 816-7.
[862] ADelt 61 (2006): 1337-8.

22. Karavelatzis plot, between Perikleous and Dosiadou Streets[863]
23. Karydakis plot, Demosthenous St. (2000)
24. Konstantinidis plot, Thoukydidou St. (1990)
25. Kozas plot, Dosiadou St. (1994-5)
26. Kyriazis House, 1A Irodotou St. (1965)
27. 68 Lachitos St.
28. Manettas plot, Athinas Sq.[864]
29. Maravelias plot, Platonos St.[865]
30. Marinos plot, 20 Lachitos St.[866]
31. K. Mavros plot, Pythagora St.[867] (1978)
32. Medieval moat
33. Minatsis plot, Menekleous St.[868]
34. Mole of the Windmills[869]
35. Nikolis plot, Ergeiou St.[870]
36. Nikolis plot, Omirou St.[871] (1991)
37. 26-28 Omirou St. (1989)
38. Oplotheke Milly ('Tholaros'), Symis Sq.[872]
39. 'Over the ancient ship-sheds.'
40. Palace of the Grand Master[873]
41. Panaitiou St., excavation of the Byzantine city wall and the conventual church of St. John of the Collachio[874]
42. Pekmetzis plot, Agisandrou St.[875]
43. 25K Perikleous St.[876]
44. Public Lavatories, Orfeos St.[877]
45. Pythagora St. (I. Kondis excavation)[878]
46. Sabihas-Kaimaktsis plot (Collachio tower), Theofiliskou St.[879]
47. St. Artemius (Sykyndy mesjid), Ergeiou St.[880]
48. St. Bernardine (St. Nicholas, Abdul Djelil or Cukur mesjud), Omirou St.[881]
49. St. Catherine (Ilk Mihrab), Perikleous St.[882]
50. St. George (Hourmali), Apollonion St.[883]
51. St. John (Kizil Kapou mesjid), Archiepiskopou Efthymiou St.
52. St. Mark (Satri Celebi mesjid), Menandrou St.[884]
53. St. Mary of the Borgo, corner of Aristotelous and Alhadeff Streets[885]
54. St. Mary of the Castle, Megalou Alexandrou Sq.[886]
55. 'St. Mary of Victory', Peisirodou Sq.[887]
56. St. Michael (Demirli), Athinas Sq.[888]

---

863 ADelt 47 (1992): 671-3.
864 ADelt 49 (1994): 819.
865 ADelt 32 (1977): 356; ADelt 34 (1979): 412; ADelt 42 (1987): 583-4.
866 ADelt 43 (1988): 652-3.
867 Archaeological diary 107.
868 ADelt 46 (1991): 504; ADelt 47 (1992): 674-5; ADelt 48 (1993): 571-2.
869 ADelt 54 (1999): 991-4' ADelt 56-59 (2001-4): 391-3' ADelt 63 (2008): 1342-4.
870 ADelt 56-59 (2001-4): 370-372.
871 Archaeological diaries 274 and 313.
872 ADelt 56-59 (2001-4): 388-90.
873 ADelt 43 (1988): 647-50; ADelt 54 (1999): 987.
874 ADelt 45 (1990): 511-4; ADelt 46 (1991): 497-9; ADelt 47 (1992): 670-1; ADelt 48 (1993): 569-70; ADelt 49 (1994): 815-6; ADelt 50 (1995): 821-3; ADelt 52 (1997): 1150; ADelt 53 (1998): 994; ADelt 54 (1999): 987-8; ADelt 56-59 (2001-4): 379-81; ADelt 61 (2006): 1338.
875 ADelt 44 (1989): 510-6; ADelt 45 (1990): 507-10; ADelt 46 (1991): 502; ADelt 56-59 (2001-4): 370.
876 ADelt 42 (1987): 675.
877 ADelt 32 (1977): 356-7.
878 PAE 1951: 225-34.
879 ADelt 43 (1988): 651-2.
880 ADelt 46 (1991): 496-7; ADelt 47 (1992): 673-4.
881 ADelt 42 (1987): 656-7.
882 ADelt 47 (1992): 673.
883 ADelt 30 (1975): 373; ADelt 37 (1982): 407-10; ADelt 38 (1983): 399-400; ADelt 42 (1987): 664-5; ADelt 52 (1997): 1151; ADelt 53 (1998): 992-3; ADelt 56-59 (2001-4): 374-5.
884 ADelt 42 (1987): 669-70; ADelt 53 (1998): 992-3.
885 ADelt 52 (1997): 1151-2; ADelt 56-59 (2001-4): 383.
886 ADelt 25 (1970): 518-527.
887 ADelt 42 (1987): 670-2; ADelt 53 (1998): 1001; ADelt 54 (1999): 989; ADelt 56-59 (2001-4): 383.
888 ADelt 42 (1987): 666-669; ADelt 45 (1990): 510-1.

57. St. Spyridon (Kavakli mesjid), Athinas Sq.[889]
58. SS Constantine & Helena (Kadi mesjid), Menekleous St.[890]
59. SS Theodore (Hudai mesjid), Omirou St.[891]
60. Sofokleous Sq. (1976)
61. 149-151 Sokratous side-street, trial trench[892]
62. Theofiliskou St.[893] (1984 ff.)
63. Tsimettas plot, 35 Aristotelous St.[894]
64. Unidentified church of Kisthiniou St.[895]
65. Unidentified church of Thiseos St.[896]
66. Valakis Building, Megalou Alexandrou Sq. (2000)
67. Villaragut Mansion, Ippoton St.[897]
68. Villiers Mansion, Ippoton St.[898]
69. Zarifis House, 3 Theophiliskou St. (1994)

Suburbs

1. Faneromeni (1954)
2. Karakonero (1969/1982)
3. Monte Smith, 'Vrysi Nymfis'
4. 'Bel Passo' (M. Petridi St.)

Countryside

1. Dormition, Mesanagros[899]
2. Basilica II, Charaki
3. Ioannidis plot, Trianda (1991)[900]
4. Kambouropoulos plot, Trianda[901]
5. Konstantinou plot, Lagou, Rodou Lindou Avenue, 11th km (1967)[902]
6. Kymisala, Monolithos (1968)[903]
7. Kyroniatis, Maritsa (1984)[904]_
8. St. George Chostos, Lindos (1971)[905]
9. Anonymous Byzantine church (narthex tomb), Phileremos, Trianda (1936)[906]
10. Sancuary of Apollo Erethimios, Tholos (1993-2012)[907]
11. Sugar mill, Charaki (1991-98)[908]
12. Tsambikakis plot, Kremasti[909]
13. Zourarakis plot, Rodou-Lindou Avenue, 7th km (1976)[910]
14. 'Stavrotholi', Paradissi (1973)

[889] ADelt 30 (1975): 373; ADelt 39 (1984): 337-40.
[890] ADelt 46 (1991): 499-502; ADelt 47 (1992): 677-8; ADelt 53 (1998): 991-2.
[891] ADelt 53 (1998): 1000.
[892] ADelt 47 (1992): 675.
[893] ADelt 46 (1991): 503-4.
[894] ADelt 27 (1972): 688-689; ADelt 29 (1974): 982.
[895] ADelt 52 (1997): 1155; ADelt 53 (1998): 1000; ADelt 54 (1999): 989; ADelt 56-59 (2001-4): 381-3.
[896] ADelt 52 (1997): 1152-5; ADelt 53 (1998): 996-9; ADelt 54 (1999): 989-91.
[897] ADelt 44 (1989): 519-20; ADelt 49 (1994): 816; ADelt 56-59 (2001-4): 366, 368; ADelt 62 (2007): 1320-1.
[898] ADelt 34 (1979): 465.
[899] ADelt 34 (1979): 475-7; ADelt 35 (1980): 571-4.
[900] ADelt 43 (1988): 660-1.
[901] ADelt 52 (1997): 1155-7.
[902] 'Archaeological diary of Trianda'.
[903] Archaeological diary 32: 117.
[904] Archaeological diary 8: 104-105.
[905] Old Inv. Nos: PVE 2606b, a/a 1305; PVE 2636b, a/a 1306; a/a 1307.
[906] Livadiotti and Rocco 1996: 40.
[907] Triantafyllidis 2015.
[908] Kollias and Michaelidou 1997; ADelt 54 (1999): 995-6.
[909] ADelt 42 (1987): 616-7, 684-5.
[910] Archaeological diary 93: 80.

Coin finds of the period 498-1522[911]

I. New town of Rhodes

1. Ancient acropolis
Pentanummium with christogram (**134**)
Heraclius: follis (**538**)
11th c. anonymous follis, type I (**1061**)
Hospitaller 15th c. obols (**2937**, NB 1106)
Hospitaller 15th c. obol imitation (NB 701)

2. Angelidis plot, St. Kotiadi St. (1982)
Heraclius: follis (**394**)

3. M. Angelou plot, Sk. Zervou St. (1960)
Hospitaller 15th c. obol (NB 306)

4. Aivalis plot, Theotokopoulou St. (1965)
11th c. anonymous follis, type B (**923**)

5. Amygdalas plot, Laïka Ayiou Ioannou (1966)
Heraclius: follis (**566**)

6. Anastasiadis plot, corner of Nikitara and Athinagora Streets (1964-5)
Heraclius: follis (**495**)

7. Atsidis plot, Alexandrou Papagou St.
Heraclius: follis (**579**)

8. Avgerinos plot, Navarinou St. (1974)
Pentanummium with christogram (**126**)
Justin II: pentanummium (**211**)

9. Ayakatsikas plot, corner of Lindou Avenue and Gregoriou 5ou St. (1973-6)
Heraclius: follis (**387**)
Alexius I (**1183**)
Hospitaller 15th c. obols (NB 887, 888)

10. Ayakatsikas plot, Kodringtonos St. (1979)
Heraclius: follis (**568**)

11. Bekir-Minettos plot, corner of Diagoridon and Kennedy Streets (1973-4)
Pentanummium with christogram (**139**)
Maurice: quarter follis (**269**)
Heraclius: follis (**412**)

12. Charalambous plot, corner of Venetokleon and St. Kazoulis Streets (1963)
Heraclius: follis (**389**)

13. City wall, junction of Kanellopoulou and Grigoriou 5ou Streets (1977)
Justin II: half follis (**228**)
Heraclius: follis (**401**, **547**)
Isaac II (**1268**)

---

[911] Within parentheses the Catalogue number of each coin; if the figure is preceded by the letters NB and not in bold type, it refers to a specimen from the inventory of the Ephorate which has not been included in the catalogue. The type of a coin is not mentioned if it is the only one of a particular ruler found on Rhodes, such as the signed folles of the 11th century, the tetartera of Alexius I and the trachea of Isaac II and Alexius III. Similarly underlined coins belong to a specific assemblage or hoard (no distinction between bold and regular script.)

14. Damianos plot, Charalambous St. (1962-4)
Anastasius I: follis (**7**)
Maurice: follis (**284**)
Heraclius: folles (**455, 501**)
Latin imitative, small module, type C (**1389**)

15. Diagoras Stadium, Vyronos St. (1967)
Hospitaller 15th c. obol (NB 3947)

16. Dontas-Dilaverakis plot, Parthenopis St. (1973-4)
Hospitaller 14th c. obol (NB 807)

17. Doxopoulos plot, Antisminarchou Volonaki St. (1973-4)
11th c. anonymous follis, type B (**977**)

18. Emboriko Epimelitirio (TEE) plot, Ethelonton Dodekanision St. (1961-3)
Heraclius: follis (**939**)

19. Emmanouïl plot, Charalambous St. (1962-4)
Heraclius: follis (**657**)

20. Ethnikis Trapezis plot, Kyprou Sq.
Justinian I: half follis (**606**)
Heraclius: follis (**526**), *half follis* (**658**)
Phocas follis imitation (**848**)

21. Filippou plot, Navarinou St. (1976)
Justin I: pentanummium (**44**)
Pentanummium with christogram (**65**)
Justin II: pentanummium (**189**)
Phocas: half follis (**317**)
Heraclius: follis (**410**)
Constans II: folles (**780, 782**)
Latin imitative, small module, type A (**1346**)

22. Fotaras-Despotakis plot, Kanellopoulou St. (1974)
Maurice: quarter follis (**270**)
Hospitaller 15th c. obol imitations (NB 1073, 1075)

23. Ganotakis plot, Cheimarras St. (1965)
Maurice: follis (**258**)
Heraclius: follis (**555**)

24. Geniki Techniki plot, Ayiou Ioannou St. (1994)
Anastasius I: pentanummium (**17**)
Justin I: follis (**34**)
Heraclius: folles (**429, 660**)
Constans II: follis (**793**)

25. Geronikolas-Doulgaroglou plot, Laïka Ayiou Ioanni (1960)
Anastasius I: follis (**36**)

26. Gerontas plot, Aeschini St. (Kizil Tepe, 1981)
Overstruck denier c. 1400 (**2049**)
Hospitaller 15th c. obol (NB 1148)

27. Giahias plot, Lindou Avenue (1967)
11th c. anonymous follis, type C (**1020**)

28. Giakras-Hatzimichalis plot, M. Petridi St. (1975)
Heraclius: follis **(457)**
Latin imitative, small module, type A **(1370)**

29. Giallousis plot, Kanellopoulou St. (1974-1975)
Constans II: follis **(795)**

30. Giamis plot (Hotel Despo), G. Lambraki St. (1966)
Constans II: follis **(808)**

31. Giannakopoulos-Voudouris plot, corner of Kennedy and Cheimarras Streets (1979-81)
Pentanummium with christogram **(55)**

32. Gikas plot, corner of Pindou and Th. Sofouli Street (1968)
Heraclius: follis **(395)**

33. Greek Tourist Organization (EOT) plot, corner of Ethnarchou Makariou and Alexandrou Papagou Streets (1959)
Justin II: half follis **(233)**

34. Hastas plot, corner of Kanada and Bevin Streets (1968)
Gavalas Successors [1294-1304?] **(1690)**

35. Hatziandreou plot, corner of P. Mela and Cheimarras Streets (1968 ff.)
Anastasius I: pentanummium **(14)**, *minimi* **(19, 20, 21, 22, 23, 24, 25, 26, 27, 28, 29)**
Pentanummia, 1st half of 6th c. **(348, 349, 352)**
Justin I: follis **(30)**, half-follis **(40)**, *pentanummia* **(45, 46, 53)**
Pentanummia with christogram **(123, 156)**
Justinian I: **(122)**
Justin II: follis **(238)**, *half follis* **(169)**, *dodecanummium* **(221)**, *pentanummia* **(174, 175, 179, 183, 185, 193, 196)**
Maurice: follis **(275)**
Phocas: half follis **(310)**, *quarter follis* **(319)**, *pentanummium* **(326)**
6th c. pentanummium (NB 619)
Dodecanummium, 2nd half of 6th c. **(375)**
6th-7th c.: quarter follis **(844)**
Heraclius: folles **(392, 517, 557, 567, 573, 612)**, *half follis* **(686)**, *quarter follis* **(687)**
Constans II: folles **(760, 790, 819)**, *half follis* **(826)**, *dodecanummium* **(833)**, *quarter follis* **(830)**
Dodecanummium 7ου αι. **(847)**
11th c. anonymous folles, type B **(914, 971)**
11th c. anonymous follis, type C **(1013)**
Romanus IV **(1104)**
Alexius I **(1142)**
Gavalas Successors [1261-43?] **(1567)**, **(1645)**
Hospitaller 14th c. deniers **(1815, 1860, 1861, 1711)**
Hospitaller 14th c. obols **(2749, 2750, 2751, 2763, 2776, 2777, 2816, 2861, 2868)**
Pins denier **(1881)**
Naillac overstrike **(2301)**
Hospitaller 15th c. obols (NB 359, 362, 3937)
Hospitaller 15th c. obol imitations **(3054**, NB 354)
Lucca **(3134)**, *Sicily* **(3171)**

36. Hatzioannou plot, Lindou side-street (1990)
Heraclius: follis **(496)**

37. Hatzistamatis plot, Agias Anastasias St. (1965)
Heraclius: follis **(706)**
Hospitaller 15th c. obol (NB 336)

38. Hotel 'Soleil', corner of Dimokratias and E. Venizelou Streets (1959-63)
Pentanummium with christogram (**147**)
Justin II: half follis (**172**), *pentanummium* (**368**)
Heraclius: folles (**442, 626**), *half follis* (**598**)
Constans II: follis (**794**)
Gavalas Successors [1294-1304?] (**1621**)

39. Iatridis-Katsaras-Kakas plot, corner of Megalou Konstantinou and Garibaldi Streets (1972)
Gavalas Successors [1278-94] (**1595**)

40. Ioannidis-Salvaris-Volonakis plot, Kennedy St. (1966)
Justin II: follis (**202**)
Heraclius: half follis (**616**)
Alexius I tetarteron imitation (**1198**)

41. Kafetzidakis plot, Alexandrou Diakou St. (1962)
Constans II: follis (**787**)

42. Kaloudis plot, 15A Voulgaroktonou St. (1977)
Hospitaller 15th c. obol (NB 956)

43. Karayannis plot, P. Rodiou St.
Theodore I (**1299**)

44. Katavenakis plot, corner of Kodringtonos and Athinagora Streets (1964)
Heraclius: follis (**493**)

45. Katsaras plot, corner of Amerikis and 25 Martiou Streets (1973-5)
Pentanummium with christogram (**128**)
Half follis, 2nd half of 6th c. (**334**)
Leo Gavalas (**1514, 1515**)
Gavalas Successors [1273-8?] (**1580**)
Hospitaller 14th c. denier (**1741**)
Hospitaller 15th c. obols (**2984**, NB 911)

46. Kavasilas plot, St. Kotiadi St. (1985)
Pentanummium with christogram (**149**)
11th c. anonymous follis, type B (**936**)

47. Kazoulis-Alevras plot, Akramitou St. (1960)
Romanus I (**877**)

48. Kazoulleion Highschool for Girls, Venetokleon St. (1977)
Anastasius I: pentanummium (**16**)
Pentanummium with christogram (**47**)
Justin II: pentanummia (**181, 195**)
Heraclius: follis (**578**)
11th c. anonymous follis, type K (**1081**)
Hospitaller 14th c. denier (**1816**)
Hospitaller 15th c. obol (NB 4192)

49. Kiousoglou plot, 29 Ethelonton Dodekanision St. (1965)
Heraclius: follis (**539**)

50. Koilias plot, 47 Ayiou Georgiou St. (1963-4)
Gavalas Successors [1294-1304?] (**1616**)

51. Konstantinidis-Kakas plot, Pavlou Mela St. (1973)
Hospitaller 15th c. obol ([NB 694])

52. Konstantinidis-Kakas plot, corner of St. Kazouli and A. Panagouli Streets (1978)
Pentanummium with christogram (**127**)

53. Kostaridis plot, corner of Vyronos and Kanada Streets (1988-91)
Pentanummium with christogram (**152**)
Justinian I: quarter follis (**88**)
Heraclius: half follis (**679**)
Gavalas Successors [1294-1304?] (**1599**)
Hospitaller 15th c. obol imitation (NB 2202)

54. Kostaridis plot, corner of P. Mela and Voreiou Ipeirou Streets (1964)
Justinian I: follis (**71**) , *half follis* (**86**)
Heraclius: follis (**420**)

55. Kouros plot, corner of Pavlou Mela and Cheimarras Streets (1978)
Heraclius: follis (**468, 492**)

56. Kozas plot, Pavlou Mela St. (1964)
Alexius I (**1161**)

57. KYP plot, Ayion Anargyron St. (1969)
Justin II: pentanummia (**208, 254**)
Phocas: half follis (**306**)
Heraclius: follis (**692**)
El Manuel I (**1216**)
Hospitaller 14th c. denier (**1715**)

58. Kypriotis plot, corner of Amarantou and 28is Oktovriou Streets (1965)
Heraclius: follis (**546**)

59. Kyramariou plot, corner of Kanada and Kolokotroni Streets (1965)
Heraclius: folles (**398, 411, 444, 651**)
11th c. anonymous follis, type C (**1030**)
Gavalas Successors [1294-1304?] (**1622**)
Hospitaller 14th c. denier (**1742**)
Hospitaller 15th c. obol imitation (**3057**)

60. Linardos plot, Agiou Ioannou St. (1979)
Maurice: quarter follis (**268**)

61. Mantas plot, corner of 33 Kanada St. and Bevin St. (1973-4)
Hospitaller 15th c. obol (NB 1037)

62. Maravelias plot, 3 R. Feraiou St. (1962)
Justin II: pentanummium (**192**)

63. Ts. Matthaiou plot, Kizil Tepe, Rodini (1979)
Hospitaller 15th c. obol (**2950**)

64. Menexelis plot, corner of P. Mela and Diagoridon Streets (1965)
Heraclius: follis (**464**)

65. 'Mnemeion Aspidos', Afroditis St. (1972)
Pentanummium of Anastasius I or Justinian I (**353**)
Pentanummium with christogram (**146**)

66. E. Moschos plot, Papalouka St. (1975)
Justin II: half follis (**170**)

67. Moustakis plot, Diagoridon St. (1968)
Justinian I: half follis (**109**)
Justin II: follis (**165**), *half folles* (**227, 231, 232**), *pentanummia* (**182, 188, 215**)
6th c. pentanummium (**356**)
Heraclius: folles (**623, 638**), *half follis* (**647**)

68. Myriallakis-Papamanolis plot, corner of Iroon Polythechneiou and I Kazouli Streets (1969-70)
Half follis, 2nd half of 6th c. (**335**)

69. Myriallis plot, Konstantinou Palaiologou St. (1972-3)
Heraclius: follis (**699**)
Latin imitative, small module, type B (**1380**)
Latin imitative, small module, type D (**1394**)

70. Neas Zilandias St. (Th. Sofouli) (1955)
Tiberius II: follis (**246**)
Gavalas Successors [1254-1258] (**1556**)

71. Oikonomidis-Ioannidis plot, 19 Th. Sofouli St.
6th c. half follis (**338**)

72. Pachos House, G. Efstathiou St. (1958)
Heraclius: folles (**386, 433, 467**)

73. Panagiotakis plot, Parthenopis St. (1980)
Heraclius: follis (**453**)
Gavalas Successors [1254-1258?] (**1555**)

74. Panopoulos plot (R26), Pindou St. (1959)
Justinian I: pentanummium (**112**)

75. Papachristodoulou plot, 17 Ethnarchou Makariou St. (1961)
Anastasius I: pentanummium (**345**)
Heraclius: follis (**478**)

76. Papachristodoulou plot, Tsaldari St. (1981)
Heraclius: follis (**506**)

77. Papadopoulou plot, Agiou Ioannou St. (1970)
Heraclius: follis (**693**)

78. Papageorgiou-Hastas-Voyatzis plot (R40), Grigoriou 5ou St. (1969)
Maurice: quarter follis (**277**)
Hospitaller 14th c. obol (**2742**)
Hospitaller 15th c. obol imitation (**3056**)

79. Papagiannakis plot, Grigoriou 5ou St. (1973)
Justin I: follis (**57**)

80. Papaioannou-Stavrias plot, Fleming St. (1979)
11th c. anonymous follis, type A2 (**896**)

81. Papapanagiotou plot, corner of Kanada and Athinagora Streets (1964-6/1991)
Heraclius: follis (**589**)

82. Papastamatis plot, corner of Pindou and Enoplon Dynameon Streets (1963-6)
Anastasius I: half follis (**8**)
Maurice: half follis (**298**)
Heraclius: follis (**472**)
Gavalas Successors [1294-1304?] (**1613**)
Hospitaller 15th c. obol (NB 3939)

83. Pappou plot, Th. Sofouli St. (1992)
Heraclius: half follis (**659**)

84. Petridis plot, corner of Iroon Polytechneiou and I. Kazoulli Streets (1966)
Phocas: quarter follis (**323**)
Heraclius: follis (**456**)

84a. Petridis plot, corner of P. Mela and Navarinou Streets (1980)
Leo Gavalas (**1525**)

85. Platis plot, P. Mela St. (1973)
6th c. follis (**329**)

86. Politou-Hatzistratis-Koutsomanolis plot, corner of Konstantinou Ydreou and Papamanoli Streets (1973)
Justin II: pentanummium (**177**)
Alexius I (**1157**)
Hospitaller 15th c. obols (**2976**, NB 1154)
Amboise denier (**3122**)

87. Rodini
Hospitaller 14th c. denier (**1736**)

88. Priest Roussos plot, Komninon side-street (1964)
Justinian I: follis (**94**)

89. Sambanis plot, P. Mela St. (1963)
Justin I: follis (**62**)
Heraclius: follis (**554**), *half follis* ([**842**])
Constans II: follis (**801**)
11th c. anonymous follis, type B (**922**)
Alexius I (**1166**)
Hospitaller 15th c. obol (NB 2169)

90. Sarikas-Moskis plot, A. Panagouli St. (1973)
Heraclius: follis (**449**)

91. Simixis plot, Cheimarras St. (1987 ff.)
Justinian I: follis (**101**)
Alexius I tetarteron imitation (**1196**)
Leo Gavalas (**1524**)
Unidentified trachy (**1485**)
Hospitaller 14th c. deniers (**1775, 1821, 1841**)
Pins denier (**1886**)
Hospitaller 14th c. obols (**2762, 2804, 2866**)
Overstruck denier c. 1400 (**2052**)

92. Skordos plot, Pindou St. (1967)
Justinian I: follis (**100**)
Maurice: follis (**279**)
Isaac II (**1250**)

93. Skoumbourdis plot, St. Kazouli St. (1981)
Heraclius: follis (**454**)

94. Soihan-Minettos plot, corner of Th. Sofouli and Cheimarras Streets (1962-4)
Phocas: half follis (**322**)
Constans II: follis (**816**)
Constans II follis imitation (**850**)
Romanus IV (**1099**)
Hospitaller 15th c. obol imitation (**2884**)

95. Sotirakis plot, P. Mela St. (1966)
Nicephorus III (**1128**)
Isaac II (**1267**)

96. Soulounias plot, Amerikis side-street (1981)
Heraclius: folles (**541, 569**)
Nicephorus III (**1119**)

97. Stavrias-Laos plot, extension of Agiou Nikolaou St. (1972)
Hospitaller 15th c. obols (NB 1086, 1087)
Famagusta (**3255**)

98. Synetairismou II development, S. Venizelou St. (1966-7)
Anastasius I: pentanummium (**15**)
Justin II: half follis (**234**)
Heraclius: folles (**390, 432, 459, 588, 642, 644**), *half follis* (**691**), *dodecanummium* (**665**)
Constans II: folles (**747, 815**)
11th c. anonymous follis, type C (**1021**)
Alexius I (**1165**)

99. Tourkalis plot, corner of Ethelonton Dodekanision and 25is Martiou Streets (1961)
Justinian I: follis (**80**)
Tiberius II: follis (**244**)
Maurice: follis (**286**), *half follis* (**287**)
6th c. dodecanummium (**372**)
Heraclius: follis (**421**), *dodecanummium* (**662**)
Constans II: follis (**784**), *half follis* (**841**)
7th c. dodecanummium imitation (**857**)
Juilly denier (**1891**)

100. Tsigaridis plot, 48 Athinagoras St. (1979)
Hospitaller 14th c. denier (**1863**)

101. Tzedakis plot, Cheimarars St. (1982)
Justinian I: quarter follis (**90**)
Justin II: pentanummia (**190, 191**)
Maurice: folles (**257, 263**)
Heraclius: folles (**494, 703**), *half folles* (**604, 713**)
Constans II: folles (**733, 772**)
Hospitaller 14th c. obols (**2743, 2803**)

102. Valakis-Volonakis plot, corner of Navarinou and Cheimarras Streets (1973-4)
Anastasius I: pentanummia (**18, [366]**)
Justin I: follis (**31**)
Pentanummia with christogram (**51, 52, 63, 64, 125, 135**)
6th c. pentanummia (**347, 359, 360, 365, 367**)
Justinian I: half folles (**85, 111**)
Justin II: follis (**205**), *half folles* (**168, 230**), *pentanummia* (**186, 187**)

Half follis, 2nd half of 6th c. (**371**)
Tiberius I: quarter follis (**251**)
Maurice: half follis (**291**), *quarter folles* (**267**)
Phocas: half follis (**304**)
Heraclius: folles (**385, 400, 404, 414, 422, 426, 438**), *half folles* (**97, 681, 690, 710, 711,** [**715**])
Constans II: follis (**835**)

103. Valsamoulis plot, Rodini (1962)
Hospitaller 14th c. denier (**1678**)

104. Venetokleion Highschool for Boys, Palaiologou St. (1970)
Maurice: pentanummium (**274**)

105. Viotechnon plot, corner of Kanada and Kolokotroni Streets (1966-8)
Maurice: half follis (**290**)

106. Water Authority (DEYAR) trench, P. Tsaldari St. (1998)
AV Manuel I (**1215**)

II. Medieval town of Rhodes

1. Argyrokastrou Square (2003 ff.)
Constans II: follis (**810**)

2. Aristofanous St.
Justin II: folles (**198, 213**)

3. Asprakis plot, Platonos St. (1976 ff.)
Justin II: pentanummium (**180**)
Heraclius: folles (**381, 465, 531**), *half follis* (**605**)
Constans II: follis (**751**)
11th c. anonymous follis, type B (**933**)
John III (**380**)
Hospitaller 14th c. denier (**1740**)

4. Auberge of the *tongue* of Spain, Ippoton St. (1998)
AV Florin (**3155**)

5. Bastion of St. George, sector of the *tongue* of Auvergne (1976/1998)
Hospitaller 15th c. obols (**2960**, NB 3383)
Amboise denier (**3113**)

6. Bastion of Carretto
Hospitaller 15th c. obols (**3026, 3027**)

7. 'Castellania' (Public Library), Ippokratous Sq.
Imitative ducat (**3266**)

8. Chrysochoou plot, 147 Menekleous St. (1988)
Heraclius: folles (**379, 591**)
11th c. anonymous follis, type B (**968**)
Romanus IV (**1110**)
Unidentified trachy (**1482**)
Leo Gavalas (**1550**)
Hospitaller 15th c. obol (NB 1221)
Famagusta (**3257**)

9. 2 Demosthenous St.
Hospitaller 14th c. denier (**1726**)

10. Gate of St. John, Fluvian bulwark and bastion of Aubusson (1992)
Constans II: follis ([**845**])
Hospitaller 15th c. obols (**2952, 2964, 2967, 2977**, NB 3979, 3981, 3984, 3985, 3986, 3989, 3990, 3991, 3993, 3994)
Majorca (**3224**)

11. Gate of St. Paul (2003)
11th c. anonymous follis, type B (**999**)
Alexius I tetarteron imitation (**1191**)
Amboise denier (**3116**)

12. Gavoyannis plot, 147D Menekleous St. (1977)
Pentanummium with christogram (**148**)
Justin II: pentanummium (**242**)
Maurice: quarter follis (**266**)
Heraclius: folles (**469, 473, 477, 497, 500, 533, 542, 544, 565, 586, 587, 590**), *half follis* (**608**), *quarter follis* (**620**)
Constans II: folles (**724, 735, 741, 776**), *half follis* (**829**)
Gavalas Successors [1294-1304?] (**1614**), *[1304-7?]* (**1631**)
Tornesello (**3301**)

13. Giouloglou Plot, corner of Apellou and Protogenous Streets (S. chapel of St. Mary of the Castle) (1992)
Romanus I (**881**)
Gavalas Successors [1278-94?] (NB 4057)

14. Haliloglou plot, Athinas Sq. (1992)
Justin I: follis (**39**)
Justin II: half follis (**235**)
Maurice: folles (**259, 278**)
Phocas: half follis (**305**), *pentanummium* ([**325**])
Heraclius: 6νούμμιο (**669**)
Constans II: folles (**752, 807**), *half folles* (**771, 828**)
11th c. anonymous follis, type B (**958**)
Nicephorus III (**1125**)
Latin imitative, large module, type A of Copnstantinople (**1315**)
Latin imitative, small module, type A (**1362, 1363**, [**1438**])
Latin imitative, small module, type G (**1427**)
Latin imitative, small module (**1496**)
[Local] imitative trachy (**1477**)
Leo Gavalas (**1521**)
Gavalas Successors [1258-61?] (**1566**), *[1273-8?]* (**1573**), *[1278-94?]* (**1586**), *[1294-1304?]* (**1606, 1617**), *[1304-7?]* (**1634**), (**1640**),
Hospitaller 14th c. denier (**1865**)
Hospitaller 14th c. obol (**2801**)
Hospitaller 15th c. obols (**2944, 2988**, NB 3719, 3723, 3732, 3734)
Hospitaller 15th c. obol imitations (NB 3721, 3730)
Aubusson denier (**3079**)

15. M. Hasapoglou plot, Platonos St. (1964-9)
Anastasius I: pentanummium (**12**)
Pentanummium with christogram (**145**)
Justin II: follis (**160**)
Heraclius: folles (**537, 705**)
Theophilus (**864**)
11th c. anonymous follis, type B (**942**)
Hospitaller 14th c. denier (**1872**)
Overstruck denier c. 1400 (**463**)

Hospitaller 15th c. obols (**2938**, NB1038, 1039, 1041, 1042)
Palestine (**3142**)

16. Hatzilazarou plot, corner of Pythagora and Sofokleous Streets (1987)
Heraclius: follis (**466**)

17. Holy Apostles (Imaret), corner of Ippodamou and Sokratous Streets (1987 ff.)
Phocas: quarter follis (**324**)
Heraclius: follis (**559**)
Constans II: follis (**727**)
Hospitaller 15th c. obols (NB 4080, 4081, 5237, 5359)
Hospitaller 15th c. obol imitations (NB 4079, [4082], 4439)

18. Holy Trinity (Dolapli), Dimosthenous St. (1979)
Anastasius I: pentanummium (**13**)
Follis of Justin I or Justinian I (**108**)
Justin II: half follis (**229**)
6th c. pentanummium (**363**)
Heraclius: follis (**446**)
Manuel I: half tetarteron (**1241**)
Latin imitative, small module, type F (**1408**)
Leo Gavalas (**1513, 1516**)
Gavalas Successors [1258-61?] (**1564**), *[1278-94?]* (**1590**)
Hospitaller 14th c. denier (**1796**)
Hospitaller 14th c. obol (**2756**)
Hospitaller 15th c. obols (**2939, 2966, 2987**, NB 578, 580, 582, 594, 595, [596], 597, 600, 1715)
Hospitaller 15th c. obol imitations (NB 576, 584, 602)
Aubusson deniers (**3071, 3086, 3101, 3106**)

19. Hospice of St. Catherine, corner of Thiseos St. and Peisidorou Sq. (1988 ff.)
Justin I: pentanummium (**42**)
Gavalas Successors [1294-1304?] (**1600**)
Hospitaller 15th c. obol imitation (NB 3809)
Aubusson denier (**3059**)
France (**3140**)

20. Installation of drain network in the medieval town (DEPOS)
Pentanummium with christogram (**158**)
Maurice: half folles (**294, 299**)
Constans II: follis (**768**)
Latin imitative, small module, type A (**1342**)
Gavalas Successors [1304-7?] (**1628**)
Hospitaller 15th c. obols (NB 4158, 4160, [4359], 4379, 4380, 5233)
Hospitaller 15th c. obol imitations (NB 4161, 4309, 4310)
Aubusson denier (**3098**)
Venice (**3158**), *Sicily* (**3172, 3201**)

21. 21 Ipparchou St.
Gavalas Successors ([**1646**])

22. Karavelatzis plot, between Perikleous and Dosiadou Streets (1992 ff.)
6th c. pentanummium (**343**)
Alexius I (**1150**)
Manuel I: Bi (**1227**)
Latin imitative, small module, type G (**1437**)
[Andronicus I of Trebizond] (**1305**)
Hospitaller 15th c. obols (NB 4827, 4828, 4829, 4830, 4831, 4832, [5358])
Venice (**3162**)

23. Karydakis plot, Demosthenous St. (2000)
Gavalas Successors [1250-4?] (**1562**)
Hospitaller 14th c. deniers (**1835, 1871**)
Hospitaller 14th c. obol (**2775**)
Pins denier (**1890**)
Hospitaller 15th c. obols (**2963, 3005**, NB 6077, 6079, 6080, 6081, 6082, 6083, 6084, 6085, 6086, 6087, 6090, 6091, 6094, 6097, 6099, 6100)
Hospitaller 15th c. obol imitations (NB 6074, 6089)
Sicily (**3214, 3216**), *tornesello* (**3278**)

24. Konstantinidis plot, Thoukydidou St. (1990)
Justin II: pentanummium (**178**)
Heraclius: follis (**441**), *half follis* (**611**)
Constans II: folles (**779, 805**), *half follis* (**832**)
Leo VI (**872**)
11th c. anonymous follis, type B (**980**)
Romanus IV (**1113**)
hd11th c. anonymous follis, type K (**1079**)
Alexius I (**1156, 1158, 1178**)
Manuel I: Bi (**1234**)
Latin imitative, large module, type A Of Thessalonica (**1322**)
Latin imitative, small module, type A (**1340, 1371, 1372**)
Latin imitative, small module, type F (**1410**, [**6035**])
Latin imitative, small module, type G (**1423, 1433**)
Latin imitative, small module (**1464**)
Leo Gavalas (**1531, 1532, 1533**)
Gavalas Successors [1278-94?] (**1588**), *[1294-1304?]* (**1602**), (**1639, 6027**)
Hospitaller 14th c. deniers (**1867, 1897**)
Hospitaller 15th c. obols (**3004**, NB 6019)
Aubusson denier (**3061**)
Armenia (**3151**), *Sicily* (**3183, 3219**), *Naples* (**3221**), *Cyprus* (**3249**), *tornesello* (**3293**), *unidentified* (**3313**)

25. Kozas plot, Dosiadou St. (1994-5)
Heraclius: AV (**378**)
Constans II: folles (**737, 738**)
Latin imitative, small module, type G (**1428**)
Latin imitative, small module (**1503**)

26. Kyriazis House, 1A Irodotou St. (1965)
Heraclius: follis (**399**)

27. 68 Lachitos St.
Hospitaller 15th c. obol (NB 3936)

28. Manettas plot, Athinas Sq. (1994 ff.)
Anastasius I: follis I (**3**)
6th c. quarter follis (**342**)
Latin imitative, small module, type F (**1409**)
Gavalas Successors [1273-8?] (**1576**) ([**1647**])
Hospitaller 14th c. obol (**2794**)
Hospitaller 15th c. obol (NB 4586)

29. Maravelias plot, Platonos St. (1977 ff.)
Anastasius I: follis I (**6**)
Pentanummium with christogram (**130**)
Justinian I: decaexanummium (**116**)
2nd half of 6th c.: quarter folles (**341**), *dodecanummia* (**373, 374**)
Phocas: dodecanummium (**320**)

Heraclius: folles (**383**, **418**, **462**, **540**, **550**, **560**, **574**, **1632**, **1743**), *dodecanummium* (**668**)
Constans II: folles (**729**, **737**, **738**, **761**, **769**, **806**, **813**, **824**), *half follis* (**822**)
Romanus I (**879**)
11th c. anonymous follis, type A1 (**888**)
11th c. anonymous folles, type B (**937**, **938**, **939**, **940**, **941**)
11th c. anonymous follis, type C (**1011**)
Romanus IV (**1108**, **1109**)
11th c. anonymous follis, type H (**1051**)
11th c. anonymous follis, type J (**1072**)
Alexius I (**1153**, **1163**)
Alexius I tetarteron imitation (**1192**)
John II (**1214**)
Manuel I: Bi (**1229**, **1231**, **1232**)
Isaac II (**1271**, **1272**)
Latin imitative, small module, type A (**1330**, **1344**, **1345**)
Latin imitative, small module, type G (**1428**, **1503**)
Latin imitative, small module (**1447**, **1495**)
Local imitative trachy (**1473**)
John Gavalas (**1544**)
Gavalas Successors [1261-73?] (**1571**), *[1278-94?]* (**1583**, **1584**, **1585**), *[1294-1304?]* (**1615**, **1623**), ([NB4200])
Hospitaller 14th c. deniers (**1702**, **1713**)
Hospitaller 14th c. obols (**1330**, **2753**, **2783**, **2830**)
Overstruck denier c. 1400 (**2055**)
Hospitaller 15th c. obols (NB 963, 975, 984, 997, 1012, 1013, 4198, 4569, 4577)
Hospitaller 15th c. obol imitations (NB 961, [1014,] 3996, 4568)
Sicily (**3191**), *Rome* (**3227**), *tornesello* (**3285**)

30. Marinos plot, 20 Lachitos St. (1988)
Hospitaller 15th c. obols (NB 793, 4605, 4606, 4608, 4609, 4610)
Hospitaller 15th c. obol imitation (NB 792)
Cyprus (**3247**), *tornesello* (**3300**), *denier tournois* (**3321**)

31. K. Mavros plot, Pythagora St. (1978)
Heraclius: follis (**513**), *half follis* (**714**)
Latin imitative, small module (**1457**)
Gavalas Successors [1261-73?] (**1572**), *[1273-8?]* (**1581**)
Hospitaller 14th c. denier (**1862**)
Naillac overstrike (**2302**)
Hospitaller 15th c. obols (**2975**, **3002**)
Tornesello (**3286**)

32. Medieval moat, sector of the *tongue* of Italy
Heraclius: follis (**627**)

33. Minatsis plot, Menekleous St. (1991 ff.)
Justin I: follis (**37**)
Pentanummium with christogram (**143**)
Justin II: pentanummium (**197**)
Heraclius: folles (**529**, **532**, **545**, **583**, **580**, **581**)
Constans II: folles (**796**, **802**, **814**, **820**)
Constans II follis imitation (**851**)
11th c. anonymous folles, type B (**945**, **946**, **947**, **948**, **949**, **950**, **951**, **952**, **953**, **954**, **988**)
11th c. anonymous folles, type C (**1032**, **1033**, **1034**)
11th c. anonymous follis, type D ([**1037**])
11th c. anonymous folles (**1136**, **1137**)
Romanus IV (**1106**)
Trebizond (**1206**)
John II (**1212**)

Manuel I: Bi (**1236**)
Isaac II (**1270**)
Alexius III (**1289**)
Faithful copy, large module, type C (**1310**)
Latin imitative, large module, type C of Thessalonica (**1326**)
Latin imitative, small module, type A (**1373, 1374**)
Latin imitative, small module (**1448,** [**1459, 1497**], **1499**)
John III (**1301**)
Gavalas Successors [1254-1258] (**1559**), *[1294-1304?]* (**1627**), (**1641**)
Hospitaller 14th c. deniers (**1790, 1812, 1819**)
Hospitaller 14th c. obol (**2787**)
Hospitaller 15th c. obols (**2927, 2940,** NB 3403, 3405, 3407, 3408, 3409, 3710, 3714, 4600, 4680)
Hospitaller 15th c. obol imitations (NB 3410, 3414, 3713)
Aubusson denier (**3110**)

34. Mole of the Windmills (1999 ff.)
11th c. anonymous follis, type B (**983**)
Isaac II (**1281**)
Trachy (**1490**)
John Gavalas (**1543**)
Gavalas Successors [1250-4?] (**1546**), *[1294-1304?]* (**1611**), (**1651**)
Hospitaller 14th c. deniers (**1679, 1770, 1771, 1781, 1724, 1793, 1808**)
Juilly deniers ([**1773, 1900**])
Hospitaller 14th c. obol (**2809**)
Hospitaller 15th c. obol (**2970,** NB 5186)
Hospitaller 15th c. obol imitations (NB [5183], 5327)
Aubusson deniers (**3063, 3095**)
Armenia (**3149** AR), *Venice* (**3159, 3160**), *Sicily* (**3206**), *imitative tornesello* (**3304**)

35. Nikolis plot, Ergeiou St. (2001)
Pentanummia of Anastasius or Justin I (**131, 144, 157**)
Heraclius: folles (**511, 519**)
Constans II: follis (**837**)
11th c. anonymous follis, type C (**1018**)
11th c. anonymous follis, type I (**1058**)
Alexius I tetartera imitations (**1199, 1204**)
Manuel I: tetarteron (**1238**)
Andronicus I (**1245**)
Alexius III (**1291**)
Gavalas Successors [1250-4?] (**1551**), *[1304-7?]* (**1630**)
Hospitaller 14th c. deniers (**1681, 1827**)
Overstruck denier c. 1400 (**2054**)
Naillac overstrike (**2315**)
Hospitaller 15th c. obols (**3028,** NB 4811, 6047, 6048, 6056, 6063, 6064, 6066, [6067], 6068)
Hospitaller 15th c. obol imitations (NB 6070, 6071)
Aubusson denier (**3069**)
Cyprus (**3251** AR), *Chios* (**3265**), *tornesello* (**3296**)

36. Nikolis plot, Omirou St. (1993)
Heraclius: follis (**634**)
Latin imitative, small module, type G ([**1449**])
Sicily (**3208**)

37. 26-28 Omirou St. (1989)
Latin imitative, small module, [type G] (**1449**)

38. Oplotheke Milly (Tholaros), Symis Sq.
Alexius I (**1145**)

Gavalas Successors [1278-94?] (**1587**)

39. 'Over the ancient ship-sheds.'
Heraclius: follis (**520**), *half follis* (**614**)
Leo Gavalas (**1538**)

40. Palace of the Grand Master
Heraclius: follis (**683**)
Amboise denier (**3112**)

41. Panaitiou St., excavation of the Byzantine city wall and the conventual church of St. John of the Collachio (1990 ff.)
Justinian I: follis (**119**)
Maurice: half follis (**292**)
Heraclius: folles (**417, 510, 530, 536, 584**)
Constans II: folles (**739, 770, 778**)
Constans II follis imitation (**855**)
11th c. anonymous follis, type A2 (**913**)
11th c. anonymous follis, type B (**992**)
Alexius III (**1285**)
Trachea (**1483**, NB 4859)
Theodore I (**1298**)
Leo Gavalas (**1536**)
Gavalas Successors [1261-1273?] (**1569**), *[1278-1294?]* (**1591, 1593, 1594**), *[1294-1304?]* (**1610, 1626**), *[1304-7?]* (**1637**), (**1569, 1654**)
Hospitaller 14th c. deniers (**1695, 1696, 1697, 1727, 1728, 1767, 1768, 1769, 1780, 1782, 1783, 1797, 1806, 1810, 1838, 1866, 1822, 1823, 1825, 1852, 1887**)
Hospitaller 14th c. obols (**2760, 2766, 2767, 2780, 2790, 2796, 2808, 2818, 2835, 2836, 2844, 2852, 2863, 2867, 2869, 2870, 2871, 2872, 2878, 2879, 2882**)
Overstruck deniers c. 1400 (**2058, 2062, 2070**)
Naillac overstrike (**2308**)
Hospitaller 15th c. obols (**2923, 2929, 2932, 2946, 2962, 2980, 2985, 2992, 2993, 2994, 2995, 2996, 2997, 2998, 2999, 3000, 3003, 3008, 3009, 3010, 3011, 3017, 3018, 3019, 3020, 3021, 3022, 3023, 3032, 3033, 3034, 3035, 3037,** NB 4150, 4152, 4153, 4154, 4156, 5280, 5282, 5290, [5293], 5294, 5297, 5300, 5302, 5303, [5305], [5309], 5311, 5602, 5614, 5645, 5651, 5653, 5655, 5657, 5658, 5659, 5660, 5661, 5662, 5663, 5664, 5665, 5667, 5668, 5669, 5670, 5673, 5674, 5679, 5682, 5683, 5684, 5685, 5687, 5688, 5690, 5692, 5693, 5694, 5696, 5697, 5699, 5701, 5702, 5703, 5704, 5705, 5706, 5707, 5708, 5709, 5711, 5722, 5723, 5731, 5735, 5736, 5738, 5739, 5740, 5741, 5742, 5743, 5746, 5747, 5748, 5749, 5750, 5751, 5752, 5754, 5755, 5756, 5757, 5758, 5759, 5760, 5762, 5764, 5765, 5766, 5767, 5769, 5771, 5772, 5773, 5774, 5775, 5776, 5777, 5778, [5779], 5782, 5784, 5786, 5788, 5789, 5790)
Hospitaller 15th c. obol imitations (**3045, 3046, 3050, 3051, 3053**, NB 5287, 5288, 5295, 5299, 5310, 5603, 5616, 5618, 5620, 5621, 5622, 5623, 5625, 5626, 5627, 5628, 5629, 5630, 5631, 5632, 5635, 5636, 5637, 5638, 5639, 5640, 5641, 5642, 5643, 5644, [5646], 5647, [5648], 5649, [5650], 5652, [5654], 5672, 5726, 5727, 5728, [5729]
Aubusson deniers (**3058, 3065, 3077, 3104**)
Palestine (**3144**), *Rome* (**3228**), *Cyprus* (**3253**), *Famagusta* (**3258**), *Mytilene* (**3263**), *Chios* (**3264**), *Ancona* (**3235**), *Venice* (**3165, 3271, 3273, 3274, 3275, 3276, 3298, 3305**), *Naples* (**3223**), *Sicily* (**3167, 3168, 3174, 3175, 3196, 3210, 3212**), *unidentified* (**3316, 3319,** NB 5277)

42. Pekmetzis plot, Agisandrou St. (1989 ff.)
Pentanummia with christogram (**49, 58, 129, 137, 138, 151, 153**)
Justinian I: follis (**74**)
Maurice: follis (**261**), *half follis* (**289**)
Heraclius: folles (**391, 437, 440, 443, 447, 448, 461, 474, 479, 498, 499, 527, 575, 592, 622, 799**), *half folles* (**600, 613, 615, 619, 709**), *dodecanummium* (**667**), *quarter folles* (**648, 688**), *hexanummia* (**670, 671**)
Constans II: folles (**728, 732, 740, 744, 749, 753, 754, 809, 812**), *half follis* (**827**), *quarter follis* (**831**)
Constants II follis imitations (**852, 853**)
7th c. quarter follis (**846**)
11th c. anonymous follis, type A2 (**900**)

11th c. anonymous folles, type B (**617, 934, 935, 959, 960, 961, 962, 963, 964, 965, 966, 967, 985, 989, 990, 991, 994, 995, [998], 1001**)
11th c. anonymous folles, type C (**1004, 1007, 1016, [1017], 1025, 1027, 1028, 1031**)
Romanus IV (**1097, 1102, 1103, 1111, 1112**)
11th c. anonymous follis, type H (**1047**)
11th c. anonymous follis, type I (**1053**)
Nicephorus III (**1120, 1129**)
11th c. anonymous folles, type J (**1067, 1068**)
11th c. anonymous folles, type K (**1080, 1082, 1083, 1085, 1087**)
Trebizond (**1205**)
Alexius I (**1152, 1154, 1162, [1164], 1169, 1175, 1179, 1184**)
Alexius I tetartera imitations (**1193, 1200**)
John II (**1210**)
Manuel I: tetartera (**1240, 1243**), *Bi* (**1220, [1221], 1225, 1228, 1229, 1230, 1235**)
Andronicus I (**[1246]**)
Isaac II (**1255, 1257, 1259, 1261, 1264, 1265, [1280]**)
Faithful copy, type B (**1306**)
Latin imitative, large module, type C of Constantinople (**1319**)
Latin imitative, large module, type F of Constantinople (**1332**)
Latin imitative, small module, type A (**1339, 1364**)
Latin imitative, small module, type B (**1323, 1375, 1377**)
Latin imitative, small module, type C (**1388**)
Latin imitative, small module, type D (**1393**)
Latin imitative, small module, type E (**1402, 1404**)
Latin imitative, small module, type G (**1418, 1419, 1421**)
Latin imitative, small module (**1441, 1461, 1501**)
[Local] imitative trachy (**1469**)
Leo Gavalas (**1529, 3756**)
John Gavalas (**1300**)
Gavalas Successors [1273-8?] (**1574**), *[1278-94?]* (**1592, 1596**), *[1294-1304?]* (**1605**)
Hospitaller 14th c. deniers (**1720, [1730], 1837**)
Juilly denier (**1892**)
Hospitaller 14th c. obols (**2745, 2758, 2759, 2789, 2864**)
Hospitaller 14th c. obol imitation (**2885**)
Hospitaller 15th c. obols (NB 3790)
Aubusson deniers (**3070, 3096**)
Isaac Comnenus of Cyprus: tetarteron (**1248**), *trachy* (**1247**)
Lucca (**3135**), *denier tournois* (**3139**)

43. 25K Perikleous St.
Hospitaller 15th c. obol imitation (NB 4514)

44. Public Lavatories, Orfeos St. (1977)
Hospitaller 15th c. obol (NB 1065)
Tornesello (**3302**)

45. Pythagora St. (I. Kondis excavation) (1951)
Justinian I: follis (**81**)
11th c. anonymous follis, type B (**979**)

46. Sabihas-Kaimaktsis plot (Collachio tower), Theofiliskou St. (1988/1991)
Heraclius: follis (**507**)

47. St. Artemius (Sykyndy mesjid), Ergeiou St. (1987 ff.)
Justin II: pentanummium (**176**)
11th c. anonymous follis, type B (**986, 987**)
11th c. anonymous follis, type C (**1015**)
Romanus IV (**1107**)

Alexius I (**1147, 1171**)
John II (**1213**)
Isaac II (**1249**)
Latin imitative, small module, type G ([**1450**])
Hospitaller 14th c. deniers (**1778, 1779, 1800, 1801, 1846, 1847, 1848, 1850, 1851, 1868,** [**1869**], **1874, 1877, 4749**)
Hospitaller 14th c. denier imitation (**1849**)
AR Heredia (**1662**)
Hospitaller 15th c. obols (**2920, 2981,** NB 4685, 4687, 4688, 4691, 4693, 4697, 4699, 4700, 4701, 4702, 4703, 4705, 4706, 4710, 4711, 4712, 4713, 4718, 4720, 4724, 4725, 4726, 4727, 4728, 4730, 4731, 4732, 4733, 4734, 4735, 4736, 4737, 4738, 4740, 4743, 4744, 4745, 4748, 4751, 4754, 4756, 4759, 4760, 4762, 4765, 4766, 4767, 4769, 4773, 4775, 4778, 4779, 4780, 4781, 4782, 4783, 4793, 4796, 4797, 4800, 4801)
Hospitaller 15th c. obol imitations (NB 4698, 4704, 4708, 4709, 4719, 4722, 4741, 4753, 4755, 4758, 4763, 4764, 4771, 4776, 4784, 4785, 4794, 4795, 4799, 4803)
Amboise deniers (**3123, 3127**)
Minorca (**3225**), *Sicily* (**3209**) *Cyprus* (**3248**), *Mytilene* (**3261, 3262**), *torneselli* (**3294, 3295**), *unidentified* (**3314, 3315**)

48. St. Bernardine (St. Nicholas, Abdul Djelil or Cukur mesjud), Omirou St. (1987)
Constans II: follis (**725**)
Hospitaller 14th c. deniers (**1803, 1901**)
Hospitaller 14th c. obol (**2798**)
Hospitaller 14th c. obol imitation ([NB 3999])
Overstruck denier c. 1400 (NB 3998)
Hospitaller 15th c. obols (NB 4000, 4005, 4006, 4008, 4009, 4010, 4012, 4013, 4812, 4814, 4815, 4816, 4818, 4821)
Hospitaller 15th c. obol imitations (NB 4007, 4011)
Aubusson deniers (**3080, 3081, 3082**)
Sicily (**3184**), *unidentified* (**3311**)

49. St. Catherine (Ilk Mihrab), Perikleous St. (1992)
Pentanummium with christogram (**154**)
6th c. dodecanummium (**370**)
Hospitaller 15th c. obol (NB 4029)
Hospitaller 15th c. obol imitation (NB 4682)
Amboise denier (**3125**)

50. St. George (Hourmali), Apollonion St. (1982 ff.)
Anastasius I: pentanummium (**361**)
Justinian I: pentanummium (**113**)
6th-7th c. half follis (**117**)
Heraclius: folles (**423, 503, 514, 661, 697**)
Constans II: folles (**746, 785**), *half follis* (**825**)
11th c. anonymous follis, type B (**932**)
11th c. anonymous follis, type C (**1006**)
Manuel I: Bi (**1233**)
Latin imitative, small module, type G (**1436**)
Leo Gavalas (**1511, 1512**)
John Gavalas (**1541**)
Gavalas Successors [1261-1273] (**1568**), (**1642**)
Hospitaller 14th c. obols (**2741, 2761, 2810, 2819, 2827**)
Hospitaller 14th c. deniers (**1817, 1831, 1895**)
Hospitaller 15th c. obols (**2986, 3030,** NB 507, 510, 512, 517, 518, 521, 1059, 4516)
Aubusson denier (**3085**)

51. St. John (Kizil Kapou mesjid), Archiepiskopou Efthymiou St.
11th c. anonymous follis, type D (**1038**)
Amboise denier (**3124**)

52. St. Mark (Satri Celebi mesjid), Menandrou St. (1987)
Justin II: pentanummium (**210**)

Maurice: quarter follis (**272**)
Constans II: follis (**783**)
Gavalas Successors [1254-8] (**1561**), *[1278-94]* (**1582**), *[1294-1304]* (**1603**), *[1307-9]* (**1636, 1638**), *?* (**1575, 1648, 1649**)
Hospitaller 14th c. deniers (**1776, 1777, 1791, 1844, 1845**)
Hospitaller 14th c. obols (**2764, 2765, 2795, 2805, 2831, 2832, 2833, 2853**)
AR Heredia (**1661**)
Overstruck denier c. 1400 (**2061**)
Hospitaller 15th c. obols (NB 4613, 4616, 4617, 4619, 4620, 4621, 4622, 4627, 4629, 4630, [4631], 4633, 4636, 4640, 4644, 4647, 4650, 4651, 4653, 4654, 4656, 4665)
Hospitaller 15th c. obol imitations (**3044**, NB 4637)
Aubusson denier (**3062**)
Amboise denier (**3132**)
England (**3141**), *pope Sixtus IV* (**3230**), *Cyprus* (**3242**)

53. St. Mary of the Borgo, corner of Aristotelous and Alhadeff Streets (1994-6)
Constans II: follis (**789**)
Hospitaller 14th c. deniers (**1725, 1772, 1798, 1799, 1820, 1839, 1840, 1875, 1898, 1899**)
Pins deniers (**1884, 1885**)
Hospitaller 14th c. obols (**2792, 2793, 2826, 2880, 2824, 2825**)
Overstruck denier c. 1400 (**2059**)
Hospitaller 15th c. obols (**2823, 2862, 2926, 2953, 2956**, NB 4299, [4303], 4304, [4311], 4314, 4316, 4322, 4323, 4329, 4331, [4332], 4335, 4336, 4340, 4343, 4346, 4350, 4351, [4353, 4354, 4356], 4357, 4361, 4364, 4366, 4367, 4376, 4377, 4383, 4387, [4389], 4392, 4393, [4395,] 4396, 4397, 4400, 4822, 4823, 4824, 4825, 5279)
Hospitaller 15th c. obol imitations (NB 4298, 4300, 4308, [4319], 4321, 4325, 4355, 4365, 4368, 4369, 4370, 4373, 4374, 4378, 4385, 4388, 4394)
Aubusson deniers (**3073, 3088, 3089, 3090, 3094**)
Amboise deniers (**3130, 3131**)
Sicily (**3202, 3203, 3204, 3205**), *Ancona* (**3234**), *torneselli* (**3290, 3291, 3292**)

54. St. Mary of the Castle, Megalou Alexandrou Sq. (1970)
Justin II: pentanummia (**240, 241**)
Maurice: pentanummium (**273**)
Heraclius: folles (**562, 572, 650, 692, 698**)
Constans II: follis (**734**)
Constans II follis imitations (**849, 856**)
Theophilus (**862, 863, 865**)
Basil I (**869**)
Constantine VII (**874**)
Romanus I (**878**)
11th c. anonymous follis, type A1 (**886**)
11th c. anonymous folles, type A2 (**895, 897, 909, 910, 911**)
11th c. anonymous folles, type B (**919, 926, 927, 928, 929, 930, 931**)
11th c. anonymous folles, type C (**1010, 1012, 1024**)
11th c. anonymous follis, type D (**1035**)
11th c. anonymous follis, type F (**1043**)
11th c. anonymous folles, type H (**1046, 1048, 1052**)
11th c. anonymous folles, type I (**1056, 1059, 1060, 1063, 1065**)
Nicephorus III (**1122, 1123, 1126, 1131**)
11th c. anonymous folles, type J (**1069, 1070, 1071**)
11th c. anonymous folles, type K (**1077, 1078, 1086, 1088, 1089, 1090**)
Trebizond (**1207, 1208, 1209**)
Alexius I (**1140, 1141, 1142, 1143, 1144, 1160, 1167, 1168, 1172, 1174, 1181, 1182, 1185, 1186, 1187**)
Alexius I tetarteron imitation (**1195**)
John II (**1211, 1307**)
Manuel I: tetarteron (**1237**)
Isaac II (**1277**)
Alexius III (**1284, 1288**)

Faithful copy, type C (**1308**)
Latin imitative, small module, type A (**1432, 1440**)
Latin imitative, small module (**1443, 1446, 1465**)
Local imitative trachea (**1472, 1475**)
Trachea (NB 410, 422)
Hospitaller 14th c. deniers (**1737, 1789**)
Hospitaller 15th c. obols (**2935, 2955, 2968, 2983,** NB 403, 404, 405, 407, 428)
Hospitaller 15th c. obol imitation (NB 430)
Ill. Byzantine (**1130, 1133, 1134, 1135, 1488,** NB 391, 392, 393, 398, 419, 433, 466, 476)
Normandy (**3138**), [*Crusader*] (**3143**), *Achaia* (**3307**), *Sicily* (**3190**), *tornesello* (**3283**)

55. 'St. Mary of Victory', Peisirodou Sq. (1987 ff.)
Heraclius: follis (**640**)
Gavalas Successors (**1653,** [NB 5247])
Hospitaller 14th c. denier (**1824**)
Overstruck denier c. 1400 (**2057**)
Hospitaller 15th c. obols (**2959, 2965, 2971,** NB 559, 560, 562, [5240], 5243)
Hospitaller 15th c. obol imitations (NB 4016, 5244)
Venice (**3166, 3297**), *Sicily* (**3189, 3215**)

56. St. Michael (Demirli), Athinas Sq. (1987 ff.)
Pentanummium with christogram (**136**)
Follis [498-537] (**331**)
Justin II: half follis (**224**), *pentanummia* (**184, 216**)
Heraclius: folles (**425, 528**)
Constans II: folles (**791, 821**)
Nicephorus II (**884**)
11th c. anonymous folles, type B (**943, 996, 997, 1000**)
11th c. anonymous follis, type F (**1042**)
11th c. anonymous follis, type G (**1045**)
Michael VII (**1117**)
Nicephorus III: El (**1118**)
11th c. anonymous follis, type J (**1073**)
11th c. anonymous follis, type K (**1074**)
Alexius I (**1173, 1176**)
Alexius I tetarteron imitation (**1201**)
Manuel I: El (**1217**), *Bi* (**1222**)
Alexius III (**1283**)
Latin imitative, small module, type A (**1347, 1348, 1369**)
Latin imitative, small module, type B (**1379**)
Latin imitative, small module, type C (**1392**)
Latin imitative, small module, type D (**1400**)
Latin imitative, small module, type E (**1403, 1405**)
Latin imitative, small module, type G (**1424, 1425, 1435**)
Latin imitative, small module (**1442, 1458, [1494]**)
Trachea (**1341, 1343, 1486, 1505, 1506**)
Leo Gavalas (**1537**)
Gavalas Successors [1250-4] (**1547, 1548, 1552, 1553, 1554**), *[1254-8]* (**1557**), *[1261-73]* (**1570**) *[1273-8]* (**1577, 1578, 1579**), *[1294-1304]* (**1604, 1612**), *[1304-7]* (**1629, 1633**), ? (**1643, 1644, 1652, 1655**)
Villaret deniers (**1676, 1677**)
Hospitaller 14th c. deniers (**1680, 1682, 1683, 1684, 1694, 1698, 1699, 1700, 1729, 1731, 1784, 1785, 1786, 1788, 1794, 1804, 1811, 1813, 1814, 1818, 1826, 1828, 1829, 1830, 1832, 1834, 1842, 1843, 1853, 1854, 1855, 1856, 1857, 1870, [1873], [1876], 1883**)
Pins deniers (**[1883], 1888, 1889**)
Juilly deniers (**[1896], 1902**)
Hospitaller 14th c. obols (**2744, 2746, 2747, 2754, 2768, 2769, 2771, 2772, 2773, 2774, 2778, 2779, 2781, 2782, 2797, 2799, 2812, 2820, 2837, 2838, 2839, 2840, 2841, [2842], 2843, 2845, 2851, 2855, 2873, 2770, 2846, 2847, 2848, 2860, 2875, 2877, 2800, 2806, 2813, 2814, 2849, 2850, 2854, 2857, 2865, 2881,** NB 1182, 5443, 5444, 5445)

Hospitaller 14th c. obol imitations (**1878**)
Overstruck deniers c. 1400 (**2050, 2053, 2056, [2063], 2064, 2065, 2066, 2067, 2068, 2069, 2071, 2072, 2073**)
Naillac obol (**2082**)
Naillac overstrikes (**2305, 2306, 2307, 2309, 2310, 2311, 2312, 2313, 2314**)
Hospitaller 15th c. obols (**2921, 2922, 2925, 2928, 2930, 2933, 2943, 2945, 2947, 2948, 2949, 2957, 2958, 2978, 2979, 2982, 2989, 2990, 2991, 3002, 3007, 3014, 3015, 3016, 3036**, NB 904, 905, 1173, 1174, 1186, 1188, 1189, 1195, 1201, 1202, 1203, 1205, 1206, 1208, 1218, 1219, 5189, 5191, 5194, 5203, 5360, 5370, 5376, 5380, 5381, 5386, 5387, 5388, 5390, 5394, 5395, 5396, 5397, 5398, 5399, 5412, 5413, 5414, 5415, 5416, 5417, 5418, 5419, 5422, 5425, 5428, 5429, 5433, 5434, 5435, 5436, 5437, 5446, 5452, 5455, 5456, 5458, 5461, 5462, 5463, 5464, 5465, 5466, 5468, 5469, 5470, 5473, 5476, 5477, 5484, 5485, 5486, 5487, 5488, 5489, 5490, 5491, 5492, 5493, 5497, 5498, 5506, 5508, 5509, 5510, 5519, 5520, 5522, 5524, 5525, 5526, 5527, 5528, 5529, 5532, 5535, 5538, 5542, 5543, 5544, 5545, 5546, 5547, 5548, 5552, 5558, 5559, 5560, 5563, 5565, 5567, 5568, 5569, 5570, 5571, 5578, 5579, 5580, 5582, 5583, 5584, 5585, 5593, 5594, 5598, 5600, 5863, 5865, 5866, 5870, 5875, 5877, 5878, 5879, [5883], 5889, 5892, 5901, 5902, 5903, 5904, 5905, 5925, 5931, 5932, 5933, 5934, 5935, 5937, 5966, 5970, 5971, 5972, 5974, 5975, 5976, 5978, 5979, 5981, 5986, 5988, 5999)
Hospitaller 15th c. obol imitations (**3040, 3041, 3042, 3043, 3047, 3049, 3052, 3055**, NB 1182, 1185, 1204, 5370, 5375, 5385, 5389, 5421, 5431, 5432, 5460, 5474, 5479, 5480, 5500, 5505, 5531, 5533, 5537, 5540, 5557, 5561, 5562, 5564, 5573, 5586, 5587, 5599, 5848, 5862, 5872, 5874, 5880, 5881, 5882, 5885, [5893], 5896, 5899, 5906, 5907, 5911, 5912, 5913, 5914, 5915, 5916, 5922, [5980], 5985, 5996)
Aubusson deniers (**3064, 3066, 3068, 3075, 3083, 3091, 3092, 3093, 3103**,)
Amboise deniers (**3114, 3126, 3129**)
Chartres (**3137**), *Genoa* (**3153**), *Venice* (**3156** AV, **3163**), *Sicily* (**3173, 3177, 3178, 3179, 3182, 3211, 3213, 3217, 3218, 3277, 3280**), *Naples* (**3222**), *Cyprus* (**3179, 3239, 3240**), *Famagusta* (**3259**), *torneselli* (**3268, 3269, 3270, 3282, 3287, 3299**), *Lepanto* (**3306**), *unidentified* (**3317, 3318**)

57. St. Spyridon (Kavakli mesjid), Athinas Sq. (1984 ff.)
Justin I: half follis (**59**)
Pentanummium with christogram (**142**)
Justinian I: half follis (**98**)
Heraclius: follis (**654**)
Romanus IV (**1115**)
Alexius I tetarteron imitation (**1203**)
Latin imitative, small module, type C (**1390, 1391**)
Latin imitative, small module, type E (**1406**)
Latin imitative, small module, type F (**1411**)
Latin imitative, small module, type G (**1454, 1455**)
Leo Gavalas (**1535**)
Hospitaller 14th c. deniers (**1750, 1774, 1787**)
Hospitaller 14th c. obols (**[2874], 2786, 2802, 2828**)
Overstruck denier c. 1400 (**2060**)
Hospitaller 15th c. obols (**3001, 3012, 3024, 3025**, NB [1137], 1138, 1140, 4465, 4466, 4468, 4471, 4473, 4474, 4475, 4479, 4485, 4488, 4489, 4490, 4495, 4496, 5831, 5832, 5834, 5835, [5837])
Hospitaller 15th c. obol imitations (NB 1139, 4467, 4469, 4470, [4477], [4478], 4486, [4492,] 4494, 5817, 5826, 5827, [5828])
Aubusson denier (**3074, 3109**)
Amboise denier (**3121**)
Venice (**3161**), *Sicily* (**3176, 3207**), *imitative ducat* (**3267** AV)

58. SS Constantine & Helena (Kadi mesjid), Menekleous St. (1991 ff.)
6th c. quarter follis (**339**)
Phocas: follis (**315**), *quarter folles* (**314, 318**)
Heraclius: follis (**551**), *half folles* (**602, 618, 621, 798**)
Constans II: folles (**811, 818**), *dodecanummium* (**834**)
11th c. anonymous follis, type B (**957**)
11th c. anonymous folles, type C (**1022, 1026**)
11th c. anonymous follis, type H (**1050**)
Nicephorus III (**1121**)
Alexius I (**1149, 1170**)
Manuel I: half tetarteron (**1242**)

Isaac II (**1269, 1273, 1274, 1275, 1276, 1279**)
Alexius III (**1295, 1290, 1294, 1292, 1297, 1296**)
Latin imitative, large module, type C of Constantinople (**1317, 1318**)
Latin imitative, large module, type D/E of Constantinople (**1320**)
Latin imitative, large module, type B of Thessalonica (**1324, 1325**)
Latin imitative, large module, type C of Thessalonica (**1327, 1328**)
Faithful copies, type C (**1311, 1312, 1313**)
[Andronicus I of Trebizond] (**1304**)
Latin imitative, small module, type A (**1331, 1333, 1334, 1335, 1336, 1337, 1338, 1349, 1350, 1351, 1352, 1353, 1354, 1355, 1356, 1357, 1358, 1359, 1360, 1361**)
Latin imitative, small module, type B (**1376, 1378, 1381, 1382, 1383, 1384, 1385, 1386, 1387**)
Latin imitative, small module, type D (**1395, 1396, 1397, 1398, 1399**)
Latin imitative, small module, type E (**1401, 1407**)
Latin imitative, small module, type G (**1412, 1413, 1414, 1415, 1416, 1417, 1426, 1429, 1431, 1434**, [**1451**], [**1452**], [**1453**], **3661**)
Latin imitative, small module (**1456, 1460, 1462, 1463, 1493**, [**1498**], [**1500, 1502, 1504**])
Leo Gavalas (**1520, 1523, 1527, 1528**)
Local imitative trachea (**1466, 1467, 1468, 1471, 1476**)
Unidentified trachea (**1479, 1480, 1481, 1492**)
Ill. trachea (**1507, 1508, 1509, 1510**, NB 3607)
Gavalas Successors [1254-8] (**1560**)
Hospitaller 14th c. deniers (**1685, 1686, 1687, 1688, 1689, 1690, 1691, 1692, 1693, 1701, 1703, 1704, 1705, 1706, 1707, 1708, 1709, 1712, 1714, 1716, 1717, 1718, 1719, 1721, 1722, 1723, 1747, 1748, 1749, 1751, 1752, 1753, 1754, 1755, 1756, 1757, 1758, 1759, 1760, 1761, 1762, 1763, 1792, 1807, 1836**)
Hospitaller 14th c. obols (**2757, 2821, 2822, 2785, 2788**, [NB 3570])
Overstruck deniers c. 1400 (**2051**)
Hospitaller 15th c. obols (**2919, 2934, 2941, 2961, 3031**, NB 3445, 3457, 3458, 3459, 3460, 3461, 3463, 3467, 3478, 3506, 3507, 3512, 3515, 3516, 3517, 3530, 3531, 3533, 3534, 3536, 3537, 3538, 3539, 3543, 3545, 3546, 3548, 3550, 3553, 3556, 3560, 3565, 3566, 3567, 3574, 3576, 3577, 3578, 3585, 3587, 3588, 3589, 3594, 3595, 3627, 3633, 3634)
AR Lastic (**1665**)
Hospitaller 15th c. obol imitations (**2942**, NB 3446, 3509, 3511, 3513, 3514, 3522, 3527, 3528, 3529, 3532, 3535, 3544, 3549, 3558, 3563, 3564, 3568, 3575, 3582, 3583, 3584, 3590, 3632)
Ill. deniers (NB 3456, 3462, 3510, 3591)
Aubusson deniers (**3060, 3078, 3087, 3102, 3105, 3107**)
Amboise deniers (**3115, 3118, 3119, 3120, 3128**)
Armenia (**3150, 3152**), *Sicily* (**3194, 3195**), *Cyprus* (**3245**), *Mytilene* (**3260**), *tornesello* (**3279**)

59. SS Theodore (Hudai mesjid), Omirou St. (1998)
6th-7th c. follis (**839**)
Juilly denier (**1894**)
Hospitaller 14th c. deniers (**1764, 1765, 1766**)
Hospitaller 14th c. obol (**2817**)
Hospitaller 15th c. obol (NB 4130)
Hospitaller 15th c. obol imitation (**3048**)

60. Sofokleous Sq. (1976)
Pentanummium, 1st half of 6th c. (**355**)
Constans II: follis (**767**)
Hospitaller 14th c. denier (**1882**)
Sicily (**3192**)

61. 149-151 Sokratous side-street (trial trench) (1992)
11th c. anonymous follis (**1139**)

62. Theofiliskou St. (1984 ff.)
Local imitative trachy (**1470**)
Gavalas Successors [1258-61?] (**1565**), *[1304-7?]* (**1635**)
Hospitaller 15th c. obols (NB4043, 4044)

Hospitaller 15th c. obol imitations (NB 4045, 4046, 4047)
Sicily (**3181**), *imitative tornesello* (**3303**)

63. Tsimettas plot, 35 Aristotelous St. (1972)
Justin II: pentanummium (**4039**)
Hospitaller 14th c. denier (**1893**)
Hospitaller 14th c. obol (**2752**)
Naillac overstrike (**2303**)
Hospitaller 15th c. obols (NB 669, 670, 3968, 3973, 3975, 4227, 4231, 4236, 4237)
Hospitaller 15th c. obol imitations (NB 2159, 3969, 3970, [3971, 3972,] 3977, 4223, 4228, 4229, 4230, 4232, 4233, 4234, 4235)
Aubusson denier (**3108**)
Amboise denier (**3133**)
Sicily (**3169, 3199, 3200**), *tornesello* (**3288**), *unidentified* (**3312**)

64. Unidentified church of Kisthiniou St. (2000 ff.)
Pentanummium with christogram (6006)
Romanus IV (**1114**)
Alexius I ([**1487**])
Hospitaller 14th c. denier (**1805**)
Hospitaller 14th c. obols (**2815, 2834**)
Hospitaller 15th c. obols (**2951, 3029**, NB [4806], 4807, 6007, 6015, 6016, 6018)
Hospitaller 15th c. obol imitation (NB 6009)
Aubusson denier (**3076**)

65. Unidentified church of Theseos St. (1998)
Justin II: follis (**218**)
Half follis, 2nd half of 6th c. (**337**)
Maurice: half follis (**297**)
Heraclius: folles (**483, 489, 512, 552, 676, 707**)
11th c. anonymous follis, type B (**970**)
Latin imitative, small module, type A (**1368**, [**1439**])
Latin imitative, small module, type F (**1444**)
Trachy (**1491**)
Hospitaller ([NB 4107])
Hospitaller 15th c. obols (NB 4101, 4102)
Venice (**3164**), *Cyprus* (**3238**)

66. Valakis Building, Megalou Alexandrou Sq. (2000)
11th c. anonymous follis, type B (**993**)

67. Villaragut Mansion, Ippoton St. (1988 ff.)
Hospitaller 15th c. obol imitation (NB 5328)

68. Villiers Mansion, Ippoton St. (1979)
11th c. anonymous follis, type C (**1009**)
John III (**1302**)
Hospitaller 15th c. obol (NB 607)

69. Zarifis House, 3 Theophiliskou St. (1994)
AV Sequin of grand master Milly (**1666**)

III. Suburbs

1. Faneromeni (1954)
Justin II: follis (**167**)

2. Karakonero (1969/1982)
Maurice: half follis (**295**)
Heraclius: follis (**643**)
Constans II: follis (**763**)
Leo Gavalas (**1519, 1526**)
Sicily (**3187**)

3. Monte Smith, 'Vrysi Nymfis'
11th c. anonymous follis, type K (**1075**)

4. 'Bel Passo' (M. Petridi St.)
Heraclius: half follis (**603**)

IV. Excavations in the countryside

1. Basilica II, Charaki
Heraclius: half follis (**708**)
11th c. anonymous folles, type B (**992**)

2. Dormition, Mesanagros
Justin I: follis (**35**)
Phocas: half follis (**307**)
Heraclius: follis (**416**)
Constans II: folles (**773, 781**)
Latin imitative, large module, type B of Constantinople (**1316**)

3. Ioannidis plot, Trianda (1991)
Hospitaller 15th c. obol (NB4463)

4. Kambouropoulos plot, Trianda
Phocas: AV (**301**)
Heraclius: folles (**388, 471, 475, 476, 480, 485, 491, 508, 516, 518, 534, 535, 549, 553, 556, 576, 594, 601, 653, 677, 702**)
Constans II: follis (**730**), *half follis* (**823**)
11th c. anonymous folles, type B (**981, 982**)

5. Konstantinou plot, Lagou, Rodou Lindou Avenue, 11th km
Justin II: half follis (**222**)
Heraclius: follis (**694**)

6. Kymisala, Monolithos
Justinian I: follis (**102**)

7. Kyroniatis, Maritsa_
Faithful copy, type C (**1314**)

8. St. George Chostos, Lindos
Heraclius: folles (**595, 675**)
Andronicus I: trachy (**1244**)

9. Anonymous Byzantine church (narthex tomb), Phileremos, Trianda
Pentanummium, 2nd half of the 6th c. (**369**)
Latin imitative, small module, type A (**1365, 1366, 1367**)

[Local] imitative trachy (**1478**)
Leo Gavalas (**1518**)
John Gavalas (**1542**)

10. Sanctuary of Apollo Erethimios, Tholos
Anastasius I or Justin I: pentanummium (**364**)
Justin I: minimus (**56**)
Maurice: half follis (**288**)
Heraclius: folles (**521, 522, 628**)
Constans II: follis (**755**)
Type B anonymous folles (**969, 975**)
11th c. anonymous follis, type E (**1039**)

11. Sugar mill, Charaki
Hospitaller 15th c. obol imitation (NB 5350)

12. Tsambikakis plot, Kremasti
Justin I: follis (**32**)

13. Zourarakis plot, Rodou-Lindou Avenue, 7th km
Heraclius: follis (**558**)

14. 'Stavrotholi', Paradissi
Hospitaller 15th c. imitation (NB 1067)

V. Chance Finds from the Countryside

1. Afandou
Justin II: follis (**199**)

2. Archangelos
pentanummium with christogram (**124**)
Justinian I: follis (4121), *half follis* (**87**), *pentanummium* (**91**)
Maurice: folles (**262, 280**)
Phocas: half follis (**313**)
Heraclius: folles (**460, 599, 625, 636, 649**), *half follis* (**610**)
Constans II: folles (**745, 775, 788**)
Constans II: follis or imitation. (**736**)
11th c. anonymous folles, type A2 (**898, 906**)
11th c. anonymous follis, type B (**920**)
Constantine X (**1091**)
Romanus IV (**1100**)
Nicephorus III (**1127**)
Manuel I: trachy (**1224**)
Isaac II (**1251, 1256**)
Alexius III (**1282, 1286**)
Gavalas Successors [1254-8?] (**1558**)
Hospitaller 14th c. deniers (**1734, 1858, 1859**)
Hospitaller 15th c. obols (**2973**, NB 85, 86, 262, 265)
Hospitaller 15th c. obols or imitations (NB 43, 44, 66)
Aubusson denier (**3100**)
Cypriot deniers: Janus (1398-1432) (**3244**), *James I* (1382-98) (**3243**)
Foreign deniers (**3321**, NB 264), *denier tournois* (**3309**)
Justin I: half follis (**41**), *follis* (**38**)
<u>Kerami, 1995</u>
Heraclius: follis (**482**)
Latin imitative, large module, type A of Thessalonica (**1321**)
Gavalas Successors [1294-1304?] (**1618**)

<u>Parish Church Sacristy</u>
[Local] imitative trachy (**1474**)
Leo Gavalas (**1539**)
Gavalas Successors (**1657**)
Hospitaller 14th c. obol (NB 6105)
Hospitaller 14th c. deniers (NB 6106, 6107, 6108, 6109, 6126, 6136)
Hospitaller 15th c. obols (NB 6110, 6111, 6113, 6114, 6115, 6116, 6118, 6119, 6120, 6121, 6122, 6123, 6125, 6127, 6128, 6129, 6130, 6131, 6132, 6133, 6135)
Hospitaller 15th c. obol imitations (NB 6112, 6117, 6124, 6134)
Aubusson deniers (NB 6137, 6138, 6139)
Cyprus: denier (**3250**), *sixain* (**3254**)
Tornesello of A. Contarini (1367-82) (**3272**)
Pope John XXII (Macerata 1316-34) (**3231**)
Ravenna (1232-1375) (**3233**), *[Sicily]* (**3220**), *[Italian]* (**3320**)

3. Arnitha
11th c. anonymous follis, type K (**1076**)

4. Asklipio
Heraclius: follis (**674**)

5. Ayios Isidoros, Vrochorio
Heraclius: follis (**481**)

7. Foundoukli
Isaac II (**1260**)

8. Kalathos
Justinian I: follis (**95**)

9. Kalavarda
Heraclius: follis (**397**)

10. Kalythies
Constans II: follis (**765**)
<u>Between Kalythies and Psinthos</u>
Alexius I (**1146**)

11. Kamiros
Heraclius: follis (**434**)
Hospitaller 15th c. obol (NB 4059)

12. Kattavia
Heraclius: half follis (**685**), *follis* (**504**)
Basil I: AV (**886**)

13. Kolympia
Maurice: follis (**282**)

14. Koskinou
Pins denier (**1880**)

15. Lardos
Justinian I: follis (**106**)
Justin II: follis (**201**)
[Lardos]
Justinian I: follis (**120**)
Justin II: pentanummium (**239**)

Tiberius II: follis (**249**), *triacontanummium* (**247**), *pentanummium* (**252**)
Maurice: half follis (**296**)
Heraclius: folles (**409, 561, 637**), *half folles* (**609, 712**)

16. Lindos
Basil I: AV (**867**)
Constantine VII (**873**)
Isaac II (**1258**)
Gavalas Successors [1304-7?] (**1632**)

17. Maritsa
11th c. anonymous follis, type A2 (**905**)
Latin imitative, small module, type G (**1422**)

18. Massari
Constans II: AV (**716**)

19. Monolithos
Justinian I: follis (**339**)
Heraclius: follis (**632**)

20. Paradissi
AR Tram (**3145, 3146, 3147, 3148**)

21. Pastida
11th c. anonymous follis, type A2 (**894**)

22. Plimmyri
11th c. anonymous follis, type B (**918**)

23. Trianda (Ialysos)
Heraclius: half follis (**647**)
11th c. anonymous follis, type A2 (**899**)
Phileremos
Constans II: follis (**804**)

24. Vati
Heraclius: follis (**577**)

25. Yennadi
Justinian I: follis (**82**), *half follis* (**977**)
[Justin II]: half follis (**173**)
Half follis, 1st half of 6th c. (**336**)
Heraclius: folles (**450, 515**)
Kyramitsi
Heraclius: follis (**563**)
Constantine X (**1092**)

Selected contexts

I. Coins from the Gavoyannis plot, Menekleous St., May/June 1977 (site II.12)

522-537	Pentanummium with christogram of Justin I or Justinian I (NB865: ?)
566-578	Pentanummium of Justin II (**242**: CON/[A])
582/602	Quarter follis of Maurice (**266**: CON/B)
642-648	Follis of Constans II (**735**)
1250-1309	Rhodian Æ of the Gavalas successors (**1614, 1631**)
1353 ff.	*Tornesello* (**3301**)

Coin assemblage from space Δ (18 pieces):

HERACLIUS		
12 folles		
year 15	1	(**469**: CON/E)
years 15-19	1	(**473**: CON/A)
year 20	1	(**477**: CON/A)
year 23	2	(**500**: CON/B, **497**: CON/Γ)
year 26	1	(**533**: CON/Δ)
years 20-29	3	(**542**: CON/A, **544**: CON/A, **565**: CON/E)
years 30-31	1	(**587**: CON/B)
year 31	2	(**586**: CON/A, **590**: CON/E)
Half follis		
year 30	1	(**608**: CON/Δ)
Quarter follis		
years 1-19	1	(**620**: CON/A)
CONSTANS II		
3 folles		
year 1	1	(**724**: A)
year 2	1	(**741**: Γ)
year 3	1	(**776**: A)
Quarter follis		
year 20	1	(**829**: A)

II. Coins from the Kambouropoulos plot, Agias Paraskevis St., Trianda, 1997 (site IV.4)

AV tremissis of Phocas (**301**)

HERACLIUS		
21 folles		
year 3	2	(**388**[*]: CON/E, **653**[**]: KYZ/A)
year 4	1	(**702**[*]: ?/B)
year 16	1	(**471**[*]: CON/Γ)
year 20	4	(**475**: CON/A, **476**[*]: CON/A, **480**[*]: CON/B, **677**[***]: ΘEC/E)
year 2[1]	1	(**491**[**]: CON/Δ)
year 2[2]	1	(**594**[*]: CON/A)
year 24	1	(**508**[*]: CON/Γ)
year 25	3	(**525**[**]: CON/Γ, **516**: CON/A, **518**[**]: CON/A)
year 26	2	(**534**[*]: CON/Δ, **535**[*]: CON/E)
years 20-29	5	(**549**: CON/Γ, **553**: CON/Γ, **556**[**]: CON/Δ, **485**[*]: CON/?, **576**[***]: CON/?)

Half follis

year 20 (**601**[*]: CON/[B])

---

[*] Ossuary 1.
[**] Ossuary 2.
[***] Ossuary 3.

CONSTANS II
Follis
year 1-2 (**730***: ?)
Half follis
(**823***: Δ)

11th c. anonymous folles, type B or imitations
981, 982

III. Excavation of grave T8, Minatsis plot, walled town of Rhodes; 12 August 1992 (site II.33)

14 worn and clipped 11th century folles
Class B anonymous folles (**945, 946, 947, 948, 949, 950, 951, 952, 953, 954**)
2 Class C anonymous folles (**1032, 1033**)
2 11th c. illegible folles (**1136, 1137**)

3 12th-century regularly clipped trachea, diam. 16mm (after 1200?)
Manuel I (**1236**)
Isaac II (**1270**)
Alexius III (**1289**)

IV. Excavation of shaft grave B, SS Constantine and Helena (north aisle), walled town of Rhodes; September/ October 1992 (site II.58)

Issues *c.* 1200-1240‡
4 clipped trachea of Isaac II (**1273, 1274, 1276, 1279**)
5 clipped trachea of Alexius III (**1290, 1292, 1294, 1296, 1297**)
2 Latin imitatives, large module, type C of Constantinople (**1317, 1318**)
1 Latin imitatives, large module, type B of Thessalonica (**1325**)
1 Latin imitatives, large module, type C of Thessalonica (**1327**)
3 faithful copies, type C (**1311, 1312, 1313**)
1 trachy of Andronicus I of Trebizond (**1304**)
16 Latin imitatives, small module, type A (**1333, 1334, 1335, 1337, 1338, 1349, 1350, 1351, 1352, 1354, 1355, 1356, 1358, 1359, 1360, 1361**)
7 Latin imitatives, small module, type B (**1376, 1378, 1382, 1383, 1384, 1385, 1387**)
4 Latin imitatives, small module, type D (**1395, 1396, 1398, 1399**)
2 Latin imitatives, small module, type E (**1401, 1407**)
9 Latin imitatives, small module, type G (**1412, 1414, 1415, 1416, 1417, 1429, 1430, 1431, 1434**)
1[+4] Latin imitatives, small module (**1456, [1493, 1500, 1502, 1504]**)
4 [+1] [local] imitatine trachea (**1466, 1467, 1468, 1471, [1476]**)
4 unidentified trachea (**1479, 1480, 1481, 1492**)
5 illegible trachea (**1507, 1508, 1509, 1510,** NB 3607)

---

* Ossuary 1.
** Ossuary 2.
*** Ossuary 3.

‡ In the same shaft grave, which was 3.9 metres deep, were also found:
2 ancient Rhodian coins
3 Roman coins
2 quarter folles of Phocas (**314, 318**)
1 follis and a half follis of Heraclius (**551, 621**)
2 folles and a dodecanummium of Constans II (**798, 818, 834**)
2 11th c. anonymous folles, type C (**1022, 1026**)
1 11th c. anonymous follis, type H (**1050**)
1 signed follis of Nicephorus III (**1121**)
2 tetartera of Alexius I (**1149, 1170**)
1 half tetarteron of Manuel I (**1242**)
44 Hospitaller coins
11 Ottoman coins
19+ illegible pieces
1 reckoning counter
3 coins of Leo Gavalas (**1520, 1523, 1528**)

V. Conventual church of St. John, Panaitiou St., walled town, burial with grave offerings, 14-18 May 1995 (site II.41)

	Depth		
	-1 to -1.37 m	-1.37 to -1.60 m	-1.60 to -1.75 m
Aubusson deniers	**3065**, **3104**	3077	-
15th c. obols, variants of the type CONUENTUS RhODI/ MAGISTER OSPITALIS	**3018**, **3019**, **3020**, **3032**, **3033**, NB 5614, 5651, 5655, 5662, 5664, 5666, 5668, 5669, 5670, 5674, 5682, 5687, 5691, 5693, 5694, 5697, 5703, 5704, 5705, 5706, 5707, 5708, 5709	**3034**, **3035**, NB 5722, 5723, 5731, 5735, 57385739, 5740, 5743, 5746, 5747, 5749, 5750, 5751, 5752, 5755, 5756, 5757, 5758, 5760, 5762, 5764, 5766	**3022**, **3023**, **3037**, NB 5771, 5773, 5774, 5775, 5776, 5777, 5778, 5782, 5784, 5786, 5788
15th c. obols, variants of the type CONUENTO RhODI/ OSPITALIS IERVSALEM	**2992**, **2993**, **2994**, **2995**, **3008**, **3009**, **3010**, **3011**, NB 5653, 5658, 5696	**2996**, **2997**, **2998**, **3003**	**2999**, **3000**
15th c. obols, variants of the type MAGISTRI OSPITAL[/ IEROSALEMITANI...	2932	**2946**, NB 5754	**2923**, **2929**
15th c. obol, type MAGISTER OSPITALI/ [OSPITALI]S S IO...	NB 5645	2962	-
15th c. obol, type CONUENTUS RhODI/ IE[RVSALEMITARhODI	2985	-	-
15th c. obol, type MAGISTER OSPITA/ MAGISTER OSPITAL	-	2963	-
Illegible 15th c. obols	NB 5661, 5657, 5660, 5663, 5665, 5667, 5673, 5679, 5683, 5684, 5685, 5688, 5690, 5692, 5699, 5701, 5702, 5711	NB 5736, 5741, 5742, 5748, 5759, 5765	NB 5769, 5772, 5789, 5790
15th c. imitative obols	**3045**, **3046**, **3050**, **3051**, **3053**, NB 5616, 5618, 5620, 5621, 5622, 5623, 5625, 5626, 5627, 5628, 5629, 5630, 5631, 5632, 5635, 5636, 5637, 5638, 5639, 5640, 5641, 5642, 5643, 5644, 5647, 5649, 5652, 5672	NB 5726, 5727, 5728	-
15th c. obols or imitations	NB 5646, 5648, 5650, 5654, 5659	NB 5729, 5767	NB 5779
14th c. obols	-	**2780**, **2844**, **2867**	2308
Foreign coins	**3167**, **3253** (AR), **3271**, **3263**, **3264**, **3223**, **3235**, NB 5613	**3165**, **3168**, **3174**, **3175**, **3212**, **3274**, **3275**, **3305**, **3319**	-
Total	108	56	24

Maps

I. Location of excavated sites and properties. New town of Rhodes

II. Location of excavated sites and properties. Medieval town of Rhodes

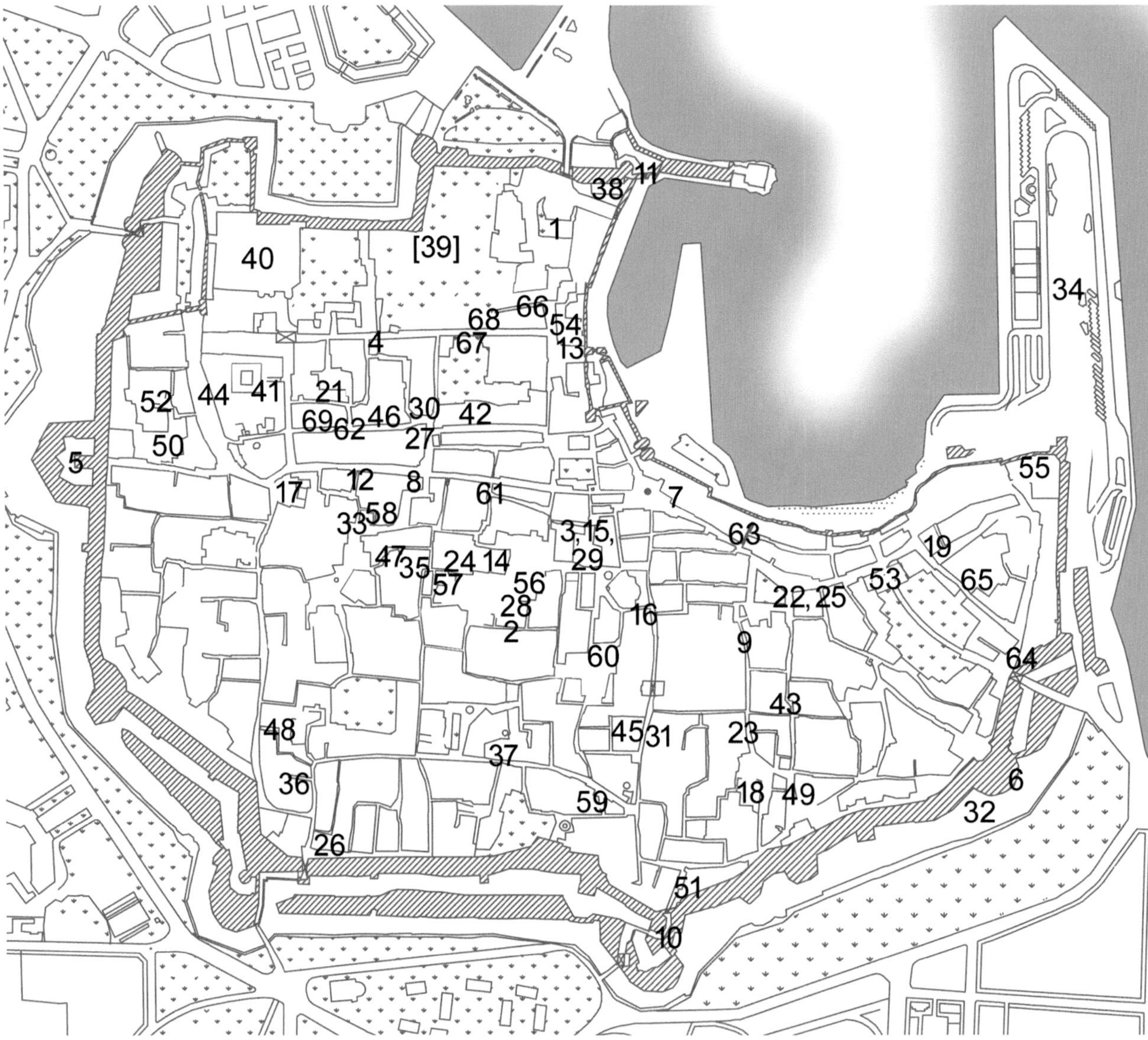

Geographical distribution of coin finds

III. Rhodes town, 6th and 7th c.

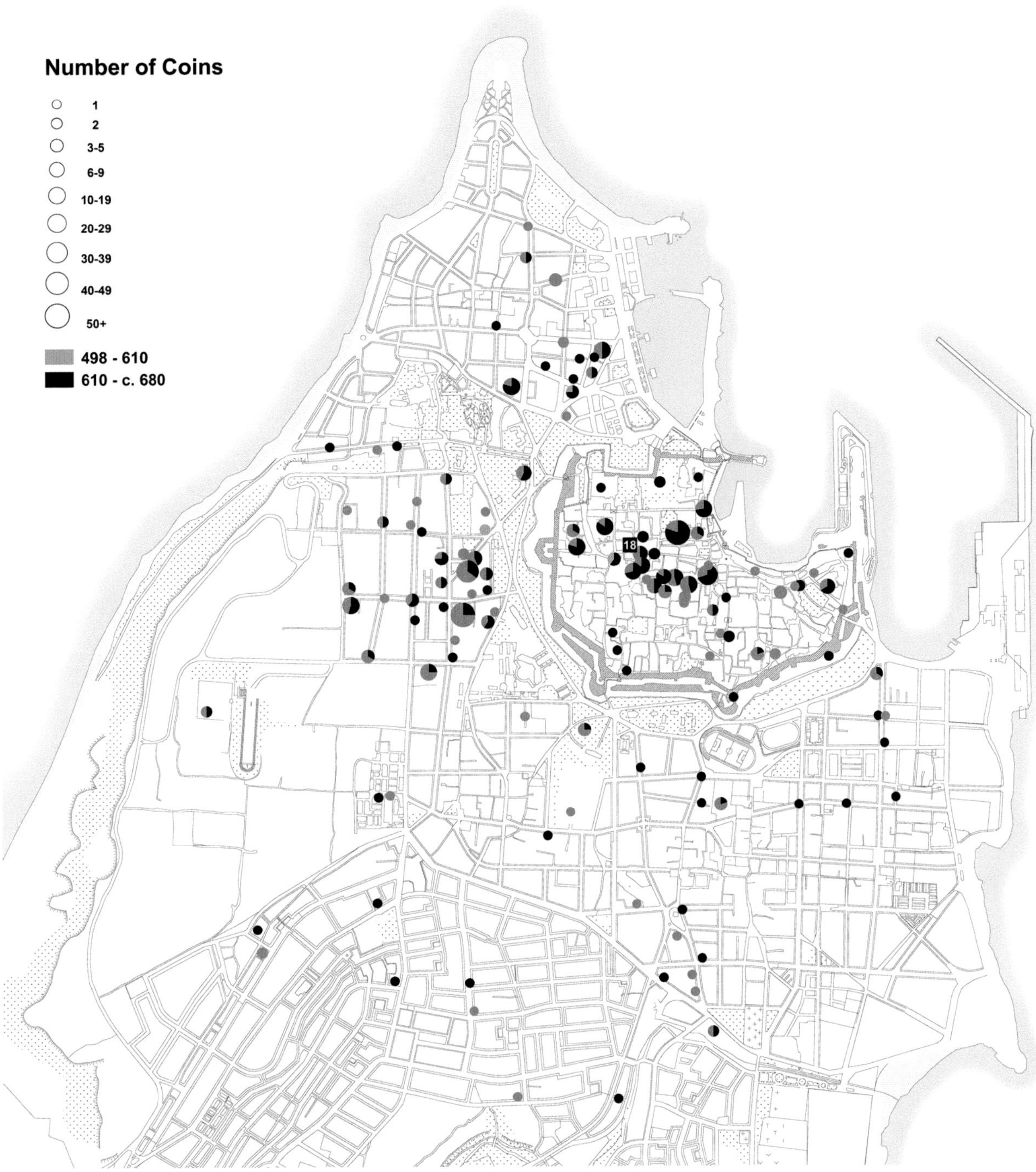

IV. Medieval town of Rhodes, 969-1092

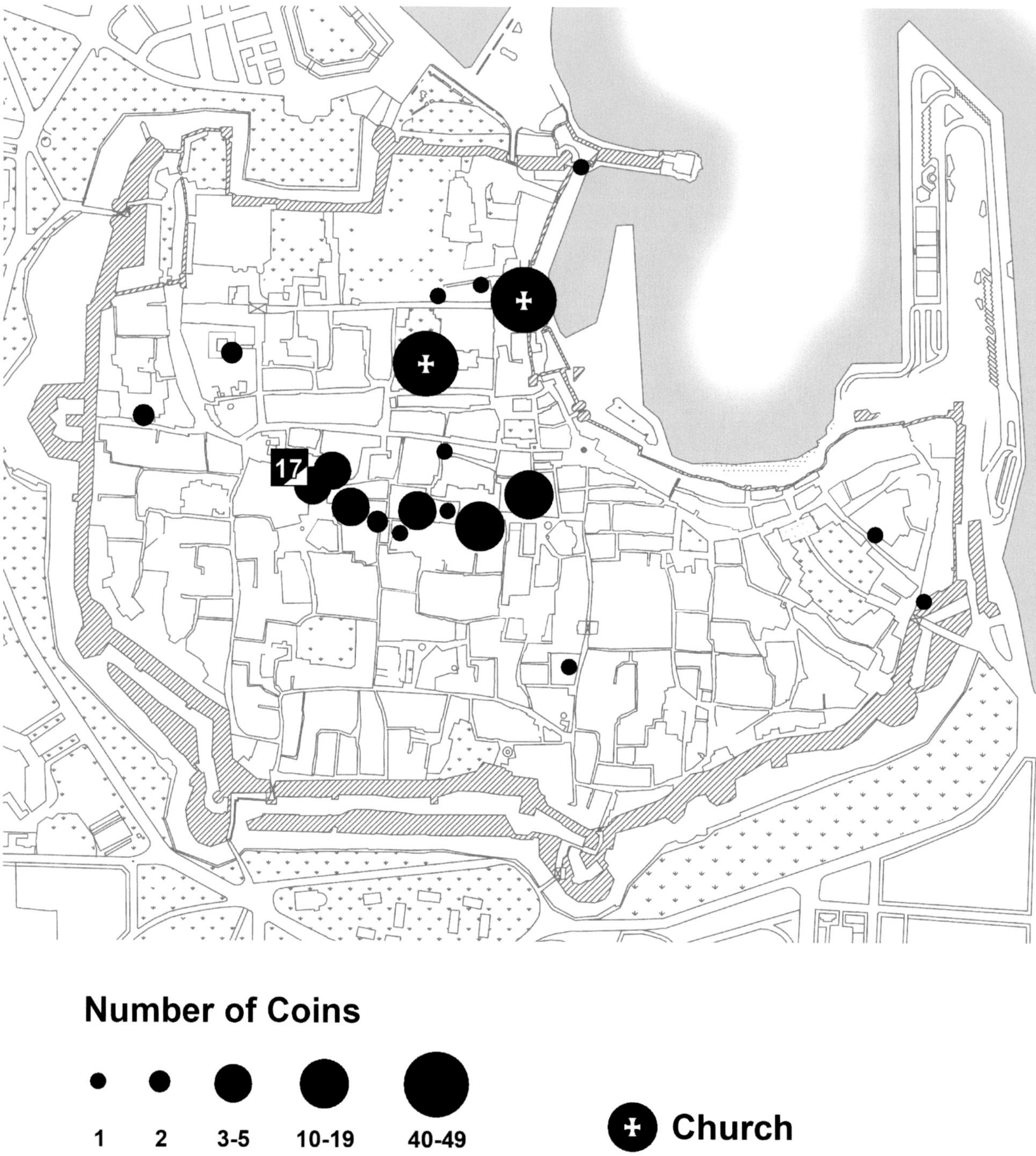

V. Medieval town of Rhodes, 1204-1309

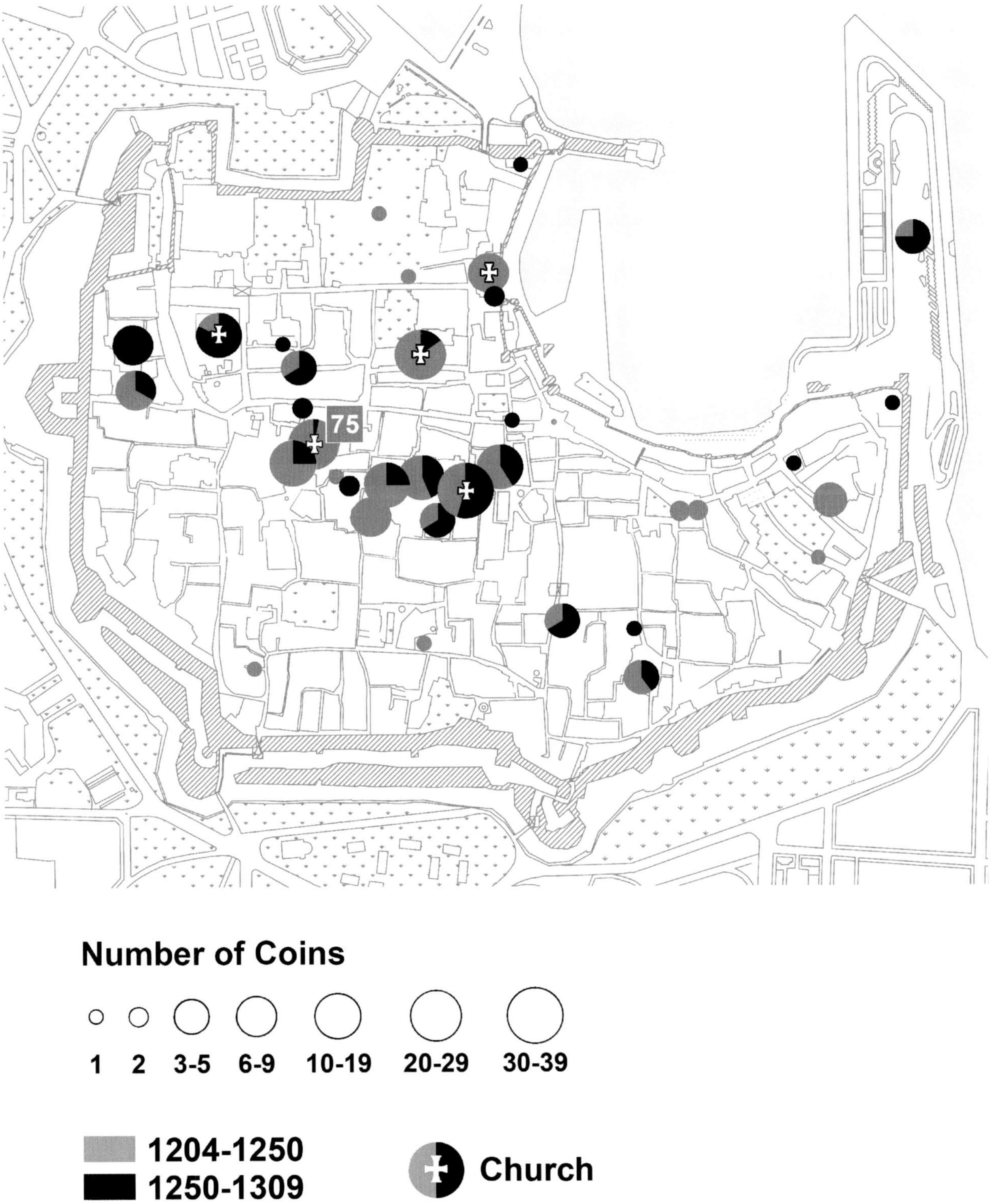

VI. Medieval town of Rhodes, 1309-1522

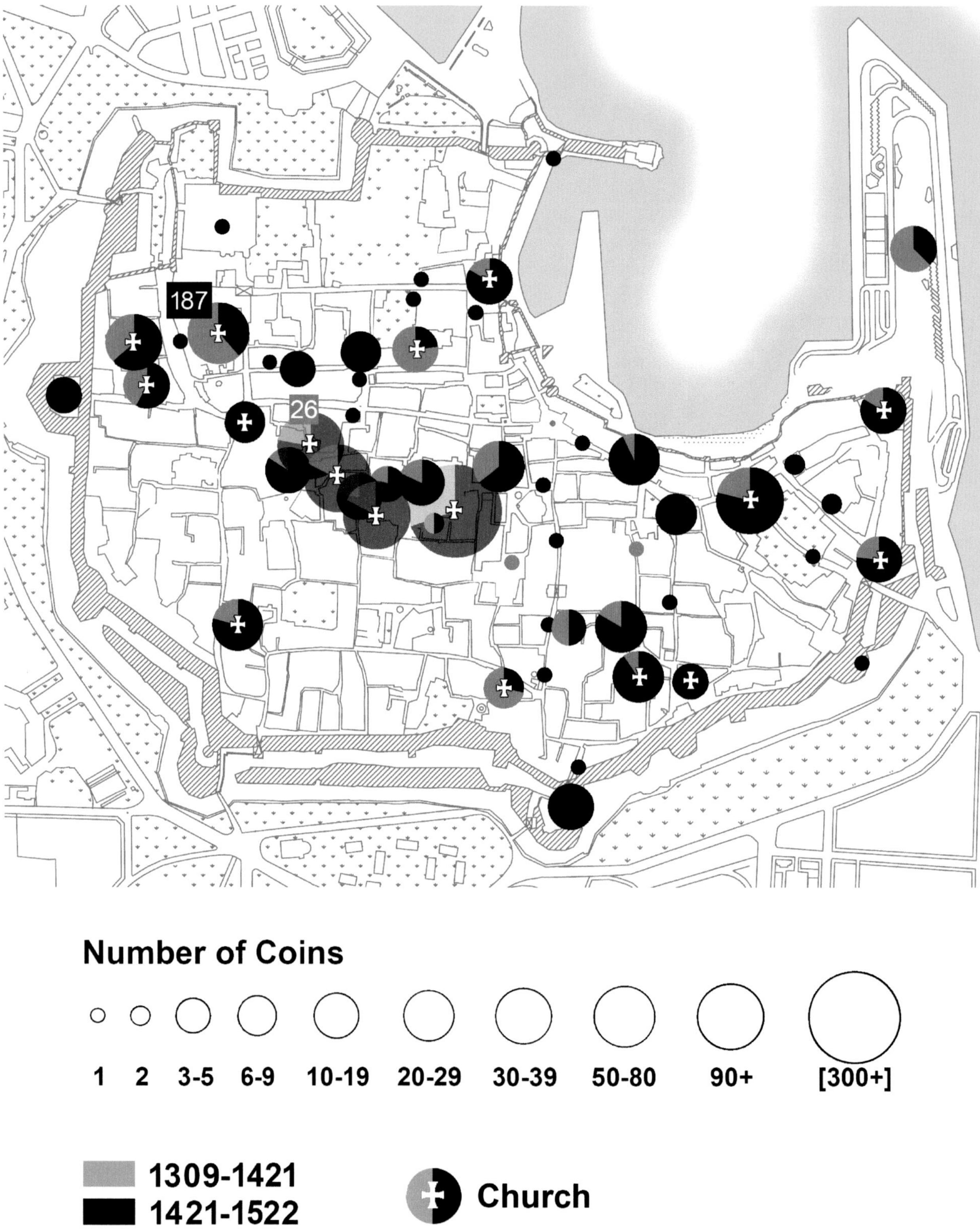

VII. New town of Rhodes, c. 680-1522

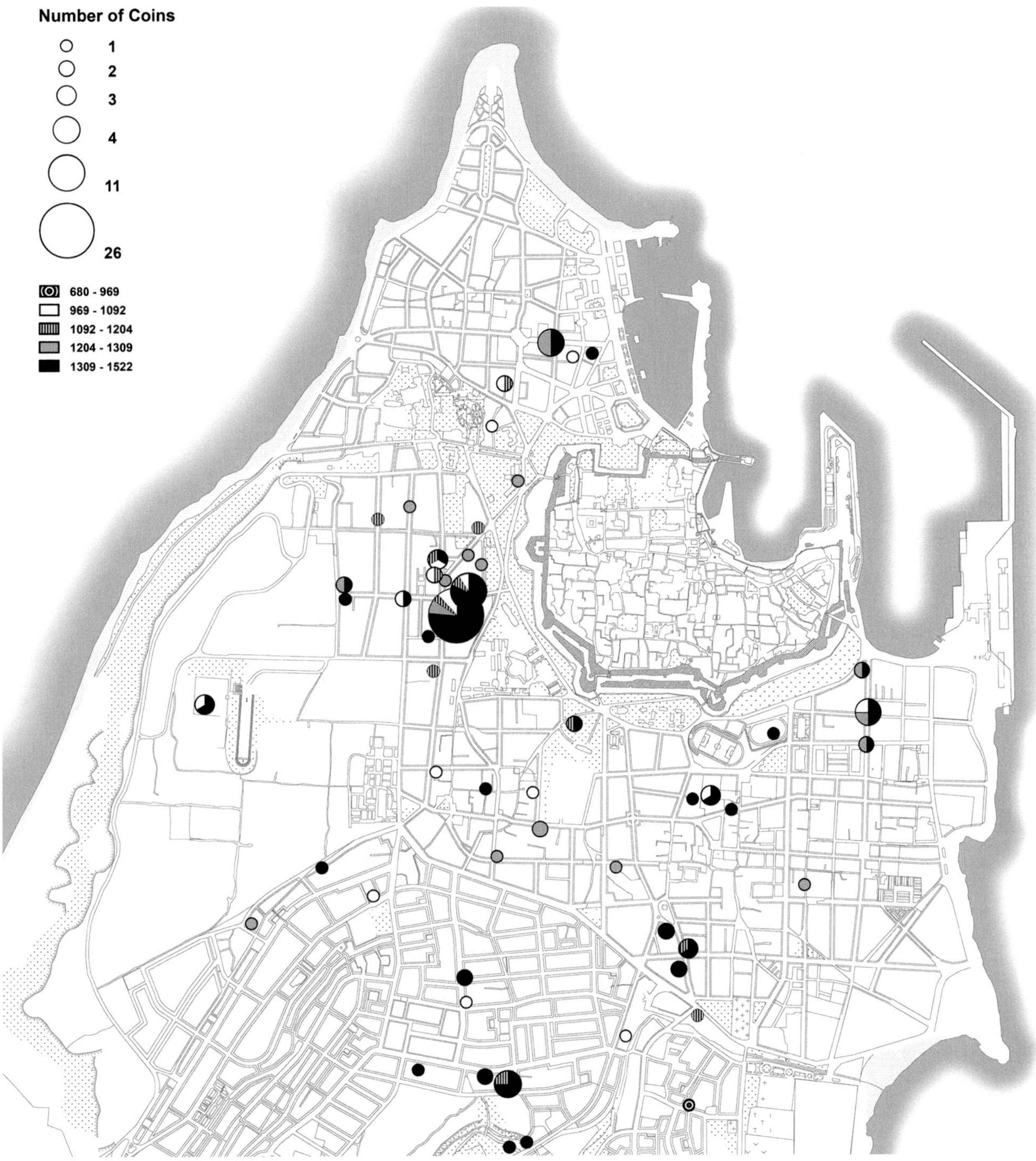

VIII. Island of Rhodes, the countryside

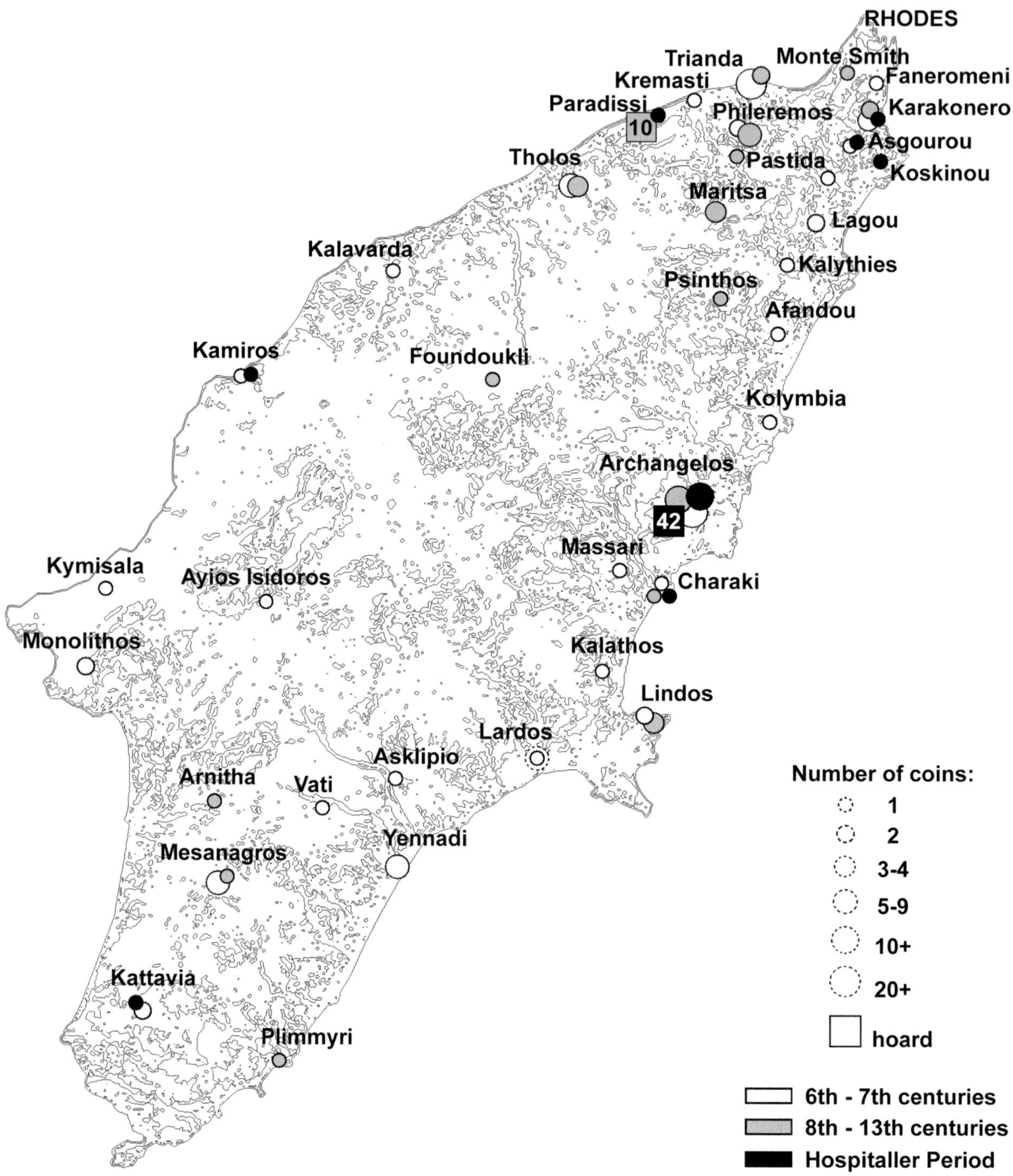

Mapping bases
Town maps: *Municipal Urban Planning Bureau*
Adaptation: V. Ayakatsikas, M. Mitton, A. M. Kasdagli
Island of Rhodes: *Google Earth*
Adaptation: A. M. Kasdagli

The Catalogue and Plates

The Catalogue contains almost all the Byzantine coins from Rhodes entered in the inventory of the Ephorate of Antiquities of the Dodecanese up to 2014, the silver and gold Hospitaller coins, the Hospitaller site finds up to 1421, a selection of the 14th century obols and overstruck deniers of the period 1377-1421 derived from the two major Hospitaller hoards (in order to establish types and variants), a selection of 15th century site finds (also to establish basic types) and all billon and foreign coins. A total of 3,354 coins are included in the Catalogue, as follows:

- 1,497 Byzantine coins and 'imitations'
- 160 13th-century coins minted in Rhodes
- 1,476 Hospitaller coins
- 221 foreign coins

'PL.' and 'PLS' in the text indicate the relevant Plates, and figures in bold type indicate Catalogue numbers. In the Catalogue, the number of each coin is followed by the number ('NB' number) of the Ephorate internal inventory within parentheses. Then follow the diameter, weight and, in the Byzantine section and Hospitalled gold and silver, the relation of reverse to obverse axis. The description of individual coins in the Byzantine section is brief and complemented by a reference to the most relevant bibliography; in the petty coinage of the Hospitaller period the legible part of the legend is also included. The provenance of each coin, if known, is displayed with reference to the relevant Site Map, the List of Excavated Properties and Sites and the Coin Finds, all found in the Appendices section: for example, II.51 in the last column of the Catalogue is the church of St. John in the Medieval town of Rhodes; while V refers to the Chance Finds from the Countryside section of the Coin Finds Appendice.

A few catalogued coins are missing from the relevant Plates, due to technical problems, but none of them are of particular significance. Equally, a few measurements are missing from the Catalogue, because the coins were inaccessible. The identification manuals used for the Catalogue were the *Moneta Imperii Byzantini* (MIB) and Dumbarton Oaks series (DOC) for the imperial Byzantine coins; Schlumberger's *Numismatique de l'Orient latin* for the medieval mint of Rhodes; and for foreign coins Metcalf's *Coinage of the Crusades and the Latin East in the Ashmolean Museum Oxford* along with a variety of other publications, most notably the Corpus Nummorum Italicorum (CNI) series and the Grierson and Travaini volume on South Italy, Sicily and Sardinia.

Catalogue

PLATE 1

				ANASTASIUS I, 491 - 518		
1 (371)	39	17.6	6	Follis. Constantinople, 512-517. *Stars* ✶.	MIB I, 27	
2 (84)	34	16.7	7	Follis. Constantinople, off. A, 512-517. *Stars* ✶.	»	
3 (4583)	33	16.1	6	Follis. Constantinople, off. E, 512-517. *Stars* ✶. *Corr.*	»	II.28
4 (4444)	34	14.6	6	Follis. Constantinople, off. E, 512-517. *Stars* ✶.	»	
5 (4545)	33	14	6	Follis. Constantinople, off. E, 512-517. *Stars* ✳.	»	?V
6 (981)	34	15.2	6	Follis. Constantinople, off. E, 517-518. *Stars* ✶.	MIB I, 30	II.29
7 (3862)	33	11.2	6	Follis. Constantinople, off. E, [517-518]. *Stars* ✶. *Corr.*	MIB I, [30]	I.14
8 (338)	19	5.1	6	Half follis. Constantinople, off. A, 507-512. *Stars* ✶.	MIB I, 32	I.82
9 (4869)	23	2.7	[6]	Half follis, 507-512. *Corr.*	MIB I, 31/32	
10 (3950)	29	9.4	7	Half follis. Constantinople, off. A, 512-517.	MIB I, 33	I
11 (302)	21	4	6	Quarter follis. Constantinople, off. Δ, 512-518. *Rev.* ...CORD. *Corr.*	[MIB I, 36]	I/II

PLATE 2

12 (496)	11	2.1	7	Pentanummium. Constantinople, off. B, 512-518.	MIB I, 39	II.15
13 (604)	12	2.1	1	»	»	II.18
14 (622)	13	2.5	6	»	»	I.35
15 (3944)	13	1.6	7	»	»	I.98
16 (4194)	12	1.9	6	Pentanummium. Constantinople, off. E, 512-517.	MIB I, 38	I.48
17 (4561)	14	2.8	7	Pentanummium. Constantinople, off. [B], 512-517. *Corr.*	»	I.24
18 (833)	13	2.5	6	Pentanummium. Constantinople, off. [A], 518-522.	MIB I, 44	I.102
19 (623)	10	0.7	6	Minimus, 491-518.	MIB I, 40	I.35
20 (628)	9	0.9		»	»	I 35
21 (660)	8	1		»	»	I.35
22 (661)	9	0.7		»	»	I.35
23 (4279)	10	0.2		»	»	I.35
24 (4280)	9	0.3		»	»	I.35
25 (4281)	8	0.1		»	»	I.35
26 (4282)	9	0.3		»	»	I.35
27 (4283)	10	0.8		»	»	I.35
28 (4384)	9	0.5		»	»	I.35
29 (4285)	9			»	»	I.35

PLATE 3

				JUSTIN I, 518 - 527		
30 (535)	34	18.4	0	Follis. Constantinople, off. E, 512-517. *Stars* ✶.	MIB I, 11	I.35
31 (818)	32	15.6	6	Follis. Constantinople, off. E, 518-522. *Stars* ✶.	»	I.102
32 (286)	34	17	6	Follis. Constantinople, off. E, 518-522. *Stars* ✳.	»	IV.12
33 (191)	31	14.8	1	Follis. Constantinople, off. Γ, 518-522. Stars ✶. Worn.	»	
34 (4557)	32	16.2	1	Follis. Constantinople, off. E. Stars ✶. 518-522. *Worn.*	»	I.24
35 (1842)	32	16.6	6	Follis. Constantinople, off. A, 518-522. *Worn.*	MIB I, 11/12	IV.2
36 (4190)	30	14.6	7	Follis. Constantinople, off. Δ. Star ✶., 522-527.	[MIB I, 12]	I.25
37 (4591)	31	12.2	7	Follis. Constantinople. *Corr.*	MIB I, 12/13	II.33
38 (179)	30	18.7	7	Follis. Constantinople, off. E, 518-522.	MIB I, 13	V.2
39 (3742)	30	15.2	6	Follis. Constantinople, off. Γ, 518-522.	[MIB I, 13]	II. 14
40 (650)	25	9.5	6	Half follis. Constantinople, off. E, 518-522.	MIB I, 18	I. 35
41 (98)	25	7.1	6	»	»	V.2
42 (3811)	12.8	2.14	6	Pentanummium. Constantinople, off. B, 518-522. *Worn.*	MIB I, 25	II.19
43 (140)	13	2.5	1	Pentanummium. Constantinople, off. Γ, 518-522.	»	
44 (1080)	12.8	2.14	1	Pentanummium. Constantinople, off. Γ, 518-522. *Worn.*	»	I.21

45 (617)		2.4		Pentanummium. Constantinople, off. Γ, 518-522.	MIB I, 27	I.35
46 (627)	12	2.3	6	Pentanummium. Constantinople, off. Δ, 518-522.	»	I.35
PLATE 4						
47 (952)	13	1.7	6	Pentanummium with christogram. Constantinople, off. A, 522-527.	MIB I, 33	I.48
48 (1103)	13	1.4		Pentanummium with christogram. Constantinople, off. A, 522-527. *Obv. ill.*	»	
49 (945)	13	1.7	6	Pentanummium with christogram. Constantinople, off. [A], 522-527.	»	II.42
50 (90)	14	1.3	6	Pentanummium with christogram. Constantinople, off. B, 522-527.	MIB I, 32	I/II
51 (830)	13	2.5	3	Pentanummium with christogram. Constantinople, off. Γ, 522-527.		I.102
52 (813)	15	2.2	6	Pentanummium with christogram. Constantinople, [off. Γ], 522-527.	»	I.102
53 (624)	12	1.5	6	Pentanummium with christogram. Constantinople, off. Δ, 522-527. *Worn.*	»	I.35
54 (5348)	14	2.4	6	»	»	
55 (808)	13	1.8	6	Pentanummium with christogram. Off. [Δ], 522-527.	»	I.31
56 (10174)	8.7	0.4		Minimus.	MIB I, 34	IV.10
57 (1098)	32	15.2	7	Follis. Nicomedia (NIKM), 518-522. *Obv. ill.*	MIB I, 38a	I.79
58 (3817)	14	2.7		Pentanummium with christogram. Nicomedia, [522-537]. *Corr.*	MIB I, 47	II.42
59 (1143)	28	4.4	10	Half follis. Antioch, off. A. *Corr.*	MIB I, 61	II.57
60 (4183)	27	7.4	6	Half follis. Thessalonica, 518-522.	MIB I, 71	II.32
61 (142)	30	12.2	6	Follis. [Constantinople], off. Γ, [518-522]. *Worn.*	MIB I, [14]	
62 (278)	32	13.7	6	Follis. *Rev. corr.*	MIB I, 11-12	I.88
63 (814)	12	2	6	Pentanummium with christogram, 522-527.	MIB I, 32/33	I.102
64 (831)	12	1.8	7	Pentanummium with christogram.	MIB I, 33	I.102
65 (1079)	16	1.3	6	Pentanummium with christogram. *Worn.*	»	I.21
PLATE 5						
				JUSTINIAN I, 527 - 565		
66 (3)	20	4.4	6	AV Solidus. Constantinople, off. I, 542-565.	MIB I, 7	I/II
67 (17)	20	4.4	6	»	»	
68 (20)	21	4.4	6	»	»	
69 (21)	25	4.4		AV Solidus. Constantinople, off. [I], 542-565.	»	
70 (23)	20	4.5	6	AV Solidus. Constantinople, off. Z, 542-565.	»	I/II
71 (3861)	29	18	6	Follis. Constantinople, off. E, 527-532.	MIB I, 87	I.54
72 (4860)	43	20.7	5	Follis, year XII. Constantinople, off. E, 538/539.	MIB I, 95a	
73 (230)	40	21.6	7	Follis, year XIII. Constantinople, off. Γ, 539/540.	MIB I, 95	
74 (3792)	42	21.2	6	Follis, year XIII. Constantinople, off. Δ, 539/540.	»	II.42
75 (68)	39	22.7	6	Follis, year XЧ. Constantinople, off. B, 541/542.	MIB I, 95a	
76 (821)	39	23.4	6	Follis, year XЧ. Constantinople, off. B, 541/542.	»	
77 (311)	38	18.8	7	Follis, year XЧ. Constantinople, off. [B], 541/542.	»	I/II
PLATE 6						
78 (347)	36	18.9	6	Follis, year XЧ. Constantinople, 542/543. *Pierced rim.*	MIB I, 95[f]	I/II
79 (4121)	41	22.5	6	Follis, year XЧ. Constantinople, off. B, 541/542.	MIB I, 95a	V.2
80 (321)	36	18.2	7	Follis, year XЧI. Constantinople, off. E, 542/543.	»	I.99
81 (1166)	40	18.6	6	Follis, year XX. Constantinople, off. Δ, 546/547.	»	II.45
82 (59)	36	18.7	0	Follis, year XXI. Constantinople, off. B, 547/548.	»	V.25
83 (2177)	32	17.4	6	Follis, year XXЧII. Constantinople, off. E, 553/554.	»	
84 (50)	33	16.9	6	Follis, year XXXIIII. Constantinople, off. B, 560/561.	MIB I, 95[a]	
85 (854)	23	9.3	6	Half follis. Constantinople, off. Γ, 527-537.	MIB I, 90	I.102
86 (3889)	26	9.6	0	Half follis. Constantinople, off. A, 527-537. *Stars* ✶.	»	I.54

87 (706)	29	10	6	Half follis, year XЧ. Constantinople, off. A, 541/542.	MIB I, 96	V.2

PLATE 7

88 (2199)	16	4		Quarter follis, year XЧ. Constantinople, 541/542. *Obv. ill.*	MIB I, 99	I.53
89 (196)	20	5.3	6	Quarter follis, year XXIIII. Constantinople, off. Δ, 550/551.	MIB I, 100	
90 (1127)	16	2.7	6	Quarter follis, year XXXIIII. Constantinople, 560/561.	MIB I, 99	I.101
91 (2162)	17	1.7	0	Pentanummium. Constantinople, off. Δ, 538-542.	MIB I, 103a	V.2
92 (235)	12	2	7	Pentanummium. Constantinople, off. +, 542-552.	MIB I, 103b	
93 (144)	42	21.6	6	Follis, year XIII. Nicomedia, off. A, 539/540.	MIB I, 114	
94 (331)	41	24.2	6	Follis, year XIII. Nicomedia, off. B, 539/540.	MIB I, 114	I.88
95 (136)	36	19.5	7	Follis, year XIIII. Nicomedia, off. A, 543/544.	»	V.8
96 (178)	34	15.5	6	Follis, year X... Nicomedia, 541-565.	»	I/II
97 (842)	30	10.4		Half follis, year XIII. Nicomedia, 539/540.	MIB I, 116a	I.102
98 (4525)	31	11	6	Half follis, year XЧ. Nicomedia, 541/542. *Corr.*	MIB I, 116b	II.57
99 (69)	26	8.9	6	Half follis, year XXX[Ч]III, 559-561. Nicomedia.	MIB I, 116a	

PLATE 8

100 (3860)	39	21.6	6	Follis, year XЧ. Cyzicus, off. A, 541/542. *Pierced rim.*	MIB I, 120a	I.92
101 (4455)	36	20	6	Follis, year XXII. Cyzicus, off. A, 551/552.	»	I. 91
102 (339)	35	16.3	4	Follis, year XXЧ. Cyzicus, off. B, 551/552.	»	IV. 6
103 (168)	34	14.6	5	Follis. Antioch, off. [Γ], 528-537. *Worn.*	MIB I, 127-30	
104 (100)	35	19.8	4	Follis, year XXI. Antioch, off. Δ, 547/548.	MIB I, [148]	
105 (162)	33	15.2	4	Follis, year XXIIII. Antioch, off. E, 550/551.	MIB I, 146b	
106 (1)	34	18.6	0	Follis, year XXX. Antioch, off. B, 556/557.	MIB I, 147-8	V. 15
107 (270)	33	18.8	5	Follis, year XXXIII. Antioch, off. Δ, 559/560.	»	
108 (586)	32	16.2		Follis, year XXXϚI. Antioch, off. A, 553/554.	MIB I, 150-1	II. 18

PLATE 9

109 (1030)	26	8.5		Half follis. Antioch, off. Γ, 532-537.	MIB II, 135	I. 67
110 (826)	27	7.1	0	Half follis. Antioch, 528-532.	MIB I, 134	V. 25
111 (820)	34	9.4	11	Half follis, year XXXII. Antioch, 558/559.	MIB I, 154a	I. 102
112 (4191)	16	2.1	6	Pentanummium. Antioch, 557-562.	MIB I, 161	I. 74
113 (4518)	16	2.5	5	Pentanummium. Antioch, 557-562. *Worn.*	»	II.50
114 (234)	15			Pentanummium. Antioch, 562-565.	MIB I, 163	
115 (297)	15	3.7	6	Dodecanummium, 527-565. *Obv. ill.*	MIB I, 165[1]	I/II
116 (1008)	21	5.5		Decaexanummium, 538-557. *Corr.; obv. ill.*	MIB I, 169	II.29
117 (1052)	23	5.9	7	Half follis. Thessalonica (TES), 562-565.	MIB I, 180	II.50
118 (293)	12	1.5	0	Pentanummium. Sicily, [552-565].	MIB I, 246	I/II
119 (5260)	29	15.5	6	Follis, 527-538. *Corr.*	Cf. MIB I, 83	II.41
120 (153)	31	14.9	7	Follis, year XЧIII[I], 545/546. *Corr.*	MIB I, 95	
121 (690)	27	9.6	7	Half follis, year XX, 546/547.	Cf. MIB I, 96	I/II
122 (611)	24	6.7	7	Half follis, year XXX, 556/557. *Corr.*	»	I.35

PLATE 10

				Pentanummia with Christogram, 522-537		
123 (4287)	13	2.3	6	Off. A or E.	MIB I, 32/93	I.35
124 (182)	14	2	7	Off. A.	MIB I, 32 ff.	V.2
125 (845)	13	2.3	6	»	MIB I, 32	I.102
126 (900)	12	1.8	6	»	MIB I, 32/93	I.8
127 (902)	12	1.5	6	»	»	I.52
128 (913)	15	2.5	6	Off. [A].	»	I.45
129 (920)	14	0.9		Off. [A]. *Corr.*	»	II.42
130 (992)	14	2.1		Off. A. *Obv. ill.*	»	II.29
131 (6072)	14	2.7	0	Off. A.	»	II.35
132 (91)	15	1.9	0	Off. B.	»	I/II

133 (340)	14	2	6	Off. B.	MIB I, 32/93	I/II
134 (700)	13	1.7	7	»	MIB I, 32 ff.	I.1
135 (815)	15	1.9	6	»	MIB I, 32/93	I.102
136 (903)	13	2	7	»	»	II.56
137 (3814)	12	2.2	6	»	»	II.42
138 (3815)	14	2.3	7	Off. B. *Worn.*	»	II.42
139 (1049)	15	1.3	6	Off. B. *Obv. ill.*	»	I.11
140 (4114)	13	1.7	6	Off. B. *Worn.*	»	
141 (4246)	13	2.4	6	»	»	
142 (4482)	13	2.2	6	Off. B.	»	II.57
143 (4597)	12	1.6		Off. B. *Worn.*	»	II.33
144 (6062)	13	1.8	6	Constantinople, off. Γ. *Worn.*	»	II.35
145 (498)	13	1.6	7	*Worn.*	»	II.15
146 (683)	11	1.4	6		»	I.65
147 (803)	12	1.4		*Obv. ill.*	MIB I, 32 ff.	I.38
148 (865)	12	1.2	6		MIB I, 32/93	II.12
149 (954)	13	2.2		*Illegible.*	»	I.46
150 (2166)	12	1.6		*Worn.*	»	
151 (2197)	12	1.6		»	»	II.42
152 (2201)	14	2.1		»	»	I.53
153 (3816)	13	1.8		»	»	II.42
154 (4027)	13	0.6		»	»	II.49
155 (4112)	14	1.9		»	»	
156 (4286)	13	1.7		»	»	I.35
157 (6043)	11	1.2	6	»	»	II.35
158 (5235)	13	1.9	6	*Incomplete.*	»	II.20
159 (6006)	13	1.2		*Corr.*	»	II.64

PLATE 11

				JUSTIN II, 565 - 578		
160 (494)	30	13.7	7	Follis, [year II]. Constantinople, off. Δ, [566/567].	MIB II, 43	II.15
161 (189)	32	11.8	1	Follis, year Ч. Constantinople, off. E, 569/570.	MIB II, 43a	
162 (4296)	29	12.1	7	Follis, year Ϛ. Constantinople, off. Δ, 570/571.	»	
163 (72)	33	13.3	6	Follis, year ЧIII. Constantinople, off. E, 573/574.	MIB II, 43	I.87
164 (171)	29	7.8	6	Follis. Constantinople, 565-578. *Corr.*	»	
165 (1029)	35	13.7	6	Follis, year II. Constantinople, off. Δ, [566/567]. *Corr.*	MIB II, 43a	I.67
166 (4184)	29	13.7	7	Follis, year IIII. Constantinople, off. E, 568/569. *Corr.*	»	I.49
167 (4275)	35	12.6	6	Follis. [Constantinople], 565-578. *Corr., [overstruck].*	MIB II, [43]	III.1
168 (817)	23	5.8	7	Half follis, year [Ч]. Constantinople, off. Δ, [569/570].	MIB II, 44	I.102
169 (4276)	24	5.7	0	Half follis, year Ч. [Constantinople, off. A].	»	I.35
170 (307)	25	4.9	7	Half follis, year Ч. Constantinople, off. B, 569/570.	»	I.66
171 (313)	25	5.9	7	Half follis, year ϚI. Constantinople, off. Δ, 571/572.	MIB II, 44d	I/II
172 (798)	27	6.5	6	Half follis, year ϚIII. Constantinople, off. B, 570/571.	MIB II, 44a	I.38
173 (715)	23	6.7	1	Half follis, year XII. Constantinople, off. Δ, 576/577.	MIB II, 44	V.25

PLATE 12

174 (4122)	17	2.5	6	Pentanummium. Constantinople, off. A.	MIB II, 45	I.35
175 (4278)	15	1.8	6	»	»	I.35
176 (4666)	15	1.8	0	Pentanummium. Constantinople, off. A/Δ.	»	II.47
177 (1158)	16	1.4	1	Pentanummium. Constantinople, off. B.	»	I.86
178 (4048)	15	1.8	6	»	»	II.24
179 (655)	15	1.7	7	Pentanummium. Constantinople, off. Γ.	»	I.35
180 (893)	17	2.5	6	»	»	II.3
181 (950)	18	1.5	7	»	»	I.48
182 (1034)	18	2.4	1	»	»	I.67

183 (3915)	16	2.5	8	Pentanummium. Constantinople, off. Γ.	MIB II, 45	I.35
184 (5495)	15	1.5	7	»	»	II.56
185 (613)	16	1.7	7	Pentanummium. Constantinople, off. Δ.	»	I.35
186 (846)	16	2	1	Pentanummium. Constantinople, off. [Δ].	»	I.102
187 (852)	17	1.5	1	Pentanummium. Constantinople, off. Δ.	»	I.102
188 (1035)	15	2.1	0	»	»	I.67
189 (1082)	27	1.9	6	»	»	I.21
190 (1122)	15	1.7	6	»	»	I.101
191 (1130)	15	0.9	1	Pentanummium. Constantinople, off. [Δ].	»	I.101
192 (3914)	16	1.4	1	Pentanummium. Constantinople, off. Δ.	»	I.62
193 (663)	15	1.9	1	Pentanummium. Constantinople, off. +.	»	I.35
194 (688)	16	1.4	7	»	»	I/II
195 (949)	14	1.2	1	»	»	I.48
196 (4019)	16	2.1	8	»	»	I.35
197 (4596)	17	1.6	0	»	»	II.33
198 (4186)	29	14.6	6	Follis, year II. Nicomedia, off. A, 566/567.	MIB II, 46	II.2
199 (2179)	31	15.2	6	Follis, year III. Nicomedia, off. B, 567/568.	MIB II, 46b	V.1
200 (225)	28	12.1	7	Follis, year Ч. Nicomedia, off. B, 569/570.	MIB II, 46a	I/II
201 (5130)	31	12.2	7	»	MIB II, 46	V.15
202 (3863)	29	11.8	7	Follis, year ϚI. Nicomedia, off. B, 571/572.	MIB II, 46a	I.40

PLATE 13

203 (103)	29	13	2	Follis, year Ϛ[III]. Nicomedia, off. A, 570-574.	MIB II, 46	
204 (82)	31	13.1	5	Follis, year X. Nicomedia, off. A, 574/575.	MIB II, 43	I/II
205 (847)	30	13.3		Follis, year XI. Nicomedia, off. A, 575/576.	MIB II, 46	I.102
206 (3397)	28	8.4	6	Follis. Nicomedia, 565-578. *Corr.*	»	
207 (241)	25	6.3	1	Half follis, year Ч, 569/570. Nicomedia.	MIB II, 44a	
208 (501)	14	1.5	6	Pentanummium. [Nicomedia], 566-578.	MIB II, [49]	I.57
209 (3916)	13	1.4	7	Pentanummium. Nicomedia, 566-578.	MIB II, 49	
210 (4661)	13	1.4	10	»	»	II.52
211 (901)	16	2.2	0	»	»	I.8
212 (237)	29	11.7	6	Follis, year X... Cyzicus, off. A, 574-578.	MIB II, 50	I/II
213 (4187)	29	14.6	6	Follis, year Ϛ]III. Cyzicus, off. B, 572/573.	MIB II, 46	II.2
214 (4509)	30	11.7	5	Follis, year X[Ч... [Cyzicus], off. A or Δ, [565/578]. KV[illegible] *Corr.*	»	
215 (1033)	16	1.4	5	Pentanummium. Cyzicus.	MIB II, 53	I.67
216 (1179)	15	1.7	0	Pentanummium. Cyzicus. *Corr.*	»	II.56
217 (4039)	15	2	7	Pentanummium. Cyzicus.	»	II.63
218 (4094)	30	11.6	5	Follis, year Ч. Antioch, off. Γ.	MIB II, 56-57	II.65
219 (192)	25	5.7	5	Half follis. Antioch. *Worn.*	MIB II, 60a	
220 (5352)	19	3.3	6	Quarter follis. Antioch, off. Γ, 569-578. *Worn.*	MIB II, 63	
221 (618)	16	2.9	5	Dodecanummium, 565-578.	MIB II, 67	I.35

PLATE 14

222 (3890)	23	5.5	6	Half follis, year III. Thessalonica (TES), 567/568. *Corr.*	MIB II, 68[b]	IV.5
223 (151)	20	4.7	6	Half follis. Thessalonica (TES), 568-578. *Worn.*	MIB II, 70[a]	
224 (5857)	20	6.2	6	Half follis, year Δ. Thessalonica (TES), 568/569. *Worn.*	MIB II, 70a	II.56
225 (242)	20	3.4	6	Half follis. Thessalonica (TES), off. E, 569/570. *Corr.*	MIB II, 70[a]	
226 (351)	22	5.3	4	Half follis. Thessalonica (TES), off. E, 568-578. *Corr.*	MIB II, 70[c/e]	
227 (3891)	24	6.2	5	Half follis, year XII. Thessalonica (TES), 576/577.	MIB II, 70e	I.67
228 (1071)	23	5.1	6	Half follis, year [Ч].Thessalonica (TES), [569/570]. *Corr.*	MIB II, 77	I.13
229 (583)	22	5.6	6	Half follis, year [ЧI]. Thessalonica (TES), [570/571].	MIB II, 70a	II.18
230 (849)	20	5	6	Half follis, year IIII. Thessalonica, 568/569.	MIB II, 70a	I.102
231 (1031)	22	5.5	6	Half follis, year H. Thessalonica (TES), 572/573.	»	I.67
232 (1032)	21	5.7	6	Half follis, year [XII]. Thessalonica (TES), 576/577.	MIB II, 70f	I.67

233 (1165)	26	5.1	6	Half follis, year E. Thessalonica (TES), 569/570.	MIB II, 70a	I.33
234 (3895)	25	5.4	6	Half follis, year XI. Thessalonica (TES), 575/576.	MIB II, 70e	I.98
235 (3743)	21	5.1	6	Half follis. Thessalonica, 568-578. *Corr.*	MIB II, 70c	II.14
236 (4202)	21	4.1	6	Half follis. Thessalonica (TES), 568-578. *Worn.*	MIB II, 70	
237 (4113)	12	1.5		Pentanummium. Thessalonica [Θ], 568-578. *Obv. ill.*	[MIB II, 72]	
238 (356)	28	10.3	1	Follis. *Corr.*	[MIB II, 43]	I.35
239 (159)	14	1.9	1	Pentanummium.	MIB II, [45]	
240 (394)	13	0.6	7	Pentanummium. *Corr.*	»	II.54
241 (401)	16	2.1	7	Pentanummium, off. [A].	»	II.54
242 (866)	13	0.9		Pentanummium, off. [A]. *Corr.*	»	II.12
243 (4290)	16	1.2		Pentanummium. *Corr.*	Cf . MIB II, 45	
PLATE 15						
				TIBERIUS II, 578 - 582		
244 (325)	36	12.3	7	Follis, year Ч. Constantinople, off. E, 578/579.	MIB II, 25	I.99
245 (226)	27	11.2	7	Follis, year Ϛ. Constantinople, off. E, 579/580.	»	
246 (805)	28	9.5	6	Follis, year ϚII. Constantinople, off. [E], 581/582.	»	I.70
247 (157)	29	10.4	7	Triacontanummium. Nicomedia, off. A.	MIB II, 36	
248 (294)	24	4.3	6	Quarter follis. Nicomedia.	MIB II, 39	I/II
249 (154)	32	12.6	5	Follis, year ϚI. Antioch, 580/581.	MIB II, 47	
250 (220)	19	2.2	6	Quarter follis.	MIB II, 31	
251 (856)	20	3.3	6	Quarter follis.	»	I.102
252 (160)	18	1.4	1	Pentanummium.	Cf. MIB II, 33A	
253 (3917)	17	2.2	7	Pentanummium.	Cf. MIB II, 33	
254 (3918)	16	1.5	1	Pentanummium.	»	I.57
PLATE 16						
				MAURICE, 582 - 602		
255 (3391)	31	9.7	0	Follis, year II. Constantinople, off. E, 583/584.	MIB II, 65-67	
256 (75)	30	9.5	1	Follis, year [X...] Constantinople, off. Γ, 582-584.	MIB II, 65B	I.87
257 (551)	33	11.8	7	Follis, year Ϛ. Constantinople, off. Γ, 587/588.	MIB II, 67D	I.101
258 (1134)	36	11.1	0	Follis, year Ϛ]II. Constantinople, off. B, 589/590.	MIB II, 67D	I.23
259 (5175)	31	11.8	6	Follis, year ϚII. Constantinople, off. B, 589/590.	»	II.14
260 (104)	31	12.5	1	Follis, year ϚII. Constantinople, 589/590.	»	
261 (3821)	32	9.9	7	Follis, year XI, 592/593. *Constantinople, but dress similar with Heraclius [Class 1] from Nicomedia.*	[MIB III, 174]	II.42
262 (710)	30	9.9	6	Follis, year XX. Constantinople, off. B, 601/602.	MIB II, 66	V.2
263 (552)	27	5.1	6	Follis, year XX. Constantinople, off. Γ, 601/602. *Corr.*	»	I.101
264 (76)	22	3.2	6	Half follis, year ϚIII. Constantinople, off. Δ, 590/591. *Corr.*	MIB II,[70]	I.87
265 (2247)	22	2.3	7	Half follis, year X... Constantinople, off. Γ, [595-601]. *Corr.*	MIB II, 71	
PLATE 17						
266 (860)	19	2.9	6	Quarter follis. Constantinople, off. B.	MIB II, 71	II.12
267 (855)	21	3.1	6	Quarter follis. Constantinople, off. Γ.	MIB I, 73D	I.102
268 (1136)	16	1.2	6	Quarter follis. Constantinople, off. Γ.	MIB II, 73	I.60
269 (1050)	21	2.6		Quarter follis. Constantinople, off. E. *Obv. corr.*	»	I.11
270 (1076)	17	3.4		Quarter follis. Constantinople, off. E. *Worn.*	»	I.22
271 (4293)	18	2.6	6	Quarter follis. Constantinople off. E.	»	
272 (4645)	18	2	7	Quarter follis. Constantinople, off. Δ. *Corr.*	MIB II, 73C/D	II.52
273 (402)	21	1.4	7	Pentanummium. Constantinople, off. B, 582-602	MIB II, 74	II.54
274 (3913)	16	1.7	7	Pentanummium. Constantinople, off. +, DNTI...RIC.	»	I.104
275 (3865)	30	12.4	6	Follis, year III. Nicomedia, off. A, 584/585.	MIB II, 75A	I.35
276 (2142)	31	11.4	7	Follis, year X. Nicomedia, off. B, 591/592.	MIB II, 75/76	
277 (527)	18	2.1	7	Quarter follis, Nicomedia, 582-602. И *in the exergue.*	Cf. MIB II, 82	I.78
278 (3740)	31	12	6	Follis, year IIII. Cyzicus, off. A, 585/586.	MIB II, 84-85	II.14

279 (3870)	30	11.2	0	Follis, year IIII. Cyzicus, off. A, 585/586.	MIB II, 84-85	I.92
280 (709)	31	12.6	1	Follis, year ϚII. Cyzicus, off. A, 589/590.	MIB II, 85	V.2
281 (47)	36	13.4	6	Follis, year XX. Cyzicus, off. B, 601/602. *Pierced rim.*	MIB II, 86D	

PLATE 18

282 (675)	30	10.9	6	Follis, year Ϛ. Antioch, 586-588.	MIB II, 95	V.13
283 (2161)	34	12.8	6	Half follis, year Ч. Antioch, [586/587].	»	
284 (3864)	29	12.4	6	Follis, year ЧIII. Antioch, off. Γ, 589/590.	MIB II, 96C	I.14
285 (4201)	30	9.7	6	Follis, year ЧIII. Antioch, off. Γ, 589/590.	MIB II, 96	
286 (320)	28	11.5	0	Follis, year XЧ. Antioch, off. Γ, 596/597.	MIB II, 96C	I.99
287 (326)	22	3.8	6	Half follis, year [Ч]. Antioch, [586/587]. *Corr.*	MIB II, 97	I.99
288 (10171)	22	5.1	6	Half follis, year XX. Antioch, 601/602.	MIB II, 99A	IV.10
289 (3828)	22	4.7	6	Half follis, year XIII. Antioch, 594/595.	MIB II, 99	II.42
290 (3948)	19	2.8	6	Quarter follis, year [XЧIIII]. Antioch, 600/601.	MIB II, 102	I.105
291 (843)	23	6.7		Half follis, year I. Thessalonica (TES), 582/583.	MIB II, 110	I.102
292 (5275)	23	5.1	6	Half follis, year XX. Thessalonica (TES), 601/602.	MIB II, 110-113	II.41
293 (118)	32	12.3	6	Follis, year XX. Thessalonica, off. B, 601/602; but in the exergue is read ...+A. *Struck on follis of Justin II.*	MIB II, 109	
294 (5234)	21	4.1	7	Half follis, year III. off. B, 584/585.	Cf. MIB II, 69	II.20
295 (537)	13	5.5	7	Half follis, year [ЧI], off. A, [587/588]. *Corr.*	»	I/II
296 (158)	25	6	6	Half follis, year Ϛ, off. A, 587/588. *Corr.*	»	
297 (4091)	24	5.6	6	Half follis, year [Ч]III, 582-601. *Worn.*	»	II.65
298 (3894)	22	4.8	0	Half follis, year XX, 601/602. *Corr.*	»	I.82
299 (5236)	22	2.6	6	Half follis. *Corr.*	»	II.20

PLATE 19

				PHOCAS, 602 - 610		
300 (15)	18	1.5	7	AV Tremissis, 602-610.	MIB II, 26/27	I/II
301 (4058)	17	1.4	6	AV Tremissis, 602-610.	»	I/II
302 (165)	31	12.4	7	Follis, year II. Constantinople, off. B, 603. *Struck on coin of Nicomedia.*	MIB II, 60	I/II
303 (4243)	31	10.9	11	Follis, year Ϛ. Constantinople, off. A, 603-610. *Struck on coin of year X.*	»	
304 (841)	23	6	7	Half follis. Constantinople, off. B, 603-610.	MIB II, 65b	I.102
305 (3735)	24	4.8	7	Half follis. Constantinople, 603-610. *Overstruck by unidentified die.*	MIB II, 65a	II.14
306 (3888)	24	5.6	[6]	Half follis. Constantinople, off. [Γ], 602-610. *Worn.*	MIB II, 65	I.57
307 (1843)	28	5.1	6	Half follis. Constantinople, 602-610. *Worn, obv. ill.*	»	IV.2
308 (4863)	23	4	5	Half follis, 602-610. *On the exergue [COZ]; worn.*	»	
309 (143)	33	10.1	7	Follis, year Ч. Nicomedia, off. A, 606/607.	MIB II, 64a/65a	
310 (4022)	26	5.4	1	Half follis, year Ч. Nicomedia, off. B, 606/607.	MIB II, 73	I.35

PLATE 20

311 (268)	32	12.5	6	Follis, year I. Cyzicus, off. B, 602/603.	MIB II, 75	
312 (3886)	24	5.8	6	Half follis. Cyzicus, off. A, 603-610.	MIB II, 78	
313 (70)	26	5.3	6	Half follis. Cyzicus, off. B, 607-610. *Overstruck on older coin.*	MIB II, 80a	V.2
314 (3596)	17	1.4	6	Quarter follis. Nicomedia or Cyzicus, 602-610.	MIB II, 74/81	II.58
315 (3438)	28	9.1	6	Follis, year II. Antioch, 603/604.	MIB II, 83b	II.58
316 (147)	29	9	0	Follis, year Ч. Antioch, 606/607.	MIB II, 83a	
317 (1078)	24	5.6	0	Half follis, έτους Ч. Antioch, 606/607.	MIB II, 85	I.21
318 (3448)	16	1.8	6	Quarter follis, year III. Antioch, 604/605.	MIB II, 87	II.58
319 (4274)	18	2.6	5	Quarter follis, year I. Antioch, 602-610.	MIB II, 87	I.35
320 (977)	13	1.3		Dodecanummium, 602-610.	MIB II, 90[5]	II.29
321 (114)	24	2.9	0	Follis. [Antioch], 602-603. *Corr.*	MIB II, 83/60	
322 (3887)	24	5	7	Half follis, year III. [Nicomedia], 603-610. *Worn.*	MIB II, 73	I.94
323 (3876)	18	2.6	0	Quarter follis, 602-610.	Cf. MIB II, 66	I.84

324 (4083)	19	3.4	7	Quarter follis, 602-610. *Corr.*	Cf. MIB II, 66	II.17
325 (3745)	14	1.3	6	Pentanummium, 602-610.	MIB II, 74/81	
326 (626)	14	1.6	6	Pentanummium, 602-610.	»	I.35

PLATE 21

				UNCERTAIN		
327 (315)	10	0.9	6	AR. Frontal bust / CN		I/II
328 (271)	31	14.9	1	Follis. Constantinople, 507-538.	Cf. MIB I, Anast. 23	
329 (679)	30	9.2	6	Follis. Constantinople, 498-536. *Corr.*	Cf. MIB I, Anast. 23	I.85
330 (77)	22	4.8	1	Follis, year ϚII[I]. *Fragment, worn.*		I.87
331 (5856)	24	7.3		Follis, 498-536. *Illegible, pierced rim.*		II.56
332 (4247)	24	7.7	6	Half follis of Justin I or Justinian I. Nicomedia, off. B, 518-538.	Cf. MIB I, Justin 61	
333 (249)	23	7.7	7	Half follis of Justin I or Justinian I, 518-538.	Cf. MIB I, Justin 61	
334 (908)	22	5.3		Half follis of Justin II or Maurice, year II. Thessalonica (TES), 566-584.	MIB II, 68/112B	I.45
335 (3900)	20	4.9	6	Half follis of Justin II, Tiberius II or Maurice. Thessalonica, 568-684. *Corr., scratched.*	Cf. MIB II, Justin 70	I.68
336 (716)	25	8.9	6	Half follis, 507-532.	Cf. MIB I, Anast. 32	V.25
337 (4095)	23	3.1		Half follis. [Nicomedia], 2nd half of 6th c. *Corr.*		II.65
338 (285)	21	2		Half follis. *Corr.*		I.71
339 (3626)	21	2.2		Quarter follis of Tiberius II or Phocas, 578-610. *Corr. Obv. ill.*	Cf. MIB II, Tib. 31	II.58
340 (4115)	19	3.4	2	Quarter follis, [off. Δ]. *Worn.*		I/II
341 (4571)	20	4.5	6	Quarter follis of Tiberius II or Phocas, 578-610.	Cf. MIB II, Tib. 31	II.29
342 (4588)	17	2.7	6	Quarter follis [Constantinople]. *Worn.*		II.28

PLATE 22

343 (5320)	16	2	7	Pentanummium of Anastasius I, Justinian I or Maurice. Constantinople, off. Δ.	Cf. MIB I, Anast. 37	II.22
344 (4291)	13	2	6	Pentanummium of Anastasius I, Justin I or Maurice, 517-602.	Cf. MIB I, Anast. 54	
345 (310)	12	1.7	7	Pentanummium of Anastasius I, Justin I or Justinian I, 512-552.	Cf. MIB I, Anast. 37	I.75
346 (317)	14	1.8	6	Pentanummium, 512-565.	Cf. MIB I, Anast. 37 ff.]	I/II
347 (829)	12	1.7	[1]	Pentanummium, off. A, 512-602.	MIB I, Anast. 37	I.102
348 (4020)	17	1.5		Pentanummium, off. B. *Corr.*	Cf. MIB I, Justin 25	I.35
349 (653)	11	1.6	6	Pentanummium, off. [Γ], 512-552.	Cf. MIB I, Anast. 37	I.35
350 (1104)	12	2	6	Pentanummium, off. Γ, 512-602.	»	
351 (4500)	16	1.3		Pentanummium, off. B or Δ, 512-602. *Corr.*	Cf. MIB I, Anast. 37	
352 (677)	12	1.6	0	Pentanummium of Anastasius I or Justin I. Constantinople, off. A, 517-522.	Cf. MIB I, Anast. 39	I.35
353 (682)	15	1.9	6	Pentanummium of Anastasius I or Justin I. Constantinople, off. Γ, 517-522.	Cf. MIB I, Anast. 39	I.65
354 (630)	14	1.9	6	Pentanummium of Anastasius I or Justin I. Constantinople, off. Δ, 517-522.	»	I.35
355 (1090)	12	2	6	Pentanummium of Anastasius I or Justin I. Constantinople, off. Δ, 512-522.	»	II.60
356 (1036)	11	0.5	1	Pentanummium. Off. A, the letter sidewise.		I.67
357 (4501)	15	0.7	6	Pentanummium, 6th c. *Corr.*		
358 (2164)	12	2.3	6	Pentanummium of Anastasius I or Justin I, off. B, 512-522.	Cf. MIB I, Anast. 37	
359 (857)	17	1.4	6	Pentanummium		I.102
360 (858)	11	1.5	[6]	Pentanummium. *Corr.*		I.102
361 (516)	10	0.7		Minimus.		II.50
362 (536)	13	1.3		? Pentanummium. *Corr.*		I.35
363 (593)	14	0.5	6	Pentanummium. Constantinople, off. Δ.		II.18

364 (4052)	13	0.9	0	Pentanummium of Anastasius I or Justin I. Constantinople, off. Δ, 512-522.	Cf. MIB I, Anast. 37	IV.10
365 (834)	11	1.7		Pentanummium. Nicomedia, off. A. *Obv. ill.*		I.102
366 (835)	12	2.5	7	Pentanummium [Anastasius I], off. B		I.102
367 (836)	11	1.7	0	Pentanummium, off. Γ.		I.102
368 (1797)	16	0.9		Pentanummium [Justin II]. *Corr.*		I.38
369 (3959)	18	1.9		Pentanummium, 2nd half of 6th c. *Illegible, bent.*		IV.9
370 (4028)	13	2.7	0	Dodecanummium, 522-578.	Cf. MIB I, Justin 68	II.49
371 (816)	15	3.6	0	Dodecanummium. *Obv. ill.*		I.102
372 (324)	14	1.8	11	Dodecanummium of Maurice or Phocas, 582-610. *Profile bust.*	Cf. MIB II, Maur. 106	I.99
373 (988)	14	2	11	»	»	II. 9
374 (990)	12	1.9	6	Dodecanummium of Maurice or Phocas, 582-610. *Profile bust.*	Cf. MIB II, Maur. 106	II.29
375 (631)	14	1.8		Dodecanummium. *Obv. ill.*		I.35
376 (685)	12	2.1		Dodecanummium. *Corr.*		I/II

PLATE 23

				HERACLIUS, 610 - 642		
377 (32)	20	4.3	6	AV Solidus, 616-622.	MIB III, 14	I/II
378 (2389)	20	4.4	6	AV Solidus, off. I, 616-622.	MIB III, 11	II.[25]
379 (3872)	29	11	7	Follis, year II. Constantinople, off. A [Class 1], 611/612. *Corr.*	MIB III, 158	II.8
380 (892)	33	4.4	6	Follis, year II. Constantinople, off. E [Class 1], 611-613.	»	II.3
381 (898)	28	10.6		Follis, year II. Constantinople, off. E [Class 1], 611/612.	»	II.3
382 (243)	30	9.4	1	Follis, year III. Constantinople, off. A [Class 1], 612/613.	»	
383 (4573)	31	13	1	Follis, year III. Constantinople, off. Γ [Class 1], 612/613. *Overstruck on coin of Justin II, year X...*	»	II.29
384 (240)	31	11.3	7	Follis, year III. Constantinople, off. Δ [Class 1], 612/613. *Overstruck on coin of Phocas, year Ч[I].*	»	
385 (850)	32	6.8	7	Follis, year III. Constantinople, off. Δ. [Class 1], 612/613.	»	I.102
386 (3871)	30	10.8	1	Follis, year III. Constantinople, off. Δ [Class 1], 612/613. *Overstrike.*	»	I.72
387 (886)	32	14.3	7	Follis, year III. Constantinople, off. [Δ]. [Class 1], 612/613.	»	I.9
388 (4408)	30	11.2	5	Follis, year III. Constantinople, off. E. [Class 1], 612/613.	»	IV.4
389 (1160)	33	11.7		Follis. Constantinople, off. B [Class 1].	»	I.12

PLATE 24

390 (3869)	32	10.4	[7]	Follis. Constantinople, off. Γ [Class 1], 612/613. *Second overstrike.*	»	I.98
391 (3823)	34	12.7	6	Follis. Constantinople, off. Δ [Class 1], 612/613. *Overstruck on coin of Maurice, year XX, Nicomedia, off. A.*	»	II.42
392 (4123)	32	10.6	5	Follis. Constantinople, off. Δ [Class 1], 612/613. *Overstruck on coin of Phocas, year IIII, Constantinople.*	»	I.35
393 (2141)	32			Follis. Constantinople off. E [Class 1], 612/613.	»	
394 (550)	33	11.7	1	Follis, year [II]. Constantinople, off. Γ [Class 2], 611-613. *Overstruck on coin of [Phocas], year [Ч], Constantinople.*	MIB III, 159b	I.2
395 (365)	35	12.1	1	Follis, year II. Constantinople, off. A. [Class 2], 611/612. *Overstrike.*	»	I.32
396 (222)	29	9.8	1	Follis, year III. Constantinople, off. A [Class 2], 612/613. *Overstrike.*	»	
397 (113)	34	10.5	1	Follis, year III. [Constantinople off. A, Class 2], 612/613. *Overstruck on coin of Phocas; and that on older coin of year Ϛ.*	MIB III, [160b]	V.9
398 (917)	34	11.8	6	Follis, year III. Constantinople, off. [A] [Class 2], 612/613. *Overstruck on coin of Phocas.*	MIB III, 160	I.58
399 (370)	28	9.05	1	Follis, year III. Constantinople, off. B [Class 2], 612/613.	MIB III, 159/ 160	II.26

400 (848)	31	10	0	Follis, year III. Constantinople, off. B [Class 2], 612/613. *Overstruck on coin from Antioch.*	MIB III, 160b	I.102
401 (1069)	32	10.3	6	Follis, year III. Constantinople, off. B [Class 2], 612/613. *Overstruck on coin of Phocas from Constantinople.*	MIB III, 160	I.13
PLATE 25						
402 (4295)	30	11	8	Follis, year III. Constantinople, off. B [Class 2], 612/613. *Overstrike.*	MIB III, 159	
403 (89)	30	11.3	6	Follis, [year III]. Constantinople, off. B [Class 2], 612/613. *Overstrike.*	MIB III, 160[b]	I/II
404 (812)	30	11.7	1	Follis, year [III]. Constantinople, off. B [Class 2], 612/613. *Overstruck on coin of Justin II, year ϚIIII.*		I.102
405 (4242)	32	11.3	6	Follis, year III. Constantinople, off. [B] [Class 2], 612/613. *Corr.*	MIB III, 160	I/II
406 (7)	33	11.3	7	Follis, year III. Constantinople, off. Γ [Class 2], 612/613. *Overstruck on coin of Phocas from Constantinople; and that on older coin of year ЧI.*	MIB III, 160b	I/II
407 (54)	30	10.6	8	Follis, year III. Constantinople, off. Γ, [Class 2], 612/613.	MIB III, 159a	I/II
408 (74)	30	10.9	1	Follis, year III. Constantinople, off. Γ [Class 2], 612/613.	MIB III, 160b	
409 (152)	35	10	7	Follis, year III. Constantinople, off. Γ [Class 2], 612/613.	»	
410 (1077)	31	12.3	1	Follis, year III. Constantinople, off. Γ [Class 2], 612/613. *Overstruck on coin of Justin II, year ϚI.*	MIB III, 159/160b	I.21
411 (919)	34	11.9	6	Follis, year [III]. Constantinople, off. Γ [Class 2], 612-615. *Overstruck on coin of Phocas.*	MIB III, 160	I.59
412 (1048)	30	9.7	6	Follis, year II[I]. Constantinople, off. Δ [Class 2], 613-616. *Worn, overstruck on coin of [Phocas] from Constantinople.*	MIB III, 159/ 160b	I.11
413 (244)	32	12.8	1	Follis, year III. Constantinople, off. E [Class 2], 612/613. *Overstruck on older coin of year XI.*	MIB III, 160	
414 (838)	33	9.9		Follis, year III. Constantinople, off. E [Class 2], 612/613. *Overstrike.*	MIB III, 160b	I.102
415 (4294)	28	9.7	1	Follis, year III. Constantinople, off. E [Class 2], 612/613. *Overstruck on coin of Phocas, year ϚIII.*	MIB III, 160	
416 (1839)	30	8.7	1	Follis, year III. Constantinople, off. E [Class 2], 612/613. *Overstruck on coin of Phocas. Worn.*	MIB III, 159/ 160b	IV.2
PLATE 26						
417 (5264)	33	10.6	7	Follis, year III. Constantinople [Class 2], 612/613. *Overstruck on coin of Phocas. Corr.*	MIB III, 159	II.41
418 (1109)	31	9.7	1	Follis, year IIII. Constantinople, off. Γ [Class 2], 613/614. *Overstrike.*	MIB III, 160a	
419 (2150)	34	8.7	7	Follis, year IIII. Constantinople, off. Γ [Class 2], 613/614.	»	
420 (3874)	33	11.6	6	Follis, year IIII [Class 2]. Constantinople, off. Γ, 613/614. *Overstruck on coin of Phocas, year [II], Nicomedia.*	MIB III, 160	I.54
421 (341)	30	9.54	0	Follis, year IIII. Constantinople, off. Δ [Class 2], 613/614. *Overstruck, probably on coin of Phocas [type with m].*	MIB III, 159/160	I.99
422 (828)	32	12.6	7	Follis, year IIII. Constantinople, off. Δ [Class 2], 613/614. *Overstruck, probably on coin of Phocas.*	MIB III, 160	I.102
423 (1053)	33	10.8	7	Follis, year IIII. Constantinople, off. Δ [Class 2], 613/614. *Overstruck, probably on coin of Maurice, from Nicomedia.*	»	II.50
424 (163)	31	11.1	4	Follis, year IIII. Constantinople [Class 2], 613/614. *Overstruck on coin of Phocas, [Cyzicus, off. A.]*	MIB III, 159/160	
425 (5858)	28	10.4	1	Follis, year IIII. Constantinople [Class 2], 613/614. *Overstruck on coin of Phocas from Antioch.*	MIB III, 160	II.56
426 (853)	31	12.4	1	Follis, year Ч. Constantinople, off. Δ [Class 2], 614/615. *Overstruck on coin of Justin II from Nicomedia, off. B.*	MIB III, 159/160b	I.102
427 (3878)	31	11.6	0	Follis, year Ч. Constantinople, off. Δ [Class 2], 614/615. *Overstruck on coin of Maurice from Constantinople, off. Δ.*	MIB III, 160	
428 (3877)	34	10	0	Follis, year Ч. Constantinople, off. Δ [Class 2], 614/615. *Overstruck on coin of Phocas from Constantinople, off. Δ.*	»	

429 (4559)	33	11.9	8	Follis, year Ч. Constantinople, off. Δ [Class 2], 614/615. *Overstruck on coin of Phocas from Nicomedia.*	MIB III, 160b	I.24

PLATE 27

430 (255)	34	10.6	7	Follis, year [Ϛ]. Constantinople, off. Γ [Class 2], 615/616. *Overstruck on coin of Maurice, year XX.*	MIB III, 159	
431 (4248)	30	8.7	1	Follis, year [Ϛ]. Constantinople, off. Γ [Class 2], 615/616. *Overstruck on coin of Phocas.*	»	
432 (3951)	34	10.7	1	Follis, year Ϛ. Constantinople, off. Δ [Class 2], 615/616. *Overstruck on coin of Phocas, year IIII, Constantinople. Corr.*	MIB III, 160	I.98
433 (3883)	29	8	7	Follis, year Ϛ. Constantinople, off. E [Class 2], 615/616. *Overstruck on coin of Phocas.*	»	I.72
434 (4507)	30	11.5	2	Follis, year Ϛ. Constantinople. [Class 2], 615/616. *Overstruck on coin of Justin II.*	MIB III, 160	V.11
435 (796)	34	12.5	7	Follis, year Ϛ. Constantinople, off. [A] [Class 2], 615/616. *Overstruck on coin of Phocas, year Ϛ, Nicomedia.*	MIB III, 159	I.18
436 (1009)	32	9.7	7	Follis, year Ϛ [Class 2], 615/616. *Overstruck on coin of Phocas, year [Ч], Constantinople; and that on older coin.*	MIB III, 160	II.29
437 (3751)	29	11.5	7	Follis, year Ϛ. Constantinople, off. E [Class 2], 615/616. *Overstruck on coin of Justin II, year Ч. Corr.*	»	II.42
438 (837)	33	11.6	6	Follis. Constantinople, off. A [Class 2], 613-615. *Overstruck on coin of Phocas from Nicomedia, off. B.*	MIB III, 160a	I.102
439 (3382)	32	6.7	6	Follis. Constantinople, off. A [Class 2], 613-615. *Overstrike; corr.*	MIB III, 160b	I/II
440 (3826)	30	10.8	1	Follis. Constantinople, off. A [Class 2], 613-615. *Overstruck on coin of Phokas from Constantinople; and that on coin from Nicomedia.*	MIB III, 160	II.42
441 (6028)	31	13.6	7	Follis. Constantinople, off. [A or Δ] [Class 2], 613-615. *Overstruck on older coin dated c. 507-532. Corr.*	MIB III, 159	II.24

PLATE 28

442 (802)	32	10.6	7	Follis. Constantinople, off. B [Class 2], 613-615. *Overstruck on coin of Justin II from Constantinople, year Ч.*	MIB III, 159/160a	I.38
443 (3824)	31	10.7	6	Follis. Constantinople, off. B [Class 2], 613-615. *Overstruck on coin of Phocas, year Ч. Worn.*	MIB III, 159/160	II.42
444 (918)	35	10.8	7	Follis, year [...I]I. Constantinople, off. Δ [Class 2], 613-615. *Overstruck on coin of Phocas from Constantinople.*	»	I.59
445 (2149)	34	11.2	7	Follis. Constantinople, off. A [Class 2], 613-615.		
446 (590)	30	9.1	7	Follis. Constantinople, off. Δ [Class 2], 613-615.		II.18
447 (925)	32	9.1	6	Follis. Constantinople, off. Δ [Class 2], 613-615. *Overstrike; corr.*	MIB III, 159/160	II.42
448 (4546)	32	10.3	7	Follis. Constantinople, off. Δ [Class 2], 613-615. *Overstruck on coin of Phocas, year IIII, Nicomedia mint.*	MIB III, 160b	II.42
449 (1085)	29	10.5	7	Follis. Constantinople, off. E [Class 2], 613-615. *Overstrike.*	MIB III, 160a	I.90
450 (60)	32	10.2	7	Follis. Off. [E] [Class 2], 613-615. *Overstruck on coin of Phocas.*	»	V.25
451 (190)	32	10.8	6	Follis. Constantinople [Class 2], 613-615. *Overstrike.*	»	
452 (219)	28	9.9	7	Follis [Class 2], 613-615. *Overstruck on coin of Phocas. Shifted die.*	MIB III, 159-61	
453 (1152)	31	11.4	1	Follis [Class 2]. Constantinople, 613-615. *Overstruck on coin of Maurice from Antioch, off. Γ.*	MIB III, 159/160b	I.73
454 (2117)	33	10	6	Follis [Class 2]. Constantinople, 613-615. *Overstruck on coin of Phocas.*	»	I.93
455 (3873)	33	11.4	1	Follis [Class 2], 613-615. *Overstruck on coin of Phocas, year Ч, Nicomedia mint.*	MIB III, 160	I.14
456 (3875)	33	10.2	1	Follis. Constantinople [Class 2], 613-615. *Overstruck on coin of Phocas from Nicomedia.*	»	I.84

PLATE 29

457 (810)	34	10.6	6	Follis, year Ч. Constantinople [Class 3], 614/615.	MIB III, 161	I.28

458 (4861)	26	6.9	1	Follis, year ЧI[. Constantinople [Class 3], 615/616.	MIB III, 161	
459 (3885)	32	11	7	Follis, year Ϛ. Constantinople, off. A [Class 3], 615/616. *Overstruck on coin of Phocas.*	»	I.98
460 (260)	29	6.1	1	Follis, year ϚI. Constantinople, off. A [Class 3], 616/617.	»	[V.2]
461 (930)	28	8.9	1	Follis, year [Ч]III[I]. Constantinople, off. Γ [Class 3], 617-619.	»	II.42
462 (985)	30	9.2	7	Follis, year X. Constantinople, off. A [Class 3], 619/620. *Corr.*	»	II.29
463 (1047)	27	7.3		Follis, year X. Off. A [Class 3], 619/620. *Obv. ill.*	»	II.15
464 (335)	25	7.3	1	Follis, year X. Constantinople, off. E [Class 3], 619/620.	»	I.64
465 (899)	27	7.4	1	Follis, year X[Ч]. Constantinople, off. Γ [Class 3], [624].	»	II.3
466 (5273)	29	7.5	1	Follis. Constantinople [Class 3], 615-624. *Overstrike; corr.*	»	II.16
467 (3884)	31	9.8	7	Follis. Constantinople, off. E [Class 3], 615-624. *Overstruck on coin of Antioch, year Ч.*	»	I.72
PLATE 30						
468 (545)	25	3.9	1	Follis. Constantinople [Class 3/4], 615-629.	MIB III, 161-3	I.55
469 (869)	24	6.6	1	Follis, year XЧ. Constantinople, off. E [Class 4], 624/625.	MIB III, 162	II.12
470 (148)	25	6.1	7	Follis, year XϚ. Constantinople, off. Γ [Class 4], 625/626.	»	
471 (4410)	26	5.7	1	»	»	IV.4
472 (1161)	28	7.5	1	»	»	I.82
473 (868)	26	5.4	7	Follis. Constantinople, off. A [Class 4], 624-629.	»	II.12
474 (5798)	25	5.1	8	Follis. Constantinople, off. Δ [Class 4], 624-629.	»	
475 (4120)	31	9.4	8	Follis, year XX. Constantinople, off. A [Class 5], 629/630.	MIB III, 164b	IV.4
476 (4406)	29	12	6	Follis, year XX. Constantinople, off. A [Class 5], 629/630. *Overstrike or shifted die.*	»	IV.4
477 (867)	34	11.7	6	Follis, year XX Constantinople, off. A [Class 5], 629/630.	MIB III, 164b	II.12
478 (309)	30	3.5	1	Follis, year XX. Constantinople, off. B [Class 5], 629/630. *Corr.*	MIB III, 164	I.75
479 (3822)	36	9.4	7	Follis, year XX. Constantinople, off. B [Class 5], 629/630. *Overstrike; corr.*	»	II.42
480 (4404)	31	10.6	7	Follis, year XX. Constantinople, off. B [Class 5], 629/630.	»	IV.4
PLATE 31						
481 (5204)	33	8.6	7	Follis, year XX. Constantinople, off. B [Class 5], 629/630.	»	V.5
482 (3967)	34	10.1	1	Follis, year XX. Constantinople, off. Δ [Class 5], 629/630. *Overstruck on coin of year* IIII. *Corr.*	»	V.2
483 (4087)	32	10.6	7	Follis, year XX. Constantinople, off. [Δ] [Class 5], 629/630. *Overstruck on coin of year* IIII. *Corr.*	»	II.65
484 (233)	35	9.7	7	Follis, year XX. Constantinople, off. [E] [Class 5], 629/630.	»	
485 (4403)	32	9.9	5	Follis. Constantinople [Class 5], 629-639. *Overstrike.*	»	IV.4
486 (105)	31	8.4	6	Follis, year [X]XI. Constantinople, off. A [Class 5], 630/631. *Overstruck on coin of Heraclius, year* III.	MIB III, 164[b]	
487 (4173)	29	10.9	6	Follis. Constantinople, off. A [Class 5], 629-639. *Overstruck on older coin (*M*); and that on another (*...X...*)*	MIB III, 164	II
488 (2154)	32	8.7	1	Follis. Constantinople, off. A [Class 5], 629-639.	MIB III, 164b	
489 (4090)	28	7.8	6	Follis, year XXII. Constantinople, off. A [Class 5], 631/632.	MIB III, 164[a]	II.65
490 (276)	31	7.3	6	Follis, year [ ]XII. Constantinople, off. B [Class 5], 631/632. *Overstrike.*	MIB III, 164b	
491 (4119)	28	8.3	6	Follis, year XX[I. Constantinople, off. Δ [Class 5], [630/631]. *Corr.*	MIB III, 164a	IV.4
492 (546)	30	5.3	7	Follis, year XXIII. Constantinople, off. A [Class 5], 632/633. *Overstruck on older coin [from Constantinople, year* X*].*	MIB III, 164b	I.55
493 (953)	24	4.9	7	Follis, year XXIII. Constantinople, off. A [Class 5], 632/633.	»	I.44
494 (1126)	26	6.4	6	Follis, year XXIII. Constantinople, off. A [Class 5], 632/633.	»	I.101
PLATE 32						
495 (3898)	27	7.3	0	Follis, year XXIII. Constantinople, off. A [Class 5], 632/633. *Star at l. of obv. field.*	MIB III, 164b	I.6

496 (4452)	25	5.7	1	Follis, year XXIII. Constantinople, off. A [Class 5], 632/633. *Worn.*	MIB III, 164b	I.36
497 (872)	25	5.4	6	Follis, year XXIII. Constantinople, off. B [Class 5], 632/633.	»	II.12
498 (3827)	27	6.2	6	Follis, year XXIII. Constantinople, off. B [Class 5], 632/633.	MIB III, 164b[2]	II.42
499 (933)	27	4.5	6	Follis, year [XXIII]. Constantinople, off. Γ [Class 5], 632/633. *Countermark.*	MIB III, [165]	II.42
500 (873)	26	5.8	6	Follis, year XXIII. Constantinople, off. Γ [Class 5], 632/633.	MIB III, 164b	II.12
501 (2171)	24	4	[0]	Follis, year XXIII. Constantinople, off. Δ [Class 5], 632/633. *Overstrike.*	MIB III, 164	I.14
502 (73)	24	4.5	0	Follis, year XXIII. Constantinople, off. Δ [Class 5], 632/633.	»	I.87
503 (1051)	27	4	7	Follis, year XXII[I]. Constantinople, off. Δ [Class 5], 632/633. *Overstrike.*	MIB III, 164b	II.50
504 (4510)	28	6.5	1	Follis, year XXIII. Constantinople [Class 5], 632/633. *Corr.*	MIB III, 164	V.12
505 (51)	22	4.5	1	Follis, year XXIII[I]. Constantinople, off. B [Class 5], 632-634.	MIB III, 164[b]	
506 (2116)	24	5.3	6	Follis, year XXIII[I]. Constantinople, off. B [Class 5], 632-634.	MIB III, 164c	I.76
507 (4447)	26	5.7	7	Follis, year XXIIII. Constantinople, off. B [Class 5], 633/634.	MIB III, 164c	II.46
508 (4412)	26	4.5	7	Follis, year XXIIII. Constantinople, off. Γ [Class 5], 633/634.	MIB III, 164b	IV.4
509 (1016)	26	6.5	6	Follis, year XXIII[I]. Constantinople, off. Δ [Class 5], 632-634.	MIB III, 164[c]	II.29
510 (5265)	25	5	6	Follis, year [ ]XIIII. Constantinople, off. Δ [Class 5], 633/634.	»	II.41

PLATE 33

511 (6039)	26	6.3	7	Follis, year XXI... Constantinople, off. A [Class 5], 630-639.	MIB III, 164a	II. 5
512 (4093)	26	7.2	7	Follis, year XXI... Constantinople, off. Γ [Class 5], 630-639.	»	II.65
513 (1019)	26	4.8		Follis, year [X]XI... Constantinople [Class 5], 630-639. *Corr.*	MIB III, 164	II.31
514 (1055)	24	5	0	Follis, year XX[I.... Constantinople, off. B [Class 5], 630-639. *Worn.*	MIB III, 164d	II.50
515 (717)	22	4.2	6	Follis, year XXЧ. Constantinople, off. A [Class 5], 634/635.	MIB III, 164	V.25
516 (4414)	27	5.5	7	Follis, year XXЧ. Constantinople, off. A [Class 5], 634/635. *Worn.*	MIB III, 164d	IV.4
517 (4273)	23	3.8	7	Follis, year XXЧ. Constantinople, off. A [Class 5], 634/635. *Worn.*	»	I.35
518 (4416)	24	3.9	7	Follis, year XXЧ. Constantinople, off. A [Class 5], 634/635. *Worn.*	MIB III, 164	IV.4
519 (6050)	23	6	7	Follis, year XXЧ. Constantinople, off. [A] [Class 5], 634/635. *Corr.*	MIB III, 164b	II.35
520 (3949)	27	5.4	1	Follis, year XXЧ. Constantinople, off. B [Class 5], 634/635.	MIB III, 164	II.39
521 (10170)	27	5.3	0	Follis, year XXЧ. Constantinople, off. B [Class 5], 634/635.	MIB III, 164d	IV.10
522 (10172)	27	5.3	1	Follis, year XXЧ. Constantinople, off. B [Class 5], 634/635.	MIB III, 164d	IV.10
523 (61)	24	5.1	1	Follis, year XXЧ. Constantinople, off. Γ [Class 5], 634/635.	MIB III, 164e	V.25
524 (291)	24	5	1	Follis, year XXЧ. Constantinople, off. Γ [Class 5], 634/635.	MIB III, 164[d]	V.16
525 (4118)	23	3.8	7	Follis, year XXЧ. Constantinople, off. Γ [Class 5], 634/635. *Worn.*	MIB III, 164b	IV.4
526 (332)	26		6	Follis, year XXЧ. Constantinople, off. Δ [Class 5], 634/635.	MIB III, 164e	I.20
527 (3835)	26	5.9	7	Follis, year X]X[Ч. Off. E [Class 5], 634/635.	MIB III, [173]	II.42

PLATE 34

528 (5369)	26	5.8	7	Follis, year [XXЧ...]. Constantinople, off. Γ [Class 5], 634-639. *Worn.*	MIB III, 164a	II.56
529 (4595)	24	5.8	6	Follis, year XXЧ... Constantinople, off. Δ [Class 5], 634-639. *Corr.*	MIB III, 164	II.33
530 (5262)	27	4.7	5	Follis, year XXϚ. Constantinople, off. [A] [Class 5], 635/636. *Corr.*	MIB III, 164e	II.41
531 (896)	25	6	7	Follis, year XXϚ. Constantinople, off. Γ [Class 5], 635/636.	MIB III, [165]	II.3

532 (3418)	26	3.8	6	Follis, year XXϚ. Constantinople, off. Δ [Class 5], 635/636.	MIB III, 164	II.33
533 (878)	27	5	5	»	MIB III, 164b	II.12
534 (4413)	25	6.6	5	Follis, year XXϚ. Constantinople, off. Δ [Class 5], 635/636. *Worn.*	MIB III, 164c	IV.4
535 (4417)	25	6	8	Follis, year XXϚ. Constantinople, off. E [Class 5], 635/636. *Overstruck on older coin, year* X.	MIB III, 164	IV.4
536 (5261)	27	5.2	7	Follis, year XXϚ. Constantinople, off. E [Class 5]. *Corr.*	»	II.41
537 (495)	26	6.3	6	Follis, year XX[Ϛ. Worn. Constantinople, off. E [Class 5], [635/636].	»	II.15
538 (703)	25	4.4		Follis, year X]X[Ϛ. [Constantinople], off. B [Class 5], [635/636]. *Corr.*	»	I.1
539 (333)	27	5.8	7	Follis, year XXX. Constantinople, off. A [Class 5], 639/640.	»	I.49
540 (4567)	26	4.8	1	Follis, year XX[X]. Constantinople, off. A [Class 5], [639/640]. *Overstrike.*	MIB III, 164b	II.29
541 (329)	27	7.2	6	Follis, year [X]XX. Constantinople, off. Δ [Class 5], 639-640.	MIB III, 164a	I.96
542 (876)	23	4	6	Follis, year XX... Constantinople, off. A [Class 5], 631-639.	MIB III, 164d	II.12
543 (2127)	28	4.4		Follis, year XX... Constantinople, off. A [Class 5], 629-639. *Worn.*	MIB III, 164b/c	

PLATE 35

544 (877)	27	5	7	Follis. Constantinople, off. A [Class 5], 631-639.	MIB III, 164d	II.12
545 (3420)	26	5.8	7	»	»	II.33
546 (3906)	21	5.3	5	Follis. Constantinople, off. A [Class 5], 631-639. *Corr.*	MIB III, 164[d]	I.58
547 (1070)	24	5.5	7	Follis. Constantinople, off. B [Class 5], 631-639.	MIB III, 164[d]	I.13
548 (3392)	27	6.4	6	Follis. Constantinople, off. B [Class 5], 631-639.	MIB III, 164d	
549 (4415)	25	4.7	1	Follis [year XX...] Off. Γ [Class 5], 631-639. *Worn.*	MIB III, 164[d]	IV.4
550 (964)	27	6.3	7	Follis. Constantinople, off. Γ [Class 5], 631-639.	MIB III, 164d	II.29
551 (3441)	26	5.8	7	Follis. Constantinople, off. Γ [Class 5], 631-639. *Countermark.*	MIB III, 164	II.58
552 (4088)	27	6.2	7	Follis. Constantinople, off. Γ [Class 5], 631-639. *Corr.*	MIB III, 164c	II.65
553 (4405)	28	6.9	5	Follis. Constantinople, off. Γ [Class 5], 631-639.	MIB III, 164	IV.4
554 (1145)	28	3.4		Follis. Constantinople, off. Γ, 631-639. *Corr., incomplete.*	»	I.89
555 (290)	25	5.7	7	Follis, year XX... Constantinople, off. Δ [Class 5], 631-639.	MIB III, 164	I.23
556 (4402)	31	9.8	7	Follis, year XX... Constantinople, off. Δ [Class 5], 629-631. *Overstruck on coin of Phocas.*	MIB III, 164b	IV.4
557 (4272)	27	5.6	7	Follis, year [XX...]. Constantinople, off. Δ, 631-639. *Overstrike.*	MIB III, 164	I.35
558 (1796)	24	5.4	7	Follis, year XX[... Constantinople, off. Δ [Class 5], 631-639. *Overstruck on coin of Phocas.*	»	I/II
559 (4084)	24	5.2	7	Follis. Constantinople, off. Δ [Class 5], 631-639. *Corr.*	MIB III, 164b	II.17
560 (4572)	26	5.9	7	Follis, year XX... Constantinople, off. E [Class 5], 631-639. *Bent; in two pieces.*	MIB III, 164	II.29

PLATE 36

561 (156)	27	5.8	7	Follis, year XX[. Constantinople, off. E [Class 5], 631-639. *Worn.*	MIB III, 164	
562 (390)	20	2.2	7	Follis, year [X]X[... Constantinople, off. E, 631-639.		I.54
563 (57)	27	6.1	6	Follis. Constantinople, off. E, [Class 5], 631-639.	MIB III, 164d	
564 (247)	23	5	7	Follis. Constantinople, off. E, [Class 5], 631-639.	»	
565 (875)	25	6.6	6	Follis. Constantinople, off. E [Class 5], 631-639.	MIB III, 164e	II.12
566 (889)	25	6.4	7	Follis. Constantinople, off. E [Class 5], 631-639.	MIB III, 164d	I.7
567 (629)	25	4.8	6	Follis. Constantinople, off. [E] [Class 5], 631-639.	MIB III, 164b	I.35
568 (890)	21	3.6	7	Follis. Constantinople, off. E [Class 5], 631-639. *Corr.*	MIB III, 164d	I.10
569 (330)	29	6.2	6	Follis. Constantinople [Class 5], 631-639. *Corr.*	MIB III, 164	I.96
570 (348)	32	8.5	7	Follis. Constantinople [Class 5], 629-639. *Corr.*		
571 (500)	23	5.1	[7]	Follis, year XXII... Constantinople [Class 5], 631-639. *Overstrike; corr.*		I.57

572 (467)	23	2.6	6	Follis. Constantinople [Class 5], 631-639. *Corr.*	MIB III, 164d	II.54
573 (651)	29	7.1	6	Follis. Constantinople [Class 5], 629-639. *Overstrike; worn.*	MIB III, 164a	I.35
574 (1006)	26	5.3	0	Follis. Constantinople [Class 5], 631-639. *Corr.*	MIB III, 164b	II.29
575 (3833)	26	4.7	6	Follis. Constantinople [Class 5], 631-639. *Corr.*	»	II.42
576 (4411)	27	4.7	7	Follis. Constantinople [Class 5], 631-639. *Worn.*	MIB III, 164	IV.4
577 (211)	20	6.5	0	Follis. Constantinople [Class 5], 631-639. *Corr.*	»	V.24
578 (4195)	21	3.8	1	Follis. Constantinople [Class 5], 631-639. *Corr.*	»	I.48
PLATE 37						
579 (5230)	24	4.8	5	Follis, year [X]XXΘ. Constantinople, off. B [Class 6], 639/640.	MIB III, 167	I.7
580 (4593)	23	5.1	7	Follis, year XXXΘ. Constantinople, off. A [Class 6], 639/640. *Overstruck on coin of Heraclius [Class 3/4]. Countermark.*	»	II.33
581 (4594)	22	3.9	7	Follis, year XXXΘ. Constantinople, off. A [Class 6], 639/640.	»	II.33
582 (657)	25	4.8	6	Follis, year XXXΘ. Constantinople, off. Γ [Class 6], 639/640.	»	
583 (3419)	25	2.2	6	Follis. Constantinople, off. [B] [Class 6], 639-641.	MIB III, 166/7	II.33
584 (5263)	24	3.7	6	Follis, year [XXX]. Constantinople, off. E [Class 6], 639/640.	»	II.41
585 (1002)	26	5.3	7	Follis, ...Θ. Off. E [Class 6], 639-641.	MIB III, 167	II.29
586 (874)	23	4	6	Follis, year XXXI. Constantinople off. A [Class 6], 640/641.	MIB III, 166	II.12
587 (871)	25	3.3	7	Follis, year XXX[I. Constantinople, off. B [Class 6], 640/641.	»	II.12
588 (3902)	25	6.4	5	Follis, year XXXIΘ. [Constantinople, off. [B] [Class 6], 640/641.	MIB III, 167	I. 98
589 (1099)	25	4.3	7	Follis, year XX... Constantinople, off. E [Class 6], 639-641.	MIB III, 166/7	I. 81
590 (870)	25	4.2	6	»	»	II. 12
591 (1223)	24	4.7	6	Follis. Constantinople, off. E [Class 6], 639-641.	»	II. 8
592 (3834)	24	3.4	6	Follis, year XX[X]. Constantinople [Class 6], 639-641.	»	II. 42
593 (2151)	28	...		Follis. Constantinople, off. A.		
594 (4407)	28	4.3		Follis, year ...X[II]... Constantinople, off. A, 639-641. *Corr.*	MIB III, 167	IV. 4
595 (665)	27	6.4	1	Follis. Constantinople [Class 2], 613-616. *Worn.*	MIB III, 160	V. 16
PLATE 38						
596 (2246)	25	5.3	7	Triacontanummium, year XX. Constantinople, off. B, 629/630.	MIB III, 168	
597 (204)	26	4	1	Triacontanummium, year XX. Constantinople, off. Δ, 629/630.	MIB III, 168a1	
598 (799)	23	4.6	1	Half follis, year [ϚIII]. Constantinople, off. Γ.	MIB III, 170	I.38
599 (37)	18	2.4	1	Half follis, year [X]. [Constantinople, off. A/Δ, 619/620].	MIB III, 170[a]	V.2
600 (927)	25	4.5	7	Half follis. Constantinople, off. E [Class 3], 615-629.	MIB III, 170	II.42
601 (4418)	23	3.6	1	Half follis, year XX. Constantinople, off. [B], 629/630.	MIB III, 171	IV.4
602 (3449)	27	5.9	2	Half follis, year XX. Constantinople, off. Γ, 629/630.	MIB III, 171a	II.58
603 (680)	24	4.2	6	Half follis, year XX. Constantinople, off. Γ, 629/630.	MIB III, 171e	III.4
604 (553)	18	1.7	0	Half follis, year XXII, Constantinople, off. B, 631/632.	»	I.101
605 (897)	22	3.7	7	Half follis, year XXII, Constantinople, off. [A/Δ], 631/632.	MIB III, 171a	II.3
606 (287)	20	2.7	7	Half follis, year XXIII. [Constantinople], 632/633.	MIB III, 171	I.20
607 (2147)	19	2.6	6	Half follis, year XXIII. Constantinople, off. B, 632/633.	»	
608 (882)	18	2.7	6	Half follis, year XX[X]. Constantinople, off. Δ, 639/640.	MIB III, 171	II.12
609 (1121)	18	1.1	6	Half follis, year XXX. Constantinople, off. Γ, 639/640.	MIB III, 171a	I/II
610 (133)	24	1.8	7	Half follis. [Constantinople, off. A/Δ], 615-639. *Worn.*	MIB III, 170/1	V.2
611 (6029)	18	1.2	8	Half follis, year [XX...] Constantinople [Class 5], 629-639. *Corr.*	MIB III, 171	II.24
612 (697)	21	3.2	7	Half follis, year XX... Constantinople, 629-639.	»	I.35
613 (3812)	21	3.5	8	Half follis, year X..., 629-639 *Corr.*	»	II.42

614 (3897)	26	3.9	7	Half follis. Constantinople, off. A [Class 5], 629-639.	MIB III, 171	II.39
615 (928)	24	3.7	7	Half follis. Constantinople, off. Δ [Class 5], 629-639. *Countermark (c. 633).*	»	II.42
PLATE 39						
616 (3899)	4.6	3.3	6	Half follis. Constantinople, year X... Constantinople, off. Δ [Class 5], 629-639. *Overstruck on older coin, year. [X]III...*	»	I.40
617 (5250)	23	2.1	6	Half follis, year XX... Constantinople, off. A, 629-41. *Worn, thin flan.*	MIB III, 171a	II.42
618 (3455)	18	3.3	7	Half follis, year XX... Constantinople, 629-639. *Ill. countermark.*	MIB III, 170	II.58
619 (931)	23	2.4	6	Half follis. Constantinople. *Broken.*		II.42
620 (883)	20	1.8	8	Quarter follis. Constantinople, off. A, 610-629. *Corr.*	MIB III, 172	II.12
621 (3518)	17	2.6	6	Half follis. Constantinople, 629-639. *Partly ill.*	MIB III, 170/1	II.58
622 (3825)	28	11.1	8	Follis, year I. Nicomedia, off. A [Class 1], 610/611. *Overstrike.*	MIB III, 174	II.42
623 (3866)	33	11	8	»	»	I.67
624 (4445)	30	11.4	7	»	»	
625 (10)	32	11.5	7	Follis, year II. Nicomedia, off. A [Class 1], 611/612.	»	V.2
626 (797)	31	10.6	7	Follis, year III. Nicomedia, off. B [Class 1], 612/613. *Overstruck on coin of Maurice, year ϚI.*	»	I.38
627 (4073)	30	11.3	6	Follis, year III. Nicomedia, off. A [Class 2], 612/613.	»	II.32
628 (10175)	34	11.5	7	Follis, year III. Nicomedia, off. A [Class 2], 612/613. *Overstruck on coin of Tiberius II, year ЧI (579/80), Constantinople mint.*	MIB III, 175/ MIB II, 25	IV.10
629 (221)	31	11	6	Follis, year III. Nicomedia, off. B [Class 2], 612/613.	MIB III, 175	
630 (4505)	33	11.1	7	Follis, year III. Nicomedia, off. B [Class 2]. 612/613. *Overstruck on coin of Phocas. Shifted die.*	»	
631 (239)	31	10.7	7	Follis, year IIII. Nicomedia, off. A, [Class 2], 613/614. *Overstruck on coin of Constantinople.*	»	
PLATE 40						
632 (644)	29	10.2	6	Follis, year IIII. Nicomedia, off. A [Class 2], 613/614.	MIB III, 175a	V.19
633 (4535)	28	10.2	7	»	MIB III, 175	I
634 (4542)	31	8.8	6	Follis, year [IIII]. Nicomedia, off. A [Class 2], 613/614. *Worn.*	»	II.36
635 (161)	35	10.3	6	Follis, year IIII. Nicomedia, off. B, [Class 2], 613/614. *Overstruck on coin of Phocas; and that on coin of Maurice.*	MIB III, 175a	
636 (63)	33	10	7	Follis, year III[I]. Nicomedia, off. B, [Class 2], 612-614. *Overstruck on coin of Phocas.*	»	V.2
637 (155)	33	14.4	7	Follis, year IIII. Nicomedia, off. B [Class 2], 613/614.	MIB III, 175	
638 (3882)	32	10.8	7	»	»	I.67
639 (4506)	30	10.1	7	Follis, year IIII. Nicomedia, off. B [Class 2], 613/614. *Overstruck on coin of Phocas. Corr.*	MIB III, 175a	?V
640 (554)	29	8.4	8	Follis. Nicomedia, off. A [Class 2], 613-615. *Overstrike.*	MIB III, 159	II.55
641 (3396)	28	10.9	7	Follis. Nicomedia, off. A [Class 2], 613-615. *Two understrikes.*	MIB III, 175	
642 (3879)	29	10.2	7	Follis. Nicomedia, off. A [Class 2], 613-615.	»	I.98
643 (1084)	31	10.3	6	Follis. Nicomedia, off. B [Class 2], 613-615. *Overstruck on coin of Phocas.*	»	III.2
644 (3901)	25	5.9	76	Follis, year ЧI[I. Nicomedia, off. B [Class 3], 615-624.	»	I.98
645 (2126)	30	6.7		Follis, year Ϛ[II]. Nicomedia, off. A [Class 3, 617/618]. *Overstruck on coin of Phocas.*	MIB III, 176	
646 (253)	24	4.9	7	Follis, year XϚI. Nicomedia, off. B [Class 4], 624-629.	MIB III, 177	
PLATE 41						
647 (3893)	25	5.7	6	Half follis, year [III]. Nicomedia [Class 1], 611-613. *Worn.*	MIB III, 179	I.67
648 (3820)	15	2.5		Quarter follis. Nicomedia, 610-615. *Corr.*	MIB III, 180	II.42
649 (36)	31	10.7	5	Follis, year II. Cyzicus, off. A [Class 1], 611/612.	MIB III, 184	V.2

650 (470)	31	8.5	6	Follis, year II. Cyzicus, off. A [Class 1], 611/612.	MIB III, 184	II.54
651 (916)	29	11.7	5	Follis, year II. Cyzicus, off. B [Class 1], 611/612.	»	I.59
652 (150)	27	10.9	6	Follis, year II. Cyzicus, off. B [Class 1], 611-613.	»	I/II
653 (4401)	36	9.9	6	Follis, year III. Cyzicus, off. A [Class 1], 612/613. *Overstruck on coin of Nicomedia.*	»	IV.4
654 (4476)	31	10.5	6	Follis, year III. Cyzicus, off. A [Class 1], 612/613. *Corr.*	»	II.57
655 (145)	35	11.3	5	Follis, year III. Cyzicus, off. A [Class 1], 612/613. *Overstruck on coin of Nicomedia.*	»	
656 (8)	31	10.7	7	Follis, year III. [Cyzicus], off. B [Class 1], 612/613. *Overstruck on coin of Phocas.*	MIB III, 175	
657 (3892)	23	5	6	Half follis, year II. Cyzicus, off. A [Class 1], 611/612.	MIB III, 187	I. 19
PLATE 42						
658 (292)	24	6.2	1	Half follis, year ϚI. Seleucia (SEL), off. A, 616/617.	MIB III, 194	I. 20
659 (4297)	19	2.9	5	Half follis, year ЧIII. Seleucia (SEL), 618/619. *Corr.*	MIB III, 197	I.83
660 (4558)	24	6.2	1	Follis, year ЧII. Isaura (ICAVP), off. A, 616/617.	MIB III, 196	I.24
661 (1061)	22	10	6	Follis. Neapolis, 629-*c.* 631. *Countermark (c. 633).*	MIB III, X23	
662 (323)	17	4.1	1	Dodecanummium, 613-618.	MIB III, 200	I.99
663 (115)	18	4.5	0	»	MIB III, 200a	I/II
664 (296)	17	3.8	7	Dodecanummium, [type 1a], 613-618.	MIB III, 200	I/II
665 (3942)	15	4.4	1	Dodecanummium, 613-618.	MIB III, 202a	I.98
666 (534)	20	5.8		Dodecanummium, 632-641.	MIB III, 208	I.35
667 (3829)	22	6.3	10	»	MIB III, 208-9	II.42
668 (959)	19	9.3	6	»	MIB III, 209	II.29
669 (3725)	13	2.1		Hexanummium, 613-618.	MIB III, 210	II.14
670 (3813)	14	1.1		»	»	II.42
671 (3819)	15	1.8		»	»	II.42
672 (5712)	14	1.8		»	»	II.41
PLATE 43						
673 (2178)	28	9.1	5	Follis, year Ч. Thessalonica (ΘEC), off. B, 614/615. *Overstrike.*	MIB III, 220	
674 (713)	35	10	5	Follis, year Ч. Thessalonica (ΘEC), off. B, 614/615.	»	V.4
675 (666)	31	7.1		Follis, year ЧI. Thessalonica (ΘEC), off. B, 615/616. *Pierced rim.*	MIB III, 220/222	V.16
676 (4092)	31	10.4	11	Follis, year ЧIII. Thessalonica (ΘEC), off. B, 617/618. *Overstruck on coin of Phocas (*XXX*), year* III*, Constantinople mint; and that on older coin (*M*), year* ϤI...	MIB III, 220	II.65
677 (4117)	31	10.8	5	Follis, year [X]X. Thessalonica (ΘEC), off. E, 629/630.	»	IV. 4
678 (4864)	21	4.6	6	Half follis. Thessalonica (on the exergue TES), 612/613. *Overstrike.*	MIB III, 226	
679 (2198)	19	2.4	6	Half follis, year III. Thessalonica (ΘEC), 612/613. *Corr.*	MIB III, 228	I. 53
680 (3896)	20	3.5	5	Half follis, year [IIII]. Thessalonica (ΘEC), 613/614. *Corr.*	MIB III, 227/8	I. 82
681 (844)	23	4.8	6	Half follis, year Ч. Thessalonica (ΘEC), 614/615.	MIB III, 228	I. 102
682 (135)	22	3.4	6	Half follis, year ЧIII. Thessalonica (ΘEC), off. A, 617/618.	MIB III, 227	
683 (5354)	22	4	6	Half follis, year ЧI[I]III. Thessalonica (on the exergue ΘEC). AИИO. *Obverse from follis die.*	MIB III, 227/228	II. 40
684 (141)	20	4	6	Half follis, year X. Thessalonica (ΘEC), 619/620.	MIB III, 228	
685 (4085)	19	3.2		Half follis, year X. Thessalonica, 619/620.	MIB III, 228[1]	V. 12
686 (4021)	21	1.8	5	Half follis, year X[Ϛ].Thessalonica (ΘEC), 625/626. *Corr., incomplete.*	MIB III, 229	I.35
687 (355)	16	2.4	7	Quarter follis, year III. Thessalonica, 612/613.	MIB III, 231	I.35
688 (926)	16	2.2	5	Quarter follis, year III. Thessalonica, 612/613.	»	II.42
689 (3941)	17	2.1	6	Quarter follis, year ЧIII. Thessalonica, 617/618.	MIB III, 232	
690 (832)	15	1.8	6	Quarter follis, year ЧIIII. Thessalonica [Class III], 618/619.	»	I.102
691 (3946)	20	6	11	Half follis, indictio E. Carthage, 616/617.	MIB III, 234	I.98

PLATE 44

692 (450)	32	10.4	1	Follis, year II[I] [Class 2], 613-616. *Worn.*	MIB III, 159/ 160b	II.54
693 (3880)	35	12.6	8	Follis, year III [Class 2], 612/613. *Overstruck on coin of Maurice, year ЧII.*	MIB III, [159]	I.77
694 (3881)	33	9.4	1	Follis, year III [Class 2], 612/613. Off. [A]. *Overstruck on coin of Maurice from Cyzicus.*	MIB III, 160	IV.5
695 (2128)	30			Follis, year IIII. Off. B [Class 1], 613/614. *Overstruck on coin of Phocas, year III.*	Cf. MIB III, 158	
696 (312)	30	11.3	6	Follis, year IIII. Off. B [Class 2], 613/614. *Overstruck on coin of Phocas, year Ϛ.*	[MIB III, 160b]	
697 (514)	30	8.3	7	Follis, year Ϛ. Off. A [Class 2], 615/616. *Worn.*		II.50
698 (378)	31	5.5	6	Follis [Class 2], 613-616. *Overstrike, incomplete.*	MIB III, 160	II.54
699 (693)	30	6.7		Follis [Class 2], 613-616. *Corr., incomplete.*	»	I.69
700 (2163)	29			Follis [Class 2], 613-616.	»	I
701 (4185)	31	11.4	1	Follis [Class 2], 613-616. *Overstruck on coin of Phocas, year III, Constantinople, off. Γ.*	»	II.32
702 (4409)	28	8.7	7	Follis, year IIII. Off. B [Class 2], 613-616. *Overstruck on coin of Phocas from Nicomedia.*	»	IV.4
703 (1128)	30	7.4		Follis. Constantinople, Off. E [Class 5], 629-632. *Corr.*	MIB III, 164	I.101
704 (2148)	34			Follis.		
705 (1044)	31	8.1		Follis, [610-635]. *Corr.*		II.15
706 (3867)				Follis. [Class 2], 613-615. *Illegible.*		I.37
707 (4089)	25	4.2		Follis. Off. A, 613-615. *Countermark, Grierson's type F (c. 633). Corr.*	MIB III, 173	II.65

PLATE 45

708 (5272)	24	3.9	6	Half follis, year [Ч]. Off. B [Class 2], 615-629. *Corr.*	MIB III, 170	IV. I
709 (5799)	24	2.9	1	Half follis, year [XX...], 629-639. *Worn, incomplete.*	[MIB III, 171]	II.42
710 (839)	24	3.2	6	Half follis, [616-624]. *Corr., broken.*	MIB III, 170	I.102
711 (840)	20	3.3	0	Half follis, [616-624]. *Corr, broken.*	»	I.102
712 (1120)	19	2.4		Half follis, [616-624]. *Corr.*	»	I/II
713 (1129)	19	1.3		Half follis. Off. [A], 613-629. *Corr, incomplete.*	MIB III, 170/188	I. 101
714 (1026)	20	2.4	6	Half follis. *Corr.*		II.31
715 (851)	22	3.1	6	Half follis, [610-612]. *Corr.*	MIB III, 169	I.102

PLATE 46

CONSTANS II, 642 - 668

716 (24)	19	4.4	6	AV Solidus, off. Γ, 651-664.	MIB III, 23	V.18
717 (26)	20	4.5		AV Solidus, off. Θ, 651-664.	MIB III, 24	
718 (18)	20	4.5	6	AV Solidus [Class VI, Grierson], off. Θ, but without Θ in exergue.	MIB III, 35	
719 (19)	19	4.4	6	AV Solidus [Class VI, Grierson].	[MIB III, 38[1]]	
720 (22)	20	4.4	6	AV Solidus [Class VI(a), Grierson], off. B.	»	
721 (5)	17	2.1	6	AV Semissis.	MIB III, 50	
722 (16)	19	1.4	7	AV Tremissis, 642-668.	MIB III, 51	
723 (1706)	17	1.4		AV Tremissis, 642-668.	»	
724 (881)	22	4.2	7	Follis [Class 1].	MIB III, 162	
725 (4819)	27	5.2	5	Follis. Off. A or Δ [Class 1]. *Overstrike.*	MIB III, 162c	
726 (272)	22	5.2	1	Follis [Class 1]. Off. Γ, 642.	MIB III, 162	
727 (4438)	24	2.5		Follis. Off. E [Class 1], 642. *Corr.*	»	II.17
728 (3836)	24	3.3	7	Follis, year I. Off. I [Class 1], 642/643.	MIB III, 162b	II.29
729 (4566)	22	4.5	5	Follis, year I [Class 1], 642/643.	MIB III, 162	II.29
730 (4419)	25	3.3	7	Follis [Class 1].	MIB III, 162b	

PLATE 47

731 (52)	21	2.9	0	Follis [Class 1 or 4] or imitation.	MIB III, 162/167	

732 (3837)	25	2.9	0	Follis [Class 1 or 4], 642-648. *Corr.*	MIB III, 162/167	II.42
733 (1132)	21	2.1		»	»	I.101
734 (432)	22	1.9	6	Follis [Class 1 or 4], 642-648. *Corr., incomplete.*	»	II.54
735 (859)	22	2.3	7	Follis [Class 1 or 4], 642-648. *Corr.*	»	II. 12
736 (4522)	25	3.3		Follis [Class 1 or 4], 642-648. *Overstrike; worn.*	»	V. 2
737 (4578)	24	4.2	6	Follis [Class 1 or 4], 642-648. *Overstrike.*	»	II.29
738 (4579)	24	2.7	7	Follis [Class 1 or 4], 642-648. *Countermark? Worn.*	MIB III, 162/167	II.29
739 (5267)	23	4.4	1	Follis [Class 1 or 4], 642-648. *Worn.*	MIB III, 162b/ 167b	II.41
740 (3838)	23	4.5	7	Follis, year II[I]. Off. Γ [Class 2], 642-648. *Worn.*	MIB III, 163	II.42
741 (880)	23	4.8	7	Follis, year [II]. Off. Γ [Class 2], 642-648.	»	II.12
742 (658)	21	2.6	7	Follis [Class 2], year II. Off. [E], 642-648. *Corr.*	»	
743 (107)	25	4.9	7	Follis [Class 2], 642-648. *Overstrike.*	»	
744 (5800)	24	4.8	6	Follis [Class 2], 642-648.	»	II.42
PLATE 48						
745 (64)	30	7.1	6	Follis. Off. A [Class 2bis], 643/644. *Overstrike.*	MIB III, 166	V.2
746 (506)	28	4.3	7	Follis. Off. A [Class 2bis], 643/644. *Overstrike*	»	II.50
747 (4168)	21	8.8		Follis. Off. B [Class 2bis], 643/644. *Worn.*	»	I. 98
748 (5251)	24	5	7	Follis. Off. B [Class 2bis], 643/644.	»	II. 42
749 (3830)	24	4.7	7	Follis, year III. Off. B [Class 2bis], 643/644.	»	II. 42
750 (41)	24	4.7	8	Follis. Off. Δ [Class 2bis], 643/644.	»	V. 2
751 (895)	26	4.3	7	Follis, year III. Off. Δ [Class 2bis], 643/644. *Overstruck, possibly on coin of Heraclius, perhaps Class 5 or 6.*	»	II. 3
752 (3736)	23	4	8	Follis. Off. Δ [Class 2bis], 643/644. *Corr.*	»	II. 14
753 (3831)	25	6.3	8	Follis, year III. Off. Δ [Class 2bis], 643/644.	»	II. 42
754 (3832)	23	3.9	1	Follis, year III. Off. Δ [Class 2bis], 643/644.	»	II. 42
755 (10178)	23	3.4	7	Follis, [year III]. Off. Δ [Class 2bis], 643/644. *Overstrike.*	»	IV. 10
756 (4110)	24	4.2		Follis. Off. Δ [Class 2bis], 643/644. *Corr.*	»	
757 (106)	26	4.8	7	Follis. Off. E [Class 2bis], 643/644. *Overstruck on coin of Heraclius, Class 6.*	»	
758 (172)	23	4.3	1	Follis. Off. E [Class 2bis], 643/644. *Overstrike.*	»	
759 (173)	25	4.7	9	»	»	
760 (696)	26	5.8	1	»	»	I. 35
761 (1017)	24	5.1	7	Follis, year [III]. Off. E [Class 2bis], 643/644. *Corr.*	»	II. 29
762 (1108)	24	5.2	7	Follis, year [III]. Off. E [Class 2bis], 643/644.	»	
PLATE 49						
763 (4189)	26	5.9	1	Follis, year III. Off. E [Class 2bis], 643/644. *Overstruck on coin of Nicomedia.*	»	III. 2
764 (4867)	23	3.8	6	Follis, off. E [Class 2bis], 643/644.	»	
765 (195)	23	4.6	7	Follis, year III. Off. [E] [Class 2bis], 643/644.	»	V. 10
766 (4245)	22	5.3	1	Follis, year III[I]. Off. E [Class 2bis], 643/644. *Corr.*	»	II
767 (1091)	22	5.9	7	Follis, off. [E] [Class 2bis], 643/644. *Overstrike.*	»	II. 60
768 (5231)	28	5.4	6	Follis, off. E [Class 2bis], 643/644. *Overstrike.*	»	II. 20
769 (1003)	25	5.5	6	»	»	II. 29
770 (5266)	28	5.4	6	Follis [Class 2bis], 643/644. *Overstrike; corr.*	»	II.41
771 (3741)	27	4.5	6	Follis [Class 2bis], 643/644. *Overstruck, possibly on coin of Heraclius.*	»	II.14
772 (1131)	24	3.2	6	Follis, year [II ...] [Class 2bis], 643/644.	»	I.101
773 (1841)	24	4.6	6	Follis, [Class 2bis], 643/644. *Worn.*	»	IV.2
774 (3904)	21	2.9	7	Follis, year III [Class 2bis], 643/644.	»	
775 (40)	23	3.4	7	Follis [Class 3], 643-645.	MIB III, 164	V.2
776 (879)	25	4.3	7	»	»	II.12
777 (353)	24	5.6	6	Follis, year Ч, off. [A] [Class 4], 646/647.	MIB III, 167b	I
778 (4836)	25	3.5	1	Follis [Class 4], 645-651.	»	II.41

PLATE 50

779 (4049)	24	5.6	6	Follis, year [Ч...] [Class 4], 645-648.	MIB III, 167	II.24
780 (1081)	21	4.7	7	Follis, year Ч. Off. Γ [Class 4], 645/646.	»	I.21
781 (1840)	27	6.4	7	Follis [Class 1 or 4], 642-648.	»	IV.2
782 (108)	25	5.6	7	Follis, year Ϛ [Class 4], 642-651. *Overstruck on coin of Heraclius, year* XX.. *[Class 5]*	»	I.21
783 (4623)	19	2.7	8	Follis, year ϚI [Class 4], 647/648.	»	II.52
784 (328)	24	4.1	7	Follis, off. [B] [Class 4], 645-648.	MIB III, 167d	I.99
785 (1054)	23	4.9	0	Follis [Class 4], 645-648.	MIB III, 167	II.50
786 (1107)	26	5	1	Follis [Class 4], 645-648. *Overstruck on coin of Heraclius [Class 3 or 4].*	»	
787 (202)	29	4.8	1	Follis [Class 4], 645-648. *Overstruck on coin of Heraclius, year XXXI, off.* Δ *[Class 6].*	»	I.40
788 (71)	21	3.8	1	Follis [Class 4], 645-648.	»	V.2
789 (4313)	23	3.4	1	»	»	II.53
790 (3905)	23	4	7	Follis [Class 4], 645-648. *Corr.*	»	I.35
791 (5859)	27	5.6	7	Follis. Off. Γ [Class 5], 651-655.	MIB III, 170	II.56
792 (2248)	20	4.4	8	Follis, year XIII. Off. Δ [Class 5], 653/654.	»	
793 (4560)	22	3.2	7	Follis, year XIIII. Off. E [Class 5], 654/655.	»	I.24
794 (801)	20	2.3	1	Follis, year XЧ. Off. A [Class 5], 655/656.	MIB III, 170c	I.38
795 (809)	21	1.9	7	Follis. Off. [Γ] [Class 5], 651-655. *Corr.*	»	I.29
796 (3421)	21	2.9	0	Follis [Class 5], 651-655. *Countermark* .	»	II.33
797 (109)	21	3.2	0	Follis. Off. Δ [Class 5], 651-655.	»	
798 (3619)	26	4.9	0	Follis [Class 5], [651-658]. *Overstruck on half-follis of Heraclius, year XX, Constantinople, off. B.*	»	II.58

PLATE 51

799 (3840)	22	1.5	0	Follis. Off. A [Class 5 or 6], 651-655.	MIB III, 170/172	II.42
800 (3907)	18	2.4	1	Follis. Off. Δ [Class 5-8], 651-658.	MIB III, 170-174	
801 (277)	23	3.1	1	Follis. Off. Δ [Class 6], 655-658.	MIB III, 172c	I. 89
802 (4602)	20	2.1	1	Follis, year XЧ. Off. A [Class 6], 655/656.	MIB III, 172	II. 33
803 (298)	20	2.8	6	Follis, year X[Ч] [Class 6], 655-657. *[Arabic] countermark.*	»	I/II
804 (4238)	26	5.3	7	Follis, year X[Ч] [Class 6], 655-657.	»	V. 23
805 (6032)	20	2.5	7	Follis [Class 6], 655-657. *[Countermark]. Corr.*	»	II. 24
806 (965)	22	3.5	6	Follis, year XIII or XЧI, 655-657. [Class 7]	MIB III, 173	II. 29
807 (3737)	21	1.6	8	Follis, year XЧI. Off. A [Class 7], 656/657. *Corr.*	»	II. 14
808 (3903)	25	2.4	0	Follis, year XЧII. Off. E [Class 7], 657/658. *Corr.*	MIB III, 173[d]	I. 30
809 (3841)	22	2.4	1	Follis. Off. [A], [Class 7], 655-658.	MIB III, 173	II.42
810 (10164)	21	1.9	6	Follis [Class 7], 655-658.	»	II.1
811 (3440)	23	3.9	6	Follis [?Class 7], 655-658 *Overstruck on coin of Heraclius [Class 5].*	»	II.58
812 (948)	18	1.7	7	Follis [Class 9], 659-664.	MIB III, 175	II.42
813 (1000)	24	3.4	6	Follis. Off. Γ [Class 9], 659-664.	»	II.29
814 (3427)	25	3.5	6	Follis, year IΘ [Class 9], 659/660.	»	II.33
815 (3908)	21	2.2	11	Follis [Class 9], 659-664.	»	I.98

PLATE 52

816 (704)	23	3.8	0	Follis [Class 11], 668.	MIB III, 177	I.94
817 (1159)	21	3.4	0	»	»	
818 (3659)	20	4	0	»	MIB III, 177a	II.58
819 (4277)	23	4.2	1	Follis [Class 11], 668. *Countermark* .	MIB III, 177	I.35
820 (4592)	22	4.7	7	»	»	II.33
821 (5339)	14	2.5		Follis [?Class 11], [668]. *Corr.*	[»]	II.56
822 (1004)	20	3	7	Half follis. Off. A, [642-643].	MIB III, 180	II.29
823 (4420)	21	2.7	1	Half follis. Off. Δ, 642-657.	MIB III, 180/183	IV.4

824 (1010)	15	1.6	1	Half follis. Off. Δ [Class 2bis], 643-645. *Corr.*	MIB III, 181	II.29
825 (515)	20	2.1	7	Half follis, 643-647.	»	II.50
826 (3910)	19	2.3	7	Half follis. Off. B, 643-7. *A in rev. upper field?*	»	I.35
827 (3839)	21	2.8	0	Half follis. Off. Δ, 642-647. *Overstrike.*	»	II.42
828 (3729)	22	1.6		Half follis, 654-658. *Incomplete.*	MIB III, 183	II.14
829 (884)	22	3.2	1	Quarter follis, year XX. Off. A, 660/661.	MIB III, 186	II.12
830 (3909)	20	2.3	1	Quarter follis. Off. A, 659-665.	»	I.35
831 (932)	22	2.5	1	Quarter follis. Constantinople, off. Δ, 659-665.	»	II.42
832 (4050)	18	1.9		Quarter follis. Constantinople, 659-665. *Rev. ill.; incomplete.*	»	II.24
833 (620)	17	7.6		Dodecanummium, 645-646.	MIB III, 189	I.35
834 (3447)	19	8.5	6	»	MIB III, 189-90	II. 58
835 (819)	22	3.1	11	Follis. Off. A. *Cointermark* Ꝁ.		I. 102
836 (2155)	20	1.4		Follis. *Corr.*		
837 (6049)	18	3.3		»		II. 35

PLATE 53

				7TH CENTURY UNCERTAIN		
838 (4868)	25	4.8		Follis [?Heraclius, Class 3] *Corr.*	[MIB III, 161]	
839 (4125)	28	8.8		Follis. *Corr. ill.*		II.59
840 (4244)	28	4.9	7	Follis [?Heraclius, Class 2], year [ЧI] or imitation. Off. Γ.		
841 (327)	21	2.4		Half follis [Constants II or imitation]. *Corr.*		I. 99
842 (1146)	16	0.7		Half follis [?Heraclius]. *Corr., incomplete.*		I.89
843 (4204)	17	5		Quarter follis. *Ill.*		
844 (5357)	16	1.7		Quarter follis. *Obv. ill.* I, ANNO l. *Corr.*	Cf. MIB II, Tib. 56	I.35
845 (4031)	15	2	1	Follis [Constans II]. *Corr., incomplete.*		II.10
846 (3818)	17	1.9	7	Quarter follis [Maurice]. *Corr.*	MIB II, 72/ 82	II.42
847 (625)	15	2.6		Dodecanummium. *Obv. ill.*		I.35
				IMITATIONS OF 7TH CENTURY COINS		
848 (1135)	26	1.1	1	Imitation of follis of Phocas. Thin flan.		I.20
849 (424)	20	1.3	11	Imitation of Class 1/4 follis of Constans II. *Thin flan.*		II.54
850 (3389)	22	3.1	6	Similar.		I.94
851 (3417)	21	1.1	6	Similar.		II.33
852 (3842)	22	2.9	11	Similar.		II.42
853 (3843)	19	1.7	0	Similar.		II.42
854 (3911)	20	1.3	4	Similar. *Incomplete.*		
855 (5268)	20	1		Imitation of Class 2bis follis of Constans II. *Thin flan. Countermark* Ꝁ. *Obv. ill.*		II.41
856 (434)	22	3.3	0	[Imitation of] Class 7 follis of Constans II. Off. [A]. *AИИO.*		II.54
857 (322)	12	1.6	5	[Imitative] dodecanummium. Profile bust. ꓭ+I	Cf. MIB III, X49	I.99

PLATE 54

				JUSTINIAN II, 685-695/ 705-711		
858 (2118)	19	4.28		AV Solidus [Grierson Class III]. Off. Θ, 692-695.	MIB III, 8a	
				ANASTASIUS II, 713-715		
859 (295)	24	4.6		Follis.	MIB III, 28	I/II
				NICEPHORUS I, 802-811		
860 (197)	23	5.6	6	Follis [Class 1], 802-803.	Grierson 1982, Pl. 38, 699	
				MICHAEL II, 820-829		
861 (2144)	23			Follis [Class 2].	DOC 3.1, Pl. 14, 8.5	
				THEOPHILUS, 829-842		
862 (438)	29	6.7	6	Follis. *Corr.; doubled die.*	DOC 3.2, Pl. 23, 14	II.54

863 (421)	26	4.7	6	Follis [Type 2a], 831-842.	DOC 3.2, Pl. 24, 15a	II.54
864 (1045)	27	2.8		Follis, 831-842. *Corr.*	DOC 3.2, Pl. 24 ff.	II.15
865 (381)	20	2.4		Follis, 831-842. *Corr., broken, incomplete.*	»	II.54
				BASIL I, 867-886		
866 (2)	20	4.26		AV Solidus, [870].	DOC 3.2, Pl. 30, 2a	V.12
867 (10184)	21	4.34	6	AV Solidus.		V.16
868 (4498)	26	3.7	5	Follis [Class 5]. *Corr.*	DOC 3.2, Pl. 33, 12.1	
869 (397)	27	5.5	2	Follis. *Worn.*	DOC 3.2, Pl. 32, 10	II.54

PLATE 55

				LEO VI, 886-912		
870 (48)	26	6.9		Follis. Class 3.	DOC 3.2, Pl. 35, 8	
871 (248)	23	5.7	5	Follis. *Worn; obv. ill.*	»	
872 (4051)	30	7.9		Follis. Class 3. *Corr.*	»	II.24
				CONSTANTINE VII, 913-959		
873 (714)	25	4.3	6	Follis [Class 1], 914-919.	DOC 3.2, Pl. 38, 22	V.16
874 (465)	21			Follis [Class 5], 945-950. *Corr., obv. ill.*	DOC 3.2, Pl. 39, 26	II.54
				ROMANUS I, 920-944		
875 (164)	25	6.4	6	Follis. *Worn.*	DOC 3.2, Pl. 38, 25a	
876 (214)	27	5.8	5	Follis.	»	
877 (303)	26	6.	[5]	Follis. *Corr., obv. ill.*	DOC 3.2, Pl. 38, 23-25	II.47
878 (412)	25	5.1	6	Follis. *Corr., obv. ill.*	»	II.54
879 (1007)	25	8	5	Follis. *Worn.*	»	II.29
880 (2145)	25			Follis.	»	
881 (4056)	23	3.7	6	Follis. *Worn.*	»	II.13
882 (4862)	27	4.2	6	Follis. *Pierced rim.*	»	
				NICEPHORUS II, 963-969		
883 (139)	23	6.4	7	Follis.	DOC 3.2, Pl. 91, 8	
884 (5363)	24	4.1	5	Follis. *Obv. corr.*	DOC 3.2, Pl. 91, 7-8	II.56
				IMITATION		
885 (6045)	20	1.7	5	Copper copy of solidus of Constantine VII or Nicephorus II. *Pierced rim.*	DOC 3.1, cf. Pl. 37, 15.26	II.35

PLATE 56

				ANONYMOUS FOLLES, 969-1092		
				Follis. Class A1, 969-976		
886 (463)	27	8.1	[4]	Follis.	DOC 3.2, Pl. 48, A1	II.54
887 (672)	27	5.3	5	Follis.	»	
888 (991)	24	4.7	[6]	Follis. *Overstrike.*	»	II.29
889 (1105)	25	5.4	6	Follis. *Overstrike.*	»	
				Class A2, 976-1028		
890 (110)	30	15	6	Follis. Var. 3.	DOC 3.2, Pl. 49	
891 (111)	32	11.3	7	Follis. Var. 3. *Worn, pierced rim.*	»	
892 (575)	36	15	6	Follis. Var. 3.	»	
893 (3381)	33	10.7	5	Follis. Var. 3.	»	
894 (711)	31	9.3	5	Follis. Var. 3 or 5.	»	V.21
895 (443)	31	12	6	Follis. Var. 8. *Worn.*	»	II.54
896 (1101)	32	12.7		Follis. Var. 12, 21 or 34. *Worn.*	DOC 3.2, Pl. 48	I/II
897 (444)	30	10.4	6	Follis. Var. 14b or 24. *Worn.*	DOC 3.2, Pl. 51	II.54
898 (119)	36	13.5	6	Follis. Var. 9 or 22	DOC 3.2, Pl. 50	[V.2]

PLATE 57

899 (198)	35	16	6	Follis. Var. 27.	DOC 3.2, Pl. 52	V.23
900 (3759)	34	16.3	6	Follis. Var. 31. *Above rev. legend* · · · *instead of* · ♦ ·	DOC 3.2, cf. Pl. 52	II.42

901 (215)	29	8.3	6	Follis. Var. 32.	DOC 3.2, Pl. 52	
902 (223)	28	9.3	7	Follis. Var. 39.	DOC 3.2, Pl. 53	
903 (112)	28	9.5	4	Follis. Var. 41.	»	
904 (99)	29	9.5	6	Follis. Var. 41.	»	
905 (177)	33	8.9	7	Follis. Var. 47.	DOC 3.2, Pl. 53, 47	V.17
906 (120)	29	9.5	6	Follis. *Worn, pierced at centre.*	DOC 3.2, Pl. 51, 24	[V.2]
907 (193)	26	8.1	5	Follis. *Worn.*	DOC 3.2, Pl. 53, 40	
908 (246)	28	8.7	5	Follis. Var. 14, 22, 35 or 41. *Obv. worn.*	DOC 3.2, Pl. 53, 41	
909 (379)	26	3.8	5	Follis. *Corr., incomplete.*	DOC 3.2, Pl. 50 ff.	II.54
910 (426)	26	8.1	5	Follis. *Worn.*	DOC 3.2, cf. Pl. 51, 24	
911 (490)	26	3.8		Follis. *Corr., incomplete; obv. ill.*	DOC 3.2, Pl. 51 ff.	II.54
912 (647)	33	16.3	5	Follis. Var. 14. *Worn.*	DOC 3.2, Pl. 50, 14	

PLATE 58

913 (5269)				Follis. *Worn.*		II.41
				Class B, 1028-1034		
914 (662)	30	13.1		Follis. *Overstruck on type A2,14/27.*	DOC 3.2, Pl. 55 - Pl. 50,14/27	I.35
915 (216)	29	11.3	5	Follis.	DOC 3.2, Pl. 55	
916 (238)	28	8.7	0	Follis.	»	
917 (352)	31	9.8	5	Follis.	»	
918 (62)	32	10	5	Follis. *Corr.*	»	V.22
919 (489)	28	6.3	6	Follis. *Corr., incomplete.*	»	
920 (9)	20	3.4		Follis. *Worn, clipped; obv. ill.*	»	V.2
921 (149)	21	4.6		»	»	
922 (280)	21	2		»	»	I.89
923 (284)	24	3.7		»	»	I/II
924 (300)	20	2.1	0	»	»	I/II
925 (316)	22	2.9	6	»	»	I/II
926 (373)	25	4.2		»	»	II.54
927 (417)	21	3.2	6	»	»	II.54
928 (445)	21	6		»	»	II.54
929 (448)	22	5	6	»	»	II.54
930 (449)	23	2.7		Follis. *Corr., clipped, broken; obv. ill.*	»	II.54
931 (452)	22	3.3		Follis. *Corr., clipped; obv. ill.*	»	II.54
932 (511)	27	3.3		Follis. *Worn, broken, bent.*	»	II.50

PLATE 59

933 (891)	22	5.1		*Worn; obv. ill.*	DOC 3.2, Pl. 55	II.3
934 (937)	20	3.6		»	»	II.42
935 (944)	25	4.9	6	Follis. *Worn; clipped.*	»	II.42
936 (955)	22	6.1		Follis. *Worn; obv. ill.*	»	II.29
937 (957)	24	5.9		»	»	II.29
938 (958)	23	5.5		»	»	II.29
939 (976)	23	3.2		»	»	II.29
940 (982)	25			»	»	II.29
941 (996)	22	4.3		»	»	II.29
942 (1046)	24	5.9		Follis. *Corr., clipped; obv. ill.*	»	II.15
943 (1198)	21	4.4		Follis. *Clipped; obv. ill.*	»	II.56
944 (2130)	23	4.6		Follis. *Worn, clipped.*	»	
945 (2183)	24	5		»	»	II.33
946 (2184)	23	3.8		»	»	II.33
947 (2185)	22	4.4		»	»	II.33
948 (2186)	24	4.7		»	»	II.33

949 (2187)	24	4.1		Follis. *Worn, clipped.*	DOC 3.2, Pl. 55	II.33
950 (2188)	22	3.1		»	»	II.33
951 (2189)	21	3.7		»	»	II.33
952 (2190)	22	3		»	»	II.33
953 (2191)		4		»	»	II.33

PLATE 60

954 (2195)	20	2.6		Follis. *Worn, clipped.*	DOC 3.2, Pl. 55	II.33
955 (2249)	24	5		Follis. *Worn, clipped; obv. ill.*	»	
956 (2250)	23	5.4	6	Follis. *Worn, clipped.*	»	
957 (3629)	23	4.9		Follis. *Worn, clipped; obv. ill. Counterstrike?*	»	II.58
958 (3733)	22	4.6		Follis. *Worn, clipped; obv. ill.*	»	II.14
959 (3769)	24	4.3		»	»	II.42
960 (3770)	23	4.7	6	Follis. *Worn, clipped.*	»	II.42
961 (3771)	23	4.4		Follis. *Worn, clipped; obv. ill.*	»	II.42
962 (3773)	22	4.2		»	»	II.42
963 (3774)	19	3.7		»	»	II.42
964 (3775)	21	5.1		»	»	II.42
965 (3776)	23	4		»	»	II.42
966 (3777)	23	3.5	6	Follis. *Worn, clipped.*	»	II.42
967 (3778)	22	3.9	6	»	»	II.42
968 (3943)	21	4.3		Follis. *Worn, clipped; obv. ill.*	»	II.8
969 (4053)	21	3.6		»	»	IV.10
970 (4096)	20	3.7		»	»	II.65
971 (4124)	23	5.5		»	»	I.35
972 (4174)	26	8.1		»	»	II
973 (4175)	21	3.4		»	»	II
974 (4176)	20	2.5	6	Follis. *Worn, clipped.*	»	II
975 (10176)	23	5.4		Follis. *Worn, clipped; obv. ill.*	»	IV.10

PLATE 61

976 (676)	22	3.3		Follis. *Worn, clipped; obv. ill.*	DOC 3.2, Pl. 55	I/II
977 (806)	24	5		»	»	I/II
978 (4178)	23	4.7		»	»	II
979 (4179)	23	4.6		»	»	II.45
980 (4251)	24	5.2		Follis. *Worn, clipped.*	»	II.24
981 (4421)	22	6.6		»	»	IV.4
982 (4422)	23	4.9		Follis. *Worn, clipped; obv. ill.*	»	IV.4
983 (4428)	23	4.9		Follis. [Class B]. *Worn, clipped.*	»	II.34
984 (4515)	23	2.8		Follis. *Star visible on obv. r. edge and letters in field from earlier strike. Thin flan. Clipped.*	»	II
985 (4517)	21	3.8		Follis. *Worn, clipped; obv. ill.*	»	II.42
986 (4667)	23	5.2		»	»	II.47
987 (4668)	21	3.9		»	»	II.47
988 (4678)	22	4.4		»	»	II.33
989 (5222)	22	3.7		Follis. *Worn, clipped.*	»	II.42
990 (5223)	20	3		»	»	II.42
991 (5249)	20	2.2		Follis. *Worn, clipped; obv. ill.*	»	II.42
992 (5270)	24	6.9	5	»	»	II.41
993 (5319)	24	3.9		»	»	II.66
994 (5323)	22	3.7		»	»	II.42
995 (5324)	20	3		»	»	II.42
996 (5365)	25	2.9	6	Follis. *Worn, clipped.*	»	II.56
997 (5366)	22	4.1		Follis. *Worn, clipped; obv. ill.*	»	II.56

PLATE 62						
998 (5806)	23	3.4	5	Follis. *Worn, clipped.*	DOC 3.2, Pl. 55	II.42
999 (5842)	20	3.9	5	Follis. *Worn, clipped; obv. ill.*	»	II.11
1000 (5853)	22	6	5	Follis. *Worn, clipped.*	»	II.56
1001 (5794)	23	3.7	[5]	Follis. *Worn, clipped; obv. ill.*	»	II. 42
1002 (3919)	20	3		Follis. »	»	
1003 (3920)	22	3.9		Follis. *Worn, clipped.*	»	
				Class C, 1034-1041		
1004 (5229)	31	8.4		Follis. *Worn, clipped. Overstrike.*	DOC 3.2, Pl. 60, C	II.42
1005 (4177)	23	4.6		Follis. *Worn, clipped.*	»	II
1006 (1062)	30	8.1		Follis. *Overstruck on Class B.*	»	II.50
1007 (3762)	29	5.2	6	Follis. *Corr., in two pieces. Overstrike?*	»	II.42
1008 (4210)	28	4.2	5	Follis. *Worn, clipped.*	»	
1009 (609)	29	5.4	5	Follis. *Corr., incomplete.*	»	II.68
1010 (474)	23	5.2	6	Follis. *Worn, clipped. Overstrike.*	»	II.54
1011 (4562)	24	4.7		Follis. *Worn, clipped; obv. ill.*	»	II.29
1012 (460)	25	4.8	5	»	»	II.54
1013 (4271)	23	3.1		»	»	I.35
1014 (301)	20	2.7	6	»	»	I/II
1015 (4676)	21	3.3		Follis. *Worn, clipped.*	»	II.47
PLATE 63						
1016 (4548)	25	5.9		Follis. *Worn, clipped; obv. ill.*	DOC 3.2, Pl. 60, C	II.42
1017 (5807)	28	5.5	5	Follis. *Worn, clipped.*	»	II.42
1018 (6040)	25	5.3	6	»	»	II.35
1019 (299)	25	6.6		Follis. *Worn, clipped; obv. ill.*	»	I/II
1020 (2174)	24	4.8		Follis. *Worn, clipped.*	»	I/II
1021 (3921)	25	5.8	7	Follis. [Class C]. *Worn, clipped; obv. ill.*	»	I.98
1022 (3617)	30	3.4		Follis. *Worn, clipped; obv. ill.*	»	II.58
1023 (6073)	23	3.8		Follis. *Worn, clipped.*	»	II
1024 (447)	22	3.3	6	Follis. *Worn, clipped; obv. ill.*	»	II.54
1025 (3772)	23	4.3		»	»	II.42
1026 (3618)	23	5		Follis. [Class C]. *Worn, clipped; obv. ill.*	»	II.58
1027 (3767)	23	5		»	»	II.42
1028 (3768)	23	4.7		»	»	II.42
1029 (176)	21	3.8		Follis. *Worn, clipped; obv. ill.*	»	
1030 (3387)	21	3.8		»	»	I.59
1031 (923)	21	2.4		Follis. *Corr., incomplete.*	»	II.42
1032 (2193)	20	3.4		Follis. *Worn, clipped.*	»	II.33
1033 (3429)	23	3.8		Follis. *Worn, clipped; obv. ill.*	»	II.33
1034 (2192)	23	3.8		Follis. *Worn, clipped.*	»	II.33
				Class D, 1052-1055		
1035 (377)	27	5.1	5	Follis. *Overstruck on type C.*	DOC 3.2, Pl. 60	II.54
PLATE 64						
1036 (4249)	26	4.3	6	Follis.	DOC 3.2, Pl. 60	
1037 (4679)	24	3.6	11	Follis. ?Imitation. *S reversed.*	»	II.41
1038 (532)	29	4.8	6	Follis. *Throne back absent.*	»	I/II
				Class E, 1059-1067		
1039 (10173)	29	6.6	6	Follis.	DOC 3.2, Pl. 61	IV.10
1040 (2131)	30	8.3		Follis. *Doubled die.*	»	
				Class F, 1059-1067		
1041 (251)	28	6.6	5	Follis.	DOC 3.2, cf. Pl. 61	
1042 (5367)	29	7.3	5	Follis.	»	II.56

1043 (451)	27	3.6	[11]	Follis. *Overstrike; corr.*	DOC 3.2, cf. Pl. 61	II.54
				Class G, 1068-1071		
1044 (4508)	30	9.2		Follis.	DOC 3.2, Pl. 61	
1045 (5338)	27	7.4	5	Follis. *Pierced rim.*	»	II.56
				Class H, 1071-1078		
1046 (376)	23	4	6	Follis. *Worn.*	DOC 3.2, cf. Pl. 68	II.54
1047 (934)	25	4.8	6	Follis. *Worn.*	»	II.42
1048 (471)	26	1.9	11	Follis. [Class H]. *Worn. Thin flan.*	»	II.54
1049 (314)	27	5.8	5	Follis. *Worn.*	»	I/II
1050 (3442)	23	3.7	6	Follis. *Worn.*	»	II.58
1051 (4563)	25	4.9		Follis. *Overstruck on follis of Theophilus. Corr.*	DOC 3.2, cf. Pl. 68 H/ DOC 3.1, Pl. 24	II.29
PLATE 65						
1052 (457)	25	3.3	6	Follis. *Worn.*	DOC 3.2, Pl. 68	II.54
				Class I, 1078-1081		
1053 (3753)	26	3.9	6	Follis.	DOC 3.2, Pl. 68, I	II.42
1054 (245)	26	5.2	6	Follis.	»	
1055 (49)	24	4.2	6	Follis.	»	
1056 (492)	28	4.8	5	Follis. *Worn.*	»	II.54
1057 (3388)	24	4.5	6	Follis.	»	I.69
1058 (6042)	23	3	6	Follis. *Overstrike.*	»	II.35
1059 (413)	24	3.7	6	Follis. *Worn.*	»	II.54
1060 (461)	25	3.7	6	Follis. *Worn.*	»	II.54
1061 (702)	23	3.3	6	Follis. *Worn, slightly bent.*	»	I.1
1062 (174)	23	3.9	5	Follis. *Worn; pierced rim.*	»	
1063 (388)	25	1.4		Follis. [Class I]. *Worn, incomplete.*	»	II.54
1064 (4109)	20	1.8	6	Follis. *Corr.*	»	II.65
1065 (456)	25	2.7	6	Follis. [Class I]. *Overstrike; worn.*	»	II.54
PLATE 66						
				Class J, 1081-*c.* 1086		
1066 (228)	26	3	11	Follis.	DOC 3.2, Pl. 68, J	
1067 (3764)	24	5.4			»	II.42
1068 (5228)	27	3.8	5	Follis. *Overstruck on follis of Nicephorus III.*	»	II.42
1069 (454)	22	6.3	11	Follis.	»	II.54
1070 (455)	24	4.5	0	Follis. *Overstruck on follis of Nicephorus III.*	»	II.54
1071 (366)	25	4.9		Follis. [Class J]. *Worn.*	»	II.54
1072 (967)	26	4.9	0	Follis. *Corr.*	»	II.29
1073 (5854)	29	12.1	5	Follis. *Overstruck on follis of Constantine X.*	DOC 3.2, cf. Pl. 64, 8	II.56
				Class K, *c.* 1087-1092		
1074 (5867)	29	3.7	5	Follis.	DOC 3.2, Pl. 68	II.56
1075 (308)	26	5.6	5	Follis. *Overstrike.*	»	III.3
1076 (80)	22	5.8	0	Follis.	»	V.3
1077 (440)	26	3.6	5	Follis. *Overstrike.*	»	II.54
1078 (416)	24	6.1	0	Follis.	»	II.54
1079 (6030)	28	3.8		Follis. *Overstrike,probably on type J. Corr.*	»	II.24
1080 (3761)	27	5.4		Follis. *Corr.; obv. ill.*	»	II.42
1081 (4196)	28	4.6		Follis. *Corr.; obv. ill.*	»	I.48
PLATE 67						
1082 (5226)	29	7.4		Follis. *Overstruck on type J.*	DOC 3.2, Pl. 68	II.42
1083 (5227)	25	6.2	5	Follis.	»	II.42
1084 (2129)	26	5.7		Follis.	»	II
1085 (5797)	26	6.3	11	Follis.	»	II.42

1086 (478)	22	0.9	2	Follis. *Thin flan.*	DOC 3.2, Pl. 68	II.54
1087 (941)	24	4.9	6	Follis.	»	II.42
1088 (479)	23	5	6	Follis. *Worn.*	»	II.54
1089 (436)	21	3.4	0	Follis.	»	II.54
1090 (380)	20	2.5		Follis. *Worn; obv. ill.*	»	II.54
				CONSTANTINE X, 1057-1067		
1091 (38)	28	6.1	6	Follis. *Worn.*	DOC 3.2, Pl. 64, 8	V.2
1092 (56)	27	6.5	7	Follis. *Worn, pierced at centre.*	DOC 3.2, Pl. 64, 9	
1093 (170)	30	11.1	5	Follis.	»	
1094 (218)	28	7	4	Follis.	»	
1095 (217)	29	11	5	Follis.	»	

PLATE 68

				ROMANUS IV, 1068-1071		
1096 (4866)	26	5.3	6	Follis.	DOC 3.2, Pl. 65, 8	
1097 (5793)	24	3.4	6	Follis. *Worn, clipped; obv. ill.*	»	II.42
1098 (2252)	23	4.3	5	Follis. *Worn, clipped.*	»	
1099 (3390)	21	4.2	5	Follis. *Worn, clipped; obv. ill.*	»	I.94
1100 (130)	22	3.2		Follis. *Worn; obv. ill.*	»	[V.2]
1101 (252)	22	3.4		Follis. *Worn, clipped; obv. ill.*	»	
1102 (5795)	21	3.5	6	Follis. *Worn, clipped; obv. ill.*	»	II.42
1103 (929)	23	4.4	6	Follis. *Worn, clipped.*	»	II.42
1104 (632)	20	2.5		Follis. *Worn, clipped; obv. ill.*	»	I.35
1105 (643)	22	3.6	6	Follis. *Worn, clipped; obv. ill.*	»	
1106 (3428)	21	2.2	6	Follis. *Worn, clipped; obv. ill.*	»	II.33
1107 (4669)	18	2.6		Follis. *Worn, clipped.*	»	II.47
1108 (4565)	18	2.4		Follis. *Worn, clipped.*	»	II.29
1109 (978)	19	3.2		Follis. *Worn, clipped; obv. ill.*	»	II.29
1110 (1222)	22	3		Follis. *Worn, clipped; obv. ill.*	»	II.8
1111 (3765)	21	2.9		Follis. *Worn, clipped; obv. ill.*	»	II.42
1112 (3766)	20	3		Follis. *Worn, clipped; obv. ill.*	»	II.42
1113 (4252)	21	4		Follis. *Worn, clipped; obv. ill.*	»	II.24
1114 (4804)	20	3.4		Follis. *Worn, clipped; obv. ill.*	»	II.64
1115 (5818)	21	4.5	6	Follis. *Worn, clipped; obv. ill.*	»	II.57
				MICHAEL VII, 1071-1078		
1116 (229)	25	6.2	5	Follis.	DOC 3, 2, Pl. 67, 14[a]	
1117 (5337)	27	6.9	7	Follis. *Overstruck on follis of Romanus IV.*	»	

PLATE 69

				NICEPHORUS III, 1071-1081		
1118 (33)	30	...		[El] Histamenon.	DOC 3.2, Pl. 69, 3a	I/II
1119 (3805)	28	2.67	6	[El] Histamenon. *Incomplete.*	DOC 3.2, Pl. 69, 3a1	I.96
1120 (942)	24	6	6	Follis.	DOC 3.2, Pl. 70, 9	II.42
1121 (3443)	23	5.4	6	»	»	II.58
1122 (481)	23	5.2	6	Follis. *Worn.*	»	II.54
1123 (482)	23	4.1	6	Follis.	»	II.54
1124 (4188)	27	5.8	7	Follis. *Overstruck on type H.*	»	II.2
1125 (5178)	26	5.1	5	Follis. *Overstruck on types of Romanus IV and Michael VII.*	»	II.14
1126 (453)	26	6.1	6	Follis. *Overstrike; shifted die.*	»	II.54
1127 (39)	27	5.1		Follis. *Overstrike.*	»	V.2
1128 (288)	25	6.9	7	Follis.	»	I/II
1129 (3763)	24	5.3	0	»	»	II.42
1130 (472)	24	4.2	6	Follis. *Corr.*	»	II.54

1131 (435)	22	1.4	6	Follis. *Overstrike.*	DOC 3.2, Pl. 70, 9	II.54
PLATE 70						
				11TH CENTURY - UNCERTAIN		
1132 (2253)	28	9.8		Follis of Constantine X (Class 2) or Michael VII, 1059-1078. *Overstruck on follis of Constantine X (Class 1).*	Cf. DOC 3.2, Pls. 64, 8-9/ 67, 14	
1133 (458)	23	2.3	5	Follis. Obv. [Christ] enthroned; Rev. cross with foliate base.		II.54
1134 (473)	24	4.3		Follis. *Corr.*		II.54
1135 (491)	24	3.1		Follis of Alexius I or of Trebizond, type III, *c.* 1100. *Corr.; rev. ill.*	DOC 4.2, Pls. 2, 19/ 25, (3)	II.54
1136 (2194)	21	3		Anonymous follis. *Ill.*		II.33
1137 (2196)	24	2.6		Follis, possibly early Crusader issue. *Worn, ill.*		II.33
1138 (2251)	22	4.2		Anonymous follis, Class B or imitation, [1028-1034]. *Worn, clipped.*	Cf. DOC 3.2, Pl. 55, B	
1139 (5813)	21	3.6		Class C anonymous follis, or follis of Romanus IV, [1034-1071]. *Worn, clipped, ill.*		II.61
				ALEXIUS I, 1092-1118		
1140 (386)	15	0.7	6	Bi Tetarteron. Constantinople, 2nd Coinage. *Incomplete.*	DOC 4.2, Pl. 6, 33	II.54
1141 (437)	22	2.2	0	Bi Tetarteron. Constantinople, type C. *Corr., incomplete.*	DOC 4.2, Pl. 6, 34	II.54
1142 (475)	21	3.4	6	Bi [Tetarteron. Constantinople, type C.] *Corr.*	»	II.54
1143 (395)	20	2.2	6	Bi Tetarteron. Constantinople, type D. *Worn.*	DOC 4.2, Pl. 6, 35	II.54
1144 (446)	16	1	6	Bi Tetarteron. Constantinople, type D. *Worn, incomplete.*	»	II.54
PLATE 71						
1145 (5845)	22	3.6	5	Tetarteron. Thessalonica, 2nd Coinage.	DOC 4.2, Pl. 6, 38	II.38
1146 (718)	22	4.2	6	Tetarteron. Thessalonica, 2nd Coinage. *Worn.*	»	V.10
1147 (4671)	19	2.4	5	»	»	II.47
1148 (654)	19	2.7	6	»	»	I.35
1149 (3620)	21	1.9	6	»	»	II.58
1150 (4833)	19	3.3	5	Tetarteron. Thessalonica, 2nd Coinage. *Corr.; pierced rim.*	»	II.22
1151 (572)	18	2.8	0	Tetarteron. Thessalonica, 2nd Coinage. *Worn.*	»	
1152 (5325)	19	1.6		Tetarteron. Thessalonica, 2nd Coinage.	»	II.42
1153 (968)	19	2.7	6	Tetarteron. Thessalonica, 2nd Coinage. *Worn.*	»	II.29
1154 (5224)	19	1.6		Tetarteron. Thessalonica, 2nd Coinage.	»	II.42
1155 (4111)	22	3.1		Tetarteron. Thessalonica, 3rd Coinage. *Worn.*	DOC 4.2, Pl. 6, 39	
1156 (4254)	18	2.7		»	»	II.24
1157 (1157)	19	2.1		Tetarteron. Thessalonica, 3rd Coinage. *Worn.*	»	I.86
1158 (6031)	20	2.2	1	Tetarteron. Thessalonica, 3rd Coinage. *Overstrike.*	»	II.24
1159 (717*)	...	...		Tetarteron. Thessalonica, 3rd Coinage. *Worn, incomplete.*	»	
1160 (389)	19	2.6		Tetarteron. Thessalonica, 3rd Coinage. *Worn.*	»	II.54
1161 (334)	19	1.3	6	Tetarteron. Thessalonica, 3rd Coinage.	»	I/II
1162 (3781)	21	1.5	6	Tetarteron. Thessalonica, 3rd Coinage. *Corr., incomplete.*	»	II.42
1163 (3997)	20	2.3		Tetarteron. Thessalonica, 3rd Coinage. *Corr.*	»	II.29
PLATE 72						
1164 (5808)	21	2.6	0	Tetarteron. Thessalonica, 4th Coinage. *Overstruck on coin of 3rd Coinage.*	DOC 4.2, Pl. 6, 39	II.42
1165 (3945)	21	2.7	6	Tetarteron. Thessalonica, 4th Coinage. *Overstrike or countermark.*	DOC 4.2, Pl. 7, 40	I.98
1166 (279)	20	2.5	0	Tetarteron. Thessalonica, 4th Coinage. *Incomplete.*	»	I.89
1167 (396)	19	2.8	6	Tetarteron Thessalonica, 4th Coinage. *Worn, incomplete.*	»	II.54
1168 (483)	19	3.1	11	Tetarteron. Thessalonica, 4th Coinage. *Worn.*	»	II.54
1169 (3779)	18	2.4	6	Tetarteron. Thessalonica, 4th Coinage. *Corr.*	»	II.42
1170 (3444)	23	3.3		Tetarteron. Thessalonica, 4th Coinage. *Overstrike.*	»	II.58
1171 (4670)	19	3.1	5	Tetarteron. Thessalonica, 4th Coinage. *Worn.*	»	II.47
1172 (480)	19	2.8	7	Tetarteron. Thessalonica, 4th Coinage. *Worn, incomplete.*	»	II.54

1173 (5364)	22	3.2	11	Tetarteron. Thessalonica, 4th Coinage.	Cf. Zervos 2009, IIIa	II.56
1174 (487)	21	3	6	Tetarteron. Thessalonica, 4th Coinage or imitation. *Corr., incomplete.*	DOC 4.2, cf. Pl. 7, 40	II.54
1175 (4549)	21	0.9		Tetarteron. Thessalonica, 4th Coinage or imitation. *Corr., incomplete.*	»	II.42
1176 (1191)	18	2.2		Tetarteron. Thessalonica, 4th Coinage or imitation. *Corr., incomplete.*	DOC 4.2, cf. Pl. 7, 40	II.56
1177 (571)	20	2.8	6	Tetarteron. Thessalonica, 4th Coinage or imitation.	»	
1178 (4253)	19	2.8	0	Tetarteron. Thessalonica, 4th Coinage or imitation.	»	II.24
1179 (947)	20	2.4	[0]	Tetarteron. Thessalonica, 4th Coinage or imitation. *Incomplete.*	»	II.42
1180 (169)	21	1.7		Tetarteron. Thessalonica, 4th Coinage or imitation. *Corr., incomplete.*	»	
1181 (485)	20	1.8	0	Tetarteron. Thessalonica, 4th Coinage or imitation. *Corr.*	»	II.54
1182 (469)	19	1.5	6	Tetarteron. Thessalonica, 4th Coinage.	»	II.54
PLATE 73						
1183 (885)	19	3		Tetarteron. Thessalonica, 4th Coinage. *Worn.*	»	I.9
1184 (5802)	18	2		Tetarteron. [Thessalonica, 4th Coinage]. *Corr., incomplete; obv. ill.*	»	II.42
1185 (486)	17	1.4		Tetarteron. [Thessalonica, 4th Coinage]. *Corr., incomplete.*	»	II.54
1186 (488)	19	1.5	0	»	»	II.54
1187 (415)	21	2		»	»	II.54
1188 (6)	21	2.4		Tetarteron [Thessalonica, 4th Coinage]. *Worn.*	»	I/II
1189 (4865)	17	2.2	6	Half tetarteron. Uncertain mint.	DOC 4.2, Pl. 7, 45a	
1190 (3923)	22	3.5	0	Imitative tetarteron of 4th Coinage of Thessalonica. *Cross at l. of rev. field.*	Cf. Papadopoulou 2005, Pl. 13, 7-8	I
1191 (5844)	21	2.5	6	Imitative tetarteron of 4th Coinage of Thessalonica. *Cross at l. of rev. field.*	»	II.11
1192 (4574)	21	2	7	Imitative tetarteron of 4th Coinage of Thessalonica.	Cf. Zervos 2009, IIIb	II.29
1193 (5801)	21	1.7	11	Imitative tetarteron of 4th Coinage of Thessalonica. *Corr.*	»	II.42
1194 (368)	22	1.3	10	Imitative tetarteron of 4th Coinage of Thessalonica. *Worn.*	Cf. Papadopoulou 2005, Pl. 13, 2	I/II
1195 (484)	19	3.1	11	Imitative tetarteron of 4th Coinage of Thessalonica. *Corr.*	Cf. DOC 4.2, Pl. 7, 40	II.54
1196 (4462)	22	4.1		Imitative tetarteron of 4th Coinage of Thessalonica. *Worn.*	»	I.91
1197 (656)	21	4.7		»	»	
1198 (3922)	20	2.5	6	»	»	I.40
1199 (6051)	18	2.2	0	Imitative tetarteron of 4th Coinage of Thessalonica. *Corr.*	»	II.35
1200 (3780)	20	3.3	0	Imitative tetarteron of 4th Coinage of Thessalonica. *Worn.*	»	II.42
1201 (5362)	21	2.9	5	Imitative tetarteron of 4th Coinage of Thessalonica. *Obv. corr.*	»	II.56
1202 (567)	20	2		Imitative tetarteron of 4th Coinage of Thessalonica. *Corr., incomplete.*	»	
1203 (5819)	21	2.9		Imitative tetarteron of 4th Coinage of Thessalonica. *Worn.*	»	II.57
1204 (6044)	25	5.3		Coarse follis-size copy of 4th Coinage of Thessalonica tetarteron.	»	II.35
PLATE 74						
				FOLLES OF TREBIZOND, 1081 ff.		
1205 (3760)	23	2.3	7	Follis, type 2, 1081-1090. *Doubled die.*	DOC 4.2, Pl. 25, (2)	II.42
1206 (4598)	30	6	1	Follis, type 3, 1081-1090.	DOC 4.2, Pl. 25, (3)	II.33
1207 (477)	24	2.9	6	Follis, type 3, 1081-1090. *Corr., clipped; rev. ill.*	»	II.54
1208 (414)	20	1.4	0	Follis, type 7, 1098-1103. *Corr., incomplete, clipped.*	DOC 4.2, Pl. 25, (7)	II.54
1209 (468)	24	2.8	6	Follis, type 8, 1098-1103.	DOC 4.2, Pl. 25, 8.1	II.54
				JOHN II, 1118-1143		
1210 (3844)	29	4.1	6	Bi Trachy. Constantinople, 2nd Coinage, var. A.	DOC 4.2, Pl. 9, 10a	II.42
1211 (464)	21	2	6	Tetarteron. Constantinople, type A. *Corr., incomplete.*	DOC 4.2, Pl. 10, 12a	II.54

1212 (3423)	18	2.6	11	Tetarteron, τύπος A. *Rev. corr.*	DOC 4.2, Pl. 10, 12a	II.33
1213 (4672)	18	2.9	6	Tetarteron, τύπος A.	»	II.47
1214 (4564)	21	3.9	6	Tetarteron. Thessalonica.	DOC 4.2, Pl. 10, 14a	II.29
				MANUEL I, 1143-1180		
1215 (4071)	29	4.30	6	AV Hyperpyron. Constantinople, var. II, 1152-*c.* 1160. *Bent, doubled die.*	DOC 4.2, Pl. 10, 1b5	I.106
1216 (606)	31	3.25	6	El Trachy, 1st Coinage, var. B, 1143-1152. *Doubled die.*	DOC 4.2, Pl. 12, 2b	I.57
1217 (34)	33	4.70		El Trachy. Constantinople, 2nd Coinage, var. B, 1152- *c.* 1160.	DOC 4.2, Pl. 12, 3b	II.56
1218 (35)	34	4.44	6	El Trachy. Constantinople, 2nd Coinage, var. B, 1152- *c.* 1160.	»	II.56

PLATE 75

1229 (3845)	31	4.8	5	Bi Trachy. Constantinople, 4th Coinage, var. Da, 1167-80.	DOC 4.2, Pl. 15, 13i	II.42
1220 (4551)	28	4.4		Bi Trachy. Constantinople, 4th Coinage, 1167-80.	DOC 4.2, Pl. 15, 13	II.42
1221 (5809)	30	4.1	5	Bi Trachy. Constantinople, 4th Coinage, var. Da, 1167-80.	DOC 4.2, Pl. 15, 13i	
1222 (5851)	29	3.8	5	Bi Trachy. Constantinople, 4th Coinage, 1167-80. *Corr., flattened.*	DOC 4.2, Pl. 15, 13	II.56
1223 (188)	27	3.4	6	Bi Trachy. Constantinople, 4th Coinage, 1167-80. *Worn, gilded.*	»	
1224 (678)	30	3.3	5	Bi Trachy. Constantinople, 4th Coinage, 1167-80.	»	V.2
1225 (3847)	29	3	6	Bi Trachy. Constantinople, 4th Coinage, 1167-80. *Clumsily flattened.*	»	II.42
1226 (269)	28	2.6		Bi Trachy. 4th Coinage, 1167-80. *Pierced rim.*	»	
1227 (4032)	26	2.3	[6]	Bi Trachy. 4th Coinage, 1167-80. *Neatly clipped; corr.*	»	II.22
1228 (938)	19	1.3	4	Bi Trachy. 2nd Coinage, 1143 ff. *Doubled die; clipped.*	DOC 4.2, Pl. 16, 11	II.42
1229 (960)	19	0.9	[6]	Bi Trachy. 3rd Coinage. *Clipped, worn, flattened; obv. ill.*	DOC 4.2, Pl. 16, 12	II.29
1230 (936)	21	0.8	6	Bi Trachy. 3rd Coinage. *Clipped, corr., incimplete.*	»	II.42
1231 (979)	16	0.6	6	Bi Trachy. 3rd Coinage. *Clipped, worn.*	»	II.29
1232 (973)	16	0.6		Bi Trachy. 3rd Coinage. *Clipped, worn.*	»	II.29
1233 (1063)	20	1.2		Bi Trachy. 4th Coinage. *Clipped, corr.*	DOC 4.2, Pl. 15, 13	II.50
1234 (4269)	19	1		»	»	II.24
1235 (924)	17	0.8	5	[Bi] Trachy. 4th Coinage. *Clipped, worn.*	»	II.42
1236 (2180)	16	0.6	[6]	Bi Trachy or imitation. 4th Coinage. *Clipped.*	»	II.33

PLATE 76

1237 (374)	23	5	5	Tetarteron. Constantinople, 1st Coinage, 1143-52.	DOC 4.2, Pl. 16, 14	II.54
1238 (6052)	18	2	0	»	»	II.35
1239 (167)	23	5	5	Tetarteron. Constantinople, type D, *c.* 1160-4. *Variant of emperor's dress.*	DOC 4.2, Pl. 16, 17a	
1240 (922)	22	6	5	Tetarteron. Thessalonica, type A, 1152-*c.* 1160.	DOC 4.2, Pl. 16, 18	II.42
1241 (587)	17	2.5	6	Tetarteron. Thessalonica, type B. *Worn.*	DOC 4.2, Pl. 16, 19	II.18
1242 (3597)	17	1.8	5	Half tetarteron. Uncertain mint, type A, 1143-52.	DOC 4.2, Pl. 16, 22	II.58
1243 (3782)	18	1.1	6	Half tetarteron. Uncertain mint, type B, 1152-*c.* 1160. *Clipped.*	DOC 4.2, Pl. 16, 23	II.42
				ANDRONICUS I, 1183-1185		
1244 (664)	28	3.4	5	Bi Trachy. Constantinople, var. B. *Pierced rim.*	DOC 4.2, Pl. 17, 3b	V.16
1245 (6038)	28	3	5	Bi Trachy. Constantinople, var. B.	»	II.35
1246 (5803)	21	1.4	6	Trachy [or Latin imitative, large module, type I]. *Incomplete.*	DOC 4.2, Pl. 17, 3/ Hendy, 26, 6	
				ISAAC COMNENUS OF CYPRUS, 1184-1191		
1247 (3846)	31	3.2	6	Trachy [Nicosia], type A. *Incomplete.*	DOC 4.2, Pl. 18, 2	II.42
1248 (3783)	20	3.2	6	Tetarteron [Nicosia], type C.	DOC 4.2, Pl. 19, 8	II.42
				ISAAC II ANGELUS, 1185-1195		
1249 (4437)	29	4.14	6	El Trachy, var. A *but ∴ at l. side of throne.*	DOC 4.2, Pl. 20, 2	II.47
1250 (375)	26	3.9	5	Bi Trachy, var. Db, *but pellets at the tips of the asterisk's rays, and single dot at upper part of* loros.	DOC 4.2, Pl. 21, 3h	I/II

1251 (31)	30	3.5		[Bi] Trachy or faithful copy, type B. *Worn; obv. ill.*	DOC 4.2, Pls. 21 3/ 26, 2	V.2
1252 (175)	27	3.5	6	Bi Trachy, var. C.	DOC 4.2, Pl. 21, 3f	
PLATE 77						
1253 (2254)	26	2.9	6	Bi Trachy. *Single dot at upper part of* loros.	DOC 4.2, Pl. 21, 3	
1254 (199)	26	2.7	6	Bi Trachy. *Flattened.*	»	
1255 (940)	28	2.2	6	Bi Trachy. *Worn, incomplete.*	»	II.42
1256 (122)	26	2.4	0	Bi Trachy. *Worn.*	»	[V.2]
1257 (3850)	25	2.4	6	Bi Trachy, var. Ab. [*Clipped.*] *Doubled die.*	DOC 4.2, Pl. 21, 3b	II.42
1258 (4523)	26	2.4	5	Bi Trachy. [*Clipped.*]	DOC 4.2, Pl. 21, 3	V.16
1259 (3849)	21	2	6	Bi Trachy, *c.* 1200. *Neatly clipped.*	»	
1260 (273)	21	2	5	»	»	V.7
1261 (4552)	22	1.9		»	»	II.42
1262 (283)	21	1.9	6	»	»	?I
1263 (282)	22	1.7	6	Bi Trachy, var. D, *c.* 1200. *Neatly clipped.*	DOC 4.2, Pl. 21, 3g/h	?I
1264 (935)	22	1.6	6	Bi Trachy, *c.* 1200. *Neatly clipped.*	DOC 4.2, Pl. 21, 3	II.54
1265 (5796)	22	1.3	6	»	»	II.42
1266 (227)	18	1.7	5	Bi Trachy, var. Cb, *c.* 1200. *Neatly clipped. Flattened.*	DOC 4.2, Pl. 21, 3f	
1267 (289)	17	1.1	5	Bi Trachy. *Clipped, small size.*	DOC 4.2, Pl. 21, 3	I/II
1268 (1072)	17	1.1		Bi Trachy,var. Ab. *Clipped, small size.*	DOC 4.2, Pl. 21, 3b	I.13
1269 (3621)	21	0.7	6	Bi Trachy. *Clipped, small size.*	DOC 4.2, Pls. 21, 3/ 26, 2	II.58
1270 (2181)	16	0.7	6	»	Cf. DOC 4.2, Pl. 21, 3	II.33
1271 (972)	15	0.9	6	Bi Trachy. *Clipped, small size.*	DOC 4.2, Pl. 21, 3	II.29
1272 (993)	16	0.9	6	»	»	II.29
1273 (3672)	17	0.8		Bi Trachy. *Clipped, small size. Corr.*	»	II.58
1274 (3707)	14	0.6	6	Bi Trachy, var. D. *Clipped, small size.*	DOC 4.2, Pl. 21, 3g/h	II.58
1275 (3623)	14	0.5	0	Bi Trachy. *Clipped.*	DOC 4.2, Pls. 21, 3/ 26, 2	II.58
1276 (3679)	14	0.3	[6]	Bi Trachy. *Clipped. Corr., obv. ill.*	DOC 4.2, Pl. 21, 3	II.58
1277 (385)	12	1	6	Trachy or imitation. *Clipped.*	Cf. DOC 4.2, Pl. 21, 3	II.54
1278 (1181*)	14	1	3	Trachy or faithful copy, type B. *Clipped.*	DOC 4.2, Pl. 26, 2	II.33
1279 (3670)	24	1.2		Trachy or faithful copy, type B. *Corr., incomplete.*	DOC 4.2, Pl. 21, 3	II.58
1280 (946)	...	...		Trachy or faithful copy, type B. *Clipped.*	»	
1281 (4436)	15	0.5		Trachy. *Clipped. Obv. ill.*	»	II.34
PLATE 78						
				ALEXIUS III, 1195-1203		
1282 (129)	27	2.8		Bi Trachy, var. B ff. *Flattened.*	DOC 4.2, cf. Pl. 23, 3d	[V.2]
1283 (5855)	27	2.6	5	Bi Trachy.	DOC 4.2, Pl. 23, 3	II.56
1284 (442)	23	1.7	6	Bi Trachy. *Clipped.*	»	II.54
1285 (5316)	25	1.3	6	»	»	II.41
1286 (121)	20	1.3	6	Bi Trachy, var. A. *Neatly clipped.*	»	[V.2]
1287 (281)	22	1.2	6	Bi Trachy, var. A. *4 dots at upper part of* loros. *Neatly clipped.*	»	?I
1288 (462)	17	1.1	6	»	»	II.54
1289 (2182)	16	0.7	6	Bi Trachy, var. A. *Clipped, small size.*	»	II.33
1290 (3652)	15	0.6	6	»	»	II.58
1291 (6057)	13	0.7	5	Bi Trachy. *Clipped, small size.*	»	II.35
1292 (3657)	18	0.7	6	Bi Trachy. *Clipped.*	DOC 4.2, Pl. 23, 3	II.58
1293 (3953)	12	0.6	5	Bi Trachy or faithful copy, type C. *Clipped.*	DOC 4.2, Pls. 23, 3 /26, 3	II.40
1294 (3655)	13	0.4	6	Bi Trachy. *Clipped, corr.*	DOC 4.2, Pl. 23, 3	II.58
1295 (3625)	13	0.3	6	»	»	II.58
1296 (3666)	13	0.3	0	Bi Trachy. *Clipped. Preserves head of Constantine.*	»	II.58

1297 (3665)	14	0.2	6	Bi Trachy. *Preserves figure of Constantine. 4 dots at upper part of* loros. *Clipped.*	DOC 4.2, Pl. 23, 3a-3c	II.58
				THEODORE I, 1204-1221		
1298 (5318)	28	2.9		Bi Trachy. Nicaea, type A, 1205-1212. *Corr., obv. ill.*	DOC 4.2, Pl. 27, 5	II.41
1299 (5317)	21	0.6		Bi Trachy. Nicaea, type A. *Incomplete, emperor visible; obv. ill.*	Cf. DOC 4.2, Pl. 27, 5	I.43
				JOHN III, 1221-1254		
1300 (3855)	20	1.1		Bi Trachy. Magnesia, type A^2. *Clipped.*	DOC 4.2, Pl. 28, (9)	II.42
1301 (4599)	23	0.8		Bi Trachy. Magnesia, type A^2. *Clipped, corr.*	»	II.33
1302 (610)	19	1.7		Tetarteron. Magnesia, type C.	DOC 4.2, Pl. 34, 58	II.68

PLATE 79

				THEODORE COMNENUS DUCAS OF THESSALONICA, 1224-1230		
1303 (4524)	25	2.2		Bi Trachy. Thessalonica, type A	DOC 4.2, Pl. 48, 4	
				ANDRONICUS I GIDO OF TREBIZOND, 1222-1235		
1304 (3609)	21	1.3		Bi Trachy (Latin imitative, type H). *Clipped.*	Cf. DOC 4.2, L, 8	II.58
1305 (4835)	20	0.7		Bi Trachy (Latin imitative, type H). *Clipped, corr., incomplete.*	»	II.22
				FAITHFUL COPIES OF BYZANTINE TRACHEA		
1306 (4553)	25	1.2		Faithful copy, type B, ? *c.* 1200-1202. *[Clipped.]*	DOC 4.2, Pl. 26, 2	II.42
1307 (423)	26	2.7	5	Faithful copy, type B, ? *c.* 1200-1202. *No throne on the obv.*	»	II.54
1308 (441)	25	3.3	6	Faithful copy, type C, ? c. 1202-15.	DOC 4.2, Pl. 26, 3	II.54
1309 (2255)	27	4.1		Faithful copy, type C, ? c. 1202-15.	»	
1310 (3431)	24	2.6		Faithful copy, type C, ? c. 1202-15.	DOC 4.2, Pl. 26, 3c.1	II.33
1311 (3608)	25	2.7		Faithful copy, type C. *[Clipped.]*	DOC 4.2, Pl. 26, 3	II.58
1312 (3643)	27	2.1		Faithful copy, type C. *Corr.*	»	II.58
1313 (3667)	25	1.2		Faithful copy, type C. *Corr.*	»	II.58
1314 (3965)	25	2.5	7	Faithful copy, type C. *Pierced rim.*	»	IV.7

PLATE 80

				LATIN IMITATIVE TRACHEA, 1204 ff.		
1315 (3749)	29	3.4		Latin imitative, large module. Constantinople, type A. *Corr.*	DOC 4.2, Pl. 48, 1	II.14
1316 (1838)	33	3.9		Latin imitative, large module. Constantinople, type B.	DOC 4.2, Pl. 49, 2	IV.1
1317 (3658)	17	0.2		Latin imitative, large module. Constantinople, type C. *Clipped.*	DOC 4.2, Pl. 49, 3	II.58
1318 (3706)	20	0.7		»	»	II.58
1319 (3853)	18	0.5	6	»	»	II.42
1320 (3628)	14	0.8		Latin imitative, large module. Constantinople, type D or E.	DOC 4.2, Pl. 49, 4/5	II.58
1321 (3807)	27	1.3		Latin imitative, large module. Thessalonica, type A. *Incomplete, flattened.*	DOC 4.2, Pl. 52, 24	V.2
1322 (6033)	28	2.3		Latin imitative, large module. Thessalonica, type A. *Corr.*	»	II.24
1323 (3848)	25	1.3		Latin imitative, large module. Thessalonica type B. *Clipped.*	DOC 4.2, Pl. 52, 25	II.42
1324 (3622)	22	1.5		»	»	II.58
1325 (3650)	19	0.7		»	»	II.58
1326 (3432)	16	0.7		Latin imitative, large module. Thessalonica, type C. *Clipped.*	DOC 4.2, Pl. 52, 26	II.33
1327 (3611)	20	1		»	»	II.58
1328 (3641)	19	0.8		»	»	II.58

PLATE 81

1329 (684)	21	1.4	5	Latin imitative, small module, type A.	DOC 4.2, Pl. 52, 30	I/II
1330 (1001)	22	1.6	6	»	»	II.29

1331 (3599)	21	1.5		Latin imitative, small module, type A.	DOC 4.2, Pl. 52, 30	II.58
1332 (4550)	22	2.1		»	»	II.42
1333 (3616)				»	»	II.58
1334 (3646)				»	»	II.58
1335 (3647)				»	»	II.58
1336 (3673)				»	»	II.58
1337 (3689)				»	»	II.58
1338 (3692)				»	»	II.58
1339 (3795)				»	»	II.42
1340 (4265)				»	»	II.24
1341 (5372)				»	»	II.56
1342 (4381)				»	»	II.20
1343 (5850)				Latin imitative, small module, type A.	»	II.56
1344 (966)				»	»	II.29
1345 (970)				»	»	II.29
1346 (1083)	22	0.7		Latin imitative, small module, type A. *Split.*	»	I.21
1347 (1211)	22	1.8		Latin imitative, small module, type A.	»	II.56
1348 (1213)	19	1.2		»	»	II.56
1349 (3612)	23	1.1		Latin imitative, small module, type A. *Corr., incomplete.*	»	II.58
1350 (3613)	25	1.5		Latin imitative, small module, type A. *Corr.*	»	II.58
1351 (3614)	21	1.2		»	»	II.58
1352 (3615)	19	1		»	»	II.58
1353 (3640)	29	1.6		»	»	II.58

PLATE 82

1354 (3644)	19	1.7		Latin imitative, small module, type A.	DOC 4.2, Pl. 52, 30	II.58
1355 (3663)	23	1.4		Latin imitative, small module, type A. *Corr.*	»	II.58
1356 (3664)	17	1		»	»	II.58
1357 (3674)	21	0.9		»	»	II.58
1358 (3690)	21	0.5		Latin imitative, small module, type A. *Corr., incomplete.*	»	II.58
1359 (3691)	21	1.4		Latin imitative, small module, type A. *Corr.*	»	II.58
1360 (3693)	20	0.7		Latin imitative, small module, type A. *Corr., incomplete.*	»	II.58
1361 (3694)	19	0.4		»	»	II.58
1362 (3744)	20	1.7		»	»	II.14
1363 (3748)	23	1.5		Latin imitative, small module, type A. *Corr.*	»	II.14
1364 (3796)	23	1.3		Latin imitative, small module, type [A].	»	II.42
1365 (3956)	19	0.9	6	Latin imitative, small module, type A.	»	IV.9
1366 (3957)	18	1.4		»	»	IV.9
1367 (3958)	21	1.3		»	»	IV.9
1368 (4103)	1	1.2		Latin imitative, small module, type A. *Corr., incomplete, in two pieces.*	»	II.65
1369 (6005)	21	1.6		Latin imitative, small module, type A. *Corr., incomplete.*	»	II.56
1370 (811)	20	1.4		Latin imitative, small module, type A.	»	I.28
1371 (4267)	20	1.5		»	»	II.24
1372 (4268)	19	0.8		»	»	II.24
1373 (3430)	20	0.9		»	»	II.33
1374 (3436)	21	0.9		»	»	II.33

PLATE 83

1375 (3797)	24	1.7		Latin imitative, small module, type B.	DOC 4.2, Pl. 53, 31	II.42
1376 (3676)	23	0.8		Latin imitative, small module, type B. *Incomplete.*	»	II.58
1377 (3800)	24	1.9		Latin imitative, small module, type B.	»	II.42
1378 (3683)	23	0.5		Latin imitative, small module, type B. *Corr., incomplete.*	»	II.58
1379 (1220)	22	1.4		Latin imitative, small module, type B.	»	II.56
1380 (692)	19	1.4		Latin imitative, small module, type B.	»	I.69

1381 (3604)	22	1.0		Latin imitative, small module, type B. *Corr.*	DOC 4.2, Pl. 53, 31	II.58
1382 (3645)	21	1.3		Latin imitative, small module, type B. *Overstrike on Latin imitative, large module type B of Constantinople.*	»	II.58
1383 (3651)	16	0.9		Latin imitative, small module, type B.	»	II.58
1384 (3696)	17	0.8		»	»	II.58
1385 (3675)	18	0.8		»	»	II.58
1386 (3598)	19	1.4		»	»	II.58
1387 (3695)	21	1.3		»	»	II.58
1388 (3798)	21	1.5		Latin imitative, small module, type C.	DOC 4.2, Pl. 53, 32	II.42
1389 (3925)	22	1.4	6	»	»	I.14
1390 (4527)	18	0.6	5	»	»	II.57
1391 (4529)	18	0.6		»	»	II.57
1392 (1212)	22	1.5		»	»	II.56

PLATE 84

1393 (3799)	25	1.4		Latin imitative, small module, type D. *Corr., bent.*	DOC 4.2, Pl. 53, 33	II.42
1394 (691)	18	1.3		Latin imitative, small module, type D.	»	I.69
1395 (3698)	20	1.1		Latin imitative, small module, type D. *Corr.*	»	II.58
1396 (3699)	17	0.8		Latin imitative, small module, type D. *Corr., bent.*	»	II.58
1397 (3600)	21	1.3		Latin imitative, small module, type D.	»	II.58
1398 (3671)	21	1		Latin imitative, small module, type D. *Corr.*	»	II.58
1399 (3697)	20	0.8		»	»	II.58
1400 (5852)	22	1.1	6	Latin imitative, small module, type D.	»	II.56
1401 (3700)	18	1		Latin imitative, small module, type E.	DOC 4.2, Pl. 53, 34	II.58
1402 (3801)	23	1.2		Latin imitative, small module, type E.	»	II.42
1403 (5371)	23	1	5	»		II.56
1404 (3851)	24	1.3	6	Latin imitative, small module, type E. *Incomplete.*	»	II.42
1405 (3966)	19	0.9		»	»	II.56
1406 (4480)	17	0.6		Latin imitative, small module, type E. *Corr.*	»	II.57
1407 (3677)	18	1		»	»	II.58
1408 (579)	19	0.5	[6]	Latin imitative, small module, type F.	DOC 4.2, Pl. 53, 35	II.18
1409 (4590)	18	0.9		Latin imitative, small module, type F. *Corr.*	»	II.28
1410 (6034)	16	0.3		Latin imitative, small module, type F. *Corr., incomplete.*	»	II.24
1411 (5820)	19	0.9		Latin imitative, small module, type F. *Corr.*	»	II.57

PLATE 85

1412 (3610)	19	0.8		Latin imitative, small module, type G. *Incomplete.*	DOC 4.2, Pl. 53, 36	II.58
1413 (3642)	21	1		Latin imitative, small module, type G. *Corr., incomplete; obv. ill.*	»	II.58
1414 (3648)	24	2		»	»	II.58
1415 (3649)	19	0.7		»	»	II.58
1416 (3686)	21	0.7		Latin imitative, small module, type G. *Corr.*	»	II.58
1417 (3702)	17	0.5		Latin imitative, small module, type G. *Corr., obv. ill.*	»	II.58
1418 (3802)	20	1		Latin imitative, small module, type G. *Worn.*	»	II.42
1419 (3803)	25	1.3		»	»	II.42
1420 (687)	21	1.6		»	»	I/II
1421 (3852)	21	1.1		Latin imitative, small module, type G. *Incomplete; only the saint visible.*	»	II.42
1422 (3954)	21	1.2		Latin imitative, small module, type G.	»	
1423 (4266)	21	1.7		»	»	II.24
1424 (5379)	20	1		Latin imitative, small module, type G. *Corr.*	»	II.56
1425 (5991)	19	1		»	»	II.56
1426 (3624)	19	0.9		Latin imitative, small module, type G. *Corr., incomplete.*	»	II.58
1427 (3738)	21	1.6		Latin imitative, small module, type G. *Corr., in two pieces.*	»	II.14
1428 (4580)	21	1.6		Latin imitative, small module, type G. *Corr.*	»	II.25

1429 (3660)	18	0.9		Latin imitative, small module, type G. *Corr.*	DOC 4.2, Pl. 53, 36	II.58
1430 (3661)	17	0.5		Latin imitative, small module, type G. *Corr., incomplete.*	»	II.58
1431 (3662)	20	0.7		Latin imitative, small module, type G. *Corr.*	»	II.58
1432 (387)	20	0.7		Latin imitative, small module, type G. *Corr., incomplete, in two pieces.*	»	II.54
1433 (6036)	21	1.7		Latin imitative, small module, type G. *Corr.*	»	II.24
1434 (3668)	19	0.6		»	»	II.58
1435 (1215)	19	1.5		Latin imitative, small module, type G.	»	II.56
1436 (1064)	22	0.4		Latin imitative, small module, type G. *Corr., incomplete.*	»	II.50
1437 (4834)	19	0.9		Latin imitative, small module, type G.	»	II.22

PLATE 86

1438 (3746)	19	0.7		Latin imitative, small module, [type A]. *Corr.*		II.14
1439 (4098)	20	0.4		Latin imitative, small module, [type A]. *Corr., incomplete, in two pieces.*		II.65
1440 (383)	18	1.1	6	[Latin imitative, small module, type A.] *Corr., worn.*		II.54
1441 (3858)	19	1.2		Latin imitative, small module, type A or C. *Uniface (obv.)*		II.42
1442 (5197)	16	0.9		Latin imitative, small module, [type B-E]. *Corr.*		II.56
1443 (367)	21	1.1		»		II.54
1444 (4097)	23	1.4		Latin imitative, small module, [type F]. *Corr.*		II.65
1445 (6035)	22	1		Latin imitative, small module, [type F].		II.24
1446 (425)	20	0.8		Latin imitative, small module, [type F-G].		II.54
1447 (969)	19	0.6		»		II.29
1448 (3433)	21	1.3		»		II.33
1449 (4603)	20	1.5		Latin imitative, small module, [type G]. *Corr.*		II.33
1450 (4673)	22	1.3	0	Latin imitative, small module, [type G.]		II.47
1451 (3637)	24	1.3		Latin imitative, small module, [type G]. *Corr.*		II.58
1452 (3602)	22	0.8		Latin imitative, small module, [type G].		II.58
1453 (3638)	21	0.7		»		II.58
1454 (4481)	19	1.3		Latin imitative, small module, [type G]. *Corr.*		II.57
1455 (4528)	17	0.6		»		II.57
1456 (3678)	21	1		Latin imitative, small module. *Corr., incomplete.*		II.58
1457 (1023)	17	0.7		»		II.31
1458 (1214)	16	0.7		Latin imitative, small module. *Ill.*		II.56
1459 (3435)	19	1.7		»		II.33
1460 (3601)	23	1		Latin imitative, small module. *Corr.*		II.58
1461 (939)	23	2.1		Latin imitative, small module. *Ill.*		II.42
1462 (3593)	19	0.9		»		II.58
1463 (3636)	18	0.7		Imitative, small module. *Rev. emperor with* akakia. *Corr., incomplete.*		II.58
1464 (4270)	20	0.8		Imitative, small module. *Rev. hip length emperor, dress of Isaac II, holds* labarum *l.*, globus cruciger *r. Obv. ill. Corr.*		II.24
1465 (420)	17	0.3		Imitative, small module. *Rev. emperor in dress of Isaac II, Corr., incomplete.*		II.54

PLATE 87

LOCAL IMITATIVE TRACHEA
c. 1221 ff.

1466 (3653)	20	1		Imitative A_{p}. *Obv. [Facing bust of Christ]. Rev.* Theotokos *crowns emperor. Corr., incomplete.*	DOC 4.2, cf. Pls 27, 5/ 50, 8	II.58
1467 (3654)	18	1.1		Imitative A_{p}. *Corr.*	»	II.58
1468 (3688)	21	1.6		Imitative A_{p}. *Corr., incomplete.*	»	II.58
1469 (3854)	20	1.5		Imitative A_{p}. *Corr.*	»	II.42
1470 (4042)	23	1		».	»	II.62
1471 (3704)	19	0.5		Imitative A_{p}.	»	II.58

1472 (384)	22	1		Imitative A_p. *Corr., incomplete.*	DOC 4.2, cf. Pls 27, 5/ 50, 8	II.54
1473 (986)	19	0.6		Imitative A_p. *Corr., clipped.*	»	II.29
1474 (6140)	19	1		»	»	V.2
1475 (382)	18	0.6		Imitative A_p. *Worn, incomplete.*	»	II.54
1476 (3709)	20	0.5		Imitative. *Rev. Standing emperor in dress of John III. Clipped.*	Cf. DOC 4.2, Pl. 33, 42-44	II.58
1477 (3750)	20	1		*Imitative* B_p, *Obv. [Frontal bust of Christ]. Rev. half-length emperor holds [*labarum*] l.,* globus cruciger *r. Clipped.*	Cf. DOC 4.2, Pl. 31, 20/22	II.14
1478 (3955)	24	0.9		*Imitative* B_p, *Corr., clipped; obv. ill.*	»	IV.9
				UNIDENTIFIED TRACHEA		
1479 (3669)	20	0.6		Trachy [of Theodore I], 1204 ff. *Corr., incomplete.*	Cf. DOC 4.2, Pl. 28, 7-8	II.58
1480 (3708)	20	0.8		Trachy [of Theodore I], [1204-1222]. *Obv. Bust of Christ. Rev. [Theodore I] l. and military saint r. holding between them* globus cruciger. *Clipped.*	Cf. DOC 4.2, Pls 27, 5/ 31, 28	II.58
1481 (3705)	21	0.5		Imitation of coin of Alexius III, 1204 ff. *Corr., incomplete.*	DOC 4.2, cf. Pl. 23, 3	II.58
1482 (3926)	28	2.4	6	Trachy [of John III], 1222 ff. *Obv. Saint holds lance l. and shield r. rosette at l. field. Rev. emperor and military saint hold [cross with long staff] betw. them. Broken.*		II.8
1483 (4135)	20	1.2		Imitative, 1204 ff. *Rev.* Theotokos *crowns emperor.*		II.41
1484 (3804)	24	1.2		Imitative. *Corr., incomplete, overstrike.*	Cf. DOC 4.2, Pl. 49, 6	II.42
1485 (4499)	28	2.4	5	Imitative, 1204 ff. *Rev. Emperor with dress of Isaac II. Possibly other figure at r.*	Cf. DOC 4.2, Pl. 21, 3	I.91
1486 (5483)	11	0.5		*Obv. Bust of Christ. Fragment.*		II.56

PLATE 88

				UNCERTAIN TETARTERA		
1487 (6012)	20	1.4	0	[Alexius I, 1095-1118]. *Obv. Bust of Christ. Rev. [Imperial bust]. Corr., half.*	Cf. DOC 4.2, Pl. 6, 33	II.64
1488 (372)	20	2.1	0	*Obv. Military saint. Rev. Blessing cross.*		II.54
1489 (4226)	16	0.8		Tetarteron or coin of Mytilene (Dorino Gattilusio, 1428-49). *Obv. Letter B visible at r. field next to standing figure or cross. Corr.*	Cf. Metcalf (1995), Pl. 45, 1168	
				ILLEGIBLE TRACHEA		
1490 (5184)	30	3.5		*Rev. Emperor, possibly other figure r. Corr., incomplete.*		II.34
1491 (4099)	23	0.7		*Rev. ...C ΔE... Corr., fragment.*		II.65
1492 (3656)	23	1.3		*Obv. Enthroned figure. Rev. Emperor. Corr.*		II.58
1493 (3685)	22	1.5		[Latin imitative, small module.] *Corr.*		II.58
1494 (5588)	21	0.7		»		II.56
1495 (987)	19	0.7		»		II.29
1496 (3747)	19	0.9		»		II.14
1497 (3434)	20	0.6		»		II.33
1498 (3603)	18	0.6		»		II.58
1499 (3426)	18	1		»		II.33
1500 (3687)	19	0.6		[Latin imitative, small module.] *Corr., incomplete.*		II.58
1501 (3794)	17	0.7		»		II.42
1502 (3682)	17	0.4		[Latin imitative, small module.] *Rev. Lower edge of long garb visible. Corr., incomplete.*		II.58
1503 (4581)	18	0.9		[Latin imitative, small module.] *Corr.*		II.25
1504 (3684)	11	0.2		[Latin imitative, small module.] *Corr., incomplete.*		II.58
1505 (5192)	22	1.6		Imitative. *Rev.* Theotokos *crowns emperor. Corr.*		II.34
1506 (5923)	22	0.7		*Corr., incomplete; in two pieces.*		II.56
1507 (3701)	19	0.4		Incomplete; in two pieces.		II.58
1508 (3680)	15	0.3		Clipped; corr., incomplete.		II.58
1509 (3681)	11	0.2		»		II.58

1510 (3703)	14	0.2		Fragment.		II.58

PLATE 89

				LEO GAVALAS, [1204]-1240		
1511 (522)	17	0.8	1	**A.** *Obv.* ...A]IC/[P]OΓ[/...ΛAC *Rev.* [+O]... /ΛOC.../BAC.../...	Schl. VIII, 18	II.50
1512 (523)	16	1	0	*Obv.* .../CAP.../BAΛ... *Rev.* ...Δ]OY/[ ]OCTOV/BACI[Λ	»	II.50
1513 (588)	18	0.9	10	*Obv.* KAIC/]APOΓ[/BAΛA[*Rev.* OΔOY/ΛOCTOV/BACI[	»	II.18
1514 (910)	19	0.6	3	*Obv.* [KAIC/CAPO[.../BAΛA[C] *Rev.* [+]/OΔO.../ O]C... /... [CI]...	»	I.45
1515 (912)	19	0.9	11	*Obv.* K.../CAPO.../BAΛA[*Rev.* .../ΛOC.../BACI.../+	»	I.45
1516 (1717)	17	0.8	1	*Obv.* K.../[C]APOΓA/]AΛA[*Rev.* .../ΛOCTOV/BACIΛ[E]/+	»	II.18
1517 (3756)	18	0.9	3	*Obv.* KAI/CAP·O.../]BAΛ... *Rev.* .../C TOY/BACIΛE[/+	»	II.42
1518 (3960)	18	10.4	4	*Obv.* K.../APOΓ[/[B]AΛAC/[+] *Rev.* .../OCTOV/[BACI...	»	IV.9
1519 (539)	17	0.8	2	*Obv.* KAI[C/CAPO[/]BAΛA[*Rev.* +/OΔOY/ΛOCTOV[/ACIΛE	»	III.2
1520 (3639)	17	0.8	1	*Obv.* .../...POΓA/[ ]AΛAC *Rev.* .../...[O]C.../BACIΛ[/+	»	II.58
1521 (3731)	17	1.5	10	*Obv.* KAI/CAP.../BAΛ... *Rev.* .../OCTOY/BACI...	»	II.14
1522 (1718)	17	0.9	7	*Obv.* [+] /.../BAΛAC *Rev.* .../...CTOV/BACIΛ[*Slightly bent.*	»	
1523 (3508)	18	0.6	1	*Obv.* KAI.../CAP[O.../]AΛAC *Rev.* ...ΔO.../]CTOV/...ACIΛE/+ *Corr., incomplete.*	»	II.58
1524 (4457)	17	0.8	1	**A**$_1$ *Obv.* KAI/CAPO[ΓA]/BAΛ... *Rev.* OΔOY/ΛOCTOV/BACIΛ[	»	I.91
1525 (1151)	19	1.2		**B.** *Obv.* KAIC/CAP O' ΓA/BAΛAC *Rev.* +/O' Δ]OŶ/TOŶBA/CIΛE'S/+	»	
1526 (538)	18	1.6	10	*Obv.* KAIC]/CAPO[Γ../BAΛA[*Rev.* .../TOVB[/CIΛE/+]	»	III.2
1527 (3561)	18	1	3	*Obv.* KAIC/CA[PO /BA... *Rev.* +/OΔOŶ/TOŶB.../CIΛE...	»	II.58
1528 (3605)	18	0.8	2	*Obv.* KAIC/[C]AP·O[Γ] /BAΛA *Rev.* +/OΔOŶ/TOŶBA/CIΛE[C]	»	II.58
1529 (3755)	18	0.9	7	*Obv.* KAI/[C]AP·O.../[BA]... *Rev.* +/...ΔOŶ/]OŶBA/CIΛES/+	»	II.42
1530 (3928)	20	1.2	4	*Obv.* KAIC /CAPOΓA/BAΛAC *Rev.* +/O.../TOŶBA/CIΛES/+	»	I
1531 (4255)	18	1		*Obv.* .../...APOΓA/[B]AΛAC *Rev.* ...O.../TOŶ [B.../CIΛE[/+	»	II.24
1532 (6025)	18	1.6	8	*Obv.* +KAIC/CAP·OΓA/...[C *Rev.* ...Y/...BA/...ES	»	II.24
1533 (6024)	18	0.9	9	*Obv.* [+KAIC/]AP·O.../...AΛ... *Rev.* .../TOŶBA/CIΛE[*Corr.*	»	II.24
1534 (681)	18	0.9	8	*Obv.* KAIC/]POΓA/]AΛAC *Rev. Indistinct.*	»	
1535 (4526)	18	0.9	3	*Obv.* KAIC/CAP.../BAΛAC *Rev.* ...TOŶBA...	»	II.41
1536 (4840)	18	0.8	7	*Indistinct. Overstrike [similar dies]*	»	II.41
1537 (5849)	19	1.5	2	*Obv.* KAI[C/CAP·O... *over* ...OY/...TOVB/...IΛES *Rev.* +/OΔOY[Λ]/...OYB... *over* ...AP.../BAΛ...		II.56

PLATE 90

1538 (3929)	19	0.8	3	**C.** *Obv.* [+]/KAIC/]APOΓA/...AC *Rev.* OΔ.../ΛOC.../BACIΛ	»	II.39
1539 (6141)	18	0.8		**D.** *Obv.* KAIC/CAPOΓA/BAΛAC *Rev.* +OΔOY/...CTOVBA/CIΛE[C	»	V.2
				JOHN GAVALAS, 1240-1250		
1540 (3393)	16	0.9	7	*Obv.* [✳]GƆI⚜/OΓABA/ ∵ ΛAC˙ *Rev.* +/ AVΘEN/THCTHC/POΔOY/+	Schl. VIII 19	
1541 (524)	17	0.7		*Obv.* ✳GƆI⚜/OΓABA/ ∵ Λ... *Rev.* ...ΘEN/THCTHC/POΔOY/+	»	
1542 (3961)	18	0.8	8	*Obv.* ✳GƆI⚜/OΓABA/ ∵ ΛAC˙ *Rev.* OAVΘEN/THCTHC/POΔOY/+	»	
1543 (4164)	16	0.5	10	*Obv.* .../OΓA.../ ∵ ΛAC˙ *Rev.* ...ΘE/...HC.../... *Incomplete.*	»	II.34
1544 (974)	19	1		*Obv.* ✳/...ΓA/... *Rev.* .../TH.../...ΔOY/+ *Overstrike.*	»	II.29

PLATE 91

				GAVALAS SUCCESSORS, 1250-1309		
1545 (1720)	17	0.7		**1.** *A: Cross potent, pellet in each quarter. B: B.* [1250-1254]		
1546 (5188)	15	0.6		[Similar.] *Rev. ill.*		II.34
1547 (5202)	18	0.6		Similar.		II.56
1548 (1216)	17	1		**2.** *A: B, crosslet with a pellet in each quarter r.* *B: B, five-pointed star l.*	Cf. Schl. VIII 29	II.56
1549 (3399)	18	1.3		Similar.	»	1954
1550 (3927)	17	0.4		Similar.	»	II. 8
1551 (6054)	18	0.7	1	Similar.	»	II. 35
1552 (5199)	18	1		[Similar.] *Cross on side A indistinct.*	»	II. 56
1553 (5201)	18	0.5		**2b.** *A: B, crosslet pommy r.* *B: B, [star l.]*		II. 56
1554 (5196)	17	0.8		**3.** *A & B: From the vertical of a cross issue two B, te one below turned left. In upper l. quarter a star of six rays; In lower r. quarter a saltire pommy. Corr., [overstrike.]*	Schl. XIX 18. Cf. MEC 14, Pl. 319, 322	II.56

PLATE 92

1555 (1153)	16	0.6		**4.** *A: Within circle of pellets, pair of facing Bs composed of strings of pearls with a thin outline, separated by a crosslet pommy; pellet within loops of each B. B: Fleur-de-lys within circle of pellets.* [1254-1258]	Schl. VIII 25	I.73
1556 (804)	20	0.8		Similar. *Overstruck by B + on side A and B on side B.*	»	I.70
1557 (1190)	16	0.6		Similar.	»	II.56
1558 (2165)	16	1		Similar.	»	V.2
1559 (3425)	15	0.6		Similar.	»	II.33
1560 (3439)	15	0.8		Similar.	»	II.58
1561 (4655)	15	0.5		Similar.	»	II.52
1562 (6076)	17	0.7		Similar. *Corr.*	»	II.23
1563 (504)	16	0.3		**5.** *A: Within circle of pellets, a pair of facing Bs separated by a cross potent; within the upper loops a pellet, within the lower loops a rosette composed of central pellet and dots. B: Within circle of pellets,* Π *and* Λ *[or* A*] flanking a fleur-de-lys. Corr.* [1258-1261]	Schl. XX 27	II
1564 (603)	18	0.3		**6a** *A: Within circle, a cross between facing Bs with loops [decorated with rosettes of dots]. B: Clumsy fleur-de-lys. Corr., incomplete.*	Cf. Schl. IX 11	II.18
1565 (5814)	17	0.5	10	**6b** *A: Pair of facing Bs separated by a cross; stars above and below. B: [*Π*] and* Λ *flanking a fleur-de-lys.*	»	II.62
1566 (3716)	16	0.2	3	**6c** *A: Within a circle of pellets [B], star l. B: Within circle of pellets,* Π *and [*Λ*] flanking a fleur-de-lys.*	»	II.14
1567 (364)	23	1.4		**7.** *A:* Π *and* Λ *(or* A*) flanking Latin cross, all recorated with thorny projections. B: Within circle,* B *with tall vertical, star l.* [1261-1273]	Cf. Schl. IX 7	I.35
1568 (4451)	16	0.7		Similar. *Clipped.*	»	II.50
1569 (4837)	20	1.4		Similar.	»	II.41
1570 (5921)	15	0.5		**8.** *A: Cross [potent with thorny projections]. B:* B, *perhaps on of a pair arranged back-to-back.*	Cf. Schl. VIII 29	II.56
1571 (4199)	17	0.3		Similar. *Overstruck on type with cross with outwards-facing B in each quarder. Corr.*	»	II.29
1572 (1018)	15	0.4		**9.** *A:* ΠA *ligature and* Λ. *B: [*B*]. Folded flan.*	Cf. Schl. VIII 31	II.31

PLATE 93

1573 (3717)	21	1.2		**10.** *A:* B C *[within circle of pellets]. B:* X M *[within circle of pellets]. Abbreviation stroke above.* [1273-c. 1278]	Schl. XIX 14	II.14
1574 (3757)	14	0.3	2	Similar. *[Clipped.]*	»	II.42
1575 (4658)	17	0.6		»	»	II.52
1576 (4587)	16	0.7		Similar.	»	II.28

1577 (5200)	17	0.8		[Similar.] *Side A ill.*	Schl. XIX 14	II.56
1578 (5847)	15	0.7		Similar. *[Clipped.]*	»	II.56
1579 (5930)	16	0.4		Similar. *[Clipped.]*	»	II.56
1580 (907)	16	0.8		Similar. *On side A star below.*	»	
1581 (1021)	15	0.7		*A:* B C *[within circle of pellets]. B:* X M *[within circle of pellets]. Abbreviation stroke.*	»	II.31
1582 (4642)	16	0.3		**11.** *A:* B C, *crosslet above. B: [*Α*], [*Λ*], [*Π*], [*Β*] in quarters of cross. Within circle.* [*c.* 1278-94]	Schl. VIII 22	II.52
1583 (971)	16	0.3		Similar. *Corr.*	»	II.29
1584 (995)	15	0.3		»	»	II.29
1585 (1005)	16	0.4	0	Similar.	»	II.29
1586 (3715)	16	0.3		Similar. *Corr, incomplete.*	»	II.14
1587 (5846)	15	0.5		Similar.	»	II.38
1588 (6026)	16	0.3		»	»	II.24
1589 (4057)	15	0.5		[Similar.] *Side A ill.*	»	II.13
1590 (599)	18	1.7		**12.** *A:* B C *back-to-back. B:* Α, Π, *[..., ... in the quarters of cross] within circle. Near the edge* B *visible from overstrike.*		II.18
1591 (4134)	19	0.7		**13a** *A: Cross, ouwards-turned* B *in each quarter. B: Standing emperor holding* labarum *and the letters* ΠΑ *from circumferential inscription r. Local countermark.*	Schl. IX 4	II.41
1592 (921)	14	0.5		[Similar]. *[Overstruck.] Different die from the rest of the type. Side B ill.*	»	II.42
1593 (3401)	17	0.9		Similar. *Countermark.*	»	II.41
1594 (3402)	16	0.6		»	»	II.41
1595 (3932)	20	1.1		»	»	I.39
1596 (3758)	19	1.2		**13b** *A: Cross, ouwards-turned* B *in each quarter, accompanied by varying number of dots. B: Standing emperor holding [*labarum*], circumferential* AVTOK*; within circle.*	»	II.42
1597 (1721)	18	0.8		Similar. *Worn.*	»	

PLATE 94

1598 (3380)	24	2.6	8	AR Dirhem. *Obv.* Kalima *in two lines separated by tendril knotted in the middle. Rev: Islamic inscription in five lines. Sultanate of Rum. Local countermark.* [*c.* 1278-94]		
1599 (2200)	16	0.6		**14.** *A: Cross potent, pellet in each corner. Within circle. B: Pair of* Bs *back-to-back, star above. Within circle. Doubled die, doublestruck.* [1294-1304]		I.53
1600 (3808)	17	0.9		Similar.		II.19
1601 (4209)	14	0.3		[Similar.] *Side A ill.*	»	
1602 (4256)	19	1		Similar.	»	II.24
1603 (4646)	17	0.5		»	»	II.52
1604 (5368)	17	0.7		»	»	II.56
1605 (5804)	16	0.5		*A & B: Cross potent. Broken, incomplete.*		II.42
1606 (3720)	21	1.3		**15.** *A: Latin cross with splayed base and horizontal bar in the form of a* B *turned downwards; Pellet below. B: Ill.*	DOC 5.2, cf. Pl. 33, 558	II.14

PLATE 95

1607 (674)	17	0.6		**16.** *A:In the quarters of a cross four* Bs *disposed slantwise, turned inwards to form a lozenge; within a circle. B: In the quarters of a cross the letters* Ο, Θ, Δ *and* Γ *disposed radially clockwise, except in the case of* Γ, *which is placed normally at lower right; within a circle.* [1294-1304]	Cf. Schl. VIII 30	
1608 (3930)	17	0.7		Similar.	»	
1690 (3931)	17	0.7		Similar. *Suspicion of older striking with very faint* B *turned outwards in the quarter of the* O. *The die of side B probably idebtical with the previous specimen's.*	»	I.34
1610 (4136)	17	0.5		Similar. *Overstruck as a Hospitaller coin: the initial crosslet of the inscription and part of a beaded circle are visible on side B.*	»	II.41
1611 (4431)	17	0.6		Similar.	»	II.34

1612 (5195)	17	0.8	Similar.	Cf. Schl. VIII 30	II.56
1613 (337)	20	-	**17.** *A: In the quarters of a cross four* Bs *disposed slantwise, turned inwards to form a lozenge; within a circle. B: In the quarters of a cross the letters* O, Θ, Δ *and* C *disposed radially.* [1294-1304]	Schl. VIII 30	I.82
1614 (862)	20	0.9	Similar.	»	II.12
1615 (999)	19	0.6	»	»	II.29
1616 (2170)	19	...	»	»	I.50
1617 (3722)	17	0.6	»	»	II.14
1618 (3806)	18	1.3	»	»	V.2
1619 (4786)	17	0.9	Similar. *Within circle [of pellets].*	»	
1620 (349)	21	1.3	**18.** *A & B: Cross, ouwards-turned* B *in each quarter.*	Schl. VIII 23	
1621 (800)	20	1.3	Similar.	»	I.38
1622 (914)	20	1.5	»	»	I.59
1623 (980)	20	1.8	»	»	II.29
1624 (1719)	16	0.4	Similar. *Corr.*	»	
1625 (4208)	20	0.8	Similar.	»	
1626 (5258)	21	0.9	»	»	II.41
1627 (3424)	20	0.5	*A & B: Cross, ouwards-turned* B *in each quarter.Overstruck on type 17.*	»	II.33
PLATE 96					
1628 (5232)	17	0.5	**19a** *A: In the quarters of a cross four pellets and, further out, four* Bs *disposed slantwise, turned inwards, forming a lozenge; within border of four cusps. B: Within a border of four cusps monogram with two* Bs *back-to-back joined by an* N. *The lower loop of the* B *on the r. indistinct, perhaps due to a second strike. Pellets decorate the loops of the* Bs *and the wedges above and below the joining stroke of the* N. *Within border. Corr.* [*c.* 1304-1307]	Cf. Schl. IX 3	II.20
1629 (5382)	17	0.4	[Similar.] *Corr.*	»	II.56
1630 (6059)	15	0.5	[Similar.] *Worn.*	»	II.35
1631 (861)	16	0.5	**19b** *A: In the quarters of a cross four four* Bs *disposed slantwise, turned inwards, forming a lozenge. B: Within border monogram with two* Bs *back-to-back joined by an* N. *From the middle of the* B *on the r. projects the vertical of a horizontal* T. [*c.* 1304-1307]	Cf. Schl. XIX 12	II.12
1632 (1102)	15	0.6	Similar.	»	V.16
1633 (1194)	15	0.5	»	»	II.56
1634 (3726)	15	0.5	[Similar.] *Side B ill.*	»	II.14
1635 (4026)	16	0.7	**19c** *A: In the quarters of a cross four four* Bs *disposed slantwise, turned inwards, forming a lozenge. Border of four cusps within circle. B: monogram with two* Bs *back-to-back joined by an* И. *Border of four cusps.* [*c.* 1304-1307]		II.62
1636 (4624)	15	0.7	**20.** *A: In the quarters of a cross four four carelessly disposed* Bs. *B: In the quarters of a cross four four* Bs *disposed slantwise, forming a lozenge.* [*c.* 1307-1309]	Cf. Schl. VIII 24/ XIX 13	II.24
1637 (5601)	19	1.1	Similar.	»	II.41
1638 (4635)	18	0.5	Similar. *On side B the letters turned inwards.*	»	II.52
			UNRELATED TYPES, 1250-1309)		
1639 (4257)	14	0.5	**21.** *A: Monogram [*H *and* E*]. B: Monogram [*R *and* E*].*		II.24
1640 (3718)	16	0.6	**22.** *A:* A *or monogram* AΓ. *B: [Cross].*	Schl. VIII 21	II.14
1641 (4601)	17	0.7	*A: [Figure.] B: [Monogram (?*KA*) or part of imperial dress].*		II.33
			LOCAL ISSUES, ILLEGIBLE (not illustrated)		
1642 (526)	16	0.4	Ill.		II.50
1643 (1172)	18	0.6	Gavalas?		II.56
1644 (1193)	14	0.2	Corr.		II.56
1645 (3924)	14	0.3	*Standing figure on one side. ?Flattened trachy.*		I.35
1646 (4241)	17	0.5			II.21

1647 (4589)	14	0.2		B *on one side. Fragment.*		II.28
1648 (4648)	16	0.4		Worn.		II.52
1649 (4652)	13	0.1		Corr.		II.52
1650 (4839)	18	0.5		[Cross, letters in quarters.]		II.41
1651 (5187)	16	0.8		Ill.		II.34
1652 (5198)	17	0.8		*On one side cross,* [O] *in quarter.*		II.56
1653 (5241)	14	0.4		Ill.		II.55
1654 (5259)	15	0.6		*On one side* B *possibly with* C *or* B *r., crosslet between.*		II.41
1655 (5895)	16	0.7		*On one side* B. *Corr.*		II.56
1656 (6027)	15	0.2		Corr.		II.24
1657 (6142)	15	0.8		Ill.		V.2

PLATE 97

				HOSPITALLER AR - AV		
1658 (1813)	27	3.81		AR Gigliato of Elion de Villeneuve, 1332-46. *Obv.* ✠ ·FR: ЄLIOП':D: VILAПOVA·D'I ˙GRACIA *Rev.* ✠˙OSPTAL':S:IOhIS·IRLП·OT': RODI·	Metcalf 1995, Pl. 46, 1183	
1659 (4133)	21	1.44		AR Asper of Elion de Villeneuve, 1332-46. *Obv.* ✠ · FR: ЄLIOПVS: DЄI:GR[ACIA] *Rev.* ✠ MAR· OSPITALIS·IRLПI·	Metcalf 1995, Pl. 46, 1187-1190	II.41
1660 (1722)	18			AR Tierce of Juan Fernandez de Heredia, 1376-96. *Obv. At r. field castle and, below,* G. ✠ IOh... [Є]R[Є] ... DI... *Rev.* ✠OSPITALIS ·I...SI[ ]RI	Cf. Schl. X 10	II
1661 (4634)	20	1.18	3	AR Tierce of Juan Fernandez de Heredia, 1376-96. *Obv.* ✠FIOhЄS[ ]ЄRA[ ]D[ ]DGR[A... *Rev.* ✠ OSPITALI...S...	»	II.52
1662 (4674)	19	1.04	0	Tierce of Juan Fernandez de Heredia, 1376-96. *Obv.* ✠FIOhЄS hЄRA... GRA... *Rev.* ...ITALIS[.]S : IhOIS IЄR...	»	II.47
1663 (6104)	19	1.18	11	AR Tierce of Juan Fernandez de Heredia, 1376-96. *Obv. [? Rosette] below the cross.* G *missing below the castle.* ...DGRAMA· *Rev.* ✠OSPIT... [IOIS] ...	»	IH
1664 (608)	19	1.12	3	AR Tierce of Philibert de Naillac, 1396-1421. *Obv.* ... [ПЄIL] ... *Rev.* ✠OSPIT[A... Ih·D] ... *Worn*	Schl. X 12	II.68
1665 (3437)	22	1.60	3	AR Giannetto of Jean de Lastic, 1437-1454. *Obv.* ✠F:IOhS:D:LЄSTIC:MAGIST: *Rev.* ✠:OSPITALIS:S:IOhS:IRLMI:R:	Metcalf 1995, Pl. 48, 1220	II.58
1666 (2376)	22	3.55		AV Sequin of Jacques de Milly, 1454-61. *Obv.* ·RЄGISISTЄ DVCT - ·SIT·T·XPЄ·DATQTV- · *Rev. Under the banner* M/R. *On lower section of staff* G. S|·|I|O|h|S|·|B|· ·F·IΛCOBUS·D· ... V-	Cf. Schl. X 19	II.69
1667 (4556)	22	3.51	6	AV Sequin of Fabrizio del Carretto, 1513-21. *Obv.* ·RЄGIS ˙ISTЄ·DV - ·SIT·T·XPЄ·DΛT; QTV· *Rev. Under the banner* M|F|⊗. ·S|I|O|Λ|П|П|I -F·FΛBRICII·D·CΛ Λ. *Exergue.*	Cf. Schl. XI, 14	
1668 (3376)[a]	36	8.67		AR Lira of Fabrizio del Carretto, 1513-21. *Obv. In field* F-C. ЄCCЄ◦AGПVS◦ DЄI[ ]QVITOLIS ◦P◦MV◦ *Rev.* ✠F FABRICII·DЄCAR[RЄ]TTO⁝MAGПVS⁝M⁝RO	Schl. XI, 11	Rhodes Town/ 1994
1669 (3377)	29	3.65		AR Half lira of Fabrizio del Carretto, 1513-21. *Obv. In field* F-C. ЄCCЄ◦ AGПVS◦D-[ЄI]QVITOLIS◦P˙ *Rev.* ✠F·FABRICII·DЄ· CARRЄTTO ·MAGП[I]M[·] R[·]	Cf. Schl. XI 16	Rhodes Town/ 1994
1670 (1167)[b]	29	5.05	8	AR Half lira of Fabrizio del Carretto, 1513-21. *Obv. In field* F-C. ЄCCЄ◦ AGПVS◦D-ЄI◦QVITOLIS◦P˙ *Rev.* ✠F◦FABRICII◦DЄ◦ CARRЄTTO◦ MAGП◦M◦	»	Rhodes Town/ 1990
1671 (1168)	29	5.07	7	AR Half lira of Fabrizio del Carretto, 1513-21. *Obv. In field* F-C. ЄCCЄ◦ AGПVS◦D-ЄI◦QVITOLIS◦P˙ *Rev.* ✠F◦FABRICII◦DЄ◦ CARRЄTTO◦MAG◦M	»	Rhodes Town/ 1990
1672 (1169)	30	5.09	4	AR Half lira of Fabrizio del Carretto, 1513-21. *Obv. In field* F-C. ЄCCЄ◦ AGПVS◦D-ЄI◦QVITOLIS◦P˙ *Rev.* ✠F◦FABRICII◦DЄ◦ CARRЄTTO◦MAG◦M	»	Rhodes Town/ 1990

1673 (1170)	30	5.06	10	AR Half lira of Fabrizio del Carretto, 1513-21. *Obv. In field* F-C. ƐⱭⱭƐ· ĦGNVS·Ɒ-ƐI·ⱭVITOLIS·P *Rev.* +F·FĦBRIⱭII·ƊƐ· ⱭĦRRƐTTO·MĦGN·M·R·	Cf. Schl. XI, 16.	Rhodes Town/ 1990
1674 (1171)	29	5.15	11	AR Half lira of Fabrizio del Carretto, 1513-21. *Obv. In field* F-C. ƐⱭⱭƐ° ĦGNVS°Ɒ-ƐI°ⱭVITOLIS°P˙ *Rev.* +FFA̅BRICII⁝ƊƐ CA̅RRƐTTO⁝MA̅GNVS˙M˙R·	»	Rhodes Town/ 1990
1675 (4555)	29	5.10	1	AR Half lira of Fabrizio del Carretto, 1513-21. *Obv. In field* F-C. ƐⱭⱭƐ° ĦGNVS°Ɒ-ƐI°ⱭVITOLIS°P˙ *Rev.* +F°FĦBRIⱭII°ƊƐ°ⱭĦRRƐTTO·MĦGN·M·RO	»	

PLATE 98

Bi Deniers of Foulques de Villaret, 1309-1317 (Schl. IX 12)

Obv.: Castle three-towered within beaded circle. Rev.: Cross pattee within beaded circle.

1676 (5908) 18, 0.4 *Obv.:* +SⱭ...IOhA̅IS·B· *Rev.:* ... A̅]GR·hOSP...· *Corr., incomplete.* II.56
1677 (6003) 17, 0.5 *Corr., incomplete.* II.56

14th Century Anonymous Bi Deniers, Type I (Schl. X 3)

Obv.: Janua, dot to r., within smooth circle. Rev.: Cross pattee within smooth circle.

1678 (3933) 15, 0.7 *Obv.:* +ⱭIV...[R]ODI *Rev.:* +ⱮA̅GR·hOSPITA̅L' I.103
1679 (5180) 15, 0.2 *Obv.:* +...VIS·RODI *Rev.:* +ⱮA̅GR[ ]hOSPI... II.34
1680 (6002) 15, 0.6 *Obv.:* +ⱭIVIS·RODI *Rev.:* +ⱮA̅GR·hOSPI[T]A̅L' II.56
1681 (6046) 15, 0.7 *Obv.:* +ⱭIVIS·RODI *Rev.:* +ⱮA̅GR·hOSPITA̅L' II.35
1682 (5989) 15, 0.7 *Obv.:* +ⱭIVIS·RODI *Rev.:* +ⱮA̅GR·hOSPITA̅L' II.56
1683 (5924) 16, 0.7 *Obv.:* +ⱭIVIS·RODI *Rev.:* +ⱮA̅GR·hOSPITA̅L' II.56
1684 (5917) 16, 0.7 *Obv.:* +ⱭIV... *Rev.: Dot below cross,* ...R·hOSPITA̅L' *Corr.* II.56
1685 (3481) 16, 0.5 *Obv.:* ...IVIS·RODI· *Rev.:* +ⱮA̅GR·hOSPI[T]A̅L' II.58
1686 (3483) 15, 0.6 *Obv.:* +ⱭIVIS[·]RODI[·] *Rev.:* +ⱮA̅GR·hOSPITA̅L' II.58
1687 (3485) 16, 0.5 *Obv.:* +ⱭIVS·RODI *Rev.:* +ⱮA̅GR·hOSPITA̅L' *Incomplete.* II.58
1688 (3486) 15, 0.6 *Obv.:* +ⱭIVIS·RODI *Rev.:* +ⱮA̅GR·hOSPITA̅L' II.58
1689 (3492) 16, 0.6 *Obv.:* +ⱭIVIS·RODI· *Rev.:* +ⱮA̅GR·hOSPIT[A̅L'] II.58
1690 (3493) 16, 0.5 *Obv.:* +ⱭIV[S]...DI *Rev.:* +ⱮA̅GR·hOSPIT... II.58
1691 (3494) 15, 0.6 *Obv.:* +ⱭIVIS·RODI *Rev.:* +ⱮA̅GR·hOSPITA̅L' II.58
1692 (3500) 14, 0.5 *Obv.:* [+]ⱭIVS·RO[DI] *Rev.:* [+Ɱ]A̅GR·hOSPITA̅L' II.58
1693 (3501) 15, 0.6 *Obv.:* [+Ɑ...IS·RODI *Rev.:* +[ⱮA̅]GR·hOSPITA̅L II.58
1694 (5378) 15, 0.7 *Obv.:* +ⱭIVIS·RODI *Rev.:* +ⱮA̅GR·hOSPITA̅L' II.56
1695 (4841) 15, 0.6 *Obv.:* [+]ⱭIVIS·RO[I] *Rev.:* +ⱮA̅GR·h[O]...[T]A̅L' II.41
1696 (4845) 15, 0.5 *Obv.:* +ⱭIVIS·RODI *Rev.:* +ⱮA̅GR[ ]hOSPITA̅L' II.41
1697 (5289) 15, 0.5 *Obv.:* +ⱭIVIS·RODI *Rev.:* +ⱮA̅GR·hOSPIT... II.41
1698 (5918) 15, 0.7 *Obv.:* +ⱭIV...RODI *Rev.:* +ⱮA̅GR·hOSPITA̅L' *Corr.* II.56
1699 (5928) 15, 0.6 *Obv.:* +ⱭIVIS·RODI *Rev.:* +ⱮA̅GR·hOSPITA̅L' II.56
1700 (5997) 16, 0.6 *Obv.:* +ⱭIVIS·RODI *Rev.:* +ⱮA̅GR·hOSPI[TA̅]L' *Worn.* II.56
1701 (3482) 15, 0.5 *Obv.:* +...[I]S·RODI *Rev.:* +ⱮA̅GR·hO...A̅L' II.58
1702 (983) 14, 0.6 *Obv.:* +ⱭIVI[ ]·RODI *Rev.:* [ ]ⱮĦGR·hOSPITĦL' II.29
1703 (3450) 16, 0.6 *Obv.:* +ⱭIVIS·RODI *Rev.:* +ⱮA̅GR·hOSPIT[A̅L'] II.58
1704 (3469) 16, 0.6 *Obv.:* +ⱭIVIS·RODI *Rev.:* +ⱮA̅GR·hOSPITA̅L' II.58
1705 (3471) 15, 0.5 *Obv.:* +[Ɑ]IVIS·RODI *Rev.:* +[ⱮA̅GR]·hOSPITA̅L' II.58
1706 (3472) 15, 0.6 *Obv.:* +ⱭIVIS·RODI *Rev.:* +ⱮA̅GR·hOSPITA̅L' II.58
1707 (3473) 15, 0.5 *Obv.:* +ⱭIVIS·RO[D]I *Rev.:* +ⱮA̅GR·hOSPITA̅L' II.58
1708 (3475) 16, 0.4 *Obv.:* [+Ɑ]IVIS·R... *Rev.:* +ⱮA̅GR·hO...[A̅]L' II.58
1709 (3476) 15, 0.5 *Obv.:* +ⱭIVIS·ROD[*Rev.:* +Ɱ...R·hOSPITA̅L' II.58
1710 (502) 15, 0.9 *Obv.:* +ⱭIVI[S]RODI *Rev.:* +ⱮA̅G...hOSPITA̅[L]
1711 (615) 15, 0.6 *Obv.:* +Ɑ...VIS·RODI *Rev.:* +[Ɱ]...R·hOSPITA̅L'' I.35
1712 (3479) 15, 0.5 *Obv.:* +ⱭIVIS·RODI *Rev.:* +ⱮA̅GR·hOSPITA̅L' II.58
1713 (998) 15, 0.6 *Obv.:* ...ⱭIVIS·RODI[*Rev.:* +...R·hOSPITA̅L'' II.29
1714 (3477) 15, 0.2 *Obv.:* +ⱭIVIS·RODI *Rev.:* +ⱮA̅GR·hOSPITA̅L' II.58
1715 (499) 14, 0.6 *Obv.:* [+]ⱭIVIS·RODI *Rev.:* +ⱮA̅GR·hOSPITA̅L'
1716 (3489) 15, 0.5 *Obv.:* +ⱭIVIS·RODI *Rev.:* +ⱮA̅GR·hOSPITA̅L' II.58
1717 (3490) 15, 0.5 *Obv.:* +ⱭIVI...RODI *Rev.:* [+]ⱮA̅GR·hOS[P]... II.58
1718 (3503) 16, 0.3 *Obv.:* ...VIS·RODI *Rev.:* ...GR[·hO]SPITA̅L' *Incomplete.* II.58
1719 (3580) 14, 0.5 *Obv.:* +...IS·RODI *Rev.:* +ⱮA̅[GR]hOS[PI]TA̅L' II.58

[a] For this hoard see Kasdagli 2006: 325-338.
[b] For this hoard see Kasdagli 1992: 53-60.

PLATE 99

1720 (3784) 16, 0.6 *Obv.:* +CIVIS·RODI *Rev.:* +MĀGR·hOSPITĀL' II.42
1721 (3495) 16, 0.5 *Obv.:* +CIVIS[·R]ODI *Rev.:* +MĀGR·hOSPIT[ĀL'] II.58
1722 (3496) 15, 0.6 *Obv.:* +CIVIS·RODI *Rev.:* +MĀGR·hOSPITĀ[L] II.58
1723 (3497) 16, 0.7 *Obv.:* +CIVIS...DI *Rev.:* +M[ĀGR·h]OSPITĀ[L] II.58
1724 (5322) 15, 0.4 *Obv.:* +CIVIS·RODI *Rev.:* ...[Ā]GR·hOSPITĀ[L'] II.34
1725 (4358) 15, 0.5 *Obv.:* +[ ]IVIS·RODI *Rev.:* +MĀGR·hOSPI[T]... II.53
1726 (4512) 15, 0.5 *Obv.:* +...IVIS·RODI *Rev.:* +MĀG...hOSPITĀ[L'] *Incomplete* II.9
1727 (4842) 14, 0.6 *Obv.:* +CIVIS·RODI *Rev.:* +MĀGR·hOSPITĀL' II.41
1728 (4844) 15, 0.6 *Obv.:* +CIVIS·RODI *Rev.:* +MĀGR·h[O]... II.41
1729 (5440) 16, 0.5 *Obv.:* +CIVIS·RODI *Rev.:* +MĀGR·hOSPITĀL' II.56
1730 (5810) 16, 0.7 *Obv.:* +C...S·RODI *Rev.:* [ ]MĀGR·hOSPI...
1731 (5886) 16, 0.6 *Obv.:* +CIVIS·RODI *Rev.:* +MĀGR·hOSPITĀL' *Corr., incomplete.* II.56
1732 (101) 14, 0.6 *Obv.:* +CIVI[S·]RODI· *Rev.:* +MĀGR·hOSPITĀL'
1733 (146) 15, 0.6 *Obv.:* +...S·RODI *Rev.:* +MĀ...hOSPITĀL'
1734 (180) 15, 0.5 *Obv.:* ...IVIS·RO... *Rev.:* +M[Ā]...SPITĀ[L] V.5
1735 (186) 14, 0.5 *Obv.:* ...IS·ROD[ ] *Rev.:* +[ĀG]·hOSPITĀL'
1736 (305) 15, 0.6 *Obv.:* +CIVIS·RODI· *Rev.:* +MĀGR·hOSPITĀL' I.87
1737 (427) 15, 0.4 *Obv.:* +CIVI...DI *Rev.:* [+]MĀGR·hOSP... II.54
1738 (503) 15, 0.5 *Obv.:* +C...VI[S]...ODI *Rev.:* +MĀ[ ]R[ ]hOS[ ]ITĀL'·
1739 (686) 14, 0.6 *Obv.:* +CIVIS·R...I *Rev.:* ...hOSPITĀ... II
1740 (894) 15, 0.7 *Obv.:* +CIVIS[·]RODI *Rev.:* +MĀGR·hOSPITĀL'' II.3
1741 (906) 15, 0.5 *Obv.:* +CIVIS[·]RODI *Rev.:* +MĀGR[·]hOSPITĀL'' I.45
1742 (915) 15, 0.8 *Obv.:* +CIVIS[]RODI *Rev.:* +MĀGR·hOSPITĀL'' I.59
1743 (1116) 14, 0.3 *Obv.:* +C...S...[OD]I *Rev.:* + M[Ā]...[SPIT]Ā[L]
1744 (1133) 15, 0.6 *Obv.:* +CIVIS·R[hO]DI *Rev.:* + MĀGR·hO[SPITĀL] II
1745 (1708) 15, 0.7 *Obv.:* +CIVIS·RODI *Rev.:* +[M]...·hOSPITĀL''
1746 (2124) 14, 0.6 *Obv.:* +CIVIS·RODI[˙] *Rev.:* +MĀGR·hOSPITĀL''
1747 (3451) 15, 0.6 *Obv.:* +...VIS·RODI *Rev.:* +MĀGR·hOSPITĀL' II.58
1748 (3452) 15, 0.5 *Obv.:* +CIVIS·RODI *Rev.:* +MĀGR·hOSPITĀ[L'] II.58
1749 (3468) 15, 0.6 *Obv.:* +CIVIS·RODI *Rev.:* +MĀGR·hOSPITĀL' II.58
1750 (5825) 15, 0.5 *Obv.:* +CIVS·RODI[◦] *Rev.:* +MĀGR[]hOSPIT[Ā]L' *Corr., incomplete.* II.57
1751 (3470) 15, 0.6 *Obv.:* +CIVIS·RODI *Rev.:* +MĀGR·hOSPITĀL' II.58
1752 (3474) 15, 0.7 *Obv.:* [+C]IVIS·RODI *Rev.:* +MĀGR·hO...[Ā]L' II.58
1753 (3480) 15, 0.3 *Obv.:* +CIVIS...DI *Rev.:* +MĀ...SPITĀL' *Broken, incomplete.* II.58
1754 (3484) 16, 0.4 *Obv.:* ...VIS·ROD[I] *Rev.:* +M...SPITĀL' *Incomplete.* II.58
1755 (3487) 16, 0.6 *Obv.:* +CIVIS·RODI *Rev.:* +MĀGR·hOSPITĀL' II.58
1756 (3488) 16, 0.5 *Obv.:* ...IVS·RODI *Rev.:* +M[Ā]...[h]O[S]...T[Ā]L' *Incomplete.* II.58
1757 (3491) 15, 0.5 *Obv.:* +...S·RODI *Rev.:* +MĀGR·hO... *Corr.* II.58
1758 (3498) 15, 0.5 *Obv.:* +CIVIS·R[ODI] *Rev.:* +MĀGR·hOS... *Incomplete.* II.58
1759 (3499) 15, 0.5 *Obv.:* +C...IS·RODI *Rev.:* +MĀGR·hOSPITĀ[L] II.58
1760 (3502) 15, 0.6 *Obv.:* +...V...·RODI *Rev.:* [M]...R·hOSPITĀ[L] II.58
1761 (3504) 14, 0.5 *Obv.:* +CIVIS·RO... *Rev.:* +...R·hOSPITĀL' *Incomplete.* II.58
1762 (3505) 14, 0.5 *Obv.:* +CIVI...RODI *Rev.:* +M[ ]GR·hOSPITĀL' II.58
1763 (3521) 15, 0.4 *Obv.:* [+CI]VIS·RODI[] *Rev.:* +MĀ[G]...hOSPITĀL' II.58
1764 (4127) 16, 0.5 *Obv.:* +CIVIS...ODI *Rev.:* +M...[·h]OSPITĀL'· II.59

PLATE 100

1765 (4128) 15, 0.6 *Obv.:* +CI... *Rev.:* +...hOSPITĀ[L] II.59
1766 (4129) 14, 0.6 *Rev.:* +M...TĀL' II.59
1767 (4145) 14, 0.3 *Obv.:* +C...DI *Rev.:* +...SPITĀL' II.41
1768 (4146) 16, 0.3 *Obv.:* +C...ODI· *Rev.:* +...SPITĀL' II.41
1769 (4147) 14, 0.5 *Obv.:* +C... *Rev.:* ...OS... II.41
1770 (4165) 15, 0.6 *Obv.:* ...ROD... *Rev.:* +MĀG... II.34
1771 (4166) 15, 0.5 *Obv.:* +... *Rev.:* +...ITĦL' II.34
1772 (4302) 14, 0.3 *Obv.:* [C]IVI[S]...RODI *Rev.:* +MĀG...SP...[L'] *Incomplete.* II.53
1773 (4432) 14, 0.5 *Obv.:* [ ]CIVIS... *Rev.:* [ ]M[Ā]GR[·]hOSP... II.53
1774 (4483) 12, 0.2 *Obv.:* ...RODI *Rev.:* +MĀGR·h... *Incomplete.* II.57
1775 (4513) 14, 0.5 *Obv.:* +...V...ODI *Rev.:* +M...[R·]hOS... I.91
1776 (4618) 16, 0.7 *Obv.:* +C...S·RODI· *Rev.:* +M[ ]GR·hOSPITĀL' *Corr.* II.52
1777 (4625) 15, 0.4 *Obv.:* ...DI *Rev.:* +...GR·h...ITĀ[L'] *Corr.* II.52
1778 (4689) 14, 0.4 *Obv.:* +CI[U]IS·RODI *Rev.:* ...GR·OSPIT[ĦL] II.47
1779 (4792) 14, 0.2 *Obv.:* +...ODI *Rev.:* +M...ĀL' *Corr., incomplete.* II.47
1780 (4856) 16, 0.4 *Obv.:* +CI[ ]IS·RODI *Rev.:* ...OSPI... *Corr.* II.41

1781 (5179) 14, 0.5 *Obv.:* ...S·RODI *Rev.:* +MĀGR[]hOSP... *Corr., incomplete.* II.34
1782 (5286) 15, 0.7 *Obv.:* +CIVIS·RO... *Rev.:* +MĀGR·hO[S]PITĀL' II.41
1783 (5306) 14, 0.4 *Obv.:* +CIVIS·ROD[ ] *Rev.:* +MĀGR·[hOS]PITĀL' *Corr., incomplete.* II.41
1784 (5517) 14, 0.4 *Obv.:* +[C]...[DI] *Rev.:* +MĀG... *Corr., incomplete.* II.56
1785 (5590) 15, 0.6 *Obv.:* [ ]CIVIS·RODI[] *Rev.:* ...R·hOSPIT... *Corr.* II.56
1786 (5596) 15, 0.3 *Obv.:* ...VIS[·]RODI[*Rev.:* ...[Ā R]... *Corr., incomplete.* II.56
1787 (5816) 15, 0.4 *Obv.:* [ ]CIVIS·[R]... *Rev.:* ...hOSPI... *Corr., incomplete.* II.57
1788 (5926) 15, 0.3 *Obv.:* +CIVI...DI *Rev.:* +M...[PIT[ ]L' *Corr., incomplete.* II.56
1789 (459) 14, 0.2 *Obv.:* ...IS·... *Rev.:* ...OSPITĀ... *Fragmented, incomplete.*
1790 (3411) 14, 0.4 *Obv.:* ...IVI[S]... *Fragmented, incomplete.* II.33
1791 (4641) 15, 0.4 *Obv.:* [ ]CIVIS·...I[] *Rev.:* [+]M...GR... *Corr.* II.52
1792 (3524) 16, 0.3 *Obv.:* +CIV...ODI *Rev.:* ...[h]O... *Corr.* II.58
1793 (4086) 15, 0.5 *Obv.:* ...[S]·R... *Rev.:* [M]Ā...[S]PIT[Ā]... *Worn.* II.34
1794 (5900) 15, 0.6 *Obv.:* ...S·RO[DI] *Corr.* II.56
1795 (102) 14, 0.5 *Obv.:* +CIVIS·RODI· *Rev.:* +MĀGR[]hOSPITĀ[L]
1796 (601) 11, 0.2 *Rev.: [Annulets in quarters 1 & 4],* ...[PIT]Ā[L]... *Corr., incomplete.* II.18
1797 (4151) 14, 0.4 *Obv.:* [ ]CIV... *Rev.:* ...R[]hOSPI... *Worn, clipped.* II.41
1798 (4327) 15, 0.4 *Obv.:* ...VI...ODI[*Rev.: Ill. Corr., incomplete.* II.53
1799 (4390) 15, 0.5 *Obv.:* ...VIS... *Rev.:* ...[P]... *Corr.* II.20
1800 (4686) 13, 0.2 *Obv.:* ...·ROD... *Rev.:* +M...TAL'· *Corr., incomplete, overstruck.* II.47
1801 (4798) 15, 0.4 *Obv.:* [+C]...ODI *Rev.:* ...SPITĀ[L] *Corr., incomplete.* II.47
1802 (346) 14, 0.4 *Obv.:* +·CIV[ ]S·ROD[*Rev.:* ...ITA... II
1803 (4001) 13, 0.4 *Obv.:* +[ ]IV...I· *Rev.:* +M[A]...OSPIT[AL'] *Worn, clipped.* II.48

PLATE 101

1804 (5514) 15, 0.4 *Obv.:* +C...RODI[ ] *Rev.:* ...[G]R[:hOS... *Corr., incomplete.* II.56
1805 (6011) 15, 0.3 *Obv.:* +...VIS:...I *Rev.:* +M...[SP]... *Corr., incomplete.* II.64
1806 (4157) 14, 0.5 *Obv.:* ...IS... *Rev.:* +...[G]...TĀL' II.41
1807 (3586) 15, 0.2 *Obv.:* ...VIS·R[O]... *Rev.:* ...[R·hOS]... *Corr., incomplete.* II.58
1808 (4435) 14, 0.2 *Obv.:* ...IVI... *Corr., incomplete.* II.34
1809 (4749) 13, 0.3 *Corr., incomplete.* II.47
1810 (4855) 14, 0.4 *Obv.:* +CI...DI *Rev.:* +...GR[·]hO... *Corr.* II.41
1811 (5406) 13, 0.5 *Obv.:* ...ODI[] *Corr., incomplete.* II.56

14th Century Anonymous Bi Deniers, Type II
Obv.: Janua, dot to r.; within beaded circle. Rev.: Cross pattee; within beaded circle.

1812 (3412) 14, 0.7 *Obv.:* [ ]CIU... *Rev.:* ...[AGR]... II.33
1813 (5408) 14, 0.3 *Obv.:* ...UI...DI[·] *Rev.: Corr.* II.56
1814 (5516) 14, 0.4 *Obv.:* +CI[U]S·[R]... *Rev.:* ...GR[·]O...TA[ ] *Corr., incomplete.* II.56
1815 (621) 14, 0.6 *Obv.:* +CIVIS·R[D]I· *Rev.:* +MAGR...ITAL·[hO P]IT[L] I.35
1816 (951) 14, 0.6 *Obv.:* ... VIS... *Rev.:* +MAGR... II.48
1817 (1057) 15, 0.7 *Obv.:* + · CIVIS·R[ ]DI· *Rev.:* +MAGR·hOSP... II.50
1818 (1200) 13, 0.4 *Obv.:* +CI[U]...ODI: *Rev.:* +...OSPITAL II.56
1819 (3406) 14, 0.3 *Obv.:* +CI[ ]IS·RODI· *Rev.:* +...GR[ ]OS... II.33
1820 (4348) 14, 0.5 *Obv.:* +CIVI...RO... *Rev.:* ...PITA[L *Corr.* II.53
1821 (4454) 13, 0.5 *Obv.:* +CIVI...ODI[·] *Rev.:* ...·hOS... I.91
1822 (4851) 14, 0.5 *Obv.:* +...ODI[·] *Rev.:* ...OS... *Corr.* II.41
1823 (4854) 14, 0.3 *Obv.:* +...ODI· *Rev.:* ...S... *Corr., incomplete.* II.41
1824 (5242) 14, 0.4 *Obv.:* ...ODI[:] *Rev.:* ...GR·hOSPI... II.55
1825 (5283) 14, 0.3 *Obv.:* ...IS...[OD] *Rev.:* ...R·OS[P]... *Corr., incomplete.* II.41
1826 (5494) 13, 0.4 *Obv.:* Janua, +C... *Rev.:* ...OSPIT[A] *Corr.* II.56
1827 (6058) 14, 0.5 *Obv.:* [ ]CIV[S]...DI *Rev.:* +M...T[A] *Corr., incomplete.* II.35
1828 (5550) 13, 0.5 *Obv.:* +...ODI· *Rev.:* ...[R]OSPI... *Corr.* II.56
1829 (5869) 15, 0.3 *Obv.:* ...S...OD... *Rev.:* [ ]MA... *Corr., incomplete.* II.56
1830 (5983) 15, 0.3 *Obv.:* +...ODI· *Rev.:* ...AGR...ITA... *Corr., incomplete, overstruck.* II.56
1831 (1056) 15, 0.3 *Obv.:*...OD[*Brockage; broken. Rev.:* [ ]M[Ā]...OS...[TĀL] II.50
1832 (1181) 14, 0.3 *Obv.:* ...VIS... *Rev.:* + M[A]...[O]S... II.56
1833 (2125) 15, 0.5 *Obv.:* ...I...I[] *Rev.:* ...R·hO...T...
1834 (5944) 13, 0.3 *Obv.:* ...[IS]... *Rev.: Corr., incomplete.* II.56
1835 (6096) 13, 0.3 *Obv.:* +...ODI *Rev.:* ...SP... *Corr., incomplete.* II.23
1836 (3562) 13, 0.4 *Obv.:* ...[V]...I... *Corr., incomplete.* II.58
1837 (3793) 12, 0.3 *Clipped, corr., incomplete.* II.14
1838 (4149) 13, 0.4 *Clipped, corr., incomplete.* II.41
1839 (4318) 14, 0.4 *Obv.:* ...VI... *Rev.:* ...[AL]... *Corr.* II.53

1840 (4330) 13, 0.3 *Obv.:* [ ]ᗅIV... *Rev.:* ✠... *Corr., incomplete.* II.53
1841 (4456) 13, 0.6 *Obv.:* ...[IVI]... *Rev.:* ✠ᗰᗩG...[OS]... *Worn.* I.91
1842 (5383) 14, 0.5 *Corr., incomplete.* II.56
1843 (5400) 14, 0.2 *Obv.:* [✠ᗅ]IVIS·RODI *Rev.:* ✠ · [ᗰᐱG]... *Corr., incomplete.* II.56
1844 (4657) 13, 0.3 *Obv.:* ...ᗅI... *Corr., incomplete.* II.52
1845 (4643) 13, 0.3 *Rev.:* ...Tᗩ... *Corr.* II.52
1846 (4694) 14, 0.4 *Obv.:* ...ODI *Rev.:* ...[ᗩGR]· O... *Worn.* II.47
1847 (4714) 15, 0.3 *Obv.:* ...ODI[ ] *Rev.:* ...·h... *Corr.* II.47

PLATE 102
1848 (4747) 13, 0.4 *Corr., clipped.* II.47
1849 (4752) 13, 0.3 *Rev.:* ✠...[SPITᗩL']... *Worn.* II.47
1850 (4774) 13, 0.2 *Obv.:* ✠ᗅIU... *Corr., incomplete.* II.47
1851 (4802) 13, 0.4 *Obv.:* ✠ · ᗅ... *Rev.:* ✠ᗰ...I[T]... *Corr.* II.47
1852 (5304) 13, 0.4 *Rev.:* ...ᗩG... *Corr., incomplete.* II.41
1853 (5572) 13, 0.2 *Obv.: Annulet within Janua. Rev.:* [✠]...*Corr., incomplete.* II.56
1854 (5577) 12, 0.2 *Obv.:* [✠]... *Rev.:* ...[L]... *Corr., incomplete.* II.56
1855 (5591) 13, 0.3 *Corr., incomplete.* II.56
1856 (5592) 12, 0.3 *Rev.:* ✠ᗰ[ᐱ]GR... *Corr., incomplete.* II.56
1857 (5939) 10, 0.1 *Corr., incomplete.* II.56
1858 (67) 13, 0.3 *Obv.:* ...[DI] *Rev.:* ... [S]PIT... *Worn.* V.2
1859 (261) 12, 0.6 *Obv.:* ✠ᗅI...[D]I· *Rev.:* [✠]ᗰᗩGR·h[O]... *Worn.* V.2
1860 (358) 15, 0.5 *Obv.:* [+]ᗅI...IS... *Rev.:* ✠ᗰ...OSPIT... *Worn.* I.35
1861 (4024) 15, 0.6 *Obv.:* ✠ ·...VIS... *Rev.:* ✠...[T]ᗩ[L'◦]...I.35
1862 (1020) 14, 0.5 *Rev.:* [+]...Tᗩ[ ]... *Worn, corr.* II.31
1863 (1068) 14, 0.4 *Obv.:* +...*[Overstrike] Rev.:* ...hOSPIT... *Worn.* I.100
1864 (3394) 14, 0.6 *Obv.:* ✠...S·RODI *Rev.:* ✠ᗰ...SPITᗩ[L']. *Worn.*
1865 (3739) 12, 0.2 *Obv.:* ...VIS... *Rev.:* ...GR·... *Fragment.* II.14
1866 (4155) 13, 0.3 *Obv.:* ...I... *Rev.:* ...[ᗩ]GR... *Corr., incomplete.* II.41
1867 (4263) 14, 0.4 *Obv.:* ✠ᗅI...DI *Rev.:* ...ᗩGR·[ ]OS... *Corr.* II.24
1868 (4723) 13, 0.2 *Rev.:* ...I... *Corr., incomplete.* II.47
1869 (4757) 15, 0.3 *Obv.:* ✠...· *Corr., fragmented, incomplete.* II.47
1870 (1180) 12, 0.2 *Worn, incomplete* II.56
Uncertain
1871 (6093) 9, 0.1 *Obv.:* ✠...[L] *Fragment, corr.* II. 23
1872 (1043) 11, 0.1 *Obv.:* ...[ᗅ]...· *Incomplete. Worn, incomplete.* II. 15
1873 (1175) 15, 0.3 *Obv.:* ...IS... *Rev.: Cross. Fragmented, incomplete.* II. 56
1874 (4715) 13, 0.3 *Worn, incomplete.* II. 47
1875 (4317) 0.06 *Fragment.* II. 53
1876 (1177) 14, 0.4 *Corr., incomplete.* II. 56
1877 (4717) 11, 0.1 *Corr., incomplete.* II. 47
Imitation
1878 (5943) 13, 0.2 *Obv.: [Janua,]* ...I *Rev.: Cross, dot below,* ...ᐱGR·O... *Corr., incomplete.* II. 56

PLATE 103
Signed deniers of Roger de Pins, 1355-1365 (Schl. X 6)
Obv.: Janua, dot to r., pinecone l.; within beaded circle. Rev.: Cross pattee within beaded circle.
1879 (224) 12, 0.6 *Obv.:* + · ᗅI...DI· *Rev.:* ...ᗩGR·...
1880 (257) 18, 0.7 *Obv.:* [+]...RODI· *Rev.:* [+ᗰ]...[I]. V. 14
1881 (361) 14, 0.4 *Obv.:* + · ᗅI...S·R... *Rev.:* ...GR[ ]O... I. 35
1882 (1092) 14, 0.2 *Obv.:* [✠ᗅ]...I... *Rev.:* ... · O... II. 60
1883 (1176) 14, 0.3 *Corr., incomplete.* II. 56
1884 (4301) 15, 0.5 *Obv.:* + · ᗅ...DI· *Rev.:* ...L· II. 53
1885 (4344) 14, 0.4 *Obv.:* ...DI·*Rev.:* ...PITᗩ[L] II. 53
1886 (4459) 14, 0.5 *Obv.:* ...S·ROD... *Rev.:* ✠ᗰ[ᐱ]G... I. 91
1887 (5248) 13, 0.3 *Corr., incomplete.* II. 41
1888 (5403) 13, 0.4 *Obv.:* ...ODI *Rev.:* ...OSPIT... *Corr., incomplete.* II. 56
1889 (5595) 14, 0.4 *Obv.:* ...ODI[·] *Rev.:* ...[S]... *Incomplete.* II. 56
1890 (6092) 13, 0.4 *Obv.:* ✠ · ᗅ...DI· *Rev.:* ...Tᗩ[L *Corr., incomplete.* II. 23

Signed deniers of Robert de Juilly, 1373-1377
Obv.: Janua with verticals topped by needles (†*), dot to r., within smooth circle. Rev.: Cross pattee within smooth circle.*
1891 (319) 15, 0.7 *Obv.:* +[·]ᗅI[VI]S[·]RODI⊕ *Rev.:* +ᗰᐱGR·hOSP[TᐱL] I. 99
1892 (943) 15, 0.6 *Obv.:* +[:]ᗅIVIS : RODI⊕ *Rev.:* [ ]ᗰᐱGR·hOSPITᐱ... II. 42

1893 (698) 14, 0.5 *Obv.:* +...RODI❀ *Rev.:*]MĀGR:h... II. 63
1894 (4126) 14, 0.5 *Obv.:* + : CIVIS : RODI[❀] *Rev.:* +MĀGR·hOSPIT... II. 59
1895 (1058) 14, 0.4 *Obv.:* ...IS·ROD[I *Rev.:* ...hOSPITAL· II. 50
1896 (1192) 13, 0.4 *Obv.: Janua, [annulet within,]* ...DI *Rev.:* [+]M[G]RhO[S]... II. 56
1897 (4261) 13, 0.4 *Obv.:* +[:]CIVIS[:]R... *Rev.:* ...[GR]hOS...ITĀ... II. 24
1898 (4341) 15, 0.3 *Obv.:* [CI]... / +... *Rev.:* ...[R] :... *Corr., incomplete.* II. 53
1899 (4349) 14, 0.5 *Obv.:* ...DI[*Rev.:* +MĀGR[h]... *Worn, incomplete.* II. 53
1900 (4429) 14, 0.4 *Rev.:* +MĀGR:h... II. 34
1901 (4813) 14, 0.3 *Rev.:* ...:...R... *Corr., incomplete.* II. 48
1902 (5439) 15, 0.3 *Obv.:* +...IS:R...I[❀] *Rev.:* [+]MĀGR...SPI... *Corr., incomplete.* II. 56

PLATE 104

Overstruck deniers, c. 1377-1400[a]

Obv.: Coarse châtel, annulet within, initial crosslet of legend under base; within beaded circle. Rev.: Cross pattee, annulets in two opposed quarters; within beaded circle.

1903 (2083) 14, 0.4 *Obv.:* +...OS... / *cross,* ...I... *Rev.: Annulets in quarters 1 & 4,* +IERUSĀL... / *janua, dot r.* [+] C...[L·] IH
1904 (3093) 14, 0.4 *Obv.:* +[MA]...ROSPE *Rev.: Annulets in quarters 1 & 4,* +IERUS[AL]E[M]I· / ...C]I... IH
1905 (3160) 14, 0.6 *Obv.:* +MAST[ ]IO.../ *[cross] Rev.: Annulets in quarters 1 & 4,* +[ERO]SA... IH
1906 (3148) 15, 0.6 *Obv.:* ...IOS... *Rev.: Annulets in quarters 1 & 4,* +IER[S]ALE... / *[janua]* IH
1907 (7560) 14, 0.6 *Obv.:* +MAST[ ]IOS[PI]T / *cross Rev.: Annulets in quarters [1 & 4],* ...RUSA... IH
1908 (7520) 14, 0.4 *Obv.:* +M[A]...ROSP... / *[cross] Rev.: Annulets in quarters 1 & 4,* [ ]IERUSA[L... / *[janua]* ...IV[I... IH
1909 (7566) 14, 0.2 *Obv.:* +M[A]STR... *Rev.: Annulets in quarters 2 & 3,* +...R[US]...EMI[T] / ...OD... IH
1910 (7591) 14, 0.4 *Obv.:* [+MASTROSPE / *cross Rev.: Annulets in quarters 1 & 4,* +IERUSALEMI[T] / *[janua]* IH
1911 (7599) 14, 0.3 *Obv.:* +MASTROSPE *Rev.: Annulets in quarters 1 & 4,* +IER...ALEMI IH
1912 (7581) 16, 0.6 *Obv.:* +MASTIOS[PE / *cross Rev.: Annulets in quarters 1 & 4,* +IER[U]SALEMIT IH
1913 (2040) 15, 0.4 *Obv.:* [M]ASTRIO... / *janua,* +CI...[I·] *Rev.:* / *cross,* +M...PITAL· IH
1914 (3074) 15, 0.5 *Obv.:* +MASTRIO... / ...ODI[*Rev.: Annulets in quarters 2 & 3,* +IR[U]S...NI / ...R... / *cross.* IH
1915 (3088) 16, 0.5 *Obv.:* ...PET / ...PITAL' *Rev.: Annulets in quarters 2 & 3,* ...RUS... / *janua,* ...IS·RODI[·] IH
1916 (3091) 14, 0.5 *Obv.:* +...OSPE[*Rev.: Annulets in quarters 1 & 4,* ...ERUSA... / ...SP... IH
1917 (3135) 15, 0.3 *Obv.:* +MA...T... *Rev.: Annulets in quarters 2 & 3,* [ ]IE[ ]USA... / *[janua],* ...ODI· IH
1918 (3147) 14, 0.5 *Obv.:* +MAST...[E]T / ...IS· *Rev.:* ...I... / +MAG... IH
1919 (7602) 14, 0.4 *Obv.:* +MASTRI... / *[cross] Rev.: Annulets in quarters 2 & 3,* +IE... / *[janua]* IH
1920 (2084) 15, 0.4 *Obv.:* +...OS[PET] / *janua, dot r.,* +·C...· *Rev.: Annulets in quarters 1 & 4,* [+]IER...[A]...[M / +MAG... IH
1921 (3080) 15, 0.4 *Obv.:* [ ]MASTRI... / ...A... *Rev.: Annulets in quarters 1 & 4,* +I...A... / ...[O]... IH
1922 (3117) 14, 0.3 *Obv.:* +M...IOSPE[TA] / ...[V]IS[ ]R[O]... *Rev.:* / ...AG...I... IH
1923 (3124) 14, 0.4 *Obv.:* ...RIOSPE / ...GR[ ]O... *Rev.:* / *janua, dot r.,* +[·]C...I· IH
1924 (3138) 14, 0.6 *Obv.:* / *cross,* ...[GR hOS]PIT... *Rev.: Annulets in quarters [1 & 4],* [+IE U]... / +[ ]CI...DI· IH
1925 (3156) 16, 0.7 *Obv.:* +[M]AS...OSPE *Rev.: Annulets in quarters 1 & 4,* ...ERUS[ALEM]IT / ...[SPI]... IH
1926 (3163) 14, 0.5 *Obv.:* +MASTRI[O]... *Rev.: Annulets in quarters 1 & 4,* [ ]IERU[S]... IH
1927 (7745) 14, 0.4 *Obv.:* +MAS... / + · ... I · *Rev.: Annulets in quarters 1 & 4,* ...ERUSALE... / ...[P]IT... IH
1928 (2106) 14, 0.4 *Obv.:* +MAST[R]IOS...T *Rev.: Annulets in quarters 2 & 3,* +IERU... / ...DI IH
1929 (3071) 15, 0.5 *Obv.:* +MA...[P]... / ...C... IH
1930 (3108) 15, 0.6 *Obv.:* +MAS...[PET] / +M[ ]GR... *Rev.: Annulets in quarters 2 & 3,* +IE[R]...MIT / *janua,* + · C...DI IH
1931 (3189) 15, 0.4 *Obv.:* +MAST...[P]ET *Rev.: Annulets in quarters 2 & 3,* +IERU... · / *janua, dot r.* IH
1932 (7567) 14, 0.4 *Obv.:* [ ]MAST[RIOSPIT] / *cross. Rev.: Annulets in quarters 1 & 4,* +IER[U]S[A]... / IH
1933 (7611) 15, 0.6 *Obv.:* ...TRIOSPE[/ ...PIT... *Rev.: Annulets in quarters 1 & 4,* ...RU...MI[T] / *[janua,]* +...[I]S...ODI IH
1934 (7820) 13, 0.3 *Obv.:* +MASTRIOSPE[T] *Rev.: Annulets in quarters 1 & 4,* [IE]RUSA... / *[janua]* IH
1935 (9617) 14, 0.5 *Obv.:* ...AST...OSPE[T *Rev.: Annulets in quarters 2 & 3,* ...ERUS[A]LEMI[KH
1936 (9630) 14, 0.4 *Obv.:* ...OSPET *Rev.: Annulets in quarters [2 & 3],* [IE]...LEMIT KH
1937 (1250) 15, 0.5 *Obv.:* +M...TALI *Rev.: Annulets in quarters 1 & 4,* +S·... IH
1938 (3186) 15, 0.6 *Obv.:* +MASTR... / ...PITĀL... *Rev.: Annulets in quarters 2 & 3,* +IRU...[N]I IH
1939 (3271) 16, 0.5 *Obv.:* +MASTRIO... / [+]...[CE] *Rev.: Annulets in quarters 1 & 4,* +S... / +... IH
1940 (7825) 16, 0.6 *Obv.:* +M[A]STR...T[*Rev.: Annulets in quarters 1 & 4,* + S :...hR[L]M[·] IH
1941 (9590) 15, 0.6 *Obv.:* ...+MA[STR]O[S[PETAL] / ...[O]D... *Rev.:* ...S:... / ...GRO... KH
1942 (9766) 15, 0.4 *Obv.: Small châtel, dot within,* +MASTR...TAL *Rev.: Annulets in quarters 1 & 4,* +S ·... KH
1943 (9768) 13, 0.7 *Obv.: Small châtel,* ...TAL / *cross. Rev.: Annulets in quarters 1 & 4,* +S ·... KH
1944 (9769) 14, 0.5 *Obv.: Small châtel,* +M...TAL *Rev.: Annulets in quarters 1 & 4,* +S ·... / *[janua,] dot r.,* ...[U]... KH

[a] At the end of an entry: IH=Italian Hoard; KH=Kamiros Hoard.

1945 (9770) 15, 0.6 *Obv.: Small châtel, [dot within,]* ✠ⲘĦSTRIS[Ⲛ...L] / *janua. Rev.: Annulets in quarters 1 & 4,* ✠S · [IO]...Ⲙ KH

PLATE 105

1946 (2061) 15, 0.4 *Obv.:* [Ⲙ]ĦST[RI]... / *cross,* ✠[Ⲙ]... *Rev.: Annulets in quarters 1 & 4,* ...[U]...ЄⲘ / *janua,* ♠ *l.*, IH

1947 (2069) 15, 0.4 *Obv.:*...ĦSTRIOS... / *cross,* [✠]Ⲙ... *Rev.:* ...I... / *janua,* ♠ *l.*, ...[RO]DI[IH

1048 (3012) 14, 0.4 *Obv.:* ✠Ⲙ...SPЄT / *janua,* ♠ *l. Rev.:* ...Ⲛ·[hO]... / *cross,* ...TĦ[L] IH

1949 (3013) 15, 0.5 *Obv.:* / *janua, dot r., [*♠ *l.,]* ...[U]IS·... *Rev.:* / ✠...I IH

1950 (7545) 14, 0.4 *Obv.:*...STRI[OSP]... / *janua, [*♠ *l.] Rev.: Annulets in quarters 1 & 4,* ✠...LЄⲘIT/ ...IT... *Incomplete.* IH

1951 (7659) 14, 0.5 *Obv.:* ✠[Ⲙ]ĦS...T / ...[GR·h]...L[I] *Rev.: Annulets in quarters 1 & 4,* ...RUS[Ħ]... / *janua,* ♠ *l.*, ...DI[◦] IH

1952 (7665) 15, 0.5 *Obv.:* ✠Ⲙ...TRIO...[Є] / *janua,* ♠ *l. Rev.: Annulets in quarters 1 & 4,* ✠IЄRUS...[:]I / *cross* IH

1953 (9618) 16, 0.6 *Obv.:* ...ĦST... / *cross,* ✠Ⲙ...[L'] · *Rev.: Annulets in quarters 1 & 4,* ...RUS... / *janua, [dot r.,]* ♠ *l.*, ...IS·RO... KH

1954 (9684) 15, 0.7 *Obv.:* ...ĦS... / *janua, dot r.,* ♠ *l.*, ✠[ ]IVIS·RODI *Rev.: Annulets in quarters 1 & 4,* ✠IЄR...[ⲘI ·] KH

1955 (9709) 14, 0.5 *Obv.:* ✠...SPЄT / *cross. Rev.: Annulets in quarters 1 & 4,* [ ]IЄRUS[ĦLЄ]ⲘIT / *janua, dot r.,* ♠ *l.*, [ ] Ⲥ... KH

1956 (9717) 14, 0.4 *Obv.:* / *[*♠ *l.,]* ✠...DI · *Rev.:* / *cross,* ... IT[Ħ]L' · KH

1957 (9722) 14, 0.5 *Obv.:* ...TROS[P... / *cross,* ✠Ⲙ... *Rev.: Annulets in quarters 2 & 3,* ...LЄⲘ... / *janua,* ♠ *l.*, ...ODI... KH

1958 (3069) 14, 0.4 *Obv.:* ...T...[U] ... / [ ]ⲤIVIS :... *Rev.:* / [ ]ⲘĀGR[:]hO[S]PI... IH

1959 (3178) 15, 0.4 *Obv.:* ✠...PЄT / *cross,* ... ĀGR·hOSPI... *Rev.: Annulets in quarters 1 & 4,* ✠...[ЄⲘ] / ✠ : ⲤIVIS :... IH

1960 (7539) 14, 0.5 *Obv.:* ✠[Ⲙ]... / *janua, [annulet within,] dot r.,* ✠ⲤIVIS:RODI✠ *Rev.: Annulets in quarters 2 & 3,* [✠]... IT/ *cross,* ...SPITĀ... IH

1961 (7711) 16, 0.6 *Obv.:* ✠ⲘĦS... / janua, ✠ ·...R[ ]DI✠ *Rev.:* / [cross,] [ ]ⲘĀGR... *Doubled die.* IH

1962 (1273) 15, 0.5 *Obv.:* ✠ⲘĦ...O... / *cross,* ✠...R·hOSPIT[ĀL·] *Rev.: Annulets in quarters 2 & 3,*]IЄ... / *[janua, dot r.]* ✠·ⲤIVIS·RO[DI·] IH

1963 (3158) 15, 0.6 *Obv.:* [ ]ⲘĦST[R]... / *cross,* ...GR[:]OSPI[T]... *Rev.:* / ✠ · Ⲥ...[R]...I· IH

1964 (9647) 15, 0.6 *Obv.:* ✠Ⲙ[ ]S... / *cross,* ...GR... *Rev.:* ...[S]... / ✠[:]ⲤI...D... KH

1965 (9697) 15, 0.4 *Obv.:* / ✠ : Ⲥ...ODI[*Rev.: Annulets in quarters 2 & 3,* ✠I...[Ħ] / ✠ⲘĦGRO[S... KH

1966 (3022) 15, 0.5 *Obv.:* ...OSP... / *[janua], dot r.* ✠ⲤIVI[S]...DI *Rev.:* ...[Є]Ⲙ... / *cross,* ✠ⲘĦGR... IH

1967 (3142) 16, 0.6 *Obv.:* / *[cross,]* ✠ⲘĀG... *Rev.: Annulets in quarters 1 & 4,* ✠IЄ[R]...[Є]ⲘIT / *[janua],* ✠ⲤIV...I IH

1968 (7515) 16, 0.4 *Obv.:* ...[TR]OS[P]... / *janua,* ✠ⲤI... *Rev.: Annulets in quarters 1 & 4,* ✠IЄRUSĦLЄⲘIT/ *cross,* ...[Ā] GR·hOS[PI]... *Corr.* IH

1969 (7528) 15, 0.7 *Obv.:* ✠...OSP... / *cross,* ✠[Ⲙ]...[ITĦ]L' *Rev.: Annulets in quarters 1 & 4,* ...ĦLЄⲘI[/ *[janua],* ...ISR[OD]I

1970 (7544) 15, 0.4 *Obv.:* ✠Ⲙ[ĦS]... / *janua, dot r.,* ✠ · ⲤIV...I · *Rev.: Annulets in quarters 1 & 4,* ...ĦLЄ.../ *cross,* [✠] ⲘĦ...[PITĦL] IH

1971 (7737) 15, 0.4 *Obv.:* ✠Ⲙ...SPЄ / ✠ · Ⲥ... *Rev.:* / *cross,* ...[Ā]GR·hOSPI... IH

1972 (7784) 16, 0.7 *Obv.:* [ⲘĦ]STR... / *cross,* ✠ⲘĀGR·hO[S]...ĀL' *Rev.:* / *[janua,]* ✠ · ⲤIV]... IH

1973 (8158) 13, 0.5 *Obv.:* ...OSPЄ[/ *janua, dot r.,* ✠ · ⲤI... *Rev.:* ...[L◦]... / ✠ⲘĦ...ĦL IH

1974 (9601) 15, 0.4 *Obv.:* ...RIOS... / ...IVI[S] · ROD... *Rev.:* / *cross,* ✠ⲘĀGR·hOS...[Ā]L' KH

1975 (9607) 15, 0.5 *Obv.:* ...RI · OS... / *janua, dot r., [*♠ *l.,]* ✠ⲤIVIS·RODI · *Rev.: Annulets in quarters 1 & 4,* ✠...[ЄⲘ]... / ✠ⲘĀGR·hOSPITĀL' KH

1976 (9807) 15, 0.5 *Obv.:* ✠Ⲙ...[I] / ✠[ⲘĀG]R·hOSPITĀL' *Rev.: Annulets in quarters 2 & 3,* ✠IЄR... / *[janua,] dot r.,* ✠ⲤIVIS[R... IVI... KH

PLATE 106

1977 (2052) 15, 0.5 *Obv.:* ✠... / *cross,* ✠Ⲙ...OSPITĦ[ ] *Rev.: Annulets in quarters 1 & 4,* ✠...ⲘI· / ✠Ⲥ[ ]UIS...[·] IH

1978 (2066) 14, 0.4 *Obv.:* ...[R]:OSP... *Rev.: Annulets in quarters [2 & 3],* ...ЄⲘ... / ✠◦...Ⲛ...[T]◦ IH

1979 (2113) 13, 0.5 *Obv.:* ...T[RI]... / ✠·Ⲙ...· *Rev.: Annulets in quarters 1 & 4,* ✠... / ...VI[S·]RO... IH

1980 (3085) 15, 0.5 *Obv.:* / ✠ · ⲤI[U]IS...[DI]· *Rev.:* / *[cross],* ✠Ⲙ...R·hOSPIT[Ħ... IH

1981 (3098) 16, 0.6 *Obv.:* ...STR... / *cross,* ✠...SPI...[L] · *Rev.: Annulets in quarters 2 & 3,* ...Є...LЄⲘ... /✠ · Ⲥ[IV]...I· IH

1982 (3100) 14, 0.3 *Obv.:* ...SPЄ / *janua, dot r.,* ...VIS·ROD... *Rev.: Annulets in quarters 2 & 3,* ...ĦLЄ... / ✠ · ⲘĦG... IH

1983 (3101) 15, 0.4 *Obv.:* ...T... / *janua, dot r.,* ...IUIS·R[O]DI[*Rev.:* / *cross,* ...ĦGR...PITĦ[L IH

1984 (3102) 15, 0.4 *Obv.:* ✠ⲘĦST... / ...DI[*Rev.:* ✠ · ⲘĦG...L·' IH

1985 (3107) 15, 0.6 *Obv.:* / *cross,* ✠ⲘĦGR... *Rev.:* / *janua,* ✠ · Ⲥ[I]...ODI· IH

1986 (3112) 14, 0.5 *Obv.:* ...ĦSTRIOS[P]... / ✠ⲘĦG... *Rev.: Annulets in quarters 2 & 3,* ...LЄⲘ... / ✠ · ⲤI...· IH

1987 (3129) 15, 0.5 *Obv.:* [Ⲙ]ĦSTRIO... / ✠ · ⲤIV... *Rev.: Annulets in quarters 2 & 3,* ✠IЄ...ⲘI[T] / *cross,* ✠...GR · OS... IH

1988 (3173) 14, 0.6 *Obv.:* / ✠ · M...[L'] · *Rev.: Annulets in quarters 2 & 3,* ...RUS... / ✠...DI[IH
1989 (3191) 14, 0.4 *Obv.:* [✠]MA...[T] / *janua,* ✠°CI... *Rev.: Annulets in quarters 1 & 4,* ✠IERUS... / *cross,* [ ]MAG... IH
1990 (3194) 14, 0.5 *Obv.:* ...AST...OSP... / *cross,* ...[R h]O... *Rev.: Annulets in quarters 1 & 4,* ✠[ ]ERUSALE[M]IT[N] / *janua,* ✠°CI... IH
1991 (7530) 15, 0.6 *Obv.:* ✠[ ]ASTR... / ✠...° *Rev.: Annulets in quarters 1 & 4,* ✠...MIT/ ...OD... IH
1992 (7546) 16, 0.6 *Obv.:* ✠... / *cross,* [✠]MAGR·h...TAL' *Rev.: Annulets in quarters 2 & 3,* ✠IERUS...IT/ *janua,* ✠CI... [IS·] IH
1993 (7549) 14, 0.4 *Obv.:* [✠]AST... / ✠°C[I... *Rev.: Annulets in quarters 2 & 3,* [ ]IERU.../ *cross,* ...A... IH
1994 (7555) 14, 0.5 *Obv.:* ✠MASTRIOS[P]... / ... AL' · *Rev.: Annulets in quarters 1 & 4,* ...USA... / *janua,* ✠ · CI... IH
1995 (7557) 14, 0.6 *Obv.:* [ ]M... / *cross,* ✠MA...SPITA[L *Rev.:* / *janua,* ✠°CIV...ODI° IH
1996 (7571) 14, 0.3 *Obv.:* ...RIOSP... / ...AL' *Rev.: Annulets in quarters [2 & 3],* ...[E]... / ✠ • C...• IH
1997 (7592) 15, 0.6 *Obv.:* [✠...ROSP... / *janua,* ✠ · CI... *Rev.: Annulets in quarters 1 & 4,* ✠IERUSAL[EM... / *cross with annulets in opposite corners* IH
1998 (7601) 16, 0.3 *Obv.:* ✠[ ]AST...OS... / *[cross,]* ...R·OSP... *Rev.: Annulets in quarters [2 & 3],* ...E[R]... / *[janua,]* ✠ · CIV...I · IH
1999 (7624) 15, 0.4 *Obv.:* ✠M... / *janua,* ✠ • C[I]...• IH
2000 (7628) 14, 0.3 *Obv.:* ✠M...IOSPE *Rev.:* / ✠ · CI[V]...[DI] · IH
2001 (7637) 15, 0.5 *Obv.:* [ ]MASTR... / *janua, dot r.,* ✠ · CIV...DI · *Rev.: Annulets in quarters [1 & 4],* [✠]IERU... / *cross,* ✠MA...[IT]A[LI] IH
2002 (7642) 14, 0.5 *Obv.:* ✠...SPET / *janua, dot r.,* ...UIS·RO[D... *Rev.: Annulets in quarters [1 & 4],* [ ]IER... / *cross,* ✠...R·hOSPIT... IH
2003 (7648) 15, 0.4 *Obv.:* ✠M...PET / ✠M[ ]GR...AL *Rev.:* / *[janua,]* ✠ · CI...DI IH
2004 (7658) 15, 0.4 *Obv.:* ...I · O... / *janua,* [✠] · CI[UI]... *Rev.: Annulets in quarters 1 & 4,* ...SALEM... / ...G... IH
2005 (7662) 16, 0.7 *Obv.:* ...TRIO... / ✠ ° ... ° *Rev.:* ...·... / *cross,* ...[PI]TA[L IH
2006 (7664) 15, 0.6 *Obv.:* ✠MAS... / *janua,* ✠ · CI...DI *Rev.: Annulets in quarters 2 & 3,* ...USALEMI · / *cross,* ...AGR·hO... IH
2007 (7670) 15, 0.5 *Obv.:* ...T... / [✠ · C...· *Rev.:* / ...TA[L IH
2008 (7696) 15, 0.4 *Obv.:* / *cross,* ...ALI ° *Rev.:* / ✠ ° CI... IH
2009 (7738) 14, 0.4 *Obv.:* ...RIO... / ...R·O... *Rev.: Annulets in quarters 1 & 4,* ✠IER... / ✠ · C...I · IH
2010 (7750) 15, 0.3 *Obv.:* ✠MASTRI · ...[ET] *Rev.: Annulets in quarters [1 & 4],* [✠IE]...[ALE]... / ✠CIUIS·[R]... IH
2011 (7761) 15, 0.4 *Obv.:* ✠MAS[T]... / ...OD... *Rev.:* / ✠ · [M]...· IH
2012 (7782) 15, 0.3 *Obv.:* ✠...OSPE *Rev.: Annulets in quarters [1 & 4],* [✠]...[LE]MI / *janua, dot r.,* [C]I[U]... IH
2013 (7789) 15, 0.3 *Obv.:* ✠MAST... / *cross,* ...GR·O... *Rev.: Annulets in quarters 1 & 4,* [ ]IER[U]... / ✠ ° CI...° IH
2014 (7844) 14, 0.6 *Obv.:* ✠...T / *cross,* ✠MAGR[h]O... *Rev.: Annulets in quarters 1 & 4,* ...[U]SA... / ✠ · CIV...I[:] IH
2015 (7847) 15, 0.5 *Obv.:* [ ]MASTR... / cross, ✠MAGR·O... *Rev.: Annulets in quarters 1 & 4,* ✠I[E]...[LE]MIT / ✠CIU... IH
2016 (8236) 16, 0.4 *Obv.:* ✠[M]...SPE / [ ]MAG... *Rev.: Annulets in quarters 1 & 4,* ✠IE[R]... / *janua,* ✠ · C...DI IH
2017 (8242) 15, 0.4 *Obv.:* ...S[ ]R... / *janua, dot r.,* ...I[U]...·... IH
2018 (8260) 15, 0.4 *Obv.:* [✠M]...T... / *janua, dot r.,* ✠ · CIV... *Rev.: Annulets in quarters 1 & 4,* ...S... / [✠M]AGR · OS...[L] IH
2019 (8266) 15, 0.5 *Obv.:* ...OS... / *janua, dot r.,* ...IUIS · RO... *Rev.:* ...S... / *cross,* ✠MAGR[· h]... IH
2020 (9611) 15, 0.5 *Obv.:* / ✠ ·...RODI · *Rev.: Annulets in quarters [1 & 4],* ...ALEMI... / ...[S]PIT[AL KH
2021 (9625) 15, 0.5 *Obv.:* ...T...[E]... / [✠] · CI... *Rev.: Annulets in quarters 2 & 3,* ✠IE... / ...AGROSPI... KH

PLATE 107

2022 (9643) 15, 0.6 *Obv.:* ✠[A]ST... *Rev.: Annulets in quarters 1 & 4,* ...U... / *janua,* ✠ · C...[S]· ... *Doubled die.* KH
2023 (9644) 14, 0.5 *Obv.:* [MA T... / *[janua, dot r.,]* ...CIU... *Rev.:* / ...G[R]...ITA[L KH
2024 (9653) 15, 0.4 *Obv.:* ✠MAS[T]... / ...OSPI[T...· *Rev.: Annulets in quarters 1 & 4,* [ ]IERUSA... / ✠ · CI...· KH
2025 (9687) 15, 0.5 *Obv.:* ✠[A]ST[R... / ✠ · I...I · *Rev.: Annulets in quarters [2 & 3],* ...[MIT]... / ...OSPIT... KH
2026 (9694) 15, 0.4 *Obv.* ✠...TROSPET / *cross. Rev.: Annulets in quarters [2 & 3],* ✠M... / *[janua],* ✠ ° C[I... KH
2027 (9704) 15, 0.6 *Obv.* / *[janua,]* ✠ · CIVIS ·...· *Rev.: Annulets in quarters 2 & 3,* ✠IERU... / ...AGR · OSP... / ...OS... KH
2028 (9706) 14, 0.4 *Obv.:* ...E[ ] / *cross,* ✠MA[ ]R[·]hOSPITAL' *Rev.:* / *[janua,] dot r.,* [ ] · CIV...RODI[KH
2029 (9708) 15, 0.4 *Obv.:* ✠[M]A...T · / ...OSPIT... *Rev.:* ...[US]ALE[M / ... IUI... KH
2030 (9733) 15, 0.3 *Obv.:* ✠MAST[RIO... / *cross,* ✠M[ ]GR · O[S... *Rev.: Annulets in quarters 1 & 4,* ...ERUSA...I... / *janua, dot r.,* ✠ · CIVIS·ROD[I KH
2031 (9736) 15, 0.4 *Obv.:* ✠MAST[R... / [ ]MAG...PITA[L *Rev.: Annulets in quarters 1 & 4,* ...RUSAL... / ✠ · CI...ODI[ ] KH
2032 (9791) 15, 0.4 *Obv.:* ✠...T / ...[OSPITA... *Rev.:* ...SAL[E]... / ✠ · CI[V...R]ODI · KH
2033 (9818) 15, 0.4 *Obv.:* / *janua,* ✠ · C...· *Rev.: Annulets in quarters 2 & 3,* ✠IER[U]... KH
2034 (9820) 14, 0.3 *Obv.:* / *Dot r.,* [✠] · CIVI... *Rev.: Annulets in quarters 2 & 3,* ...US... / ...OSPIT[AL KH
2035 (9828) 15, 0.4 *Obv.:* ✠M[A]...AL' *Rev.: Annulets in quarters 2 & 3,* ✠I[ ]RU... / *janua, dot r.,* ✠CI[U... KH
2036 (9848) 15, 0.4 *Obv.:* ✠...OSPET / *cross,* ...GR · O... *Rev.:* / ✠ · C...· KH

2037 (9849) 15, 0.4 *Obv.:* ✠[ ]Ħ... / *cross,* ✠ · ᗰĦ... *Rev.: Annulets in quarters 2 & 3,* [ ]IЄRUSĦLЄ... / *[janua], dot r.,* ...RODI[KH
2038 (9867) 15, 0.5 *Obv.:* ✠ᗰĦST...Є / *cross,* ...GROSPIT... *Rev.: Annulets in quarters 1 & 4,* ✠I...[L]Є[ ]I / *janua,* ...[R]ODI° KH
2039 (9868) 13, 0.4 *Obv.: Small châtel,* ...SP[Є... / ✠...DI° *Doubled die. Rev.:* ...USĦL... / ...[P]ITĀ[I] KH
2040 (2046) 17, 0.7 *Obv.:* ✠ᗰĦST[R]... / ✠·... I·RI·[S·] *Rev.: Annulets in quarters 1 & 4,* ✠[IЄ]...ᗰIT / ✠... /...[ON]... IH
2041 (3188) 16, 0.3 *Obv.:* ✠ᗰ... / *[foreign]* ...[DI]...[N]... *Rev.: Annulets in quarters 2 & 3,* ...ЄRUSĦLЄ... / ...·S·... IH
2042 (3254) 16, 0.3 *Obv.:* ✠...ЄT / ✠IOhĦNN[ĦD...TI... *Rev.:* / ✠...LЄTSIΩI...NĦ] *Incomplete.* IH
2043 (7517) 16, 0.5 *Obv.:* ...STR... / *cross cantonned with radiately placed fleurs-de-lys,* ...LЄTSIΩI... *Rev.: Annulets in quarters 1 & 4,* ...SĦLЄᗰ / ...NĦDЄI[G... *Corr.* IH
2044 (7598) 15, 0.5 *Obv.:* ✠...OSP... / ...RĀDV[S... *Rev.: Annulets in quarters [1 & 4],* ...[ᗰ]IT /...[hE]N[R... IH
2045 (7708) 14, 0.5 *Obv.:* [ᗰ]ĦSTR... / ✠ · S[I]... · *Rev.: Annulets in quarters 2 & 3,* ✠IЄL·...ЄᗰI· IH
2046 (8253) 16, 0.3 *Obv.:* ...[SP]ЄΠ[Ħ *Rev.:* / ✠ · [OSN]...S ·...O · / ...★ IH
2047 (8271) 14, 0.4 *Obv.:* [✠]...[S]PЄ[T] *Rev.: Annulets in quarters 1 & 4,* [ ]IЄRUSĦL... /...[IO]LANV[S... IH
2048 (9780) 14, 0.3 *Obv.: Small châtel,* ✠ᗰ...[Ħ]I *Rev.: Annulets in quarters 1 & 4,* ✠IЄ...LЄᗰIT / ...DV... KH

PLATE 108

2049 (1147) 14, 0.2 *Obv.:* ✠...ST[R]SPЄ *Rev.:* ...S · ... I. 26
2050 (1184) 14, 0.2 *Obv.:* [✠]...[ST]R[ ]OS[PЄ[/ *cross. Rev.:* ...[N]... / *[janua], annulet r.*
2051 (3465) 15, 0.5 *Rev.: Annulets in quarters 1 & 4,* ✠[I]ЄRUSĦ... II. 58
2052 (4460) 14, 0.4 *Obv.:* ✠...OSPЄT I. 91
2053 (5994) 14, 0.5 *Obv.:* ✠ᗰĦST...DI / *cross,* ...[·]OSPIT[Ħ]... *Rev.: Annulets in quarters 1 & 4,* ✠IЄ...[ᗰIT] / ...S·RODI II. 56
2054 (6065) 16, 0.6 *Obv.:* ...[O]SP... *Rev.: Annulets in quarters 1 & 4,* ...R... II. 35
2055 (962) 11, 0.2 *Clipped, corr.* II. 29
2056 (1196) 14, 0.4 *Obv.:* ...Ħ[T]... / ✠...· *Rev.:* ...O·... / ...RO... II. 56
2057 (4035) 14, 0.4 *Rev.:* ...LЄ...[Ħ]LIS... *Corr.* II. 55
2058 (4148) 15, 0.6 *Obv.:* ...[I]TS... *Rev.:* ...ĦL[O]... II. 41
2059 (4347) 14, 0.3 *Obv.:* ...[ST]R... *Rev.: Annulets in quarters [2 & 3],* [✠IR]OS... *Corr., incomplete.* II. 53
2060 (4491) 13, 0.2 *Corr., incomplete.* II. 57
2061 (4659) 14, 0.4 *Obv.:* ✠ᗰ...[Є]TĦ II. 52
2062 (4857) 14, 0.2 *Corr., incomplete.* II. 41
2063 (5392) 15, 0.6 *V. worn. Uncertain ident.* II. 56
2064 (5430) 15, 0.4 *Obv.:* ...T *Corr., incomplete.* II. 56
2065 (5459) 14, 0.3 *Obv.:* ...ᗰĦST...[S]... *Corr.* II. 56
2066 (5482) 15, 0.3 *Obv.:* ...S...[I]OSP... *Rev.: Annulets in quarters [2 & 3],* ...ЄR... *Corr.* II. 56
2067 (5518) 15, 0.6 *Obv.:* / ✠Ω... *Rev.: Annulets in quarters 2 & 3,* ✠IЄRUSĦ... *Worn.* II. 56
2068 (5549) 13, 0.4 *Corr.* II. 56
2069 (5569) 12, 0.2 *Corr., incomplete.* II. 56
2070 (5811) 13, 0.5 *Obv.:* ...ᗰĦ...STЄ...ĦL... *Rev.:* ...US...Ħ... / ✠... *Corr., incomplete.* II. 41
2071 (5864) 15, 0.4 *Obv.:* ✠ᗰ...T... *Rev.:* ...[Ħ]... *Corr., incomplete.* II. 56
2072 (5868) 14, 0.4 *Obv.: Ill. [Brockage.] Rev.:* ... *Corr., incomplete.* II. 56
2073 (5964) 14, 0.4 *Obv.:* / ...ĦGR·h... *Rev.:* / *[janua]. Worn.* II. 56

First signed type of Philibert de Naillac, 1396-1421
Obv.: Naillac arms (two lions passant guardant in pale, a label) within beaded circle. Rev.: Maltese cross within beaded circle, annulets in two opposed quarters.

2074 (2330) 15, 0.7 *Obv.:* ✠... S · IOĦ *Rev.: Annulets in quarters 2 & 3,* ✠IO...ROLI IH
2075 (3050) 16, 0.5 *Obv.:* ✠... S · IOĦ *Rev.: Annulets in quarters 2 & 3,* ✠...[N]ЄS·IЄROLI IH
2076 (6168) 15, 0.7 *Obv.:* ...O[P]... *Rev.: Annulets in quarters 1 & 4,* ✠O... · S · ...Ħ IH
2077 (6169) 15, 0.7 *Obv.:* ✠OSP...·[I]... *Rev.: Annulets in quarters 2 & 3.* ✠...[I]O... · IЄRO... IH
2078 (8319) 17, 0.6 *Rev.: Annulets in quarters 2 & 3,* ✠IO[Ħ]...IЄ KH
2079 (8320) 16, 0.4 *Rev.:* ...IЄ / *[lion rampant]* KH
2080 (9584) 15, 0.4 *Obv.:* ...[I]O *Rev.: Annulets in quarters 2 & 3,* ✠IO...[ЄS...I] KH
2081 (9586) 16, 0.4 *Rev.: Annulets in quarters 2 & 3,* ...[ITSL]... KH
2082 (1183) 15, 0.3 *Rev.: Annulets in quarters 2 & 3* II. 56

PLATE 109

First signed type of Naillac, overstruck by later issues
Obv.: Clumsy châtel, initial crosslet of legend under base. Rev.: Cross pattee, annulets in two opposed quarters.

2083 (3031) 16, 0.6 *Obv.: Annulet within châtel,* ...SPITĦ·ᗰ... / *Naillac arms. Rev.: Annulets in quarters 1 & 4,* ✠...L·S·O IH
2084 (3064) 17, 0.6 *Obv.:* ✠IO · IhRL · ᗰ · [O] / *Naillac arms. Rev.:* ...h[O]SP... IH

2085 (3283) 16, 0.6 *Obv.: / Naillac arms,* ✠… · IO… *Rev.: Annulets in quarters [1 & 4],* ✠O… IH
2086 (3351) 17, 0.4 *Obv.:* [✠]…ᗰ · … *Rev.: Annulets in quarters 2 & 3,* …· [O]…[IO · Ih]…[OS]… IH
2087 (7600) 17, 0.7 *Obv.:* …[O]S…OSPƐ… */ Naillac arms / cross. Rev.: Annulets in quarters 2 & 3/* …·[I]ƐROLI IH
2088 (7951) 17, 0.6 *Obv.:* …S · I… */ Naillac arms,* …· O[*Rev.:* …[· IO]… IH
2089 (7974) 16, 0.8 *Obv.:* ✠IO ·…ᗰ · O*/ cross. Rev.: / Naillac arms.* IH
2090 (7975) 16, 0.6 *Obv.:* …O[·]… */ [Naillac arms.] Rev.:* …[Ꭿ]S… IH
2091 (8020) 15, 0.4 *Obv.:* ✠hOS…S */ [Naillac arms.] Rev.:* …L…[I] ·…· IH
2092 (8077) 16, 0.5 *Obv.:* ✠[h]…[I]Lᗰ[*/ cross. Rev.:* …L · S · I… */ [Naillac arms.]* IH
2093 (8189) 16, 0.5 *Obv.:* ✠…Lᗰ */ [Naillac arms,]* ✠… *Rev.:* …ͲᎯ[L]… / …ƐR… IH
2094 (8224) 16, 0.7 *Obv.:* …*/ [Naillac arms,]* …I[Ɛ]ᗰ / …· I *Rev.:* ✠hO[S]…[I] / [I]ƐRO… IH
2095 (10045) 16, 0.7 *Obv.:* …*/ cross, annulets in opposite quarters, [/]*…· Ih… *Rev.: / Naillac arms.* KH
2096 (10079) 16, 0.6 *Obv.:* ✠[IO]…ᗰ · O / …[hOSP]… */ Naillac arms.* KH
2097 (10119) 16, 0.5 *Obv.:* …·Ih… / …*[cross, annulets ° in opposite quarters.] Rev.:* …S[PI]… / …IhR… */ Naillac arms* KH
2098 (10146) 16, 0.5 *Obv.:* ✠IO… */ cross, annulets in opposite quarters,*…IƐR[OS… *Rev.: / Naillac arms.* KH

Second signed type of Philibert de Naillac, 1396-1421
Obv.: Clumsy châtel, dot within; initial crosslet of legend under base; in beaded circle. Rev.: Maltese cross, annulets in quarters 2 & 3; in beaded circle.

2099 (1678) 16, 0.8 *Obv.:* ✠PhIBƐR… *Rev.:* …S]Ꭿ[L]… / … ∾·IƐR… IH
2100 (7855) 16, 0.6 *Obv.:* ✠ PhI[BƐR]T…[I]… *Rev.:* …OSPITᎯL · S · [I]… IH
2101 (7856) 15, 0.4 *Obv.:* ✠PhI[BƐ]…[I · ᗰ]. *Rev.:* ✠…[OՌ]I IH
2102 (7857) 16, 0.4 *Obv.:* ✠[ ]hIBƐRT…[ᗰ]. *Rev.:* …ƐS · IƐ… IH
2103 (7866) 16, 0.6 *Obv.:* ✠P…[· Ɛ ·] RͲI[· ᗰ]. *Rev.:* [✠]IOᎯ[ՌƐ]S…S / ✠…[L] IH
2104 (7868) 16, 0.6 *Obv.:* ✠PhIBƐ[ ]ͲI · [ᗰ] / … *Rev.:* I[OᎯ]ՌƐS · [Ꭿ]… IH
2105 (7875) 15, 0.6 *Obv.:* ✠Ph[ ]BƐRͲI · [ᗰ]. *Rev.:* ✠IOᎯՌƐS · [Ɛ]ROLI IH
2106 (8006) 16, 0.6 *Obv.:* ✠ …BƐRͲI[ᗰ] · ᗰ *Rev.:* ✠[h]O… / …[Ͳ]ƐS ·… IH
2107 (8047) 16, 0.4 *Obv.:* ✠…Ɛ✠[BƐ]ͲI · ᗰ… *Rev.:* …OS[P]… / …S · [I]… IH

Related issues
Naillac overstrikes. Obv.: Clumsy châtel, dot within; in beaded circle. Rev.: Maltese cross, annulets in two opposite quarters; in beaded circle.

2108 (1337) 17, 0.8 *Obv.:* IO[Ꭿ]… *Rev.: Annulets in quarters 2 & 3,* ✠OSPIͲ… IH
2109 (2019) 16, 0.5 *Obv.:* …[ᎯՌ]ƐS·IƐ… / ✠…IT…[L]… *Rev.: Annulets in quarters 1 & 4,* ✠IO·IhRLᗰ·… IH
2110 (3259) 16, 0.6 *Obv.:* …[Ռ]ƐS · IƐ… *Rev.: Annulets in quarters [1 & 4],* ✠[O · IO · IIhՌ]… IH

PLATE 110

Anonymous overstrikes of Philibert de Naillac, 1396-1421
Clumsy châtel, dot within, initial crosslet of legend under base; within beaded circle. Rev.: Cross pattee, annulets in two opposed quarters; within beaded circle.

Major hoards

2111 (1543) 17, 0.5 *Obv.:* ✠O[ ]IͲ·S… *Rev.: Annulets in quarters 1 & 4,* ✠OSPI… IH
2112 (1998) 16, 0.5 *Obv.:* ✠O[Ռ]… B[O]… *Rev.: Annulets in quarters 2 & 3,* …SPIͲ… IH
2113 (2001) 16, 0.4 *Obv.:*…Ͳ·SBO… *Rev.: Annulets in quarters 1 & 4,* ✠…[hO]…L·S·… */ cross.* IH
2114 (2003) 17, 0.8 *Obv.:* …·SBO… *Rev.: Annulets in quarters 2 & 3,* ✠O[S]…T·… */ cross.* IH
2115 (3299) 16, 0.6 *Obv.:* [✠]O[ ] · … · Sh[ ]OS… *Rev.: Annulets in quarters 2 & 3,* ✠OS · T…[ᗰ]O / ✠…L IH
2116 (3322) 15, 0.4 *Obv.:* ✠O…Ͳ · S[B]… *Rev.:* …OSPI[T]… IH
2117 (8007) 15, 0.5 *Obv.:* ✠OՌIͲ · SB[I] · ᗰ[*Rev.:* …OS[P]IͲ[Ꭿ… IH
2118 (8012) 15, 0.5 *Obv.:* ✠OՌIͲ · SBO…Ꭿ *Rev.:* ✠O[·]…S · I✠hO[S]… IH
2119 (8084) 15, 0.6 *Obv.:* …SB[O… / …RO[D… *Rev.:* …hOS… / …L[ᗰ]… / …Ɑ… IH
2120 (8099) 16, 0.6 *Obv.:* …ՌIͲ · SB[O… *Rev.: Annulets in quarters 2 & 3,* ✠…LI IH
2121 (9906) 16, 0.5 *Obv.:* ✠OՌI…[Lᗰ… / …I[Ɛ]… *Rev.: Annulets in quarters 1 & 4,* ✠OSPIͲ…ƐS[I]O IH
2122 (9946) 17, 0.7 *Obv.:* [ ]OՌIͲ… *Rev.: Annulets in quarters [2 & 3],* ✠OS[P]…· S · IO · IH
2123 (9993) 16, 0.5 *Obv.:* [ ]OՌIͲ · S… / …S · *Rev.:* …ᎯL[ ]S · IO… / …SPI… IH
2124 (10052) 16, 0.5 *Obv.:* [ ]O…SBO… / [✠]… *Rev.:* /✠hO[S]…· I IH
2125 (10059) 17, 0.7 *Obv.:* [✠O]ՌI[Ͳ… [/]IO[ᎯՌ]… *Rev.:* / ✠[h]…ᎯL · S · IO… IH
2126 (10066) 16, 0.8 *Obv.:* [OՌI]Ͳ · S… / ✠…[LI] *Rev.:* …ͲᎯL · / …· IO…
2127 (1700) 16, 0.7 *Obv.:* …ՌIͲ·SB[O]… *Rev.: Annulets in quarters 2 & 3,* ✠IO[ ]IhRL·[ᗰ·O] IH
2128 (2026) 16, 0.6 *Obv.:* ✠O…Ͳ·SB[O]… *Rev.: Annulets in quarters [1 & 4],* [✠]IO… IH
2129 (2034) 17, 0.6 *Obv.:* …ՌIͲ·S[B]… *Rev.: Annulets in quarters 2 & 3,* [✠]IO·[IhRL]… IH
2130 (3282) 16, 0.5 *Obv.:* ✠OՌI…SP…]… *Rev.: Annulets in quarters [1 & 4],* …IO · …[RLᗰ]… IH
2131 (3318) 15, 0.3 *Obv.:* ✠OՌIͲ · SB]… · [Lᗰ]… *Rev.: Annulets in quarters 1 & 4,* ✠IO · Ih[RL]…O IH
2132 (8053) 16, 0.6 *Obv.:* ✠O[Ռ]… / …[S]BO… *Rev.: Annulets in quarters 2 & 3,* ✠IO · I[h]… / …[I]OᎯ[Ռ]✠[h] · L IH
2133 (9893) 17, 0.5 *Obv.:* ✠OՌIͲ · S[B]O… *Rev.: Annulets in quarters 1 & 4,* ✠IO · Ih[RLᗰ] · [ ] IH
2134 (9899) 18, 0.4 *Obv.:* ✠O[Ռ]…SB[O]… *Rev.: Annulets in quarters 1 & 4,* ✠IO · [I]…L[ ]ᗰ · IH
2135 (9903) 16, 0.5 *Obv.:* …IͲ · SB[O… *Rev.:* …IO… / ✠OS… IH

2136 (9921) 16, 0.5 *Obv.:* ✠OΠIΠ · S[B]O[· I… *Rev.: Annulets in quarters 1 & 4,* ✠…[h]RLM · O · IH
2137 (9994) 17, 0.5 *Obv.:* ✠O[Π]…M… *Rev.: Annulets in quarters 1 & 4,* ✠MAGR[✪]… / ✠SPIT… KH
2138 (3355) 17, 0.5 *Obv.: [Annulet within]* ✠hO[S]PITA… *Rev.: Annulets in quarters 2 & 3,* ✠S[·]…hRLM IH
2139 (7898) 14, 0.3 *Obv.:* ✠…L · S *Rev.: Annulets in quarters 1 & 4,* ✠S · [I]… IH
2140 (7905) 16, 0.5 *Obv.:* ✠hOS[P]… / …OS… *Rev.: Annulets in quarters 2 & 3,* ✠[S]…[A]LM IH
2141 (7916) 16, 0.5 *Obv.:* ✠hO[S]PIΠA[L *Rev.: Annulets in quarters [2 & 3],* [S] · IO · Ih[ ]LM · IH
2142 (7945) 16, 0.5 *Obv.:* [ ]OSPIΠAL / …IO… IH

PLATE 111

2143 (7957) 16, 0.5 *Obv.:* ✠…IΠAL… *Rev.: Annulets in quarters 1 & 4,* ✠[S] · I…[Π] · / …h… IH
2144 (7996) 15, 0.5 *Obv.:* ✠h[O]…A[L] · *Rev.: Annulets in quarters 1 & 4,* ✠S ·…·… IH
2145 (8063) 16, 0.4 *Obv.:* ✠…LI / …[S]… *Rev.: Annulets in quarters 1 & 4,* [✠]S · IO · I… /]S · IO… IH
2146 (8229) 14, 0.5 *Obv.:* ✠OSPIΠA[L… *Rev.: Annulets in quarters 1 & 4,* ✠S · IO · IhRL[ ] IH
2147 (1352) 17, 0.4 *Obv.:* ✠hOSP[IT]A… / …GR·OSP… *Rev.: Annulets in quarters 1 & 4,* ✠IO·IhRL… IH
2148 (1534) 17, 0.6 *Obv.:* …SPIΠAL·[*Rev.: Annulets in quarters 1 & 4,* ✠[I]O·IhRL…O[] IH
2149 (1537) 16, 0.5 *Obv.:*]hOSPIΠ[A]L[*Rev.: Annulets in quarters 1 & 4,* ✠[IO]·IhRL… IH
2150 (1677) 17, 0.4 *Obv.:*]hOSPIΠAL[*Rev.: Annulets in quarters 1 & 4,* ✠IO·…[D] IH
2151 (2009) 15, 0.5 *Obv.:* ✠hOSPIΠAL / …◦… *Rev.: Annulets in quarters 2 & 3,* ✠IO·IhRLM / cross. IH
2152 (2020) 17, 0.4 *Obv.:* [✠]hO[SP]I·… *Rev.: Annulets in quarters [2 & 3],* [✠]…IhR…· IH
2153 (2022) 17, 0.8 *Obv.:*]hOSPIT… *Rev.: Annulets in quarters 1 & 4,* [✠]IOIhRL…· IH
2154 (2025) 15, 0.6 *Obv.:* …PI[T]… / …SPI… *Rev.: Annulets in quarters 1 & 4,* [✠]…I[ ]RLM IH
2155 (3033) 15, 0.4 *Obv.:* ✠OSPIT… *Rev.: Annulets in quarters 1 & 4,* ✠IO·…M·O IH
2156 (3035) 14, 0.5 *Obv.:*]hOSPIT… *Rev.: Annulets in quarters 1 & 4,* ✠IO·IhR… IH
2157 (3037) 15, 0.4 *Obv.:* ✠O…AL[·]… / …S… *Rev.: Annulets in quarters 1 & 4,* ✠S·IO·… IH
2158 (3038) 15, 0.3 *Obv.:* ✠[h]OSPI…[·] M[*Rev.: Annulets in quarters 1 & 4,* ✠ IO·I…[M]… IH
2159 (3222) 16, 0.6 *Obv.:* …hOSPI[T]… *Rev.: Annulets in quarters 1 & 4,* ✠IO · I… · *Doubled die.* IH
2160 (3295) 16, 0.6 *Obv.:* …O…IT… *Rev.: Annulets in quarters 1 & 4,* …O · IhRL[M]… IH
2161 (3345) 14, 0.3 *Obv.:* ✠hOSPI… *Rev.: Annulets in quarters 1 & 4,* ✠IO · [Ih]… IH
2162 (7872) 15, 0.5 *Obv.:* ✠hOS[P]I[TA]… *Rev.: Annulets in quarters 2 & 3,* ✠…IO · I]hR]LM IH
2163 (7940) 16, 0.4 *Obv.:* [ ]hO…[Π] … *Rev.: Annulets in quarters [1 & 4],* [ ]IO · IhRL[M / ✠O…A IH
2164 (7954) 17, 0.7 *Obv.:* [✠OSPI]… / …[L] · S ·… *Rev.:* …RLM… IH
2165 (7969) 16, 0.7 *Obv.:* ✠…IΠA[I / …[S]… *Rev.: Annulets in quarters 1 & 4,* ✠IO · IhR[L… / *[châtel]* IH
2166 (7973) 15, 0.4 *Obv.:* ✠IO · I[h]…M · O *Rev.:* …IΠA… IH
2167 (7977) 16, 0.4 *Obv.:* ✠hO[S]…Π…A *Rev.: Annulets in quarters 1 & 4,* ✠[I]O ·…M · [D] IH
2168 (7995) 16, 0.4 *Obv.:* …PIΠA… *Rev.: Annulets in quarters 1 & 4,* ✠[· IO]…· O IH
2169 (7997) 15, 0.4 *Obv.:* [✠]hOS… *Rev.: Annulets in quarters 1 & 4,* ✠IO · [I]…[M] IH
2170 (8008) 17, 0.8 *Obv.:* ✠[h]…[A]L · / ✠… *Rev.: Annulets in quarters 1 & 4,* ✠IO ·… IH
2171 (8017) 17, 0.5 *Obv.:* [ ]hOSPIΠ[A… *Rev.: Annulets in quarters 1 & 4,* ✠IO…[RL]M · O / …OS… IH
2172 (8022) 16, 0.4 *Obv.:* ✠hOSPI…[· S] *Rev.: Annulets in quarters 1 & 4,* ✠IO · IhRL[M]O IH
2173 (8029) 15, 0.5 *Obv.:* ✠[h]…PIΠAL *Rev.:* …hRL[M]… IH
2174 (8042) 16, 0.7 *Obv.:* ✠[h]…AL · M *Rev.: Annulets in quarters 2 & 3,* ✠IO[IhR]…[OL] IH
2175 (8054) 15, 0.4 *Obv.:* ✠hOSPI…L ·[A] *Rev.: Annulets in quarters 1 & 4,* ✠IO[ ]IhRLM… / ✠… IH
2176 (8066) 15, 0.5 *Obv.:* ✠hOS… / …h… / …· IЄ[R]… *Rev.: Annulets in quarters 1 & 4,* ✠…M · O / ✠… IH
2177 (8076) 15, 0.4 *Obv.:* …OS[PI]…AL *Rev.: Annulets in quarters 1 & 4,* ✠…IhR…[D] / …[IOΠ]… IH

PLATE 112

2178 (8080) 15, 0.4 *Obv.:* ✠[h]…L · S[ ] *Rev.:* …· IhRL ·… *Incomplete.* IH
2179 (8086) 15, 0.6 *Obv.:* ✠…PIΠAL[· M *Rev.:* [ ]IO · IhRL[M IH
2180 (8094) 17, 0.4 *Obv.:* …OSPIΠA[L *Rev.: Annulets in quarters 1 & 4,* [✠]IO · I[h]L[M]O IH
2181 (8108) 16, 0.6 *Obv.:* [✠]hOSP… / [✠OS]… *Rev.: Annulets in quarters 2 & 3,* ✠S · IO ·…LM / …[LM… IH
2182 (8144) 14, 0.4 *Obv.:* ✠[hO PIΠ]… / …[OS]… *Rev.: Annulets in quarters 2 & 3,* ✠…I[h]…[LM] IH
2183 (8154) 15, 0.4 *Obv.:* ✠…ΠAL / …[SP]… *Rev.: Annulets in quarters 1 & 4,* ✠…LM IH
2184 (8182) 15, 0.4 *Obv.:* ✠hOS… [/ · α… *Rev.:* …IhR… / *[cross with annulets in opposite quarters.]* IH
2185 (8198) 16, 0.4 *Obv.:* ✠hO[S… / …[A ·] *Rev.:* …O · IhRLM… IH
2186 (8201) 18, 0.6 *Obv.:* ✠hO…AL / …[Π]… *Rev.:* …IO · Ih… IH
2187 (9892) 17, 0.5 *Obv.:* …PIΠALO… *Rev.:* [ ]IO · Ih[RLM ·]… / …IO… KH
2188 (9894) 16, 0.6 *Obv.:* …· O[SPIΠA]… *Rev.: Annulets in quarters 1 & 4,* ✠IO · IO… KH
2189 (9901) 15, 0.5 *Obv.:* ✠…[Π]AL / …IT… *Rev.: Annulets in quarters [1 & 4],* [✠I]O · I… / ✠α… KH
2190 (9909) 16, 0.6 *Obv.:* ✠hO… / …[Є]… [/] ΠAL / …[A]… *Rev.: Annulets in quarters [1 & 4],* [ ]IO · IhRLM ·… / …L… KH
2191 (9911) 17, 0.6 *Obv.:* ✠[hOS…ΠA]L / …[OSP]… *Rev.:* …RL[M… / …AL · KH
2192 (9915) 15, 0.4 *Obv.:* …PI[Π]A… / …[M]A… *Rev.: Annulets in quarters 1 & 4,* ✠IO · O[S]… · O · KH
2193 (9935) 16, 0.4 *Obv.:* ✠[hO]SPIΠAL · S *Rev.: Annulets in quarters 1 & 4,* ✠IO · I[h]RLM · O / …α… KH
2194 (9937) 16, 0.7 *Obv.:* / …OSPI… / ✠… *Rev.: Annulets in quarters 1 & 4,* ✠IO ·…RLM · O · KH

2195 (9944) 15, 0.3 *Obv.:* ✠hOSPI… *Rev.: Annulets in quarters 1 & 4,* ✠IO ·…ᗰ · O[·]. KH
2196 (9947) 17, 0.6 *Obv.:* [ ]hOS…ΑL / …ЄS… / …[G]R… *Rev.: Annulets in quarters 1 & 4,* ✠IO · Ih…· O · KH
2197 (9949) 15, 0.5 *Obv.:* [ ]hOS…[TΑ… O: *Rev.: Annulets in quarters 1 & 4,* ✠IO · I[hR]…O · KH
2198 (9956) 17, 0.8 *Obv.: Small châtel,* ✠hO…RLᗰ / …OSPI… *Rev.: Annulets in quarters 1 & 4,* ✠IO ·…ᗰ · O · / ✠OS… KH
2199 (10030) 14, 0.4 *Obv.:* ✠[I]OSP[I]ΑL[ ] *Rev.: Annulets in quarters 2 & 3,* ✠[ ]O · IhRLᗰ / ✠ᗰ… KH
2200 (10056) 15, 0.4 *Obv.:* ✠hOSPITΑL *Rev.:* …[O ·]IhR[L]ᗰ KH
2201 (10090) 15, 0.5 *Obv.:*]hOSPI…Α… *Rev.:* …O · IhR… / …[OD]… KH
2202 (10103) 16, 0.6 *bv.:* ✠hOS[ ]I…· IO *Rev.: Annulets in quarters 1 & 4,* ✠IO ·…[O] / …L… KH
2203 (10120) 15, 0.6 *Obv.:* ✠hO… *Rev.: Annulets in quarters 1 & 4,* ✠…Ih…Lᗰ *Doubled die.* KH
2204 (1335) 16, 0.3 *Obv.:* ✠IO[˙.]IhRLᗰ[˙.]O[˙.] *Rev.: Annulets in quarters 2 & 3,* [✠h]…[Α]L · S[·] IH
2205 (1349) 16, 0.5 *Obv.:* ✠[IO]·Ih…·O *Rev.: Annulets in quarters 2 & 3,* ✠[hOSPI]TΑL · S ·[IH
2206 (1692) 16, 0.5 *Obv.:* ✠IO·IhRL[ᗰ] · O *Rev.:* …OS…TΑ… IH
2207 (1701) 16, 0.5 *Obv.:* ✠IO·IhRLᗰ ·[O] *Rev.: Annulets in quarters 2 & 3,* ✠[h]OSPIT…[L] IH
2208 (2014) 14, 0.4 *Obv.:* ✠…·hRLᗰ · O *Rev.:* [✠]…hOSPITΑL[ᗰ / *cross.* IH
2209 (3063) 15, 0.4 *Obv.:* ✠IO · I[hR] · ᗰ · [O] *Rev.:* …[ΑL] ·… IH
2210 (3067) 16, 0.6 *Obv.:* ✠IO…hRL · ᗰ · [O] *Rev.: Annulets in quarters 1 & 4,* ✠[hOSPI]… IH
2211 (3068) 16, 0.5 *Obv.:* ✠IO · I…L · [ᗰ] · O *Rev.: Annulets in quarters 1 & 4,* ✠hO… IH

PLATE 113

2212 (3198) 15, 0.5 *Obv.:* ✠IO · Ih[RL…[O] *Rev.: Annulets in quarters [2 & 3],* ✠…TΑ… / ✠…L· IH
2213 (3199) 16, 0.7 *Obv.:* ✠IO · Ih… · [O]… *Rev.: Annulets in quarters 2 & 3,* ✠h…PI / ✠… *Doubled die.* IH
2214 (3213) 16, 0.4 *Obv.:* …Ihᗰ…[ᗰ ·]… / …[*Rev.:* …[TΑL]… / ✠OS… IH
2215 (3255) 17, 0.5 *Obv.:* ✠…Lᗰ…[h] *Rev.: Annulets in quarters 2 & 3,* ✠OSPITΑL ·… IH
2216 (3335) 17, 0.6 *Obv.:* ✠IO · Ih… · O / [✠]… *Rev.:* …ΑL · … IH
2217 (3361) 16, 0.6 *Obv.:* ✠IO · Ih…✠O : [Ꭰ] *Rev.:* ✠hOS… / …[RO]…
2218 (7882) 17, 0.4 *Obv.:* ✠…· IhRLᗰ · O *Rev.: Annulets in quarters 2 & 3,* ✠hOSPI… IH
2219 (7907) 16, 0.5 *Obv.:* ✠[ ]O · IhRLᗰ · O *Rev.: Annulets in quarters 2 & 3,* ✠…OSPI…L… / ✠…OS… IH
2220 (7935) 17, 0.6 *Obv.:* ✠IO · Ih…ᗰ · O *Rev.:* …ΑL · S… / …[T]ΑS… IH
2221 (7941) 16, 0.5 *Obv.:* ✠IO · IhR…· O / …[O]… *Rev.: Annulets in quarters 2 & 3,* ✠hOSP… IH
2222 (7952) 16, 0.4 *Obv.:* …IhRLᗰ… *Rev.: Annulets in quarters 1 & 4,* ✠[hOS]…[I]S IH
2223 (7959) 14, 0.5 *Obv.:* ✠IO…· ᗰ · O *Rev.:* …[h]OSP[TΑ]… IH
2224 (7966) 14, 0.4 *Obv.:* ✠IO · IhRLᗰ · O *Rev.:* …TΑL… / …SP… / …T… IH
2225 (7992) 15, 0.6 *Obv.:* ✠IO…[L · ᗰ] · O / ✠IO… *Rev.:* …T[ ]LS · IO[ ] ·… IH
2226 (7993) 16, 0.5 *Obv.:* ✠IO ·…[R]…· [O] *Rev.:* …hOSP… IH
2227 (7998) 15, 0.5 *Obv.:* ✠IO · Ih[RL]… / …O[SPIT]… *Rev.:* …OSPITΑ[ ] ·… IH
2228 (7999) 14, 0.4 *Obv.:* ✠IO · Ih[L]ᗰ · O *Rev.: Annulets in quarters 2 & 3,* ✠[h]…TΑL ·… IH
2229 (8004) 17, 0.5 *Obv.:* ✠IO · IhRL[ᗰ] · O *Rev.:*…OSPITΑL · S… IH
2230 (8030) 15, 0.5 *Obv.:* [✠]IO… / …PIT… *Rev.:*…PITΑ[L / ·… VI[S… IH
2231 (8121) 17, 0.7 *Obv.:* …O · IhRLᗰ… *Rev.:* …SPIT… / …[· h]OS… IH
2232 (8134) 15, 0.4 *Obv.:* ✠IO · IhRLᗰ[O] *Rev.: Annulets in quarters 2 & 3,* ✠hOSPI[T]… / ✠… IH
2233 (8135) 15, 0.6 *Obv.:* ✠IO · IhRLᗰ · [ ] *Rev.: Annulets in quarters 2 & 3,* ✠hOS…T[Α]L[ ]S IH
2234 (8138) 15, 0.4 *Obv.:* ✠IO · IhR[ᗰ O] *Rev.: Annulets in quarters [2 & 3],* [ ]OSPITΑL[·IH
2235 (8141) 15, 0.4 *Obv.:* ✠[ ]O · Ih…ᗰ · [O] *Rev.:* [ ]hOSP…[L] ·…/ *cross.* IH
2236 (8156) 15, 0.6 *Obv.:* ✠IO · IhRL… *Doubled die. Rev.: Annulets in quarters 2 & 3,* ✠OS…IO · IH
2237 (8169) 14, 0.4 *Obv.:* …[IO] · I[RL[·]ᗰ · O[*Rev.: Annulets in quarters [1 & 4],* …PITΑ… IH
2238 (8205) 15, 0.5 *Obv.:* ✠…RL · ᗰ · O *Rev.: Annulets in quarters 2 & 3,* ✠[ ]OSPITΑ[L… KH
2239 (9785) 15, 0.2 *Obv.:* [ ]IO · IhR[L]ᗰ · *Rev.:* …[Α]… / …GR[h]… KH
2240 (9895) 17, 0.7 *Obv.:* ✠IO · IhRL · ᗰ · O *Rev.: Annulets in quarters 2 & 3,* ✠OSP…[ΛL]… KH
2241 (9912) 16, 0.5 *Obv.:* ✠IO · IhRL… *Rev.: Annulets in quarters 2 & 3,* ✠O ·…ΑL / …· IOS… KH
2242 (9917) 15, 0.5 *Obv.:* …O · I[ ]RL… / …Α[L] *Rev.: Annulets in quarters 2 & 3,* [✠OS]P… / …Α… KH
2243 (9924) 17, 0.6 *Obv.:* ✠… / …[I] / …IhRL[ᗰ O]… / …Α… *Rev.:* / ✠[OS]PIT…S · / …ΑL KH
2244 (9945) 17, 0.6 *Obv.:* [ ]IO · I[ ]RL · ᗰ · [O] *Rev.:* …[SPI]… KH
2245 (9962) 15, 0.5 *Obv.:* ✠…RLᗰ *Rev.: Annulets in quarters 2 & 3,* ✠OS…IO · / … ITΑL KH
2246 (10019) 16, 0.7 *Obv.:* ✠…· IhRL… *Rev.: Annulets in quarters [2 & 3],* ✠[h]…Α[LI]S KH
2247 (10080) 15, 0.4 *Obv.:* ✠ …hR…[ᗰ] · O *Rev.: Annulets in quarters 2 & 3,* ✠[hOSP]…Α[L… KH
2248 (10127) 14, 0.3 *Obv.:* ✠IO[ ]I[ ]RL[ ]ᗰ *Rev.:* …SPI[T… / [✠I… KH
2249 (10159) 15, 0.4 *Obv.:* ✠IO · I[h]…ᗰ · O *Rev.: Annulets in quarters [2 & 3],* ✠hOSPITΑ… IH

PLATE 114

2250 (3291) 15, 0.5 *Obv.:* …IO · IhR… *Rev.: Annulets in quarters [2 & 3],* …IO · Ih[R]… IH
2251 (7878) 16, 0.5 *Obv.:* ✠IO · IhRL… *Rev.: Annulets in quarters 1 & 4,* ✠IO · IhRL… IH
2252 (7926) 17, 0.8 *Obv.:* ✠IO · IhRLᗰ · O *Rev.: Annulets in quarters 1 & 4,* ✠ · IO · IhRLᗰ · O IH
2253 (8122) 15, 0.3 *Obv.:* ✠IO · Ih…· O *Rev.: Annulets in quarters 2 & 3,* ✠[IO]… IH

2254 (9943) 16, 0.3 *Obv.:* [✠]O · IhRLM... *Rev.: Annulets in quarters 1 & 4,* ✠IO · IhRLM... KH
2255 (3207) 15, 0.5 *Obv.:* ✠hO · I[R]... · I... *Rev.:* ✠I O · I... · ...R[L M] · O IH
2256 (3240) 15, 0.4 *Obv.:* ✠h...hR[LM]... *Rev.: Annulets in quarters 1 & 4,* ✠IO ·... IH
2257 (3241) 15, 0.5 *Obv.:* ✠hO · ...hRL[M]... *Rev.: Annulets in quarters 1 & 4,* ✠IO · IhRL... *Doubled die.* IH
2258 (7869) 16, 0.5 *Obv.:* ✠hO · IhR[L]M · *Rev.: Annulets in quarters 1 & 4,* ✠[ ]O · IhR[L]M · [O] · IH
2259 (7870) 16, 0.5 *Obv.:* ✠hO · Ih...M *Rev.: Annulets in quarters 1 & 4,* ✠IO · I...LM... IH
2260 (7922) 17, 0.5 *Obv.:* ✠hO...· [Oh]... *Rev.: Annulets in quarters [1 & 4],* [✠]IO · IhRL... / ...[IT]... IH
2261 (8014) 15, 0.4 *Obv.:* ✠h...[LM] / [✠...·] *Rev.: Annulets in quarters [1 & 4],* [ ]IO · Ih... [/ ...[AG]... IH
2262 (8023) 15, 0.5 *Obv.:* ✠hO · I[Oh]...M *Rev.: Annulets in quarters [1 & 4],* ...[O] · IhRLM... IH
2263 (8037) 15, 0.6 *Obv.:* ✠hO · [I]...[M *Rev.: Annulets in quarters 2 & 3,* ✠IO · Ih... IH
2264 (8056) 16, 0.6 *Obv.:* ✠hO...[R]LM / ✠...[S] · IOA *Rev.:* ...· IhRLM... / ✠IO[h]...LIhO IH
2265 (8092) 15, 0.4 *Obv.:* [✠hO · I]... *Rev.: Annulets in quarters [2 & 3],* [✠IO] · I[ ]R... / ...O... IH
2266 (8105) 15, 0.3 *Obv.:* ✠h[O] · [hR]... *Rev.: Annulets in quarters 1 & 4,* ✠IO · IhRL...O · *Incomplete.* IH
2267 (8111) 16, 0.6 *Obv.:* ✠hO · [ ]hRL[*Rev.: Annulets in quarters 1 & 4,* ✠IO · I...O · IH
2268 (8148) 14, 0.5 *Obv.:* ✠hO · Ih... *Rev.: Annulets in quarters 1 & 4,* ✠IO · I...M · [O] IH
2269 (8165) 16, 0.4 *Obv.:* ✠hO[ ]IhRLM *Rev.: Annulets in quarters 1 & 4,* ✠IO · IhRLM · O[ ]IH
2270 (8170) 15, 0.5 *Obv.:* ✠hO · I[hRL... *Rev.: Annulets in quarters 1 & 4,* [ ]hO · Ih[RL... IH
2271 (8173) 15, 0.4 *Obv.:* ✠hO... [/] ...DI... [/] ...L... *Rev.: Annulets in quarters 1 & 4,* ✠IO · I...[M] IH
2272 (8185) 16, 0.3 *Obv.:* ✠hO · IhRLM *Rev.: Annulets in quarters [1 & 4],* [✠IO] · I... IH
2273 (8203) 16, 0.5 *Obv.:* [ ]hO · [I]h... *Rev.:*...IO · / ...OS[P]... / ...· M... IH
2274 (9955) 16, 0.6 *Obv.: Small châtel,* ✠h[O ·]...RLM *Rev.: Annulets in quarters [1 & 4],* ...LM · O[KH
2275 (9957) 17, 0.6 *Obv.: Small châtel,* ✠hO...RLM / ...[I]RO·... *Rev.: Annulets in quarters 1 & 4,* ✠IO · Ih...O · KH
2276 (9964) 18, 0.5 *Obv.: Small châtel,* ✠hO ·IhRL[ ] *Rev.: Annulets in quarters 1 & 4,* ✠IO · I[hR]LM · O KH
2277 (9972) 15, 0.4 *Obv.:* ✠hO...S *Rev.: Annulets in quarters 1 & 4,* ✠hOSPI[TAL]I KH
2278 (10035) 17, 0.6 *Obv.: Small châtel,* ✠[hO...hR]... *Doubled die. Rev.: Annulets in quarters 1 & 4,* ✠IO ·...[L] KH
2279 (10157) 16, 0.6 *Obv.: Small châtel,* ✠hO · IhRL[M] *Rev.: Annulets in quarters 2 & 3,* ✠[I]O...[R]L[M] ·... KH

PLATE 115

2280 (1696) 15, 0.6 *Obv.:* ✠h...TAL...S *Rev.: Annulets in quarters 1 & 4,* ✠hOSPIT...I IH
2281 (3030) 18, 0.9 *Obv.:* ✠...OSPITALI[*Rev.: Annulets in quarters 1 & 4,* ...OSPITA[I] / ✠O... IH
2282 (3047) 16, 0.5 *Obv.:* [✠h]O... *Rev.:*...h]OS[P... *Worn.* IH
2283 (3233) 16, 0.7 *Obv.:* ✠h[O]...LM *Rev.:* ✠OS... / ...RLM · O IH
2284 (3288) 16, 0.6 *Obv.:* ✠hOSPITAL · S *Rev.: Annulets in quarters 1 & 4,* ✠...OSPITAI IH
2285 (3309) 15, 0.6 *Obv.:* ✠hOSPI... *Rev.: Annulets in quarters 1 & 4,* ✠h...[A]... IH
2286 (3313) 16, 0.6 *Obv.:* [✠OSPN] · OS... / ...[MO]... / ... [ROD]... *Rev.: Annulets in quarters 1 & 4,* ✠ OS[P]...IT... IH
2287 (3337) 16, 0.4 *Obv.:* ✠...TAL... *Rev.:* ...OSPIT... IH
2288 (3350) 16, 0.4 *Obv.:* ✠hO · ... / ✠OS... *Rev.: Annulets in quarters 1 & 4,* ✠hO... IH
2289 (3360) 15, 0.4 *Obv.:* ✠hO · ...[T]... *Rev.: Annulets in quarters 1 & 4,* ✠hOS...[L]I / ...AG... IH
2290 (7924) 15, 0.4 *Obv.:* κοκκ. εσωτ., [ ]hO[ ]PIT[L ·... / ... *Rev.:* [✠]OS...[L]... IH
2291 (7968) 16, 0.5 *Obv.:* [ ]hOS[II]...L... *Rev.:* ✠[h]O...· / ...O[SP]... IH
2292 (8088) 15, 0.3 *Obv.:* ✠O...L · S *Rev.: Annulets in quarters 1 & 4,* ✠[h]O[S]...ITA[L IH
2293 (8100) 16, 0.5 *Obv.:* ✠O...[AL ·] / ✠O[S... *Rev.: Annulets in quarters 2 & 3,* ✠OS... / [✠]... IH
2294 (8115) 15, 0.4 *Obv.:* [ ]hOSPIT... / ...PIT... / ...G... *Rev.: Annulets in quarters 2 & 3,* ✠[hO]...[S ·]... / ...[S ·] IH
2295 (8179) 16, 0.5 *Obv.:* ✠h[S]PIT[AL]...[I] · *Rev.:* ...A[L]S...
2296 (8219) 15, 0.5 *Obv.:* [✠hO]... *Rev.: Annulets in quarters 1 & 4,* ✠[ ]OSPITA[I]. IH
2297 (9913) 16, 0.5 *Obv.:* [✠]hOSPI...L ·... / ...I...[R]O... *Rev.: Annulets in quarters 1 & 4,* ✠h...TA[h / ... IVI... KH
2298 (9954) 16, 0.3 *Obv.:* ✠hOSP... / ...I... *Rev.: Annulets in quarters 1 & 4,* ✠hOSPIT[LI] *Doubled die.* KH
2299 (10047) 15, 0.4 *Obv.:* [ ]hOS[P... / ...S · O[SP... *Rev.: Annulets in quarters 1 & 4,* ✠hO[S]...LI KH
2300 (10087) 14, 0.6 *Obv.: Small châtel, annulet within,* ✠hO...[R]...[M] *Rev.: Annulets in quarters 1 & 4,* ✠hO... [/] ...IT[ ]L KH

Site Finds

2301 (614) 14, 0.5 *Obv.: Coarse châtel,* ...MA... *Rev.: Annulets in quarters 2 & 3,* ✠OSP...M · O ... *Naillac overstrike.* I.35
2302 (1024) 14, 0.2 *Obv. Châtel, annulet within, initial crosslet below base,* ✠hO... *Rev.: Annulets in quarters [1 & 4],* ...TL *Naillac overstrike.* I.31
2303 (2160) 15, 0.2 *Obv.:* ...Ɛ... *Rev.: Annulets in quarters 2 & 3,* ...D[I]... II.63
2304 (4222) 15, 0.4 *Obv.:* ✠...Ih[R]... *Rev.: Annulets in quarters 1 & 4,* ✠...
2305 (5404) 16, 0.6 *Rev.:* ...IO... *Corr.* II.56
2306 (5507) 15, 0.2 *Obv.:* ...[h]... *Corr., incomplete.* II.56
2307 (5576) 14, 0.1 *Rev.:* ...G... *Fragment, corr.* II.56
2308 (5770) 14, 0.1 *Obv.:* ✠...[L]... *Corr., incomplete.* II.41
2309 (5920) 15, 0.3 *Corr.* II.56
2310 (5963) 16, 0.5 *Obv.:* ...[h·hO]... *Rev.:* ...[AL·]... *Corr.* II.56
2311 (5965) 17, 0.4 *Obv.:* ✠[I].../ ✠OS[PIT]... *Rev.:* ...S... *Worn.* II.56
2312 (5995) 16, 0.5 *Obv.: [Annulet within]. Rev.:* ...[TR]... II.56

2313 (5496) 16, 0.5 *Worn.* II.56
2314 (5998) 17, 0.5 *Obv.:* ✠... / ✠ᗰ·ShO... *Rev.:* ✠hOS...·S...[I]... *Worn.* II.56
2315 (6061) 16, 0.6 *Obv.:* ✠...SI...[O ·] *Rev.: Maltese cross,* ...[R]S·I[ ]ROL... / ...[ᗰ]... II.35

PLATE 116

14th Century Anonymous Obols *c.* 1350-1377 (major hoards)

Obv.: Châtel, annulet, platelet or dot within; in beaded circle. Rev.: Cross pattee, annulets or platelets in opposite quarters; within beaded circle.

2316 (2500) 16, 0.7 *Obv.: Dot within,* ...[◦]RODI[◦] *Rev.: Annulets in quarters 1 & 4,* ...R·OSPI... IH
2317 (2534) 15, 0.6 *Obv.: Dot within,* ...IVITΛS[ ]RODI... *Rev.: Annulets ◦ in quarters 1 & 4,* ✠...R·OSPITHLIS[ ]. IH
2318 (2570) 16, 0.5 *Obv.: Dot within,* ✠ᑕIV...DI *Rev.: Annulets in quarters 1 & 4,* ✠[ᗰ] ...OSPITΛ[L]IS[ ]. IH
2319 (1629) 17, 0.6 *Rev.: Annulets in quarters 1 & 4,* ✠ᗰ...ITH[L]I[∵]. IH
2320 (6772) 16, 0.3 *Obv.: Platelet within,* ✠ᑕI...S◦RODI *Rev.: Annulets ◦ in quarters 1 & 4,* ✠ᗰΛG[R] ...[THLI ∵]... *Worn.* IH
2321 (6971) 16, 0.4 *Obv.: [Dot within,]* ✠ᑕIV...◦R[OD]I *Rev.: Annulets ◦ in quarters 1 & 4,* ✠ᗰΛGR◦OSPITH[L]I :· *Worn.* IH
2322 (8745) 16, 0.6 *Obv.: Dot within,* ✠ᑕIVITΛS◦RODI *Rev.: Annulets ◦ in quarters 1 & 4,* ✠ᗰΛGR◦OSPITHL[I ∵]... *Worn.* IH
2323 (1330) 16, 0.6 *Obv.: [Dot within,]* ✠ᑕIVITΛ...ODI *Rev.: Annulets in quarters 1 & 4,* ✠...GR...ITHLI.˙ IH
2324 (1328) 16, 0.4 *Obv.: Dot within,* ✠ᑕIVITΛ...RODI *Rev.: Annulets in quarters 1 & 4,* ✠ᗰHGR◦OSPIT[HL]IS· IH
2325 (6844) 16, 0.8 *Obv.: Dot within,* ✠ᑕIVITΛS◦RODI *Rev.: Annulets ◦ in quarters 1 & 4,* ✠ᗰHGR◦OSPITHLIS· *Worn.* IH
2326 (8920) 18, 0.5 *Obv.: Dot within,* ✠ᑕ[IVIT]ΛS◦RODI *Rev.: Annulets* [◦] *in quarters 1 & 4,* ✠ᗰHGR◦OSPIT[HL]IS· *Corr.* KH
2327 (6850) 16, 0.5 *Obv.: Dot within,* ✠ᑕIVITΛS◦RODI *Rev.: Annulets in quarters 1 & 4,* ✠ᗰHGR[◦]O[S]PITHLI· *Worn.* IH
2328 (6886) 16, 0.4 *Obv.: Dot within,* ...IVIT...◦ROD[I *Rev.: Annulets ◦ in quarters* 1 & 4, ✠...R[◦]OSPITHLI· *Worn.* IH
2329 (6891) 15, 0.6 *Obv.: Dot within,* ✠ᑕIV...ODI *Rev.: Annulets* [◦] *in quarters 1 & 4,* ✠ᗰH...OSPIT[HL]I· *Worn.* IH
2330 (6924) 16, 0.4 *Obv.: Dot within,* ✠ᑕ...RODI *Rev.: Annulets* [◦] *in quarters 1 & 4,* [✠ HGR◦]OS[PI]...I· *Worn.* IH
2331 (1331) 17, 0.6 *Obv.: Dot within,* ...VITΛS◦RᑕD[*Rev.: Annulets in quarters 1 & 4,* ✠...R◦OSPITHLIS· IH
2332 (8774) 16, 0.3 *Obv.: Dot within,* ✠ᑕI[IT]...RᑕDI *Rev.: Annulets ◦ in quarters 1 & 4,* ✠ᗰH... ◦OS[ ]IT[HLIS] *Worn.* IH
2333 (8816) 16, 0.4 *Obv.: Dot within,* ✠ᑕIV...ᑕDI *Rev.: Annulets ◦ in quarters 1 & 4,* ✠ᗰHGR◦OSP...[H]... *Worn.* IH
2334 (1326) 16, 0.4 *Obv.: Dot within,* ✠ᑕIVITΛS[◦]RODI *Rev.: Annulets in quarters 1 & 4,* [✠ᗰHG...SPITHL∴ IH
2335 (2397) 18, 0.6 *Obv.: Dot within,* ✠ᑕIVITΛS◦RODI *Rev.: Annulets ◦ in quarters 1 & 4,* ✠ᗰHGR·OSPITH[L˙]. IH
2336 (6786) 16, 0.7 *Obv.: Dot within,* ✠ᑕIVIT[ΛS]RODI *Rev.: Annulets ◦ in quarters 1 & 4,* ✠ᗰΛGR·OS...THL∵ *Worn.* IH
2337 (6797) 16, 0.4 *Obv.: Dot within,* ✠ᑕIVITΛS◦RODI *Rev.: Annulets ◦ in quarters 1 & 4,* ✠ᗰHG[R]OSPITHL∵ *Worn.* IH
2338 (2480) 16, 0.7 *Obv.: Dot within,* ✠ᑕIVI...S◦RODI *Rev.: Annulets in quarters 1 & 4,* ✠ᗰHGR[·]OSPITHL∴ IH
2339 (1325) 16, 0.6 *Obv.: Dot within,* ✠ᑕIVITΛS[ ]RODI[ ]*Rev.: Annulets in quarters 1 & 4,* ✠[ᗰ]GR...PITHL∴ IH

PLATE 117

2340 (1370) 15, 0.5 *Obv.: Dot within,* ✠ᑕIVIT...RᑕDI *Rev.: Annulets in quarters 1 & 4,* ✠...GR[OS]...THLI[·.]. IH
2341 (7050) 16, 0.3 *Obv.:* ✠[ ]IV[IT]...ODI *Rev.: Annulets ◦ in quarters 1 & 4,* ✠ᗰHG[ ]◦OSPIT[HL]I∵ *Corr., incomplete.* IH
2342 (7067) 17, 0.6 *Obv.:* ✠ᑕIVIT...ODI *Rev.: Annulets in quarters 1 & 4,* ✠[ᗰ]HGR[O]SPITHLI∵ *Corr.* IH
2343 (7069) 17, 0.4 *Obv.:* [ ]ᑕIVITΛS◦ROD... *Rev.: Annulets* [◦] *in quarters 1 & 4,* ✠ᗰHG...[OS]PITHLI∵ *Corr.* IH
2344 (1327) 16, 0.4 *Obv.: Dot within,* [✠ᑕI]...RODI *Rev.: Annulets in quarters 1 & 4,* ✠ᗰHGR◦...THLI[ ]. IH
2345 (2503) 18, 0.7 *Obv.: Dot within,* ✠ᑕ...TΛS◦RODI *Rev.: Annulets in quarters 1 & 4,* ✠ᗰHGR◦O...HLI[IH
2346 (2589) 16, 0.4 *Obv.: Dot within,*]ᑕIVIT...ODI... *Rev.: Annulets* [◦] *in quarters 1 & 4,* ✠ᗰ...R◦OSPITHLI[∷]. IH
2347 (6975) 17, 0.5 *Obv.: [Dot within,]* ✠ᑕIV...[S◦]RO[ ]I *Rev.: Annulets ◦ in quarters 1 & 4,* ✠ᗰΛGR◦O...T[HL]S: *Worn.* IH
2348 (2513) 16, 0.7 *Obv.: Dot within,* ✠ᑕIV...[DI]... *Rev.: Annulets in quarters 1 & 4,* ✠ᗰ...IS[.:]. IH
2349 (2388) 17, 0.6 *Obv.: Annulet within,* ✠ᑕIVITΛS[:]RODI[·]*Rev.: Annulets in quarters 1 & 4,* ...ΛGR◦OSPITΛ[L IH
2350 (6442) 16, 0.5 *Obv.: Annulet within,* ✠ᑕIVITΛS◦RODI *Rev.: Annulets* [◦]*in quarters 1 & 4,* ✠ᗰΛGR◦OSPITΛL[◦]... *Worn.* IH
2351 (6988) 17, 0.4 *Obv.: [Dot within,]* ✠ᑕIVIT...RODI *Rev.: Annulets ◦ in quarters 1 & 4,* ✠ᗰΛGR◦OSPITΛ[L *Worn.* IH
2352 (6449) 17, 0.5 *Obv.: Annulet* [◦]*within,* ✠ᑕ...ODI *Rev.: Annulets in quarters 1 & 4,* ✠ᗰΛG...Λ[L◦] *Worn.* IH
2353 (8473) 15, 0.4 *Obv.: Annulet ◦ within,* ✠ᑕIVI...[R]ODI *Rev.: Annulets in quarters 1 & 4,* ✠[ᗰΛGR◦O]PIT[ΛL◦ *Worn.* KH
2354 (2415) 17, 0.4 *Obv.: Platelet within,* ✠ᑕIVI...S◦RODI *Rev.: Annulets in quarters 1 & 4,* ✠ᗰΛGR[◦]OSPITΛ[L˙] IH
2355 (6984) 17, 0.7 *Obv.: [Annulet within,]* ✠ᑕIVIT...RODI *Rev.: Annulets ◦ in quarters 1 & 4,* ✠ᗰΛGR◦OSPITHL[◦] *Worn.* IH
2356 (1575) 16, 0.4 *Obv.: Platelet within,* ✠ᑕIVITΛS◦RODI *Rev.: Annulets in quarters 1 & 4,* ✠ᗰΛGR◦OSPI[TΛL]◦ IH
2357 (1887) 17, 0.5 *Obv.: Platelet within,* ✠ᑕIVIT[ ]S◦RODI *Rev.: Annulets in quarters 1 & 4,* ✠ᗰΛ[GR]OSPITΛ[L]... IH
2358 (2461) 17, 0.4 *Obv.: Platelet within,* ✠ᑕIVIT[Λ]S◦RO... *Rev.: Annulets in quarters 1 & 4,* ✠ᗰΛG...PITΛL◦ IH
2359 (8648) 16, 0.5 *Obv.: Platelet within,* ✠ᑕIVIT[ΛS R]ODI *Rev.: Annulets ◦ in quarters 1 & 4,* ✠[Λ]GR◦OSPIT[ΛL◦]... *Worn.* KH

2360 (8653) 16, 0.5 *Obv.: Platelet within,* ✠CIVIT…RODI *Rev.: Annulets in quarters 1 & 4,* [MΛ]GR… *Worn.* KH
2361 (8659) 16, 0.6 *Obv.:* ✠CIV[I]…DI° *Rev.: Annulets ° in quarters 1 & 4,* …[G]R°OSPIT… *Corr.* KH
2362 (8950) 16, 0.5 *Obv.:* …ITΛ… *Rev.: Annulets ° in quarters 1 & 4,* …R°OS[P]… *Corr.* KH

PLATE 118

2363 (2750) 17, 0.6 *Obv.: Annulet* [°]*within,* ✠CIVITAS[°]… *Rev.: Annulets in quarters 1 & 4,* ✠MA…AL· IH
2364 (2803) 17, 0.6 *Obv.: Annulet ° within,* ✠C[I]…I *Rev.: Annulets in quarters 1 & 4,* ✠[M]AGR°O…AL· IH
2365 (6499) 16, 0.5 *Obv.: Annulet ° within,* ✠…AS°[R]O… *Rev.: Annulets ° in quarters 1 & 4,* ✠…[O]PITAL· *Worn.* IH
2366 (6286) 17, 0.8 *Obv.: Annulet ° within,* ✠CI…[°]RODI *Rev.: Annulets ° in quarters 1 & 4,* [✠M]…AL· *Worn.* IH
2367 (6287) 16, 0.4 *Obv.: Annulet ° within,* …AS[°]… *Rev.: Annulets in quarters 1 & 4,* [✠MA]…L· *Worn.* IH
2368 (8357) 16, 0.5 *Obv.: Annulet ° within,* ✠CIV…I *Rev.: Annulets ° in quarters 1 & 4,* ✠…TAL· *Worn.* KH
2369 (1476) 15, 0.3 *Obv.: Annulet ° within,* ✠CIVITAS°…DI *Rev.: Annulets ° in quarters 1 & 4,* ✠MAG…SPITA[L]. IH
2370 (2778) 16, 0.5 *Obv.: Annulet within,* …ITAS… *Rev.: Annulets ° in quarters 1 & 4,* ✠M…[R O]SPITAL· IH
2371 (6304) 17, 0.7 *Obv.: Annulet ° within,* ✠CIVIT…ODI / …[S]PITAL… *Rev.: Annulets ° in quarters* 1 & 4, …ITAL· *Worn, clipped.* IH
2372 (8346) 17, 0.6 *Obv.: Annulet ° within,* …[IV]ITAS°…[DI *Rev.: Annulets* [°]*in quarters 1 & 4,* ✠[M]AGR°…A[L *Worn.* KH
2373 (8525) 16, 0.6 *Obv.: Annulet ° within,* ✠CIVI…[°]RODI *Rev.: Annulets ° in quarters 1 & 4,* ✠MAGR°OSPI… *Worn.* KH
2374 (1516) 17, 0.4 *Obv.: Annulet within,* ✠CIVIT[A]S°RODI *Brockage. Rev.: Annulets in quarters 1 & 4,* ✠MAGR[·]OSPIT[A]LI[∵] IH
2375 (1938) 16, 0.3 *Obv.: Annulet ° within,* …AS°R[O]DI[*Rev.: Annulets in quarters 1 & 4,* ✠[M]…TAL∵ IH
2376 (7119) 16, 0.5 *Obv.:* ✠CIV…[D]I *Rev.: Annulets ° in quarters* 1 & 4, ✠[M]AGR·OSPITAL∵ *Corr.* IH
2377 (8415) 16, 0,7 *Obv.: Annulet ° within,* [✠]CIV…[AS]… *Rev.: Annulets in quarters 1 & 4,* ✠MAG…AL· *Worn.* KH
2378 (2631) 16, 0.6 *Obv.:* ✠CI…S°RODI[ ] *Rev.: Annulets in quarters 1 & 4,* ✠MAGR[ ]OSPITA[L]∵ IH
2379 (2747) 16, 0.7 *Obv.: [Annulet within,]* …AS°R… *Rev.: Annulets in quarters 1 & 4,* ✠MAGR·[OS]PI[T]AL∵ IH
2380 (8411) 17, 0.6 *Obv.: Annulet* [°]*within,* ✠CIV…[A]S… *Rev.: Annulets ° in quarters 1 & 4,* ✠…[R]OSPITAL∵ *Worn.* KH
2381 (8521) 16, 0.5 *Obv.: Annulet within,* ✠CI…DI *Rev.: Annulets ° in quarters 1 & 4,* …AG… *Worn.* KH
2382 (9577) 15, 0.7 *Obv.: [Platelet within,]* ✠…[R]ODI *Rev.: Annulets ° in quarters 1 & 4,* ✠[M]…[L∵]… *Worn.* KH
2383 (1517) 17, 0.6 *Obv.: Annulet within,* ✠C…[ROD]I *Rev.: Annulets in quarters 1 & 4,* …ΛGR°OSPITA[LI·]. IH
2384 (6435) 15, 0.5 *Obv.: Annulet ° within,* ✠CI[V]…S°R[OD]I *Rev.: Annulets ° in quarters* 1 & 4, ✠MΛGR°OSP[I]TALI[·] *Worn.* IH
2385 (9031) 16, 0.5 *Obv.: Annulet ° within,*…S°RODI *Rev.: Annulets ° in quarters 1 & 4,* …SPI[ ]A[L]I[*Corr.* KH
2386 (1762) 17, 0.6 *Obv.: Annulet ° within,* ✠CIVI…ODI *Rev.: Annulets ° in quarters 1 & 4,* ✠MAG…ITALI· IH
2387 (6460) 16, 0.5 *Obv.: Annulet ° within,* ✠CI[V]…ODI *Rev.:* δακτ. ° *in quarters 1 & 4,* ✠M…OSP…A[L]I· *Worn.* IH
2388 (8536) 17, 0.5 *Obv.: Annulet ° within,* ✠CIV…I *Rev.: Annulets in quarters 1 & 4,* …GR· OSPITA[LI] *Corr.* KH

PLATE 119

2389 (2749) 15, 0.6 *Obv.: Annulet* [°] *within,* ✠CI[V]…[°RO]… *Rev.: Annulets* [°] *in quarters* 1 & 4, ✠MΛGR[ ]O[S]…LI∵ IH
2390 (2815) 17, 0.6 *Obv.: Annulet within,* ✠CI…RODI *Rev.: Annulets in quarters 1 & 4,* ✠MΛG[R]…A[L]I[∵]. IH
2391 (2980) 16, 0.5 *Obv.: Annulet within,* …[AS RODI]… *Rev.: Annulets ° in quarters 1 & 4,* ✠MΛGR°OSPIT[ ]LI∵ IH
2392 (6429) 15, 0.4 *Obv.: Annulet within,* ✠CI…[S°]RO[ ]I[*Rev.: Annulets ° in quarters 1 & 4,* ✠MΛGR°OS…[LI·]. *Worn.* IH
2393 (6577) 16, 0.5 *Obv.: Annulet ° within,* ✠CIVI…ROD… *Rev.: Annulets ° in quarters 1 & 4,* ✠MΛGR°…TALI· *Worn.* IH
2394 (8384) 16, 0.5 *Obv.: Annulet within,* [ ]CIV[ITA]S°R… *Rev.: Annulets ° in quarters 1 & 4,* ✠MΛGR°OS…[AL]I∵ *Worn.* KH
2395 (8522) 16, 0.6 *Obv.: Annulet ° within,* ✠CIVI…S°RODI *Rev.: Annulets ° in quarters 1 & 4,* ✠[MΛ]GR°OSPITALI[ ] *Corr.* KH
2396 (2811) 16, 0.4 *Obv.: Annulet ° within,* ✠…S°RODI *Rev.: Annulets in quarters 1 & 4,* ✠MΛGR°OSPITA·S· IH
2397 (6447) 17, 0.8 *Obv.: Annulet ° within,* ✠CIV…S°RO[D]I *Rev.: Annulets ° in quarters 1 & 4,* ✠MΛGR°OSPITALS[:] *Worn.* IH
2398 (6539) 18, 0.6 *Obv.: Annulet* [°]*within,* ✠…S°RODI *Rev.: Annulets ° in quarters 1 & 4,* ✠MΛGR°O…S: *Worn.* IH
2399 (8524) 16, 0.7 *Obv.: Annulet ° within,* ✠CI…AS°RODI *Rev.: Annulets ° in quarters 1 & 4,* ✠[M]GR°OSPIT[ALI ·] *Worn.* KH
2400 (8874) 15, 0.7 *Obv.: Annulet within,* …[A]S°RO… *Rev.: Annulets ° in quarters 1 & 4,* ✠M…R…PITA·S: *Corr.* KH
2401 (1738) 18, 0.5 *Obv.: Annulet ° within,* ✠C…S[°]RODI *Rev.: Annulets ° in quarters 1 & 4,* ✠MΛ[ ]R°OSPITA·S[ ]. IH
2402 (1900) 17, 0.5 *Obv.: [Annulet] within,* [✠]CIVIT… *Rev.: Annulets ° in quarters 1 & 4,* ✠MΛGR°OSPITA·'S IH
2403 (8890) 17, 0.7 *Obv.: [Dot within,]* [ ]CIVIT…[R]…S *Rev.: Annulets ° in quarters 1 & 4,* ✠MΛ[R]°OSPITA·S *Worn.* KH
2404 (8918) 17, 0.5 *Obv.: Annulet ° within,* ✠CIVI[T S]°RO[DI] *Rev.: Annulets in quarters 1 & 4,* ✠M…[R]°[O]… A·'S *Doubled die; worn.* KH
2405 (2647) 15, 0.3 *Obv.:*…TAS°RO[D… *Rev.: Annulets in quarters 1 & 4,* ✠MΛGR°[O]…[A·]S IH

2406 (8899) 16, 0.5 *Obv.: Dot within,* [ ]Ɑ[ ]VIT[ ]S[]RODI *Rev.: Annulets ◦ in quarters 1 & 4,* ✠ᗰĀG[R]...SPIT[FLI]S[*Corr.* KH
2407 (2816) 16, 0.5 *Obv.: Annulet* [◦] *within,* ✠ⱭIVI...[DI]... *Rev.: Annulets in quarters 1 & 4,* ✠...R[◦]OS...IS[∷]. IH
2408 (1910) 17, 0.6 *Obv.:*...VITAS[◦]...*Rev.: Annulets in quarters 1 & 4,* ✠ᗰ[A]...[FL]IS∷ IH
2409 (8544) 16, 0.6 *Obv.: Annulet within,* ✠Ɑ...I *Rev.: Annulets ◦ in quarters 1 & 4,* ✠...SPIT[FLIS] *Worn.* KH
2410 (8878) 17, 0.6 *Obv.: Annulet within,* ✠Ɑ...S[◦]R[ODI] *Rev.: Annulets in quarters 1 & 4,* [✠ᗰ]A...OS...FLIS∷ *Worn.* KH

PLATE 120
2411 (2593) 18, 0.6 *Obv.:* ✠ⱭIVI...S◦RODI· *Rev.: Annulets in quarters 1 & 4,* ✠ᗰ...R·OS...ĀL· IH
2412 (2646) 16, 0.5 *Obv.: Dot within, dot r.,* ✠ⱭIVIT...ODI· *Rev.: Annulets in quarters 1 & 4,* ✠ᗰĀGR·OS...Ā[L]... IH
2413 (6996) 17, 0.7 *Obv.: [Annulet within,] dot r.,* ✠ⱭIVITĀS◦RODI· *Rev.: Annulets ◦ in quarters 1 & 4,* ✠ᗰĀGR·OSPIT[Ā]L · *Worn.* IH
2414 (9039) 16, 0.7 *Obv.: Annulet ? within, dot r.,* ✠ⱭIVI...DI· *Rev.: Annulets ◦ in quarters 1 & 4,* ...ĀGR...SPIT... *Worn.* KH
2415 (1627) 16, 0.4 *Obv.:* ✠ⱭIVIT... *Rev.: Annulets in quarters 1 & 4,* ✠ᗰĀG[R]...ITFL[ ]. IH
2416 (8720) 16, 0.4 *Obv.: Annulet ◦ within, dot r.,* ✠[Ɑ]...S◦RODI· *Rev.: Annulets ◦ in quarters 1 & 4,* ✠...G...O...[L]I· *Corr.* KH
2417 (8462) 16, 0.3 *Obv.: Annulet within,* ✠ⱭI[V]...I· *Brockage. Rev.: Annulets in quarters 1 & 4,* ✠ᗰĀ...[PITFL]I· *Corr.* KH
2418 (9484) 17, 0.5 *Obv.: Dot r.,* ✠Ɑ...ĀS◦RODI· *Rev.: Annulets in quarters 1 & 4,* ✠ · ᗰ[Ā R◦]OSPIT[FL]I· *Worn.* KH
2419 (6272) 17, 0.6 *Obv.: Annulet ◦ within, dot r.,* ✠Ɑ...TĀS◦RODI· *Rev.: Annulets ◦ in quarters 1 & 4,* ✠ᗰĀGR[✿]OS[PI]T[FL]I[*Worn.* IH
2420 (2734) 18, 0.6 *Obv.: Annulet within, dot r.,* ✠ⱭIVITĀ[S◦]RODI· *Rev.: Annulets in quarters 1 & 4,* ✠[·]ᗰĀ[G]R✿OSPIT[FL]I· IH
2421 (2736) 16, 0.7 *Obv.: Annulet within, dot r.,* ✠ⱭIVIT[Ā]S◦RODI· *Rev.: Annulets in quarters 1 & 4,* ✠ᗰĀGR✿OSPIT[FL]I· IH
2422 (6464) 16, 0.4 *Obv.: Annulet ◦ within, dot r.,* ✠Ɑ...[T]Ā[S]R[ ]DI · *Rev.: Annulets ◦ in quarters 1 & 4,* ✠ · ᗰ[ ]GR[✿]...FLI· *Worn.* IH
2423 (1322) 16, 0.4 *Obv.: Dot r.,*...VIT[ ]S[]RO[D... *Rev.: Annulets in quarters 1 & 4,* ✠...OSPITFLI· IH
2424 (2827) 16, 0.6 *Obv.: Annulet within,* ✠ⱭIVITA...ODI◦ *Rev.: Annulets in quarters 1 & 4,* ✠ᗰAGR·OSPITALI· IH
2425 (2834) 16, 0.6 *Obv.: Annulet within,* ✠[ ]IVITAS◦RODI◦ *Rev.: Annulets* [◦]*in quarters 1 & 4,* ✠ᗰAGR·OSPITALI· IH
2426 (6397) 16, 0.6 *Obv.: Annulet within,* ✠ⱭIVIᗰAS[◦]RODI[◦] *Rev.: Annulets ◦ in quarters 1 & 4,* ✠ᗰAGR·OSPITA[L]I· *Worn.* IH
2427 (2833) 16, 0.6 *Obv.: Doubled die.* δακτ. εσωτ., ✠ⱭIVITAS◦RODI[◦] *Rev.: Annulets in quarters 1 & 4,* ✠ᗰAGR◦OS[ ]ITA[L]I· IH
2428 (2839) 16, 0.7 *Obv.: Annulet within,* ✠...VITA[S]...[O]DI◦ *Rev.: Annulets* [◦] *in quarters 1 & 4,*...AGR◦OS...TALI· IH
2429 (6381) 16, 0.5 *Obv.: Annulet within,* [✠]...[TAS R]ODI◦ *Rev.: Annulets ◦ in quarters 1 & 4,* ✠ᗰAGR◦[O]...[FL]I· *Worn.* IH
2430 (6389) 16, 0.6 *Obv.: Annulet within,* ✠Ɑ...ITA...ODI◦ *Rev.: Annulets ◦ in quarters 1 & 4,*...[R◦]OSPITA[L]I· *Worn.* IH
2431 (7059) 16, 0.5 *Obv.: [Annulet within,]* ✠...ITAS◦RO●I[◦] *Rev.: Annulets in quarters 1 & 4,* ✠ᗰAGR[◦O P]ITA[LI ·˙] *Worn.* IH
2432 (8662) 16, 0.4 *Obv.: [Annulet within,]* ✠ⱭIVIT[A]S...[D]I◦ *Rev.: Annulets ◦ in quarters 1 & 4,* [ᗰAGR]◦O[ ]PI... *Worn.* KH
2433 (8879) 16, 0.4 *Obv.: Annulet* [◦]*within,* ✠[Ɑ]...ITAS◦RODI◦ *Rev.: Annulets ◦ in quarters 1 & 4,* ✠ᗰ...R[◦]OSPITALIS *Worn.* KH
2434 (9083) 15, 0.5 *Obv.: Annulet within,* ✠ⱭIVIT...DI◦ *Rev.: Annulets ◦ in quarters 1 & 4,* ✠ᗰAGR◦...[FLIS·] *Worn.* KH
2435 (7252) 17, 0.5 *Obv.: Annulet ◦ within,* ✠ⱭIV[I]TAS◦RODI◦ *Rev.: Platelets in quarters 1 & 4,* [ᗰ]AGR◦OSPI[T... *Worn.* IH
2436 (9175) 16, 0.6 *Obv.: Platelet within,* ...TAS...ODI◦ *Rev.: Platelets in quarters 1 & 4,*...R◦O[S]...IS[] *Corr.* KH
2437 (9176) 17, 0.5 *Obv.: Platelet within,* ...ITAS...[IS] *Rev.: Platelets in quarters 1 & 4,* ✠...R◦O...S *Corr.* KH

PLATE 121
2438 (775) 17, 0.6 *Obv.: Dot within,* ✠ⱭIVITAS◦RODI☘ *Rev.: Platelets in quarters 1 & 4,* ✠ᗰAGR◦OSPITALI◦ IH
2439 (780) 16, 0.5 *Obv.: Dot within,* ✠ⱭIVITAS◦RODI☘ *Rev.: Platelets in quarters 1 & 4,* ✠ᗰAGR◦OSPITA[L]I◦ IH
2440 (9250) 17, 0.3 *Obv.: Dot within,* ✠ⱭIVITAS◦RODI☘ *Rev.: Platelets in quarters 1 & 4,* ✠ᗰA[G...S]PITALI◦ *Worn.* KH
2441 (778) 17, 0.5 *Obv.: Dot within,* ✠[ⱭI[ ]ITAS◦RODI☘ *Rev.: Platelets in quarters 1 & 4,* ✠ᗰ[AGR]OSPIT[AL]IS[IH
2442 (7083) 17, 0.7 *Obv.:* ✠ⱭIVITA...ODI☘ *Rev.: Platelets in quarters 1 & 4,* ✠ᗰAGR◦OSPITA[L]IS *Corr.* IH
2443 (7267) 17, 0.5 *Obv.: [Dot within,]* ...[T]AS◦RODI[☘]*Rev.: Platelets in quarters 1 & 4,* ✠ᗰAG...ALIS *Worn.* IH
2444 (7280) 16, 0.5 *Obv.: [Annulet within,]* ✠[Ɑ]VITA[S◦]RODI☘ *Rev.: Platelets in quarters 1 & 4,* ✠ᗰAGR◦OSPIT[L]IS[·] *Worn.* IH
2445 (9238) 17, 0.4 *Obv.: Dot within,* ...TAS◦RODI[☘] *Rev.: Platelets in quarters 1 & 4,* ✠...SPITALI[*Worn, incomplete.* KH
2446 (776) 17, 0.5 *Obv.: Dot within,* ✠ⱭIVITAS[◦]RODI☘ *Rev.: Platelets in quarters 1 & 4,* ✠ᗰAGR·OSPITA[L]IS· IH

2447 (2317) 16, 0.5 *Obv.: Dot within,* ✠...S·RODI⚘ *Rev.: Platelets in quarters 1 & 4,* ✠MĦGR·OSPI... IH

2448 (7274) 17, 0.4 *Obv.: Dot within,* ✠CIVITĦ[S]...DI⚘ *Rev.: Platelets in quarters 1 & 4,* ✠MΛGR·O...Ħ[LIS *Worn, incomplete.* IH

2449 (9172) 17, 0.6 *Obv.:* ✠CIVITĦ...ODI√ *Rev.: Platelets in quarters 1 & 4,* ✠MĦG...[PITĦLI]S· *Worn.* KH

2450 (9222) 17, 0.5 *Obv.: Dot within,* ✠CIVITĦS[ ]RODI⚘*Rev.: Platelets in quarters 1 & 4,* ✠[ ]ĦGR· OSPITĦ[L]S· *Worn.* KH

2451 (9230) 18, 0.8 *Obv.: Dot within,* ✠CIVITĦS◦RODIS⚘ *Rev.: Platelets in quarters 1 & 4,* ✠MĦGR· OSPITĦLIS· *Worn.* KH

2452 (2864) 18, 0.5 *Obv.: Annulet within,* ✠CI...TΛS◦RODI⸰ *Rev.: Annulets ◦ in quarters 1 & 4,* ✠MΛGR[·O]PITΛ[L S] IH

2453 (8839) 17, 0.4 *Obv.: Annulet within,* ✠CI[V]...DI ⸰ *Rev.: Annulets ◦ in quarters 1 & 4,* ✠MΛ[G]...TΛLIS *Corr.* KH

2454 (8485) 17, 0.7 *Obv.: Annulet ◦ within,* ✠CIVI...ODI⸰ *Rev.: Annulets ◦ in quarters 1 & 4,* [✠]...R· OSPITΛLI[S *Corr.* KH

2455 (2391) 16, 0.7 *Obv.: Platelet within,* ✠CIVITΛ...RODI⸰ *Rev.: Annulets in quarters 1 & 4,* ...ΛGR[·]OSPITΛLIS[IH

2456 (6769) 16, 0.3 *Obv.: Platelet within,* [✠]C[I]VITΛS[ ]RODI⸰ *Rev.: Annulets in quarters 1 & 4,* [✠]MΛGR·OSPITΛ[LIS] *Worn.* IH

2457 (8951) 16, 0.4 *Obv.:* ✠C...ΛS◦RODI[⸰] *Rev.: Annulets ◦ in quarters 1 & 4,* [✠]M[Λ]GR· O[S]PI[TΛ... *Worn.* KH

2458 (2874) 16, 0.6 *Obv.: Annulet ◦ within,* ✠C...[S◦]RODI⸰ *Rev.: Annulets in quarters 1 & 4,* ✠MΛGR·OSPITĦLIS[IH

2459 (2878) 17, 0.6 *Obv.: Annulet* [◦]*within,* ✠CIVI...S◦[R]ODI⸰ *Rev.: Annulets in quarters 1 & 4,* [✠]MΛGR·OSP[I]T[ĦL]IS[ ] IH

2460 (6217) 17, 0.6 *Obv.: Annulet ◦ within,* ✠CI[ ]ITΛS◦RODI⸰ *Rev.: Annulets ◦ in quarters 1 & 4,* ✠[M]GR[ ]OSPIT[ĦL]IS *Worn.* IH

2461 (6260) 16, 0.6 *Obv.: Annulet* [◦]*within,* ✠CIVITΛS◦[ROD]I⸰ *Rev.: Annulets ◦ in quarters 1 & 4,* ✠M[ΛGR]OSPIT[ĦL]IS *Worn.* IH

PLATE 122

2462 (1552) 16, 0.6 *Obv.: Platelet within,* ✠CIVIT...DI⸰ *Rev.: Annulets in quarters 1 & 4,* ✠M...SPI[TĦL]IS[·] IH

2463 (1591) 16, 0.7 *Obv.: Platelet within,* ✠...ΛS◦...**D**I⸰ *Rev.: Annulets in quarters 1 & 4,* ✠...GR·OS...[ĦL]IS IH

2464 (2395) 16, 0.5 *Obv.: Platelet within,* ✠CI...S◦RO**D**I⸰ *Rev.: Annulets ◦ in quarters 1 & 4,* ✠[M]...R[OSP]ITĦLIS[IH

2465 (2507) 15, 0.3 *Obv.: Platelet within,* ✠CIV...DI⸰ *Rev.: Annulets ◦ in quarters 1 & 4,* ...ΛGR·OSPIT... IH

2466 (2614) 17, 0.5 *Obv.: [Platelet within,]* ✠CIVITΛS[◦]RO[D]I⸰ *Rev.: Annulets* [◦] *in quarters 1 & 4,* ✠MΛGR[•]OS...[L]I[·] IH

2467 (2857) 16, 0.5 *Obv.: Annulet ◦ within,* ✠CI...[TΛ]...ODI⸰ *Rev.: Annulets in quarters 1 & 4,* ✠MΛ[G ◦]OS[P T]ΛLI· IH

2468 (2860) 16, 0.5 *Obv.: Annulet ◦ within,* ✠C...ΛS◦RODI⸰ *Rev.: Annulets in quarters 1 & 4,* ✠MΛGR[·]O...[L]I· *Incomplete.* IH

2469 (2862) 16, 0.7 *Obv.: Annulet* [◦]*within,* ✠...[R]ODI⸰ *Rev.: Annulets ◦ in quarters 1 & 4,* ✠MΛG[R]...LI· IH

2470 (8484) 17, 0.3 *Obv.: Annulet ◦ within,* ✠[ ]I[V]ITΛS...ODI⸰ *Rev.: Annulets ◦ in quarters 1 & 4,* ✠MΛGR[ ]OSPITΛ[L]I[·] *Worn.* KH

2471 (8501) 16, 0.5 *Obv.: Annulet ◦ within,* ✠CI...[S R]ODI⸰ *Rev.: Annulets in quarters 1 & 4,* ✠[M]GR◦OSPIT[ΛLI] *Worn.* KH

2472 (9033) 16, 0.5 *Obv.: Annulet ◦ within,* [✠]IVITΛS[ ]RODI[*Rev.: Annulets ◦ in quarters 1 & 4,*...ΛGR[ ]OSPIT[ĦL *Worn.* KH

2473 (9102) 16, 0.5 *Obv.: Annulet ◦ within,* ✠...[ΛS]◦ROD... *Rev.: Annulets ◦ in quarters 1 & 4,* ✠M...PITĦLI *Worn.* KH

2474 (1963) 16, 0.6 *Obv.: Annulet ◦ within,* ✠CIVIT[ ]S...[O]DI⸰ *Rev.: Annulets in quarters 1 & 4,* ✠MΛGR[ ]OSPITĦLI◦ IH

2475 (2879) 16, 0.5 *Obv.: Annulet ◦ within,* ✠...[ΛS◦RO]DI⸰ *Rev.: Annulets in quarters 1 & 4,* ✠MΛ...[O]SPI[TΛ]LI◦ IH

2476 (8506) 15, 0.5 *Obv.: Annulet ◦ within,* ✠CI...[ΛS◦R D]I⸰ *Rev.: Annulets in quarters 1 & 4,* [✠]M[Λ]G...OS[PITΛ]LI◦ *Worn.* KH

2477 (9432) 16, 0.4 *Obv.: Annulet ◦ within,* ...S◦RODI[⸰] *Rev.: [Annulets] in quarters 1 & 4,* ✠M...SPITΛLI[ ] *Worn.* KH

2478 (8482) 15, 0.4 *Obv.: Annulet ◦ within,* ✠CI...[ΛS]◦RODI⸰ *Rev.: Annulets in quarters 1 & 4,* ✠[M G]R◦OSPITΛL[ ]◦ *Worn.* KH

2479 (6192) 17, 0.5 *Obv.: Annulet* [◦]*within,* ✠CI...◦RO...[⸰] *Rev.: Annulets ◦ in quarters 1 & 4,* ✠[M]...R·OSP...ΛLIS *Worn.* IH

2480 (753) 16, 0.5 *Obv.: Annulet ◦ within,* ✠CI...IS⸰ *Rev.: Platelets in quarters 1 & 4,* ✠M...OSPIT[Λ... IH

2481 (1987) 17, 0.4 *Obv.: Annulet ◦ within,* ✠C...[O]DI⸰ *Rev.: Platelets in quarters 1 & 4,* ✠MΛGR◦OSPITΛ[L]I◦ IH

2482 (2355) 14, 0.4 *Obv.: Annulet ◦ within,* ✠C... ΛS[ ]RODI⸰ *Rev.: Platelets in quarters 1 & 4,* ✠M...[O]SPITΛ[L]I[S IH

2483 (7247) 18, 0.4 *Obv.: [Annulet within,]* ✠CI...ODI⸰ *Rev.: Platelets in quarters 1 & 4,* ✠MΛGR[ ]OS...TΛ[L]I[◦] *Worn.* IH

2484 (9452) 16, 0.7 *Obv.: Annulet ◦ within,* ...RO... *Rev.: Annulets in quarters 1 & 4,* ✠...ΛLI◦ *Worn.* KH

2485 (7248) 15, 0.5 *Obv.: Annulet within,* ✠...[◦]RODI⸰ *Rev.: Platelets in quarters 1 & 4,* [ ]M[Λ]G[R]OS[P]TΛ[L... *Worn.* IH

2486 (7276) 17, 0.6 *Obv.: Annulet within,* ✠C...ODI⸰ *Rev.: [Platelets] in quarters 1 & 4,* ✠MΛG...OSPITΛL · *Worn.* IH

PLATE 123

2487 (1760) 16, 0.4 *Obv.: Annulet within,* +...VITΛS°RODI[°] *Rev.: Annulets in quarters 1 & 4,* +MΛGR°OSP...[AL]IS IH
2488 (2843) 16, 0.6 *Obv.: Annulet* ° *within,* +CIVITΛS...DI[°] *Rev.: Annulets* ° *in quarters 1 & 4,* +[M]...OSPITALIS IH
2489 (2844) 17, 0.7 *Obv.: Annulet* ° *within,* +[C]...ΛS[°]...DI[°] *Rev.: Annulets in quarters 1 & 4,* +M[Λ]...[°]...S IH
2490 (6493) 16, 0.7 *Obv.: Annulet* ° *within,* +[ ]IVITΛS°R[ ]DI[·] *Rev.: Annulets* ° *in quarters 1 & 4,* +M[Λ]G...[AL]IS *Worn.* IH
2491 (1449) 18, 0.6 *Obv.: Annulet within,* +CIVIT[ ]S°...[O]DI·°· *Rev.: Annulets in quarters 1 & 4,* +M[Λ]G...OSPIT·LIS IH
2492 (6232) 16, 0.4 *Obv.: Annulet* ° *within,* +CI...°RODI·°· *Rev.: Annulets* ° *in quarters 1 & 4,* [ ]MΛ[ ]R...[PIT·]LIS *Worn, incomplete.* IH
2493 (8850) 17, 0.5 *Obv.: Annulet* ° *within,* +CI...RODI ·°· *Rev.: Annulets* ° *in quarters 1 & 4,* ...GR°OSPIT·LIS *Worn, incomplete.* KH
2494 (1947) 18, 0.5 *Obv.: Annulet within,* +CI...TΛ[S]...S *Rev.: Annulets in quarters 1 & 4,* ...GR°OSPIT·LIS[ ] IH
2495 (3005) 16, 0.3 *Obv.: Annulet within,* +CI...RO... *Rev.: Annulets in quarters 1 & 4,* +MΛGR[·]OSPIT·[L]S IH
2496 (8857) 17, 0.5 *Obv.: Annulet* ° *within,* ...ΛS°ROD... *Rev.: Annulets* ° *in quarters 1 & 4,* +MΛG...[AL]IS· *Worn.* KH
2497 (8868) 16, 0.5 *Obv.: Annulet* ° *within,* +CIVI[T]...RODI ·°· *Rev.: Annulets* ° *in quarters 1 & 4,* +MΛGR°OSPI[TL]IS· *Worn.* KH
2498 (6233) 16, 0.5 *Obv.: Annulet* ° *within,* +[ ]IVIT[Λ]...RODI·°· *Rev.: Annulets* ° *in quarters 1 & 4,* ...[Λ]GR°OSPIT·LIS *Worn.* IH
2499 (6488) 17, 0.5 *Obv.: Annulet* ° *within,* +CIVIT[Λ]S[°]RODI[·°·] *Rev.: Annulets in quarters 1 & 4,* +M...R°OSPIT·[L] I·S *Worn.* IH
2500 (2867) 15, 0.5 *Obv.: Annulet* [°] *within,* +C...[ΛS]°R[ODI]·°· *Rev.: Annulets* ° *in quarters 1 & 4,* +M...[R°]OSPIT[A]L° IH
2501 (6226) 17, 0.5 *Obv.: Annulet* ° *within,* +CIVIT...ODI·°· *Rev.: Annulets* ° *in quarters 1 & 4,* +MΛGR°OS[PIT]L[°] *Worn.* IH
2502 (6239) 15, 0.4 *Obv.: Annulet* ° *within,* +C[I]...RODI·°· *Rev.: Annulets* ° *in quarters 1 & 4,* +MΛGR...[L]° *Worn.* IH
2503 (6319) 16, 0.5 *Obv.: Annulet* ° *within,* +CI[V]ITΛS°ROD[I] *Rev.: Annulets in quarters 1 & 4,* +[MΛ]R[°]OSPITAL° *Worn.* IH
2504 (2854) 16, 0.6 *Obv.: Annulet within,* +...[Λ]S°RODI·°· *Rev.: Annulets in quarters 1 & 4,* +MAG...[AL]I∴ IH
2505 (8512) 16, 0.4 *Obv.: Annulet* ° *within,* +CI...ODI·°· *Rev.: Annulets* [°] *in quarters 1 & 4,* +MAG...[°]OSPIT... *Worn.* KH
2506 (8643) 16, 0.4 *Obv.: Annulet* ° *within,* +C...[Λ]...RODI·°· *Rev.: Annulets* ° *in quarters 1 & 4,* +MAG...S[ ]IT[A... *Corr.* KH

PLATE 124

2507 (1631) 16, 0.6 *Obv.: [Dot within,]* ...S *Rev.: Annulets* ° *in quarters 1 & 4,* +M...SPITAL· IH
2508 (2483) 16, 0.6 *Obv.: Dot within,* +CIVITAS[°]...IS *Rev.: Annulets in quarters 1 & 4,* +MAGR[ ]OS[P]ITAL· IH
2509 (6865) 16, 0.6 *Obv.: Dot within,* +CIVITA...IS *Rev.: Annulets* ° *in quarters 1 & 4,* +MAGR[ ]OSPI[ ]A[L]· *Worn.* IH
2510 (6849) 16, 0.6 *Obv.: Dot within,* +...S *Rev.: Annulets in quarters 1 & 4,* +[M]...TAL · *Worn.* IH
2511 (6938) 17, 0.8 *Obv.: Dot within,* ...S°R... *Rev.: Annulets* ° *in quarters 1 & 4,* +...ITAL[·]*Worn.* IH
2512 (1361) 17, 0.4 *Obv.: Dot within,* +CIVIT[A]...[·] *Rev.: Annulets in quarters 1 & 4,* +MAG[ ]·OSPITALI· IH
2513 (8706) 15, 0.5 *Obv.: Dot within,* +CIVIT...IS *Rev.: Annulets* ° *in quarters 1 & 4,* +MA[GR]O[S]PIT[A... *Worn.* KH
2514 (9098) 17, 0.7 *Obv.: Dot within,* ...TAS°R... *Rev.: Annulets* ° *in quarters 1 & 4,* +MA[G]...I· *Worn.* KH
2515 (1844) 15, 0.6 *Obv.: Dot within,* +CIVITAS...DIS *Rev.: Annulets in quarters 1 & 4,* +MΛGR°OSPITALI∵ IH
2516 (2518) 16, 0.5 *Obv.: Dot within,* +CIVITAS...IS[ ] *Rev.: Annulets in quarters 1 & 4,* +MΛGR°OSPITALI[∵] IH
2517 (6774) 17, 0.4 *Obv.: Dot within,* +CIVITA[S°]RODIS *Rev.: Annulets* ° *in quarters 1 & 4,* +MΛGR°O...[AL]I∵ *Worn.* IH
2518 (2343) 17, 0.5 *Obv.: Dot within,* +CIVITAS°RODI[*Rev.: Platelets in quarters 1 & 4,* +MAGR·OSPITA[L]IS· IH
2519 (2347) 17, 0.6 *Obv.: Dot within,* ...IVIT...[RO]DI[S *Rev.: Platelets in quarters 1 & 4,* [M]AGR...SPIT[AL]... IH
2520 (7288) 16, 0.3 *Obv.: Dot within,* +CI...S[°]RODIS *Brockage. Rev.: Platelets in quarters 1 & 4,* +MAGR·OS...[AL]IS· *Worn.* IH
2521 (9179) 17, 0.8 *Obv.: Dot within,* ...AS°RODIS *Rev.: Platelets in quarters 1 & 4,* ...ALIS[·]*Worn.* KH
2522 (9190) 16, 0.5 *Obv.: Dot within,* +CIVITAS°RODIS *Rev.: Platelets in quarters 1 & 4,* +MAGR· OSPITA[L]IS· *Worn.* KH
2523 (9185) 16, 0.5 *Obv.: Dot within,* +CI...S *Rev.: Platelets in quarters 1 & 4,* +MAGR°...[AL]IS *Worn.* KH
2524 (2516) 17, 0.5 *Obv.: Dot within,* +CIVIT...R...S *Rev.: Annulets in quarters 1 & 4,* +MΛGR°OSPITALS: IH
2525 (2560) 16, 0.5 *Obv.: Dot within,* +CIVIT...S *Rev.: Annulets* ° *in quarters 1 & 4,* +M...OSPITALS: IH
2526 (6780) 17, 0.6 *Obv.: Dot within,* +CIV...IS *Rev.: Annulets* ° *in quarters 1 & 4,* +MΛGR°OS...ALS: *Worn.* IH
2527 (2484) 17, 0.5 *Obv.: Dot within,* +CIVIT...DIS *Rev.: Annulets in quarters 1 & 4,* +MΛGR°OSPIT...S IH
2528 (2536) 18, 0.9 *Obv.: Dot within,* +CIVIT...RODIS *Rev.: Annulets in quarters 1 & 4,* +MΛGR°OSPIT[AL]S[ ] IH
2529 (6872) 16, 0.5 *Obv.: Dot within,* +CIV[ITA]...DIS *Rev.: Annulets* ° *in quarters 1 & 4,* +MΛGR°...IT[AL·˙S] *Worn.* IH
2530 (8707) 17, 0.7 *Obv.: Dot within,* +CI...S *Rev.: Annulets* ° *in quarters 1 & 4,* +M...[O]SPIT[ALS... *Corr.* KH
2531 (8829) 16, 0.4 *Obv.: Dot within,* +CIVIT...S *Rev.: Annulets* ° *in quarters 1 & 4,*...[Λ]GR°O[SPITALS... *Worn* KH.
2532 (9119) 16, 0.6 *Obv.: Annulet within,* +CIVITAS°R... *Rev.: Annulets in quarters 2 & 3,* +MΛGR[°]O[SP]IT... *Corr.* KH

PLATE 125

2533 (1884) 16, 0.6 *Obv.: Platelet within,* ✠... ĦS·RODIS˙ *Rev.: Annulets in quarters 1 & 4,* ✠ᗰɅGR∘OSPI... IH
2534 (6682) 17, 0.4 *Obv.: Platelet within,* ✠ⲤIVIT...ODIS· *Rev.: Annulets in quarters 1 & 4,* ...GR∘O... *Worn.* IH
2535 (8699) 17, 0.4 *Obv.: [Platelet within,]* ✠ⲤI...TĦS·RODIS· *Rev.: Annulets* [∘] *in quarters 1 & 4,* ...[Ʌ]GR∘OSPITɅĿ[*Worn.* KH
2536 (6671) 17, 0.4 *Obv.: Platelet within,* ✠ⲤIVITĦS·RODIS· *Rev.: Annulets* ∘ *in quarters 1 & 4,* ✠ᗰɅGR[ ]OSPITɅĿI[] *Worn.* IH
2537 (9532) 15, 0.3 *Obv.: [Platelet within,]* ...IVITĦS... *Rev.: Annulets in quarters 1 & 4,* ✠[ᗰ]...TɅĿI∘ *Corr., incomplete.* KH
2538 (1458) 16, 0.5 *Obv.: [Platelet within,]* ✠ⲤI[V]...[S]RODIS· *Rev.: Annulets* ∘ *in quarters 1 & 4,* ✠ᗰɅGR∘...ITɅLI∘ IH
2539 (2653) 16, 0.4 *Obv.: [Platelet within,]* ✠ⲤI...S...S· *Rev.: Annulets in quarters 1 & 4,* ...ɅGR∘SP... IH
2540 (2707) 16, 0.5 *Obv.: [Platelet within,]* ✠ⲤI...ODIS· *Rev.: Annulets in quarters 1 & 4,* ✠ᗰɅG...Ʌ[Ŀ]I∘ IH
2541 (6607) 16, 0.5 *Obv.: Platelet within,* ✠ⲤIVITĦS[∘]RODIS · *Rev.: Annulets in quarters 1 & 4,* [✠]ᗰɅ[G]...OS[PIT]ɅĿI[∘] *Worn.* IH
2542 (9008) 16, 0.5 *Obv.: Annulet* ∘ *within,* ✠ⲤI... *Rev.: Annulets in quarters 1 & 4,* [✠]ᗰɅGR∘SP[I... *Corr., incomplete.* KH
2543 (1641) 16, 0.6 *Obv.: Platelet within,* ✠ⲤIVITĦS·RODIS· *Rev.: Annulets in quarters 2 & 3,* ✠ᗰ[Ʌ]...[O]SPIT[L]I∘ IH
2544 (2449) 17, 0.5 *Obv.: Platelet within,* ✠ⲤI...TĦS·RODIS[*Rev.: Annulets in quarters 2 & 3,* ✠...[G]R·OSPITɅ[D]I∘ IH
2545 (6467) 15, 0.7 *Obv.: Annulet* ∘ *within,* ✠ⲤI...[D]IS· *Rev.: Annulets in quarters 2 & 3,* ✠[ᗰ]...SPIT[Ʌ]LI∘ *Worn.* IH
2546 (6722) 15, 0.6 *Obv.: Platelet within,* ✠ⲤI...ODIS· *Rev.: Annulets in quarters 2 & 3,* ✠ᗰɅG[R OSPITɅL]I∘ *Worn.* IH
2547 (6730) 16, 0.4 *Obv.: Platelet within,* ...O... *Rev.: Annulets in quarters 2 & 3,* [✠]...[TɅ]ĿI∘ *Worn.* IH
2548 (9118) 16, 0.5 *Obv.: Platelet within,* ✠ⲤIVIT[Ħ]...DIS· *Rev.: Annulets in quarters 2 & 3,* ✠...GR· OSP...I[∘]*Worn.* KH
2549 (9147) 16, 0.7 *Obv.: Platelet within,* ✠ⲤIVITĦS·R[ ]DIS· *Rev.: Annulets* ∘ *in quarters 2 & 3,* ✠ᗰɅGR[·]OSPI[T Ŀ]I∘ *Worn.* KH
2550 (9449) 16, 0.5 *Obv.: Annulet* ∘ *within,*...S·ROD... *Rev.: Annulets in quarters 2 & 3,* ✠...GR· OSP...[LI∘] *Worn.* KH
2551 (733) 16, 0.4 *Obv.: Annulet within,* ✠... *Rev.: Annulets in quarters 2 & 3,* ✠...TɅĿI[⸰] IH
2552 (1577) 17, 0.6 *Obv.:* ✠[Ⲥ]...TĦS·RODIS· *Rev.: Annulets in quarters 2 & 3,* ✠ᗰ...SPITɅĿI⸰ IH
2553 (1614) 16, 0.3 *Obv.: Platelet within,* ✠ⲤIVIT[ĦS·]RODIS[·] *Rev.: Annulets in quarters 2 & 3,* ✠ᗰɅGR...TɅĿI[∘] IH
2554 (1625) 16, 0.6 *Obv.: Platelet within,* [ ]ⲤIVITĦS[·RODI·] *Rev.: Annulets in quarters 2 & 3,* ✠[ᗰ]GR·O...[Ʌ]LI⸰ IH
2555 (2914) 17, 0.6 *Obv.: Annulet within,* ✠Ⲥ[I]...S·RO[DIS·] *Rev.: Annulets in quarters 2 & 3,* ✠ᗰ...[LI⸰] IH
2556 (6716) 15, 0.3 *Obv.: Platelet within,* ✠ⲤIVIT[Ħ]... *Rev.: Annulets in quarters 2 & 3,* ✠...[Ʌ]ĿI⸰ *Worn.* IH
2557 (9125) 16, 0.4 *Obv.: Platelet within,* ✠[ⲤI]...S·RODIS· *Rev.: Annulets in quarters 2 & 3,* ✠ᗰɅGR[·]OS...I⸰ *Worn.* KH

PLATE 126

2558 (2922) 16, 0.6 *Obv.: Annulet within,* ✠Ⲥ...S·RODIS˙ *Rev.: Annulets in quarters 1 & 4,* ✠ᗰĦGR∘OSPITɅĿI∘ IH
2559 (6306) 18, 0.4 *Obv.: Annulet* ∘ *within,* ✠ⲤIVIT[ ]S·RODIS[˙] *Rev.: Annulets in quarters 1 & 4,* ✠ᗰĦGR[]OSPITɅĿI∘ *Worn.* IH
2560 (2933) 17, 0.7 *Obv.: Annulet* [∘] *within,* ✠ⲤIVI...RODIS˙ *Rev.: Annulets* ∘ *in quarters 1 & 4,* ✠ᗰɅGR·OSP...[ĦĿ]IS IH
2561 (2963) 17, 0.6 *Obv.: Annulet within,* ✠ⲤI[VI]...S∘ROD[I]... *Rev.: Annulets in quarters 1 & 4,* [ᗰ]ɅGR·OSPI...ĿIS[] IH
2562 (3001) 17, 0.5 *Obv.: Annulet* [∘] *within,* ✠ⲤI...DI[*Rev.: Annulets in quarters 1 & 4,* ✠ᗰɅ...ITĦĿIS[IH
2563 (2945) 16, 0.5 *Obv.: Annulet within,* ✠ⲤI...RODIS[] *Rev.: Annulets in quarters 1 & 4,* ✠ᗰ[Ʌ]...[T]ɅLI∘ IH
2564 (1867) 15, 0.4 *Obv.: Dot within,* ✠Ⲥ...RODIS⁖ *Rev.: Annulets in quarters 1 & 4,* ✠ᗰ...[∘]...IT[ĦL·] IH
2565 (6852) 16, 0.5 *Obv.: Dot within,* ✠ⲤI...ĦS∘RODIS⁖ *Rev.: Annulets* ∘ *in quarters 1 & 4,* [✠ᗰĦ]GR[∘]...TĦL· *Worn.* IH
2566 (8628) 15, 0.4 *Obv.: Dot within,* ✠Ⲥ...[ODI]S⁖ *Rev.: Annulets* ∘ *in quarters 1 & 4,* ✠ᗰĦ...[L *Corr.* KH
2567 (8633) 15, 0.5 *Obv.: Dot within,* ✠[Ⲥ]...TĦ[S]RODIS⁖ *Rev.: Annulets* ∘ *in quarters 1 & 4,* ✠[ĦGR]∘OS...TĦ[L *Worn.* KH
2568 (1564) 15, 0.5 *Obv.: Platelet within,* ✠ⲤIVIT...DIS⁖ *Rev.: Annulets in quarters 1 & 4,* ✠ᗰɅGR...PIT[ɅL]... IH
2569 (2675) 16, 0.5 *Obv.: [Dot within,]* ✠Ⲥ...ĦS∘RODIS⁖ *Rev.: Annulets in quarters 1 & 4,* ✠ᗰĦGR...ĦĿI· IH
2570 (2705) 17, 0.6 *Obv.: Dot within,* ✠Ⲥ...DIS⁖ *Rev.: Annulets in quarters 1 & 4,* ✠ᗰĦ[GR]...[L]I· IH
2571 (7313) 17, 0.6 *Obv.: Dot within,* ✠ⲤIVITĦS[∘]RODIS[⁖] *Rev.: Annulets* ∘ *in quarters 1 & 4,* ✠ᗰĦGR...SPIT... *Worn.* IH
2572 (1916) 16, 0.7 *Obv.:* ✠ⲤIVIT...[D]IS⁖ *Rev.: Annulets in quarters 1 & 4,* ...ɅGR∘OS[PI]... IH
2573 (6972) 15, 0.5 *Obv.: Dot within,* ✠ⲤIVIT...DIS⁖ *Rev.: ?Annulets in quarters 1 & 4,* ✠ᗰɅGR∘OSPITĦ[L]I⁖ *Worn. IH*
2574 (6973) 16, 0.6 *Obv.:* ✠ⲤIVITĦS[∘]RODIS⁖ *Rev.: Annulets* ∘ *in quarters 1 & 4,* ✠ᗰɅGR∘O[ ]PITĦĿI[⁖] *Worn.* IH
2575 (7137) 17, 0.5 *Obv.:* [ ]ⲤIVIT[Ħ]...IS[*Rev.: Annulets* ∘ *in quarters 1 & 4,* ✠ᗰɅGR∘OSPITĦ[Ŀ]I[⁖] *Worn.* IH
2576 (2322) 17, 0.4 *Obv.: [Dot within,]* ✠Ⲥ[ ]VI...IS⁖ *Rev.: Platelets in quarters 1 & 4,* ✠ᗰĦGR...[S] IH
2577 (2323) 16, 0.6 *Obv.: Dot within,* ✠[Ⲥ]VITĦ[S]RODIS⁖ *Rev.: Platelets in quarters 1 & 4,* ✠ᗰĦ...[S]PI...[Ŀ]IS IH
2578 (7046) 16, 0.6 *Obv.: Dot within,* ✠Ⲥ...ĦS∘RODIS ⁖ *Rev.: [Platelets] in quarters 1 & 4,* [✠]ᗰĦGR∘OSPI... *Corr.* IH
2579 (7315) 16, 0.5 *Obv.: Dot within,* ✠ⲤI...IS⁖ *Rev.: Platelets in quarters 1 & 4,* ✠ᗰĦG...[ĦLI]S *Worn.* IH
2580 (7314) 18, 0.5 *Obv.: Dot within,* ✠ⲤIVITĦS∘RODIS⁖ *Rev.: Platelets in quarters 1 & 4,* ✠ᗰĦGR·OS[PIT]ĦLIS˙*Worn.* IH
2581 (9201) 17, 0.7 *Obv.: Dot within,* ...TĦS∘RODIS[*Rev.: Platelets in quarters 1 & 4,* ✠ᗰ[ ]G...OS[P]TĦLIS *Worn.* KH

PLATE 127

2582 (769) 17, 0.5 *Obv.: Dot within,* +CI...TAS°RODIS° *Rev.: Annulets in quarters 1 & 4,* +MA...SPITALIS IH

2583 (2301) 15, 0.6 *Obv.: Dot within,* +CIVITAS°RODIS[ ] *Rev.: Platelets in quarters 1 & 4,* +MAGR°OSPITA[L]IS· IH

2584 (2316) 16, 0.7 *Obv.: Dot within,* +CIVI...RODIS° *Rev.: Platelets in quarters 1 & 4,* +MAGR·O[S]...TA[L]IS· IH

2585 (2359) 16, 0.8 *Obv.: Dot within,* +CIVITAS[ ]RODIS° *Rev.: Platelets in quarters 1 & 4,* +MAGR°OSPITALI[IH

2586 (7497) 16, 0.3 *Obv.: Dot within,* +CI...AS°RODIS° *Rev.: Platelets in quarters 1 & 4,* +MAGR[O]...[A]LIS *Worn.* IH

2587 (7504) 16, 0.6 *Obv.: Dot within,* +CIVITAS°R...IS° *Rev.: Platelets in quarters 1 & 4,* +[M]AGR[O]SPITALIS *Worn.* IH

2588 (7511) 17, 0.4 *Obv.: Dot within,* +CI...TAS°R[ ]DIS° *Rev.: Platelets in quarters 1 & 4,* +...[G]R°OSP...LIS[*Worn.* IH

2589 (771) 16, 0.7 *Obv.: Dot within,* +CIVITAS°RODIS° *Rev.: Platelets in quarters 1 & 4,* +MA[R]...[S]PITA[L]I[IH

2590 (2321) 17, 0.5 *Obv.: Dot within,* +CIVIT...·...[D]IS° *Rev.: Platelets in quarters 1 & 4,* +MAGR°OSPI...∴ IH

2591 (9239) 17, 0.6 *Obv.: Dot within,* ...IVITAS[°]ROD... *Rev.: Platelets in quarters 1 & 4,* +MAGR°OS[PI]TA[LI∴ *Worn.* KH

2592 (2333) 16, 0.5 *Obv.: Dot within,* ...TAS°R[O... *Rev.: Platelets in quarters 1 & 4,* +MAGR·OS... IH

2593 (1816) 16, 0.7 *Obv.: Dot within,* +CIVI...RODIS° *Rev.: Platelets in quarters 1 & 4,* +[M GR]OSPIT...S° IH

2594 (7507) 16, 0.6 *Obv.: Dot within,* +CI...[S]°RODIS° *Rev.: Platelets in quarters 1 & 4,* +MAGR[O]SPI...S° *Worn.* IH

2595 (9194) 16, 0.6 *Obv.: Dot within,* [ ]CIVITAS°ROD... *Rev.: Platelets in quarters 1 & 4,* +MAGR°OSP...LIS° *Worn.* KH

2596 (9219) 16, 0.7 *Obv.: Dot within,* +CIVIT...IS° *Rev.: Platelets in quarters 1 & 4,* +...IS° *Worn.* KH

2597 (1492) 16, 0.4 *Obv.: Annulet within,* +CIVITĀRODIS *Rev.: Annulets in quarters 1 & 4,* +MĀGR[ ]OSPITĀ[L] IH

2598 (6349) 17, 0.5 *Obv.: Annulet within,* +CIVITĀRODIS *Rev.: Annulets ° in quarters 1 & 4,* +MĀGR·OS[PITĀL *Worn.* IH

2599 (8342) 16, 0.5 *Obv.: Annulet ° within,* +CIVIT...IS *Rev.: Annulets ° in quarters 1 & 4,* +MĀGR· OSP...ĀL · *Doubled dies; worn.* KH

2600 (8569) 18, 0.6 *Obv.: Annulet ° within,* +CIVITĀRODIS *Brockage. Rev.: Annulets in quarters 1 & 4,* +MĀG[R] · OSPITĀ[L ·] *Worn.*

2601 (8582) 17, 0.3 *Obv.: Annulet ° within,* +CI...TĀRODIS *Rev.: Annulets ° in quarters 1 & 4,* +M[Ā]GR· OS...[ĀL] · *Worn.* KH

2602 (8576) 15, 0.5 *Obv.: Annulet ° within,* +CI...S *Rev.: Annulets ° in quarters 1 & 4,*...[Ā]GR...IT[AL *Worn.* KH

2603 (8586) 18, 0.7 *Obv.: Annulet within,*+CIVITĀRO[D]IS *Rev.: Doubled die. Annulets in quarters 1 & 4,* +MĀG... OSPIT[AL... *Worn, cracked.* KH

2604 (6485) 16, 0.5 *Obv.: Annulet ° within,* +C...[Ā]RODIS *Rev.: Annulets* [°] *in quarters 1 & 4,* ...PIT[AL]...*Worn.* IH

2605 (7024) 16, 0.5 *Obv.:* +C...ODIS[·]*Rev.: Annulets ° in quarters 1 & 4,* +MĀGR...I° *Worn.* IH

2606 (9029) 16, 0.6 *Obv.: Annulet ° within,* +CI...RODI[S *Doubled die. Rev.: Annulets in quarters 1 & 4,* +MĀG...ITALI° *Worn.* KH

2607 (1589) 17, 0.4 *Obv.:* +C...RODIS *Rev.: Annulets ° in quarters 1 & 4,* +M...OSPITĀLI[∴] IH

PLATE 128

2608 (6341) 17, 0.6 *Obv.: Annulet ° within,* +[C]...ITĀ...[O]DIS *Rev.: Annulets in quarters 1 & 4,* + · M[ ]GR✪O...[ĀL]I· *Worn.* IH

2609 (6357) 16, 0.4 *Obv.: Annulet* [°] *within,* +CI...DIS[ ] *Doubled die. Rev.: Annulets in quarters 1 & 4,* ...✪OSPIT[A]... *Worn.* IH

2610 (6481) 16, 0.5 *Obv.: Annulet within,* ...VI[ ]Ā...DIS[*Rev.: Annulets ° in quarters 1 & 4,* + · M[Ā]...[✪]OSPI[AL]I· *Worn, incomplete.* IH

2611 (7209) 17, 0.5 *Obv.:* +CIVITĀRODIS *Rev.: [Annulets] in quarters 1 & 4,* +MAGR°OSPI...LI[∴] *Corr.* IH

2612 (7107) 17, 0.4 *Obv.:* ...IVIT[Ā]... *Rev.: Annulets in quarters 1 & 4,* ...GR°OSPIT[AL]... *Corr.* IH

2613 (8393) 17, 0.5 *Obv.: Annulet ° within,* +CIVIT[Ā]...[D]IS *Rev.: Annulets ° in quarters 1 & 4,* +MĀG[R°] OSPITALI∴*Worn.* KH

2614 (8577) 17, 0.5 *Obv.: Annulet ° within,* +CIV...[ĀRO]DIS *Rev.: Annulets ° in quarters 1 & 4,* +MAGR[°]O...[TALI∴] *Worn.* KH

2615 (1486) 16, 0.6 *Obv.: Annulet within,* +CIV[I]TĀRODIS *Rev.: Annulets in quarters 1 & 4,* +MĀGR°OSPITALIS IH

2616 (2920) 17, 0.4 *Obv.: Annulet within,* +C[I] ...ĀR[D]S *Rev.: Annulets in quarters 1 & 4,* ...[ĀG]R°OS...LI[IH

2617 (2906) 16, 0.4 *Obv.: Annulet* [°] *within,* +CIVIT...RODIS *Rev.: Annulets ° in quarters 1 & 4,* +MAG...[OS]PITĀL∴ IH

2618 (2907) 17, 0.5 *Obv.: Annulet within,* +C...[R]ODIS *Rev.: Annulets in quarters 1 & 4,* +...O[SPIT]ĀL∴ IH

2619 (6312) 17, 0.7 *Obv.: Annulet ° within,* +CI[V]ITĀRODIS *Rev.: Annulets ° in quarters 1 & 4,* +MĀGR·OSP...[L∴] *Worn.* IH

2620 (8552) 16, 0.5 *Obv.: Annulet ° within,* +C...DIS *Rev.: Annulets ° in quarters 1 & 4,* +MĀG...ĀL∴ *Worn.* KH

2621 (8359) 16, 0.4 *Obv.: Annulet ° within,*...[Ā]RODIS *Rev.: Annulets in quarters 1 & 4,* +MĀ...ĀL∴ *Worn.* KH

2622 (2908) 16, 0.4 *Obv.: Annulet within,* +[C]IVIT[Ā]RODIS *Rev.: Annulets ° in quarters 1 & 4,* +MĀGR[°]OS[PITĀ]L∴ IH

2623 (6352) 16, 0.6 *Obv.: Annulet ° within,* +CIVIT...RODIS *Rev.: Annulets ° in quarters 1 & 4,* +MĀGR·OSPITĀL∴*Worn.* IH

2624 (6613) 16, 0.4 *Obv.: Platelet within,* +CIVITĀ[R]DIS *Rev.: Annulets ° in quarters 1 & 4,* +[M]Ā[G]...OSPITĀL∴ *Worn.* IH

2625 (6614) 16, 0.5 *Obv.: Platelet within,* +CIVITĀRODIS *Rev.: Annulets in quarters 1 & 4,* +MĀGR·OSPI[T L∴] *Worn.* IH

2626 (6615) 17, 0.5 *Obv.: [Platelet within,]* +CIVIT[ĀR]ODIS *Rev.: Annulets ◦ in quarters 1 & 4*, 1 & 4, +[ ]ĀGR…TĀ[L] *Worn.* IH
2627 (1584) 17, 0.4 *Obv.: Platelet within,* +CIVITĀRODIS *Rev.: Annulets in quarters 1 & 4,* +MĀGR·OSPITĀL IH
2628 (2443) 17, 0.4 *Obv.: Platelet within,* +CIVI…ODIS *Rev.: Annulets in quarters 1 & 4,* +MĀGR…PITĀL IH
2629 (8619) 17, 0.7 *Obv.: Platelet within,* +…VI[T]…ODIS *Rev.: Annulets ◦ in quarters 1 & 4,* +MĀGR· O…L *Worn.* KH
2630 (1587) 18, 0.4 *Obv.: Platelet within,* +C…TĀRODIS *Rev.: Annulets in quarters 1 & 4,* +MĀGR·O…[Ā]L IH

PLATE 129

2631 (1488) 16, 0.5 *Obv.: Annulet within,* …IVITĀRODIS *Rev.: Annulets in quarters 1 & 4,* …ĀGR[ ]OSPITĀLI[◦] IH
2632 (8324) 16, 0.6 *Obv.: Annulet within,* +CIVI[ ]ĀRODIS *Rev.: Annulets ◦ in quarters 1 & 4,* +M…R◦OSPITĀ[L]◦ *Corr.* KH
2633 (8325) 16, 0.5 *Obv.: Annulet ◦ within,* +CIVITĀRODI[ ] *Rev.: Annulets ◦ in quarters 1 & 4,* +MĀGR◦OSPITĀL[◦] *Corr.* KH
2634 (8611) 17, 0.7 *Obv.: Annulet ◦ within,* +CIVI[TĀ]ODIS *Rev.: Annulets ◦ in quarters 1 & 4,* [+ Ā]GR◦OSPIT[ĀL◦] *Worn.* KH
2635 (2917) 17, 0.5 *Obv.: Annulet within,* +CIVITĀ…DIS *Rev.: Annulets in quarters 1 & 4,* +M[ ]GR◦OSP[I]…L◦ IH
2636 (2419) 17, 0.6 *Obv.: Platelet within,* +CIVITĀRODIS *Rev.: Annulets in quarters 1 & 4,* +MĀGR◦OSPITĀL◦ IH
2637 (2421) 18, 0.5 *Obv.: Platelet within,* +CIVI[T]…R…S *Rev.: Annulets in quarters 1 & 4,* +MĀGR…SPITĀ[L] IH
2638 (6624) 16, 0.6 *Obv.: Platelet within,* +CIV…RODIS *Rev.: Annulets in quarters 1 & 4,* +M[ĀG]R[◦]OS[PIT]ĀL◦ *Worn.* IH
2639 (6320) 17, 0.5 *Obv.: Annulet ◦ within,* +CIVIT…[O]DIS *Rev.: Annulets ◦ in quarters 1 & 4,* +M[Ā]…OSPIT[L]I◦ *Worn.* IH
2640 (6354) 17, 0.6 *Obv.: Annulet ◦ within,* +CIV…RODIS *Rev.: Annulets ◦ in quarters 1 & 4,* +…OSPITĀLI· *Worn.* IH
2641 (6378) 16, 0.5 *Obv.: Annulet* [◦] *within,* +CI[V]TĀRODIS *Rev.: Annulets ◦ in quarters 1 & 4,* +M[ ]GR◦OSPITĀLI· *Worn.* IH
2642 (8549) 15, 0.4 *Obv.: Annulet ◦ within,* +CIVIT…DIS[] *Rev.: Doubled die. Annulets* [◦] *in quarters 1 & 4,* +M[Ā]…◦OSPIT[Ā]LI· *Corr.* KH
2643 (2433) 17, 0.6 *Obv.: Platelet within,* +…RODIS *Rev.: Annulets ◦ in quarters 1 & 4,* …PITĀLI[ ] IH
2644 (6631) 17, 0.5 *Obv.: Platelet within,* +CIVITĀRODIS *Rev.: Annulets ◦ in quarters 1 & 4,* +MĀGR◦OSPITĀLI· *Worn.* IH
2645 (6476) 16, 0.6 *Obv.: Annulet ◦ within,* …IVITĀRO[D… *Rev.: Annulets* [◦] *in quarters 1 & 4,* +MĀG…[T˙]LIS· *Worn.* IH
2646 (2912) 16, 0.7 *Obv.: Annulet within,* +CIVITĀ…DIS *Rev.: Annulets in quarters 1 & 4,* +MĀ…SPIT˙LI[IH
2647 (8883) 16, 0.5 *Obv.: Annulet ◦ within,* +CIVITĀRODIS *Rev.: Annulets ◦ in quarters 1 & 4,* +M[Ā…TL]IS[*Worn.* KH
2648 (1550) 16, 0.6 *Obv.: Platelet within,* +CIVIT[Ā]…S *Rev.: Annulets in quarters 1 & 4,* +MĀ…[T˙]LIS· IH
2649 (8870) 17, 0.4 *Obv.: Platelet within,* +CI…TĀRODIS *Rev.: Annulets ◦ in quarters 1 & 4,* +MĀG…OSPI[TL]IS[ ] *Worn.* KH
2650 (8888) 16, 0.6 *Obv.: [Platelet within,]* +CIVIT[Ā]RODIS *Rev.: Annulets ◦ in quarters 1 & 4,* [+]…PIT˙LIS· *Worn.* KH
2651 (8849) 15, 0.6 *Obv.: Annulet ◦ within,* +CIV[ITĀ]RODIS *Rev.: Annulets ◦ in quarters 1 & 4,* +M…[O]SPITHLIS *Worn.* KH
2652 (2932) 18, 0.5 *Obv.: Annulet within,* +CIVITĀR[ ]DIS *Rev.: Annulets in quarters 1 & 4,* [+]MĀGR[·]SPITHLIS IH
2653 (6313) 16, 0.6 *Obv.: Annulet ◦ within,* +CIV[IT]…[R]ODIS *Rev.: Annulets ◦ in quarters 1 & 4,* +MĀGR·OSPITHL[I *Worn.* IH

PLATE 130

2654 (1763) 17, 0.4 *Obv.: Platelet within,* +[CI]VITĀRODIS *Rev.: Annulets in quarters 1 & 4,* +[ ]ĀGR]…PITHLIS IH
2655 (2425) 17, 0.6 *Obv.: Platelet within,* +CI…RODIS *Rev.: Annulets ◦ in quarters 1 & 4,* +MĀGR[ ]OSPIT[HL]IS IH
2656 (2439) 16, 0.5 *Obv.: Platelet within,* +…TĀRODIS *Rev.: Annulets in quarters 1 & 4,* …GR·OSPIT[HL]IS IH
2657 (6646) 17, 0.4 *Obv.: Platelet within,* +CIVI[TĀR]…IS *Rev.: Annulets ◦ in quarters 1 & 4,* +…[GR·OS]PITHLIS *Worn.* IH
2658 (6648) 16, 0.4 *Obv.: Platelet within,* +CIVIT…[D]IS *Rev.: Annulets ◦ in quarters 1 & 4,* +MĀGR·O…ITHLIS *Worn.* IH
2659 (8897) 17, 0.5 *Obv.: Platelet within,* +CIV…ODIS *Rev.: Annulets ◦ in quarters 1 & 4,* +M[Ā]…THLIS *Worn.* KH
2660 (6473) 16, 0.6 *Obv.: Annulet within,* +CIV…ĀRODI[ ] *Doubled die. Rev.: Annulets in quarters 1 & 4,* +MĀGR◦O…[T]ĀLI◦ *Worn.* IH
2661 (8337) 15, 0.4 *Obv.: Annulet ◦ within,* +CIV[IT]…IS *Rev.: Annulets in quarters 1 & 4,* +MĀGR[OS]ITĀL◦ *Worn.* KH
2662 (8339) 16, 0.5 *Obv.:* +CIVI[T]…DIS *Rev.: Annulets in quarters 1 & 4,* +M…OSPI…LI◦ *Worn.* KH
2663 (8338) 16, 0.4 *Obv.: Platelet within,* +C…RODIS *Rev.: Annulets in quarters 1 & 4,* +M…SPITĀLI◦ *Worn.* KH
2664 (8612) 16, 0.6 *Obv.: [Platelet within,]* +CIVIT…IS *Rev.: Annulets ◦ in quarters 1 & 4,* +…OSPI…[LI◦] *Corr.* KH
2665 (8858) 18, 0.5 *Obv.: Platelet within,* +CIVIT[ĀRO]DIS *Rev.: Annulets ◦ in quarters 1 & 4,* +MĀGR· OSPI[T]…S *Worn.* KH
2666 (8885) 16, 0.5 *Obv.: Platelet within,* +[C]IVIT[Ā…D]IS *Rev.: Annulets ◦ in quarters 1 & 4,* +MĀG…S *Corr.* KH
2667 (9011) 16, 0.7 *Obv.: Platelet within,* +CI[V… *Rev.: Annulets ◦ in quarters 1 & 4,*…R ·O…T[ĀL… *Worn.* KH
2668 (6641) 15, 0.3 *Obv.: Platelet within,* +CIV[IT]ĀRO… *Rev.: Annulets ◦ in quarters 1 & 4,* +MĀGR◦OS[P]…IS *Worn.* IH

2669 (6702) 15, 0.6 *Obv.: Platelet within,* +CIVITΛ]RO[ ]IS *Rev.: Annulets ◦ in quarters 1 & 4,* +M...R...TΛ[LIS] IH

PLATE 131

2670 (2728) 15, 0.6 *Obv.: Annulet [◦] within,* [ ]SIVITAS... *Rev.: Annulets [◦] in quarters 1 & 4,* ...AGR·OSP... IH
2671 (2729) 17, 0.7 *Obv.: Annulet [◦] within,* +S...ITAS[◦]...I· *Rev.: Annulets [◦] in quarters 1 & 4,* +...GR·O...ALI· IH
2672 (6500) 16, 0.6 *Obv.: Annulet ◦ within,* ...IVITA[S]◦ROD... *Rev.: Annulets ◦ in quarters 1 & 4,* +...R·OSPITA[L]I *Worn.* IH
2673 (6545) 15, 0.8 *Obv.: Annulet [◦] within,* [ ]SIVITAS[◦]ROD[*Rev.: Annulets ◦ in quarters 1 & 4,*...T[A]... *Worn.* IH
2674 (8418) 15, 0.7 *Obv.: Annulet within,* +SIVITA...DI· *Rev.: Annulets ◦ in quarters 1 & 4,* +M[A]GR · OS...LI· *Worn.* KH
2675 (8469) 15, 0.5 *Obv.: Annulet ◦ within,* +SIVITA...RODI· *Rev.: Annulets [◦] in quarters 1 & 4,* ...R· OSPIT[A... *Corr.* KH
2676 (6563) 16, 0.5 *Obv.: Annulet ◦ within,* +SIVIT[A]...ODI· *Rev.: Annulets ◦ in quarters 1 & 4,* ...GR·OS[PITAL]... *Worn.* IH
2677 (8419) 16, 0.6 *Obv.: Annulet within,* +SI[V]ITAS... *Rev.: Annulets in quarters 1 & 4,* +M[ ]GR[◦]O[S...L]I· *Corr.* KH
2678 (8431) 16, 0.3 *Obv.: Annulet ◦ within,* [ ]SIVITAS◦RO[D... *Rev.: Annulets ◦ in quarters 1 & 4,* +MAGR[◦]OSPITA... *Worn.* KH
2679 (2725) 16, 0.6 *Obv.: Annulet [◦] within,* [ ]SIVITAS◦ROD... *Rev.: Annulets [◦] in quarters 1 & 4,* +MAGR◦OSPITA[L]· IH
2680 (6538) 18, 0.6 *Obv.: Annulet ◦ within,* ...I...AS[◦]RO... *Rev.: Annulets ◦ in quarters 1 & 4,* +MA...ITAL · *Worn.* IH
2681 (9438) 15, 0.5 *Obv.: Annulet ◦ within,* +SIVITAS◦R...IS *Rev.: Annulets in quarters 1 & 4,* +MA[ ]R◦...AL · *Worn.* KH
2682 (2318) 15, 0.5 *Obv.: Annulet within,* +SIVI...RODI· *Rev.: Platelets in quarters 2 & 3,* +MAGR·OSPI[T]LIS[IH
2683 (8425) 17, 0.6 *Obv.: Annulet [◦] within,* +SIVITA[ ]◦RODI⁚· *Rev.: Annulets ◦ in quarters 1 & 4,* [ ]MAGR·OSPIT... *Worn, doubled die.* KH
2684 (8432) 16, 0.5 *Obv.: Annulet ◦ within,* +SIVITAS[◦]...[I⁚·] *Rev.: Annulets [◦] in quarters 1 & 4,* ...OSPIT... *Worn.* KH

PLATE 132

Late types

Obv.: Châtel, dot within and thick verticals topped by needles (✝*), triangular roof topped by dot, with another dot within (*⧊*); in beaded circle. Rev.: Maltese cross, platelets in opposite quarters; within beaded circle.*

2685 (7372) 16, 0.7 *Obv.:* +CIVITΛS:RODI *Rev.: Platelets in quarters 2 & 3,* +MΛGR[·]...PITΛL IH
2686 (7428) 16, 0.6 *Obv.:* +CIVIT[ ]S:RODI *Rev.: Platelets in quarters 2 & 3,* [+]MΛGR:[OS]PITΛ[L IH
2687 (9363) 16, 0.7 *Obv.:* +CIVITΛS:RODI *Rev.: Platelets in quarters 2 & 3,* +[Λ]R:OSPITΛL *Corr.* KH
2688 (7460) 16, 0.6 *Obv.:* +...S:ROD[I *Rev.: Platelets in quarters 2 & 3,* ...G...PITAL'·˙] *Corr.* IH
2689 (7487) 17, 0.8 *Obv.:* ...IVITΛS:... *Rev.: Platelets in quarters 2 & 3,* +M...TAL'·˙ *Worn.* IH
2690 (9395) 16, 0.8 *Obv.:* ...IVITΛS:RO[D *Rev.: Platelets in quarters 2 & 3,* ...:OSPITAL'·˙ *Worn.* KH
2691 (9411) 16, 0.5 *Obv.:* +CIVITΛS:R[O]DI *Rev.: Platelets in quarters 2 & 3,* +MAG...[S]PITAL'·˙ *Worn.* KH
2692 (1287) 16, 0.6 *Obv.:* +CIV...RODI *Rev.: Platelets in quarters 2 & 3,* +MΛGR:OS[PITΛ[L]I· IH
2693 (7466) 17, 0.5 *Obv.:* +[C]VITΛS:RODI *Rev.: Platelets in quarters 2 & 3,* +MΛG...[LI·] *Worn.* IH
2694 (9392) 16, 0.7 *Obv.:* +CIVITΛ...[O]DI *Rev.: Platelets in quarters 2 & 3,* +MΛ...PITΛLI· *Worn.* KH
2695 (1244) 15, 0.4 *Obv.: Doubled die. Rev.: Platelets in quarters 1 & 4,* IH
2696 (2214) 16, 0.4 *Obv.:* ...IVI... *Rev.: Platelets in quarters 1 & 4,* +[ ]ΛG...SPITΛ[LI] IH
2697 (2232) 17, 0.4 *Obv.:* ...IVI...ROD[*Rev.: Platelets in quarters 1 & 4,* ...PITΛ... IH
2698 (2259) 16, 0.5 *Obv.:,* ...:ROD[*Rev.: Platelets in quarters 1 & 4,* ...PITΛ[L IH
2699 (1279) 16, 0.5 *Obv.:* +CIVITΛS:RODI· *Rev.: Platelets in quarters 2 & 3,* +[MA]GR[:]O[SPIT]... IH
2700 (2216) 17, 0.5 *Obv.:* +CIVITΛS:R... *Rev.: Platelets in quarters 2 & 3,* +M...[R·]OSPITΛL IH
2701 (2219) 17, 0.6 *Obv.:* [ ]CIVITΛS:RODI· *Rev.: Platelets in quarters 2 & 3,*]MΛGR·OSPITΛ... IH
2702 (9273) 16, 0.5 *Obv.:* ...IVI[T]...ODI· *Rev.: Platelets in quarters 2 & 3,* +MΛ...L *Corr., incomplete.* KH
2703 (9274) 15, 0.5 *Obv.:* +CIVITΛ...I· *Rev.: Doubled die. Platelets in quarters 2 & 3,* ...ΛGR· OSPITΛ[L] *Worn.* KH
2704 (9277) 17, 0.5 *Obv.:* +CIV...O[D]I· *Rev.: Platelets in quarters 2 & 3,* +...ITΛ[L] *Corr.* KH
2705 (9283) 15, 0.5 *Obv.:* ...VITΛS:RODI· *Rev.: Platelets in quarters 2 & 3,* +...SPITΛL *Corr.* KH
2706 (9284) 15, 0.7 *Obv.:* +[ ]IVIT[Λ]...DI· *Rev.: Platelets in quarters 2 & 3,*]MΛG...[IT]ΛL'[ ] *Worn.* KH

PLATE 133

Obols of Raymond Berenger, 1365-1373

Obv.: Châtel, annulet; in beaded circle. Rev.: Cross pattee, annulets in opposite quarters; within beaded circle.

2707 (1776) 17, 0.6 *Obv.: Annulet ◦ within,* +C...TAS◦RODISƱ *Rev.: [Annulets in quarters 2 & 3],* +MΛ[R]◦SP...Λ[L]I◦ IH
2708 (2722) 17, 0.5 *Obv.: Annulet [◦] within,* +... SƱ *Rev.: [Annulets in quarters 2 & 3],* +M[ΛG]R◦SP[I]... IH
2709 (2723) 15, 0.4 *Obv.: Annulet [◦] within,* ... SƱ *Rev.:*]MΛGR◦S... IH
2710 (6171) 16, 0.5 *Obv.: Annulet ◦ within,* +...◦RODISƱ *Rev.: Annulets in quarters 2 & 3,* +MΛ...[I]TΛ[LI] IH
2711 (6172) 18, 0.6 *Obv.: Annulet ◦ within,* ...S◦R...[I]SƱ *Rev.: Annulets in quarters 1 & 4,* [+]M...R◦S... IH
2712 (6173) 16, 0.3 *Obv.: Annulet [◦] within,* +...DI[S]Ʊ *Rev.: Annulets in quarters 1 & 4,* ...R◦SPIT... IH
2713 (6249) 17, 0.6 *Obv.: Annulet ◦ within,* +...AS◦R...ISƱ *Rev.: Annulets in quarters [1 & 4],* [ ]MΛG...SPI[T]... IH
2714 (6250) 16, 0.5 *Obv.: Annulet ◦ within,* +C...[ ]R...Ʊ *Rev.: Annulets in quarters 2 & 3,* +MΛ...I[TΛ]I◦ *Incomplete.* IH

2715 (7227) 17, 0.6 *Obv.:* ✠…◦RODIS *Doubled die. Rev.: [Annulets in quarters 2 & 3],* ✠M[Λ]…SPITΛLI◦ *Worn.* IH
2716 (8318) 16, 0.5 *Obv.: Annulet ◦ within,* ✠C…[I]S *Rev.: Annulets in quarters 1 & 4,* …[G]R◦SPIT… *Worn.* KH
2717 (9566) 15, 0.4 *Obv.: Dot within,* …RODIS *Rev.: [Annulets in quarters 1 & 4],* …[ITΛ]… *Worn.* KH
2718 (731) 18, 0.5 *Obv.: Annulet within,* ✠CIVITH…ODIS *Rev.:* ✠MΛGR· OSP…ΛLI IH
2719 (1734) 17, 0.4 *Obv.: Annulet ◦ within,* ✠CIV… *Rev.: Annulets in quarters 2 & 3,* …Λ… IH
2720 (1777) 16, 0.4 *Obv.: Annulet ◦ within,* ✠CIVIT[H]… *Rev.: Annulets in quarters 2 & 3,* [ ]MΛGR[ ]OSP… IH
2721 (2720) 16, 0.5 *Obv.: Annulet ◦ within,* ✠CIV…S *Rev.: Annulets in quarters 2 & 3,* [ ]MΛGR· OS[I]… IH
2722 (2721) 16, 0.6 *Obv.: Annulet ◦ within,* ✠C…[R]ODIS *Rev.: Annulets in quarters 2 & 3,* …[O]SP…[L]I IH
2723 (2724) 18, 0.3 *Obv.: Annulet within,* ✠…[◦ROD]IS *Rev.: Annulets in quarters 2 & 3,* [M]Λ[GR]…ΛLI[I IH
2724 (6170) 16, 0.4 *Obv.: Annulet ◦ within,* ✠C…[R]ODIS *Rev.: Annulets in quarters 2 & 3,* ✠…LI IH
2725 (6174) 17, 0.5 *Obv.: Annulet [◦] within,* ✠CI[V]ITHS… *Rev.: Annulets in quarters 2 & 3,* ✠M…R·…ITΛLI[ ] *Cancelled.* IH
2726 (6175) 16, 0.8 *Obv.: Annulet ◦ within,* ✠…S…S *Rev.: Annulets in quarters 2 & 3,* ✠MΛGR·[OSP]… IH
2727 (6176) 15, 0.3 *Obv.: Annulet ◦ within,* ✠C…[S] *Rev.: Annulets in quarters 2 & 3,* ✠MΛGR·O[S]… IH
2728 (6177) 16, 0.5 *Obv.: Annult ◦ within,* ✠C[I]… *Rev.: Annulets in quarters 2 & 3,* …[OSP]ITΛ[L]… IH
2729 (6178) 16, 0.7 *Obv.: Annulet ◦ within,* ✠CIVITHS◦…DIS *Rev.: Annulets in quarters 2 & 3,* …GR·OS…[LI◦] IH
2730 (6179) 15, 0.3 *Obv.: Annulet ◦ within,* ✠C…IS *Rev.: Annulets in quarters 2 & 3,* ✠MΛGR·O[S]… IH
2731 (1778) 16, 0.5 *Obv.: Annulet ◦ within,* ✠…ODIS *Rev.: [Annulets in quarters 2 & 3],* … IH
2732 (2723) 15, 0.4 *Obv.: Annulet [◦] within,* … S *Rev.:* [ ]MΛGR◦S… IH
2733 (8315) 17, 0.4 *Obv.: Annulet ◦ within,* ✠…RODIS *Rev.: Annulets in quarters [2 & 3],* ✠MΛ…TΛ[LI] *Worn.* KH
2734 (8316) 16, 0.5 *Obv.: Annulet ◦ within,* ✠[CI]…[I]S *Rev.: Annulets in quarters 2 & 3,* …OS…Λ[L]I[ ] *Worn.* KH
2735 (8317) 16, 0.5 *Obv.: Annulet ◦ within,* ✠C…[I]S *Rev.: Annulets in quarters 2 & 3,* ✠[Λ]…LI[◦] *Worn.* KH
2736 (9433) 16, 0.6 *Obv.: Annulet ◦ within,* ✠CIVIT… *Rev.: Annulets in quarters 2 & 3,* …[ΛG]R[·]OS… *Corr.* KH
2737 (9434) 15, 0.5 *Obv.: Annulet ◦ within,* ✠…S *Rev.: Annulets in quarters 2 & 3,* …IT… *Worn.* KH
2738 (9435) 17, 0.5 *Obv.: Annulet ◦ within,* ✠CIVITHS◦…S *Rev.:* ✠[ ]ΛGR· OSP…ΛLI[*Worn.* KH
2739 (9451) 16, 0.3 *Obv.: Annulet ◦ within,* ✠CI…ROD…[] *Rev.: Annulets in quarters 2 & 3,* ✠MΛG… *Worn.* KH
2740 (9573) 17, 0.4 *Obv.: Annulet within,* ✠C[V T]HS[◦]… *Rev.: Annulets in quarters 2 & 3,* [✠]…GR·[OSPI]TΛ… *Worn.* KH

PLATE 134

14th Century Anonymous Obols *c.* 1350-1377, (Site finds)

Obv.: Châtel, annulet, platelet or dot within; in beaded circle. Rev.: Cross pattee or Maltese, annulets with platelets in opposite quarters; within beaded circle.

2741 (505) 16, 0.3 *Obv.: Annulet within,* [ ]CIVI[T]HS… *Rev.: Annulets in quarters 1 & 4,* ✠MHGR◦O…
2742 (528) 15, 0.6 *Obv.: Annulet within,* …HS[◦]RODI[*Rev.: Annulets,* …[PITA]… I.78
2743 (1124) 17, 0.5 *Obv.: Annulet within,* ✠CI[V]…DI◦ *Rev.: Annulets in quarters 1 & 4,* ✠MHGR·OS[P]… I.101
2744 (1210) 17, 0.4 *Obv.: Annulet within,* …[VI]…RODI[*Rev.: Annulets ◦ in quarters 1 & 4,* ✠[H]G[R]…THLI[*Corr., incomplete.* II.56
2745 (3788) 17, 0.7 *Obv.: Annulet within,* ✠CIVITHS[◦]…[DI] *Rev.: Annulets ◦ in quarters 1 & 4,* ✠MH…TH L∴ II.42
2746 (5948) 17, 0.4 *Obv.: Annulet ◦ within, dot r.,* ✠CI[ ]ITΛ[S]…ODI[◦] *Rev.: Annulets ◦ in quarters 1 & 4,* ✠[M]Λ…OSPIT… *Worn.* II.56
2747 (5956) 14, 0.3 *Obv.: Annulet within,* ✠[C]…ODI◦ *Rev.: Annulets in quarters 1 & 4,* ✠[M]HGR·OS… *Corr., incomplete.* II.56
2748 (350) 16, 0.4 *Obv.: [Dot within.] Rev.: Annulets,* …[P]ITΛ[L… *Corr., incomplete.*
2749 (357) 18, 0.4 *Obv.: Dot within,* [✠]CIVIT[A]… *Rev.: Annulets in quarters 1 & 4,* …R·OSPI… I.35
2750 (363) 18, 0.5 *Obv.: Annulet within,* ✠CIVI…IS[·] *Rev.: Annulets in quarters 1 & 4,* [✠M]ΛGR·… I.35
2751 (649) 16, 0.4 *Obv.: Annulet within,* ✠CI[VI]…[R]ODI *Rev.: Annulets in quarters 1 & 4,* ✠MΛ[ ]R·OSPITΛ[L]IS I.35
2752 (667) 15, 0.3 *Obv.: Annulet ◦ within,* [ ]CI… *Rev.: Annulets ◦ Corr.* II.63
2753 (989) 15, 0.4 *Obv.: Annulet within,* …T…RODI[ ] *Rev.: Annulets in quarters 1 & 4,* ✠M[H]GR·OSPIT[H… *Corr.* II.29
2754 (1187) 15, 0.5 *Obv.: Annulet ◦ within,* …[D]… *Rev.: Annulets ◦* II.56
2755 (1707) 16, 0.3 *Obv.: Annulet within,* [✠CIVI]… *Rev.: Annulets in quarters 1 & 4,* ✠C…H[’ ·]
2756 (1712) 16, 0.6 *Obv.: Annulet within,* ✠C…[ROD]I◦ *Rev.: Annulets in quarters 1 & 4,* ✠MH[G]R…SPI… II.18
2757 (3464) 16, 0.3 *Obv.: Annulet within,* …ODIS *Rev.: Annulets in quarters 1 & 4,* ✠…I◦ *Incomplete.* II.58
2758 (3787) 17, 0.7 *Obv.: Annulet within,* ✠C…RODI • *Rev.: Annulets ◦ in quarters 1 & 4,* ✠MΛ…[P]ITΛ[L∴] II.42
2759 (3789) 16, 0.4 *Obv.: Annulet within,* ✠CIVIT…[D]IS∵ *Rev.: Annulets ◦ in quarters 1 & 4,* ✠MΛGR[◦]OSPI…LI∵ II.42
2760 (4140) 15, 0.3 *Obv.: Annulet within. Rev.: Annulets in quarters 1 & 4,* …GR◦OSPI… *Incomplete.* II.41
2761 (4448) 16, 0.7 *Obv.: Annulet within,* ✠CIV…R[O]DI◦ *Rev.: Annulets ◦ in quarters 1 & 4,* ✠M…SPITHLI[II.50
2762 (4461) 19, 0.5 *Obv.: Annulet ◦ within,* ✠[ ]IVI… *Rev.: Annulets ◦ in quarters 1 & 4,* …SP…HLI· I.91
2763 (3935) 16, 0.4 *Obv.: Annulet within,* …IV…[] *Rev.: Annulets ◦ in quarters 1 & 4,* ✠M…TΛL◦ I.35
2764 (4626) 16, 0.3 *Obv.: Annulet within,* ✠CI[ ]IT… *Rev.: Annulets in quarters 1 & 4,* ✠MΛ… ◦…T… *Incomplete.* II.52
2765 (4628) 16, 0.3 *Obv.: Annulet within,* ✠CI… *Rev.: Annulets ◦ in quarters 1 & 4,* ✠M…IS[∵] *Worn, incomplete.* II.52
2766 (4852) 16, 0.3 *Obv.: Annulet within, [dot r.,]* ✠CIVI[T]… DI *Rev.: Annulets in quarters 1 & 4,* …GR◦OSP… *Corr., incomplete.* II.41
2767 (4853) 15, 0.2 *Obv.: Annulet within,* …IS… *Rev.: [Annulets ◦ in quarters 1 & 4,]* [✠M]…OS… *Corr., incomplete.* II.41

2768 (5373) 14, 0.5 *Obv.: Annulet within,* [ ]CI... *Rev.: Annulets in quarters 1 & 4,* ...R◦S[PI]... *Corr., incomplete.* II.56
2769 (5384) 16, 0.5 *Obv.: Annulet within,* ...ITᕼS◦RO... *Rev.: Annulets ◦ in quarters 1 & 4,* ✠ᗰᕼG...I· *Worn, incomplete.* II.56
2770 (5515) 15, 0.4 *Obv.: Annulet within,* ✠C... *Rev.: [Annulets ◦ in quarters 1 & 4,]* ...[S]PIT...I[ ] *Corr., incomplete.* II.56
2771 (5949) 16, 0.3 *Obv.: Annulet ◦ within,* ✠...S◦ROD[I *Rev.: Annulets ◦ in quarters 1 & 4,* ...GR[ ]OS[PI]... *Worn.* II.56
2772 (5950) 15, 0.3 *Obv.: Annulet ◦ within,* ✠CI[V]...[RO]... *Rev.: Annulets ◦ in quarters 1 & 4,* ...ᕼGR◦OS... *Worn, overstrike.* II.56
2773 (5960) 16, 0.2 *Obv.: Annulet ◦ within,* ...ODI... *Corr., incomplete.* II.56
2774 (5961) 16, 0.3 *Obv.: Annulet ◦ within,* [ ]C...S[◦]ROD... *Rev.: Annulets ◦ in quarters 1 & 4,* ✠...R·O[S]... *Corr., incomplete.* II.56
2775 (6095) 15, 0.3 *Obv.: Annulet within,* ...IV[I]... *Rev.: Annulets in quarters 1 & 4,* ✠[ᗰ]...IT... *Corr., incomplete.* II.23

PLATE 135
2776 (4023) 16, 0.6 *Obv.: [Annulet within,]* [ ]CIVITΛROD[IS] *Rev.: Annulets in quarters 1 & 4,* ✠ᗰΛGR[ ]SPITΛ[L∴] I.35
2777 (652) 17, 0.4 *Obv.: [Annulet within,]* ✠CIVITΛS[ ]RODI *Rev.: Annulets in quarters 1 & 4,* ✠ᗰΛGR◦OSPI... I.35
2778 (1178) 15, 0.5 *Obv.: [Annulet within,]* ...[O]DIS[.] *Rev.: Annulets ◦ in quarters 1 & 4,* ✠ᗰᕼG... II.56
2779 (1199) 16, 0.3 *Obv.: [Annulet within,]* ✠CIVI...RCDI◦ *Rev.: Annulets in quarters 1 & 4,* ...GR[◦]OSPITᕼLI[II.56
2780 (5725) 16, 0.3 *Obv.: [Annulet within,]* [ ]SIVITᕼ... *Rev.:* ✠ᗰ...ᕼĿ · *Corr.* II.56
2781 (5957) 16, 0.6 *Obv.: [Annulet within,]* ✠CIVI...[S] *Rev.: Annulets ◦ in quarters 1 & 4,* [✠]ᕼGR[ ]OSPITᕼLI... *Worn.* II.56
2782 (5958) 15, 0.4 *Obv.: [Annulet within,]* ...S◦R... *Rev.: Annulets ◦ in quarters 1 & 4,* [ ]ᗰᕼGR·OS... *Corr.* II.56
2783 (994) 15, 0.6 *Obv.: Dot within,* ✠CIV...S *Rev.: Annulets in quarters 1 & 4,* ✠ᗰ...ΛĿI◦ II.29
2784 (1709) 15, 0.4 *Obv.: Platelet within,* [✠]CIVI[Λ]S[ ]RO[D]... *Rev.: Annulets in quarters 1 & 4,* ✠ᗰΛGR◦OS...
2785 (3579) 14, 0.4 *Obv.: Platelet within,* ✠CIVITΛRODIS *Rev.: Annulets in quarters 1 & 4,* [ᗰ]...R·OSPIT[ΛL] II.58
2786 (5824) 15, 0.5 *Obv.: Platelet within,* ✠C... *Worn.* II.57
2787 (3404) 14, 0.3 *Obv.: Platelet within,* ✠CIV...S[·]*Rev.: Annulets in quarters 1 & 4,* ...[OSPITΛ]... *Corr.* II.33
2788 (3630) 16, 0.4 *Obv.: Platelet within,* ✠CIVIT...IS *Rev.: Annulets in quarters 1 & 4,* ✠ᗰΛGR...SPITΛ... II.58
2789 (3785) 17, 0.6 *Obv.: Platelet within,* ✠CI...S[◦]... *Rev.: Annulets ◦ in quarters 1 & 4,* [ᗰᕼGR·OSPI[T]... II.42
2790 (4138) 15, 0.4 *Obv.: Platelet within,* ✠C...S *Rev.: Annulets in quarters 1 & 4,* ...ᗰ...[IT]ᕼĿ... II.41
2791 (4171) 16, 0.4 *Obv.: Platelet within,* ✠CIVI[T]... *Rev.: Annulets in quarters 1 & 4,* [ ]ᗰΛ...T... *Incomplete.*
2792 (4339) 17, 0.4 *Obv.: Platelet within,* ...DIS *Rev.: Annulets in quarters 1 & 4,* ...Λ[GR]... *Corr., incomplete.* II.53
2793 (4342) 18, 0.6 *Obv.: Platelet within,* ✠C...TΛS[◦R DIS] *Rev.: Annulets ◦ in quarters 1 & 4,* ✠...ΛG...ᕼL'· *Corr.* II.53
2794 (4585) 15, 0.3 *Obv.: Platelet within,* ...OD... *Rev.:*...[P]... *Corr., incomplete.* II.28
2795 (4664) 14, 0.4 *Obv.: Platelet within,* ✠CI...S· *Rev.: Annulets ◦ in quarters 1 & 4,* ✠ᗰΛ...I◦ *Worn, incomplete.* II.52
2796 (5284) 17, 0.4 *Obv.: Platelet within,* ✠...TΛRODIS *Rev.: Annulets in quarters 1 & 4,* ✠...R·OSRI... ΛLI◦ *Corr., incomplete.* II.41
2797 (5992) 15, 0.3 *Obv.: Platelet within,* ...ᕼ[S] ◦... *Rev.: Annulets in quarters 1 & 4,* ✠ᗰᕼG[R]... II.56
2798 (4820) 16, 0.3 *Obv.: [Platelet within,]* ✠...RODI ◦̇◦ *Rev.: Annulets ◦ in quarters 1 & 4,* ✠...GR[◦]...ᕼ[Ŀ]I *Worn, incomplete.* II.48
2799 (5451) 16, 0.5 *Obv.: [Platelet within,]* [C]I...S·RO... *Rev.: Annulets,* ✠ᗰΛG[R]... *Corr., incomplete.* II.56
2800 (5947) 17, 0.3 *Obv.: [Platelet within,]* ✠CI[ ]ITΛ[S]...IS *Rev.: Annulets ◦ in quarters 1 & 4,* ✠...[GR OS]PITΛĿI· *Worn, incomplete.* II.56

PLATE 136
2801 (5177) 15, 0.2 *Obv.: Annulet within,* ✠CIVI...IS *Rev.: Annulets ◦ in quarters 1 & 4,* ...OS... ΛLI◦ *Corr., incomplete.* II.14
2802 (4497) 16, 0.4 *Obv.: Annulet ◦ within,* ...Tᕼ...ROD... *Rev.: Annulets in quarters 1 & 4,* ...GR◦O... *Worn, incomplete.* II.57
2803 (1123) 17, 0.7 *Obv.: Dot within,* ✠CI...TΛROD[IS] *Rev.: Annulets in quarters 1 & 4,* ✠ᗰΛGR...IT[ᕼĿ]I[I.101
2804 (4458) 17, 0.5 *Obv.: Dot within,* ✠...[I]TΛS◦RODI *Rev.: Annulets ◦ in quarters 1 & 4,* ✠...[ ]OSPITᕼ[L]· I.91
2805 (4663) 17, 0.6 *Obv.: Dot within,* ✠CIVIT[ᕼ]S◦RODIS∴ *Rev.: Annulets in quarters 1 & 4,* ✠ᗰᕼGR◦OS[P]...ᕼL· II.52
2806 (5955) 16, 0.4 *Obv.: Dot within,* ✠CIVIT...[O]DI *Rev.: Annulets ◦ in quarters 1 & 4,* [ ]ᗰᕼGR[ ]OSPITᕼĿI... *Corr., incomplete.* II.56
2807 (1710) 16, 0.5 *Obv.: Dot within,* [✠]CIVI[T]... *Rev.: Annulets in quarters 1 & 4,* ✠ᗰᕼGR[·]OS...
2808 (4142) 15, 0.5 *Obv.: Dot within. Rev.: Annulets. Worn.* II.41
2809 (4430) 16, 0.4 *Obv.: Dot within,* ✠C...IS *Rev.: Annulets in quarters 1 & 4,* ✠ᗰΛGR◦OS... II.34
2810 (4449) 18, 0.2 *Obv.: Dot within,* ✠CIVITᕼS...S *Rev.: Annulets ◦ in quarters 1 & 4,* ✠ᗰΛGR... ĿS: *Incomplete.* II.50
2811 (4541) 17, 0.6 *Obv.: Dot within,* ... ΛS◦ROD... *Rev.: Annulets in quarters 1 & 4,* ...ᕼGR◦OS[P]... *Worn, incomplete.* II.35
2812 (5959) 15, 0.3 *Obv.: Dot within,* ...◦R... *Rev.: Annulets in quarters 1 & 4,* ...SPI... *Corr.* II.56
2813 (5993) 16, 0.5 *Obv.: Dot within,* ...S◦[ ]ODI[*Rev.: Annulets in quarters 1 & 4,* ✠ᗰᕼG[R·OS]... II.56
2814 (6000) 15, 0.3 *Obv.: Dot within,* ✠CIVI[T]...DI *Rev.: Annulets ◦ in quarters 1 & 4,* ...ᕼG...ᕼ[L·] II.56
2815 (6010) 14, 0.3 *Obv.: Dot within,* ✠C[ ]V... *Rev.: Annulets,* ...[I]... *Worn, incomplete.* II.64
2816 (4025) 15, 0.4 *Obv.: [Dot r.,]* ...DI[ ] *Rev.: Annulets in quarters [1 & 4],* [✠ᗰΛ]... I.35

2817 (4131) 16, 0.4 *Obv.: [Dot within,]* +CIVIT[A]S... *Rev.: Annulets in quarters 1 & 4,* ...OSPITAL... *Incomplete.* II.59
2818 (4141) 16, 0.3 *Obv.: [Dot within,]* ...VI...RO... *Rev.: Annulets in quarters 1 & 4,* +MAGR[ ]OSPI... *Incomplete.* II.41
2819 (513) 17, 0.6 *Obv.:* +CI...S[∘]RODI· *Rev.: Annulets in quarters 1 & 4,* ...A[ ]R...OSP[ ]T... II.50
2820 (1207) 15, 0.4 *Obv.:* +CIVI...[D]I∘ *Rev.: Annulets* ∘ *in quarters 1 & 4,* ...AG[R∘]OS[P]... II.56
2821 (3523) 17, 0.5 *Obv.:* +C...[·] *Rev.: Annulets in quarters 1 & 4,* +MAGR·OSPIT[L ∵] *Worn.* II.58
2822 (3551) 17, 0.3 *Obv.:* +CIV...∘R...I *Rev.: Annulets in quarters 1 & 4,* +...R∘OSP...ALS *Corr., incomplete.* II.58
2823 (4305) 16, 0.3 *Obv.:* +...S∘RODI[*Rev.: Annulets in quarters 1 & 4,* +...R[ ]OSPIT[ALI] *Incomplete.* II.53
2824 (4328) 15, 0.4 *Obv.:* +CIV...DI· *Rev.: [Annulets,]* ...R·OSP... *Corr., incomplete.* II.53
2825 (4338) 15, 0.4 *Obv.:* ...S∘... *Rev.:*...A...[·S]... *Corr., incomplete.* II.53
2826 (4362) 18, 0.6 *Obv.:* +CIVIT...I· *Rev.: Annulets in quarters 1 & 4,* ...L·... *Corr.* II.20
2827 (4450) 17, 0.5 *Obv.:* ...ITA... *Rev.: Annulets* ∘ *in quarters 1 & 4,* +...TA[L]. II.50
2828 (4484) 13, 0.2 *Corr., incomplete.* II.57

2829 (4493) 16, 0.4 *Rev.: Annulets,* ...⁚... *Corr., incomplete.* II.57
2830 (4582) 15, 0.5 *Obv.:* +C...DI· *Rev.: Annulets in quarters 1 & 4,* ...TAL · *Corr.* II.29
2831 (4632) 17, 0.6 *Obv.:* ...S·RO[D]... *Rev.: Annulets* ∘ *in quarters 1 & 4,* +MAGR∘OS[ ]ITALI[*Doublestruck.* II.52
2832 (4638) 15, 0.3 *Worn.* II.52
2833 (4639) 16, 0.2 *Corr.* II.52
2834 (4805) 16, 0.5 *Obv.:* +...∘̈ *Rev.:*...OS... *Corr., incomplete.* II.64
2835 (4850) 17, 0.5 *Obv.:* +CI...S[·]RO... *Rev.: Annulets in quarters 1 & 4,* ...GR∘OS...T... *Worn, incomplete.* II.41

PLATE 137
2836 (5292) 15, 0.3 *Obv.:* +CIV...IS *Rev.: Annulets in quarters 1 & 4,* +MAGR[ ]OSPITAL[I]· *Corr.* II.41
2837 (5410) 16, 0.4 *Obv.: Annulet within,* ...S *Rev.: Annulets in quarters 1 & 4,* ...OSPIT[AL]S[*Corr.* II.56
2838 (5420) 15, 0.4 *Obv.:* +C... *Rev.: Annulets in quarters 1 & 4,* [+M]...[L] *Worn, bent.* II.56
2839 (5427) 16, 0.6 *Rev.:* +MAG... *Corr., bent.* II.56
2840 (5438) 13, 0.3 *Obv.:* ... RODI *Rev.: Annulets in quarters 1 & 4,* +M... *Corr., incomplete.* II.56
2841 (5450) 15, 0.5 *Obv.:* ...S... *Rev.: Annulets. Corr.* II.56
2842 (5513) 16, 0.5 *Obv.:* ...RO... *Corr., incomplete, bent.* II.56
2843 (5589) 15, 0.3 *Obv.:* [+]C... *Rev.: Annulets in quarters 1 & 4,* ...R∘O... *Corr., incomplete.* II.56
2844 (5732) 13, 0.1 *Rev.: Annulets in quarters 1 & 4,* ...GR[∘ O]... *Worn, fragment.* II.56
2845 (5888) 15, 0.4 *Rev.:* ...GR... *Corr., incomplete.* II.56
2846 (5898) 13, 0.3 *Obv.:* ...I...IT[A]... *Rev.: Annulets in quarters 1 & 4,* +...I∘ *Corr., incomplete.* II.56
2847 (5945) 12, 0.1 *Obv.:* ...[I]S *Rev.: [Annulets],* ...[PIT]... *Corr., incomplete.* II.56
2848 (5946) 15, 0.3 *Rev.: [Annulets] Corr., incomplete.* II.56
2849 (5951) 17, 0.5 *Rev.: Annulets in quarters 1 & 4,* ...OSP... *Worn, doublestruck.* II.56
2850 (5952) 18, 0.5 *Obv.:* +CIVIT[ ]S... *Rev.: Annulets in quarters 1 & 4,* [ ]MAGR∘OS[P]...AL[˙]S *Worn, doublestruck.* II.56
2851 (5984) 14, 0.2 *Rev.: Dot below cross. Fragment, corr.* II.56
2852 (5291) 16, 0.3 *Obv.: Annulet within,* +CIV...S·R...S· *Rev.: Annulets* ∘ *in quarters 2 & 3,* +MAGR·O[ ]PI... *Corr., incomplete.* II.41
2853 (4615) 16, 0.5 *Obv.: Dot within,* +C[IV]...S·RODIS· *Rev.: Annulets in quarters 2 & 3,* [+M]AGR·OS...A[L]I[ ] *Worn, incomplete.* II.52
2854 (5962) 15, 0.1 *Obv.:* [CI]... *Rev.: [Annulets in quarters 2 & 3],* ...GR[ ]OS... *Corr., incomplete.* II.56

PLATE 138
2855 (5377) 16, 0.4 *Obv.: Annulet within,* [ ]CIVI...[DI] *Rev.: Platelets in quarters 1 & 4,* ...R·O...S[ ] *Worn.* II.56
2856 (1182) 15, 0.5 *Obv.: Annulet within,* +CI[ ]I...S˙ *Rev.: Platelets in quarters 1 & 4,* ...GR[ ]OSPIT... II.56
2857 (5953) 16, 0.4 *Obv.: Annulet within,* ...S...OD... *Rev.: [Platelets]. Corr.* II.56
2858 (187) 17, 0.6 *Obv.: Dot within,* ...DI[⸽] *Rev.: Platelets in quarters 1 & 4,* +...[LI]... Town
2859 (1163) 15, 0.5 *Obv.: Dot within,* ...S∘RO[D]... *Rev.: Platelets in quarters 1 & 4,* +MA...IS
2860 (5910) 17, 0.4 *Obv.: Dot within,* +CIVITAS∘R...S[∘] *Rev.: Platelets in quarters 1 & 4,* +MA[ ]R[ ]OS[P]...A[L]IS *Corr.* II.56
2861 (360) 16, 0.6 *Obv.: [Dot within,]* ...A... *Rev.: Platelets.* I.35
2862 (4315) 15, 0.3 *Rev.: Platelets in quarters 1 & 4,* ... A[ ]R·O...ITAL... *Corr., incomplete.* II.53
2863 (4849) 17, 0.5 *Obv.: Dot within,* +CIVITAS∘RODI⁖ *Rev.: Platelets in quarters 1 & 4,* +M...R[·]OSPIT[AL]IS· II.41
2864 (3786) 16, 0.7 *Obv.:* ⧊, *Dot within,* +CIVITAS[ ]RODI *Rev.: Platelets in quarters 2 & 3,* +MAGR·OSPITAL'.˙ II.42
2865 (5990) 16, 0.7 *Obv.:* ⧊, +CIVITA...ODI *Rev.: Platelets in quarters 2 & 3,* +M...[:] *Corr., incomplete.* II.56
2866 (4453) 16 0.6 *Obv.:* ⧊, *Dot within,* ...AS[ ]RODI[*Rev.: Platelets in quarters 2 & 3,* [ ]MAG... I.91
2867 (5724) 16, 0.6 *Obv.:* ⧊, +CIVI...[ODI] *Rev.: Platelets in quarters 2 & 3,* ...R·O[PIT]... *Worn.* II.41
2868 (3934) 15, 0.4 *Obv.:* ⧊, *Dot within,* +CI...S[·]RODI *Rev.: Platelets in quarters 2 & 3,* +M...OSPITAL... I.35
2869 (4143) 17, 0.4 *Obv.:* ⧊, *Dot within,* +CIVI[T]... : RODI *Rev.: Annulets in quarters 2 & 3,* [M]AG...[AL .]... II.41
2870 (4144) 15 0.3 *Obv.: Dot within,* +C...IS *Rev.: Platelets in quarters 1 & 4,* ...R·OSPIT... II.41
2871 (4848) 16 0.4 *Obv.:* ⧊, *Dot within,* +CIVIT[ ]S:RODI *Rev.: Platelets in quarters 2 & 3,* ...R:OSPITA... *Corr.* II.41

2872 (4846) 15, 0.5 *Obv.:* ⛬, ...T... *Rev.: Platelets in quarters 2 & 3,* ✠...R:... *Worn, incomplete.* II.41
2873 (5374) 16, 0.6 *Obv.:* [⛬] *Rev.: Platelets. Corr.* II.56
2874 (4487) 17, 0.7 *Obv.:* ⛬, ...[ROD]... *Rev.: Platelets. Worn.* II.57
2875 (5936) 18, 0.5 *Obv.:* ⛬, *Dot within,* [ ]ⱭIV...RO... *Rev.: Platelets in quarters 2 & 3,* [ᗰ]...R:OS... *Worn, overstrike.* II.56
2876 (1164) 15, 0.5 *Obv.:* ⛬, *Dot within,* [Ɑ]I... *Rev.: Platelets in quarters 2 & 3,* ...[R[·]OSPI...
2877 (5891) 16, 0.5 *Obv.:* ⛬, *Dot within,* ✠Ɑ[IV]I... *Rev.: Platelets in quarters 2 & 3,* ...:O... *Corr., incomplete.* II.56
2878 (4847) 15, 0.4 *Obv.:* ⛬, *Dot within,* ✠ⱭIVI...RODI *Rev.: Platelets in quarters 2 & 3,* ✠ᗰ...:OS...[L⁚] *Worn, incomplete.* II.41
2879 (4139) 16, 0.3 *Obv.:* ⛬, ✠ⱭIVI...DI *Rev.: Annulets in quarters 2 & 3,* [ᗰ]ΗG...[ΗL]... *Incomplete.* II.41
2880 (4312) 14, 0.2 *Obv.:* ⛬, *Dot within,* ✠ⱭI...O... *Rev.: Platelets in quarters 2 & 3,* ✠...R:OSPI... *Corr., incomplete.* II.53
2881 (5954) 14, 0.2 *Obv.:* ⛬, *Dot within,* ...S:RO... *Rev.: Platelets in quarters 2 & 3,* ✠...GR:... *Corr., incomplete.* II.56
2882 (4858) 14, 0.1 *Obv.:* ⛬ *Rev.: Platelets in quarters 2 & 3,...P... Corr., incomplete.* II.41
2883 (205) 16, 0.7 *Obv.:* ⛬, *Dot within,* ...IVIT...[ROD *Rev.: Platelets in quarters 2 & 3,* ...OSPI[Ʌ]L[

PLATE 139
Imitative 14th century obols
Obv.: Clumsy châtel, annulet within; in beaded circle. Rev.: Maltese cross, annulets in opposite corners; in beaded circle.
2884 (2172) 16, 0.6 *Obv.: Annulet* ◦ *within. Rev.:* [ᗰΗGR]... I. 94
2885 (3752) 14 *Obv.:* [✠Ɑ]...·ROⱭI· *Rev.: Annulets in quarters 1 & 4,* [✠ᗰ]ΗG[R]... *Worn.* II.42
2886 (1495) 15, 0.5 *Obv.:* ✠ⱭIVIT[ ]S... *Rev.: Annulets in quarters 1 & 4,* ✠ᗰΗPR✿OS...[ΗL]I[Ƨ IH
2887 (1500) 15, 0.6 *Obv.:* ...VI[ΠΗ]...RO *Rev.: Annulets in quarters 2 & 3,* ✠[ᗰ]...SP[I]Π[OO]. IH
2888 (1683) 15, 0.4 *Obv.:* ...TɅS✿R... *Rev.: Annulets in quarters 2 & 3,* [✠ᗰɅGR✿...ITΗ... IH
2889 (1997) 14, 0.4 *Obv.:* ...[OIT]... *Rev.:* ΗTIPƧO... IH
2890 (2205) 17, 0.6 *Obv.:* ...ΗRODI[*Rev.: platelets in quarters 2 & 3,* ✠ᗰɅ...ɅL' IH
2891 (2961) 14, 0.3 *Obv.:* ...V... *Doubled die. Rev.: Annulets in quarters 2 & 3,* ...ΗGR[ ]OSP[I]... IH
2892 (2962) 15, 0.4 *Obv.:* ✠ⱭI...O[D]... *Rev.: Annulets in quarters 1 & 4,* ...R✿OS[P]IT... IH
2893 (3003) 15, 0.5 *Obv.:* ✠Ɑ... *Rev.: Annulets in quarters 2 & 3,* ✠ᗰΗ[GR✿]... *Doubled die.* IH
2894 (3026) 14, 0.4 *Obv.:* ...IVITR[OD]... *Rev.: Annulets in quarters 1 & 4,* ✠ᗰɅ...OɅ IH
2895 (3027) 14, 0.5 *Obv.:* ...IVITɅS✿R... *Rev.: Annulets in quarters 2 & 3,* ✠ᗰɅ[ ]ROSP... IH
2896 (3028) 16, 0.5 *Obv.:* ...IVITɅS✿ROD... *Rev.: Annulets in quarters 1 & 4,* ...ΗGR[I]OSPI... IH
2897 (3052) 14, 0.3 *Obv.: Platelet within,* [✠ⱭI...ROD]... *Rev.:* ...[GRO]... IH
2898 (3058) 15, 0.5 *Rev.: Annulets in quarters 1 & 4,* ✠...[O]R◦OS... *Overstrike.* IH
2899 (3166) 15, 0.5 *Obv.:* [ ]ⱭIVITΗS◦RDO[*Rev.:* ...[IT]. IH
2900 (3183) 15, 0.4 *Obv.:* ✠Ɑ...DO◦ *Rev.: Annulets in quarters 2 & 3,* [ ]ᗰΗGR[ ]O... IH
2901 (3328) 15, 0.4 *Obv.:* ✠[◦]ⱭI[V]...[◦] *Rev.: Annulets in quarters 2 & 3,* ✠ᗰΗGR[ ]O... *Overstrike.* IH
2902 (8027) 15, 0.3 *Obv.:* ✠ⱭIVI...◦RO[DI *Rev.:* ...[OS[Π]U[Ɵ... / ✠... *Overstrike.* IH
2903 (8043) 16, 0.6 *Obv.:* ✠Ɑ... *Rev.: Annulets in quarters 1 & 4,* ✠ᗰΗGR[ ]OS[PI]Η *Doubled dies.* IH
2904 (8146) 14, 0.4 *Obv.:* ...[Rh O] *Rev.: Annulets in quarters 2 & 3,* ✠ᗰ...[TΗL] *Overstrike.* IH
2905 (8231) 14, 0.4 *Obv.:* [✠]ⱭIVI...O[OI◦] *Rev.:* ...OƧ[PΠ]VƟ[LI·]... IH
2906 (8232) 14, 0.6 *Obv.:* [✠]ⱭIVITɅS◦RO... *Rev.:* ...O... IH
2907 (8233) 14, 0.6 *Obv.:* ...S◦RODI◦ *Rev.:* ✠ᗰ...O[ ]◦ IH
2908 (8234) 14, 0.6 *Obv.:* ...IO[I]...O... *Rev.:* ...OƧ[P]... IH
2909 (9115) 14, 0.4 *Obv.:* [ ]ⱭIV...[S· R] *Rev.: Annulets in quarters 2 & 3,* ✠ᗰ[Ʌ]...◦OS...[T] *Worn.* KH
2910 (9764) 15, 0.3 *Obv.:* ...ⱭIV...IƧ · ROD... *Doubled die. Rev.:* ✠ᗰ... *Overstrike.* KH
2911 (9765) 15, 0.5 *Obv.:* ...IVITɅ... *Rev.: Annulets in quarters 2 & 3,* ✠ᗰ...[◦]... *Overstrike.* KH
2912 (9891) 14, 0.4 *Obv.: Dot within. Rev.: Annulets in quarters 1 & 4,* ...R◦O... *Doubled dies.* KH
2913 (9918) 15, 0.4 *Obv.:* ✠Ɑ...TɅS[◦]ROD *Rev.: Annulets* ◦ *in quarters 1 & 4,* ✠ᗰ...OSPIΠ *Overstrike.* KH
2914 (9976) 15, 0.4 *Obv.:* [ ]ⱭIVITɅ... *Rev.: Annulets in quarters 1 & 4,* ✠ᗰΗGR... *Overstrike.* KH
2915 (9977) 14, 0.4 *Obv.:* ✠ⱭI... .ROD *Rev.: Annulets in quarters 1 & 4,* ✠...R◦...IΠ[ ] *Overstrike.* KH
2916 (9980) 15, 0.4 *Obv.:* ✠Ɑ...OD *Rev.: Annulets in quarters 2 & 3,* ✠ᗰ[G]... *Overstrike.* KH
2917 (9981) 15, 0.4 *Rev.: Annulets in quarters 1 & 4,* ✠ᗰ...PI... *Overstrike.* KH
2918 (9984) 15, 0.3 *Obv.:* ✠ⱭIVIΠΗƧ•[RO... *Rev.: Annulets in quarters 1 & 4,* ✠ᗰ[ɅG]R◦OƧ... *Overstrike.* KH

PLATE 140
15th Century Anonymous Obols
Obv.: Châtel; annulet or dot within; in beaded circle. Rev.: Maltese cross, annulets in opposite quarters; within beaded circle.
2919 (3466) 16, 0.4 *Obv.: Janua,* ✠ᗰɅGIS...OSPITɅLIS *Rev.: Annulets in quarters 1 & 4,* ✠...[OS]ɅLƟᗰITɅПIRODI II.58
2920 (4692) 14, 0.4 *Obv.: Janua, dot r.* ✠ᗰɅGIST...ITɅLI *Rev.: Annulets [in quarters 2 & 3],* ...TɅПIR... *Worn.* II.47
2921 (5393) 16, 0.5 *Obv.: Janua,* ✠ᗰɅGISTRIOSPITɅLIS· *Rev.: Annulets in quarters 2 & 3,* ...OSΗLIᗰITɅП[ ]RO... *Corr.* II.56
2922 (5409) 16, 0.4 *Obv.: Janua, [platelet within, dot r.]* ✠ᗰɅGIST...[Ʌ◦]S *Rev.: Annulets [in quarters 1 & 4],* ...Ʌ[L] ƟᗰIT... *Corr., incomplete.* II.56

2923 (5792) 15, 0.4 *Obv.: Janua,* ...[ISTRI]OSPITⲀĿS *Rev.: Annulets in quarters 1 & 4,* +IЄROSⲀĿЄᗰITⲀ... *Corr., incomplete.* II.41
2924 (659) 14, 0.3 *Obv.: Janua, platelet within,* [+ᗰ]ⲀGISTR[IOS]... *Rev.: Annulets in quarters 1 & 4,* [+]IЄROSⲀL[Єᗰ]...
2925 (5967) 14, 0.3 *Obv.: Janua,* +ᗰⲀGIST...IT...IS *Rev.: Annulets in quarters 1 & 4,* +IЄROSⲀ...I...ROꝹ *Corr., incomplete.* II.56
2926 (5278) 15, 0.4 *Obv.: Janua,* +ᗰⲀGI...S·IO *Rev.: Annulets,* ...[ⲀLЄ]... *Corr. [Doubled die.]* II.20
2927 (3712) 16, 0.8 *Obv.: Janua,* ...ITĦLI... *Rev.: Annulets in quarters 2 & 3,* + ·...PITⲀL...I[] II.33
2928 (5407) 14, 0.4 *Obv.: Janua, [platelet within,]* +Ɑ...TⲀĿS *Rev.: Platelets in quarters 2 & 3,* +IЄRO[S Ŀ]...IRO *Corr.* II.56
2929 (5791) 14, 0.6 *Obv.: Janua,* ...TRIOSPITⲀ[L]... *Rev.: Annulets in quarters 1 & 4,* ...ĿЄᗰITⲀȠI... *Corr.; doubled die.* II.41
2930 (5876) 17, 0.5 *Obv.: Janua, [annulet within,]* ...STRIOSPITⲀĿS *Rev.: Platelets in quarters 2 & 3,* ...SⲀĿЄᗰITⲀȠIRO... *Corr.* II.56
2931 (541) 13, 0.3 *Obv.: Janua, platelet within,* ...[Ⲁ]GISTRIOSPITⲀ... *Rev.: Platelets in quarters 2 & 3,* +IЄROS[Ⲁ]...Ⲁ[Ƞ] IRO
2932 (5615) 14, 0.4 *Obv.: Janua,* +ᗰⲀGIS...[Ŀ]S *Rev.: Platelets in quarters 2 & 3,* +IЄRO...[R]OꝹI· *Corr., incomplete.* II.41
2933 (5968) 15, 0.3 *Obv.: Janua,* +ᗰⲀGISTRIO...IT... *Rev.: Platelets in quarters 2 & 3,* +IЄ...ȠIRO *Corr.* II.56
2934 (3542) 15, 0.5 *Obv.: Janua,* ...PITⲀLS *Rev.: Platelets [in quarters 2 & 3,]* ...SⲀLЄ... *Corr., incomplete.* II.58
2935 (406) 16, 0.6 *Obv.: Annulet within,* +ᗰⲀGISTR[IOSPITⲀ]LIS *Rev.: Annulets in quarters 2 & 3,* ...ⲀLЄᗰITⲀȠIRO... II.54
2936 (579*) *Obv.: Annulet within,* +ᗰⲀG...[ST]... *Rev.: Annulets in quarters 2 & 3,* +...TⲀLIR[hO]Ꝺ:
2937 (699) 13, 0.4 *Obv.: Annulet within,* ...ⲀGISTRIOSPITⲀ[LIS *Rev.: Annulets in quarters 1 & 4,* ...IЄROSⲀLЄᗰITⲀ I.1
2938 (1040) 15, 0.4 *Obv.: [Annulet within,]* +ᗰⲀGISTRI·OSPITⲀL... *Rev.: Annulets in quarters 1 & 4,* +IЄRO[ ] ⲀLЄᗰITⲀȠIROꝹ· II.15
2939 (1714) 13, 0.4 *Obv.: Annulet within,* +...IST[RI]OSPITⲀLIS *Rev.: Annulets in quarters 2 & 3,* +IЄROSⲀLЄ[ᗰ]I[T] ⲀȠI·ROꝹ II.18
2940 (3413) 16, 0.4 *Obv.: Annulet within,* ...GISTRIOSPI...IS[] *Rev.: Annulets in quarters 1 & 4,* +IЄR[O]S[Ħ]LЄ·...Ⲁ[ȠI] ROꝹ II.33
2941 (3453) 14, 0.4 *Obv.: Annulet within,* +[ᗰ]Ħ[G]...IS[.] *Rev.: Annulets in quarters 1 & 4,* +IЄ...ROꝹI•⁚ *Corr.* II.58
2942 (3454) 14, 0.3 *Obv.: Annulet within,* +...[Ⲁ]...•⁚ *Rev.: Annulets in quarters 1 & 4. Corr.* II.58
2943 (5499) 16, 0.4 *Obv.: Annulet within,* +ᗰⲀGISTRI... *Rev.: Annulets in quarters 2 & 3,* +IЄRUSⲀĿЄᗰITⲀȠ...[O]ꝹI *Corr.* II.56
2944 (4534) 14, 0.4 *Obv.: [Annulet within,]* +ᗰⲀGISTR[ ] · O... *Rev.: Annulets in quarters 2 & 3,* +IЄRO[S]...ⲀȠIR[ ]Ꝺ[*Corr.* II.14
2945 (5523) 14, 0.5 *Obv.: Annulet within,* +ᗰⲀGI[STЄ]...IS· *Rev.: Annulets in quarters 1 & 4,* +IЄRO...ⲀȠIROꝹ *Corr.* II.56
2946 (5753) 14, 0.3 *Obv.: Annulet within,* +ᗰⲀGI[S]... *Rev.: Annulets in quarters 2 & 3,* +IЄ... ĿЄᗰITⲀ...R[ ]ꝹI: *Corr.* II.41
2947 (5969) 15, 0.3 *Obv.: Annulet ◦ within,* +ᗰⲀGISTRI... *Rev.: Annulets in quarters 2 & 3,* +IЄRO...IROꝹI: *Corr., incomplete.* II.56
2948 (5973) 15, 0.5 *Obv Annulet within,* ...SPIT[Ⲁ]...S... *Rev.: Annulets in quarters 2 & 3,* ...ЄROSO[ ]IᗰITⲀȠI[R]... *Corr., incomplete.* II.56
2949 (5977) 14, 0.4 *Obv.: Annulet within,* ...TЄ[R]OSPIT... *Rev.: Annulets in quarters 2 & 3,* [ ]IЄRUS...[RhO]... *Corr., incomplete.* II.56

PLATE 141

2950 (1150) 16, 1.1 *Obv.: Annulet within, legend crosslet below,* +...[PT]DI[·]S *Rev.: Annulets in quarters 1 & 4,* +OSPITⲀ... SSIO I.63
2951 (6014) 17, 0.7 *Obv.: Annulet within initial crosslet below,* +O....[ĦU]IS·[ ]·I *Rev.: Annulets. Incomplete.* II.64
2952 (3980) 16, 0.7 *Obv.: Dot within,* ...PI[O]S... *Rev.: Annulets in quarters 2 & 3,* +ᗰOS...IS·SI· II.10
2953 (4386) 15, 0.6 *Obv.: Dot within, initial crosslet below,* +OSPI... *Rev.: Annulets in quarters 1 & 4,*...OSPITLI II.20
2954 (4215) 14, 0.4 *Obv.: Dot within,* ...[S]IO *Rev.: Annulets in quarters 1 & 4,* +[Ɑ]...S *Worn.*
2955 (408) 17, 0.6 *Obv.: Dot within,* +...IS[...]SIO *Rev.: Annulets in quarters 2 & 3,* +O...P II.54
2956 (4382) 13, 0.5 *Obv.: Dot within,* +...SIO *Rev.: Annulets. Corr., incomplete.* II.20
2957 (5475) 15, 0.6 *Obv.: Annulet within,* +OSP... *Rev.: Annulets in quarters 1 & 4,* +OSPIT... *Corr., incomplete.* II.56
2958 (5504) 16, 0.3 *Obv.: Annulet within,* +OSP...[hⲀ]O *Rev.: Annulets in quarters 1 & 4,* +OS[PIT]... *Corr.* II.56
2959 (558) 18, 0.6 *Obv.: Annulet ◦ within,* ...[O]S... *Doubled die. Rev.: Annulets in quarters 2 & 3,* ...PITLISSIO II.55
2960 (4062) 17, 0.5 *Obv.: Dot within,* +[ ]OSP...SIO *Rev.: Annulets,* +ᗰO...SSIO II.5
2961 (3631) 16, 0.5 *Obv.: Dot within,* ...OS... *Rev.: Annulets in quarters 1 & 4,* +ᗰ[ ]S...[SS]IO *Corr., incomplete.* II.58
2962 (5761) 15, 0.4 *Obv.: Dot within,* +[ᗰ]...[R]UI *Rev.: Annulets,* ...[IS]SIO... *Corr.* II.41
2963 (6075) 17, 0.4 *Obv.: Annulet within,* +OSPIT... *Rev.: Annulets in quarters 1 & 4,* +...SIO *Worn.* II.23
2964 (3992) 16, 0.6 *Obv.: Dot within,* [ ]ᗰO[ ]I... *Rev.: Annulets in quarters 1 & 4,* +[O]...S·SI II.10
2965 (563) 16, 0.3 *Obv.:* +O...LISSIO *Rev.: Annulets in quarters 1 & 4,* +O[S]...ISSIO II.55

2966 (1713) 16, 0.6 *Obv.: Dot within,* ...OSPT... *Rev.: Annulets in quarters 2 & 3,* [M]OSPI[L]IS... II.18
2967 (3983) 15, 0.6 *Obv.:* ...TLI... *Rev.: Annulets in quarters 2 & 3,* +MOS[P]...SIO[• •] *Broken.* II.10
2968 (399) 15, 0.5 *Obv.: Dot within and inside the roof,* +...[IT L]S...SIO... *Rev.: Annulets in quarters 1 & 4,* [h]OS[P] ITLI... II.54
2969 (1025) 15, 0.7 *Obv.: Dot within,* ...[I S]...[I]O[*Rev.: Annulets in quarters 1 & 4,* [+]...ΛL *Doubled die.* II.31
2970 (4433) 16, 0.3 *Obv.: Annulet within,* ...IS... *Rev.: Annulets [in quarters 2 & 3],* ...SS... *Corr.* II.34
2971 (5245) 16, 0.7 *Obv.: Dot within,* ...OSPI[TLIS]... *Rev.: Annulets in quarters 2 & 3,* +[ ]OS...[ΛL]SSIO[ ] II.55
2972 (4181) 15, 0.3 *Obv.: Annulet within,* ...SPITſ... *Rev.: Annulets in quarters 1 & 4,* +[M]...SIO *Worn.* II.32
2973 (87) 16, 0.5 *Obv.: Platelet within,* ...S[I]O... *Rev.: Annulets in quarters 1 & 4,* +...IS·SI V.2
2974 (194) 14, 0.3 *Obv.: Dot within,* ...EN...DI[*Rev.: Annulets in quarters 2 & 3,* +OSPITAL[IS]...I...
2975 (1027) 18, 0.7 *Obv.: Dot within,* [+CO]...LI... *Rev.: Annulets in quarters 2 & 3,* [+]OSPI... II.31
2976 (1155) 13, 0.3 *Obv.: [Platelet within,]* ...E...[h]ODI[*Rev.:* [+]OSPIT[Λ... I.86
2977 (3988) 16, 0.4 *Obv.:* +...TORODI *Rev.: Annulets in quarters 1 & 4,* +OS[PITA]...M II.10
2978 (5503) 15, 0.3 *Obv.: Annulet within,* +[C]NU...O... *Rev.: Annulets in quarters 2 & 3,* +IERVSΛLE... *Corr.* II.56

PLATE 142

2979 (5391) 13, 0.2 *Obv.:* ...MΛGISTRI[S]... *Rev.: Annulets in quarters 2 & 3,* ...STERhOPTΛ... *Corr., incomplete.* II.56
2980 (5730) 16, 0.7 *Obv.: Annulet within,* [MAGI]STEROSPIT[A *Rev.: Platelets in quarters 1 & 4,* +MAGISTERO... II.41
2981 (4716) 14, 0.5 *Obv.: Dot within,* ...IST[R]IO...IS· *Rev.: Annulets in quarters 1 & 4,* +[ΛG]...TΛLI... *Corr.* II.47
2982 (5534) 15, 0.4 *Obv.: Annulet within,* +...ALISIE[RU] *Rev.: Annulets in quarters 1 & 4,* +OSPI...[L] *Corr., incomplete.* II.56
2983 (429) 14, 0.3 *Obv.: Annulet within,* +CON[U]...ODI *Rev.: Annulets in quarters 1 & 4,* +CO[N]VENT[ ]S II.54
2984 (909) 15, 0.5 *Obv.: [annulet within,]* +CON...S *Rev.:* ...ONV[E]... I.45
2985 (5700) 14, 0.4 *Obv.: Dot within,* +CONUENTU...OCI *Rev.: Annulets in quarters 1 & 4,* +IE...ΛRhO[D:] *Corr., incomplete.* II.41
2986 (508) 15, 0.4 *Obv.: [Annulet within,]* [+C]NUEN... *Rev.: Annulets in quarters 1 & 4,* ...ALISIERVSAL... II.50
2987 (605) 17, 0.6 *Obv.: Dot within,*+CO[N E]NTO...[C]I[S] *Rev.: Annulets in quarters 1 & 4,* +...TALISIERVSALE... II.18
2988 (3728) 15, 0.5 *Obv.:* [C]O...NTOROC[I]. *Rev.: Annulets in quarters 1 & 4,* +OS...ERVSALE... II.14
2989 (5454) 16, 0.6 *Obv.: [Annulet within,]* +C...ENT...[R]OCI *Rev.: Annulets in quarters 1 & 4,* ...ITALIS...RVSA... II.56
2990 (5467) 14, 0.3 *Obv.: Annulet within,* ...O[RO]... *Rev.: Annulets in quarters 1 & 4,* +OS[P]...SALE *Corr., incomplete.* II.56
2991 (5502) 14, 0.5 *Obv.: Annulet within,* ...[ONUENTU]... *Rev.: Annulets in quarters 1 & 4,* [+OSP]IT...ERVSΛLE *Corr.* II.56
2992 (5671) 14, 0.5 *Obv.: Annulet within,* +CON...[R]ODI *Rev.: Annulets [in quarters 2 & 3],* ...RVSALE... II.41
2993 (5675) 16, 0.4 *Obv.: Annulet within,* +CONUENT...[R]ODI *Rev.: Annulets in quarters 1 & 4,* ...PITALISIERVS[A]... *Corr.* II.41
2994 (5689) 15, 0.6 *Obv.: Annulet within,* +CON[U]...ODI *Rev.: Annulets in quarters 2 & 3,* [+O]...ALISIERVSALE... *Corr.* II.41
2995 (5695) 14, 0.4 *Obv.: Annulet within,* +C...[OC] *Rev.: Annulets in quarters 1 & 4,* +OSPI[T]...I...VSALEM *Corr.* II.41
2996 (5734) 16, 0.9 *Obv.:* [ ]CONU[EN]TO[R DI] *Rev.: Annulets in quarters 1 & 4,* +OSPITA...ERVSAL... *Corr.* II.41
2997 (5737) 15, 0.5 *Obv.:* [ ]CONUE... *Rev.: Annulets in quarters 2 & 3,* ...A[L]...VSALEM *Corr.* II.41
2998 (5744) 15, 0.5 *Obv.: Annulet within,* [ ]CONUE...[D]... *Rev.: Annulets in quarters 1 & 4,* ...LISIERVSAL... *Corr., incomplete.* II.41
2999 (5780) 16, 0.4 *Obv.: Dot within,* ...U[E]...[R]OC... *Rev.: Annulets in quarters 2 & 3,* ...ITALISI...VSAL... *Corr., incomplete.* II.41
3000 (5781) 16, 0.5 *Obv.:* ...ENT... *Rev.: Annulets [in quarters 1 & 4],* [+]...IEROS[*Corr., incomplete.* II.41
3001 (5836) 14, 0.5 *Obv.: Annulet within,* +CONUE...[D]I *Rev.: Annulets [in quarters 1 & 4],* ...[P]I[TALI]SIE... *Corr., incomplete.* II.57
3002 (5987) 13, 0.3 *Obv.: Annulet within,* [ ]CON... *Rev.: Annulets in quarters 1 & 4,* ...IERVSALE... *Corr., incomplete.* II.56
3003 (5745) 13, 0.1 *Obv.: Annulet within,* [C]ON[UE]... *Rev.: Annulets in quarters 1 & 4,* +...[SA]LE *Corr.* II.41

PLATE 143

3004 (6023) 16, 0.5 *Obv.: Annulet within,* +CON[UE]TORO[ ]I *Rev.: Annulets ◦ in quarters 1 & 4,* +OSPITALISIERV SALE *Corr.* II.24
3005 (6101) 15, 0.3 *Obv.: [Platelet within,] Rev.: Annulets in quarters 1 & 4,* +OSPI[TA]LISIE[R]...E *Corr.* II.23
3006 (318) 14, 0.5 *Obv.: Platelet within,* +CON...[R]OCI *Rev.: Annulets in quarters 1 & 4,* ...[TVS...]+OSPI...VSL[EM]
3007 (5521) 13, 0.3 *Obv.: Annulet within,* +C...ROD *Rev.: Annulets in quarters 1 & 4,* +OSET...LS *Corr., incomplete.* II.56
3008 (5656) 15, 0.4 *Obv.:* ...ONUEN... *Rev.: Annulets in quarters 2 & 3,* +O...ALE *Corr.* II.41
3009 (5677) 18, 0.5 *Obv.: Annulet within,* ...E...T... *Rev.: Annulets in quarters 1 & 4,* +[O]...T...AL[ ] II.41

3010 (5680) 16, 0.6 *Obv.: Annulet within,* +CONU... *Rev.: Annulets in quarters 1 & 4,* +O[PIT]ALISI... *Corr., incomplete.* II.41
3011 (5681) 12, 0.4 *Obv.: Annulet within,* +...RODI *Rev.: Annulets in quarters 1 & 4,* +OS...I *Corr.* II.41
3012 (5833) 6, 0.4 *Obv.: Annulet within,* +[CO]...[ROD]I *Rev.: Annulets in quarters 1 & 4,* +OSPITAL... *Corr.* II.57
3013 (1113) 14, 0.5 *Obv.: Annulet within,* ...[O]NUENTUSRhOC[I] *Rev.: Annulets in quarters 2 & 3,* +M[AGISTER] OSPITHIS V
3014 (5411) 15, 0.3 *Obv.: Annulet within,* +C...[R]O[DN]TI *Rev.: Annulets in quarters 2 & 3,* +MAGIST[ERhOSPITAL] *Corr., incomplete.* II.56
3015 (5423) 15, 0.5 *Obv.: Annulet within,* +CONUENT[I]...CI *Rev.: Annulets in quarters 2 & 3,* ...ROSPTAL[*Corr., incomplete.* II.56
3016 (5453) 15, 0.3 *Obv.: Annulet within,* +CONUE... / ... NUENT...*Rev.: Annulets in quarters 1 & 4,* +MAG... / ...GISTE... II.56
3017 (5666) 15, 0.5 *Obv.: Annulet within,* +CONUENTUS[R]... *Rev.: Annulets [in quarters 2 & 3],* +MAGISTERO...T[ ]LI *Corr.* II.41
3018 (5676) 16, 0.4 *Obv.: Annulet within,* +C...UENT...PT[ ] *Rev.: Annulets in quarters 1 & 4,* ...STEROSPITAL[ ] II.41
3019 (5678) 15, 0.5 *Obv.: Annulet within,* +C...NTUSRO... *Rev.: Annulets in quarters 1 & 4,* +M[A]...ALIS *Corr.* II.41
3020 (5686) 15, 0.6 *Obv.: Annulet within,* +[C]...[U]SRhOCI *Rev.: Annulets in quarters 2 & 3,* +MAGIST[E]... *Corr.* II.41
3021 (5691) 13, 0.3 *Obv.: Annulet within,* +CONUENT... *Rev.: Annulets in quarters 1 & 4,* +MAGI...TALIS *Corr., incomplete.* II.41
3022 (5785) 14, 0.5 *Obv.: Annulet within,* +CONUENT[US]... *Rev.: Annulets in quarters 2 & 3,* +M[A]...[R]OSPIT[AS] II.41
3023 (5787) 15, 0.6 *Obv.: Annulet within,* +CONUEN...SRhOCI *Doubled die. Rev.: Annulets in quarters 1 & 4,* +MAGI... [S]PITALI *Corr., incomplete.* II.41
3024 (5829) 15, 0.5 *Obv.: Annulet within,* [ ]CONUENT[US:]RO[NTI] *Rev.: Annulets in quarters 1 & 4,* +MAGIST...[T] ALI[S] *Corr.* II.57
3025 (5830) 15, 0.6 *Obv.: Annulet within,* ...NTUS·ROCI *Rev.: Annulets in quarters 1 & 4,* +MAGISTER... *Corr., incomplete.* II.57
3026 (5839) 16, 0.4 *Obv.: Annulet within,* +CONUEN...SRhODI *Rev.: Annulets in quarters 1 & 4,* +[MAGI] STEROSPITA[S] *Worn.* II.6
3027 (5840) 16, 0.6 *Obv.: Annulet within,* +CONUENTUSR[ ]NT[*Rev.: Annulets in quarters 1 & 4,* +MAGISTERO[PS] TALI *Worn.* II.6
3028 (6069) 15, 0.5 *Obv.: Annulet within,* +CONUENTU...[NT]I *Rev.: Annulets in quarters 1 & 4,* +MA[G]...[ERO] SPITALS *Worn.* II.35
3029 (6017) 16, 0.3 *Obv.: Annulet within,* +CON...TUSRONTI *Rev.: Platelets in quarters 2 & 3,* [ ]MAGIST[R]... SPITAL[I] *Corr., incomplete.* II.64
3030 (520) 17, 0.8 *Obv.: Dot within,* ...UENTUSROCI *Rev.: Annulets in quarters 1 & 4,* ...GISTERhOSP[IT] II.50
3031 (3581) 16, 0.5 *Obv.: Dot within,* +CON...ROCI *Rev.: Annulets in quarters 1 & 4,* ...GISTEROSPIT... II.58
3032 (5698) 14, 0.3 *Obv.: Dot within,* ...NUE...ROC... *Rev.: Annulets in quarters 2 & 3,* +M...T[AL]S *Corr.* II.41
3033 (5710) 13, 0.5 *Obv.: Dot within,* +CO[N]...RhODI *Rev.: Annulets in quarters 1 & 4,* ...RhOS[P]... *Worn.* II.41
3034 (5733) 17, 0.7 *Obv.: [Platelet within,]* +...ENT[U]SR[O T]I: *Rev.: Annulets in quarters 2 & 3,* +MAGISTE...TALIS *Corr.* II.41
3035 (5763) 17, 0.6 *Obv.: Dot within,* +CONUEN[T]...ONTI *Rev.: Annulets in quarters 1 & 4,* +MA...[STER...ITALI II.41
3036 (5530) 14, 0.5 *Obv.: Dot within,* ...SRhOC[ ] *Rev.: Platelets in quarters 1 & 4,* +MAGISTR... *Corr., incomplete.* II.56
3037 (5783) 15, 0.6 *Obv.: Dot within,* ...ENTU... *Rev.: Platelets,* [ ]MAGIS... *Doubled die.* II.41

PLATE 144

15th Century Anonymous Obol Imitations

Obv.: Châtel; annulet or dot within; in beaded circle. Rev.: Maltese cross, annulets in opposite quarters; within beaded circle.

3038 (1112) 15, 0.5 *Obv.: Compact châtel, annulet within,* ...[RM]ERME... *Rev.:* ...[ERM]ER...
3039 (4217) 17, 0.6 *Obv.: Compact châtel, annulet within,* ...ERM... *Rev.:* ...MERMEREME...
3040 (5442) 17, 0.6 *Obv.: Compact châtel, annulet within,* ...[M]E... *Rev.:* ...ERM... II.56
3041 (5501) 15, 0.4 *Obv.: Compact châtel, annulet within,* ...[R]M... *Rev.:* ...EhMEhM... *Worn.* II.56
3042 (5536) 17, 0.6 *Obv.: Compact châtel, annulet within,* ...ME[R]...E... *Rev.:* ...ME...ME... *Corr.; Doubled die.* II.56
3043 (5539) 16, 0.5 *Obv.: Compact châtel, annulet within,* ...ERM...ERM... *Rev.:* ...ERMERME... *Worn; incomplete.* II.56
3044 (4660) 17, 0.8 *Obv.: Compact châtel, annulet ◦ within,*...ME[ ]ME... *Rev.:* ...ETME[T]... I.91
3045 (5617) 15, 0.6 *Obv.: Compact châtel, annulet within. Rev.:* ...E[R]... *Worn.* II.41
3046 (5624) 17, 0.7 *Obv.: Compact châtel, annulet within,* ...SMSMSM... *Rev.:* ...EMSEMSEMSE... II.41
3047 (5405) 16, 0.6 *Obv.: Compact châtel, annulet ◦ within,*...[SM]... *Worn.* II.56
3048 (4132) 14, 0.4 *Obv.: Compact châtel, annulet within,* ...SVS... *Rev.:* ...[EShE]... II.59
3049 (5541) 15, 0.4 *Obv.: Compact châtel, annulet ◦ within,*...MSV... *Rev.: Annulets ◦,* ...E[TM]ES... *Worn, incomplete.* II.56
3050 (5633) 15, 0.4 *Obv.: Compact châtel, annulet within,* ...SMSV... *Rev.:* ...[V]SMES... *Corr., incomplete.* II.41

3051 (5634) 15, 0.5 *Obv.: Compact châtel, annulet within,* ...NTNTN... *Rev.:* ...SЄ[ ]SƲ...S... *Corr.* II.41
3052 (5441) 18, 0.7 *Obv.: Compact châtel,*...T...[S]S[Є]... *Rev.:*...N[ ]SLTN... II.56
3053 (5619) 17, 0.6 *Obv.: Compact châtel, annulet within,* ...[S]UT[L]Є... *Rev.:*...NЄ[Π]NЄ... *Corr.* II.41
3054 (648) 17, 0.7 *Obv.: Dot within,* ... o[ ]R... *Rev.:*... | ◦ ⲙ o ... I.35
3055 (5478) 14, 0.5 *Obv.: Dot within,* [ ] o I ... o ... *Rev.:*...T... / ...ΛXVΛ[ ]V... *Corr., overstrike.* II.56
3056 (529) 13, 0.4 *Obv.:* ...◦ (*... *Rev.:* ...◦... I.78
3057 (3386) 17, 0.5 *Obv. & Rev.: Legend with nonsense characters.* I.59

PLATE 145

Bi Deniers of Pierre d'Aubusson, *c.* 1488-1503 (Schl. X 24)

Obv.: St. John Baptist standing, holding cross on long staff l., open scroll r. Rev.: Aubusson arms (cross moline) within beaded circle.

3058 (5301) 15, 0.5 *Obv.:* ·S·IOhΛΠΠS - ·B·IЄRUL *Rev.:* ✠ · f · PЄ · ꝹΛƲB...Π·ⲙ·OSPI II.41
3059 (3810) 15, 0.3 *Obv.:* [S]· IOhΛΠ[IS] - ·B·IЄR... *Rev.:* ...·PЄ·ꝹΛƲBƲSSO[Π... II.19
3060 (3520) 16, 0.3 *Obv.:* ·S·IO...S - ·B·IЄR[Ʋ]L· *Rev.:* ...Є·ꝹΛƲBƲSSOΠ·ⲙ·OS... II.58
3061 (4262) 16, 0.4 *Obv.:* S ·IOhΛΠΠS· - ·B·IЄR[ƲL] *Rev.:* ✠ · f·PЄ·ꝹΛƲBƲSSOΠ·ⲙ·OSPIT II.24
3062 (4614) 15, 0.5 *Obv.:* ·S·IOhΛΠΠ[S] - ·B·IЄR[U] *Rev.:* ✠ · [f]...ΛƲBƲSSOΠ·ⲙ·OSPIT *Corr.* II.52
3063 (5182) 15, 0.3 *Obv.:* ·S...hΛΠΠ[S] - ·B·IЄR... *Rev.:* [✠ ·]f · PЄ·ꝹΛƲBƲSSOΠ[ ]ⲙ·OSPIT II.34
3064 (5553) 15, 0.4 *Obv.:* ·S·IOhΛΠΠS...ЄRƲ... *Rev.:* ...f] ·PЄ · ꝹΛƲBƲSSOΠ·ⲙ[ ]OS[P]... II.56
3065 (5611) 15, 0.4 *Obv.:* ·S·IO...·B·IЄR[ƲS] *Rev.:* ...·PЄ·ꝹΛƲBƲSSOΠ·ⲙ·[O]... *Corr.* II.41
3066 (5894) 14, 0.4 *Obv.:* ·S·IOhΛ...[B·]IЄRƲL *Rev.:* ✠ · f ·PЄ·ꝹΛƲ...SSOΠ·ⲙ·OSPIT II.56
3067 (556) 14, 0.5 *Obv.:* ·S·IOhΛ...[B·]...L *Rev.:* [✠]· f · Є·ꝹΛƲBƲSSOΠ·ⲙ... II.55
3068 (5897) 15, 0.4 *Obv.:* ·S·IOhΛΠΠS - ·B·... *Rev.:* ✠ · f ·PЄ·ꝹΛƲBƲSSOΠ·ⲙ·OSPIT II.56
3069 (6060) 14, 0.3 *Obv.:* ·S·IOhΛ...S - [ ]B·IЄRƲL *Rev.:* ✠...ƲBƲSSOΠ[ ]ⲙ·OSPIT II.35
3070 (5326) 15, 0.4 *Obv.:*...B·IЄRU[*Rev.:* ✠ · f · PЄ · Ꝺ[Λ]...ⲙ·OSPIT II.42
3071 (598) 15, 0.3 *Obv.:* ...·B·IЄ[ ]ƲL *Rev.:* ✠ · f ·PЄ...[ƲS]SOΠ·ⲙ·OSPIT *Incomplete* II.18
3072 (2132) 16, 0.3 *Obv.:* ·S·IOhΛ[ΠΠS]·B·I... *Rev.:* ✠ [ ]f...Λ...ƲSSOΠ·ⲙ·O... I
3073 (4371) 16, 0.4 *Obv.:* ...[B]·IЄR[ƲL] *Rev.:* ✠ · f ·PЄ·ꝹΛƲBƲSSO[Π]...OSP[TL] II.20
3074 (5838) 15, 0.4 *Obv.:* ...OhΛΠΠ[I]...ЄRƲL *Rev.:* ✠ · f ·PЄ·Ꝺ[ ]ƲBƲSSOΠ·ⲙ·OSPIT *Corr.* II.57
3075 (5938) 14, 0.4 *Obv.:* ...·B·IЄR... *Rev.:* ✠...[P]Є·ꝹΛƲ...Π·ⲙ·OS... II.56
3076 (6008) 15, 0.4 *Obv.:* ... ΛΠΠS - ·B·IЄRƲ[L] *Rev.:* ✠...·PЄ·ꝹΛ...OΠ·ⲙ·OSPIT II.64
3077 (5721) 15, 0.4 *Obv.:* [S]·IOh...ЄRƲ... *Rev.:* ...PЄ·ꝹΛ...SO... II.41
3078 (3635) 14, 0.3 *Obv.:* ... B· IЄRƲL *Rev.:* ...[Ʋ]BƲSSOΠ·ⲙ·OS... II.58
3079 (3724) 15, 0.4 *Obv.:* [S]· IOhΛΠΠS - ·B·... *Rev.:* ✠ · f·PЄ·Ꝺ·[ΛƲ]...SPIT II.14
3080 (4002) 16, 0.5 *Obv.:* [S]· IOhΛΠΠS - ·B·IЄR... *Rev.:* ...·PЄ·ꝹΛƲBƲSSO[Π]... II.48
3081 (4003) 16, 0.4 *Obv.:* [·]S·I[O]... - ·B·IЄRƲL *Rev.:* ✠ · f ·PЄ·ꝹΛƲB...SPIT II.48
3082 (4004) 14, 0.6 *Obv.:* ...ΠΠS... *Rev.:* ✠ · f ·PЄ·Ꝺ[Λ]... II.48
3083 (5860) 15, 0.3 *Obv.:* [ ]S...·B·IЄRƲL *Rev.:* ...PЄ·ꝹΛƲBƲSSO...[·]OSPIT *Corr., incomplete.* II.56
3084 (4212) 15, 0.2 *Obv.:* S ·IOhΛ...ЄR]... *Rev.:* ...ΛƲBƲSSOΠ... *Corr.*
3085 (1060) 14, 0.3 *Obv.* :...·IOhΛΠΠS - ·B·I[h]RUL *Rev.:* ✠[ ]f...Λ...ƲSSOΠ·ⲙ·O...[T] *Corr.* II.50
3086 (1711) 14, 0.2 *Obv.:* ...IRƲL *Rev.:* ✠[ ]f · PЄ·ꝹΛƲB...OΠ·ⲙ·OSPIT *Incomplete.* II.18
3087 (3606) 15, 0.4 *Obv.:* ·S·I... – [B]·IЄR[Ʋ]L *Rev.:* ✠[ ]f ·PЄ·Ꝺ...SSOΠ·ⲙ·OSPIT II.58
3088 (4306) 15, 0.3 *Obv.:* ...IOhΛΠ...- B·IЄRƲL *Rev.:* ...PЄ·ꝹΛƲ...[OS]PIT *Corr.* II.20
3089 (4334) 16, 0.4 *Obv.:* S ·IO...Π[ΠS] - ·B...[RƲ] *Rev.:* · f ·P]...ꝹΛƲBƲSSO[Π]...[ⲙ]·OS... II.53
3090 (4337) 15, 0.4 *Obv.:* [S ·IO]...*Rev.:* ...PЄ·ꝹΛƲBƲSSO[Π] *Corr.* II.53
3091 (5871) 15, 0.4 *Obv.:* ...B·I[ЄRL] *Rev.:* ...[f ·]PЄ·DΛ[ƲBƲ]...SPT *Corr., incomplete.* II.56
3092 (5402) 15, 0.4 *Obv.:* [ ]S·I...B·IЄ... *Rev.:* ✠ · [f]...OΠ·ⲙ[ ]OSPIT II.56
3093 (5457) 14, 0.4 *Obv.:* ...IЄR[S]L *Rev.:* ...SO...S[PI]... II.56
3094 (4391) 13, 0.3 *Obv.:* ... S... - ·B·IЄR[Ʋ]... *Rev.:* ✠ · f ·PЄ·ꝹΛƲB...ƲSSOΠ·ⲙ·OSP... *Corr.* II.20
3095 (5181) 13, 0.2 *Obv.:* ·S...ΛΠS... *Rev.:* ✠ · f...Π·ⲙ·OSPIT *Corr.* II.34
3096 (5225) 15, 0.4 *Obv.:* ...IЄRƲ... *Rev.:* ✠[ ]f[ ]PЄ[ ]ꝹΛ...[Π]·ⲙ·OSPIT II.42
3097 (2175) 15, 0.4 *Obv.:* ...·IOh[Λ]ΠΠS·B·I... *Rev.:* ✠ · f ·PЄ·ꝹΛ...ⲙ·OSPIT I.
3098 (4159) 15, 0.3 *Obv.:* ·S [·]O... *Corr.* II
3099 (4169) 15, 0.5 *Obv.:* [S ·IOhΛΠΠ...ЄRƲL *Rev.:* ✠ · f ·PЄ·ꝹΛƲ...R·ⲙ·OSPIT *Corr.*
3100 (65) 14, 0.6 *Rev.:* ... ꝹΛƲ... *Clipped*
3101 (577) 14, 0.4 *Obv.:* S·IO... *Rev.:* ✠ · f ·PЄ·ꝹΛƲ... *Worn.* II.18
3102 (3557) 15, 0.3 *Rev.:* ...S·I...Π·ⲙ·O[S]... II.58

PLATE 146

3103 (5554) 14, 0.3 *Obv.:* [ ]S·[IOh]ΛΠ[Π]... *Rev.:* ...·PЄ... *Corr.* II.56
3104 (5612) 12, 0.2 *Obv.:* ·S[ ]IOh[Λ]... *Rev.:* ✠...OSPIT *Corr., incomplete.* II.41
3105 (3569) 13, 0.3 *Obv.:* ...S·IOh... *Rev.:* ... [✠]...SOΠ...OSPIT *Corr.* II.58
3106 (581) 14, 0.1 *Obv.:* [ ]S·IOΠΠS...RƲL· *Rev.:* ✠[f ·]Є·ꝹΛƲBƲSSOΠ...OSP[*Incomplete.* II.18
3107 (3571) 14, 0.2 *Obv.:* ...ΛΠΠ[S]... *Rev.:* ...OΠ·ⲙ... *Corr.* II.58
3108 (668) 15, 0.3 *Obv.:* ...IO... *Corr., pierced.* II.63

3109 (1141) 14, 0.3 *Obv.:* ...·IƐRUL *Rev.:* ...S... *Corr., incomplete.* II.57
3110 (3711) 15, 0.3 *Rev.:* ...ꟿ·OS... *Broken.* II.33
3111 (4777) 12, 0.2 *Corr.* II.47

Bi Deniers of Emery d'Amboise, 1503-1512
A. (Schl. XI, 10) *Obv.: St. John Baptist standing, holding Lamb l., cross on long staff r. Rev.: Shield with Amboise arms (paly of six) within beaded circle.*
3112 (5351) 17, 0.6 *Obv.:* ƐCCƐ·ΛG[U]...[D]ƐI· *Rev.:* ✠ f ·MƐRICVS·DΆMBOI[S]... [MΛG] *Corr.* II.40
3113 (4063) 14, 0.3 *Obv.:* ƐCCƐ·ΛGUS – DƐI[ ]ƐααƐ[ ]αVI *Rev.:* ...ƐMƐRICVS... ΛMBOISƐ [ ]MΛ[G] II.5
3114 (5555) 15, 0.6 *Obv.:* ...ƐI· ƐCCƐ... *Rev.:*...ƐRICVS·DΛMBOI[S]... *Corr.* II.56
3115 (3559) 14, 0.6 *Obv.:* ...Λ[G]...α[*Rev.:* ✠.f · ƐMƐRICVS· D ...[O]...[ΛG] II.58
3116 (5843) 14, 0.7 *Obv.:* ƐCCƐ...NS - DƐI ƐCC... *Rev.:* [✠]f ƐMƐRIC[V]...[Λ]MBOISƐ·M[*Corr.* II.11
3117 (542) 15, 0.4 *Obv.:* ƐCCƐΛGNSDƐIƐCCƐαV[*Rev.:* ...f ƐMƐRICVS DΛBO[·R]·MΛ[G
3118 (3519) 15, 0.5 *Obv.:* ƐCCƐ·Λ[G]...DƐI· ƐCCƐ· αVI *Rev.:* ...[Ɛ]MƐRICVS · DΛMBOSΛ · ...[R] II.58
3119 (3554) 14, 0.5 *Obv.:* ...[D]ƐIƐCC[ ]αVI *Rev.:* ...MBOISƐ·MΛG II.58
3120 (3555) 14, 0.5 *Obv.:* ...[ɳ]US-DƐIƐCC... *Rev.:* ...f ƐM[ƐR]...DΛMBOISƐ·...[S] II.58
3121 (1142) 15, 0.4 *Obv.:* ...CƐΛGN[S]... *Rev.:* +f ...CVSD ΛM[ ]OISƐ[ ]·MΛ[II.57
3122 (1156) 12, 0.4 *Rev.:*]ƐMƐ[I.86
3123 (4696) 12, 0.2 *Obv.:* ...CƐ·ΛGU[S] – DƐI... *Rev.:*...BOSΛMΛ[G] *Corr.* II.47

B. (Schl. XI, 12) *Obv.: Paschal Lamb passant reguardant, holding cross on long staff. Exergue. Rev.: Cross potent cantoned by four saltires within beaded circle.*
3124 (533) 15, 0.4 *Obv.:* ƐCƐΛ[G]... *Rev.:* +f MƐRICVS...BOISM
3125 (4030) 13, 0.2 *Obv.:* IO... *Rev.:* +f...M...OIS·M· II.49
3126 (5556) 14, 0.4 *Obv.:* ...αα - Ɛ Άɳ... *In the exergue* ...[D]I... *Rev.:* + · f MƐRICVSDΛ[M]... *Corr.* II.56
3127 (4750) 14, 0.4 *Obv.:* ...A[Gɳ]I... *In the exergue*...[I]... *Rev.:* + f...VSDΛBOIS·M *Corr.* II.47
3128 (3572) 14, 0.5 *Obv.:* Ɛ... *In the exergue*... ·I[α] *Rev.:* ...DΛBOIS·M II.58
3129 (1217) 14, 0.4 *Obv.:* ...NVS... *In the exergue*... · OI *Rev.:* +f ƐMƐRICVS·...[O]ISM II.56
3130 (4360) 15, 0.3 *Obv.:* ...[ƐαƐ] - Λ... *In the exergue*]I[*Rev.:* ...ƐRIC...SOI... II.20
3131 (4372) 15, 0.3 *Obv.:* ...ƐαƐ... *Rev.:* +f ...OISM... *Corr., incomplete.* II.20
3132 (4649) 14, 0.3 *Obv.:* ...DƐI... *In the exergue* ...[I]... *Rev.:* +f ƐMƐRICVS...[OIS] *Corr.* II.52
3133 (671) 11, 0.1 *Corr.* II.63

PLATE 147
FOREIGN COINS
Site and stray finds
3134 (4289) 16, 0.91 AR Imperial denier, 1004-1125. Mint of Lucca. *Obv.: Monogram* H. *Rev.:* L/VC/A II.35
3135 (5805) 15, 0.65 AR Imperial denier, 1004-1125). Mint of Lucca. *Obv.: Monogram* H. *Rev.:* L/VC/A II.42
3136 (25) 28, 3.87 AV Ecu d' or à la couronne, Charles VI of France, 1380-1422
3137 (6004) 18, 0.6 Denier of Chartres. *Obv.:* Cross, ✠α...✠α...TIα... *Rev.: Stylized profile bust r. Corr., incomplete.* II.56
3138 (439) 18 Denier of Normandy II.54
3139 (3791) 19, 0.9 Bi Denier tournois. *Obv.: Cross,* ✠L[ ]DOVICVS...EX· *Rev.: Church,* ✠[T...O]...IVS... II.42
3140 (4055) 27, 2.46 AR Piéfort, John II of France, 1350-64. *Obv.: Cross,* [✠]IOhΆɳɳES[ ]REX/ [✠B]ɳD[αIT...SIT ɳOꟿ DɳI hRI]hV XP[I] *Rev.: Church within circle of 12 fleurs-de-lys in medallions,* ✠TVRONVS*CIVIS II.19
3141 (4612) 17, 1.3 AR English penny, 1180-1218. *Obv.: Crowned facing bust holding cross-bearing sceptre,* hƐNRICVSRƐX *Rev.: Double short cross cantoned by quatrefoils,* ...ILCER· ON·LVND... II.52
3142 (493) 19, 3.2 Follis of Antioch, Tancred, 1104-12. *Obv.: Bust of Tancred with sword. Rev.: Tree of Life cross cantoned by* IC/ XC/ NI/ KA.
3143 (418) 22, 1.6 [Early Crusader]. *Obv.: Inscription* AN/...X/DV[M] *in three lines overstruck on facing bust. Rev.: Inscription* [MA]R *in two lines.* II.54
3144 (4838) 14, 0.5 Crusader coin of Sidon. *Obv.: Rosette with six spokes within a circle.* II.41
3145 (11) 22, 2.98 AR Tram, Leo I, 1199-1226. *Obv.: Seated ruler holds* globus cruciger *l. and lily r. Rev.: Patriarchal cross on long staff between two lions rampant reguardant addorsed.* V.20
3146 (12) 20, 2.68 AR Tram, Leo I, 1199-1226. *Obv.: Seated ruler holds* globus cruciger *l. and lily r. Rev.: Patriarchal cross on long staff between two lions rampant reguardant addorsed.* V.20
3147 (13) 22, 2.70 AR Tram, Leo I, 1199-1226. *Obv.: Seated ruler holds* globus cruciger *l. and lily r. Rev.: Patriarchal cross on long staff between two lions rampant reguardant addorsed.* V.20
3148 (14) 20, 2.77 AR Tram, Leo I, 1199-1226. *Obv.: Seated ruler holds* globus cruciger *l. and lily r. Rev.: Patriarchal cross on long staff between two lions rampant reguardant addorsed.* V.20
3149 (4167) AR Tram, Leo I, 1199-1226. *Obv.: Seated ruler holds* globus cruciger *l. and lily r. Rev.: Patriarchal cross on long staff between two lions rampant reguardant addorsed.* II.34
3150 (3416) 19, 2 Kardez. *Corr.* II.58
3151 (6021) 18, 1.7 [Takvorin, 1375 ff.] *Rev.: Mounted ruler holding lance. Corr.* II.24
3152 (3526) 15, 0.9 *Obv.: Cross within beaded circle. Rev.: Seated ruler holds* globus cruciger *l. and lily r. Corr.* II.58

3153 (5919) 14, 0.7 Bi Genoese denier, 1139-1252, *Obv.: Cross,* [ᗡ]VNRᗅDI[·] · RᗴX. *Rev.: Janua,* ✠ · Iᗅ·NV·ᗅ· II.56

3154 (5274) 13, 0.6 Genoese minuto, 1396-1461. *Obv.: Janua. Rev.: Long cross,* CO-NR-AD-VS

3155 (4072) 20, 2.92 AV Florentine florin, 1330 ff. *Obv.: St. John the Baptist,* ✠ · S'IOHᗅ / NNIS'B, *battlemented bridge badge. Rev.: Fleur-de-lys florency,* ✠F L O R / ENTIᗅ II.4

3156 (4446) AV Venetian ducat, Andrea Contarini, 1367-82. II.56

PLATE 148

3157 (1209) 16, 0.7 Venetian quartarolo. *Obv.: Cross cantoned by fleurs de lys placed radially. Rev.:* EVZɔ II.56

3158 (4163) 16, 0.4 Venetian quartarolo. *Obv.: Cross cantoned by fleurs de lys placed radially,* ꩜✠꩜. *Rev.:* ...LDV... II.20

3159 (4441) 18, 0.6 Venetian quartarolo. *Obv.:* Cross cantoned by fleurs de lys placed radially, ✠ ·...RᗡV꩜ · *Rev.:* EVZɔ, ✠ · I...[NO] DVX *Incomplete.* II.34

3160 (4442) 14, 0.3 Venetian quartarolo, G. Dandolo, 1280-9. *Obv.: Cross cantoned by fleurs de lys placed radially,* Rᗡ... *Rev.:* EVZɔ, ...[D]ᗩND *Fragment.* II.34

3161 (4464) 15, 0.9 Venetian quartarolo. *Obv.: Cross cantoned by fleurs de lys placed radially,* O... *Rev.:* EVZɔ, ...X... *Fragment.* II.57

3162 (4826) 16, 0.5 Quartarolo του G. Dandolo, 1280-9. *Obv.: Cross cantoned by fleurs de lys placed radially,* ✠IO·DᗩN... *Rev.:* EVZɔ, ꩜.R. II.22

3163 (5190) 16, 0.5 Venetian quartarolo. *Obv.: Cross cantoned by fleurs de lys placed radially,* ✠[꩜ᗰ]ᗅRᗡV꩜ *Rev.:* EVZɔ, ...IOhᗅNN DVX II.56

3164 (4108) 15, 0.4 Venetian quartarolo. *Obv.: Maltese radiate cross with bead nestling at each finial,* ...L[E]O[L] ...DVX *Rev.:*...VENITI... *Corr.* II.65

3165 (5719) 10, 0.1 Denier, [Francesco Foscari?1423-57]. *Obv.: Cross pattee with convex ends within circle,* ✠ ·[F] R...·[F]...X *Rev.: Lion of St. Mark passant. Clipped.* II.41

3166 (5238) 17, 1.8 Venetian bagattino (1500 ff.) *Obv.: Lion of St. Mark within square. Rev.: Virgin with Child.* II.55

3167 (5606) 13, 0.6 Sicilian denier, Martin, 1402-9. *Obv.:* Eagle, ✠ᗰᗩR... *Rev.: Shield of Aragon. Corr., incomplete.* II.41

3168 (5718) 12, 0.2 Sicilian denier, Martin, 1402-9. *Corr., incomplete. Obv.: Eagle, [*✠ᗰᗩR...*] Rev.: Shield of Aragon,* ✠...I II.41

3169 (4037) Sicilian denier, Alfonso I, 1416-58. *Obv.: Eagle,* ✠ᗩL[F]ONS :D:GR. *Rev.: Shield of Aragon,* ✠Rᗴ[X] : SIᗡILI[ᗴ] II.63

3170 (4259) 14, 0.4 Sicilian denier, Alfonso I, 1416-58. *Obv.: Eagle,* ...ONS[U]... *Rev.: Shield of Aragon,* ✠...Iᗴ *Worn.* II.24

3171 (4288) 15, 0.8 Sicilian denier, Alfonso I, 1416-58. *Obv.: Eagle,* ✠[ᗩ]LF... *Rev.: Shield of Aragon,* ...X:SIᗡILIᗴ[I.35

3172 (4425) 14, 0.3 Sicilian denier, Alfonso I, 1416-58. *Obv.: Eagle,* [ᗩLF]O[N]... *Rev.: Shield of Aragon. Corr. incomplete.* II.20

3173 (5448) 16, 0.5 Sicilian denier, Alfonso I, 1416-58. *Obv.: Eagle,* ✠...[F]ONS...[ᗴ]I: *Rev.: Shield of Aragon,* ✠Rᗴ... LIᗴ[:] II.56

3174 (5716) 14, 0.6 Sicilian denier, Alfonso I, 1416-58. *Obv.: Eagle,* ✠ᗅL[F]... *Rev.: Shield of Aragon,* ✠...ᗴ: *Corr. incomplete.* II.41

3175 (5768) 15, 0.7 Sicilian denier, Alfonso I, 1416-58, Class A. *Obv.: Eagle,* ✠ᗩLFON... *Rev.: Shield of Aragon,* ✠Rᗴ... LIᗴ: *Corr. incomplete.* II.41

3176 (5822) 15, 0.5 Sicilian denier, Alfonso I, 1416-58, Class B. *Obv.: Eagle,* ✠ᗩL...S:D:G... *Rev.: Shield of Aragon between pellets,* ✠R...LI *Corr. incomplete.* II.57

3177 (5861) 14, 0.4 Sicilian denier, Alfonso I, 1416-58. *Obv.: Eagle,* ...ONS·D·... *Rev.: Shield of Aragon,* ✠... I *Corr. incomplete.* I.56

3178 (5887) 13, 0.5 Sicilian denier, Alfonso I, 1416-58. *Obv.: Eagle,* ✠ᗩ...O... *Rev.: Shield of Aragon,* ✠... *Corr. incomplete.* II.56

3179 (5929) 14, 0.4 Sicilian denier, Alfonso I, 1416-58. *Obv.: Eagle,* ...ONS:[D]... *Rev.: Shield of Aragon,* ✠... *Corr.* II.56

3180 (3978) 14, 0.4 Sicilian denier, John II, 1458-79. *Obv.: Eagle,* ✠IOᗩN... *Rev.: Shield of Aragon,* ...XSIᗡ... *Corr.*

3181 (4017) 15, 0.3 Sicilian denier, John II, 1458-79. *Obv.:* Eagle, ✠IOᗩ[N].[G]. *Rev.:* Shield of Aragon, ✠...Iᗴ II.62

3182 (5472) 16, 0.5 Sicilian denier, John II, 1458-79. *Clipped, incomplete. Obv.: Eagle,* [ ]IOᗩN[ᗴS]:D:G::/ Eagle. *Rev.: Shield of Aragon,* ✠R...[L]Iᗴ: / *Shield of Aragon,* ...ᗴX[:]... II.56

3183 (4260) 16, 0.5 Sicilian denier, John II, 1458-79. *Obv.: Eagle,* ✠IOᗩ... *Rev.: Shield of Aragon,*...IᗡILIᗴ *Worn.* II.24

3184 (4817) 15, 0.5 Sicilian denier, John II, 1458-79. *Obv.: Eagle,* ✠IOᗩ...[D:G:] *Rev.: Shield of Aragon,*...ᗴX:SIᗡILI... II.48

3185 (94) 14, 0.6 Sicilian denier. *Obv.: Eagle. Rev.: Shield of Aragon.* V.2

3186 (236) 15 Sicilian denier. *Obv.: Eagle. Rev.: Shield of Aragon.* V.2

3187 (530) 13 Sicilian denier. *Obv.: Eagle. Rev.: Shield of Aragon.* III.2

3188 (543) 14, 0.6 Sicilian denier. *Obv.: Eagle. Rev.: Shield of Aragon.*

3189 (555) 15, 0.6 Sicilian denier. *Obv.: Eagle. Rev.: Shield of Aragon.* II.55

3190 (557) 17, 0.4 Sicilian denier. *Obv.: Eagle. Rev.: Shield of Aragon.* II.54

3191 (1015) 15, 0.6 Sicilian denier. *Obv.: Eagle. Rev.: Shield of Aragon.* II.29

3192 (1097) 14, 0.3 Sicilian denier. *Worn.* II.60

3193 (3395) 14, 0.6 Sicilian denier. *Obv.: Eagle. Rev.: Shield of Aragon,* ✠[RᗴX]...ᗴ:

3194 (3540) 15, 0.4 Sicilian denier. *Obv.: Eagle. Rev.: Shield of Aragon. Corr.* II.58
3195 (3547) 14, 0.3 Sicilian denier. *Obv.: Eagle. Rev.: Shield of Aragon. Corr. incomplete.* II.58
3196 (4137) 14, 0.3 Sicilian denier. *Obv.: Eagle. Rev.: Shield of Aragon.* II.41

PLATE 149
3197 (4170) 14, 0.3 Sicilian denier. *Obv.: Eagle. Rev.: Shield of Aragon.*
3198 (4182) 14, 0.3 Sicilian denier, *Obv.: Eagle. Rev.: Shield of Aragon,* …[. IOI]
3199 (4224) 11, 0.2 Sicilian denier. *Obv.: Eagle. Rev.: Shield of Aragon. Corr. incomplete.* II.63
3200 (4225) 14, 0.5 Sicilian denier. *Obv.: Eagle.* ✠… *Rev.: Shield of Aragon,* …[. IOI] *Corr.* II.63
3201 (4307) 14, 0.5 Sicilian denier. *Rev.: Shield of Aragon,* …SIⱭI… *Folded.* II.20
3202 (4320) 14, 0.4 Sicilian denier. *Obv.: Eagle,* ✠…[D:G:] *Rev.: Shield of Aragon,* ✠…Є…LIЄ[:] II.53
3203 (4333) 14, 0.5 Sicilian denier. *Obv.: [Eagle]. Rev.: Shield of Aragon.* II.53
3204 (4363) 14, 0.4 Sicilian denier. *Obv.: [Eagle]. Rev.: Shield of Aragon.* II.20
3205 (4398) 0.2 Sicilian denier. *Obv.: [Eagle]. Rev.: Shield of Aragon. Corr. broken.* II.20
3206 (4434) 14, 0.4 Sicilian denier. *Rev.: Shield of Aragon. Folded.* II.34
3207 (4472) 15, 0.5 Sicilian denier. *Obv.: Eagle. Rev.: Shield of Aragon,* ✠…ЄX [SIⱭILIЄ] II.57
3208 (4544) 15, 0.5 Sicilian denier. *Obv.: Eagle. Rev.: Shield of Aragon,* ✠…ЄX [SIⱭILIЄ] *Corr.* II.36
3209 (4742) 14, 0.4 Sicilian denier. *Obv.: Eagle. Rev.: Shield of Aragon. Corr.* II.47
3210 (5307) 15, 0.5 Sicilian denier. *Obv.: Eagle,* …[L]OП… *Rev.: Shield of Aragon,* [R]ЄX:SI… II.41
3211 (5447) 13, 0.4 Sicilian denier. *Obv.: Eagle. Rev.: Shield of Aragon,* …ⱭIL… *Corr.* II.56
3212 (5717) 14, 0.4 Sicilian denier. *Obv.: Eagle,* …S :D:G[R]… *Rev.: Shield of Aragon,* ✠ · RЄ[X]… *Corr., incomplete.* II.41
3213 (5890) 13, 0.4 Sicilian denier, *Obv.: Eagle. Rev.: Shield of Aragon,* …X… *Corr., incomplete.* II.56
3214 (6078) 15, 0.3 Sicilian denier. *Obv.: Eagle. Rev.: Shield of Aragon. Corr. incomplete.* II.23
3215 (561) 15, 0.3 Sicilian denier. *Obv.: Eagle. Rev.: Shield of Aragon.* II.55
3216 (6088) 15, 0.7 Sicilian denier. *Obv.:* Eagle. *Rev.: Shield of Aragon. Corr.* II.23
3217 (5481) 17, 0.9 Sicilian denier, Martin, 1390-1409. *Obv.: Eagle,* ✠MΛR… *Rev.:* Cross. *Corr.* II.56
3218 (5942) 16, 0.4 Sicilian denier, Manfred, 1258-64. Messina. *Obv.: Rosette of eight spokes. Rev.:* M. *Corr.; incomplete.* II.56
3219 (4264) 15, 0.7 [Sicilian denier]. *Obv.: [Cross],* …SSIL / OLS / … *Rev.: Crowned profile bust l. Worn.* II.24
3220 (6148) 14, 0.3 [Sicilian denier] V.2
3221 (6022) 15, 0.4 Naples denier, Joanna I, 1343-81. *Obv.: Quartered arms,* [✠LVDOVIⱭ Z IOhA'D]ЄI· [GRA] *Rev.: Cross cantoned by fleurs de lys placed radially,* ✠[RЄX Z RЄGIN IЄRL ЄT]S[IⱭIL'] *Incomplete.* II.24
3222 (5512) 14, 0.3 Naples denier, René, 1435-42. *Obv.: Cross cantoned by fleurs de lys placed radially,* ✠RЄПΛTV[S]… *Rev.: Crowned R,* ✠IЄR…SIⱭIL… *Incomplete.* II.56
3223 (5608) 13, 0.6 Naples denier. *Obv.: Crowned bust,* …[OhΛЄ]… *Rev.: Coat of arms.* …[IЄ] °… *Clipped.*
3224 (3987) 19, 1.2 Dobler of Majorca, Alfonso II, 1416-1458. *Obv.: Royal bust flanked by dogs,* … US‡DЄI‡GRΛ‡R… *Rev.: Cross with long staff,* ✠ΛRΛGOПU- [ЄT]MΛ… R° II.10
3225 (4677) 17, 1.5 Diner of Minorca, Alfonso II (V of Aragon), 1412-1458. *Obv.: Royal bust l.,* +ALFONSUS:REX: *Rev.: Arms of Aragon in lozenge within quatrefoil,* +MINORICARUM: II.47
3226 (304) 16, … Portuguese dinheiro, Ferdinand I, 1367-83. *Obv.: Cross, star and crescent alternately in quarters,* ✠F:REX:PORTVGALI *Rev.: Five escutcheons in cross split circumferential legend* AL - GA - RB - II I.87
3227 (4570) 15, 0.4 Provins-type denier, *c.* 1300-1404. *Obv.: Cross,* ✠ROMΛ… *Rev.: 'Comb', crescent - star above,* …ЄNΛ… *Cancelled.* II.29
3228 (5281) 16, 0.5 Provins-type denier, *c.* 1300-1404. *Obv.: Cross, star in first quarter,* ✠ROMΛ·… *Rev.: 'Comb', crescent - star above.* II.41
3229 (266) Denier, pope Paul II, 1464-71. V.2
3230 (4611) 14, 0.8 Picciolo, pope Sixtus IV, 1471-84. *Obv.:* … VS · ✿ ·… *Rev.: Arms of della Rovere.* II.52
3231 (6146) 15, 0.5 Denier, pope John XXII, 1316-1334. Mint of Macerata. *Obv.: Cross,* ✠PPIOhANNES *Rev.:* VICES[I] MVSEC, *in the centre* $_{D}{}^{V}{}_{S}$ V.2

PLATE 150
3232 (5511) 19, 0.7 Soldo, G.-M. Visconti, 1402-12. *Obv.: Cross,* ✠ · II… *Rev.: Crowned snake,* ✠… II.56
3233 (6147) 15, 0.4 Denier of Ravenna, 1232-1375. *Obv.:* ✠ ARCIEPI∽CO, *in the centre* $_{P}{}^{V}{}_{S}$ *Rev.: Cross with ray ending in three pellets in quarters 2 & 3,*✠ DE RAVENA V.2
3234 (4352) 17, 0.5 Denier of Ancona, *c.* 1250-1350. *Obv.: Cross, stars [in quarters 1 & 4],* ✠ · S…VIR[I]Λ…VS · *Rev.: ?,* ✠✱D…ΛN[CO]✱ *Corr.* II.53
3235 (5609) 12, 0.2 Denier of Ancona, *c.* 1250-1350. *Obv.:* [$_{C}{}^{V}{}_{S}$], …·SⱭV[I]. *Rev.: Cross,* ΛNⱭO… *Corr., incomplete.* II.41
3236 (5401) 14, 0.3 Denier of Ancona, *c.* 1250-1350. *Obv.:* [$_{C}{}^{V}{}_{S}$]. *Rev.: Cross. Corr., incomplete.* II.56
3237 (10169) 16, 0.4 Denier of Ancona, *c.* 1250-1350. *Obv.:* ✠ · P[D]·SⱭV[I]RIΛ· $_{C}{}^{V}{}_{S}$, *Rev.: Cross,* ✠ · DE·ΛNⱭONΛ· II
3238 (4100) 16, 0.4 Bi Cypriot denier, Henry II, 1285-1324. *Obv.: Cross,* ✠hЄNRI…ЄI·DЄ *Rev.: Lion rampant,* …M·Є[D] ⱭhIPR II.65
3239 (5424) 14, 0.5 Bi Cypriot denier, Henry II, 1285-1324. *Obv.: Cross, pellet in each quarter. Rev.: Lion rampant,* ✠…V II.56

3240 (5597) 15, 0.6 Bi Cypriot denier, Henry II, 1285-1324. Obv.: *Cross, pellet in each quarter. Rev.: Lion rampant. Corr., incomplete.* II.56

3241 (5927) 14, 0.4 Bi Cypriot denier, Henry II, 1285-1324. Obv.: *Cross, pellet in each quarter. Rev.: Lion rampant. Corr., incomplete.* II.56

3242 (4662) 15, 0.5 Bi Cypriot denier, James I, 1382-98. Obv.: *Cross,* ✠IHQ[ ]E [R]OI DE C Obv.: *Lion rampant,* ✠E IER…[EM] II.52

3243 (88) 15, 0.4 [Bi Cypriot denier, James I, 1382-98.] Obv.: *[Lion rampant.] Rev.: Cross, crosslet in first quarter. Worn.* V.2

3244 (42) 14, 0.6 Cypriot denier, Janus, 1398-1432. Obv.: Jerusalem cross, …USR…[EC]… Rev.: *Lion rampant,* …CI[P]…[S] V.2

3245 (3592) 16, 0.4 Cypriot denier, Janus, 1398-1432. Obv.: Jerusalem cross, …X[C]… Rev.: *Lion rampant. Corr.* II.58

3246 (1115) 14, 0.3 Cypriot denier. Obv.: *Cross. Rev.: Lion rampant.*

3247 (4681) 14, 0.5 Cypriot denier. Obv.: *Cross. Rev.: Lion rampant.* II.30

3248 (4729) 16, 0.3 [Bi Cypriot denier.] Obv.: *Cross, pellet in each quarter. Corr.* II.47

3249 (6020) 11, 0.2 [Cypriot denier.] Obv.: *Cross,* ✠[EN]… Rev.: *[Lion rampant.] Corr., clipped.* II.24

3250 (6143) 14, 0.5 [Cypriot denier.] Obv.: *Cross. Rev.: Lion rampant.* V.2

3251 (6041) 20, 1.10 Cypriot AR sixain, James I, 1382-98. Obv.: *Jerusalem cross,* …BUS DEI [G… Rev.: *Lion rampant,* …USALEM CIPRI [ARM… *Corr.* II.35

3252 (519) 17, 1.77 Cypriot [AR] sixain, Janus, 1398-1432. Obv.: *Lion rampant,* ...U·S R... Rev.: *Jerusalem cross,* ...I·ME... *Clipped.* II.50

3253 (5604) 18, 1.73 Cypriot [AR] sixain, Janus, 1398-1432. Obv.: *Lion rampant. Rev.: Jerusalem cross,* ✠IO : [DEI]…[ΛI]. *Clipped.* II.41

3254 (6144) 17, 1.01 Cypriot AR sixain. Obv.: *Jerusalem cross. Rev.: Lion rampant. Corr.* V.2

3255 (1088) 14, 0,3 Famagusta denier, 1373-1464. Obv.: *Cross,* ✠DV… Rev.: *Janua,* ✠CIVIT… *Worn.* I.97

3256 (1117) 14, 0.3 Famagusta denier, 1373-1464. Obv.: *Cross. Rev.: Janua. Incomplete.*

3257 (1224) 14, 0.4 Famagusta denier, 1373-1464. Obv.: *Cross,* … Rev.: *Janua. Corr., incomplete.* II.8

3258 (5285) 15, 0.5 Famagusta denier, 1373-1464. Obv.: *Cross,* …VIΛNVE… Rev.: *Janua,* ✠CIV…AMAG II.41

3259 (6001) 15, 0.5 Famagusta denier, 1449-1458. Obv.: *Cross, X in first quarter,* ✠[CIV]…:IHNVE: Rev.: *Janua,* ✠S:IOh…:D II.56

PLATE 151

3260 (3541) 14, 0.7 Denier of Mytilene, Niccolò Gattilusio, 1459-62. Obv.: *Gothic* N, ✠[N]YDO[L]HOYS [ ]TO[MI] Rev.: *Cross, Bs back-to-back in quarters,* [✠]DOM·[N] O[S]… II. 58

3261 (4675) 15, 0.8 Denier of Mytilene, Domenico Gattilusio, 1449-59. Obv.: *Gothic* d, ✠ · D · DOM… Rev.: *Cross, Bs back-to-back in quarters,* ✠…ETELINI II. 47

3262 (4721) 15, 0.4 Denier of Mytilene. Rev.: *Cross, Bs back-to-back in quarters. Corr.* II. 47

3263 (5607) 15, 0.5 Denier of Mytilene, Domenico Gattilusio, 1449-59. Obv.: *Gothic* d, ✠ · D… Rev.: *Cross, Bs back-to-back in quarters,* …INO…E[L]… *Corr.* II. 41

3264 (5610) 12, 0.3 Denier tournois of Chios. Obv.: *Cross pattee,* …CONRΛDV… Rev.: *Church, star below,* C…[Λ]S :✱: C…I *Corr., incomplete.* II. 41

3265 (6055) 12, 0.4 *Denier tournois of Chios,* 1479-98. Obv.: *Cross with split ends,* …ONRΛDVS [RE]X[ ] Rev.: *Justiniani arms flanked by* [L] / I, ✠ CIVITΛS… *Clipped.* II. 35

3266 (789) 20, 3.56 AV Imitative ducat, Eastern type. *Obv. & Rev.: Nonsense legends.* II.7

3267 (864) 20, 3.57 AV Imitative ducat, Eastern type. Obv.: R:EGIƧIƧTEDVCAT ˙ - ˙ ƧIT.T. ⊗ PEDA·T· QTV Rev.: ∾NVENET - DV✠ - AZDRAZDV[L. II.57

3268 (5574) 14, 0.2 Tornesello, doge G. Dolfin, 1356-61. Obv.: *Cross,* …O · D[E]… Rev.: *Lion of St. Mark,* …V… *Corr., incomplete.* II.56

3269 (5449) 15, 0.6 Tornesello, doge A. Contarini, 1368-1382. Obv.: *Cross,* ✠ANDR' OTAR' DVX Rev.: *Lion of St. Mark,* ✠VEXILIFER·VENETIA II.56

3270 (5471) 16, 0.5 Tornesello, doge A. Contarini, 1368-1382. Obv.: *Cross,* …ODV[X]. Rev.: *Lion of St. Mark,* …NETI[A] II.56

3271 (5605) 16, 0.5 Tornesello, doge A. Contarini, 1368-82. Obv.: *Cross,* ✠ANDR'…A… Rev.: *Lion of St. Mark,* ✠VEXILI… ETIΛ *Corr., incomplete.* II.41

3272 (6145) 16, 0.4 Tornesello, doge A. Contarini, 1368-82. Obv.: *Cross.* ✠ANDR'OTAR DVX Rev.: *Lion of St. Mark.* …VEXIL]IFER·VENETIA V.2

3273 (5296) 16, 0.4 Tornesello, doge A. Venier, 1382-1400. Obv.: *Cross,* ✠[ANTO]…DVX. Rev.: *[Lion of St. Mark.] Corr., crumpled.* II.41

3274 (5713) 17, 0.5 Tornesello, doge A. Venier, 1382-1400. Obv.: *Cross,* [ ]AИTO' VEИERIO DV[X]. Rev.: *Lion of St. Mark,* ✠VE[XI]LIFER·VEИ…[A] II.41

3275 (5714) 15, 0.4 Tornesello, doge A. Venier, 1382-1400. Obv.: *Cross,* …TO'VE[И]ERI… Rev.: *Lion of St. Mark,* …VENE[TI]… *Corr., incomplete.* II.41

3276 (5812) 16, 0.3 Tornesello, doge A. Venier, 1382-1400. Obv.: *Cross,* ✠ANTO…DVX. Rev.: *Lion of St. Mark,* ✠…TIA *Corr., incomplete.* II.41

3277 (5909) 17, 0.6 Tornesello, doge A. Venier, 1382-1400. Obv.: *Cross,* ✠AИTO…DVX. Rev.: *Lion of St. Mark,* ✠VEXI[LI]…VEИ [ET]IA II.56

3278 (6098) 17, 0.5 Tornesello, doge A. Venier, 1382-1400. *Obv.: Cross,* ✠...VЄИЄR... *Rev.: Lion of St. Mark,* ✠VЄ[XILIF] ЄRVЄИ[ЄT]I[ ]Ꝝ *Corr., incomplete.* II.23
3279 (3525) 17, 0.5 Tornesello, doge M. Steno, 1400-13. *Obv.: Cross,* ✠[M]IϹhΛЄL ·S... [V]· DVX· *Rev.: Lion of St. Mark,* VЄXILIFЄR·VЄN... II.58
3280 (5941) 6, 0.4 Tornesello, doge M. Steno, 1400-13. *Obv.: Cross,* ✠MI[Ϲh]ΛЄL[S]TЄΠDVX. *Rev.: Lion of St. Mark,* ✠VЄXILIFЄRVЄИЄTIΛꝜ *Corr.* II.56
3281 (4540) 15, 0.5 Tornesello, doge A. Barbarigo, 1486-1501. *Obv.: Cross,* ... ΛVG[BΛ]RBΛDICO... *Rev.: Lion of St. Mark,* ...NITI... *Worn.*
3282 (5873) 14, 0.4 Tornesello, doge A. Barbarigo, 1486-1501. *Obv.: Cross,* ·ΛVC.Λ...ΛDICO·DVX. *Rev.: Lion of St. Mark. Corr.* II.56
3283 (431) 17, 0.2 Tornesello. *Obv.: Cross. Rev.: Lion of St. Mark. Half.* II.54
3284 (569) 15, 0.4 Tornesello. *Obv.: Cross. Rev.: Lion of St. Mark.*
3285 (1011) 14, 0.4 Tornesello. *Obv.: Cross. Rev.: Lion of St. Mark.* II.29
3286 (1028) 15, 0.5 [Tornesello.] *Obv.: Cross. Rev.: Lion of St. Mark.* II.31
3287 (1197) 14, 0.4 [Tornesello.] *Obv.: Cross. Rev.: Lion of St. Mark.* II.56
3288 (4038) 14, 0.2 [Tornesello.] *Obv.: [Cross.] Rev.: [Lion of St. Mark.],* ...[Λ]RCVS[]VEN... II.63
3289 (4078) 17, - Tornesello. *Obv.: Cross. Rev.: [Lion of St. Mark.] Corr., broken.* II.17
3290 (4326) 16, 0.3 Tornesello. *Corr. Obv.:* [Cross.] *Rev.: Lion of St. Mark.* II.53
3291 (4345) 13, 0.1 Tornesello. *Obv.: Cross. Rev.: Lion of St. Mark. Corr., incomplete.* II.53
3292 (4384) 15, 0.6 Tornesello. *Obv.: Cross. Rev.: Lion of St. Mark. Worn, cancelled.* II.20
3293 (4423) 12, 0.3 Tornesello. *Obv.: Cross. Worn.* II.24
3294 (4695) 15, 0.3 Tornesello. *Obv.: Cross. Rev.:* Lion of St. Mark. *Worn.* II.47

PLATE 152
3295 (4707) 15, 0.4 Tornesello. *Rev.: [Lion of St. Mark],* ...VS·[VIR... *Worn.* II.47
3296 (4809) 14, 0.6 Tornesello. *Obv.: Cross. Rev.:* [Lion of St. Mark.] *Worn.* II.35
3297 (5246) 15, 0.2 Tornesello. *Corr., incomplete. Obv.:*...[M]O[R]...O[D]... *Rev.: Lion of St. Mark.* II.55
3298 (5298) 17, 0.5 Tornesello. *Obv.:* ✠[MΛ]...LIODX. *Corr.* II.41
3299 (5575) 15, 0.4 Tornesello. *Rev.: Lion of St. Mark. Corr., incomplete.* II.56
3300 (795) 15, 0.4 Tornesello. *Clipped.* II.30
3301 (863) 15, 0.3 Tornesello. *Corr., worn.* II.12
3302 (1066) 14, 0.3 Tornesello. *Worn.* II.44
3303 (4018) 15, 0.6 Imitative tornesello. II.62
3304 (5321) 15, 0.7 Imitative tornesello. II.34
3305 (5715) 16, 0.3 Imitative tornesello. *Obv.: Cross,* ...X,XIO[I]...[ЄR]... *Rev.: Lion of St. Mark.,* ...OIV... *Corr., incomplete.* II.41
3306 (5982) 16, 0.5 Denier tournois of Lepanto, Philip of Taranto c. 1294-1310. *Obv.: Cross,* ✠ ·...[PAϹh .TΛR]DЄSPO. *Rev.: Church,* ...ΠЄ[P]ΛΠTIϹ...IS *Corr., incomplete.* II.56
3307 (400) 18, 0.3 Denier tournois of Achaia. *Corr., incomplete.* II.54
UNIDENTIFIED
3308 (1716) 16, 0.7 Denier. *Obv.: Cross with 'grain seed' placed radially in each quarter. Rev.: Shield with three bendlets,* IOANES[M]AG[O... II.44
3309 (263) 16, 0.6 Denier tournois. V
3310 (4607) 12, 0.2 Denier tournois. *Corr., incomplete.* II.30
3311 (4014) 14, 0.5 [?Kardez] *Obv.: Cross potent,* ...D]ЄI°... *Rev.: Ruler cross-legged, holds scepter and globus cruciger.* II.48
3312 (4041) 0.5 [?Gros] *Obv.:*...SSIL... *Rev.:* ...E[N... *Fraction.* II.63
3313 (4424) 16, 0.2 Denier. *Obv.: Cross, a pellet in each quarter. Worn.* II.24
3314 (4768) 15, 0.5 Denier. *Obv.: Cross, [a pellet in each quarter]. Rev.: [Five vertical spikes in a row.] Corr.* II.47
3315 (4772) 16, 0.5 Denier. *Obv.:* ...OΠ...UO... *Rev.:* ...V... *Corr.* II.47
3316 (4843) 20, 1.1 [Gros] *Obv.: Central cross, two concentric legends. Rev.:* PNC, *circumferential inscription.* II.41
3317 (5340) 15, 0.5 [Denier.] *Obv.: Standing Christ,* XC r. *Rev.: Byzantine-style emperor, holds cross-bearing sceptre r.* II.56
3318 (5551) 14, 0.4 Denier. *Corr. Obv.: Cross pattee,* ...VI... II.56
3319 (5720) 14, 0.4 Denier. *Corr., incomplete. Obv.: [Crowned shield]. Rev.: [Arms of Aragon]* II.41
3320 (6149) 15, 0.4 Denier. *Obv.:* ·F·, ...Λ·RI·[M... *Rev.: Eagle,* D[I]...ЄΠIO V.2
3321 (181) 13, 0.5 Denier. *Corr., incomplete. Obv.: [Cross]. Rev.: [Crown].* V

PLATE 153
Major hoards
3322 (566) 13, 0.6 Genoese denier. *Obv.: Long cross cutting through circumferential legend. Rev.: Janua.* IH
3323 (8305) 15, 0.5 Bi Genoese denier, 1139-1339. *Obv.:* Cross, [:]CVNR...X˙ *Rev.: Janua,* ✠ · IΛ...Λ [·] KH
3324 (6161) 15, 0.4 Portuguese real de 10 soldos, John I, 1385-1443, Lisbon mint. *Obv.: Cross with annulet in each quarter,* ✠PO✱Є...[L]GΛ[B]IIG✱ *Rev.: Arms of Portugal on floriated cross,*]IhΠS✱DЄI[G]RΛ... IH

3325 (8311) 15, 0.6 Sicilian denier, Frederick IV, 1355-77. Obv.: *Cross,* ✠G…CILIЄ: *Rev.: Crowned bust,* ✠FRI…RIC[U] KH
3326 (6158) 15, 0.7 Bi [Sicilian denier], Obv.: *Cross with annulet in each quarter,* …RMCI… *Rev.: Eagle,* [⚜C]I…ILI[Є] IH
3327 (6165) 17, 0.6 Neapolitan denier, Ladislaus, 1386-1414. Obv.: *Arms of Anjou,* ✠LADI· …S [DЄ]…CIЄ. *Rev.: Cross,* ✠[ ]V[GЄ…IЄ[RL]ЄSICI… IH
3328 (8312) 17, 1.1 Quattrino of Mantua, Francisco I, 1382-1407. Obv.: *Arms of Gonzaga,* ✠ ◦ F ◦ D ◦ GONZAGA ◦ *Rev.: [Bust],* ✠[◦]U ◦ D ◦ MANTUA ◦ KH
3329 (6162) 15, 0.4 Denier of Ravenna, 13th-14th c. Obv.: ✠ARChIEPISCO, $_{P}{}^{V}{}_{S}$ *round centrally placed pellet. Rev.: Cross with ray ending in three pellets in quarters 2 & 3,* ✠DE RAVENA IH
3330 (6163) 16, 0.4 Sesino of Ascoli, 13th-14th c. Obv.: *Cross with ray ending in three pellets in quarters 1 & 4,* ✠ · DEASCh… *Rev.:* ✠ · S · E…D'EP'CO, $_{P}{}^{V}{}_{S}$ *in the centre.*
3331 (6164) 15, 0.4 Quattrino of Bologna, 13th-14th c. Obv.: A *between four annulets placed 1:2:1,* ✠ ◦BO◦NO◦[N…◦ *Rev.:* [✠]ER◦…VDI, ORVM *round centrally placed pellet.* IH
3332 (6159) 15, 0.4 Bi Milanese denier. Obv.: *Floriated cross with pellet in each quarter,* ✠ ·[N]…PVSM…· *Rev.:* Arms of Visconti, ✠ · C[I]…[AP]…[Є]· IH
3333 (2368) 14, 0.4 [Cypriot denier, Hugh III, 1267-84]. Obv.: *Cross,* ✠… *Rev.: Lion rampant,* ✠… IH
3334 (564) 17, 0.4 Cypriot denier, Henry II Lusignan, 1285-1324. Obv.: *Cross,* ✠ hЄNRI R[ЄI] DЄ… *Rev.: Lion rampant,* .M:ЄD[C]hI[P… IH
3335 (3049) 18, 0.5 Cypriot denier, Henry II Lusignan, 1285-1324. Obv.: *Cross with pellet in each quarter,* [✠hЄNRI:RЄI:DЄ] *Rev.: Lion rampant,* [✠IRLMЄD'ChIPR] IH
3336 (8313) 16, 0.5 Cypriot denier, Henry II Lusignan, 1285-1324. Obv.: *Cross with pellet in each quarter. Rev.: Lion rampant,* …Є[DChIPR] KH
3337 (8314) 16, 0.4 Cypriot denier. *Rev.: [Lion rampant],* …RЄI DЄ… KH
3338 (719) 13, 0.6 Denier of Famagusta, 1373-1464. Obv.: *Cross. Rev.: Janua,* ✠CIVI… IH
3339 (721) 14, 0.6 Denier of Famagusta, 1373-1464. Obv.: *Cross,* …IANV… *Rev.: Janua,* ✠[C]VI[AN… IH
3340 (6166) 16, 0.5 Denier of Famagusta, 1373-1464. Obv.: *Cross,* ✠DVX·IA[NV]Є… *Rev.: Janua,* ✠CIVIT… IH
3341 (6167) 14, 0.4 Denier of Famagusta, 1373-1464. Obv.: *Cross,* … X·I[ANV]… *Rev.: Janua,* …AMA IH
3342 (8310) 16, 0.8 Denier of Famagusta, 1373-1464. Obv.: *Cross,* ✠DVX · IANVЄN. *Rev.: Janua,* ✠CIVI… IH
3343 (6157) 16, 0.6 Denier of Mytilene, Francesco II, 1384-1403. Obv.: *Gattilusio arms in circle with eight petals,* ✠ FRAN…XIU… *Rev.: Cross, four Bs back-to-back in circle with eight petals,* [✠D]O[MI]…MЄTЄLI…[✿ ·] IH
3344 (565) 16, 0.6 Denier of Chios. Obv.: *Cross pattee in beaded circle, crosslet in one quarter. Rev.: Church in beaded circle.* IH
3345 (1162) 16, 0.5 Tornesello, A. Venier, 1382-1400. Obv.: *Cross,* ✠ANT'VЄNЄRIOD… *Rev.: Lion of St. Mark,* …ILIFЄRVЄNЄTIA… IH

PLATE 154

3346 (6150) 16, 0.4 Tornesello, A. Venier, 1382-1400. Obv.: *Cross,* [✠AИ]TO'VЄИЄRIO[D]VX. *Rev.: Lion of St. Mark,* ✠V[Є]XIL…2 IH
3347 (6151) 17, 0.6 Tornesello, A. Venier, 1382-1400. Obv.: *Cross,* ✠AИTO' VЄИЄ[R]IO [:D]V[X]. *Rev.: Lion of St. Mark,* ✠VЄXILI[F]ЄRVЄИЄTIA2 IH
3348 (6152) 16, 0.6 Tornesello, A. Venier, 1382-1400. Obv.: *Cross,* ✠AИTO'VЄИЄRIO:DVX. *Rev.: Lion of St. Mark,* ✠VЄXILI[F]ЄRVЄИЄTIA2 IH
3349 (6153) 16, 0.6 Tornesello, A. Venier, 1382-1400. Obv.: *Cross,* ✠AИTO'VЄИЄRIO[ ]DVX. *Rev.: Lion of St. Mark,* [✠V] ЄXILI[F]ЄRVЄИЄTIA2 IH
3350 (6154) 17, 0.5 Tornesello, A. Venier, 1382-1400. Obv.: *Cross,* ✠AИ[TO'] VЄИЄRIO DVX… *Rev.: Lion of St. Mark,* ✠VЄXILIFЄ[R]VЄИЄTIA2 IH
3351 (6155) 17, 0.5 Tornesello, A. Venier, 1382-1400. Obv.: *Cross,* … ИЄRIODV[ ]… IH
3352 (6156) 17, 0.4 Tornesello, A. Venier, 1382-1400. Obv.: *Cross,* ✠[A]…[И]ЄRIODVX. *Rev.: Lion of St. Mark,* [✠]V[ЄX] ILIFЄRVЄИЄTIA2 IH
3353 (8307) 17, 0.6 Tornesello, A. Venier, 1382-1400. Obv.:…[T]OVЄИЄRIODV… *Rev.:* …VЄ[И]… KH

UNIDENTIFIED

3354 (6160) 15, 0.4 Denier tournois. *Corr. Obv.: Cross,* ✠C… *Rev.: Church,* ✠ ·[ ]·…[ЄI·[G]…· IH

Anastasius I

Plate 1

1

2

3

4

5

6

7

8

10

11

Plate 2

Anastasius I *(cont.)*

12 13 14 15 16 17 18

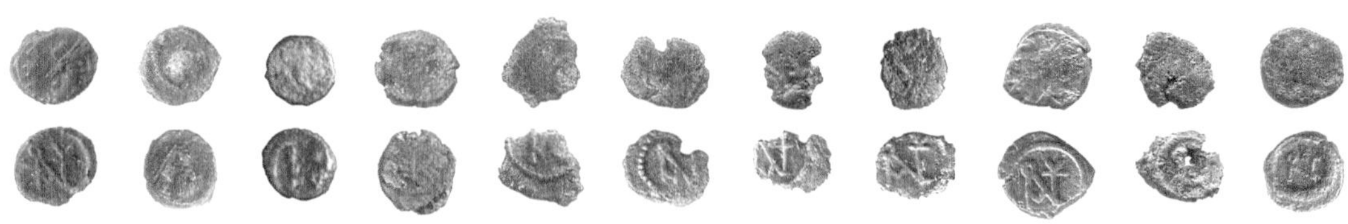

19 20 21 22 23 24 25 26 27 28 29

Plate 3

Justin I
Constantinople

30

31

32

33

34

35

36

37

38

39

40

41

42

43

44

45

46

Justin I
Constantinople *(cont.)*

47 48 49 50 51 52 53 54 55 56

Nicomedia

57

58

Antioch

59

Thessalonica

60

Uncertain

61

62

63

64

65

Plate 5

Justinian I
Constantinople

66

67

68

69

70

71

72

73

74

75

76

77

Justinian I
Constantinople *(cont.)*

Plate 6

78

79

80

81

82

84

85

86

87

Justinian I
Constantinople *(cont.)*

Plate 7

88

89

90

91

92

Nicomedia

93

94

95

96

97

98

99

Justinian I *(cont.)*
Cyzicus

100

101

102

Antioch

103

104

105

106

107

108

Justinian I
Antioch *(cont.)*

Plate 9

112 113 114

109 110 111

Thessalonica

Alexandria

115

116 117

Sicily

118
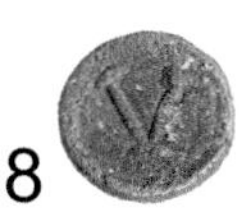

Uncertain

119 120 121 122

Pentanummia with Christogram 522-537 Constantinople

Plate 10

123 124 125 126 127 128 129 131 131

132 133 134 135 136 137 138 139 140

141 142 143 144

Uncertain

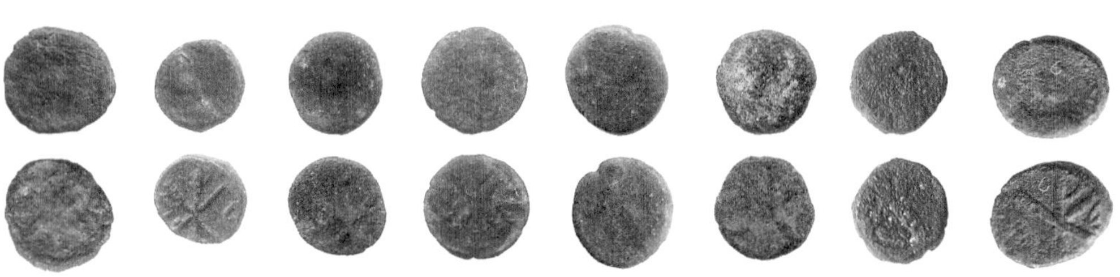

145 146 147 148 149 150 151 152

153 154 155 156 157 158 159

Justin II
Constantinople

Plate 11

160

161

162

163

164

165

166

167

168

169

170

171

172

173

Justin II

Plate 12

Constantinople *(cont.)*

174 175 176 177 178 179 180 181

182 183 184 185 186 187 188 189

190 191 192 193 194 195 196 197

Nicomedia

198 199 200 201 202

Plate 13

Justin II
Nicomedia *(cont.)*

203 204 205 206 207

208 209 210 211

Cyzicus

212 213 214 215 216 217

Antioch

218 219 220

Alexandria

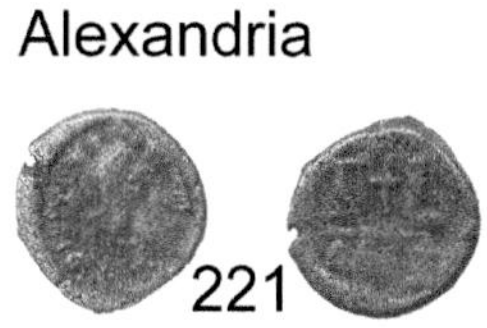

221

Justin II *(cont.)*
Thessalonica

Plate 14

222 223 224 225 226 227

228 229 230 231 232 233 234

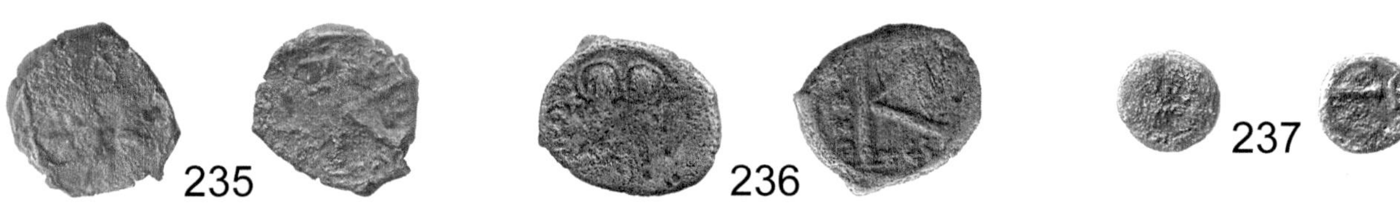

235 236 237

Uncertain

238 239 240 241 242 243

Tiberius II Constantinople

Plate 15

244

245

246

Antioch

249

Nicomedia

247

248

Uncertain

250

251

252

253

254

Maurice
Constantinople

Plate 16

255

256

257

258

259

260

261

262

263

264

265

Plate 17

Maurice
Constantinople *(Cont.)*

266

267

268

269

270

271

272

273

274

Nicomedia

275

276

277

Cyzicus

278

279

280

281

Maurice *(Cont.)*
Antioch

Plate 18

282

283

284

285

286

287

288

289

290

Thessalonica

291

292

293

Uncertain

294

295

296

297

298

299

Plate 19

Phocas
Constantinople

300

301

302

303

304

305

306

307

308

Nicomedia

309

310

Plate 20

Phocas *(cont.)*
Cyzicus

311

312

313

314

Antioch

315

316

317

318

319

Alexandria

320

Uncertain

321

322

323

324

325

326

6th Century Uncertain

Plate 21

327

328

329

330

332

333

334

335

336

337

338

339

340

341

342

6th Century Uncertain *(cont.)*

Plate 22

343 344 345 346 347 348 349 350 351

352 353 354 355 356 357 358 359 360

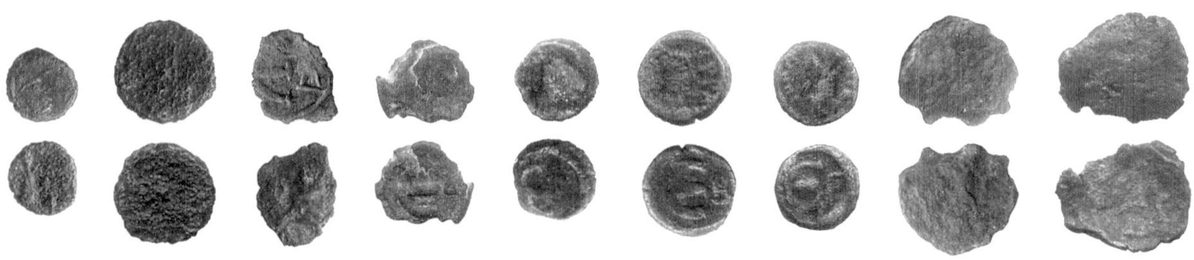

361 362 363 364 365 366 367 368 369

Egypt

370 371 372 373 374 375 376

Heraclius
Constantinople

Plate 23

377

378

Class 1 II

379

380

381

382

383

384

385

386

387

388

?

389

Heraclius
Constantinople *(Cont.)*

?

390

391

392

Class 2 [II]

394

395

396

397

398

399

400

401

Plate 25

Heraclius
Constantinople *(Cont.)*

402

403

404

405

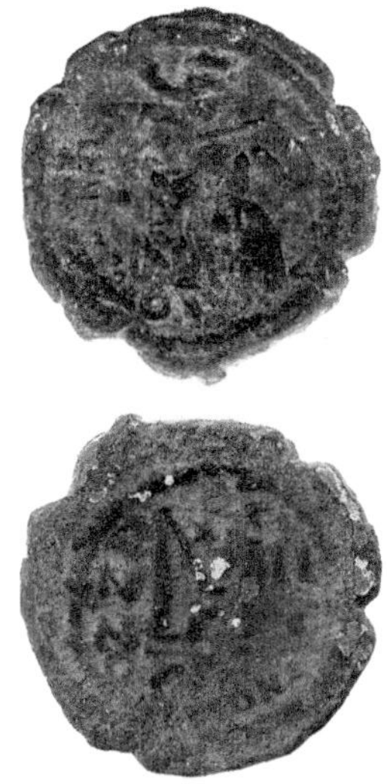
406

407

408

409

410

411

412

413

414

415

416

Plate 26

Heraclius
Constantinople *(Cont.)*

417

II

418

419

420

421

422

423

424

425

Ч

426

427

428

429

Plate 27

Heraclius
Constantinople *(Cont.)*

430

431

432

433

434

435

436

437

438

439

440

441

Plate 28

Heracliius
Constantinople *(Cont.)*

442

443

444

445

446

447

448

449

450

451

452

453

454

455

456

Plate 29

Heraclius
Constantinople *(Cont.)*

Class 3

Ч

457

ЧI

458

ς

459

ςI

460

ЧIII

461

X

462

463

464

XЧ

465

?

466

467

Heraclius
Constantinople *(Cont.)*

Plate 30

Class 3/4

468

Class 4 X Ч

469

X ϛ

470

471

472

?

473

474

Class 5 X X

475

476

477

478

479

480

Heraclius
Constantinople *(Cont.)*

Plate 31

481

482

483

484

485

XXI

486

487

488

XXII

489

490

491

XXIII

492

493

494

Heracles
Constantinople *(Cont.)*

Plate 32

495

496

497

498

499

500

501

502

503

504

505

506

507

508

509

510

Plate 33

Heraclius
Constantinople *(Cont.)*

XXI...

511

512

513

514

XXЧ

515

516

517

518

519

520

521

522

523

524

525

526

527

Heraclius
Constantinople *(Cont.)*

Plate 34

528

529

XXϛ

530

531

532

533

534

535

536

537

538

XXX

539

540

541

?

542

543

Heraclius
Constantinople *(Cont.)*

Plate 35

544 545 546 547 548 549

550 551 552 553 554 555

556 557 558 559 560

Plate 36

Heraclius
Constantinople *(Cont.)*

?

561

562

563

564

565

566

567

568

569

570

571

572

573

574

575

576

577

578

Heraclius
Constantinople *(Cont.)*

Plate 37

Class 6

580 581 582 583 584

585 586 587 588 589 590

591 592

Uncertain type

594 595

Heraclius
Constantinople *(Cont.)*

Plate 38

596

597

598

599

600

601

602

603

604

605

606

607

608

609

610

611

612

613

614

615

Plate 39

Heraclius
Constantinople *(Cont.)*

616 617 618 619 620 621

Nicomedia

622 623 624 625 626

627 628 629 630 631

Heraclius
Nicomedia *(Cont.)*

Plate 40

632

633

634

635

636

637

638

639

640

641

642

643

644

645

646

Plate 41

Heraclius
Nicomedia *(Cont.)*

647

648

Cyzicus

649

650

651

652

653

654

655

656

657

Plate 42

Heraclius *(Cont.)*

Seleucia

658 659

Isaura

660

Neapolis in Syria

661

Alexandria

662 663 664 665 666 667 668

669 670 671 672

Heraclius *(Cont.)* Thessalonica

Plate 43

673 674 675 676 677

678 679 680 681 682 683 684

685 686 687 688 689 690

Carthage

691

Heraclius *(Cont.)*
Uncertain

Plate 44

692

693

694

696

697

698

699

701

702

703

705

707

Heraclius
Uncertain *(Cont.)*

Plate 45

708

709

710

711

712

713

714

715

Constans II
Constantinople

Plate 46

716

717

718

719

720

721

722

723

Class 1

724

725

726

727

728

729

730

Constans II
Constantinople *(Cont.)*

Plate 47

Class 1/4

731 732 733 734 735

737 738 739

Class 2

740 741 742 743 744

Constans II
Constantinople *(Cont.)*

Plate 48

Class 2bis

745 746 747 748 749

750 751 752 753 754 755

756 757 758 759 760

761

762

Constans II
Constantinople *(Cont.)*

Plate 49

763

764

765

766

767

768

769

770

771

772

773

774

Class 3

775

776

Class 4

777

778

Constans II
Constantinople *(Cont.)*

Plate 50

779 780 781 782 783 784

785 786 787 788 789 790

Class 5

791 792 793 794 795 796

797

798

Constans II
Constantinople *(Cont.)*

Plate 51

Class 5/6

799

Class 5-8

800

Class 6

801 802 803 804 805

Class 7

806 807 808 809 810 811

Class 9

812 813 814 815

Constans II
Constantinople *(Cont.)*

Plate 52

Class 11

816 817 818 819 820 821

822 823 824 825 826 827 828

829 830 831 832

Alexandria

833 834

Uncertain

835 836 837

7th Century Uncertain

Plate 53

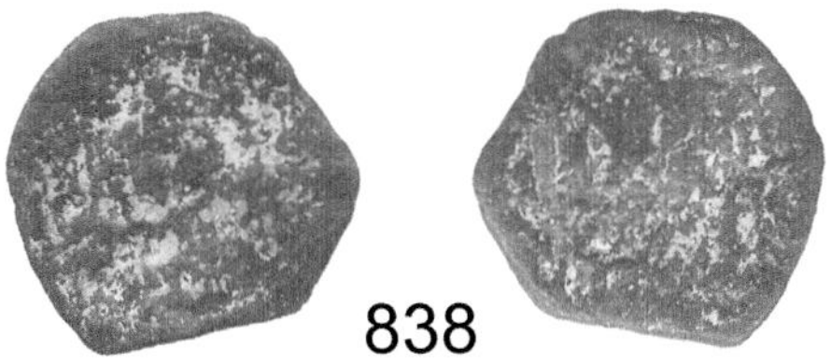
838

840

841

842

843

844

845

846

847

Imitations of 7th Century Byzantine Coins

848

849

850

851

852

853

854

855

856

857

Plate 54

Justinian II

858

Anastasius II

859

Nicephorus I

860

Michael II

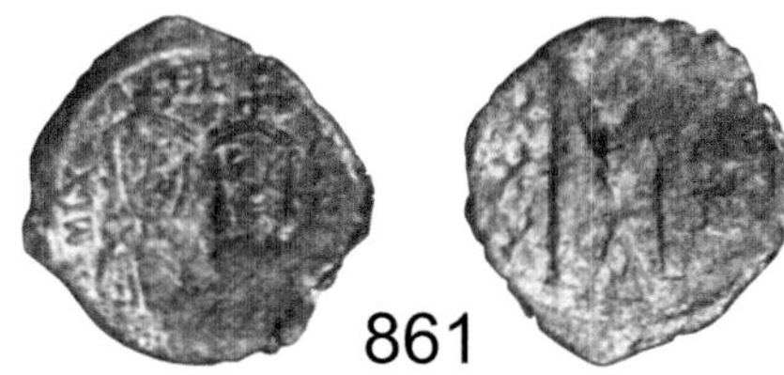

861

Theophilus

862 863

864 865

Basil I

866 867

868 869

Plate 55

Leo VI

870

871

872

Constantine VII

873

874

Romanus I

875

876

877

878

879

880

881

882

Nicephorus II

883

884

Imitation

885

A1

Plate 56

886 887 888 889

A2

890 891 892 893

894 895 896 897 898

A2 *(Cont.)*

Plate 57

899

900

901

902

903

904

905

906

907

908

909

910

911

912

A2 *(Cont.)*

Plate 58

913

B

914

915

916

917

918

919

920

921

922

923

924

925

926

927

928

929

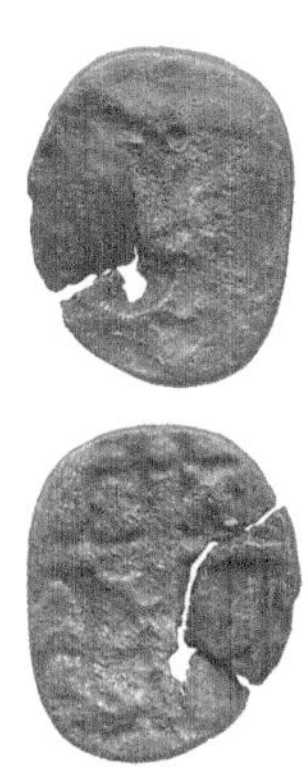

930

931

932

B *(Cont.)*

Plate 59

933 934 935 936 937 938 939

941 942 943 944 945 946

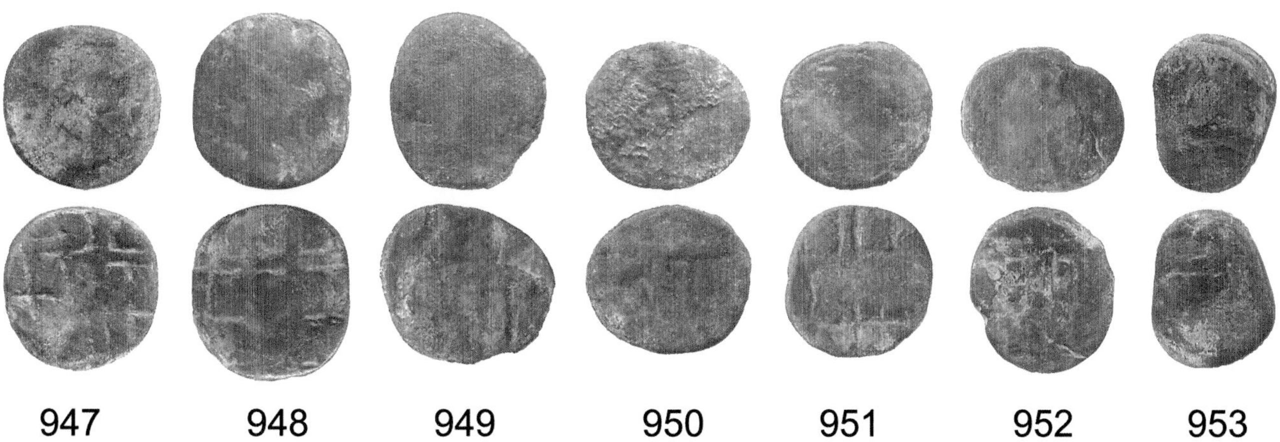

947 948 949 950 951 952 953

B *(Cont.)*

Plate 60

954 955 956 957 958 959 960

961 962 963 964 965 966 967

968 969 970 971 972 973 974

975

B *(Cont.)*

Plate 61

976 977 978 979 980 981 982

983 984 985 986 987 988 991

992 993 994 995 996 997

B *(Cont.)*

Plate 62

998 999 1000 1001 1002 1003

C

1004 1005 1006 1007 1008

1009 1010 1011 1012 1013 1014

1015

C *(Cont.)*

Plate 63

1016

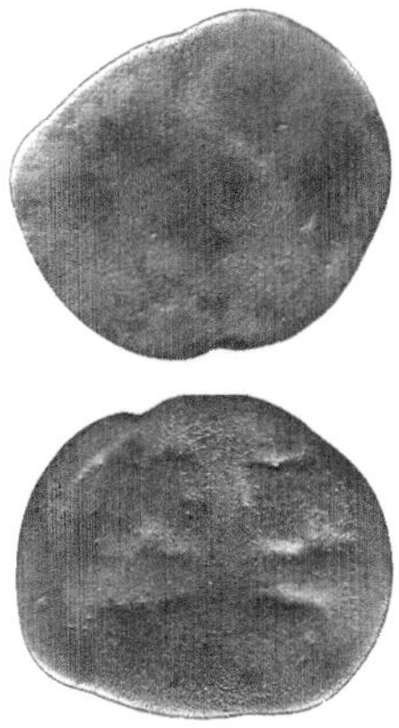
1017

1018

1019

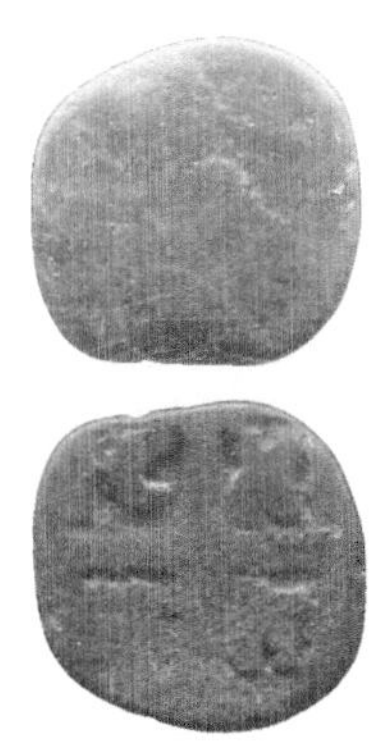
1020

1021

1022

1023

1024

1025

1026

1027

1028

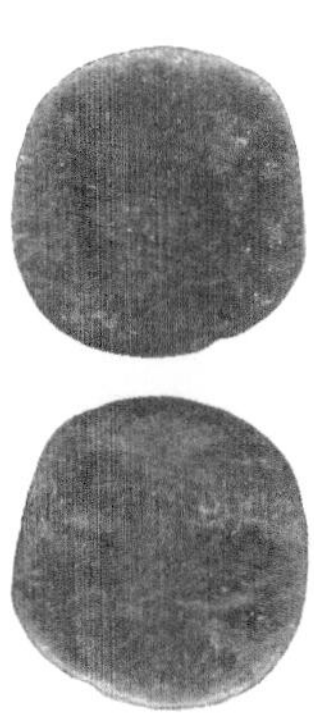
1029

1030

1031

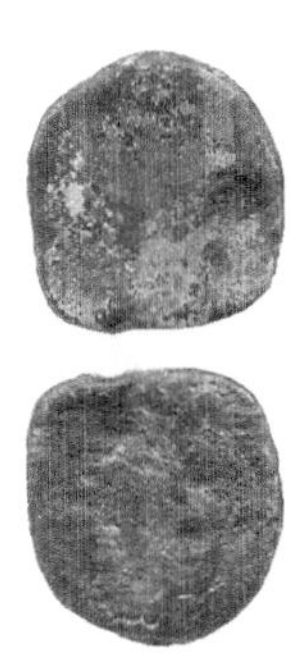
1032

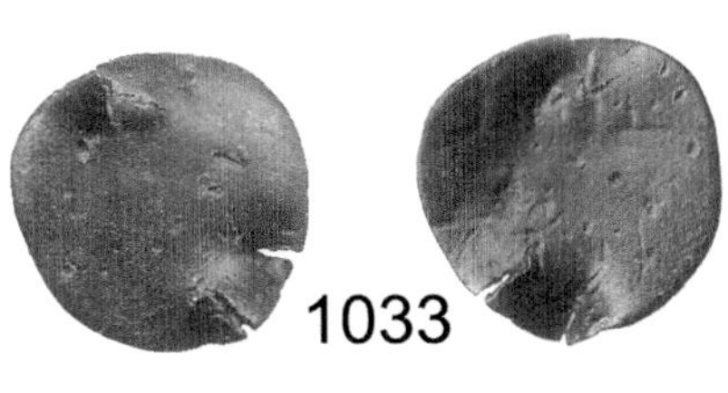
1033

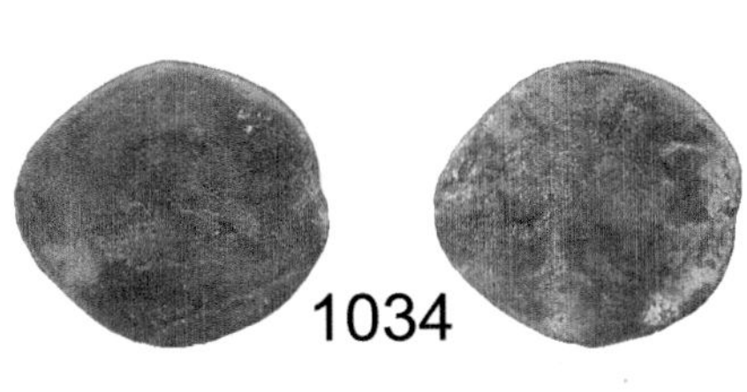
1034

C / D

1035

Plate 64

D

1036 1037 1038

E

1039 1040

F

1041 1042 1043

G

1044 1045

H

1046 1047 1048 1049 1050 1051

H *(Cont.)*

Plate 65

1053

I

1054

1055

1056

1057

1058

1059

1060

1061

1062

1063

1064

1065

1066

J

Plate 66

1066

1067

1068

1069

1070

1071

1072

1073

K

1074

1075

1076

1077

1078

1079

1080

1081

K *(Cont.)*

Plate 67

1082 1083 1084 1085 1086

1087 1088 1089 1090

Constantine X

1091 1092 1093 1094 1095

Romanus IV

Plate 68

1096 1097 1098 1099 1100 1101 1102

1103 1104 1105 1106 1107 1108 1109

1110 1111 1112 1113 1114 1115

Michael VII

1116 1117

Plate 69

Nicephorus III

1118

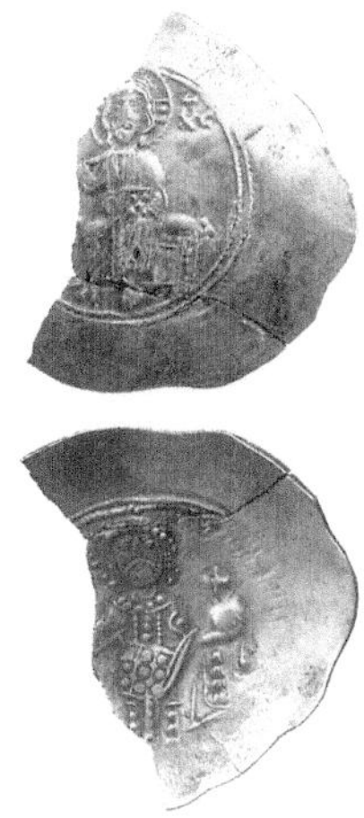
1119

1120

1121

1122

1123

1124

1125

1126

1127

1128

1129

1130

1131

Uncertain

1132 1133 1134 1135 1136 1137

 1138 

 1139 

Alexius I
Constantinople
2nd Coinage

A

1140

C

1141 1142

D

1143 1144

Alexius I *(Cont.)*

Plate 71

Thessalonica

2nd Coinage

1145 1146 1147 1148 1149 1150 1151

1152 1153

3rd Coinage

1155 1156 1157 1158 1159 1160 1161

1162

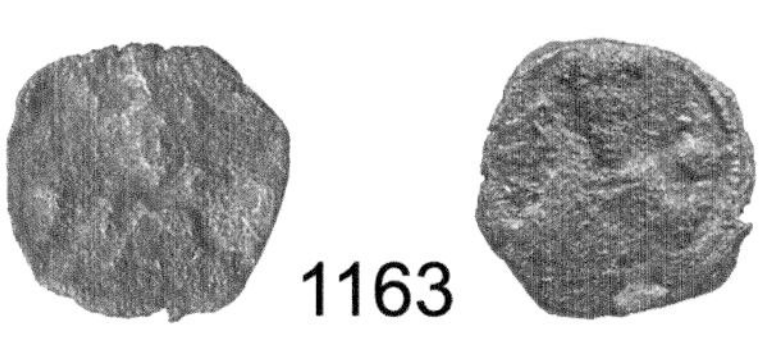

1163

Alexius I
Thessalonica *(Cont.)*
4th Coinage

Plate 72

1164 1165 1166 1167 1168 1169 1170

1171 1172

4th Coinage or imitations
a1 [IIIa?]

1173 1174 1175 1176 1177 1178 1179

a2

1180 1181 1182

Plate 73

Alexius I
Thessalonica *(Cont.)*

Worn specimens

1183 1184 1185 1186 1187 1188

Uncertain mint

1189

4th Coinage of Thessalonica Imitations

b1 b2 c d e

1190 1191 1192 1193 1194 1195

f

1196 1197 1198 1199 1200 1201 1202

g

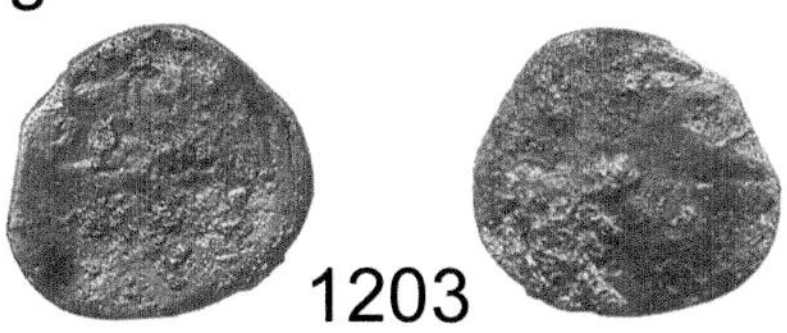

1203

h

1204

Trebizond, Gavras Period *c.* 1091-1140

2 3 7 8

1205 1206 1207 1208 1209

John II

Constantinople, 2nd Coinage, A Constantinople, A Thess.

1210

1211 1212 1213 1214

Manuel I

Constantinople, II 1st Coinage, A 2nd Coinage, A

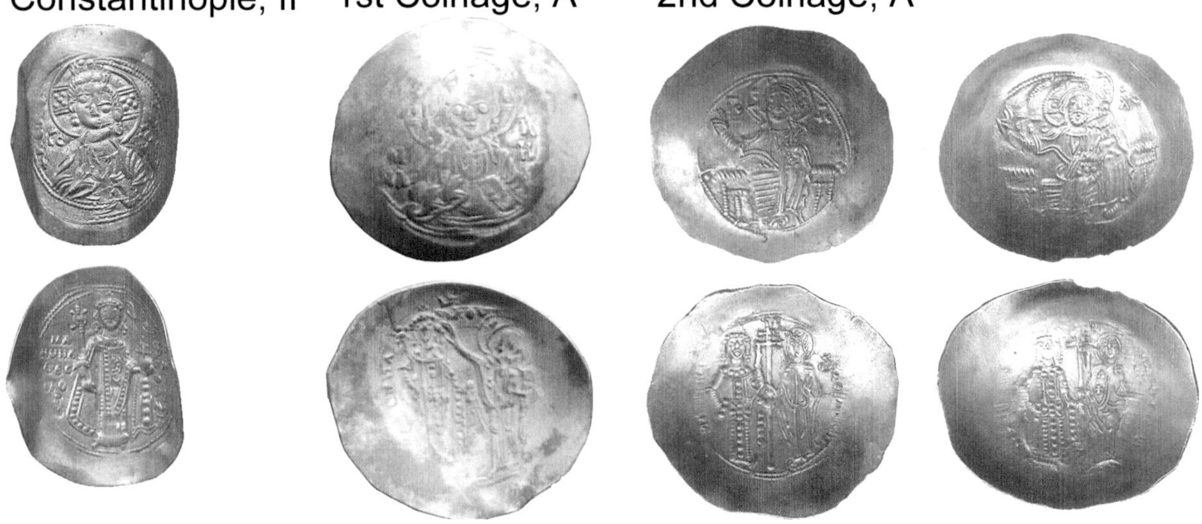

1215 1216 1217 1218

Manuel I *(Cont.)*
4th Coinage

Plate 75

1219

1220

1221

1222

1223

1224

1225

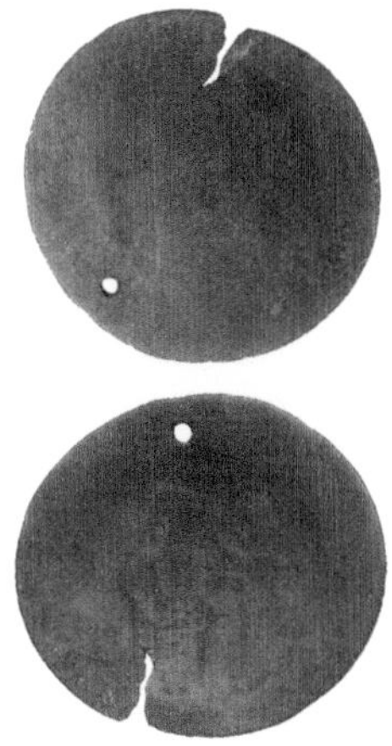
1226

1227

2nd Coinage

1228

3rd Coinage

1229

1230

1231

1232

4th Coinage

1233

1234

1235

1236

Plate 76

Manuel I *(Cont.)*

Constantinople

1st Coinage

1237

1238

D

1239

Thessalonica

A

1240

B

1241

Uncertain

A

1242

B

1243

Andronicus I

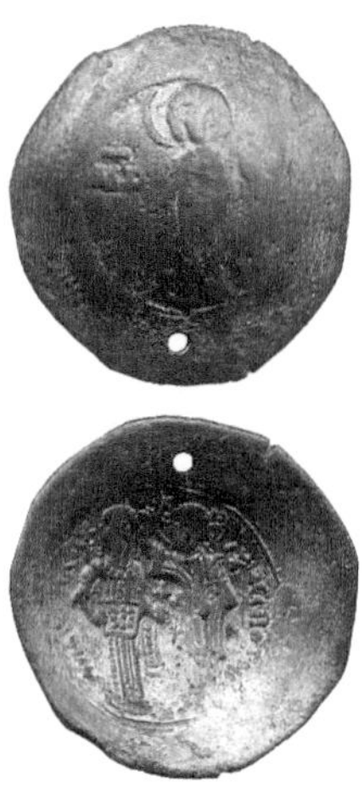

1244

1245

1246

Isaac Comnenus of Cyprus

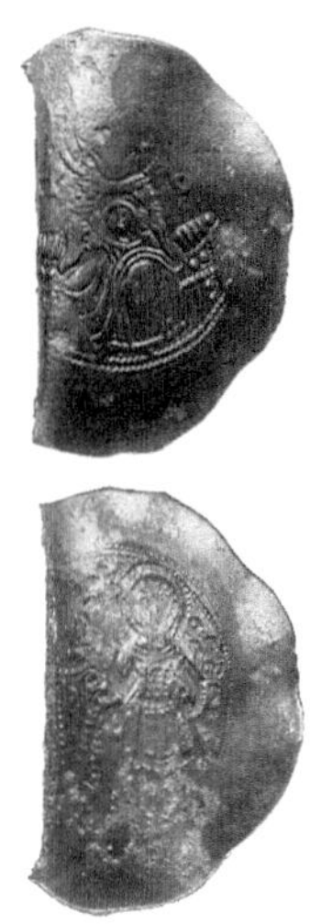

1247

1248

Isaac II

1249

1250

1251

1252

Isaac II *(Cont.)*

Plate 77

1253 1254 1255 1256 1257 1258

1259 1260 1261 1262 1263 1264 1265

1266 1267 1268 1269 1270 1271 1272

1273 1274 1275 1276 1277 1279 1280 1281

Alexius III

Plate 78

1282

1284

1285

1286

1287

1288

1289

1290

1291

1292

1293

1294

1295

1296

1297

Theodore I

1298

1299

John III

1300

1301

1302

Plate 79

Theodore Comnenus-Ducas

1303

Andronicus I Gido (Latin imitatives, type H)

1304

1305

Faithful ('Bulgarian') Imitations

B

1306

1307

C

1308

1309

1310

1311

1312

1313

1314

Plate 80

Latin Imitatives, large module
Constantinople

A

1315

B

1316

C

1317

1318

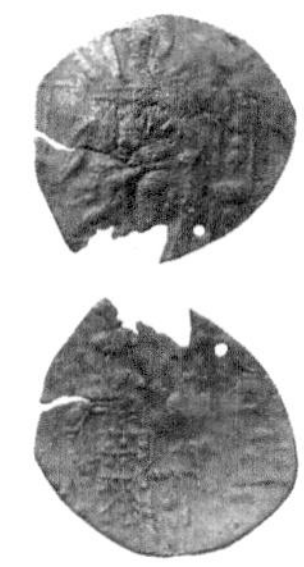

1319

D / E

1320

Latin Imitatives, large module
Thessalonica

A

1321

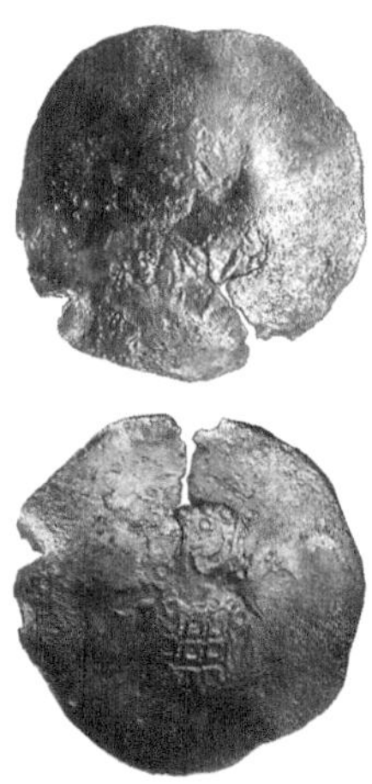

1322

B

1323

1324

1325

C

1326

1327

1328

Latin Imitatives, small module
Type A

Plate 81

1329 1330 1331 1332 1333 1334 1335

1336 1337 1338 1339 1340 1341 1342

1343 1344 1345 1346 1347 1348 1349

1350 1351 1352 1353

Plate 82

Latin Imitatives, small module
Type A *(Cont.)*

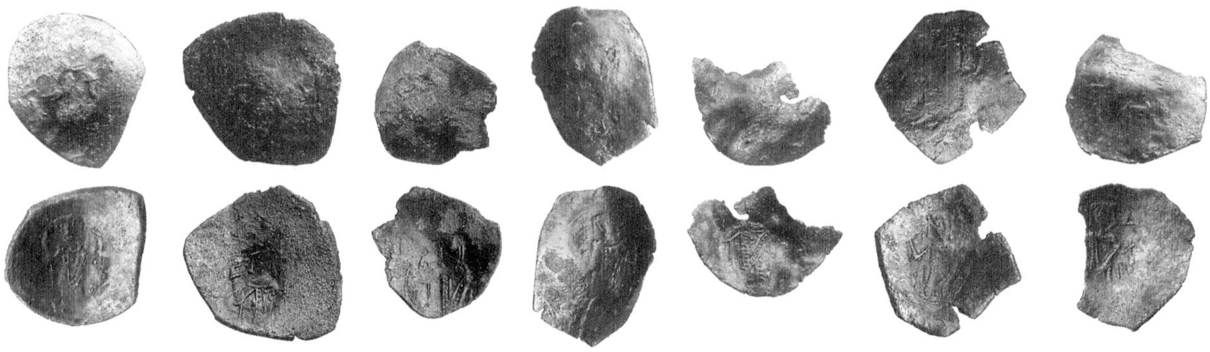

1354 1355 1356 1357 1358 1359 1360

1361 1362 1363 1364 1365 1366 1367

1368 1369 1370 1371 1372 1373 1374

Plate 83

Latin Imitatives, small module *(Cont.)*

Type B

1375 1376 1377 1378 1379 1380 1381

1382 1383 1384 1385 1386 1387

Type C

1388 1389 1390 1391 1392

Latin Imitatives, small module *(Cont.)*

Plate 84

Type D

1393 1394 1395 1396 1397 1398 1399

1400

Type E

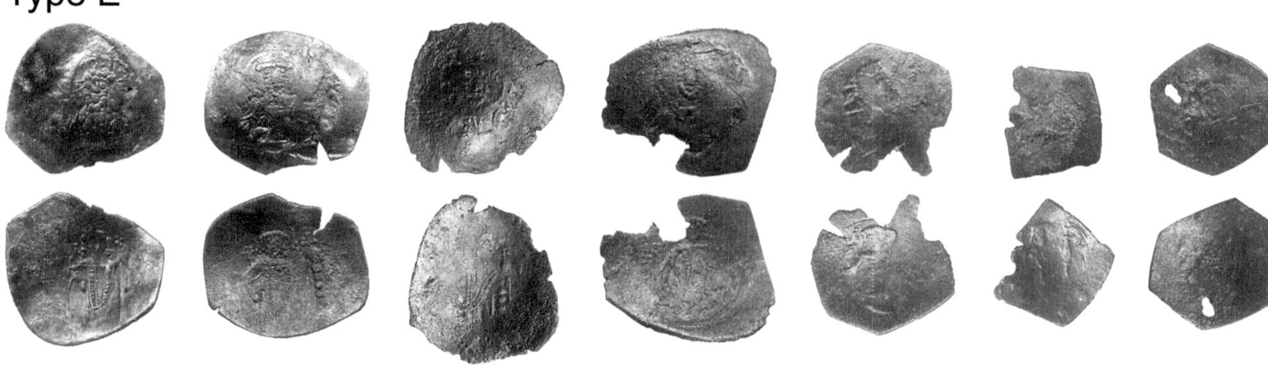

1401 1402 1403 1404 1405 1406 1407

Type F

1408 1409 1410 1411

Plate 85

Latin Imitatives, small module
Type G

1412 1413 1414 1415 1416 1417 1418

1419 1420 1421 1422 1423 1424 1425

1426 1427 1428 1429 1430 1431 1432

1433 1434 1435 1436 1437

Plate 86

Latin Imitatives, small module
Uncertain

1438 1439 1440 1441 1442 1443 1444

1445 1446 1447 1448 1449 1450 1451

1452 1453 1454 1455 1456 1457 1458 1459

1460 1461 1462 1463 1464 1465

Plate 87

Local imitative trachea, *c.* 1221 ff.

A P

1466 1467 1468 1469 1470 1471 1472

1473 1474 1475

?

1476

B P

1477 1478

Unidentified trachea

1479 1480 1481 1482 1483 1484

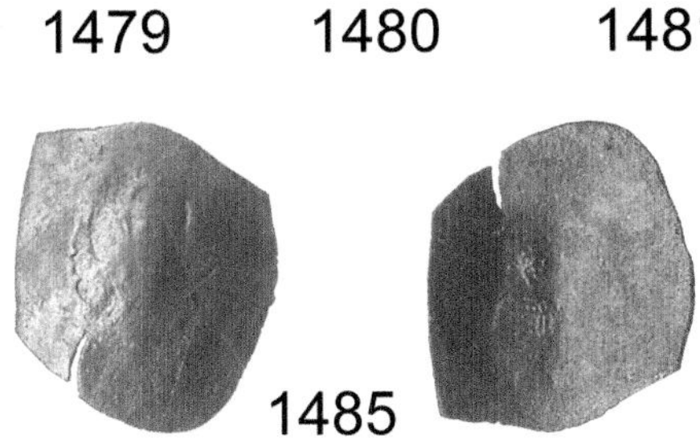

1485

1486

Uncertain tetartera

Plate 88

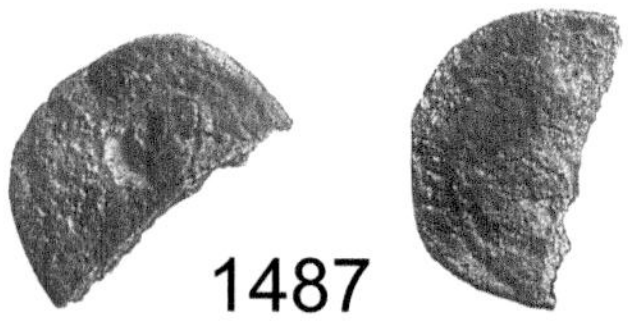

1487

1488

1489

Illegible trachea

1490

1491

1492

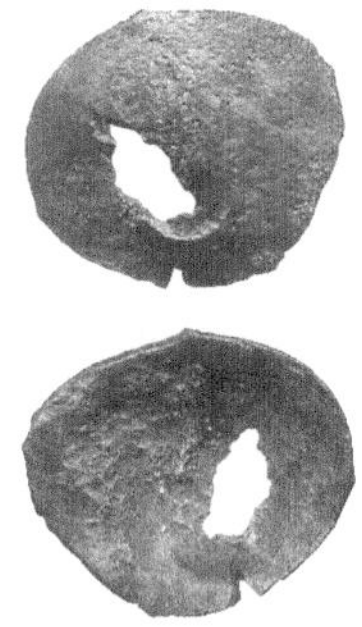

1493

1494

1495

1496

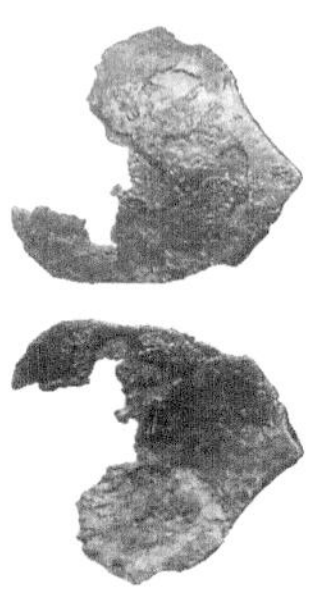

1497

1498

1499

1500

1501

1502

1503

1504

1505

1506

1507

1508

1509

1510

Leo Gavalas

Plate 89

A

1511 1512 1513 1514 1515 1516 1517 1518

1519 1520 1521 1522 1523

A1

1524

B

1525 1526 1527 1528 1529 1530 1531

1532 1533 1534 1535 1536 1537

Leo Gavalas *(Cont.)*

C

1538

D

1539

John Gavalas

1540

1541

1542

1543

1544

Plate 91

Gavalas Successors
1250-1254

1

1545 1546 1547

2

1548 1549 1550 1551 1552

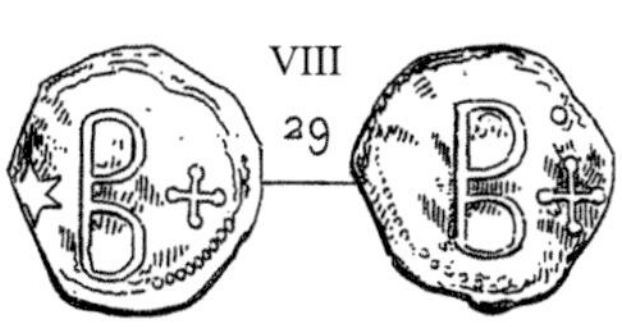

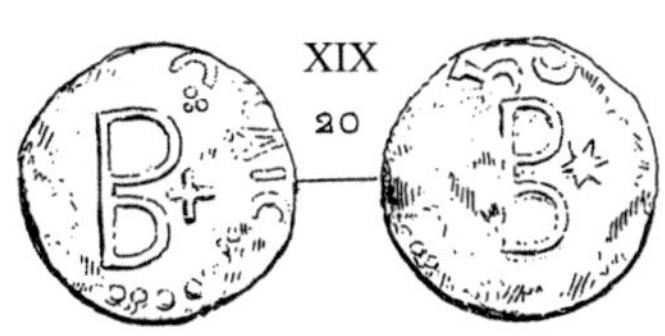

2b

1553

3

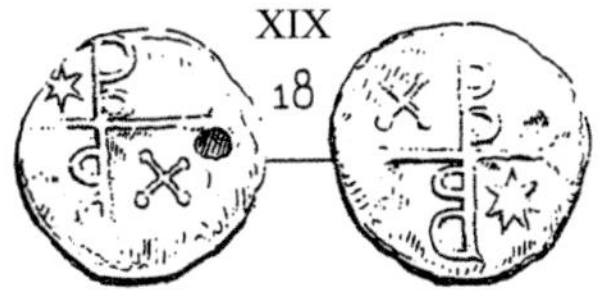

1554

Gavalas Successors *(Cont.)*

Plate 92

1254-1258

4

1555 1556 1557 1559 1560 1561 1562

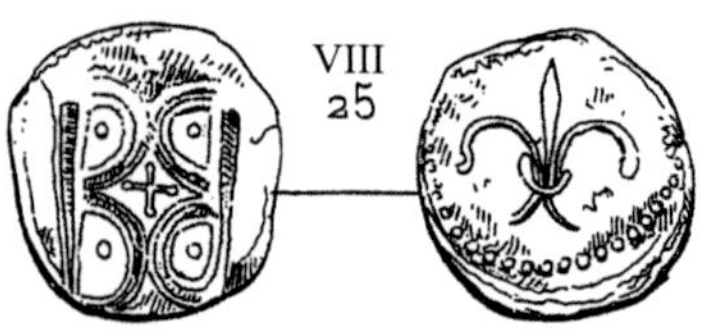

1258-1261

5

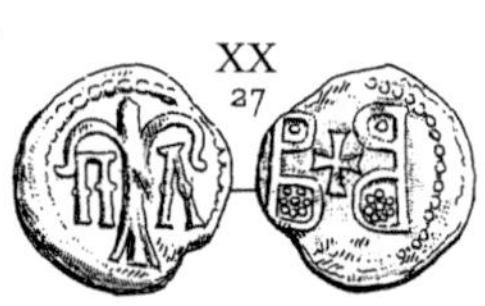

1563

6

a

1564

b

1565

c

1566

1261-1273

7

1567 1568 1569

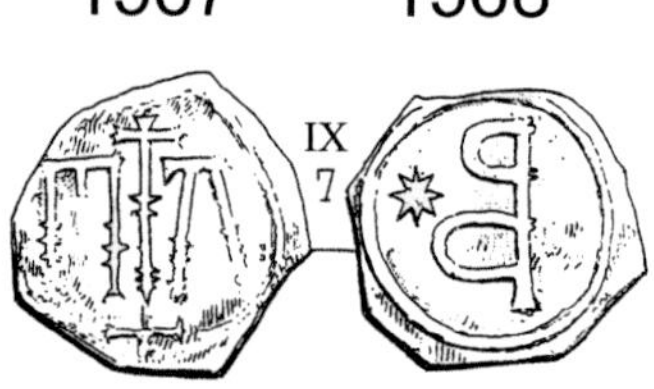

8

1570 1571

9

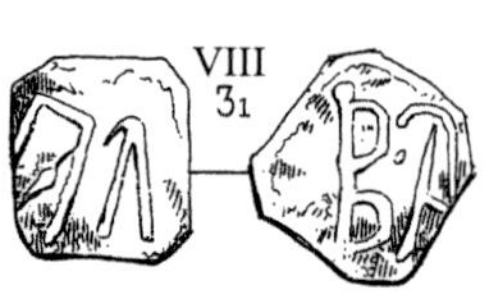

1572

Gavalas Successors *(Cont.)*

Plate 93

1273-[1278]

10

1573 1574 1575 1576 1577 1578 1579 1580

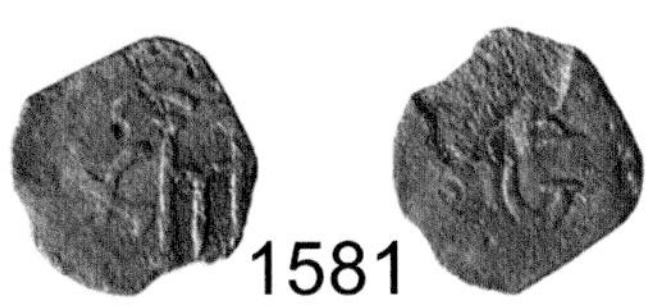

1581

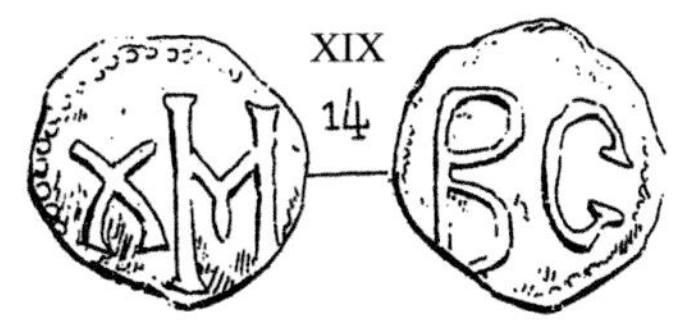

[1278]-1294

11

1582 1583 1584 1586 1587 1588

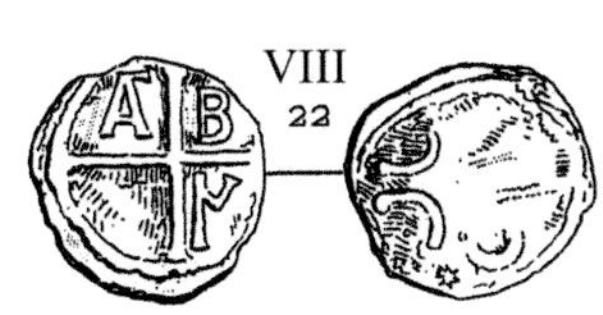

12

1590

13

a

1591 1592 1593 1594 1595

b

1596 1597

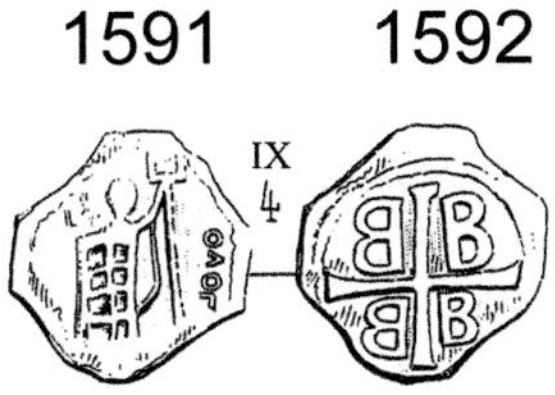

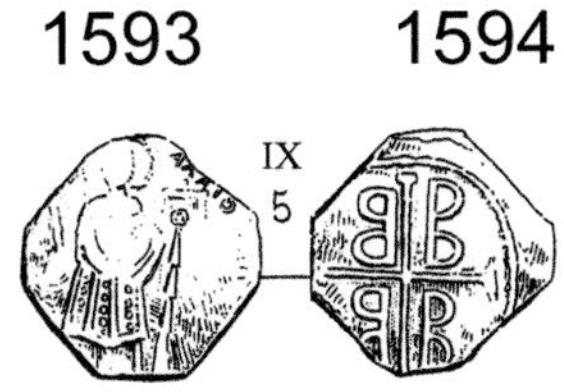

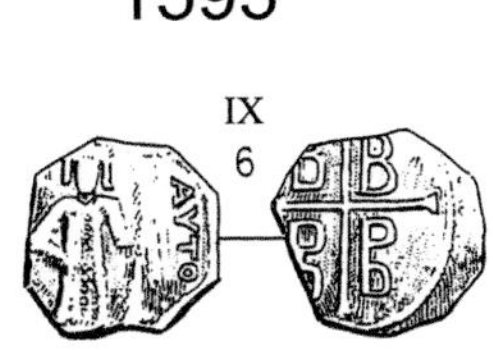

Gavalas Successors *(Cont.)*

Plate 94

Countermarked *dirhem* of the Seljuks of Rum

Mas'ud II

1598

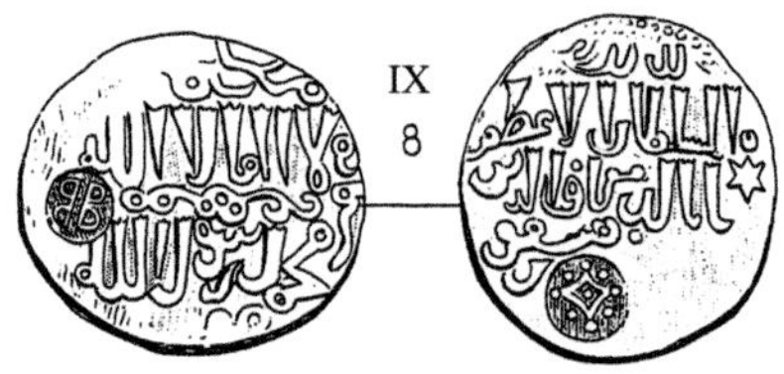

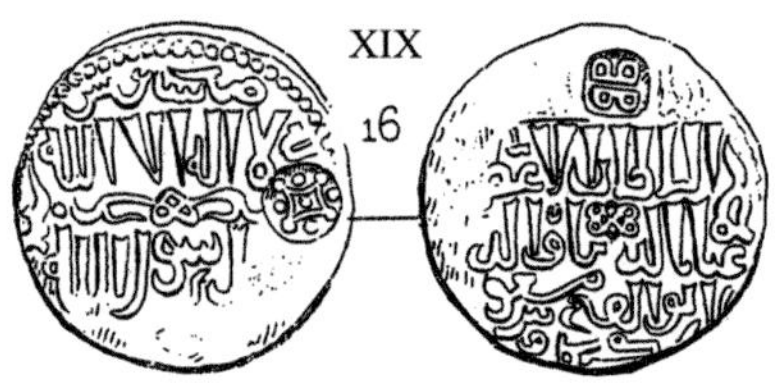

Kay-Khusru III

[1294-1304]
14

1599

1600

1601

1602

1603

1605

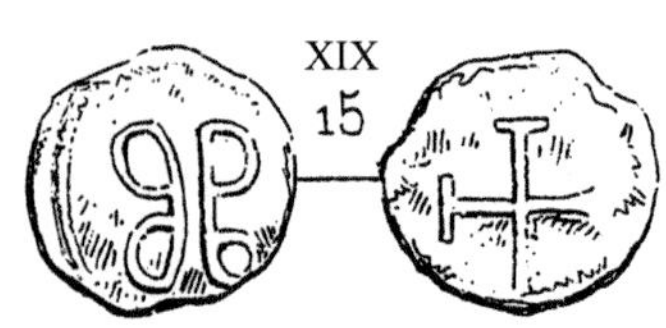

15

1606

Gavalas Successors *(Cont.)*

[1294-1304]

16

Plate 95

1607 1608 1609 1610 1611 1612

17

1613 1614 1615 1616 1617 1618 1619

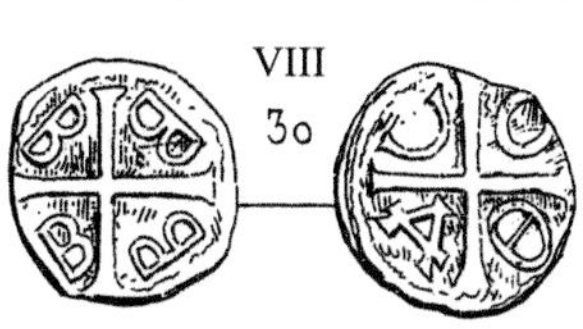

18

1620 1621 1622 1623 1624 1625 1626

1627

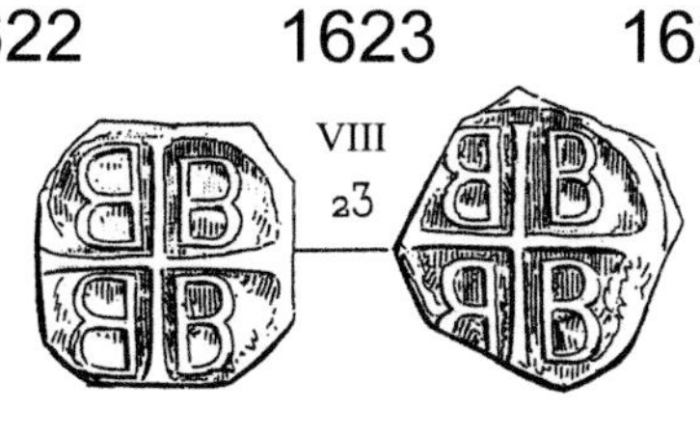

Gavalas Successors *(Cont.)*

Plate 96

[*c.*1304 - *c.*1307]

19

a

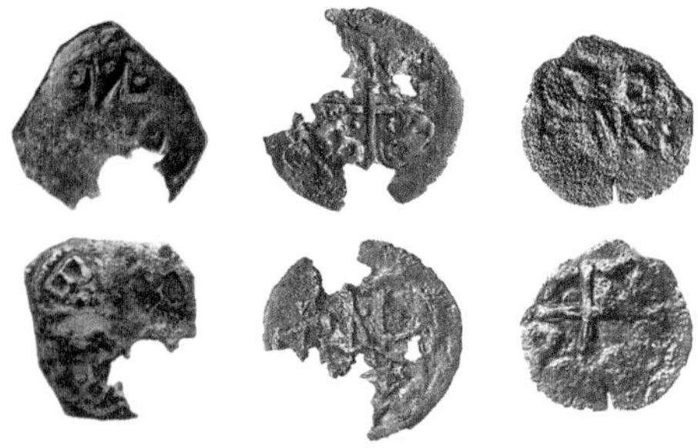

1628 1629 1630

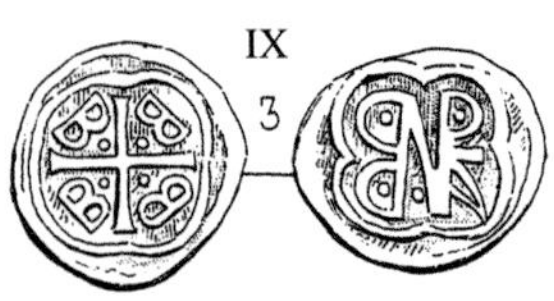

b

1631 1632 1633 1634

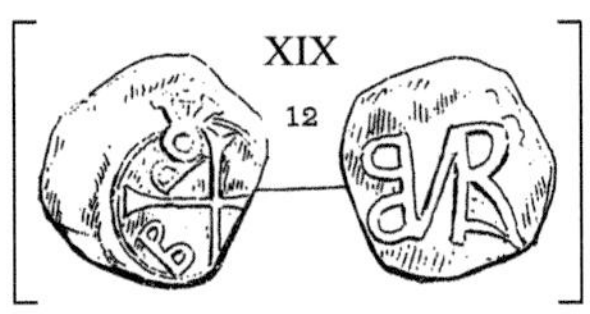

c

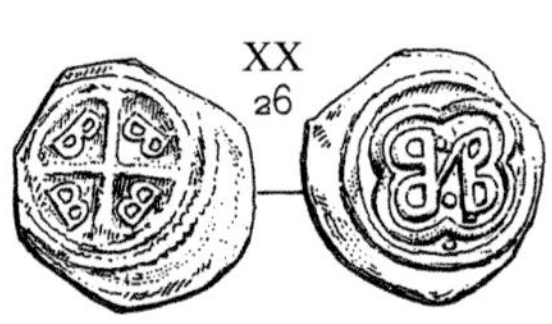

1635

[*c.*1307 - *c.*1309]

20

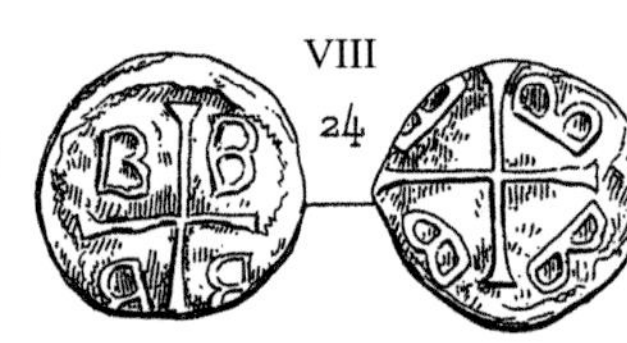

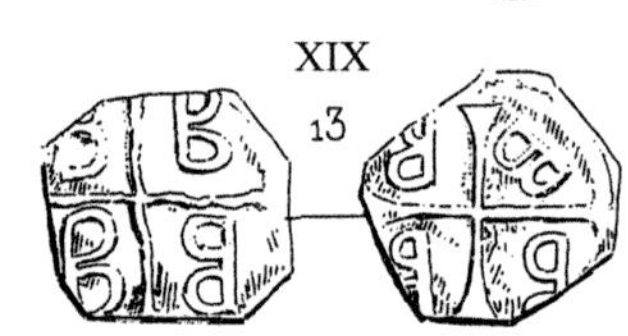

1636 1637 1638

Unrelated types

21

1639

22

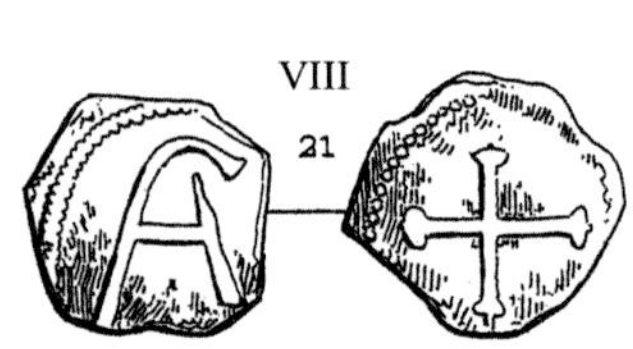

1640

1641

Hospitaller AR/AV

Plate 97

1658

1659

1660

1661

1662

1663

1664

1665

AV
1666

AV
1667

1668

1669

1670

1671

1672

1673

1674

1675

Villaret deniers

Plate 98

1676 1677

14th c. anonymous deniers, type I

1678 1679 1680 1681 1682 1683

1684 1685 1686 1687 1688 1689 1690 1691 1692

1693 1694 1695 1696 1697 1698 1699 1700 1701

1702 1703 1704 1705 1706 1707 1708 1709 1710

1711 1712 1713 1714 1715 1716 1717 1718 1719

14th c. anonymous deniers, type I *(Cont.)*

Plate 99

1720 1721 1722 1723 1724 1725 1726 1727 1728

1729 1730 1731 1732 1733 1734 1735 1736 1737

1738 1739 1740 1741 1742 1743 1744 1745 1746

1747 1748 1749 1750 1751 1752 1753 1754 1755

1756 1757 1758 1759 1760 1761 1762 1763 1764

14th c. anonymous deniers, type I *(Cont.)*

Plate 100

1765 1766 1767 1768 1769 1770 1771 1772 1773

1774 1775 1776 1777 1778 1779 1780 1781 1782

1783 1784 1785 1786 1787 1788 1789 1790 1791

1791 1792 1793

Type I, late and uncertain

1795 1796 1797 1798 1799 1800 1801 1802 1803

Plate 101

14th c. anonymous deniers, type I, late and uncertain *(Cont.)*

1804 1805 1806 1807 1808 1809 1810 1811

14th c. anonymous deniers, type II

1812 1813 1814 1815 1816 1817 1818 1819 1820

1821 1822 1823 1824 1825 1826 1827 1828 1829

1830 1831 1832 1833 1834 1835 1836 1837 1838

1839 1840 1841 1842 1843 1844 1845 1846 1847

14th c. anonymous deniers, type II *(Cont.)*

1848 1849 1850 1851 1852 1853 1854 1855 1856 1857

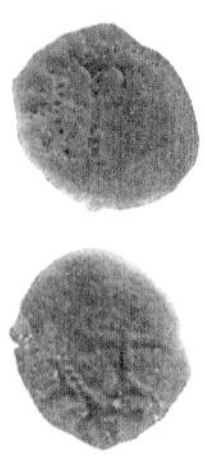        

1858 1859 1860 1861 1862 1863 1864 1865 1866

1867 1868 1869 1870

Uncertain

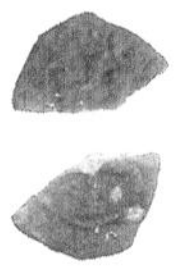      

1871 1872 1873 1874 1875 1876 1877

Imitation

1878

Plate 103

Signed deniers of Roger de Pins (1355-1365)

1879 1880 1881 1882 1883 1884 1885 1886 1887

1888 1889 1890

Signed deniers of Robert de Juilly (1373-1377)

1891 1892 1893 1894 1895 1896

1897 1898 1899 1900 1901 1902

Overstruck deniers, *c.* 1377-1400
Major hoards

Plate 104

1903 1904 1905 1906 1907 1908 1909 1910 1911

1912 1913 1914 1915 1916 1917 1918 1919 1920

1921 1922 1923 1924 1925 1926 1927 1928 1929

1930 1931 1932 1933 1934 1935 1936

1937 1938 1939 1940 1941 1942 1943 1944 1945

Overstruck deniers, *c.* 1377-1400 *(Cont.)* Major hoards

Plate 105

On Pins issue

1946 1947 1948 1949 1950 1951 1952 1953 1954

1955 1956 1957

On Juilly issue

1958 1959 1960 1961 1962 1963 1964 1965

On Anonymous Type I

1966 1967 1968 1969 1970 1971 1972 1973 1974

1975 1976

The coins have been arranged according to the orientation of the understrike .

Overstruck deniers, *c.* 1377-1400 *(Cont.)*

Plate 106

Major hoards

On Anonymous Type II

1977 1978 1979 1980 1981 1982 1983 1984 1985

1986 1987 1988 1989 1990 1991 1992 1993 1994

1995 1996 1997 1998 1999 2000 2001 2002 2003

2004 2005 2006 2007 2008 2009 2010 2011 2012

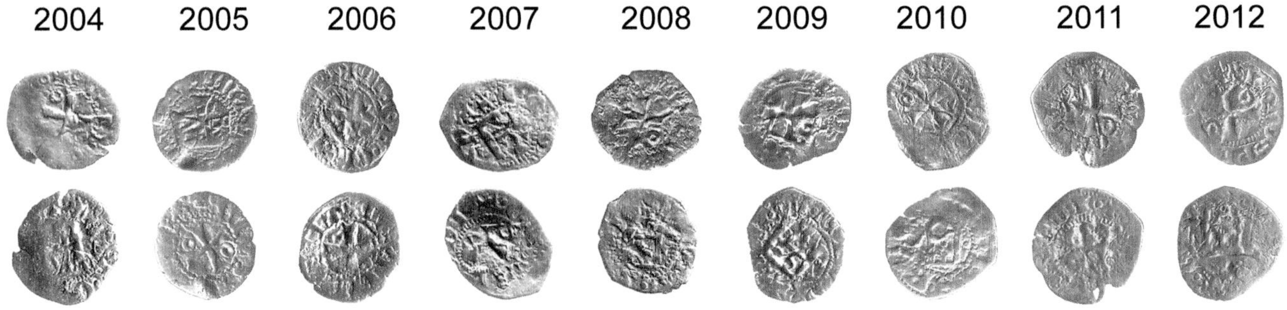

2013 2014 2015 2016 2017 2018 2019 2020 2021

The coins have been arranged according to the orientation of the understrike.

Overstruck deniers, *c.* 1377-1400 *(Cont.)* Major hoards

Plate 107

On Anonymous Type II

2022 2023 2024 2025 2026 2027 2028 2029 2030

2031 2032 2033 2034 2035 2036 2037 2038 2039

On foreign coins

2040 2041 2042 2043 2044 2045 2046 2047 2048

The coins have been arranged according to the orientation of the understrike.

Overstruck deniers, *c.* 1377-1400 *(Cont.)*
Site finds

Plate 108

2049 2050 2051 2052 2053 2054 2055 2056 2057

2058 2059 2060 2061 2062 2063 2064 2065 2066

2067 2068 2069 2070 2071 2072 2073

First Signed Type of Philibert de Naillac
Major hoards

2074 2075 2076 2077 2078 2079 2080 2081

Site find

2082

First signed Naillac type overstruck by later types
Major hoards

Plate 109

2083 2084 2085 2086 2087 2088 2089 2090

2091 2092 2093 2094 2095 2096 2097 2098

Second Signed Type of Philibert de Naillac

2099 2100 2101 2102 2103 2104 2105 2106

2107

Related Issues

2108 2109 2110

Plate 110

Anonymous Overstrikes of Philibert de Naillac, *c.* 1396-1421
Major hoards

1. ✠ONIT · S[B]O…/ ✠OSPITAL[· S · IO ·]

2111 2112 2113 2114 2115 2116 2117 2118

2119 2120 2121 2122 2123 2124 2125 2126

2. ✠ONIT · SBO… / ✠IO · IhRLM · O

2127 2128 2129 2130 2131 2132 2133 2134

9903 2136 2137

3. ✠[h]OSPITA… / ✠[·]S · IO · IhRLM ·

2138 2139 2140 2141 2142

Plate 111

Anonymous Overstrikes of Philibert de Naillac, *c.* 1396-1421 *(Cont.)*
Major hoards

3. ✠[h]OSPITA... / ✠[·]S · IO · IhRLM · *(Cont.)*

2143 2144 2145 2146

4. ✠OSPITAL · [M] / ✠IO · IhRLM · O

2147 2148 2149 2150

2151 2152 2153 2154 2155 2156 2157 2158 2159

2160 2161 2162 2163 2164 2165 2166 2167 2168

2169 2170 2171 2172 2173 2174 2175 2176 2177

Plate 112

Anonymous Overstrikes of Philibert de Naillac, *c.* 1396-1421 *(Cont.)*
Major hoards

4. ✠OSPITAL · [ɱ] / ✠IO · IhRLɱ · O *(Cont.)*

2178 2179 2180 2181 2182 2183 2184 2185 2186

2187 2188 2189 2190 2191 2192 2193 2194 2195

2196 2197 2198 2199 2200 2201 2202 2203

5. ✠IO · IhRLɱ · O / ✠[h]OSPITAL · [ɱ]

2204 2205 2206 2207 2208 2209 2210 2211

Plate 113

Anonymous Overstrikes of Philibert de Naillac, *c.* 1396-1421 *(Cont.)*
Major hoards
5. ✠IO · IhRLᗰ · O / ✠[h]OSPITᗩL · [ᗰ] *(Cont.)*

2212 2213 2214 2215 2216 2217 2218 2219 2220

2221 2222 2223 2224 2225 2226 2227 2228 2229

2230 2231 2232 2233 2234 2235 2236 2237 2238

2239 2240 2241 2242 2243 2244 2245 2246 2247

2248 2249

Anonymous Overstrikes of Philibert de Naillac, *c.* 1396-1421 *(Cont.)*
Major hoards

6. ✠IO • IhRLM / ✠IO • IhRLM

2250 2251 2252 2253 2254

7. ✠hO • IhRLM • / ✠IO • IhRLM • O

2255 2256 2257 2258 2259 2260 2261 2262 2263

2264 2265 2266 2267 2268 2269 2270 2271

2272 2273 2274 2275 2276 2277 2278 2279

Plate 115

Anonymous Overstrikes of Philibert de Naillac, *c.* 1396-1421 *(Cont.)*
Major hoards

8. ✠hOSPITAL… / ✠hOSPITAL…

2280 2281 2282 2283 2284 2285 2286 2287 2288

2289 2290 2291 2292 2293 2294 2295 2296 2297

2298 2299 2300

Site finds

2301 2302 2303 2304 2305 2306

2307 2308 2309 2310 2311 2312 2313 2314 2315

14th c. Obols

Plate 116

Obverse legend i. ✠ƆIVITΛS◦RODI

I-II

31 (#26) ✠M[ ]GR·OSPITΛLIS

2316 2317 2318

17 (#18) ✠MΛGR◦OSPITA[L]I∵

2319 2320 2321 2322

17 (#18a) ✠...GR...ITALI∴

2323

38 (#25) ✠MAGR◦OSPITALIS

2324 2325 2326

29 (#6) ✠MAGR◦OSPITALI·

2327 2328 2329 2330

39 (#29) ✠MAGR◦OSPIT[AL]IS·

2331 2332 2333

8 (#12) ✠MAGR·OSPITAL∵

2334 2335 2336 2337 2338 2339

14th c. Obols

Plate 117

Obverse legend i. +CIVITΛS◦RODI *(Cont.)*

I-II

30 (#12/20) +MHGR◦OSPITHLI·:

2340 2341 2342 2343 2344 2345

43 (#10) +MΛGR◦OSPITHLIS:

2346 2347

41 (#20b) +MHGR[ ]OSPITHLIS::

2348

III

2 (#53) +MΛGR◦OSPITΛLI◦

2349 2350 2351 2352 2353 2354 2355

2 (#149) +MΛGR◦OSPITΛLI◦

2356 2357 2358 2359 2360 2361 2362

14th c. Obols *(Cont.)*

Obverse legend ii. +CIVITAS◦RODI

6 (#41) +MAGR◦OSPITALI·

2363 2364 2365 2366 2367 2368

5 (#47) +MAGR◦OSPITALI·

2369 2370 2371 2372 2373

8 (#50) +MAGR·OSPITALI:·

2374 2375 2376 2377 2378 2379 2380 2381 2382

11 (#57) +MAGR◦OSPITA[LI·]

2383 2384 2385

21 (#64) +MAGR·OSPITALI·

2386 2387 2388

Plate 119

14th c. Obols

Obverse legend ii. +CIVITAS◦RODI *(Cont.)*

17 (#80) +MΛGR◦OSPITALI∴

2389 2390 2391 2392 2393 2394 2395

43 (#95) +MΛGR◦OSPITALS:

2396 2397 2398 2399 2400

44 (#96) +MΛGR◦OSPITAL•S

2401 2402 2403 2404

44 (#24) +MΛGR◦OSPITAL˙S

2405 2406

41 (#95d) +MAGR◦OSPITALIS::

2407 2408 2409 2410

14th c. Obols *(Cont.)*

Obverse legend iii. +CIVITĀS◦RODI·

1 (#45) +·MĀGR·OSPITĀL·

2411 2412 2413 2414

27 (#141) +·MĀGR◦OSPITALI·

2415 2416 2417 2418

28 (#143) +·MĀGR◦OSPITALI·

2419 2420 2421 2422 2423

Obverse legend iv. +CIVITAS◦RODI◦

21 (#59) +MAGR·OSPITALI·

2424 2425 2426

22 (#60) +MAGR◦OSPITALI·

2427 2428 2429 2430 2431 2432

35 (#87) +MAGR◦OSPITALIS

2433 2434

35 (#194c) +MAGR◦OSPITALIS

2435 2436 2437

14th c. Obols *(Cont.)*

Obverse legend v. +CIVITAS◦RODI∘∘

23 (#178) +MAGR◦OSPITALI◦

775 780 9250

35 (#178a) +MAGR◦OSPITALIS

778 7083 7267 7280 9238

34 (#188) +MAGR·OSPITALIS·

2446 2447 2448 2449 2450 2451

Obverse legend vi. +CIVITAS◦RODI·◦·

31 (#121) +MAGR·OSPITALIS

2452 2453 2454

31 (#163) +MAGR·OSPITALIS[

2455 2456 2457

36 (#122) +MAGR·OSPITALIS

2458 2459 2460 2461

14th c. Obols

Obverse legend vi. +ƆIVITΛS◦RODI·☼· *(Cont.)*

36 (#163c) +ⱮΛGR·OSPITΛLIS

2462 2463 2464

10 (#163b) +ⱮΛGR[◦]OSPITΛ[LI·

2465 2466

10 (#120) +ⱮΛGR◦OSPITΛLI·

2467 2468 2469 2470 2471

27a (#119) +ⱮΛGR[ ]OSPITΛLI[

2472 2473

20 (#118) +ⱮΛGR◦OSPITΛLI◦

2474 2475 2476 2477 2478

1 (#117b) +Ɱ[Λ]GR·OSPIT[Λ]L·

2479

13 (#194) +ⱮΛGR[ ]OSPITΛLI◦

2480 2481 2482 2483 2484

12 (#194a) +ⱮΛG...OSPITΛL·

2485 2486

Plate 123

14th c. Obols

Obverse legend vi. +CIVITAS◦RODI˙◦˙ *(Cont.)*

32 (#86) +MAGR◦OSPIT[AL]IS

2487 2488 2489 2490

45 (#116) +MAGR◦OSPIT˙LIS

2491 2492 2493

47 (#116a) +MAGR◦OSPIT˙LIS·

2494 2495 2496 2497

46 (#116b) +MAGR◦OSPIT·LI˙S

2498 2499

9 (#117) +MAGR◦OSPITAL◦

2500 2501 2502 2503

30 (#125) +MAGR◦OSPIT[ALI:]

2504 2505 2506

14th c. Obols *(Cont.)*

Obverse legend vii. +CIVITAS◦RODIS

5 (#2) +MAGR◦OSPITALI·

2507 2508 2509 2510 2511

29 (#7) +MAGR◦OSPI[TAL]I·

2512 2513 2514

17 (#23) +MAGR◦OSPITALI∵

2515 2516 2517

34 (#187) +MAGR·OSPITALIS·

2518 2519 2520 2521 2522

35 (#182) +[·]MAGR◦[OSPIT]ALIS

2523

43 (#24a) +MAGR◦OSPITALIS:

2524 2525 2526

44 (#24b) +MAGR◦OSPITALIS

2527 2528 2529 2530 2531

(#166) +MAGR◦O[SP]IT[A...

2532

Plate 125

14th c. Obols *(Cont.)*

Obverse legend viii. +CIVITAS·RODIS·

10 (#152) +MΛGR◦OSPI[TΛLI]

2533 2534 2535

13 (#157) +MΛGR[ ]OSPITΛLI◦

2536 2537

16 (#114) +MΛGR◦SPITΛLI◦

2538 2539 2540 2541 2542

14 (#172) +MΛGR·OSPITΛLI◦

2543 2544 2545 2546 2547 2548 2549 2550

15 (#174) +MΛGR·OSPITΛLI⁘

2551 2552 2553 2554 2555 2556 2557

14th c. Obols *(Cont.)*

Obverse legend ix. ✠CIVIT[A]S◦RODIS˙

✠CIVIT[ ]S◦RODIS
(#114a) ✠MAGR◦OSPITALI◦

2563

22a (#114b) ✠MAGR◦OSPITALI◦

2558 2559

36 (#88c) ✠MAGR·OSPITALIS

2560 2561 2562

Obverse legend x. ✠CIVITAS◦RODIS:·

5 (#1) ✠MAGR◦OSPITAL·

2564 2565 2566 2567

11 (#4) ✠MAGR◦OSPITALI·

2568 2569 2570 2571

17 (#23b) ✠MAGR◦OSPITALI[:·]

2572 2573 2574 2575

35 (#183) ✠MAGR◦OSPITALIS

2576 2577 2578 2579

34 ([#183a]) ✠MAGR·OS…ALIS˙

2580

2581

14th c. Obols *(Cont.)*

Obverse legend xi. +CIVITAS◦RODIS◦

35 (#30) +MAGR[ ]OSPITALIS

2582

35 (#185) +MAGR◦OSPITALIS

2583 2584 2585 2586 2587 2588

30a (#191) +MAGR◦OSPITALI[∴]

2589 2590 2591

42 (#192) +MAGR◦OSPITALIS◦

2592 2593 2594 2595 2596

Obverse legend xii. +CIVITĀRODIS

1 (#44a) +MAGR•OSPITALI•

2597 2598 2599 2600 2601

24 (#72) +MAGR◦OSPITALI•

2602 2603

26 (#72a) +MAGR◦OSPITALI◦

2604 2605 2606

25 (#77) +MAGR◦OSPITALI∴

2607

14th c. Obols

Obverse legend xii. +CIVITĀRODIS *(Cont.)*

28 (#143a) +MĀGR∘OSPITALI·

2608 2609 2610

30 (#80a) +MAGR◦OSPI…LI[·:]

2611 2612 2613 2614

37 (#52f) +MĀGR◦OSPITALIS

2615 2616

3 (#44) +MĀGR·OSPITĀL:

2617 2618 2619 2620 2621 2622 2623

3 (#145) +MĀGR·OSPITĀL:

2624 2625 2626

[3] (#146) +MĀGR·OSPITĀ[L]

2627 2628 2629 2630

Plate 129

14th c. Obols

Obverse legend xii. +CIVITĀRODIS *(Cont.)*

2 (#52) +MĀGR◦OSPITĀL◦

2631 2632 2633 2634 2635

2 (#151) +MĀGR◦OSPITĀL◦

2636 2637 2638

10 (#52a) +MĀGR◦OSPITĀLI·

2639 2640 2641 2642

10 (#160) +MĀGR◦OSPITĀLI·

2644 2645

47 (#52d) +MĀGR◦OSPIT'LIS·

2645 2646 2647

47 (#162) +MĀGR◦OSPI[T]'LIS[·

2648 2649 2650

36 (#52e) +MĀGR·OSPITĀLIS

2651 2652 2653

Plate 130

14th c. Obols

Obverse legend xii. +CIVITĀRODIS *(Cont.)*

36 (#88) +MAGR·OSPITALIS

2654 2655 2656 2657 2658 2659

13 (#136) +MAGR◦OSPITALI◦

2660 2661 2662

13 (#155) +MAGR◦OSPITALI◦

2663 2664

31 (#161) +MAGR·OSPITALIS

2665 2666 2667

33 (#161a) +MAGR◦OSPITALIS

2668 2669

Plate 131

14th c. Obols *(Cont.)*

Obverse legend xiii. +SIVITAS◦RODI·

21 (#127) +MAGR·OSPITALI·

2670 2671 2672 2673 2674 2675

22 (#128) +MAGR◦OSPITALI·

2676 2677 2678

5 (#130) +MAGR◦OSPITALI·

2679 2680 2681

34 (#194b) +MAGR·OSPITALIS[

2682

Obverse legend xiv. +SIVITAS◦RODI∴

21 (#131) +MAGR·OSPIT[ALI·]

2683 2684

Plate 132

14th c. Obols *(Cont.)*

Obverse legend xv. △ +CIVITAS:RODI

49 (#199) +MAGR:OSPITAL

2685 2686 2687

50 (#201) +MHGR:OSPITHL'⁚

2688 2689 2690 2691

51 (#202) +MHGR:OSPITHLI·

2692 2693 2694

[51] (#205) +MAGR:OSPITAL[

2695 2696 2697 2698

Obverse legend xvi. △ +CIVITAS:RODI·

48 (#200) +MAGR·OSPITAL[']

2699 2700 2701 2702 2703 2704 2705 2706

Plate 133

Obols of Raymond Berenger (1365-1373)
Major hoards

Obverse legend +CIVITAS◦RODISC

Reverse 16 +MAGR◦SPITALI◦

2707 2708 2709 2710 2711 2712 2713 2714

2715 2716 2717

Reverse 15 +MAGR·OSPITALI⁝

2718 2719 2720 2721 2722

2723 2724 2725 2726 2727 2728 2729 2730 2731

2733 2734 2735 2736 2737 2738 2739 2740

14th c. Obols
Site finds

Annulet within châtel/ Annulets in quarters 1 & 4 of the cross.

2741 2742 2743 2744 2745 2746 2747 2748

2749 2750 2751 2752 2753 2754 2755 2756 2757

2758 2759 2760 2761 2762 2763 2764 2765 2766

2767 2768 2769 2770 2771 2772 2773 2774 2775

Plate 135

14th c. Obols
Site finds *(Cont.)*

Annulet within châtel/ Annulets in quarters 1 & 4 of the cross.

2776 2777 2778 2779 2780 2781 2782

Platelet within châtel/ Annulets in quarters 1 & 4 of the cross.

2783 2784 2785 2786 2787 2788 2789 2790 2791

2792 2793 2794 2795 2796 2797

[Platelet] within châtel/ Annulets in quarters 1 & 4 of the cross.

2798 2799 2800

Plate 136

14th c. Obols
Site finds *(Cont.)*

Dot within châtel/ annulets in quarters 1 & 4 of the cross.

2801 2802 2803 2804 2805 2806 2807 2808 2809

2810 2811 2812 2813 2814 2815 2816 2817

2818

Uncertain obverse/ Annulets in quarters 1 & 4 of the cross.

2819 2820 2821 2822 2823 2824 2825 2826

2828 2829 2830 2830 2831 2832 2833 2834 2835

Plate 137

14th c. Obols
Site finds *(Cont.)*

Uncertain obverse/ Annulets in quarters 1 & 4 of the cross

2836 2837 2838 2839 2840 2841 2842 2843 2844

2845 2846 2847 2848 2849 2850 2851

Annulet within châtel/
Annulets in quarters 2 & 3 of the cross.

2852

Dot within châtel/
Annulets in quarters 2 & 3 of the cross.

2853

Uncertain obverse/
Annulets in quarters 2 & 3 of the cross.

2854

14th c. Obols
Site finds *(Cont.)*

Annulet within châtel/ Platelets in quarters 1 & 4 of the cross.

2855 2856 2857

Dot within châtel/
Platelets in quarters 1 & 4 of the cross.

2858 2859 2860 2861 2862 2863

Late Types (#199-202)

2864 2865 2866 2867 2868 2869 2870 2871 2872

2873 2874 2875 2876 2877 2878 2879 2882 2881

2882

2883

Plate 139

Imitative 14th c. Obols

2884 2885 2886 2887 2888 2889 2890 2891 2892

2893 2894 2895 2896 2897 2898 2899 2900 2901

2902 2903 2904 2905 2906 2907 2908 2909 2910

2911 2912 2913 2914 2915 2916 2917 2918

15th c. Obols

[1] +MAGISTRI·OSPITALIS /+IEROSALEMITANI RODI

2919 2920 2921 2922 2923 2924 2925 2926 2927

2928 2929 2930 2931 2932 2933 2934

[2] +MAGISTRI·OSPITALIS / +IEROSALEMITANI ROD

2935 2936 2937 2938 2939 2940 2941 2942 2943

2944 2945 2946 2947 2948 2949

Plate 141

15th c. Obols *(Cont.)*

+OSPITĀLIS S IO / +[M]OSPITĀLIS S IO

[3]

2950 2951

[4]

2954 2955 2956 2957 2958

2952 2953

2959 2960 2961 2962 2963

[3] or [4]

2964 2965 2966 2967 2968 2969 2970 2971 2972

2973
87

[5] +CONVENTUS ROCI
+OSPIT[A]LIS...

2974 2975 2976 2977

[6] +CONUEN...OC.../
+IERUSALE...

2978

15th c. Obols *(Cont.)*

[7]]MAGISTEROSPIT[A/
+MAGISTERO…L

2979 2980 2981

[8] +…[AL]ISIE[RU]
+OSPI…[L]

2982

[9] +CON[U]…ODI
+CO[N]VENT[ ]S

2983 2984

[10] +CONUENTU…OCI
+IE…ΛRhO[D:]

2985

[11] +CONUENT[O]ROCI / +OSPITALIS IERUSALE[M]

2986 2987 2988 2989 2990 2991 2992 2993 2994

2995 2996 2997 2998 2999 3000 3001 3002 3003

15th c. Obols

[11] +CONUENT[O]ROCI / +OSPITALIS IERUSALE[M] *(Cont.)*

3004 3005 3006 3007 3008 3009 3010 3011 3012

[12] +CONUENTUS RhOCI / +MAGISTER·OSPITALIS·

3013 3014 3015 3016 3017 3018 3019 3020 3021

3022 3023 3024 3025 3026 3027 3028 3029 3030

3031 3032 3033 3034 3035 3036 3037

Imitative 15th c. Obols

Plate 144

3038

3039

3040

3041

3042

3043

3044

3045

3046

3047

3048

3049

3050

3051

3052

3053

3054

3055

Legends with pseudo-letters

3056

3057

Plate 145

Deniers of Pierre d'Aubusson (*c.* 1488-1503)

3059 3060 3061 3062 3063 3064 3065 3066 3067

3067 3068 3069 3070 3071 3072 3073 3074 3075

3076 3077 3078 3079 3080 3081 3082 3083 3084

3085 3086 3087 3088 3089 3090 3091 3092 3093

3094 3095 3096 3098 3099 3100 3101 3102

Deniers of Pierre d'Aubusson *(Cont.)*

3103 3104 3105 3106 3107 3108 3119 3110 3111

Deniers of Emery d'Amboise (1503-1512)

A

3112 3113 3114 3115

3116 3117 3118 3119

3120 3121 3122 3123

B

3124 3125 3126 3127

3128 3129 3130 3131

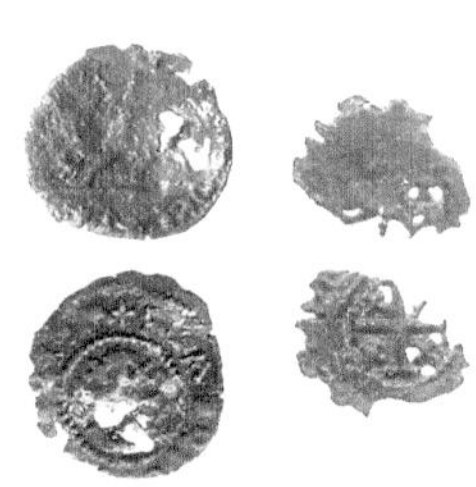

3132 3133

Plate 147

Foreign Coins. Site and stray finds.

Lucca

3134 3135

France

3136

3137 3138 3139

England

3141

Palestine

3142 3143 3144

Armenia

3145 3146 3147 3148

3149 3150 3151 3152

Genoa

3153 3154

Florence

3155

Venice

3156

Plate 148

Foreign Coins. Site and stray finds.

Venice *(Cont.)*

3157 3158 3159 3160 3161 3163 3164 3165 3166

Sicily

3167 3168 3170 3171 3172 3173 3174 3175 3176

3177 3178 3189 3180 3181 3182 3183 3184 3185 3186

3187 3188 3189 3190 3191 3192 3193 3194 3195 3196

Plate 149

Foreign Coins. Site and stray finds.

Sicily *(Cont.)*

3197 3198 3199 3200 3201 3202 3203 3204 3205 3206

3207 3208 3209 3210 3211 3212 3213 3214 3216

3217 3218 3219 3220

Naples

3221 3222 3223

Majorca

Minorca

Portugal

3224 3225 3226

Rome

3227 3228 3229 3230

Macerata

3231

Foreign Coins. Site and stray finds *(Cont.)*

Milan Ravenna Ancona

3232 3233 3234 3235 3236 3237

Cyprus

3238 3239 3240 3241 3242 3243 3244 3245 3246

3247 3248 3249 3250

3251 3252 3253 3254

Famagusta

3255 3256 3257 3258 3259

Foreign Coins. Site and stray finds *(Cont.)*

Mytilene

3260 3261 3262 3263

Chios

3264 3265

Levantine ducat imitations

3266 3267

Torneselli

3268 3269 3270 3271 3272 3273 3274 3275 3276

3277 3278 3279 3280 3281 3282 3283 3284 3285

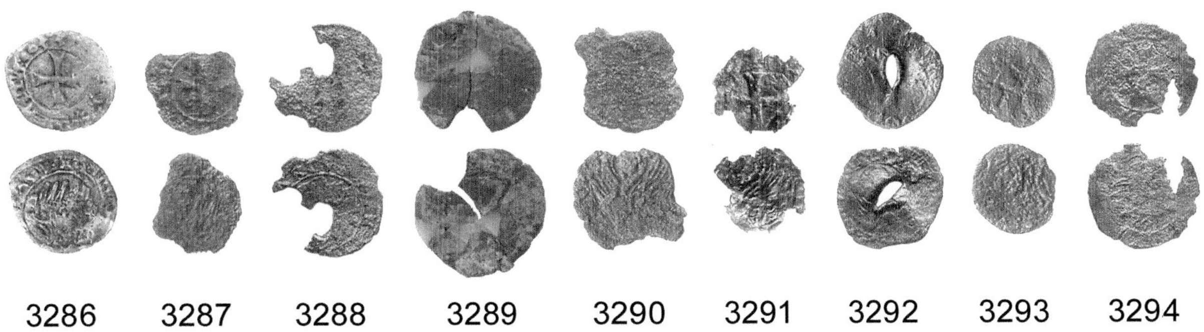

3286 3287 3288 3289 3290 3291 3292 3293 3294

Plate 152

Foreign Coins. Site and stray finds.

Torneselli *(Cont.)*

3295 3296 3297 3298 3299 3300 3301 3302

Imitations

3304

3305

Lepanto

3306

Achaia

3307

Unidentified

3308 3309 3310 3311 3312 3313 3314 3315 3317

3318 3319 3320 3321

Foreign Coins *(Cont.)*
Major hoards

Genoa Portugal Sicily Naples Mantua

3322 3323 3324 3325 3326 3327 3328

Ravenna Ascoli Bologna [Milan]

3329 3330 3331 3332

Cyprus

3333 3334 3335 3336 3337

Famagusta Mytilene Chios

3338 3339 3340 3341 3342 3343 3344

Plate 154

Foreign Coins
Major hoards *(Cont.)*

Torneselli

3346 3347 3348 3349 3350 3351 3352 3353

Unidentified denier tournois

3354

Index

N

O

Z